THE AMERICAN PRESIDENT

THE AMERICAN PRESIDENT

From Teddy Roosevelt to Bill Clinton

WILLIAM E. LEUCHTENBURG

OXFORD
UNIVERSITY PRESS

OXFORD
UNIVERSITY PRESS

Oxford University Press is a department of the University of Oxford.
It furthers the University's objective of excellence in research, scholarship,
and education by publishing worldwide. Oxford is a registered trade mark of
Oxford University Press in the UK and certain other countries.

Published in the United States of America by Oxford University Press
198 Madison Avenue, New York, NY 10016, United States of America

© Oxford University Press 2015

First edition published in 2015

Library of Congress Cataloging-in-Publication Data
Leuchtenburg, William E. (William Edward), 1922–
The American president: from Teddy Roosevelt to Bill Clinton / William E. Leuchtenburg.
    pages   cm
Includes bibliographical references and index.
ISBN 978-0-19-517616-2 (hardback : alk. paper)
    1. Presidents—United States—20th century.
    2. Presidents—United State—Biography.
3. United States—Politics and government—1901–1953.
4. United States—Politics and government—1945–1989.
5. United States—Politics and government—1989–   I. Title.
        E176.1.L377   2015
        973.09'9—dc23
            [B]
        2015014413

1 3 5 7 9 8 6 4 2

Printed in the United States of America
on acid-free paper

For Jean Anne

Editor Extraordinaire
Fount of Inspiration
Loving Companion of Three Decades

The president is not a Gulliver immobilized by 10,000 tiny cords, nor even a Prometheus chained to a rock of frustration. He is, rather, a kind of magnificent lion who can roam widely and do great deeds so long as he does not try to break loose from his broad reservation.

—Clinton Rossiter

CONTENTS

PREFACE

ONE OF MY FAVORITE CARTOONS, which appeared in a mass-circulation magazine, was called to my attention years ago, impishly, by my teenage stepson. A father is leaning over his son who is laboring over his homework, and the boy, looking up, says, "Of course, *you* were good in history. You were *there* for *most* of it."

For much the greater part of the twentieth-century American presidency, I was there. I was born in Warren Harding's administration; once received a letter from Mrs. Woodrow Wilson assigning me rights to her husband's *The New Freedom*; and, when I taught at Smith College (1949–51), lived a few doors down the block from Grace Coolidge, a lady I greatly admired.

Most of my political maturation coincided with the presidency of Franklin Delano Roosevelt. I was nine in the summer of 1932, when my parents let me stay up late to listen to the broadcast from Chicago of the Democratic National Convention that wound up nominating him, and I was twenty-two when he died. Along with millions of other Americans, I was held spellbound by his fireside chats, and his National Youth Administration program enabled me to work my way through Cornell. Subsequently, I wrote or edited eight books about FDR and his times. At the invitation of the brilliant landscape architect Lawrence Halprin, I provided quotations to be inscribed on the FDR Memorial in Washington.

In the post-Roosevelt era, especially during the thirty years I taught at Columbia, I was actively engaged in politics and, while teaching and writing, participated in the public realm. For three successive national contests starting in 1964, I worked as presidential elections analyst for NBC—first for Huntley and Brinkley, then for John Chancellor. In later years, I was on-screen for a number of presidential inaugurations: in 1985 at Ronald Reagan's second with Bill Moyers, in 1989 at George H. W. Bush's, and at both of Bill Clinton's, one of them at the CBS anchor desk with Dan Rather and Charles Kuralt.

During this period, too, I served on a committee headed by Robert Kennedy to record recollections of the presidency of John F. Kennedy; was asked to the White House for an extraordinarily lengthy (and stunningly indiscreet) interview with Lyndon Johnson; commuted to Washington for two years as a member of the National Study Commission on Records and Documents of Federal Officials after joining in the lawsuit to prevent Richard Nixon from destroying his papers; supervised the twentieth-century segment of a report for the Impeachment Inquiry Staff Investigating Charges Against Richard M. Nixon; shared a spot on the program with Gerald Ford at a conference at the LBJ Presidential Library in Austin; participated on a panel with Jimmy Carter at the Woodrow Wilson Center in Washington; provided historical material for the president's brief in *Clinton v. Jones*; and edited the microfilm collection of "Papers of the Republican Party." For more than thirty years, I have had the pleasure and privilege of working with Ken Burns on his documentary films, starting with *Huey Long* and continuing on to *The Roosevelts* (2014), which reaches back beyond FDR to Theodore Roosevelt, close to where this book begins.

Both at home and abroad, I have discussed the trajectory of the American presidency. In the United States, I have spoken at the Herbert Hoover Presidential Library in West Branch, Iowa; at the Franklin D. Roosevelt Library in Hyde Park, New York; at the John F. Kennedy Library in Boston, where I chaired a presentation by Robert Dallek of his biography of JFK, a session televised by C-SPAN; and at a conference assessing the Carter presidency at the Jimmy Carter Presidential Library in Atlanta. Overseas, I have lectured on the US presidency in venues as far apart as Oxford (where I held the Harmsworth chair), Ben-Gurion University of the Negev in Israel, and the University of Cape Town in South Africa, as well as any number of places in between, including

Paris, Berlin, and Bologna. In dedicating the opening of the first US history research institute in Russia at Moscow State University, I analyzed the nature of the US executive branch, and in the Italian city of Torino I delivered the opening address at a conference contrasting the American, Italian, and Mexican presidencies. As recently as 2011, I was keynoter at the twenty-fifth anniversary of the Roosevelt Study Center in Middelburg, Zeeland, the Netherlands, and at a conference on presidential foreign policy with representatives of twenty-seven nations at the Salzburg Global Seminar in Austria.

When, at a meeting at the University of Pennsylvania in 2004, the great scholar of medieval thought Jaroslav Pelikan, speaking for the Annenberg Foundation, asked me to write a history of the American presidency, I readily agreed, for, though it was a daunting assignment, it offered the opportunity to create the capstone of a lifetime of interest in the subject. Soon after I began, I recognized that the material was so dense I would do well to confine myself to the twentieth century for this volume. (I have, however, begun work on another book carrying the narrative from the Constitutional Convention of 1787 to 1900.)

Only one feature of Professor Pelikan's invitation struck me at first as uncongenial: he asked me not to annotate my account because the foundation wanted the book to be accessible to the widest spectrum of citizens. I was at that moment engaged in completing *The White House Looks South: Franklin D. Roosevelt, Harry S. Truman, Lyndon B. Johnson*, which, when published in 2005, had no fewer than 105 pages of endnotes, and a good number of the books I had written in the past had been heavily annotated, reflecting my research in archives in almost every state, including Alaska, and in British depositories. But I had also written books such as *The Perils of Prosperity, 1914–32* (1958) that had no notes, and was busy at that very time writing a biography, *Herbert Hoover* (2009), that was not expected to be annotated. One consideration was especially compelling. I recalled the books that long ago had attracted me to the study of history—Vernon Parrington's *Main Currents in American Thought* and Charles and Mary Beard's *The Rise of American Civilization*— masterpieces that offered overviews in which the authors present the reader their unvarnished conclusions with no notes whatsoever.

The American President explores how the American presidency in the twentieth century became a very much more powerful institution than it had ever been before and how that aggrandizement was brought about by the men who inhabited the White House. I fully recognize that political developments are not determined by the president alone—that Congress, the judiciary, state and local governments, and private actors are significant. Furthermore, I acknowledge that impersonal forces—the emergence of the United States as a world power, the demands of a national economy, the communications revolution—were highly influential. Still, I am persuaded that twentieth-century America was significantly shaped by its presidents.

That proposition might seem to be self-evident, altogether unremarkable, but it has been strongly challenged by formidable scholars. In 1988, asked to name the most overrated figure in American history, Robin Winks of Yale replied: "Nearly any of the Presidents (a group by whom we tend to organize our textbooks, as though their years somehow defined time for us) who actually did virtually nothing." He added, "Even to discuss Chester Arthur or Millard Fillmore is to overrate them." More recently, the eminent jurist Richard Posner has said, "We have learned that the President of the United States, like Tolstoy's Napoleon, is to a certain extent a cork floating on the ocean rather than the moon controlling the tides."

Such assertions have not gone unanswered. In his anthology of quotations from presidents about their experiences in the White House, Arthur Tourtellot observed: "Everyone is familiar with Charles Evans Hughes's comment 'We live under a Constitution, but the Constitution is what the judges say it is.' It may be similarly said that we live under a presidency, but the presidency is what the President thinks it is." My own response is lodged in the pages that follow: a chronicle of those not so faraway times when lions—often magnificent, sometimes feckless or perfidious—roamed the land.

THE AMERICAN PRESIDENT

PROLOGUE

EARLY IN SEPTEMBER 1901, the twenty-fifth president of the United States, William McKinley, arrived at the Pan-American Exposition in Buffalo to greet well-wishers at a festival celebrating progress and international amity. At the lake city, a fireworks display hailed him with the message WELCOME MCKINLEY, CHIEF OF OUR NATION AND EMPIRE. A Civil War hero who had enlisted in the 23rd Ohio Volunteer Regiment and fought at Antietam, he had broad popular appeal. Elected in 1896 at the climax of a historic contest with William Jennings Bryan, Major McKinley had been returned to office in 1900 in a resounding affirmation of his hold on the affections of the American people. "Now, six months into his second term, in this late, lazy summer of the first year of the twentieth century," the historian Eric Rauchway has written, "it looked as though the McKinley Administration would continue peaceably unbroken for another four years, going on as it had begun, a government devoted to prosperity and standing firm against demands that it become an engine for social betterment."

Despite the aura of contentment and tranquility, his secretary, George Cortelyou, advised McKinley to cancel his plans for a public reception because the Temple of Music was such an open venue that he would be putting himself at risk. Cortelyou's anxiety appeared to be excessive, but, in truth, there was some reason for trepidation. After an assassin cut

1

The White House, 1866. Pedestrians, including a woman in a hoop skirt, are captured by a photographer alongside Pennsylvania Avenue—a dirt thoroughfare, often muddy. *Photo by G. D. Wakely, 1866, courtesy of Mike Fitzpatrick*

down Kentucky's governor-elect, William Goebel, early in 1900, Ambrose Bierce had composed some doggerel:

> The bullet that pierced Goebel's breast
> Can not be found in all the West;
> Good reason, it is speeding here
> To stretch McKinley on his bier.

The verse appeared in one of William Randolph Hearst's newspapers, and in the spring of 1901 an editorial in another Hearst journal asserted, "If bad institutions and bad men can be got rid of only by killing, then the killing must be done." In this age of confidence, however, such rhetoric was so aberrant that McKinley brushed aside Cortelyou's plea that he call off the event. "Why should I?" he asked. "No one would wish to hurt me."

When festivities began at the Temple of Music, a domed hall likened to "a red, yellow, and blue Fabergé egg," the president's serenity seemed amply justified. The scene could not have been more tranquil. As an organist played Schumann's *Träumerei* (Reverie), hundreds of admirers queued up in hopes of getting close to the country's first citizen. McKinley himself cut a comforting figure. With his double-breasted Prince Albert coat, starched shirt, wing collar, black satin cravat, white piqué vest, striped trousers, and red carnation, he conveyed equanimity and solemnity befitting a head of state. One diplomat had informed a French journalist who was about to call on the US chief executive, "His face is as serious and distant as that of a Roman emperor."

While for some minutes McKinley shook hands with each of the fairgoers who filed by, security guards scrutinized the throng. They saw no reason to be wary of the next in line—a slender young man of middling height and unremarkable features with a bandaged right hand. They had no way of knowing, or even suspecting, that Leon Czolgosz, "set... on fire" by an Emma Goldman speech he had heard in Cleveland, thought of himself as an anarchist, though anarchists, suspecting that he was a police plant, disowned him. Whatever the source of his views, he stoked a smoldering hatred of men of wealth and power.

As McKinley reached out to him, Czolgosz pulled the trigger on a short-barreled revolver concealed in a cumbersome handkerchief wrapped

The assassination of William McKinley, 1901. Leon Czolgosz, his revolver concealed in a bandaged hand, fatally wounds the president on a September day that a Buffalo newspaper called the saddest in the city's history. *Library of Congress, LC-USZ62-5377*

around his fist. He fired twice. One bullet caromed off a button, but the other penetrated the president's stomach. Staggering among potted plants, his shirt reddened by seeping blood, McKinley expressed concern not for himself but for the assassin, who was being pummeled with fists, clubs, and rifle butts. "Don't let them hurt him," McKinley instructed Cortelyou. The man was just "some poor misguided fellow." Grievously wounded, he added, "My wife, be careful...how you tell her—oh be careful."

McKinley clung to life for eight days. At one point, surgeons announced that he was out of danger. But Czolgosz's bullet would not be denied, and, as the week drew to a close, the president knew that his hours were numbered. "Goodbye, goodbye all," he whispered to friends at his bedside. Early in the morning, murmuring the reassuring words of a beloved hymn, "Nearer My God to Thee," the president passed away. McKinley, said Secretary of State John Hay, "showed in his life how a citizen should live, and in his last hour taught us how a gentleman could die."

———

It seems odd that anyone would target McKinley—though he was the third American president in a generation to be murdered—not only because he appeared to be unprovocative, even benign, but still more because the presidency in 1901 did not begin to resemble the leviathan it was to become. Not for a generation had there been a strong leader in the White House. "The nineteenth-century American presidency," the historian Morton Keller has written, "consisted of a mountain of greatness (Lincoln) bounded on either side by lowlands of mediocrity." In explaining the US system of government to European contemporaries, the influential Russian sociologist Moisei Ostrogorski said that "after the war the eclipse of the executive was complete and definitive." The Supreme Court, in *The Floyd Acceptances* (1869), confirmed that perception by proclaiming that "officers in this government, from the President down to the most subordinate agent, had limited authority." Only in the most minimal sense could the president be thought of as head of the executive branch. He had no control over the budgets of cabinet officials who ran the major departments. They answered not to him but to chummy congressional committee chairmen with whom they colluded.

When in 1888 James Bryce summed up two decades of study of US political institutions in his classic *The American Commonwealth*, he found it necessary to devote an entire chapter to "Why Great Men Are Not Chosen President."

To that conundrum, Lord Bryce gives several answers. He begins by observing that "the proportion of first-rate ability drawn into politics is smaller in America than in most European countries" because in the United States public affairs do not seem as exciting as "the business of developing the material resources of the country." Consequently, one gets Chester Arthur, not Andrew Carnegie. Furthermore, the American voter "does not value, because he sees no need for originality or profundity, a fine culture or a wide knowledge" in presidents and is content to let "commonplace men" choose candidates who will not create a stir. Lastly, a president is not required to be exceptional because "four-fifths of his work is the same in kind as that which devolves on the chairman of a commercial company or the manager of a railway."

Three years earlier, young Woodrow Wilson had anticipated this last point in his Johns Hopkins doctoral dissertation, published as *Congressional Government*. "The business of the President, occasionally great, is usually not much above routine," he said. The presidency was "too silent and inactive, too little like a premiership and too much like a superintendency." Wilson elaborated:

> Except in so far as his power of veto constitutes him a part of the legislature, the President might, not inconveniently, be a permanent officer; the first official of a carefully-graded and impartially regulated civil service system, through whose sure series of merit-promotions the youngest clerk might rise even to the chief magistracy. He is part of the official rather than of the political machinery of the government, and his duties call rather for training than for constructive genius. If there can be found in the official systems of the States a lower grade of service in which men may be advantageously drilled for Presidential functions, so much the better.

Still, commentators found it hard to fathom how men of such parochial backgrounds could have become heads of state. Andrew Johnson, born of illiterate parents, never went to school, did not learn to read until, at thirteen, he was apprenticed to a tailor, and could not write or cipher until his wife tutored him. In his final address to Congress, Ulysses S. Grant said: "It was my fortune, or misfortune, to be called to the office of Chief Executive without any previous political training. From the age of seventeen I had never even witnessed the excitement attending a Presidential campaign but twice antecedent to my own candidacy, and at but one of them was I eligible as a voter." At the start of his tenure, Grover Cleveland, one historian has written, "knew nothing about being President and nearly nothing about the important national issues." Until he entered the national political arena, he had hardly ever left Buffalo, and he first saw Washington, DC, when he moved into the White House. Cleveland would never visit Europe, never see America west of the Mississippi.

Men of letters viewed the incumbents of their generation with contempt. In Henry James's short story "Pandora," a character says, "Hang it, . . . let us be vulgar and have some fun—let us invite the President." Henry Adams in his 1880 novel, *Democracy*, originally published anonymously, depicted his protagonist's visit to the White House: "There Madeleine found herself before two seemingly mechanical figures, which might be wood or wax, for any sign they showed of life. These two figures were the President and his wife; they stood stiff and awkward by the door, both their faces stripped of every sign of intelligence. . . . To her it had the effect of a nightmare, or of an opium-eater's vision. She felt a sudden conviction that this was to be the end of American society; its realization and dream at once. She groaned in spirit." Contemplating the arc of decline from George Washington to Grant, Adams later said, caused him to lose confidence in the Darwinian creed of progressive evolution. Grant, he declared, "had no right to exist. He should have been extinct for ages."

Historians who have echoed Adams and other jaundiced patricians in depicting the presidents of this period as dunderheads and philistines misconceived them. James Garfield cherished Goethe, and Chester Arthur spent evenings reading Thackeray. Born into poverty, Garfield, whose campaign biography, *From Canal Boy to President*, was written by Horatio Alger, had taken so readily to his studies that as a schoolboy he had kept a diary in Latin. A graduate of Williams College, he had been appointed professor of classics, then president, of what was later called Hiram College. He counted Henry Wadsworth Longfellow and William

Dean Howells as friends and kept au courant with the latest poems of Tennyson. U. S. Grant was painfully conscious of his intellectual limitations, but his *Personal Memoirs* is an American classic whose superb style won the praise of so demanding a literary critic as Edmund Wilson. A couple of presidents even took on the role of patron of belles lettres in the style of the Medici. Hayes appointed the renowned poet James Russell Lowell ambassador to Spain and named Lincoln's secretary and biographer, John Hay, assistant secretary of state. Hay went on to publish a novel, *The Bread-winners*, in 1883. Garfield so admired the aspiring novelist General Lew Wallace that he chose him to be the US envoy to Paraguay. But on reading Wallace's new novel, *Ben-Hur*, he moved him instead to Constantinople in the expectation that the writer would "draw inspiration from the modern East for future literary work."

Writers have also lumped together the post–Civil War presidents as racists and as vassals of Wall Street, but neither epithet fit Rutherford B. Hayes. Told to incorporate into his letter accepting the 1876 Republican nomination a statement of respect for "the constitutional right of local self-government," he responded that the phrase "seems to me to smack of the bowie knife and revolver," and, in the White House, he deplored the way that "by frauds, by intimidation and by violence of the most atrocious character colored citizens have been deprived of the right of suffrage—a right guaranteed by the Constitution, and to the protection of which the people of these States have been solemnly pledged." He sought the counsel of African Americans, and he appointed Frederick Douglass to be marshal of the District of Columbia. He also acknowledged that "many, if not most, of our Indian wars have had their origin in broken promises and acts of injustice on our part." After he left office, Hayes made what restitution he could by diligently expanding the educational opportunities of southern blacks through the Peabody Fund and the Slater Fund. Thanks to Hayes, the brilliant young African American W. E. B. Du Bois was able to study in Berlin.

Far from being a lackey of the robber barons, Hayes had expressed alarm as early as 1871 at "the colossal fortunes...consolidating into the hands of a few men—not always the best men—powers which threaten alike good government and our liberties," and in later years he called Standard Oil "a menace to the people," favored confiscatory inheritance taxes, and warned of the degeneration of the republic into a "government of corporations, by corporations, and for corporations." After calling out federal troops to suppress the violent railway strike of 1877 that threatened public safety, Hayes recorded in his diary, "The strikes have been put down by *force*; but now for the real remedy." Something ought to be done by measures such as "judicious control of the capitalists," he said, for "the railroad strikers, as a rule, are good men, sober, intelligent and industrious."

The sterility of these years derived less from the shortcomings of the incumbents than from the circumstances that entrapped them. It was not an easy time to be president. The generation that had lived through the Civil War knew it had participated in a grand, if awful, experience, and everything thereafter seemed anticlimactic. In J. W. De Forest's novel *Honest John Vane* (1875), a newly elected congressman innocently assumes that he will be dealing with "reform, foreign relations, sectional questions, constitutional points," only to be set straight by a longtime legislator who retorts, "All exploded, my dear sir! All gone out with Calhoun and Webster, or at the latest, with Lincoln and Stanton. All dead issues, as dead as the war." The paramount concerns of slavery and secession had been resolved, and few whites were prepared to cope with race. The issues that would preoccupy presidents in the early twentieth century—urban decay, social welfare, trusts—had not yet been born. As Hayes noted in his diary, "We are in a period when old questions are settled, and the new are not yet brought forward." Under these circumstances, as the historian Bernard Weisberger has written, "the most that could realistically be expected from presidents, other than personal integrity, would be a holding action until the country caught up with the implications of the age of steel and steam."

Presidents headed a government that was no more than a miniaturized version of a European state. In the Grant era, the size of the bureaucracy doubled, reaching one hundred thousand for the first time in 1877, and Congress created both a Department of Justice and the office of solicitor general, but most federal employees were engaged in one of just two tasks: delivering the mail or collecting customs duties. The US Army made do with twenty-five thousand officers and men, and the US Navy was pitiful. Of the thirty-seven fighting vessels in an age of armor-plate, thirty-three were of wood. "We have not six ships that would be kept at sea in war by any maritime power," Captain Alfred Thayer Mahan lamented.

In the 1880s, the United States could not intervene on behalf of Peru in the War of the Pacific because the Chilean fleet was more powerful than the American. "Never," said a British journal, "was there such a hopeless, broken-down, tattered, forlorn apology for a navy."

Little about the American government suggested an incipient superpower. Though the United States had envoys, none was of ambassadorial rank. And no foreign power sent an ambassador to Washington. The few ministers America did dispatch abroad were so ill paid that they could not accept an appointment unless they had independent incomes, especially if they hoped to support a family. In 1881, John Hay remarked that he reckoned the Foreign Service, "like the Catholic Church, calculated only for celibates." The era, the historian Justus Doenecke has observed, "was marked by uncoordinated diplomacy, amateurish emissaries, shallow rhetoric, and much public and congressional indifference." A secretary of state in this period said, "There are just two rules at the State Department: one, that no business is ever done out of business hours; and the other is, that no business is ever done *in* business hours."

Domestic affairs did not elicit much more attention. Presidents had no notion that the national government could be a dynamo for social reform, and they absorbed, by osmosis, the Social Darwinist predilections of their generation. Neither Grant in the Panic of 1873 nor Cleveland in the Crisis of 1894 thought that the federal government had any obligation to alleviate the suffering of millions of jobless. Not only Hayes but also Harrison and Cleveland did, however, call out troops that broke major strikes. No president has ever had so illustrious a pedigree as Benjamin Harrison (his ancestors included a former president of the United States, a signer of the Declaration of Independence, and a member of Parliament who ordered the execution of Charles I), but the consequence, the historian Karen Orren has written, "was an overbreeding for punctiliousness and a feeling for tradition that, as Harrison aged, made it comfortable, even satisfying, to resist the currents of his own time." Garfield disapproved of labor unions, opposed government imposition of an eight-hour day, believed, at this late date, in property qualifications for voting, and regarded women's suffrage as "atheistic, and destructive of marriage and family." But no one matched Grover Cleveland in articulating the tenets of laissez-faire or in hostility to beleaguered farmers and workers.

Cleveland expressed his doctrinal views in words that would provide libertarian orators with texts for generations to come. He offered the most chilling revelation of his attitude when in 1887 he vetoed a bill Congress had passed to provide a tiny sum for seed grain to help out Texas farmers devastated by drought. He could "find no warrant for such an appropriation in the Constitution," he said, adding sternly, "I do not believe that the power and duty of the General Government ought to be extended to the relief of individual suffering which is in no manner properly related to the public service or benefit." He further stated: "A prevalent tendency to disregard the limited mission of this power and duty should, I think, be steadfastly resisted, to the end that the lesson should be constantly enforced that though the people should support the Government, the Government should not support the people." Encouraging "the expectation of paternal care on the part of the Government...weakens the sturdiness of our national character," Cleveland warned. (This conception of a circumscribed government, however, did not deter him from sending soldiers to smash the Pullman strike.) Cleveland's tenure did see the advent of the Interstate Commerce Act of 1887 and the elevation of the Department of Agriculture to cabinet status, but the president had little or nothing to do with either development. He said of the statute creating the ICC: "The cure might be worse than the disease." A contemporary said of him: "Cleveland delighted in the little and would labor pantingly at the windlass of small things. It was this bent of the infinitesimal that led him to put in hours darkly arranging a reason to shatter some old woman's pension with the bludgeon of his veto."

No one ever caught a president with his hand in a till, but more than one reached the White House through means that do not invite scrutiny. In 1888, Benjamin Harrison won in good part because of the ministrations of his campaign chairman, Senator Matt Quay of Pennsylvania, who once recommended a constituent for the job of state treasurer in Harrisburg with the words "He understands addition, division, and silence." To bankroll Harrison's campaign, Quay resolved to place big businessmen "under the fire and fry all the fat out of them." Republicans employed the huge fund they accumulated from industrialists in closely contested Indiana, regarded as the great purchasable state. (Every now and then, it was said, an innocent Hoosier was sent to the legislature.)

Thanks to well-placed cash in a state where twenty thousand votes were for sale and there was no secret ballot, the Republican ticket narrowly prevailed. Afterward, the sanctimonious Harrison, deeply moved by his triumph, told Quay, "Providence has given us the victory." Senator Quay, relaying that remark to cronies, exclaimed, "Think of the man!" Harrison, he declared, would never know "how close a number of men were compelled to approach the gates of the penitentiary to make him president." Harrison himself later said, "When I came into power, I found that the party managers had taken it all to themselves. I could not name my own Cabinet. They had sold out every place."

McKinley had taken office at the climax of a long period of legislative dominance over the executive branch. Congress established its hegemony during the first of the postwar presidencies, and successors to Andrew Johnson never fully recovered from his ordeal. In the midst of a dispute over which branch should control Reconstruction following the assassination of Abraham Lincoln that brought Johnson to the White House, congressmen denounced the new president as a "despicable, besotted traitorous man—an incubus, who wallowed in 'the purloins and filth of treason,'" attended by minions who were "the worst men that ever crawled like filthy reptiles on the footstool of power." The embittered leader of the Radical Republicans in the House, Thaddeus Stevens, said of the president: "He is the servant of the people as they shall speak through Congress." Stevens—an unrelenting hater of his political foes—added: "Andrew Johnson must learn that...as Congress shall order he must obey. There is no escape from it. God forbid that he should have one tittle of power except what he derives through Congress and the Constitution." Another congressman, notorious for his brutal rhetoric, went even further. The central question, declared Benjamin Butler, was "whether the Presidential office (if it bears the prerogatives and power claimed for it) ought, in fact, to exist, as a part of the constitutional government of a free people."

On February 24, 1868, by a resounding vote of 126–47, the House of Representatives adopted a resolution "that Andrew Johnson, President of the United States, be impeached" for "high crimes and misdemeanors." On March 4, seven Republicans, designated as impeachment managers, delivered to the Senate eleven charges. In Butler's opening presentation in the red and gold Senate chamber, he said of Johnson: "By murder most foul did he succeed to the presidency and is the elect of an assassin to that high office, and not the people." The closing argument came from the fatally ill Thad Stevens, who, it has been said, looked like "a white old rock drying in the sun." In his statement, which had to be read for him, Stevens warned that any senator who voted to acquit "this offspring of assassination" would be "tortured on the gibbet of ever-lasting obloquy."

When the roll was called, the senators found Johnson guilty, 39–19, a tally that fell one vote shy of the two-thirds needed to convict. So Johnson remained in office, but, as the historian Albert Castel has observed, "the presidency in an institutional sense plummeted to the lowest point of power and prestige in its history." If Johnson had been ejected, his successor, under the law at that time, would have been the aggressively partisan president pro tempore of the US Senate, Ben Wade. "Had the impeachment succeeded," the historian Sir Denis Brogan has written, "had Congress tasted blood by putting one of its own...into the White House, who can say what would have happened to the presidential office?" Removal of Johnson, the political scientist Norton Long has speculated, "might have been the American analogue to the earlier English development, the political beheading of an elective king." The attempt failed only because seven moderate Republicans broke with their party to vote acquittal. So unpopular was their action that each of the five who sought reelection went down to defeat.

Schooled by this experience, the presidents who followed Johnson hunkered down at their own end of Pennsylvania Avenue. U. S. Grant deferred to Congress just as he had bowed to superiors as a fledgling army officer, when he had first learned that "Congress is the boss," in the words of the historian Bruce Catton. "The President rarely appoints," Grant said. "He merely registers the appointments of members of Congress." In his first annual message, he commented meekly, "The appropriations estimated for river and harbor improvements and for fortifications are submitted.... Whatever amount Congress may deem proper to appropriate for these purposes will be expended." Garfield showed even less interest in imposing himself in the policy realm. A president, he contended, did not have the right to "use the power of his

great office to force upon Congress his own peculiar views of legislation." Government, he believed, should do nothing save "keep the
peace" and then "stand out of the sunshine of the people."

Cleveland had so doctrinaire a conception of the separation of powers
that he all but abdicated any role in enacting legislation. Less than a year
after taking office, he stated: "I believe the most important benefit that
I can confer on the country by my presidency is to insist upon the entire
independence of the executive and legislative branches of the government. ... I have certain executive duties to perform; when that is done,
my responsibility ends." Cleveland thought it unseemly "to meddle"
when Congress was debating a bill. "It don't look as though Congress
was very well prepared to do anything," he said at one point. "If a botch
is made at the other end of the Avenue, I don't mean to be a party to it."

The young scholar Woodrow Wilson expressed a common view in
asserting that the president was "plainly bound in duty to render unquestioning obedience to Congress," which was "the dominant, nay, the
irresistible, power of the federal system." The arrogant New York senator
Roscoe Conkling instructed President-elect Garfield on the eve of his
inauguration: "Your Administration cannot be more successful than I
wish it to be." A highly respected legislator from Massachusetts, George
Frisbie Hoar, reflected that in this period "the most eminent Senators,"
such as John Sherman of Ohio, "would have received as a personal affront a private message from the White House expressing a desire that
they should adopt any course in the discharge of their legislative duties
that they did not approve. If they visited the White House, it was to
give, not to receive, advice." Sherman, who believed that "the executive
department of a republic like ours should be subordinate to the legislative department," instructed Benjamin Harrison: "The President should
touch elbows with Congress. He should have no policy distinct from
that of his party; and this is better represented in Congress than in the
Executive." Harrison took that tutelage to heart. "His conduct of his
office," the political scientist Wilfred Binkley later wrote, "leaves the distinct impression that he regarded the President as little more than an
agent of Congress."

Contemporaries did not perceive the presidents of this period as cast
in a heroic mold. Garfield, said a US senator who knew him well, was "a
grand, noble fellow, but fickle, unstable, more brains but no such will as

Sherman, brilliant like Blaine but timid and hesitating." Similarly, Rutherford B. Hayes said of Garfield: "He was not executive in his talents—not original, not firm, not a moral force. He leaned on others— could not face a frowning world." Chester Arthur, remarked the wife of Secretary of State James G. Blaine, had a talent for "seeming to do things, while never putting his hands or his mind near them." Republicans gave no thought to nominating him for another term, and so, the historian Bernard Weisberger has written, "the waters of presidential history closed behind Arthur with hardly a ripple."

If a president did harbor an inclination to take an initiative, he lacked the staff to carry it off. Cleveland, who made do with one secretary, commented that "as the executive office is now organized, it can deal, with a fair amount of efficiency, with the routine affairs of Government; but if the President has any great policy in mind or on hand, he has no one to help him work it out." When that new contraption the telephone rang at the White House, Cleveland had to answer it himself, and when there was a knock at the front door, he had to open it. (The dreary social burdens of the presidency he turned over to his sister Rose, who, as the author of a book on George Eliot's poetry, had better things to do. To keep her wits together on tedious receiving lines, she conjugated Greek verbs.)

Not infrequently, presidents had time on their hands. U. S. Grant did not turn up for work until ten in the morning, and he ended his day at three to take a carriage ride. For weeks at a time, he was not in Washington but at his seaside retreat in Long Branch, New Jersey. Chester Arthur sat at his desk only from ten to four. He took Sundays off and gave himself Monday holidays too. A White House clerk later said that Arthur "never did today what he could put off until tomorrow." Little occupied with affairs of state, Arthur thought that his most important function as president was to make a majestic impression. He moved about the capital in a red and green English landau with gold lace curtains and silver-plated lamps, his gilded coat of arms on the door, and his footman in livery. In the White House, Benjamin Harrison skipped off at midday to play with his grandchildren; on one occasion, after their pet goat got loose, the president of the United States of America, formally attired with top hat, was seen waving his cane as he raced down Pennsylvania Avenue after "Old Whiskers." When Harrison sought reelection in 1892, he holed up for weeks at Loon Lake in the Adirondacks, while his opponent, Grover Cleveland, summered in Buzzards Bay, Massachusetts.

Presidents felt no obligation to make themselves available to the citizenry or to cater to their whims. "Ah, you really must excuse me," President Arthur told a cadre of journalists. "I make it a habit not to talk politics with you gentlemen of the press.... By the way, I hope you are not *interviewing* me—I believe that is the word—or intending to quote what I have been saying. Do you know, I dislike very much to open a newspaper in the morning and find a column or so of a conversation in which I have taken part the day before." As Arthur was about to embark on a journey, one Chicago newspaperman complained to a cabinet official, "It is easier for a man to get a post-office in Indiana than it is for a reporter to get on that train." Arthur's lieutenant replied, "If one does get on, he will be dropped through the trestle...of the first bridge we reach." And when a woman asked Arthur, who once served eight vintage wines at a fourteen-course state dinner, to reform his drinking habits, he retorted, "Madam, I may be President of the United States, but my private life is nobody's damned business."

Grover Cleveland insisted upon even greater seclusion. He loathed journalists, and he let them know it. He was outraged when, after he married a pretty young woman and took her to a remote spot in the Blue Ridge for their honeymoon, reporters besieged them as they emerged from their cottage the next morning—behavior he regarded as "colossal impertinence." He would not permit the press corps to set foot in the White House. Newspapermen had to stand outside in freezing rain and sleet in hope of getting a word from an emerging caller. So determined was he to evade the press that news gathering, complained one reporter, was carried out "much after the fashion in which highwaymen rob a stage-coach." In 1893, at the time of a precarious financial crisis, surgeons surreptitiously boarded a yacht in New York's East River to remove cancerous tissue in the cigar-smoking president's mouth and to fit him with an artificial jaw. Not for nearly a quarter of a century did the country learn that the clandestine operation had taken place.

Dwarfed by Congress, often denied respect, presidents found elevation to the highest office in the land deeply disappointing. On returning from his walks about town, Harrison would look up at the White House pillars and say, "There is my jail." Not long after he went down to defeat in 1892, he told Indiana Republicans, "There never has been an hour since I left the White House that I have felt a wish to return to it." When an acquaintance from the Hudson Valley paid a call at the White House with his young son, Grover Cleveland patted five-year-old Franklin Delano Roosevelt on the head and said, "My little man, I am making a strange wish for you. It is that you may never be president of the United States."

James Garfield shared the same desolate view. "I felt like crying out in the agony of my soul against the greed for office and its consumption of my time," he said. "I have been dealing all these years with ideas. I have been heretofore treating of the fundamental principles of government and here I am considering all day whether A or B shall be appointed to this or that office." Besieged by hordes of job seekers who kept him captive in the White House, he cried, "My God! What is there in this place that a man should ever want to get into it?" The presidency, he concluded, was a "bleak mountain." Less than four months into his term, Garfield was gunned down at a Washington railway depot by a crazed assassin who was a disappointed office seeker. In tears, Robert Todd Lincoln said, "How many hours of sorrow I have witnessed in this town!"

A generation later, in his essay "The Four Lost Men," Thomas Wolfe ruminated about a period that was so unmemorable. Recalling his father's evocation of the postbellum age, Wolfe wrote of "the strange, lost, time-far, dead Americans...who were more lost to me than...the lost faces of the first dynastic kings that built the pyramids." He continued:

For who was Garfield, martyred man, and who had seen him in the streets of life? Who could believe his footfalls ever sounded on a lonely pavement? Who had heard the casual and familiar tones of Chester Arthur? And where was Harrison? Where was Hayes? Which had the whiskers, which the burnsides; which was which?...

Had Garfield, Arthur, Harrison, and Hayes been young? Or had they all been born with flowing whiskers, sideburns, and wing collars, speaking gravely from the cradle of their mother's arms the noble vacant sonorities of far-seeing statesmanship?...Had they not all been young men?...Had they not known, as we have known, the wild secret joy and mystery of the everlasting earth, the lilac dark, the savage, silent, all-possessing wilderness?...Did they not say: "Oh, there are women in the East—and new lands, morning, and a shining city?"

———

In recent years, a number of skilled historians have conceived of McKinley, long thought a dullard, as the forerunner, even the creator, of the twentieth-century presidency. He flirted with modernity by becoming the first president to ride in an automobile, the first to appear in motion pictures when Republicans featured him in a primitive campaign movie, and the first candidate to keep in touch with party strategists by telephone. He also took halting steps toward making the presidency more accessible by providing a table for reporters in an outer reception room on the second floor of the White House; twice daily, his secretary gave them briefings. In addition, he anticipated later developments in creating commissions to recommend policy on issues such as bimetallism and relations with Canada, and in naming professors to these task forces. By firing a customs official without citing any of the grounds Congress had stipulated as required for dismissal, he precipitated an important ruling, *Shurtleff v. United States* (1903), in which the Supreme Court gave a broad reading to the president's removal power. Without consulting Congress, he ordered several thousand US soldiers to Peking to quell the Boxer Rebellion (an uprising against Westerners), and he resorted to executive agreements, which sidestepped Congress, to pursue an Open Door policy in Asia.

More than any other event of the post-Lincoln era, the Spanish-American War amplified executive power. As commander in chief, McKinley set up a War Room in the White House where he scrutinized maps of the far-flung battle zones and monitored the fighting. Thanks to cable, he could get in touch with the commander of US troops in Cuba in twenty minutes. When a general dallied on embarking to combat the Spaniards, McKinley wired him, "Sail at once." In dispatching US troops to occupy Manila, he became the first president to order the American army to deploy outside the Western Hemisphere. McKinley, on his own authority, established military governments in Cuba and the Philippines, permitting no congressional supervision, and he dictated the terms of peace, including the acquisition of overseas possessions. Ratification of the Treaty of Paris made McKinley the first suzerain of a new American empire extending from the Caribbean to Asia—a realm unlike any his predecessors had ever known.

In 1900, Woodrow Wilson, registering the impact of the Spanish-American War on the White House, revised his earlier views. In a new preface to *Congressional Government*, he underscored "the greatly increased power...given the President by the plunge into international politics." When foreign affairs preoccupy the country, he wrote, "its Executive must of necessity be its guide: must utter every initial judgment, take every first step of action, supply the information upon which it is to act, suggest and in large measure control its conduct. The President of the United States is now...at the front of affairs."

The reach of McKinley's tenure, though, fell considerably short of that of twentieth-century presidents. McKinley campaigned not by barnstorming the country but by greeting visitors while seated on his front porch in Canton, Ohio, where 750,000 people stopped by. His managers screened not only the questions and comments of his callers, which had to be submitted in advance, but also his own remarks. Despite the innovations in press relations, journalists could neither interview McKinley nor quote him directly. When he entered the decrepit executive mansion in Washington—rugs threadbare, ceilings cracked, wallpaper dog-eared, the structure so dilapidated that it was feared the floors might collapse—his entire staff consisted of one secretary and eight subordinates. Shortly before the 1896 contest, Lord Bryce had noted that "the domestic authority of the President is in time of peace small," and it remained small under McKinley. Furthermore, he had only a tenuous grasp of foreign affairs, for he had never been abroad, and he was an active commander in chief largely because he had made such poor cabinet appointments that he could rely upon neither his secretary of the navy nor his hopelessly incompetent secretary of war.

At a time when farmers in the prairie states were being told to raise less corn and more hell and urban reformers were publicizing the horrors of slums and sweatshops, McKinley showed hardly a flicker of awareness that the Gilded Age was giving way to the Progressive Era. Content to rely on traditional nostrums such as the historically high Dingley Tariff of 1897 and the Gold Standard Act of 1900, he had no conception of anything remotely like the Square Deal or the Great

Society. His cabinet represented capitalism triumphant—men of substance such as the New York banker Cornelius Bliss, the lumber baron Russell Alger, the president of the First National Bank of Chicago, Lyman Gage—and, during his reign, trusts metastasized.

Born nearly two decades before the Civil War in the administration of John Tyler, McKinley inhabited the premodern era of the early republic, and he was ill suited for the role of pathbreaking tribune of the people. The crabbed Speaker of the House, "Uncle Joe" Cannon, said, "McKinley keeps his ear to the ground so close that he gets it full of grasshoppers much of the time," and the Republican editor William Allen White reflected: "McKinley, for my taste, had a little too much of the cooing dove in his cosmos. He was...too meticulous in his observation of the formalities of the political Sanhedrin....He shook hands with exactly the amount of cordiality and with precisely the lack of intimacy that deceived men into thinking well of him....His Prince Albert coat was never wrinkled, his white vest front never broken. His black string tie, or a dark four-in-hand, was always properly tied....He weighed out his saccharine on apothecary scales, just enough and no more for the dose that cheers but does not inebriate."

More than three decades after Andrew Johnson left office, the country had become increasingly urbanized and industrialized and had acquired an empire, but the executive realm remained much the same. McKinley, like Grant years before, quit his job at four in the afternoon, then napped before dinner. Some afternoons, he would harmonize with a pet parrot on "Yankee Doodle Dandy"; other times, he would watch a baseball game on the South Lawn. When the spirit moved him, he would take leave of the White House and saunter up Connecticut Avenue window-shopping. Save for an hour before bedtime, he spent most of each evening chatting with his wife and friends, frequently reading the Bible aloud. In contrast to twentieth-century first ladies, Ida McKinley—a chronic invalid and often a recluse—attracted no notice. "At the outset of the twentieth century the office of the president was but a suggestion of what it would become during the next several decades," the historian H. W. Brands has concluded. "The center of American political gravity was still well toward the eastern end of Pennsylvania Avenue."

McKinley made his greatest contribution to the growth of executive power inadvertently, when he took on Theodore Roosevelt as his running mate in 1900. Unlike McKinley, TR radiated boundless energy. Scornful of physical handicaps, including severe asthma and poor eyesight, Teddy had fought his way to an amateur boxing title, climbed the Matterhorn, transcribed birdsong in a system of phonetics he invented, and, at an early age, wrote several books, the first of them published when he was only twenty-three. Roosevelt went west, a dude called "Four Eyes" who rode horseback wearing spectacles—an aristocratic easterner who would call out to cowpokes in a high-pitched voice, "Hasten forward quickly there"—and, despite these drawbacks, earned the lifelong devotion of the wranglers of the Dakota Badlands. He showed his mettle by running a ranch, hunting grizzlies, braving blizzards, breaking stampedes, and leading a posse that captured three thieves at gunpoint.

At a time when most patricians thought it unseemly to soil themselves in the grubby political arena, Roosevelt plunged into politics because, he explained, he "intended to be one of the governing class." At twenty-three, he won election to the New York legislature, where he immediately stirred up a ruckus. "Roosevelt has the knack of doing things," an observer wrote, "and doing them noisily, clamorously; while he is in the neighborhood, the public can no more look the other way than the small boy can turn his head away from a circus parade followed by a steam calliope." He proved himself a tireless worker as civil service commissioner and showed such a flair for self-promotion as New York City police commissioner that he turned his assignment into melodramatic street theater. "It became part of the New York credo," wrote his biographer Henry Pringle, "that delinquent patrolmen watched uneasily for the approach at night of a dark figure with gleaming molars."

William James regarded his former student as an adolescent, always spoiling for a fight, who "swamps everything together in one flood of abstract bellicose emotion." In 1886, Roosevelt wanted to ready a corps of "as utterly reckless a set of desperadoes as ever sat in the saddle" for a possible fracas with Mexico, and a few years later he hoped for "a bit of a spar with Germany." One of the salutary features of a tussle with the Kaiser to which he looked forward was "the burning of New York and a few other seacoast cities" which would awaken the country to the need to build coastal defenses. As assistant secretary of the navy during the mounting crisis with Spain, he revealed how headstrong and impetuous he could be. When the secretary of the navy innocently took a few hours off, Roosevelt, briefly in authority, defied instructions by ordering Commodore George Dewey to sea at a time when America was at peace with Spain—a brash action that, when hostilities commenced, led to the routing of the Spanish fleet at Manila Bay and the acquisition of the Philippines by the United States.

After war broke out, Roosevelt resigned his post to put together a cavalry regiment of one thousand that included Dakota bronco-busters, Indians, Irish cops, yachtsmen, and Ivy League football players. Bravely, and recklessly, he led these "Rough Riders" on a bloody charge up a Cuban hill, dashing about shouting encouragement to his men while sporting a blue polka-dot handkerchief that made him a conspicuous target. "I do not want to be vain," he said, "but I do not think that anyone else could have handled this regiment quite as I have handled it." Roosevelt savored the smoke of battle. "I killed a Spaniard with my own hand—like a jack-rabbit," he boasted. After San Juan Hill, a friend wrote Colonel Roosevelt's wife to report that her husband "was just reveling in victory and gore."

War hero and figure of romance, Roosevelt moved easily into the New York governor's chair in Albany, where he alarmed Wall Street by his actions and his rhetoric. He advocated an employer's liability bill and got through the legislature measures to protect women and children, inspect tenements, and establish an eight-hour day. Announcing that he would punish corporations "organized in a spirit of mere greed for improper speculative purposes," he declared that "the man who by swindling or wrongdoing acquires great wealth for himself at the expense of his fellow, stands as low morally as any predatory nobleman." Distressed by this attitude, the head of the Republican machine in the state, US Senator Tom Platt ("the Machiavelli of Tioga County") admonished him: "I... heard from a good many sources that you were a little loose on the relations of capital and labor, on trusts and combinations, and, indeed, on those numerous questions... affecting the security of earnings and the right of a man to run his business in his own way, with due respect, of course, to the Ten Commandments and the Penal Code. Or, to get at it even more clearly, I understood that you entertained various altruistic ideas, all very well in their way, but which before they could safely be put into law needed very profound consideration."

Determined to get rid of this troublemaker, Boss Platt decided to exile him from the state by advancing him to the vice presidency in Washington. Roosevelt was dismayed. He would, he said, "a great deal rather be anything, say professor of history, than vice president." But Platt prevailed, and TR's name appeared on the victorious McKinley ticket in 1900. To the delight of most conservatives, the scheming boss had apparently sidetracked the maverick's career. Asked if he planned to attend the inauguration, Senator Platt replied, "Yes, I am going to Washington to see Theodore Roosevelt take the veil." McKinley's sponsor, the wealthy Cleveland industrialist Mark Hanna, did not share in the glee. "What is the matter with all of you?" he asked. "Don't any of you realize that there's only one heartbeat between that damned cowboy and the presidency?" Disgruntled and fearful, he told McKinley, "Now it is up to you to live."

Bridling at the absurdity of being immured in a ridiculous office, Roosevelt went glumly through the paces, taking what solace he could in rugged outdoor activities. At one point, the vice president of the United States was observed jumping off a horse into a pack of ferocious baying hounds and slaying a mountain lion with his hunting knife. As the summer of 1901 was winding down, Roosevelt, assured that the wounded McKinley was out of danger, went off on another adventure: scaling one of the highest peaks in the Adirondacks.

In the afternoon of September 13, as he was consuming a trailside lunch on the mountainside by Lake Tear of the Clouds, he spotted a park ranger, yellow telegram in hand, puffing up the steep slope on the run. The vice president knew in an instant what the appearance of the courier portended. In murdering McKinley, Czolgosz thought he was striking a blow against government. Instead, his violent deed put in place of McKinley a far more dynamic leader—the rambunctious, ambitious, pugnacious Theodore Roosevelt—a succession that significantly altered the course of the American presidency.

I

Theodore Roosevelt and William Howard Taft

ON THE FUNERAL TRAIN CARRYING the slain president to Washington, Mark Hanna spoke his mind to a journalist: "I told William McKinley it was a mistake to nominate that wild man at Philadelphia. I asked him if he realized what would happen if he should die. Now look, that damned cowboy is president of the United States." The wife of a Texas congressman, too, expressed a common anxiety. After attending "a beautiful and tender little memorial service" for McKinley, she wrote in her diary, "Above all looms the question of Roosevelt. What will it mean for the country to have him roughriding over it preaching war and the strenuous life?"

Wakening on his first morning in the White House, Theodore Roosevelt cried, "I feel bully!" Not yet forty-three, the youngest man to be president (then and ever since), he infused the office with an energy it had never known. "Roosevelt, more than any other man living," observed Henry Adams, "showed the singular primitive quality that belongs to ultimate matter—the quality that medieval theology ascribed to God—he was pure act." The contrast to his predecessor could hardly have been greater. "After McKinley's grey respectability, Roosevelt seemed a roman

Theodore Roosevelt, the first media president, exuded such a lust for life that photographers and cartoonists found him an irresistible subject. *Library of Congress, LC-USZ62-5377*

candle of exuberance and fun," the historian Lewis Gould has written. "Becoming the president in the first year of a new century...helped Roosevelt convey a symbolic sense of change and vitality."

Roosevelt had a lifelong love affair with power, and he made no effort to disguise it. "I like to have my hand on the lever," he acknowledged. Years later, he said, "I do not believe that any President has ever had as thoroughly good a time as I have had, or has ever enjoyed himself so much." To his friend Henry Cabot Lodge, he confided, "It is a dreadful thing to come into the Presidency this way; but it would be a far worse thing to be morbid about it." Not long after taking over, he wrote one of his sons, "I am of course in a perfect whirl of work and have every kind of worry and trouble—but that's what I am here for and down at bottom I enjoy it after all."

In the three-ring performance he carried on day after day, he has been likened to the circus impresario P. T. Barnum. "No other President of the United States," said one observer, "ever put on such a corking good show." The first president to be identified by his initials, TR was also the first to go down in a submarine. "Every day or two," reported a Detroit newspaper, "he rattles the dry bones of precedent and causes Senators and heads of departments to look over their spectacles in consternation." The historian Dixon Wecter later wrote, "He established a family tradition: that under a Roosevelt administration...ennui is banished from public affairs." For politics, "he became what Buffalo Bill had been to the big top," Wecter added. "Do you know the two most wonderful things I have seen in your country?" asked a British visitor, Lord Morley. "Niagara Falls and the president of the United States...both great wonders of nature."

Before, during, and after his assumption of the presidency, Roosevelt expounded his belief in lifelong commitment to ceaseless activity. "I wish to preach, not the doctrine of ignoble ease, but the doctrine of the strenuous life," he had said in 1899. "Far better it is to dare mighty things, to win glorious triumphs, even though checkered by failure, than to rank with those poor spirits who neither enjoy much nor suffer much, because they live in that grey twilight that knows neither victory nor defeat." More than a decade later, in an address at the Sorbonne, he elaborated this message:

It is not the critic who counts, not the man who points out how the strong man stumbled, or where the doer of deeds could have done better. The credit belongs to the man who is actually in the arena; whose face is marred by the dust and sweat and blood; who strives valiantly; who errs and comes short again and again, because there is no effort without error or shortcoming; who knows the great enthusiasms, the great devotions and spends himself in a worthy cause; who, at the best, knows in the end the triumph of high achievement, and who, at worst, if he fails, at least fails while daring greatly.

One could not hope to find a more zealous exemplar of this creed than Roosevelt himself. In the West, he had nabbed armed robbers, hunted cougars, and punched out a drunken bully in a barroom brawl. He expected no less of others. "I am father of three boys, and if I thought any one of them would weigh a possible broken bone against the glory of being chosen to play on Harvard's football team, I would disinherit him," he said. Disturbed by the girth of army officers, he ordered them to prove their mettle by riding ninety miles in three days. When they complained that the demand was unreasonable, he mounted a horse before dawn and rode the distance in a single day—"the last fifteen miles," he reported to one of his sons, "in pitch darkness and with a blizzard of sleet blowing in our faces." He got back to the White House that night "all covered with ice." Keenly aware of the McKinley assassination, he carried a pistol. There was no way to prevent a man from trying to take his life, the president said, "but such a man must be quicker than I am in the use of his gun."

Nor did he allow assumptions about propriety or concern about physical comfort to slow him down. Although he claimed in his first year in office, "I do but little boxing because it seems rather absurd for a President to appear with a black eye or a swollen nose or a cut lip," he did, in fact, engage in slugging exchanges with the likes of John L. Sullivan. But when a blow blinded him in one eye, he later noted, "I thought it better to acknowledge that I had become an elderly man and would have to stop boxing. I then took up jiu-jitsu." He further reported on his first year: "Four times I have broken bones in falls with horses." He also set up broadsword contests with Brigadier General Leonard Wood. Adorned in helmets, breastplate, and gauntlets, they flailed away at one another's heads with stout sticks, leaving both of them painfully bruised. An apostle of the great outdoors, he spent three days in the solitude of Yosemite with the famed naturalist John Muir and was delighted when, as they lay in the open one night, four inches of snow fell on them.

"You must always remember," said his friend the British envoy Cecil Spring-Rice, "that the President is about six." Those close to him agreed. Gifford Pinchot first encountered Roosevelt in 1899 when he arrived in Albany for an overnight visit "just as the Executive Mansion was under ferocious attack from a band of invisible Indians, and the Governor of the Empire State was helping a houseful of children to escape by lowering them out of the second-story window on a rope." The forester then engaged in a boxing bout with Roosevelt and proved his worth by knocking the governor down. Only then did they sit down to discuss the woodlands. When president, Roosevelt himself recounted, "I play bear with the children almost every night, and some child is invariably fearfully damaged in the play; but this does not seem to affect the ardor

Theodore Roosevelt and the conservationist John Muir, whom he so much admired, together survey the Yosemite Valley from Glacier Point in 1903. *Library of Congress, LC-USZ62-8672*

of their enjoyment." In a congratulatory message to Roosevelt when the president turned forty-six, Secretary of War Elihu Root told him, "You have made a very good start in life, and your friends have great hopes for you when you grow up."

He matched this hyperkinetic activity with an insatiable lust for intellectual stimulus. In the course of his life, he wrote thirty-eight books—and 150,000 letters. At bedtime, he read works on paleontology, and on a battleship en route to Panama, he relieved the monotony of the long voyage by perusing Tacitus. He extended one jocular invitation to dinner by writing, "We could discuss the Hittite empire, the Pithecanthropus and Magyar love songs, and the exact relations of the Atli of the *Volsunga Saga* to the Etzel of the *Nibelungenlied*, and of both to Attila." As a journalist later noted, Roosevelt "read Dante in Renaissance Italian, could rattle off long passages in French from the *Chanson de Roland*, made a special study of Rumanian literature, and, while President of the United States, was also honorary president of the Gaelic Literature Association."

The White House in these years approached being a salon, in part because Roosevelt made it more glamorous. Though the term "the White House" had been in vogue for a long while, the president decreed that henceforth the executive mansion would have that designation officially. Under the influence of Edith Wharton, he hired her cousin Charles Follen McKim, of the prestigious architectural firm McKim, Mead & White, to refurbish the edifice. The White House acquired an expanded "West Wing," a term that became synonymous with the functioning of the chief executive, and, in a Beaux-Arts style, McKim gave the East Room and State Dining Room a new elegance with parquet floors and painted panels.

To this more stylish White House and to other Washington venues writers and artists instinctively gravitated, with the president—an extraordinary conversationalist—their magnet. On one occasion Paderewski performed on a new Steinway, and on another Henry James, Augustus Saint-Gaudens, Henry Adams, and John La Farge came to lunch. A member of Franklin Roosevelt's Brain Trust later wrote of TR's "regaling a group of his friends with judgments on Goya, Flaubert, Dickens, and Jung, and discussions of Louis the Fat or the number of men at arms seasick in the fleet of Medina Sidonia." One writer said: "His personality so crowds the room that the walls are worn thin and threaten to burst outwards. You go to the White House, you shake hands with Roosevelt and hear him talk—and then go home to wring the personality out of your clothes." Rudyard Kipling made a point of stopping by at Washington's Cosmos Club, where, curled up in a chair, he listened with fascination to Roosevelt deliver nonstop his opinions on a range of topics from politics to literature "until the universe seemed to be spinning round and Theodore was the spinner."

Roosevelt did not compartmentalize his cultural pursuits and his political obligations but saw them as a seamless web. Moved to strike back at his critics in the Senate, he likened them to characters in Dickens's *Martin Chuzzlewit*, and he found a niche in the US Treasury for the poet Edwin Arlington Robinson. Rarely did a week go by without a pronouncement on some topic far removed from the political realm. When in his novel *White Fang* Jack London depicted a lynx killing a wolf, Roosevelt denounced him as a "nature faker" ignorant of the ways of animals. Above all, he regarded the White House as a "bully pulpit" from which he could deliver sermons to the citizenry, his parishioners.

"Pulpit" was an inspired term, for Roosevelt saw a moral dimension to every political issue. "Theodore," said Speaker Tom Reed, "if there is one thing more than another for which I admire you, it is your original discovery of the Ten Commandments." The Mexican insurgent Pancho Villa met with his disapproval because he was a "murderer and a bigamist." The president favored a "very heavy tax on the celibate and the childless" and said that the refusal of a wife to bear children "merits contempt as hearty as any visited upon the soldier who runs away in battle." Instead of evaluating the consolidation of corporate power by measuring its impact on the market, he distinguished between "good" and "bad" trusts. On completing his final term, he told a writer before sailing to Africa, "Well, I'm through now. I've done my work. People are going to discuss economic questions more and more: the tariff, currency, banks. They are hard questions, and I am not deeply interested in them; my problems are moral problems, and my teaching has been plain morality." John Hay noted in his diary: "Knox says that the question of what is to become of Roosevelt after 1908 is easily answered. He should be made a bishop."

Not without reason, Roosevelt assumed that his pronouncements would be accorded the respect due a man so broadly experienced, so widely read, but the historian Richard Hofstadter later hit the mark when he called TR "a muscular...Polonius." In no respect was Roosevelt's "tissue of philistine conventionalities" more evident than in his judgments on writers. Tolstoy, though no doubt talented, he said, was "a man of diseased moral nature, a man in whose person the devotee and debauchee alternately obtain sway." *The Kreutzer Sonata*, he maintained, was a "filthy and repulsive book." He was greatly relieved when Anna Karenina took her life because, given her wicked behavior, suicide was the only ethically appropriate course. He condemned Émile Zola for dwelling on "the lascivious, the beast side" of mankind and for describing "the unspeakable." Chaucer was "altogether needlessly filthy." When Maxim Gorky came to America with a woman to whom he was not married, the president refused to receive him.

Even those who deplored his priggish outlook, though, could not escape his presence. "He is," said Henry James, "the very embodiment of noise." His frenzied activism and his persistent moralizing led one observer to call him "an interesting combination of St. Vitus and St. Paul." The president, with his oversized ego, seized upon every opportunity for self-promotion. (In writing one of his books, Roosevelt, it was said, used "I" so many times that the publisher had to send a rush order to a foundry for more of that letter.) He made sure that he was front-page news by manipulating reporters through ploys such as releasing trial balloons and off-the-record revelations, and while his barber was lathering his face and sharpening his razor, he chatted garrulously with a half-dozen favored correspondents.

As tales of his antics and adventures circulated, Roosevelt became the first president to be treated as a media personality, so that Americans came to think it natural to follow in minute detail the exploits and most vagrant thoughts of their leader. His flashing teeth, pince-nez, bushy mustache, and frenetic gestures proved irresistible to caricaturists, and newspaper accounts about the president of the United States romping with his young sons, "the White House Gang," or about "Princess Alice," his flighty strong-willed daughter, and her lovesick suitors captivated the country. (Asked if he could not make his daughter toe the line, he replied, "I can be President of the United States, or I can control Alice. I cannot possibly do both.") One particular report—of a hunting expedition in Mississippi where Teddy Roosevelt refused to shoot a bear that guides had tied to a tree—epitomized the country's romance with him. By the time the story had made the rounds, the bear had become a cub whose life the president had spared, and children all over America knew exactly what they hoped to find under the tree on Christmas morning: a "Teddy bear."

On reading the opening passages of Roosevelt's first annual message to Congress in December 1901, the financial world breathed a sigh of relief. "The captains of industry who have driven the railway systems across this continent, who have built up our commerce, who have developed our manufactures, have on the whole done great good to our people," he declared. "The mechanism of modern business is so delicate that extreme

care must be taken not to interfere with it in a spirit of rashness or ignorance." These words, said a New York newspaper, expecting the truculence of a feisty young ex–Rough Rider, appeared to have come from "a
man of sixty, trained in conservative habits." But Roosevelt went on to
say, "It should be as much the aim of those who seek for social betterment to rid the business world of crimes of cunning as to rid the entire
body politic of crimes of violence."

The president's tergiversation opened him to gentle ribbing from the
humorist Finley Peter Dunne. Speaking in an Irish brogue, Dunne's Mr.
Dooley summed up the president's remarks: "The trusts . . . are heejous
monsthers built up be the enlightened interprise iv th' men that have
done so much to advance progress in our beloved country. . . . On won
hand I wud stamp them undher fut; on the other hand not so fast." Still,
as H. W. Brands has written, "Whatever readers made of the portents of
Roosevelt's message, there was no mistaking the tone. This wasn't McKinley
speaking; this was someone new, someone self-confidently assertive,
someone with a far grander sense of the public purpose than anyone
who had every held the presidency."

Roosevelt, indeed, conveyed the impression that he intended to reign
over a new political order. Like a chanticleer proclaiming the dawn, he
asserted: "When the Constitution was adopted, at the end of the eighteenth century, no human wisdom could foretell the sweeping changes . . .
which were to take place by the beginning of the twentieth century. At
that time it was accepted as a matter of course that the several States
were the proper authorities to regulate . . . the comparatively insignifi-
cant and strictly localized corporate bodies of the day. The conditions
are now wholly different and wholly different action is called for."

In 1902, Roosevelt shocked Wall Street by his response to a gargantuan merger. With J. P. Morgan as underwriter, James J. Hill, E. H.
Harriman, and other titans had combined the Burlington, the Great
Northern, and the Northern Pacific railroads into a system carrying
passengers and freight over thirty-two thousand miles of track and, on
Hill's ships, all the way to China. Save for U.S. Steel, this Northern Securities
Company was the largest amalgamation in the world. In creating the monster corporation, Morgan and his confederates were thumbing their
noses at the US government and supposed, with good reason, that they
could get away with it. No president had tried seriously to enforce

the Sherman Antitrust Act of 1890, especially after the Supreme Court, in its *E. C. Knight* ruling, had drained it of almost all meaning. Not once had the Department of Justice, from Harrison to McKinley, brought an action against a corporation for violation of the Sherman law. Furthermore, no one supposed in 1902 that any president, let alone a man who had chanced into office only five months before, would have the temerity to challenge J. P. Morgan. So empyrean did Morgan seem to Wall Streeters that they called him Jupiter. "The boldest man was likely to become timid under his piercing gaze," said one observer. "The most impudent or recalcitrant were ground to humility as he chewed truculently at his huge black cigar."

But on February 18, 1902, on Roosevelt's orders, the attorney general stunned financiers by launching an antitrust suit against Northern Securities as a conspiracy in restraint of trade. The *Detroit Free Press* remarked sardonically, "Wall Street is paralyzed at the thought that a President of the United States would sink so low as to try to enforce the law." With that one act, Roosevelt showed that he was his own man, not McKinley's stand-in. After the suit was filed, Morgan said to the president, "Send your man to my man and they can fix it up." By "your man" he meant the attorney general of the United States. Roosevelt was no foe of consolidation, but he meant to curb this arrogance and establish for the first time that tycoons were not the equals, let alone the superiors, of elected officials.

In 1904, the Supreme Court sustained the government by ordering Northern Securities dissolved. Roosevelt was disappointed that one of the dissenters in the 5–4 ruling was his recent appointee, Oliver Wendell Holmes Jr. In a high dudgeon, the president fumed, "I could carve out of a banana a judge with more backbone than that." But he was gratified by the result. "It was necessary to reverse the Knight case in the interests of the people against monopoly and privilege just as it had been necessary to reverse the Dred Scott case in the interest of the people against slavery," he said, and, during the 1904 campaign, Roosevelt claimed that the Northern Securities prosecution was "one of the great achievements of my administration," because "through it we emphasized...that the most powerful men in the country were held to accountability before the law." Not since Andrew Jackson had a president brought a gigantic financial agglomeration to heel. "If Roosevelt had never done anything else," the publisher Joseph Pulitzer wrote to one of the president's critics, "and if he had committed a hundred times more mistakes...he would be entitled to the greatest credit for the greatest service to the nation" because of this deed.

The demolition of Northern Securities gave Roosevelt the appellation of "trustbuster" that he has never lost, creating the mistaken impression that he was the sworn enemy of business consolidation. In his State of the Union address in December 1902, however, he declared: "Our aim is not to do away with corporations; on the contrary, these big aggregations are an inevitable development of modern industrialism, and the effort to destroy them would be futile unless accomplished in ways that would work the utmost mischief to the entire body politic." Solicitous for the American empire, he urged particular care "not to abandon the place which our country has won in the leadership of the international industrial world." When he subsequently articulated his views most fully, he scoffed at those who had been engaged in the "hopeless effort" of "restoring the country to the economic conditions of the middle of the nineteenth century." Though "they regarded themselves as radical progressives," he said, they actually were advocating a kind of "rural toryism," comparable to resorting to "the flintlocks of Washington's Continentals."

Big Business, though, found little solace in these statements. Despite his rhetoric, he followed up the Northern Securities suit with forty-four additional prosecutions, including actions against Standard Oil, the Beef Trust, the Sugar Trust, DuPont, and the New Haven Railroad. More important, Roosevelt always accompanied remarks about the inevitability of the concentration of economic power with insistence on the necessity of government regulation, a conviction that would be at the core of the doctrine of the New Nationalism he later espoused. In the same sentence in which he scoffed at "relying upon the foolish anti-trust law," he advocated "federal control over all combinations engaged in interstate commerce." In 1903, he declared: "The immediate necessity in dealing with trusts is to place them under the real, not nominal, control of some sovereign.... In my judgment this sovereign must be the national government." Subsequently, one of his most acerbic critics, the Democratic *New York World*, said that Roosevelt's largest achievement was proving that "the Government of the United States was more powerful than any aggregations of capital."

Roosevelt had created even greater consternation in corporate board-rooms that year by his reaction to a crippling strike. In May, led by John Mitchell of the United Mine Workers, well over a hundred thousand an-thracite miners walked out of the pits. Railroad operators, who owned most of the mines, refused to negotiate. They were confident they could break the union because if a critical coal shortage developed, the federal government could be counted on to bring in troops. As the deadlock continued—month in, month out, through spring and summer and into fall—with the price of anthracite (essential for heating homes) qua-drupling and coal bins emptying, the president became greatly troubled. Always anxious about the potential for social unrest, he feared that if the strike went on into winter, people would freeze and there could be con-vulsions in the cities. Yet his attorney general cautioned him that he had no legal right to intervene, and mine owners did not appear to be open to cajoling, certainly not by him. Roosevelt told Lodge: "Unfortunately, the strength of my public position . . . is also its weakness. I am genuinely independent of the big monied men in all matters where I think the interests of the public are concerned, and probably I am the first President of recent times of whom this can be truthfully said. . . . But where I do not grant any favors to these big monied men . . . , it is out of the ques-tion for me to expect them to grant favors to me."

Convinced that he could not stand idly by while a crisis developed, no matter what his advisers told him, Roosevelt decided on a bold move. On October 3, he summoned operators and union leaders to the White House. Conservative commentators were appalled, because never before had a president taken such an initiative. The *New York Journal of Commerce*, a voice of Wall Street, deplored "Mr. Roosevelt's seemingly uncontrol-lable penchant for impulsive self-intrusion." The operators were in-censed. They refused to acknowledge Mitchell's presence and demanded that the president "put an end to the anarchy in the coal fields"—even if it meant sending in soldiers as Cleveland had done. Mitchell was more reasonable. He proposed that Roosevelt appoint a commission to arbi-trate the dispute, adding: "If the gentlemen representing the operators will accept the award or decision of such a tribunal, the miners will will-ingly accept it, even if it be against our claims." The operators would not hear of such an arrangement. "Are you asking us to deal with a set of outlaws?" one of them inquired indignantly.

George Baer, who had been installed by J. P. Morgan as president of the Philadelphia and Reading Railroad, spoke for the owners. He revealed his mindset when, in a letter leaked to the press that outraged the country, he stated that "the rights and interests of the laboring man will be cared for, not by the labor union agitators, but by the Christian men to whom God, in his infinite wisdom, had given control of the property interests of the country." In addressing the president at the White House gathering, he was insulting. "The duty of the hour," he said, "is not to waste time negotiating with the fomenters of this anarchy." In fact, Baer lectured the president, he should not be dealing at all with these mutineers. Afterward, Roosevelt, distressed by the "wooden-headed obstinacy and stupidity" of men who were "utterly unable to see the black storm impending," said of Baer that "if it weren't for the high office I hold, I would have taken him by the seat of the breeches and the nape of the neck and chucked him out of that window."

Refusing to be frustrated by the mine owners, who would not accept his good faith effort at mediation, Roosevelt decided that more drastic measures were required. "I feel most strongly that the attitude of the operators is one which accentuates the need of the Government having some power of supervision . . . over such corporations," he said. "I would like to make a fairly radical experiment on the anthracite coal business to start with!" In keeping with this resolve, Roosevelt, in his capacity as commander in chief, called General J. M. Schofield to the White House and, saying that the country faced a situation akin to war, asked if the army could take over and run the mines. The general, instructed that he should pay "no heed to any authority, judicial or otherwise, except mine," told the president that he need only give the order.

That action galvanized the movers and shakers. After Secretary Root called on him in New York, J. P. Morgan brought pressure on the operators, who reluctantly agreed to arbitration but not to recognition of a union representative. They also specified the composition of the arbitration commission, including an "eminent sociologist." Roosevelt outfoxed them by naming to the sociologist slot the head of a railroad union. The miners returned peacefully to the pits, quieting alarm about a prospective fuel shortfall, and the commissioners heard testimony. In his closing argument, Baer said of the miners: "These men don't suffer. Why, hell, half of them don't even speak English." When the commission reported, it approved a pay hike and a shorter work day; though the union was denied outright recognition, it got something approximating it. And in the next inaugural parade, miners, wearing lamps on their caps, marched by the president's stand with the banner "We Honor the Man Who Settled Our Strike."

Roosevelt feared that by intervening he had set an "evil precedent," but, in fact, he prepared the way for future presidents to assert a right to intercede when a domestic conflict endangered the national interest. After the crisis dissipated, he said, "It was essential that organized capital and organized labor should thoroughly understand that the third party, the great public, had vital interests and overshadowing rights." By becoming the first chief executive to exert the power of the national government not to crush a strike but to bring about a fair outcome, Roosevelt added a new dimension to the presidency.

In 1903, overcoming fierce conservative opposition, he established a Department of Commerce and Labor that housed a Bureau of Corporations charged with investigating and exposing business malfeasance. His proposal for this bureau aroused such strident objections from stand-pat senators in his own party that it was doubtful that the measure would ever reach the floor. But at a time when it appeared to be doomed, Roosevelt announced to the press that John D. Rockefeller was masterminding the resistance. To substantiate his charge, he read out the language of what he said were Rockefeller's messages. He was fabricating. He had never seen any document, and he invented the words. But a Standard Oil official had turned out something like it, and Roosevelt created such a public outcry that Congress had no choice but to enact the law.

During his first days as president, Roosevelt shook up the Establishment in a different way by inviting the country's most highly regarded African American, Booker T. Washington, to dine at the White House. Born into slavery, Washington, who, against enormous odds, had worked his way up from menial labor in salt furnaces and coal mines to head the all-black Tuskegee Institute in Alabama, was a man of distinction. But when the white South learned of the dinner, it erupted in fury—a Memphis paper calling the event "the most damnable outrage ever perpetrated by any citizen of the United States." A US senator from South Carolina said, "The action of President Roosevelt in entertaining that nigger will necessitate our killing a thousand niggers in the South before they will learn their place again." Noting that Washington was seated at a table with the president's wife and teenaged daughter, a Richmond paper charged Roosevelt with recommending "that negroes shall mingle freely with whites in the social circle—that white women may receive attentions from negro men," and an editorialist asserted that "no Southern woman with proper self-respect would now accept an invitation to the White House." Congressman Tom Heflin of Alabama exceeded all bounds by saying that "if some Czolgosz had thrown a bomb under the table" at which Washington and the first family sat, "no great harm would have been done the country."

The most eloquent rebuttal came from an unexpected source—a large-circulation Democratic daily in New York City that usually was gratified by the commitment of the Solid South to the party. The *World* commented: "An American named Washington, one of the most eloquent, most brilliant men of the day—the President of a college—is asked to dinner by President Roosevelt. And because the pigment of his skin is some shades darker than that of others a large part of the United States is convulsed with shame and rage....Truly Liberty must smile at such broadminded logic, such enlightened tolerance. Or should she weep?"

In marked contrast to all of his predecessors since John Quincy Adams three-quarters of a century before, Theodore Roosevelt had a Hegelian conception of the primacy of the state. Like Bismarck, he conjoined imperialism with socioeconomic initiatives; like the German autocrat, too, he believed that both capital and labor should behave dutifully toward the government. A member of the Knickerbocker elite limned by Edith Wharton, the president, who had been born in a four-story Manhattan town house, nurtured a patrician's resentment of nouveau-riche interlopers. "A thousand rich bankers," he said, "cannot leave such a heritage as [Admiral] Farragut left." To define a national interest distinct from the parochial objectives of any faction, he counted on two groups: patricians like himself with a different perspective from that of the financiers, and the new class of professional bureaucrats—men such as Gifford Pinchot and James R. Garfield (the slain president's son)—who, it was supposed, acted disinterestedly, running with neither the hares nor the hounds.

Roosevelt sought to employ government as a mediating force among all elements in society. He had, he once said, a Greek horror of extremes. He saw two agents of jeopardy for the country: the mob, which could be whipped up by demagogues to overthrow cherished institutions, and the arriviste plutocracy, which, by its excessive greed, incited the mob. In explaining his goal of a "Square Deal," he declared, "We do not intend that this Republic shall ever fail as those republics of olden times failed," with "the poor plundering the rich or . . . the rich . . . exploiting the poor." He would regret, he stated, "failing on the one hand to make the very wealthiest and most powerful men in the country obey the law and handle their property . . . in the public interest; or, on the other hand . . . fail[ing] to make the laboring men in their turn obey the law, and realize that envy is as evil a thing as arrogance, and that crimes of violence and riot shall be as sternly punished as crimes of greed and cunning."

Though often classified as a progressive, Roosevelt held reformers in contempt and cast out radicals as lepers. "Sentimental humanitarians," he wrote in his biography of Senator Thomas Hart Benton, "always form a most pernicious body, with an influence for bad hardly surpassed by that of the professional criminal class," and in *Gouverneur Morris*, he dismissed Tom Paine as a "filthy little atheist." An anarchist, he maintained, was "in no shape or way a 'product of social conditions,'" for anarchism was "no more an expression of 'social discontent' than picking pockets or wife-beating." One of his best-known utterances came in the spring of 1906 when, borrowing from John Bunyan's image in *Pilgrim's Progress*, he said of magazine writers who were exposing corruption in business and government: "Men with the muckrake are often indispensable to the well-being of society, but only if they know when to stop raking the muck, and to look upward to the celestial crown above them." (Writers swiftly converted "muckraker," a term of opprobrium, into a badge of honor.)

Roosevelt expressed no less revulsion at "men of wealth" who were "careless . . . of the State, whose existence they imperil." The lives of millionaires, he said, frequently "vary from rotten frivolity to rotten vice." As a New York legislator, he had accused the financier Jay Gould of being a member "of that most dangerous of all dangerous classes, the wealthy criminal class," and as president he deplored "the damage done to our country by . . . swollen and monstrous fortunes" and railed against "the dull, purblind folly of the very rich men." In the summer of 1907, he charged that "certain malefactors of great wealth" were trying to create a panic in order to undo his regulatory policies "so that they may enjoy unmolested the fruits of their own evil-doing," and after leaving office, he disparaged plutocrats whose values "are merely those of so many glorified pawnbrokers."

He conceived of the president as the expounder and enforcer of a new morality in the commercial world. In the autumn of 1907, when he was being instructed to tone down his rhetoric in order to bolster the confidence of investors, he declared, "I regard this contest as one to determine who shall rule this free country—the people through their governmental agents, or a few ruthless and domineering men whose wealth makes them peculiarly formidable because they hide behind the breast works of corporate organization." At the same time that he reviled crusading journalists as muckrakers, he called for an inheritance tax and federal supervision of corporation stock issues, and he concluded a keynote address to a national conference on conservation by saying, "In the past we have admitted the right of the individual to injure the future of the Republic for his own present profit. The time has come for a change."

Called "America's only Nietzschean president," Roosevelt had said before entering the White House, "If this country could be ruled by a benevolent czar, we would doubtless make a good many changes for the better." He had no patience with "idiotic jealousy of the Executive." In his historical writings, he identified with the strong-willed Alexander Hamilton, who venerated the British monarchy, and scorned the Jeffersonians, who sought to fetter federal officials. As his tenure was drawing to a close, he wrote the British historian George Otto Trevelyan: "While President, I have *been* President, emphatically; I have used every ounce of power there was in the office and I have not cared a rap for the criticisms of those who spoke of my 'usurpation of power.' . . . The efficiency of this Government depends upon possessing a strong central executive, and wherever I could establish a precedent for strength in the executive, I did." On leaving office, he boasted of how many admirable deeds were "done by me without the assistance of Congress" over a course of more than seven years. "Roosevelt's all right," said the conservative Speaker of the House, "Uncle Joe" Cannon, "but he's got no more use for the Constitution than a tomcat has for a marriage license."

———

No one has ever entered the White House who loved war half so much as did Theodore Roosevelt. He was, in the words of the historian Thomas Bailey, a man of "almost pathological bellicosity." In 1904, the president declared:

> The amiable peace at any price people who in our country have been prancing about . . . are . . . men weak in body or mind, men who could not be soldiers because they lack physical hardihood or courage. There are undoubtedly large sections of the population who would become utterly appalled by slaughter in the field. In the Spanish war, our generals had to grapple with a public sentiment which screamed with anguish over the loss of a couple of thousand men, a sentiment of preposterous and unreasoning mawkishness.

Yet Roosevelt was the first governmental leader to hand the Hague Tribunal a case to adjudicate, and while he was president, not a single soldier or sailor lost his life because of one of his initiatives.

At the outset, however, TR greatly favored the warrior mode. "The America that Roosevelt dreamed of was always a sort of swollen Prussia," said H. L. Mencken. "There was always a clank of saber in his discourse; he could not discuss the tamest matter without swaggering in the best dragoon fashion." Before taking office, Roosevelt had welcomed "a new century big with the fate of mighty nations," adding: "Is America a weakling to shrink from the world work of the great world-powers? No. The young giant of the West stands on a continent and clasps the crest of an ocean in either hand." An unapologetic imperialist, he called opponents of the acquisition of an American empire "simply unhung traitors," and he admired superpowers that exercised their will over the "weak and craven." He once said, "I have always been fond of the West African proverb 'Speak softly and carry a big stick,'" and, though he rarely spoke softly, "big stick" aptly encapsulated his initial approach.

In 1903, Roosevelt elbowed aside both Germany and Great Britain. The Kaiser, exasperated by Venezuela's refusal even to acknowledge an obligation to pay its debts, had decided on a show of force. The president despised Venezuela's dictator, an "unspeakable villainous little monkey," but he bridled when the Germans imposed a blockade and bombarded coastal towns. In response, he mobilized the fleet under Admiral Dewey and issued a stern warning that an invasion would mean war with the United States. Confronted by this ultimatum, the Kaiser backed down. That same year, Roosevelt dealt forcefully with a boundary dispute between Alaska and British Columbia inflamed by the discovery of gold in the Klondike. At a time when Canadian foreign policy was determined in London, Secretary of State Hay counseled him to give priority to the need for Anglo-American amity, but the president sent in hundreds of troops. (Eventually, Roosevelt agreed to arbitration by a trinational commission, which handed down a verdict largely favorable to the United States, and he accepted the findings, though they required concessions from America too.)

Roosevelt might well have disclaimed responsibility for the conduct of US forces in putting down the Filipino revolt against American occupation, since he had inherited the operation from McKinley, but, instead, he embraced it. He rejected reports of atrocities committed by American soldiers (Mark Twain called the men "uniformed assassins") as "utterly baseless slanders." When US troops slaughtered Muslim Moros—including hundreds of women and children—inside a crater, he congratulated Major General Leonard Wood for this "brilliant feat of arms," then promoted him.

Determined to dig a canal across Central America to link the Atlantic Ocean with the Pacific, Roosevelt in January 1903 authorized Hay to offer Colombia $10 million and annual payments for a strip of land on the isthmus of its northern province, Panama, and to pay a French company $40 million for its rights to the route. The Senate quickly ratified this Hay-Herrán treaty, but the Colombian Senate, controlled by a dictator, rejected the settlement as too parsimonious. The Colombians had every right to ask for a portion of the large sum earmarked for the French, but Roosevelt, in a fury, lashed out at this "pithecoid community" of "Dagos" and "homicidal corruptionists" who were trying to "blackmail" him. "I do not think that the Bogota lot of jack rabbits should be allowed permanently to bar one of the future highways of civilization," he said. Consequently, he drafted a message proposing to Congress that the United States seize the isthmus and dredge the canal "without any further parley with Colombia."

That recommendation became moot when in November Panamanian nationalists revolted and declared that they were seceding from Colombia. The rebellion, financed by an agent for the French company and a self-interested Manhattan lawyer, was undertaken in the knowledge that Roosevelt would welcome it. On the evening before the insurrection, the USS *Nashville* had arrived in Colón, with orders from the president—in violation of long-standing treaty obligations to Colombia— "to prevent the landing of any armed force, either Government or insurgent." Despite the neutral wording, the United States was forestalling a legitimate government from holding on to a breakaway province. With unseemly haste, Roosevelt recognized the new Republic of Panama and then negotiated a treaty, not with the new government but with the French agent, giving the United States a canal zone much wider than in the original treaty. Tearfully, Panamanians submitted because they had no other option.

Roosevelt ran into a storm of criticism for his high-handed behavior, but he brazened it out. A Chicago newspaper accused him of "a rough-riding assault upon another republic over the shattered wreckage of international law," and, in TR's words, "a goodly number of the Senators even of my own party have shown about as much backbone as so many angleworms." Critics pointed out that he could have avoided this unsavory denouement by paying Colombia a reasonable sum but that he was too vainglorious to do so. Brushing aside faultfinders, Roosevelt found gratification in sailing to Panama, where, as photographers clicked their shutters, he worked the levers of a gigantic steam shovel excavating the big ditch—thereby ending the custom that a president of the United States never goes beyond its continental borders. To the end of his days, he regarded the Panama Canal as his greatest achievement. At the close of his presidency, he said of its construction: "I do not think any feat of quite such far-reaching importance had been to the credit of our country in recent years, and this I can say absolutely was my own work, and could not have been accomplished save by me or by some man of my temperament."

Still, the challenge to the legitimacy of Roosevelt's conduct remained a running sore. At a cabinet meeting after the treaty had been ratified, Roosevelt called on Attorney General Philander Knox to expatiate on the justification for his actions. "If I were you," Knox responded, "I would not let so great an achievement suffer from any taint of legality." Never able to accept even gentle wit at his expense, Roosevelt persisted: "Have I answered the charges? Have I defended myself?" Secretary Root answered, "You certainly have, Mister President. You have shown that you were accused of seduction and you have conclusively proved that you were guilty of rape."

In his autobiography, Roosevelt showed not a trace of remorse. "From the beginning to the end," he claimed, "our course was straight-forward and in absolute accord with the highest standard of international morality." But in an indiscreet address at Berkeley in 1911, he declared: "I am interested in the Panama Canal because I started it. If I had followed traditional conservative methods I would have submitted a dignified state paper of probably two-hundred pages to the Congress and the debate would be going on yet, but I took the Canal Zone and let the Congress debate, and while the debate goes on, the canal does also." In another passage in his memoir, he bragged, "I took the Isthmus, started the canal and then left Congress not to debate the canal, but to debate me."

At a time when jingoes were swelling with pride in the march of American empire under TR, the president's reputation for machismo got a fortuitous boost from a happening that had farcical aspects. In May 1904, Roosevelt learned that in Morocco, a bandit who called himself Raisuli had kidnapped a onetime resident of Trenton, New Jersey, Ion Perdicaris, and demanded from the sultan of Morocco a ransom and other concessions. Indignant at what he regarded as an affront to America, the president responded with a display of firepower and bluster more appropriate to a serious threat from a hostile foreign country. He sent seven warships and several companies of marines to the North African coast to coerce the sultan into paying the ransom and pursuing Raisuli. In the midst of these overheated efforts, the president received unsettling information: Perdicaris was not an American citizen. Still worse, Perdicaris had, long before, gotten rid of his US passport in favor of one from the Greek government. Embarrassed, Roosevelt insisted on pushing ahead on his absurd course until Hay came to his rescue with an ingenious bit of flummery. The secretary of state drafted a message addressed to the US consul in Morocco but actually intended for the ears of delegates at the 1904 Republican National Convention, to whom it would be read aloud: "We want Perdicaris alive or Raisuli dead." Overjoyed by this evidence of American gumption and delighted by the catchy phrase, which they attributed to TR, the delegates nominated the president for a new term by acclamation. That action marked the first time that a man who had entered the White House on the death of a president had been nominated for a new term by his party.

Roosevelt entered the 1904 campaign with two great assets: a weak opponent and a bagful of cash. Having lost twice in a row with William Jennings Bryan at the head of the ticket, the Democrats turned to a colorless New York judge, while industrialists poured millions into Republican coffers. (Afterwards, one of them, Henry Clay Frick, complained, "We bought the son of a bitch and then he did not stay bought.") Under these circumstances, the outcome was hardly surprising, but the

The World's Constable. With his first term drawing to an end, President Roosevelt is shown wielding a truncheon as he stands astride four continents while everyone from dark-skinned peasants to John Bull seeks his favor. *Library of Congress, LC-DIG-ds-05213*

extent of the triumph was. Sweeping every state outside the former Confederacy, Roosevelt, with a stunning 56.5 percent of the popular vote, gained the greatest margin ever received by a Republican presidential candidate. All through the capital on inaugural week, Washington could hear the pulsing beat of "There'll Be a Hot Time in the Old Town Tonight." The tune was prophetic. On March 3, 1905, his final day as McKinley's legatee, TR said: "Tomorrow I shall come into my office in my own right. Then watch out for me."

As the inaugural parade passed by the reviewing stand on Pennsylvania Avenue in March 1905, the historian Paul Boller Jr. has written, TR "grinned, smiled, laughed, nodded, waved his hat, clapped his hands, stamped his feet, swayed to the rhythm of the band music, and at times almost danced." He enjoyed the Sousa marches and the ragtime, still more the military pageantry. Spying a black cavalry regiment, he exclaimed, "Ah, they were with me at Santiago!" When a Puerto Rican battalion approached, he guyed a prominent antiexpansionist, "They look pretty well for an oppressed people, eh Senator?" Best of all was the sight of his old buddies from the Badlands, mounted on broncos and waving their slouch hats. At the end, Roosevelt cried, "It was a great success. Bully. And did you note that bunch of cowboys? Oh, they are the boys who can ride! It was all superb. It really touched me to the heart."

Buoyed by this rousing start to the new term, Roosevelt set out to chalk up legislative victories that had eluded him in the past—a course that frequently embroiled him in disputes with conservative Republican legislators and with financial titans. In particular, he aimed to discipline the marketplace. In December 1905, in the first message to Congress of his second term, Roosevelt said that the time had arrived "to assert the sovereignty of the National Government" over corporations. He followed up that provocative statement with a number of demands that, as the historian George Mowry later wrote, were "calculated to curl the hair of industrialists." Wall Street was shocked to hear that he wanted the books of railroad companies open to inspection by the government, insisted on controlling the rates railroads charged, sought to intervene in labor disputes, and advocated regulating insurance firms.

He achieved some of these goals in 1906, notably by overcoming fierce resistance to expanding the Interstate Commerce Commission's authority over railroad rates. When the Republican Old Guard balked, he collaborated with a Democrat, "Pitchfork Ben" Tillman, though he had once likened the South Carolina demagogue to Robespierre and Marat. He also hurled speech after speech against the opposition until one railway executive acknowledged that the president had so "roused the people that it was impossible for the Senate to stand against the popular demand." The Hepburn Act did not accomplish all that progressives had hoped for, but it nonetheless constituted, as Mowry observed, "a landmark in the evolution of federal control of private industry."

That same year, Roosevelt grappled with the meat packers and their allies on Capitol Hill. Appalled by passages in Upton Sinclair's *The Jungle* exposing vile practices in the slaughterhouses, he ordered a thoroughgoing investigation that resulted in a hard-hitting report. When Congress diddled, the president informed the chair of the key congressional committee that he would not publicize the findings, though they revealed "hideous" conditions, if he got the legislation he demanded. When Congress still balked, he released part of the report, sparking further indignation at the arrogance of the Beef Trust. After he intimated that he was prepared to release the rest of the report, which would have been devastating, his opponents, aware both of the public clamor and declining meat sales, agreed to negotiate. The resulting Meat Inspection Act of 1906 established federal regulation of the industry for the first time. On that same day, Roosevelt signed into law another consumer protection measure: the Pure Food and Drug Act, which struck a blow at the notorious patent medicine industry by banning adulteration and fraudulent labeling. Unimpressive by latter-day standards, these two measures created a precedent for more significant federal intervention throughout the twentieth century.

During the rest of his tenure, Roosevelt gravitated perceptibly to the left while Congress moved relentlessly to the right. In his message of December 1906, the president advocated government control of corporations, with federal regulators empowered to scrutinize their ledgers, and a year later he came out for inheritance and income taxes, workmen's compensation, and limits on labor injunctions. He followed up with a special message to Congress in January 1908 denouncing "the abuses of the criminal rich." Impugning executives of Standard Oil and the Santa Fe Railroad by name, he said, "Every measure for honesty in business that has been passed during the last six years has been opposed by these men . . . with every resource that bitter and unscrupulous craft could suggest and the command of almost unlimited money secure."

In the most compelling segment of his communication, he railed against "opponents of a just employers' liability law" who cloaked themselves in the Constitution at a time when the courts were striking down protective legislation for labor on the specious grounds that these laws infringed upon a worker's liberty of contract. "It is hypocritical baseness to speak of a girl who works in a factory where the dangerous machinery is unprotected as having the 'right' freely to contract to expose herself to dangers to life and limb," he declared. "She has no alternative but to suffer want or else expose herself to such dangers. . . . It is a moral wrong that the whole burden of risk necessarily incidental to the business should be placed with crushing weight on her weak shoulders." Before his term ended, the president was moved to say: "If the spirit which lies behind these . . . decisions obtained in all the actions of the . . . courts, we should not only have a revolution, but it would be absolutely necessary to have a revolution because the condition of the worker would become intolerable."

When the Panic of 1907 convulsed financial markets, conservatives placed the blame on TR's intemperate rhetoric. "Mr. Roosevelt," said Mark Twain, "has done what he could to destroy the industries of the country, and they all stand now in a half-wrecked condition and waiting in an ague to see what he will do next." With no notion of how to right the economy and fearful of "a general industrial smashup," the president made concessions to the House of Morgan. But he assigned responsibility for the panic to "the speculative folly and the flagrant dishonesty of a few men of great wealth." Furthermore, charging that "the reactionaries wish to take advantage of the moment by having me announce that I will abandon my policies," he pledged that he would not permit "the big financial men" to "seize the occasion . . . to escape from all governmental control."

Roosevelt, however, met obdurate resistance in Congress. Capitol Hill had greeted his new term, the historian William Harbaugh pointed out, with "studied insolence," and it became even more antagonistic thereafter. Speaker Cannon spoke for the Old Guard in the House in saying, "That fellow at the other end of the Avenue wants everything from the birth of Christ to the death of the devil." The Senate was led by an even more powerful foe: supercilious multimillionaire Nelson Aldrich of Rhode Island. Father-in-law of John D. Rockefeller Jr., Aldrich was called "Morgan's floor leader in the Senate." The president was sickened by reports of armed men with bloodhounds hunting down black workers and Italian immigrants to force them into peonage in Florida, but he could not persuade Congress to end these horrors. Congress also scuttled Roosevelt's plans to make Washington a model city by denying him authority to tear down the noisome alley dwellings and create parks and playgrounds (as well as his request to set up a whipping post for wife beaters). Frustrated and at times in despair, Roosevelt wrote a friend that "there are several eminent statesmen at the other end of Pennsylvania Avenue whom I would gladly lend to the Russian government, if they care to expend them as bodyguards for Grand Dukes wherever there was a likelihood of dynamite bombs being exploded."

To light fires under congressmen by stoking public enthusiasm for his programs, Roosevelt set up commissions that would issue reports, and he called conferences of experts in a number of fields. He appointed panels to improve housing and public health, as well as the Keep Commission to enhance government efficiency, and, at a White House Conference on the Care of Dependent Children, he strongly advocated mothers' pensions. To further river valley development, he established an Inland Waterways Commission. In 1908, he became the first president to assemble the nation's governors for a meeting when he called them to Washington to a national conservation congress at which he delivered the keynote address.

Theodore Roosevelt recorded greater accomplishments in conservation than in any other field. In contrast to McKinley, who had refused to support an ambitious Democrat-sponsored bill to fund irrigation projects in the West, Roosevelt threw his weight behind it. Under this Newlands Act, which created the Bureau of Reclamation, thirty projects got under way during his presidency, including the Roosevelt Dam in Arizona. Guided by his appointee Gifford Pinchot, the Forest Service (founded in 1905) quadrupled the acreage of woodlands in the public domain in the short space of his second term. Roosevelt created more than twice as many national parks as had all his predecessors combined—including Crater Lake in Oregon and the Mesa Verde cliff dwellings in Colorado—and he took advantage of a law he got through in 1906 to save the tract of giant sequoias that John Muir had shown him in California. In all, he added an area bigger than Texas to the public domain.

Though he was an avid hunter, the mindless slaughter of birds and animals appalled him, and he was determined to bring it to an end. At a time when buffalo were nearing extinction, he collaborated with Pawnee Bill to move the breed in the Bronx Zoo to a National Bison Range in the West. He cared particularly about birds; studying them had been his favorite avocation since boyhood. While still an undergraduate, he had coauthored his first publication, *The Summer Birds of the Adirondacks, in Franklin County, N. Y.*, and in the White House he faithfully listed the warblers he spotted in Rock Creek Park. As TR's biographer David McCullough has pointed out, "The last letter he wrote, like the first that we know of, had to do with birds." When Congress showed no interest in preserving habitat, he acted on his own to create America's first bird refuge—at Pelican Island in Florida. Before he was done, he added fifty more. He explained: "To lose the chance to see frigate-birds soaring in circles above the storm, or a file of pelicans winging their way homeward across the crimson afterglow of the sunset, or...myriad terns flashing in the bright light of midday as they hover in a shifting maze above the beach—why, the loss is like the loss of a gallery of the masterpieces of the artists of old time."

To achieve his conservation objectives, the president had to overcome—or, more often, circumvent—hostility in Congress, especially from Western delegations. One congressman, after hearing Roosevelt say that forests had to be preserved for posterity, retorted, "What has posterity ever done for me?" Instead of asking Congress to expand his authority, which he knew it was unlikely to do, the president construed statutes imaginatively, and sometimes played fast and loose with them. He saved Inscription Rock in New Mexico and the Petrified Forest in Arizona under the Antiquities Act. After Congress refused to make Grand Canyon a national park, he brashly set aside eight hundred thousand acres as a "national monument." When in 1907 the Senate added a rider to an appropriations bill forbidding the creation of any new national forests in six western states, Roosevelt defied it. He could not veto the measure, because the funds were indispensable. So, hours before his authority expired and with the legislation on his desk awaiting his signature, the president, in cahoots with Pinchot, picked out choice woodland sites. He then issued a decree sequestering more than sixteen million acres in those six states before signing the bill into law. Infuriated by this high-handed establishment of "midnight reserves," Congress struck back. After the Country Life Commission, appointed by the president in 1908, issued a thoughtful report, Congress not only ignored it but would not even provide the money to have it printed. Nor would it come up with the small sum of $20,000 to let the Inland Waterways Commission go on with its work. Furthermore, it outlawed the practice of setting up commissions—a prohibition that Roosevelt promptly announced he would flout.

In his final year in the White House, when he excoriated the "purchased politician," relations with Congress turned ugly. The attitude of legislators, the president wrote his son, was "utterly to disregard me." He, in turn, viewed the hostilities on Pennsylvania Avenue as a "war to the knife." In response to a measure curbing the activities of the Secret Service, he asserted that "the chief argument in favor of the provision was that the Congressmen did not themselves wish to be investigated by Secret Service men," adding, "This amendment has been of benefit only...to the criminal class." By 213 to 35, the House of Representatives voted to reprimand him for disrespect to the legislative branch. During his last days as president, members of Congress slipped out of a room to avoid shaking hands with him.

Though the president's attitude toward congressional obstructionists was largely justifiable, it also revealed a willfulness that Roosevelt displayed much too often, sometimes nastily. When a government worker criticized his policies in the Philippines, he fired her for "insolent insubordination," and when postal employees joined clubs promoting the political ambitions of William Randolph Hearst, he insisted that they be discharged. He ordered the Secret Service to shadow a US senator and employed private investigators who, without sanction from Congress, tapped phones. If reporters wrote something unflattering, he called their publishers to have them reassigned or enrolled them in the Ananias Club, branding them with the name of a character in the Bible who was a liar. More discreditably, he banned Socialist papers from the mail and instructed the Justice Department to sue Joseph Pulitzer and the *New York World* for libel because of the allegation that financing of the Panama Canal had been corrupt. "Pulitzer is one of these creatures of the gutter of such unspeakable degradation that to him even eminence on a dunghill seems enviable," he said. As his attorney general had warned him it would, his suit foundered and reflected badly on him. He could also be unbelievably petty. When a story in the *Boston Herald* riled him, he ordered the Weather Bureau to deny the city of Boston news of approaching storms.

Roosevelt especially shamed himself and his country in his response to an incident in 1906 when a dozen or so black soldiers shot up the town of Brownsville, Texas, injuring several whites, one of them fatally, in retaliation for mistreatment. A Texas court found no one guilty, but because none of the troops in the three segregated companies would finger the culprits, the president summarily discharged all 160 "without honor" and "forever barred from reenlistment." Among the large number drummed out without a hearing were soldiers nearing retirement, expelled pensionless after years of service. Six of the men, including a hero of the Spanish-American War, had merited a Congressional Medal of Honor. "If the colored men elect to stand by criminals of their own race, they assuredly lay up for themselves the most dreadful day of reckoning," Roosevelt declared.

Criticism of his action whipped the president into a fury. When a Senate inquiry raised doubt about the accusations, Roosevelt, unwilling to admit he had been unjust, hired private detectives who manufactured evidence to satisfy him that he had done well. At a Gridiron Club dinner, where a Republican senator accused him of behaving badly in the Brownsville episode, Roosevelt came close to going berserk. Red-faced, squinty-eyed, talking through clenched teeth, he shouted, "Some of these men were bloody butchers; they ought to be hung!" Shaking his fist at the senator, he said that passing judgment on the soldiers "is my business and . . . not the business of Congress. . . . If they pass a resolution to reinstate these men, I will veto it; if they pass it over my veto, I will pay no attention to it. I welcome impeachment." If Roosevelt showed the value of a strong president who battled for the people, he also demonstrated the danger of unbridled executive power.

Roosevelt cut an even larger figure in foreign affairs during his second term. Toward infirm Latin American republics, he was a swashbuckler. But when he dealt with the envoys of major powers, he came across as a patient, painstaking diplomat who displayed a keen grasp of geopolitics and a sophisticated sensitivity to the nuances of multinational diplomacy. He had mellowed since first taking office. At one point in his second term, he even chided "those who would lightly undergo the chance of war in a spirit of mere frivolity, or mere truculence."

Major European powers showed how highly they regarded TR when they turned to him to resolve a dangerous conflict in a country remote from American interests that once again engaged his attention: Morocco. In March 1905, the Kaiser had precipitated the crisis by giving a belligerent speech in Tangier revealing his determination to enter the race to acquire African colonies. But when war with France threatened, he persuaded the American president to convene a summit meeting in Algeciras in 1906. Though Roosevelt did not attend, he took advantage of his easy access to the Kaiser and to the French ambassador at Washington—Jules Jusserand, his tennis partner—to bring it off.

The president assumed this role reluctantly, for it distracted him from a much more salient concern: safeguarding the approaches to the Panama Canal. As the consequence of a dispute that surfaced in his first term, he not only enunciated but also acted out the boldest claim ever advanced by a president to US domination of the Western Hemisphere. When Santo Domingo reneged on its debts to European creditors because it was bankrupt, rumors circulated that France and Italy were poised to intervene and that a German flotilla had set sail for the Caribbean. In 1904, fearful of being targeted by European powers, the head of the island nation invited the United States to establish a protectorate over his benighted country, though he did so only after some prodding.

Roosevelt moved warily in 1904, an election year, but he tipped his hand on his ultimate course when in May he asked Root to read an open letter from him at a banquet in New York:

If a nation shows that it knows how to act with reasonable efficiency and decency in social and political matters, if it keeps order and pays its obligations, it need fear no interference by the United States. Chronic wrongdoing, or an impotence which results in a general loosening of the ties of civilized society, may...ultimately require intervention by some civilized nation, and in the western hemisphere the adherence of the United States to the Monroe Doctrine may force the United States, however reluctantly, in flagrant cases of such wrongdoing or impotence, to the exercise of an international police power.

By attaching this "Roosevelt Corollary," the president converted the Monroe Doctrine from a warning to European powers against intervention in the Western Hemisphere into an announcement that the United States reserved to itself the right to intervene.

In February 1905, he signed a protocol with Santo Domingo placing its collectors of customs under an American supervisor, who was to dole out roughly half of revenues to the government and half to its overseas creditors. When the Senate, distressed by this involvement, refused to ratify the pact, the president went ahead on his own by employing an executive agreement. "The Constitution did not explicitly give me power to bring about the necessary agreement with Santo Domingo," he later wrote. "But the Constitution did not forbid my doing what I did. I put the agreement into effect, and I continued its execution for two years before the Senate acted; and I would have continued it until the end of my term, if necessary, without any action by Congress."

Roosevelt brooked no criticism of either the protocol or the corollary. "What I wrote is the simplest common sense, and only the fool or the coward can treat it as aught else," he said. "It is our duty, when it becomes absolutely inevitable, to police these countries in the interest of order and civilization," he told a Philadelphia editor, and to his British friend Trevelyan he explained, "We cannot perpetually assert the Monroe Doctrine on behalf of all American republics, bad or good, without ourselves accepting some responsibility." Accused of imperial avarice, Roosevelt said that he had no more appetite for acquiring the island "than a gorged boa constrictor might have to swallow a porcupine wrong-end to." The venture was an outstanding success. Within two years, the country was financially viable, and in 1907 the Senate gave in and endorsed the protocol. But a dangerous precedent of US patriarchy had been set.

He had no compunction about telling Cuba how to behave either, for he had risked his life there. In 1906, unrest on the island prompted him to say, "Just at the moment I am so angry with that infernal Cuban

republic that I would like to wipe its people off the face of the earth."
Acting under authority of a proviso he had approved—the Platt Amendment of 1901 establishing Cuba as an American protectorate—he ordered marines to restore order. His action in sending armed forces into
a country with which the United States was at peace was highly questionable, but he told Taft: "I should not dream of asking the permission
of Congress.... You know as well as I do that it is for the enormous interest of this government to strengthen and give independence to the
executive in dealing with foreign powers." Two years later, the troops
were still there, the mission of pacification not yet fulfilled.

Roosevelt's main preoccupation in foreign affairs in his second term
came not in the Caribbean but in the Far East, where he authorized
secret negotiations with Japan—a rising power he much admired but
also feared. Under the Taft-Katsura Memorandum of 1905, amplified
by the Root-Takahira Agreement of 1908, the United States conceded
to Japan control of Korea, recognized its "paramount interest" in
Manchuria, and encouraged its efforts to lead China toward modernity,
in return for Tokyo's acquiescence in American hegemony over the
Philippines. Without notifying the Senate, he bound his country to the
Anglo-Japanese alliance. These extraordinary arrangements were made
in such total secrecy that the American people (and the US Senate) did
not learn of them until two decades later.

When in the fall of 1906 the San Francisco Board of Education jeopardized these covert arrangements by ordering all pupils of Oriental descent to attend segregated schools, Roosevelt blew a fuse. Denouncing
this action as "a wicked absurdity" and "a crime against a friendly
nation," he raised the threat of employing "all the forces, civil and military" to undo this outrage against American citizens and this insult
to Japan. After further indignities to Japanese Americans ensued, he
dispatched Secretary of War William Howard Taft to Tokyo, where he
hammered out a "Gentlemen's Agreement" committing each country to
limit entry of unwanted migrants. In this informal manner, Roosevelt,
while yielding to the xenophobes in California, managed to preserve
Japan's delicate sense of honor.

The president's assiduous efforts to cultivate Tokyo served him in
good stead when in 1906, with the Russo-Japanese War stalemated, he
decided, on his own authority, to intercede to end the bloodletting. Well

regarded by leaders in Europe and Asia, he coaxed the czar and a Japanese baron who had been his Harvard classmate to send emissaries to Portsmouth, New Hampshire, to settle their differences. When the adversaries became mulish, he asked the Kaiser and others to exert pressure. Without ever setting foot in New England, he succeeded in hammering out an agreement in 1907. For his skillful mediation, this son of Mars became the first American to win the Nobel Peace Prize.

Roosevelt never forgot, though, that to be heeded when he spoke softly he required a big stick. A disciple of Alfred Thayer Mahan, who exalted sea power, he had spent more time in his first message to Congress on the imperative of rebuilding the navy than on any other topic. By the time he left office, he had gained authorization for doubling the size of the fleet—to which were added six dreadnoughts that could blast even battleships out of the water. In December 1907, without consulting Congress or even his cabinet, he dispatched eighteen battleships, eight armored cruisers, and assorted other vessels to circumnavigate the globe. He wanted this display of America's naval might to impress upon the world that "the Pacific is as much our home waters as the Atlantic." When congressmen objected to this venture, he asserted that he would never "permit anything so fraught with menace as the usurpation of any clique of Wall Street Senators of my function as Commander-in-Chief." The Great White Fleet spent fourteen months at sea, though the president had only enough funds to get it halfway around the world. When the chair of the Naval Affairs Committee threatened to deny him further money, he retorted that should that happen, he would simply leave the pride of the US Navy stranded in mid-Pacific. "There was," he subsequently stated, "no further difficulty." On Washington's birthday 1909, only days before his final term ended, Roosevelt had the pleasure of welcoming the armada home at Hampton Roads from its epic journey.

The novelist Hamilton Basso later wrote of Theodore Roosevelt that "the lines of his life are like isobars and isotherms that trace much of the American weather to come," but a number of commentators have reckoned that these lines signified little. His presidency has struck some as resembling a rocking chair: "all motion and no progress." That view is extreme, for there were undoubtedly some advances, but, a number of historians have contended, fewer than might be supposed. "Certainly no legislation of great significance to twentieth-century American life came about under his aegis," Morton Keller has pointed out. "The proposals for business regulation and conservation that were such important parts of his Presidency hardly compare with the institutional changes of the New Deal and after." TR's cannonading, the Wisconsin senator Robert La Follette concluded in 1911, "filled the air with noise and smoke, which confused and obscured the line of action, but, when the battle cloud drifted by and quiet was restored, it was always a matter of surprise that so little had really been accomplished."

William Allen White, the maverick Kansas journalist, has spoken for many of his contemporaries in offering a spirited rejoinder. Roosevelt was a "gorgeous, fighting, laughing, loving, robust man," White said. "In his generation he was unique. Men who lived with him died without seeing his kind again." In sum, White wrote of Roosevelt: "He, more than any other man in the country, is responsible for our awakening of civic righteousness. He turned us from the materialism of Hanna into a larger and more spiritual life."

The contrast between Roosevelt and his late nineteenth-century predecessors is one not of degree but of kind. "Theodore Roosevelt," Keller has written, "was the first chief executive after Lincoln to lay claim to attention as a major figure in the mythos of the office and as an important shaper of national policy." When Gutzon Borglum carved the great stone faces on Mount Rushmore, he made room—alongside Washington, Jefferson, and Lincoln—for Theodore Roosevelt, sculpted with his hallmark pince-nez. No one since the emergence of industrial America had so single-mindedly insisted on the distinction between the entitlements of High Finance and the national interest. When, shortly after he left office, he set off on an African safari, businessmen raised a toast, "Health to the lions!" On numerous issues such as the tariff "he made more noise than progress," the historian Kathleen Dalton has acknowledged, "but his rhetoric changed minds and renamed the common ground on which American politics stood." In taking countless steps to preserve national resources, he richly earned the title of Father of Conservation. "Surely," wrote a contemporary journalist, "history will be just to Col. Roosevelt. It will call him the first American of enormous popularity and ability to question the modern industrial system."

Theodore Roosevelt passed on to his successor an office vastly enhanced from the one he had inherited from McKinley, and before turning over the reins he had one parting shot. On the eve of his departure, he told William Jennings Bryan: "When you see me quoted in the press as welcoming the rest I will have after March the 3d take no stock in it, for I will confess to you confidentially that I like my job. The burdens of this great nation I have borne up under for the past seven years will not be laid aside with relief, as all presidents have heretofore said, but will be laid aside with a good deal of regret, for I have enjoyed every moment of this so-called arduous and exacting task."

He left with the satisfaction of knowing that, however much right-wingers in the congressional leadership detested him, he continued to hold a warm spot in the hearts of Main Street Republicans. At the first mention of his name in the 1908 Republican convention, delegates hoisted a giant Teddy bear to the platform and chanted, "Four, Four, Four Years More." It took over three-quarters of an hour to quell the demonstration and make clear that TR was holding fast to a pledge he had made after his 1904 victory not to run for another term. The convention then did the next best thing: on the first ballot, it chose TR's handpicked selection for his successor, William Howard Taft.

As a candidate, though, Taft proved to be problematic. He did not want to take on the responsibilities of a chief executive, and he entered the race only because of his wife's prodding and TR's insistence. "Taft's declaration of his candidacy was so tepid, so lacking in conviction that it sounded as if he had decided *not* to run," the biographer Doris Kearns Goodwin has remarked. "You blessed old trump," Roosevelt wrote him. "I have always said you would be the greatest President, bar only Washington and Lincoln, and I feel mighty inclined to strike the exception." Bryan, trying for a third time, constituted enough of a threat that Taft abandoned his Cincinnati front porch to campaign, marking the first year that both of the major party candidates had taken the stump, but he had so little gift for politicking that Roosevelt found it necessary to tutor him. When Taft gave a speech, the president advised him, he should not offer a welter of details but paint brightly hued images. Despite his liabilities, Taft won by more than a million votes—an outcome taken to be less a personal triumph than a testament to the strength of the Republican Party and an affirmation of the performance of Theodore Roosevelt.

No one ever failed to let William Howard Taft know that he could thank Theodore Roosevelt for putting him in the White House. In a worshipful letter, he wrote the former president, who was off hunting big game in Africa: "When I am addressed as 'Mr. President' I turn to see whether you are not at my elbow. . . . I want you to know that I do nothing in the Executive Office without considering what you would do under the same circumstances and without having in a sense a mental talk with you over the pros and cons of the situation. . . . I can never forget that the power that I now exercise was a voluntary transfer from you to me." Later, he reflected, "My coming into office was exactly as if Roosevelt had succeeded himself."

Nor were people hesitant to say that he fell far short of measuring up to his predecessor. Only a year older than Roosevelt, he seemed—in his outlook, his comportment, his manner of dress—a generation older. Grossly obese at 332 pounds, he moved at a much more measured, even sluggish, pace than did the dynamic TR. "My sin," Taft himself confessed, "is an indisposition to labor as hard as I might." At public gatherings, his wife had to prod him awake; once he even fell asleep while Speaker Cannon was talking animatedly to him. Critics ridiculed him for ordering an oversized bathtub for the White House, and his corpulence made him the butt of jokes: William Howard Taft, it was said, once got up in a streetcar and offered his seat to three ladies. In contrast to Roosevelt's roughing it in the wilderness, Taft played slow-paced rounds of golf, frowned upon as an elite pursuit inappropriate for the leader of a republic.

President Taft found the White House a poor fit. He would much rather have had a seat on the US Supreme Court. "I love judges, and I love courts," he said. "They . . . typify on earth what we shall meet hereafter in heaven under a just God." He had no stomach for the political arena. Running for president "is to me a nightmare," he once said, and "politics," he told his wife, "makes me sick." Later, when he was chief justice, he confided that the Court, "next to my wife and children, is the nearest thing to my heart in life." The historian Alan Brinkley

Taft as crown prince. This 1906 magazine cover highlights how diminished he was by Theodore Roosevelt, garbed in the ermine-trimmed robe of a king. Though TR chose him as his successor, Taft never was regarded as measuring up to his powerful predecessor. *Library of Congress, LC-DIG-ppmsca-26082*

has observed: "He was a man of considerable intelligence, talent, and integrity. But he was temperamentally unsuited for the intensely political character of the presidency; and his uneasiness with the demands of the office seemed to evoke all his worst qualities—his tendency to procrastinate, his excessive legalism, even a kind of physical and intellectual laziness."

Taft could not hope to match Teddy Roosevelt's popularity, but he did have admirers who were charmed by his endearing qualities. The fleshy, mustached Taft looked, said one newspaper, "like an American bison—a gentle, kind one." William Allen White remarked on the "easy gurgle of his laugh and the sweet insouciance of his answers," and

Roosevelt advised him, "Let the audience see you smile, *always*, because...your nature shines out so transparently when you do smile—you big, generous, high-minded fellow." He and his wife also brought welcome innovations. First Lady Helen Taft created a highly popular tourist attraction in the capital by having thousands of cherry trees planted, and her husband added a new feature to the role of the president in popular culture by throwing out the first ball on Opening Day. When Taft left the White House, Will Rogers said, "We are parting with three hundred pounds of solid charity to everybody, and love and affection for all his fellow men."

He thought of himself as a progressive, and in many ways he was. He established an eight-hour day for federal employees, set up a commission to explore workmen's compensation, promoted legislation to expand the authority of the Interstate Commerce Commission, approved the creation of postal savings banks, favored a corporation excise, and advocated a constitutional amendment authorizing a federal income tax—a reform achieved with the ratification of the Sixteenth Amendment early

As he picks up a primitive telephone, William Howard Taft reveals both his bulk and his genial nature. *Library of Congress, LC-DIG-hec-15149*

in 1913. Taft launched twice as many antitrust suits in four years as the "trustbuster" Roosevelt had in nearly two terms. The Sherman Act, he declared, "is a good law that ought to be enforced, and I propose to enforce it." On his final day in office, Taft signed a measure separating a recently created government entity into two institutions—the Department of Commerce and the Department of Labor, allowing the latter to become a vigilant proponent of social justice.

Taft demonstrated, too, that even phlegmatic presidents may enlarge executive power. Despite his belief in deference to Congress, he sent not only recommendations but even drafts of bills, and he issued an executive order proclaiming his right to instruct heads of departments to withhold information from Congress if a demand was "incompatible with the national interest." Somewhat inadvertently, he precipitated a significant augmentation of presidential authority when in 1909, without congressional authorization, he withdrew large tracts of oil land from private development. With characteristic circumspection, he asked Congress to ratify his executive order retroactively, and when it did not do so, the matter became the subject of litigation. In a major ruling in *United States v. Midwest Oil Co.* (1915), more than two years after his term ended, the US Supreme Court validated Taft's order, reasoning that if Congress did not countermand a president's action it was tacitly sanctioning it. Dissenting justices objected that the decision accorded the chief executive "a power which the framers of the Constitution saw fit to vest exclusively in the legislative branch." But Justice Joseph Rucker Lamar, speaking for the Court, declared, "The President is the active agent, not of Congress, but of the Nation. He is the agent of the people of the United States, deriving all his power from them." In effect, the Court was saying that a president acquired authority not only from Article II and from statutory grants but also from prolonged silences of Congress.

He also took the first steps toward establishing presidential control of the budget. To that end, he appointed a Commission on Economy and Efficiency in 1911, and he ordered the heads of departments and agencies to route their spending requests through the White House. But Congress in 1912 forbade him to continue in this direction and told cabinet officials to flout his orders. Not long afterward, Taft lamented that "dust is accumulating on the Commission's reports." But he had made an important start toward the managerial presidency.

In his first days in office, Taft courageously entered the minefield of tariff revision—a subject that Roosevelt had ducked but many, especially midwestern farmers, wanted set to rights. In his inaugural address, he asked that "a tariff bill be drawn in good faith in accordance with the promises made before the election," and, proving his sincerity, he called Congress into special session for the first time in a generation. He anticipated that legislation would "require the advancement of few, if any," rates, but he refused to give Republicans in either house any direction. He did not believe, he said, in bothering legislators while they were at work. Untrammeled, the Senate majority leader, Nelson Aldrich, saw to it that the Payne-Aldrich Tariff of 1909 increased 600 of 847 duties. Charged with duplicity, Aldrich responded brazenly, "Where did we ever make the statement that we would revise the tariff *downward?*" Urged to veto the bill to maintain the integrity of his party, Taft, though he knew that Aldrich had bamboozled him, waffled, then signed it.

Recognizing that every one of the ten Republican votes in the Senate against Payne-Aldrich had come from the Midwest, the president set off on a trip through that region in the summer of 1909 to "get out and see the people and jolly them." He hoped to close the breach in the party, but, by inattention and imprudence, he widened it. When he should have been preparing himself vigilantly for this hazardous mission, he was lumbering after golf balls on the back nine. The ensuing expedition was a disaster. In Winona, Minnesota, the heartland of progressivism, he lauded Payne-Aldrich, which he had signed with such misgivings, as "the best tariff bill that the Republican party has ever passed, and therefore the best tariff bill that has been passed at all."

The president had already roused the suspicions of progressives by failing to retain as Secretary of the Interior Roosevelt's chum James Garfield, an ardent conservationist, and by choosing in his stead Richard Ballinger, who believed that Garfield and Gifford Pinchot had acted lawlessly in withdrawing hundreds of water-power sites on the pretext that they were needed for ranger stations. TR's followers were quick to believe Pinchot when he charged Ballinger with betraying the public trust by permitting a Morgan-Guggenheim syndicate to acquire reserved coal lands in Alaska. The quarrelsome Pinchot leveled public accusations in such a manner that he left the president with no choice save to fire him, an action certain to antagonize Roosevelt. Far from being a tool of oil and lumber barons, Taft wound up withdrawing more lands from private development than Roosevelt had in an equivalent period, and when Ballinger stepped down, Taft replaced him with a friend of Pinchot's who was highly regarded by conservationists. Still, the president came out of the Ballinger-Pinchot affair badly. A congressional investigation exonerated Taft and Ballinger, but it caught the president in a scheme to predate a letter, with the consequence that, a biographer has noted, "Taft was laid wide open to charges of being a liar and a forger."

Along with certain inclinations toward progressivism, Taft held deeply conservative beliefs, and clashes with insurgents brought them to the fore. A student of William Graham Sumner at Yale, he had been taught to be wary of the State. In 1908, he had maintained that it was not the mission of the federal government "to be spectacular in the enactment of great statutes laying down new codes of morals or asserting a new standard of business integrity." He dragged his feet on supporting a proposal for direct election of senators, and when Arizona sought admission to the union with a constitution providing for the recall of judges, Taft vetoed the legislation. (No sooner was Arizona admitted, after meeting the president's objection, than it restored the provision for recall.) He displayed no enthusiasm for the earlier Republican cause of advancing the rights of freedmen, and his wife dressed six African Americans in blue livery to serve as footmen. Moreover, he lacked the energy to bear up against special interests. One senator characterized Taft as "a large, amiable island surrounded entirely by persons who knew exactly what they wanted."

In the 1910 midterm election races, Taft allied himself with the Old Guard in a campaign to drive progressives out of the US Senate. He dispatched the vice president to Wisconsin in the hope of ousting Robert La Follette, and he joined with the Southern Pacific crowd in an attempt to get rid of Hiram Johnson in California. But both La Follette and Johnson triumphed, and in Iowa, where Taft mapped out strategy for party regulars, a resolution endorsing the president was booed down. For the first time in sixteen years, Democrats won control of the House. Still more portentously, New Jersey voters elected as their new Democratic governor the president of Princeton University, Woodrow Wilson.

Taft approached foreign affairs much more circumspectly than his predecessor, but still did not escape trouble. Under strong pressure from

Roosevelt and others to intervene in Mexico in pursuit of rogue soldiers who had crossed the US border and taken American lives, Taft said, "I seriously doubt whether I have such authority…, and if I had, I would not exercise it without express Congressional approval." Taft, however, did take some initiatives. In addition to unsuccessful attempts to foster American interests in Asia and to negotiate a reciprocity treaty with Canada, he reorganized the State Department by creating "desks" for each of the regions of the world. He also dispatched troop ships to Honduras and landed 2,700 marines in Nicaragua. But he much preferred well-tempered suasion, notably by supporting international arbitration agreements—a commitment Roosevelt dismissed as "maudlin folly" resulting from "sloppy thinking." ("The truth is," Taft riposted, "that he believes in war and wishes to be a Napoleon and to die on the battlefield.")

These gibes revealed how badly the onetime friendship between the two men had curdled. Even before Taft took office, Roosevelt had been miffed by the incoming president's determination to replace cabinet officials chosen by TR with corporation lawyers, and his doubts about the extent of his protégé's progressivism deepened after Pinchot sailed to Europe to fill his ears with tales of Taft's perfidy. The final break came when the Taft administration filed an antitrust suit against U.S. Steel reprimanding Roosevelt for his concessions to financiers during the Panic of 1907. As early as 1910, the magazine *Life*, expressing the sentiments of TR's admirers, offered a bit of verse:

> Teddy, come home and blow your horn,
> The sheep's in the meadow,
> The cow's in the corn.
> The boy that you left to tend the sheep,
> Is under the haystack fast asleep.

Egged on by his supporters and incensed at the president, Roosevelt decided to wrest the Republican nomination from Taft in 1912. "My hat is in the ring," he announced. "The fight is on, and I am stripped to the buff." Those words constituted a formidable challenge, for even though Taft had held the White House for the past three years, TR had been a much more imposing presence on the world stage. After emerging from the jungle in March 1910, he had lectured at Oxford and the Sorbonne, represented the United States at the funeral of Edward VII, searched for birds in New Forest with Sir Edward Grey, admonished the Vatican, and told the Kaiser that he was the only European sovereign who could carry a ward in Manhattan.

The imperative of proving himself more popular than his opponents put Taft at a stark disadvantage. He did not know how to reach out to the electorate, and he did not truly care to. For three years, he had kept press conferences to a minimum and had rarely sought to rally public support. "He could not be persuaded to return the greetings of a crowd, or even to turn his head ... for a sign of recognition," the historian Elmer Cornwell has written. "That he should be unaware of the need for so elementary a gesture, or unwilling to give it ... suggests how far he was from being able to exploit the potential of the office under the conditions that had obtained since the advent of the new journalism and the White House incumbency of the redoubtable Rough Rider." Taft himself acknowledged, "I have proven to be a burdensome leader and not one that aroused the multitude."

In the scramble for delegates in 1912, Taft and Roosevelt slugged it out. Roosevelt called Taft "a flubdub with a streak of the second-rate and the common in him," and a "fathead" with less brain than a guinea pig. Taking advantage of the emergence of a new institution—the presidential primary—Roosevelt demonstrated in a number of states that he was the favorite of Republican voters. Initially, the president refused to defend himself, but when he kept losing primaries, he relented, explaining, in a singularly maladroit choice of words, "Even a rat will fight when driven into a corner." His poor showing, though, turned out not to matter, for Big Bill Taft controlled the party machinery, and enough delegates did his bidding to fend off Roosevelt.

Indignant that he had been denied the nomination (he thought by foul means), Roosevelt kept his candidacy alive by becoming the standard-bearer of a new party in a campaign that never ran short of melodrama. So committed was he to "fighting for the loftiest of causes," Roosevelt told delegates to the Progressive Party convention, that he was willing at the end of the struggle to be "cast aside and left to die." He concluded: "We fight in honorable fashion for the good of mankind unheeding of our individual fates; with unflinching hearts and undimmed eyes, we stand at Armageddon and we battle for the Lord." By saying that he felt "as fit as a bull moose," the former president gave the Progressives a symbol. In 1910, in a speech at Osawatomie, Kansas, he had shocked conservatives by declaring that dissolving "the unholy alliance between corrupt business and corrupt politics is the first task of the statesmanship of the day," and in 1912 he again articulated this vision of a "New Nationalism," which regarded trusts as beneficial so long as they were controlled by a powerful government and accompanied by a program for social justice.

In Milwaukee in October, a would-be assassin horrified hundreds at a political rally by shooting Roosevelt. The former president survived only because of a metal spectacle case and a thick wad of prepared remarks in a breast pocket covering his heart. For the rest of his days, he carried a bullet inside him. Despite wrenching pain and loss of blood, the doughty warrior insisted on going through with a fifty-minute address. "Friends, I shall ask you to be as quiet as possible," he said. "I don't know whether you fully understand that I have just been shot; but it takes more than that to kill a bull moose.... Don't you make any mistake. Don't you pity me. I am all right. I am all right and you cannot escape listening to the speech." Roosevelt's courage under fire and his large following doomed Taft's already slim chance for reelection. "I think I might as well give up so far as being a candidate is concerned," the president told his wife. "There are so many people in the country who don't like me."

The schism in the GOP all but assured victory for the Democrats, if they could agree on a candidate. Champ Clark of Missouri had a majority of the delegates, but that did not suffice because ever since Van Buren, Democrats had required a two-thirds vote for nomination. In 1912, when ballot after ballot denied Clark a supermajority, the party settled on New Jersey's governor, Woodrow Wilson, who two years earlier had never held, or even run for, any political office. In the most ideologically diverse campaign in American history, Wilson distinguished his approach from Teddy Roosevelt's by advocating a "New Freedom." Counseled by the Boston reformer Louis Brandeis, who warned against the concentration of power, whether in industry or in Washington, he sought to liberate market forces to advance opportunities for entrepreneurs. "The history of liberty," Wilson maintained, "is the history of the limitation of governmental power, not the increase of it."

As Taft anticipated, he went down to a crushing defeat, receiving a meager eight electoral votes and finishing third—the only time a major party candidate has ever been so reduced. Polling just 23 percent of the ballots, he got the lowest percentage of any Republican or Democratic candidate in history. Roosevelt, the Bull Mooser, with 27 percent, did not prevail either, though he did carry six states. With the Republicans fragmented, Wilson won handily, despite receiving only 42 percent of the ballots. (In a four-way competition, the Socialist, Eugene Debs, polled nearly a million votes.)

Taft had not enjoyed a gratifying four years. "I have come to the conclusion," he said, "that the major part of the work of a President is to increase the gate receipts of expositions and fairs and bring tourists into town." His tenure, Keller has remarked, "was a pallid second act after TR's star turn." On March 4, 1913, the day that Woodrow Wilson succeeded him, Taft told him, "I'm glad to be going—this is the lonesomest place in the world." Too much was expected of the White House, he believed. In words that TR would never have thought of uttering, he reflected, "The President cannot make clouds to rain and cannot make the corn to grow, he cannot make business good." Years later, after he had fulfilled his cherished ambition to be appointed chief justice of the United States, Taft commented, "The truth is that in my present life I don't remember that I ever was President."

The Taft-TR feud simmered past their stays in the White House. In 1913, the year Taft's term ended, Roosevelt published *An Autobiography*, in which, after identifying himself with Lincoln and Andrew Jackson, he said that, unhappily, "my successor...took...the Buchanan view of the President's powers and duties." Not content with likening Taft to the inept James Buchanan, Roosevelt stated, "Whether he is highminded and wrongheaded or merely infirm of purpose, whether he means well feebly or is bound by a mischievous misconception of the powers and duties of the National Government and the President," an incumbent of the White House who adhered to "the Buchanan-Taft school" grievously impaired the office.

To underscore the contrast between his attitude and Taft's, Roosevelt presented a bold assertion of the scope of the presidency:

My view was that every officer...was a steward of the people bound actively and affirmatively to do all he could for the people, and not to content himself with the negative merit of keeping his talents undamaged in a napkin. I declined to adopt the view that what was imperatively necessary for the Nation could not be done by the president unless he could find some specific authorization to do it. My belief was that it was not only his right but his duty to do anything that the needs of the Nation demanded unless such action was forbidden by the Constitution or by the laws. Under this interpretation of executive power I did and caused to be done many things not previously done by the President.

In a series of lectures from Charlottesville to Toronto, and especially at Columbia University, that were gathered together and published in 1916 as *Our Chief Magistrate and His Powers*, Taft offered a rebuttal:

My judgment is that the view of...Mr. Roosevelt, ascribing an undefined residuum of power to the President, is an unsafe doctrine...that... might lead under emergencies to results of an arbitrary character, doing irremediable injustice to private right. The mainspring of such a view is that the Executive...is to play the part of a Universal Providence and...that anything that in his judgment will help the people he ought to do, unless he is expressly forbidden not to do it. The wide field of action that this would give to the Executive one can hardly limit.

Though disputing Roosevelt's latitudinarian claims, Taft did not hold a strict constructionist view. He acknowledged that a president could draw upon implied powers, and he found no fault with Lincoln's far-reaching actions. He stated: "The Constitution does give the President wide discretion and great power, and it ought to do so....He is no figurehead, and it is entirely proper that an energetic and active clear-sighted people, who, when they have work to do, wish it done well, should be willing to rely upon their judgment in selecting their Chief Agent, and having selected him, should entrust to him all the power needed to carry out their governmental purpose, great as it may be."

William Howard Taft's lectures have endured, however, primarily because of his reasoning on behalf of cabining executive prerogatives. In what may have been a reflection on his own experience in the White House, Taft maintained: "The truth is that great as his powers are, when a President comes to exercise them, he is much more concerned with the limitation upon them than he is affected, like little Jack Horner, by a personal joy over the big personal things he can do." Eschewing TR's role of chief legislator, he contended that "our President has no initiative in respect to legislation given him by law except that of mere recommendation, and no legal . . . method of entering into the . . . discussion of . . . proposed legislation while pending in Congress." In sum, he declared: "The true view of the Executive function is . . . that the President can exercise no power which cannot be fairly and reasonably traced to some specific grant of power or justly implied. . . . There is no undefined residuum of power which he can exercise because it seems to him to be in the public interest."

Taft was fighting a losing battle, because his successor had come to take a decidedly Rooseveltian view of the powers of his office. In lectures at Columbia University, published in 1908 as *Constitutional Government in the United States*, Wilson had said of the president: "His is the only national voice in our affairs. Let him once win the admiration and confidence of the country, and no other single force can withstand him, no combination of forces will easily overpower him. . . . He is the representative of no constituency, but of the whole people. . . . The President is at liberty, both in law and conscience, to be as big a man as he can."

As Inauguration Day, March 4, 1913, approached, Wilson elaborated these thoughts. The president, he asserted, "is expected by the nation to be a leader of his party as well as the chief executive officer of the government, and the country will take no excuses from him. He must play the part and play it successfully or lose the country's confidence. He must be the prime minister, as much concerned with the guidance of legislation as with the just and orderly execution of the law; and he is the spokesman of the nation in everything, even the most momentous and most delicate dealings of the government with foreign nations." No one who read these words could doubt that Woodrow Wilson had every intention of swiftly expanding the realm of the presidency.

2

Woodrow Wilson

THE ONLY PRESIDENT WITH A PHD, one of the first scholars to be chosen to head the American Political Science Association, Woodrow Wilson had long valued the political arena over a professor's retreat. As a sixteen-year-old, he pointed to the portrait above his desk of "Gladstone, the greatest statesman that ever lived," and announced, "I intend to be a statesman too." After taking voice lessons, he revealed to a Princeton acquaintance: "I make frequent extemporaneous addresses to the empty benches of my father's church in order to get a mastery of easy and correct and elegant expression, in preparation for the future. My topics are most of them political, and I can sometimes almost see the benches smile at some of my opinions and deliverances."

Instead of rejoicing in the success of his first book, *Congressional Government*, published in 1885, Wilson lamented to the young woman he would marry that he felt "shut out from my heart's first—primary—ambition and purpose,...a statesman's career." He confided:

> I have a strong instinct of leadership, an unmistakably ahistorical temperament, and the keenest possible delight in affairs....I have no patience for the tedious toil of what is known as "research"; I have a passion for interpreting great thoughts to the world; I should be complete if I could inspire a great movement of opinion, if I could read

the experiences of the past into the practical life of the men of today and so communicate the thought to the minds of the great mass of the people as to impel them to great political achievements.

To reach this vast audience, he was seeking to develop "a style full of life, of colour and vivacity, of soul and energy, of inexhaustible power—of a thousand qualities of beauty and grace and strength that would make it immortal."

Born in a Presbyterian manse, the son and grandson of clergymen, he moved effortlessly into the role of preacher. His biographer John Thompson has concluded that "Wilson seems to have derived from the Calvinist-Presbyterian mindset...certain psychological characteristics, including a disposition to divide the world into the elect and the damned...and a tendency toward self-righteous obstinacy when under stress in conflict situations." Freud carried these perceptions considerably farther in diagnosing Wilson as a man who subconsciously identified himself with Jesus. Since Freud did not see Wilson, and rendered his verdict on the basis of secondhand information provided him by an American envoy, that judgment must be treated with caution. But when following his 1912 victory the Democratic national chairman thought he himself deserved some of the credit, Wilson responded loftily, "Whether you did little or much, remember that God ordained that I should be the next president of the United States. Neither you nor any other mortal or mortals could have prevented that." And Wilson did later astound weary European diplomats by saying, "Why has Jesus Christ so far not succeeded in inducing the world to follow His teachings...? It is because He taught the ideal without devising any practical means of attaining it. That is why I am proposing a practical scheme to carry out His aims."

Some found Wilson's idealistic rhetoric thrilling, but a number of his contemporaries thought the "Princeton Schoolmaster" presumptuous and chilling. A Maryland politician told a bartender: "He gives me the creeps. The time I met him, he said something to me, and I didn't know whether God or him was talking." Responding to a rumor that Wilson was having an affair with a divorcée, Theodore Roosevelt commented: "It wouldn't work. You can't cast a man as Romeo who looks and acts so much like an apothecary's clerk." A veteran Washington journalist, observing that Wilson reflected "the cold analysis of the cloister," commented that "on looking back at this period, Wilson stands out, clear cut and rigid, in the sharp definite lines of a steel engraving; when I turn to Roosevelt he is revealed in strong human tints, the warm flesh tones of a Rembrandt or a Franz Hals." Wilson himself recognized how different he seemed from TR: "He is a real, vivid person. . . . I am a vague, conjectural personality, more made up of opinions and academic prepossessions than of human traits and red corpuscles." In 1914, he acknowledged to reporters that he was troubled by being regarded as "a cold and removed person who has a thinking machine inside," quickly adding, "You may not believe it, but I sometimes feel like a fire from a far-from-extinct volcano."

Wilson began his presidency in the manner he had imagined for himself as a young man. He wound up his inaugural address by saying, in the style of discourse of a prophet: "This is not a day of triumph; it is a day of dedication. Here muster, not the forces of party, but the forces of humanity. Men's hearts wait upon us; men's lives hang in the balance; men's hopes call upon us to say what we will do. Who shall live up to the great trust? Who dares fail to try? I summon all honest men, all patriotic, all forward-looking men, to my side. God helping me, I will not fail them, if they will but counsel and sustain me!"

That same day, he summoned Congress into special session, and on April 8, hardly more than a month later, he dared one of the most dramatic departures in the history of the presidency. To urge the necessity for tariff reform, he appeared before Congress in person—the first chief executive to do so since John Adams. Jefferson had abandoned the practice as too Federalist—indeed, too royalist—and for a century, that precedent had been unwritten law. It was a bold act for a newcomer to break it, and especially risky for a man who headed the party that venerated Jefferson as its patron saint. A Democratic senator protested: "I am sorry to see revived the old Federalist custom of speeches from the throne. . . . I regret all this cheap and tawdry imitation of English royalty."

Intent on asserting his leadership of the legislature by closing the distance between the White House and Capitol Hill, Wilson declared: "I am very glad indeed to have this opportunity to address the two Houses

This 1913 portrait of Woodrow Wilson conveys both his stern demeanor and his kinetic energy. He seems ready to spring into action in a year when he drove so much New Freedom legislation through Congress. *Library of Congress, LC-USZ62-20570*

directly and to verify for myself the impression that the President of the United States is a person, not a mere department of the Government hailing Congress from some isolated island of jealous power, sending messages, not speaking naturally and with his own voice—that he is a human being trying to cooperate with other human beings in a common service."

Despite the misgivings of traditionalists, Wilson's experiment made a decidedly favorable impression. "The wonder is that in seven years Theodore Roosevelt never thought of this way of stamping his personality upon his age," the *New York Times* commented. When his wife made a similar remark, Wilson replied with a laugh, "Yes, I think I put one over on Teddy." The new president was immensely pleased with himself. "The town is agog about it," he said. "It seems I have been smashing precedents almost daily ever since I got here." And he kept on doing it.

In 1914 alone, he appeared in person before Congress five times. Thereby, Wilson made an enduring contribution to the strength of the executive office. As his biographer H. W. Brands has written, "This return to long-abandoned practice...was one of the hallmarks of the Wilson presidency, and one of his lasting contributions to American governance. Ever since Wilson, a president's ability to take his message to Congress, and through Congress to the American people, has been one of his most potent tools; and the occasions on which presidents have addressed joint sessions have included some of the most memorable in American history."

Skeptics anticipated that Wilson, a professor without a day's experience in Washington, would not be able to find his way around Capitol Hill, but, with good reason, his principal biographer, Arthur Link, has called him "the parliamentary leader par excellence in the history of the American presidency." Even before he was sworn in, he huddled with power brokers in both houses of Congress, and, only hours after delivering his inaugural address, he traipsed up to the Hill to confer with the Senate Finance Committee in the President's Room in the Capitol on strategy and tactics. No chief executive since Lincoln had done that, and then only in wartime. When congressmen wavered, he installed a special telephone line so that he could badger them, and he sat in on committee hearings. He also created a Common Council Club of junior cabinet officials, including Assistant Secretary of the Navy Franklin Delano Roosevelt, to exert pressure on legislators.

In a time before air-conditioning, congressmen dreaded Washington's sultry summers, but they had taken comfort in knowing that after being elected in November, they were not expected to convene until a year from December—thirteen months away—and even then could count on escaping town in late spring. Not only had Wilson summoned Congress into early session, but he held it in Washington (save for one short break) for eighteen straight months. Never before, not even during civil war, had a Congress sat that long.

Wilson, who so admired Gladstone, pursued the British model of mobilizing the members of his party, instead of building bipartisan coalitions. For the first time, newspapers wrote of "Administration bills." Initially squeamish about using patronage to secure the votes he needed, the high-minded president soon decided to let Postmaster General Albert S. Burleson, a former Texas congressman, distribute federal jobs, and when grateful right-wing Democrats fell into line on liberal legislation, he was glad he had.

In addition to attempting to impose party discipline, at which he was remarkably successful, Wilson set out to cultivate the press, an endeavor that did not go nearly so well. Little more than a week after he took office, the president, who created a new institution by scheduling regular news conferences with the Washington press corps, invited journalists to the East Room of the White House. At these gatherings, he tried to engage in repartee, but his efforts to show that he was a regular chap fell short. He regarded reporters as "dullards," one commentator has noted, "and they sensed his condescension." Wilson started out meeting reporters each week, but he canceled that practice in 1915, ostensibly for national security reasons but more likely because he did not want to be grilled about a courtship he was carrying on soon after the death of his wife. Only rarely thereafter did he convene the press.

Throughout his presidency, Wilson relied not on the press but on his oratory to promote his programs, and, save for his indulgence in archaisms and overwrought metaphors, he carried it off brilliantly. Knowing that he could expect opposition from powerful corporate interests to tariff revision and other reforms he planned to propose, Wilson set out to build public support even before he took office by launching a blunt attack. In a talk to the Southern Society of New York in December 1912, he commented on the rumor that business leaders would deliberately foment a panic to undercut him. If any man dared to carry out such a conspiracy, he warned, "I promise him, not for myself but for my countrymen, a gibbet as high as Haman—not a literal gibbet, because that is not painful after it has been used, but a figurative gibbet, upon which the soul quivers so long as there are persons belonging to the family who can feel ashamed."

Though Wilson had grand expectations for enacting landmark legislation, he conducted a minimalist operation in the White House. He brought with him from Trenton young Joseph Tumulty for a position that would later be called chief of staff, but Tumulty never was given that designation because he was Wilson's entire staff, save for employees such as clerks. With no speechwriters and very little technical support, the president had to handcraft documents. On an old portable type-writer, he banged out diplomatic notes to be sent over the signature of the secretary of state. "Wilson," Lewis Gould has observed perceptively, "showed that it was...possible to be a strong president without becoming a modern one."

Despite these meager resources, Wilson girded for battle with Congress on behalf of the whole range of the New Freedom program, starting with his determination to scale down tariff barriers. On this issue, he knew he could count on considerable support from Democrats because free trade had been the talisman of southern planters and still carried that cachet. It was also a doctrine that Wilson cherished. "I have had the accomplishment of something like this at heart ever since I was a boy," he said. The Underwood bill breezed through the House, but in the Senate sugar and wool interests clamored for protection. With a very narrow margin of votes, the president could be expected to compromise. Instead, he made use of the party caucus to establish tariff reform as a measure Democrats were expected to support.

Through such adroit personal leadership, Wilson secured passage of the Underwood-Simmons bill with almost unanimous party backing. When the roll was called, every Democrat voted as the president wished, save for the two sugar-state senators from Louisiana, and their defection was offset by two colleagues from across the aisle. To make up for the loss of customs revenue, the act provided for an income tax, the first under authorization of the recently ratified Sixteenth Amendment. Wilson had little to do with that, but this innovation, so innocently undertaken, provided presidents in years to come with an invaluable mechanism for distributing economic gains more fairly. The law marked the first real lowering of the tariff in the United States since 1846. A London editor called it "the heaviest blow that has been aimed at the Protective system since the British legislation of Sir Robert Peel."

In June, Wilson motored up to the Hill for a second time—to promote a drastic overhaul of the banking system. Even before he took office, he had declared: "I am not indicting the bankers. They have been convicted." He called for "public, not private" control, thus making the banks "the instruments, not the masters of business," a conception that was anathema to Wall Street and conservative editors. The proposal the president favored, said the *New York Sun*, was "covered all over with the slime of Bryanism." But Wilson persisted. The Federal Reserve bill still left management of the money supply in the hands of bankers, but it provided for governmental oversight that could be amplified in years to come.

Addressing Congress in June, he told the joint session: "I have come to you, as head of the Government and as responsible leader of the party in power, to urge action now." The language seemed more appropriate for a prime minister, which is precisely how Wilson conceived of himself. As an undergraduate at Princeton, where he published an essay on "Cabinet Government in the United States," he had said of his country: "How much happier she would be now if she had England's form of government instead of the miserable delusion of the republic." Under the influence of the British theoretician Walter Bagehot, he had developed an infatuation with the parliamentary system, and especially with the office of prime minister and the conception of party solidarity.

Legislators quickly learned the full meaning of the president's emphasis on party. The bill creating the Federal Reserve System was drafted not in Congress but in the White House after Wilson met with prominent Democrats, and when it reached the House he insisted that members be bound by a party caucus. As the roll was called, all but three Democrats in the House voted for the measure. He fared even better in the Senate, where every Democrat cried "Yea." As Wilfred Binkley later wrote, "The theory of government advocated by Woodrow Wilson for thirty years was operating precisely as planned."

In January 1914, Wilson addressed a joint session of Congress yet another time to ask it to write into law the third and final feature of the New Freedom: an amplified antitrust act. The Clayton Act, approved in October, outlawed interlocking directorates, predatory price cutting, and other unfair practices. An elaboration of the 1890 Sherman law, too much was claimed for it. The statute was called, extravagantly, the "Magna Carta" of labor, but Wilson did not intend to dole out any special favors for unions, and the courts soon saw to it that the statute was more a liability for unions than an asset. Wilson maintained that the law made it possible "to check and destroy the noxious growth" of monopoly "in its infancy," but embedded in it was so much provision for judicial review that one cantankerous senator characterized it as "a sort of legislative apology to the trusts, delivered hat in hand, and accompanied by assurances that no discourtesy is intended." The law, though, did strengthen the Sherman Act by stipulating that corporation officials were criminally liable for misdeeds of their firms. Furthermore, Congress created at the same time, in accord with Wilson's demand, a Federal Trade Commission, which was authorized to monitor mergers and issue cease-and-desist orders when it found unfair methods of competition or deceptive practices such as false advertising. To the president's gratification, the FTC bill, too, won the votes of every Senate Democrat.

One additional piece of legislation suggestive of the later New Deal and Great Society revealed, by contrast, the limited range of the New Freedom, for it came not from the president but from the first lady. Critically ill, Ellen Axson Wilson had become the first woman in her position to affect legislation directly. She focused a spotlight on the vile slums that blighted African American neighborhoods only a short walk from the White House by inviting housing reformers to White House socials so that they could talk to congressmen. Moments before she died in August 1914, Congress passed the Ellen Wilson Alley Housing bill.

By dynamic leadership, Wilson had won enactment of the entire program of the New Freedom. He had given the country its first coherent banking system and had secured the first antitrust law since adoption of the original Sherman Act in 1890. In the difficult terrain of tariff reform—where Cleveland had been balked, where Roosevelt had feared to tread, where Taft had been all but impaled—Wilson had succeeded beyond every expectation. The *New York Times* stated: "President Cleveland said he had a Congress on his hands, but this Congress has a President on its back, driving it pitilessly.... Never were Congressmen driven so, not even in the days of the 'big stick.'" Chauncey Depew, who had been a powerful conservative Republican senator, concluded, "This man who was regarded as a pedagogue, a theorist, is accomplishing the most astounding practical results."

Above all, Wilson had demonstrated what many reasonable people had long doubted—that the Democratic Party could rule. In the nineteenth century, Democrats had been the party of states' rights, of aversion to national authority. One critic had asked, "Are they but an organized no?" In September 1914, the *Nation*, which for a long while had been finding fault with the Democrats, declared, "The old cry that the Republican party is the only one fit to govern the country...will not be heard this year, or, if heard, will provoke only a smile."

Unhappily, Wilson's bright beginning had one miserably dark side. The return of the Democrats to power with his victory in 1912 meant, in the words of one periodical, that "the South is in the Saddle," and southerners the president appointed to a majority of places in the cabinet carried their racist saddlebags with them. He named as secretary of the navy Josephus Daniels, who had said that "the subjection of the negro, politically, and the separation of the negro, socially, are paramount to all other considerations." Postmaster General Burleson and Secretary of the Treasury William McAdoo set out to impose racial segregation on offices, dining halls, and restrooms in federal buildings, a practice the president defended as "distinctly to the advantage of the colored people themselves." When black leaders called on him to protest, Wilson became haughty and testy. Severe pressure from the NAACP halted the procedure, but Wilson never showed any empathy toward the desire of African Americans for a share of the New Freedom. He once confessed, "I have very little ease with coloured people or they with me." When he ran for reelection in 1916, not a single black leader supported him. "You have grievously disappointed us," W. E. B. Du Bois told him.

"It would be the irony of fate," Wilson said to a friend after he was elected in 1912, "if my administration had to deal chiefly with foreign affairs." So little did the subject interest him that he felt comfortable with naming as secretary of state a parochial Nebraskan utterly without experience in the field, William Jennings Bryan, during an era when it was assumed that the most prestigious post in the cabinet should go to the leading figure in the party. Wilson came to place greater reliance, though, on an enigmatic Texan, Colonel E. M. House. The president once said: "Mr. House is my second personality. He is my independent self. His thoughts and mine are one."

Wilson hoped that foreign quarrels would stay away, but if they did cross the ocean, he planned to address them with a few simple—in fact, simplistic—assumptions. "The force of America," he maintained early in his presidency, "is the force of moral principle.... There is nothing else that she loves, and... there is nothing else for which she will contend." With little of Theodore Roosevelt's jingoism in his makeup, he sought to be a man of peace and goodwill.

Few realized in 1913 that Wilson also harbored some contrary ideas. He had been gratified that "this country has some young men who prefer dying in the ditches of the Philippines to spending their lives behind the counters of a dry goods store in our eastern cities." Subsequently, he stunned Colonel House by saying that he "did not share the views of so many of our present day statesmen that war was so much to be deprecated," for he "thought there was no more glorious way to die than in battle." It was especially troublesome that this sentiment was coupled with copybook fancies far removed from the agony of corpse-strewn battlefields. He loved to recite Shakespeare's couplet in *Henry V*:

> But if it be a sin to covet honor,
> I am the most offending soul alive.

This preoccupation with "honor" bore watching.

Latin America gave Wilson an early lesson on how difficult it was to be a moral leader in an immoral world. He approached the region determined not to be a pawn of US investors or a bullying Uncle Sam. That resolve was immediately tested when he was called upon to deal with the Mexican government of Victoriano Huerta—a general who, three weeks before Wilson took office, had staged a coup in which the Constitutionalist president, Francisco I. Madero, was murdered. American businessmen wanted Wilson to follow the British example of granting immediate recognition to Huerta, but the president took the high ground. Eschewing the customary practice of validating a coup d'etat, he refused to recognize this "government of butchers," and instead sided with Madero's heir, the Constitutionalist Venustiano Carranza, who was mounting an offensive against Huerta. Wilson promised Mexico that a "new order, which will have its foundations on human liberty and human rights, shall prevail," and, claiming for the United States the final say on whether a new regime met American standards, he announced that he would not recognize governments established by force.

The president ratcheted up his high-flown rhetoric after Huerta, with the backing of British oil interests, installed himself as dictator, but when Wilson carried his words into action, he got his fingers burned. He announced that, in support of the cause of "constitutional liberty" in Mexico, he would lead the world toward "those great heights where there shines unobstructed the light of the justice of God." To scale those heights, he asked Congress for authority to use armed forces against Huerta. Carranza made clear that he did not want any *yanquis* in his country, but Wilson was not deterred. When, in a trivial incident, a Mexican officer arrested some American sailors, the president backed an American admiral who insisted on a twenty-one-gun salute to avenge this affront to national honor.

Though he had been a longtime critic of American meddling south of the border, Wilson did not scruple at intervention. On learning that a large shipment of arms from Germany was destined for Huerta, he ordered naval forces to seize Mexico's chief port, Veracruz. He expected a peaceful occupation, but the operation resulted in the deaths of nineteen Americans and many times that number of Mexicans. Wilson, looking "preternaturally pale, almost parchmenty," was shocked that his actions had brought about the deaths of American sailors and marines, and that, instead of being hailed as a liberator, he was denounced by Mexicans—including a furious Carranza—as an invader.

Mediation by the ABC countries (Argentina, Brazil, Chile) permitted Wilson to withdraw from Mexico but did not end his vexations there. Early in 1916, another insurrectionist, Pancho Villa, who resented Wilson's support of President Carranza, struck back. After seizing sixteen American engineers from a train in Mexico and murdering them, he crossed the border into Columbus, New Mexico, in a raid that left nineteen Americans dead. Wilson retaliated by sending an expeditionary force under General "Black Jack" Pershing to pursue Villa. It failed to capture him but, by driving deep into Mexico, incensed Carranza. Though Villa was seeking to oust him, Carranza demanded that the Punitive Expedition leave his country. Chastened by his experiences, Wilson ignored the outcries of American nationalists and pursued a peaceful settlement. "There won't be any war with Mexico if I can prevent it," he said, "no matter how loud the gentlemen on the Hill yell for it." He did not want "some poor farmer's boy, or the son of some poor widow" sent into combat. Moreover, he deeply sympathized with "the age-old struggle of...poor Mexico, with its pitiful men, women, and children, fighting to gain a foothold in their own land."

During this same period, however, Wilson behaved like an old-style imperialist in the Caribbean. After a mob murdered the president of

Haiti in 1915, and violence took American lives, he sent in troops and set up a puppet government. (In 1934, US Marines were still in Port-au-Prince.) Wilson also acquiesced in a military occupation of the Dominican Republic that persisted for eight years. In addition, he got Nicaragua to agree to a treaty that so seriously compromised its sovereignty in providing for America's right to intervene that the Central American Court of Justice denounced it and the US Senate refused to ratify it.

Wilson did not always wield such a heavy hand. He acted with conspicuous courage in daring to reverse a policy that the Democratic Party leadership strongly favored. In 1912, with the Panama Canal nearing completion, Congress had enacted a law exempting US coastal shipping from canal tolls, though this was a flagrant violation of a 1901 treaty with Great Britain stipulating equal treatment of the ships of all nations. The House majority leader, however, charged that if Wilson sought to abolish the special status of the United States, he would contravene the 1912 platform on which he had been elected. Despite this weighty objection, the president asked a joint session of Congress for repeal, saying, "I shall not know how to deal with other matters of even greater ... consequences if you do not grant it to me in ungrudging measure."

Wilson threatened to resign the presidency if Congress did not comply. "In case of failure in this matter," he elaborated, "I shall go to the country, after my resignation is tendered, and ask it whether America is to stand before the world as a nation that violates its contracts." As it turned out, he did not find it necessary to take this drastic course. Though repeal would not sit well with their constituents, members of both houses of Congress fell into line. "When I think of the obstacles you have encountered and overcome in this conflict for the national honor," a friend wrote him, "the victory seems colossal."

The president carried on in this fashion by supporting his secretary of state's attempt to make amends for Theodore Roosevelt's intrusion in Panama. In an unparalleled gesture by a great power toward a small nation, Bryan negotiated a treaty paying Colombia an indemnity of $25 million, granting it free use of the canal, and, most remarkably, expressing "sincere regret." Predictably, TR was livid, and his very close friend Henry Cabot Lodge succeeded in blocking ratification. Not until 1921 did the Senate consent to the indemnity, and without the apology, but if the Wilson administration had not taken the initiative, it is unlikely this action would have come that soon.

A decolonizer, Wilson beat a retreat from the imperial ambition of TR. He played a large role in the adoption of the Jones Act of 1916 conceding self-government to the Philippines, and, in 1917, he persuaded Congress to grant US citizenship and limited self-government to the people of Puerto Rico. When Germany cast covetous eyes on the Danish West Indies, Wilson avoided a potential confrontation by arranging to purchase them from Denmark; in 1917, they were renamed the Virgin Islands. Within a decade, islanders had been granted all of the rights accruing to American citizens.

The outbreak in 1914 of the Great War (what a later generation was to call World War I) brought Wilson and the nation infinitely more grief than anything that transpired elsewhere on the globe at this time, even though the president tried to insulate America. When the guns of August boomed in Europe, he immediately proclaimed US neutrality and implored his "fellow countrymen" to be "impartial in thought as well as in action," and to "put a curb upon our sentiments." He did not want them even to cheer or hiss either side in movie theaters. In his State of the Union address in December 1914, he spoke of the European conflict as "a war with which we have nothing to do, whose causes cannot touch us." Indeed, he added, Americans ought to be "ashamed of any thought of hostility or fearful preparation for trouble." But he also had a more disquieting notion. "The real man believes that his honor is dearer than his life," he said.

Though the president was sincere in his avowals of neutrality, he pursued policies that gave an enormous advantage to Great Britain and its allies over Germany and the other Central Powers. An Anglophile, he had courted a woman by reading to her Bagehot and Burke. The imbalance, however, resulted less from bias than from Wilson's strained perception of international law. By insisting on the right of neutrals to trade with belligerents, he made America the arsenal of Great Britain, which controlled the seas. Trade with Germany and Austria dropped from $169 million in 1914 to $1 million in 1916. By contrast, trade to the Allies in 1916 totaled $3,214 million, with munitions exports rising from $40 million in 1914 to $1,290 million. Consequently, the American economy, rescued from a recession by this transatlantic traffic, became highly dependent on British orders. Not only munitions makers and financiers—who later would be called "merchants of death"—but factory workers and farmers had a huge stake in the success of the Allies.

Furthermore, Wilson judged German and British behavior by different standards. When in February 1915 Berlin announced that submarines ("U-boats" for *Unterseeboote*) would sink Allied ships without warning and that it might be hard to distinguish them from neutral vessels, he told Germany that it would be held to "strict accountability." But when the British blacklisted American firms, confiscated the cargoes of neutral vessels, intercepted American mail, and forced ships to put into English ports, all they got from the president was a slap on the wrist. The disparity, it was said, derived from the reality that British transgressions could be litigated, while lives taken by U-boats could never be restored. True enough. But British mines were no less deadly than German torpedoes. The mines did not claim American lives simply because US ships stayed out of the huge area Wilson permitted the British to designate as a war zone.

By the president's reckoning, only the Germans threatened national honor. Wilson contended that he was "constantly reminded . . . by . . . every voice that comes to me out of the body of the nation" that a "double obligation" was laid upon him: "keep us out of war" and "keep the honor of the nation unstained." In fact, "every voice" did not tell him that. But he concluded: "Do you not see that a time may come when it is impossible to do both of these things?"

Concern about U-boat depredation took a dreadful turn when, on May 7, 1915, a German submarine, on orders of its stupid and cold-blooded commander, torpedoed the queen of Britain's Cunard fleet, the *Lusitania*, killing 1,198 men, women, and children, 128 of them American. Three days later, Wilson said, "There is such a thing as a man being too proud to fight. There is such a thing as a nation being so right that it does not need to convince others by force that it is right." The very next day, he tried to squirm out of those remarks, which seemed so inadequate to the horror Americans felt at the loss of life, but he could not turn away the gale of derision they brought on. (Wilson himself realized that he had blundered. "I have a bad habit of thinking out loud," he told a friend.)

His language became much sterner when he drafted a note to Berlin denouncing the sinking of the *Lusitania*. He told the German government: "The principal fact is that a great steamer . . . carrying more than a thousand souls who had no part or lot in the conduct of the war was torpedoed and sunk without so much as a challenge or a warning, and that men, women, and children were sent to their death in circumstances unparalleled in modern warfare." He dispatched the message over the objections of Secretary of State William Jennings Bryan. The president, Bryan protested, was taking a very strong stand against U-boat warfare when he did not do so against British employment of a blockade to starve out the Germans.

Wilson's persistence eventually got the Kaiser to back down, but only after many weeks of sharp exchanges. A supercilious German reply to his first communication induced Wilson to draft a second note. He warned Berlin that persistence in these actions was "unpardonable" and would be regarded by the American government as "deliberately unfriendly" to the United States. Bryan, believing the document was irresponsibly provocative, refused to put his name to it and resigned as secretary of state. "Germany," he stated, "has a right to prevent contraband from going to the Allies and a ship carrying contraband should not rely upon passengers to protect her from attack—it would be like putting women and children in front of an army." (The cargo of the *Lusitania* included a large supply of ammunition to be employed against the Germans.) In addition to accusing Wilson of pursuing an unfair and reckless policy, Bryan told him, "Colonel House has been secretary of state, not I, and I have never had your full confidence." To replace Bryan, Wilson chose the bellicose and devious Robert Lansing. From that point on, with Bryan gone, and Lansing, House, and others avid for intervention on the side of the Allies, the president had no counselor to restrain him.

With these negotiations getting ever more ominous, word reached Washington that a U-boat had sunk a British liner, *Arabic*, taking forty-four lives, two of them American. Recognizing that he had to respond forcefully but not eager for another futile note exchange, the president hit upon the tactic of leaking word to the press that he was seriously considering a rupture in diplomatic relations. That finally got the attention of the German government, which stated that passenger vessels would no longer be sunk without warning. German shipyards, though, sped up construction of U-boats.

Early in 1916, alarmed that America was moving headlong toward intervention, Senator Thomas Gore of Oklahoma and Representative Atkins McLemore of Texas introduced resolutions warning against or forbidding US citizens from sailing on belligerent vessels destined for war zones. This precaution—sensible, even self-evident—was enacted by Congress in the 1930s. But when, in support of this safeguard, the Democratic chairman of the Senate Foreign Relations Committee wrote the president to say that he would find it hard "to consent to plunge this nation into the vortex of this world war" because of the "foolhardiness" of "our own people recklessly risking their lives on armed belligerent ships," Wilson replied, "I cannot consent to any abridgement of the rights of American citizens in any respect. . . . We covet peace, and shall preserve it at any cost but the loss of honor." In a sweeping declaration, he asserted, "Once accept a single abatement of right, and many other humiliations would follow, and the whole fine fabric of international law might crumble in our hands."

These words revealed Wilson's most grievous shortcoming as a thinker and as a leader. In privileging "honor" and in expressing solicitude for "the whole fine fabric of international law," daily disrespected by the belligerents, Wilson failed to grasp that he was putting the American people gravely at risk so that the leisured few able to afford overseas travel could indulge in it. His ratiocination, wrote the editor Walter Weyl, "is part of a curiously a priori metaphysical idealism. His world stands firmly on its head. Ideas do not rest upon facts but facts on ideas. . . . To him railroad cars are not railroad cars but a gray general thing called Transportation; people are not men and women, corporeal, gross, very human beings, but Humanity—Humanity very much in the abstract."

Told that, despite his opposition, the Gore-McLenore resolution would pass, the president once again considered resigning, but instead decided to exert relentless pressure on Congress. He sent two members of his cabinet up to the Hill with a handwritten letter in which he requested Congress to save him from "the present embarrassment" by killing the resolutions. "No other course would meet the necessities of the case." Though congressional support for the resolutions ran two to one in favor, the House voted to table because "the question...is whether we shall stand by the President in this crisis or not."

Gratified by this outcome, Wilson had to confront a new challenge overseas precisely of the sort that the Gore-McLemore resolutions had tried to forestall. In March 1916, a U-boat made a mockery of the *Arabic* promise by torpedoing an unarmed French ferry, the *Sussex*. In April, Wilson went before Congress to read an ultimatum to Berlin, and early in May, the German government gave in. Until it had enough U-boats for an effective blockade of the British Isles, it did not dare risk war with the United States. Hence, it promised that it would cease sinking merchant vessels without warning, so long as the United States also forced the British to obey international law. Ignoring that condition, Wilson accepted this "*Sussex* pledge." The German announcement came at an optimal time for the president. Fortified by the *Sussex* pledge, he entered the 1916 campaign as the leader who, while defending national honor, had preserved peace.

Wilson began his quest for another term not as a man of peace but as an enthusiast for "preparedness"—a euphemism for military buildup. Clad in a blue jacket with white duck trousers, and sporting a straw hat, he had marched at the head of a preparedness parade up Pennsylvania Avenue waving the Stars and Stripes. Sounding like no one so much as Theodore Roosevelt, he asserted that the United States should have "incomparably the greatest navy in the world," as he signed on to an ambitious plan to give America a two-ocean fleet by adding six battleships, ten cruisers, fifty destroyers, and one hundred submarines. He also advocated a one-third increase in the regular army as well as creation of a "Continental Army"—a reserve auxiliary of four hundred thousand. "Force everywhere speaks out with a loud and imperious voice," he declared.

In this spirit, Wilson instructed the keynoter at the Democratic National Convention in June 1916 to make patriotism the theme of his address—only to have something untoward happen. Partway through his oration, Martin Glynn, a former New York governor, chanced to say that he would not tax the patience of his listeners by reviewing each of the instances where conflict had been avoided, only to have delegates surprise him by rising from their seats shouting, "No, no, go on!" And each time that he recounted an occasion when a president had eschewed belligerency, Glynn would call out, "What did we do? What did we do?" and the aroused crowd would yell back, "We didn't go to war! We didn't go to war!"

On the second day of the gathering, a Kentucky senator, Ollie James, furthered this claim by noting Wilson's response to U-boat provocations: "Without orphaning a single American child, without widowing a single American mother, without firing a single gun, without the shedding of a single drop of blood, he wrung from the most militant spirit that ever brooded above a battlefield an acknowledgment of American rights and an agreement to American demands." And when William Jennings Bryan was summoned to the platform, he delighted the delegates by saying, "I join the American people in thanking God that we have a President who does not want this nation plunged into...war."

In this fashion, "He Kept Us Out of War"—a boast that referred at least as much to Mexico as to Europe—became the motif of the 1916 Democratic presidential campaign. Wilson knew full well that he could not guarantee peace, and indeed had positioned America in a way that war seemed highly likely. "I can't keep the country out of war," he confided to Secretary Daniels. "Any little German lieutenant can put us into war at any time by some calculated outrage." But he went along with the slogan. A vote for his Republican opponent, he implied, would be a mandate for war.

Republicans made this contention plausible by accusing Wilson of being fainthearted. "He first shook his fist and then his finger," said Elihu Root. Theodore Roosevelt went much further. He likened the president to Pontius Pilate, then apologized to Pilate. Wilson, he maintained, was a "demagogue, adroit, tricky, false, without one spark of loftiness in him, without a touch of the heroic in his cold, selfish and timid soul." Roosevelt, having abandoned progressivism for single-minded advocacy of an aggressive foreign policy, hoped for the Republican presidential nomination that year. "It would be a mistake to nominate me," he pontificated, "unless the country has in its mood something of the heroic." But the GOP had no intention of granting absolution to a renegade and instead plucked Charles Evans Hughes from the Supreme Court bench to be its nominee.

In his acceptance address, Wilson placed his main emphasis not on foreign affairs but on his liberal record. "We have in four years come very near to carrying out the platform of the Progressive Party as well as our own," he stated. A spurt of legislation in 1916 gave substance to his crowing. Much of the impetus for it came not from the White House but from congressional insurgents. Indeed, the president had expressed doubts about the wisdom of what became the Federal Farm Loan Act and about the constitutionality of a bill banning child labor. Moreover, he had nothing at all to do with the Revenue Act of 1916, which provided for the first federal inheritance tax and doubled income tax rates. But when legislation stalled, Wilson again went up to the President's Room in the Capitol and brought pressure on Democrats to enact the child labor measure as well as a federal workmen's compensation bill. In both instances, he succeeded.

Two other developments derived largely or wholly from Wilson's initiatives. Early in 1916, he startled the country by nominating to the US Supreme Court Louis Brandeis, the crusading Boston attorney and theoretician of the New Freedom. "When Brandeis's nomination came in yesterday, the Senate simply gasped," a confidant informed ex-president Taft. "There wasn't any more excitement at the Capitol when Congress passed the Spanish War resolution." Overcoming strenuous objections from conservatives and anti-Semites, Wilson won confirmation of the first Jew to take a seat on the Court. Later that year, when a national railroad strike loomed, the president told obdurate railroad operators, "I pray God to forgive you, I never can," and stalked out of a White House meeting. He then lent his support to the Adamson Act, which averted a disruptive strike by imposing on management an eight-hour day for employees. A measure of borderline constitutionality, it won cheers from progressives. Walter Lippmann, who in *Drift and Mastery* (1914) had skewered the New Freedom, wrote in 1916 that Woodrow Wilson headed the only party "national in scope, liberal in purpose, and effective in action.... He has fashioned the old party into something like a national liberal organization."

For all his accomplishments, Wilson recognized that in 1916 he was laboring under the decided disadvantage of being the nominee of a minority party. Four years earlier, his rivals had amassed 58 percent of the vote, and he had prevailed only because the Republican Party was fractured. The candidate of a reunited GOP in 1916 figured to be the likely victor. On Election Night, the *New York Times* pronounced Hughes the winner, for he had swept almost all of the Northeast and the Midwest, running strongly even in former Democratic bastions. On hearing the results, Wilson got set to carry out a plan he already had in place. As Gladstone might have done, he intended to resign at once and install his opponent in the White House, so that there would be no discontinuity in national leadership.

Happier tidings caused Wilson to hold back on executing this scheme. In the West, where women were singing "I Didn't Raise My Boy to Be a Soldier," devotion to the president as the peace candidate permitted him to draw nearly even in electoral votes. For days, the decision remained in doubt. Finally, in California a margin of less than four thousand out of more than a million ballots pushed Wilson over the top, making him the first Democrat since Andrew Jackson to win a second consecutive term in the White House. For close to two weeks, Hughes would not concede. When at last he did send a concession wire, Wilson quipped, "It was a little moth-eaten when it got here but quite legible." The outcome fortified Theodore Roosevelt in the sentiment he had expressed earlier: "We are passing through a thick streak of yellow in our national life."

———

Wilson approached his second term with one vaulting ambition—to prevent the United States from being dragged into the European war. He had long since concluded that the best way to keep the country out of the maelstrom was to persuade the antagonists to lay down their arms, even if it meant American commitments never given before. He had sent Colonel House shuttling between European capitals in 1915 and again in 1916 as his personal emissary to negotiate a settlement that would end the fighting, but House, a partisan of the Allies, presented Wilson's views in a way guaranteed to allow the British and French to ignore them, and then misrepresented their attitudes to the president.

The course of the war in 1916 strengthened the president's resolve. In response to the hideous bloodletting that year, especially at the Somme, which saw more than a million casualties, he declared: "If the contest must continue to proceed towards undefined ends by slow attrition until the one group of belligerents or the other is exhausted, if million after million of human lives must continue to be offered up until on the one side or the other there are no more to offer, if resentments must be killed that can never cool and despairs engendered from which there can be no recovery, hopes of peace and of the willing concert of free people will be rendered vain and idle."

In conflict with this thought, however, he nurtured a different sentiment: America might seize the opportunity to embark upon a crusade. During the recent campaign, he had said: "When you are asked, 'Aren't you willing to fight?' reply yes, you are waiting for something worth fighting for; you are not looking around for petty quarrels, but you are looking about for that sort of quarrel within whose intricacies are written all the texts of the rights of man; you are looking for some cause...in which it seems a glory to shed human blood, if it be necessary, so that all the common compacts of liberty may be sealed with the blood of free men." But this was a conception he held in reserve.

The returns had hardly been counted in the November election when he launched a peace offensive with the promise that the United States, which he declared was "ready to join a league of nations," would be an impartial mediator. He even said that "the objects which the statesmen of the belligerents have in mind in this war are virtually the same." House attempted to discourage him from this endeavor, which he believed the Allies would regard as unfriendly, and Secretary of State Lansing deliberately sabotaged it by assuring the British and the French that the president was pro-Allied. Wilson, who much later fired Lansing (for the wrong reason), ought to have sacked him then. The overtures were doomed anyway, for neither side, after sustaining such heavy losses, was willing to settle for the *status quo ante bellum* that Wilson urged.

On January 22, 1917, Wilson delivered a major address to the US Senate in which he told the European powers what America expected from them. Assigning himself the role of spokesman for the voiceless victims of never-ending carnage, he asked, in the name of "our Lord and Savior," for a "peace without victory." In the archaic phrasing into which he sometimes lapsed, he said, "I would fain believe that I am...speaking for the silent mass of mankind everywhere who have as yet had no place or opportunity to speak their real hearts out concerning the death and ruin they see to have come already upon the persons and the homes they hold most dear." Appealing to the warring nations to agree to a peace with no annexations, no indemnities, he held out to them a vision of a new world order with harmony preserved by a league of nations.

The president's thoughtfully crafted message did not generate the response he had hoped for. Though, after Wilson concluded, La Follette said, "We have just passed through a very important hour in the life of the world," Theodore Roosevelt, who had a considerably larger following, retorted sourly, "Peace without victory is the natural ideal of the man who is too proud to fight.... The Tories of 1776 demanded peace without victory. The Copperheads of 1864 demanded peace without victory. These men were Mr. Wilson's spiritual forebears." Whatever the war-weary masses may have thought of the president's oration, if they ever even learned of it, European leaders scoffed. "Peace without victory," responded Anatole France, "is bread without yeast... love without quarrels, a camel without humps, night without moon, roof without smoke, town without brothel."

At the time he spoke, Wilson had no way of knowing that Germany had already made a fateful decision: to resume unrestricted submarine warfare. The Kaiser had signed an edict, effective February 1, 1917, unleashing U-boats to sink without warning any vessel on the high seas, including unarmed merchant ships and passenger liners. The Admiralty in Berlin had concluded that, though these actions might very well draw the United States into the war, Germany could wreak so much devastation before America could intervene effectively that the Allies would be compelled to capitulate.

Once Germany flouted his ultimatum, Wilson believed that he had to retaliate, but he still sought to avoid war. It would be a "crime," he told House, for the United States to be caught up in such a fashion "as to make it impossible to save Europe afterward." He had further concerns. On February 2, he asked his cabinet, "With the terrible slaughter taking place in Europe, what effect would the depletion of manpower have upon the relations of the white and yellow races? Would the yellow races take advantage of it and attempt to subjugate the white races?" After the meeting broke up, he praised Secretary Daniels for his opposition to war, adding that he feared that intervention would mean the loss of "every reform we have won since 1912." Big Business would take control, "and neither you nor I will live to see government returned to the people. More than that, Free Speech and the other rights will be endangered." On the very next day, however, Wilson broke off diplomatic relations with Germany. There was "no alternative," he told Congress, "consistent with the dignity and honor of the United States."

In late February, the president received shocking intelligence that propelled the United States further toward war when the British passed on to the American government a document from Berlin that they had decoded. Alfred Zimmermann, the German minister of foreign affairs, they revealed, had ordered the Reich's ambassador in Mexico City to offer Carranza an alliance, in the event renewed U-boat attacks led the United States to declare war on Germany. Mexico, the telegram promised, would regain "her lost territory in Texas, New Mexico, and Arizona." Inducements would also be offered Japan. The communication, a New York newspaper declared, was "final proof that the German government has gone stark mad."

To win the approval of Congress for arming merchant ships, Wilson, calculatedly, released the text of the Zimmermann Telegram, and the House of Representatives, in a fury at the Germans, approved the measure overwhelmingly. In the Senate, however, a cadre of eleven talked the bill to death, at a session in which feelings ran so high that one of the foremost antiwar leaders, Robert La Follette, carried a loaded pistol into the chamber to protect himself. Unfairly and self-righteously, Wilson said afterward, "A little group of willful men, representing no opinion but their own, have rendered the great Government of the United States helpless and contemptible." The very next day, on the slim authority of an 1819 piracy statute, he ordered US merchant ships fitted with arms.

Wilson still hesitated to plunge America into "this vast gruesome contest of systemized destruction," but when on March 19 U-boats sank three US merchant vessels, he saw no other recourse. On the following day at a session with the president, every member of the cabinet—even Daniels, ostensibly a pacifist—agreed. Wilson decided on belligerency not only in retaliation for German provocations but also because he desired a seat at the peace table so that he could shape postwar arrangements. If America remained neutral, the most he could expect, he said, was to "call through a crack in the door." The time had come, he had stated in his inaugural address two weeks earlier, for America to step onto the world stage. "We are provincials no longer," he declared.

On the night of April 2, Wilson went before Congress, called into emergency session, to ask it to affirm that a state of war existed between the United States and the German empire. He began by stressing the horrors wrought by U-boats, which had sunk ships "ruthlessly... without... mercy for those on board," even "hospital ships and ships carrying relief to the sorely bereaved and stricken people of Belgium." He went on to say that "there is one choice we cannot make, we are incapable of making: we will not choose the path of submission and suffer the most sacred rights of our nation and our people to be ignored or violated."

Framing the resolve to go to war in universal terms, the president vowed "to fight... for the ultimate peace of the world and for the liberation of its peoples, the German peoples included: for the rights of nations great and small and the privilege of men everywhere to choose their way of life.... The world must be made safe for democracy." He wound up his half-hour address with a memorable peroration:

> It is a fearful thing to lead this great peaceful people into war, into the most terrible and disastrous of all wars, civilization itself seeming to be in the balance. But the right is more precious than peace, and we shall fight for the things which we have always carried nearest our hearts—for democracy, for the right of those who submit to authority to have a voice in their own governments, for the rights and liberties of small nations, for a universal dominion of right by such a concert of free peoples as shall bring peace and safety to all nations and make the world itself at last free. To such a task we can dedicate our lives and our fortunes, everything that we are and everything that we have, with the pride of those who know that the day has come when America is privileged to spend her blood and her might for the principles that gave her birth and happiness and the peace which she has treasured. God helping her, she can do no other.

That final sentence, many recognized, derived from Martin Luther: "God helping me, I can do no other." When he finished, the House exploded in lusty cheers, earsplitting clapping, and rebel yells. Hours later in the White House, Wilson said to Tumulty, "My message tonight was a message of death for our young men. How strange it seems to applaud that."

Congress made quick work of acting. On April 4, the Senate debated the war resolution for thirteen hours, with La Follette demolishing Wilson's claim that the Allies sought the triumph of democracy, and the esteemed Nebraska senator George Norris charging, "We are going into war upon the command of gold." But when the roll was called, only six votes were cast against war. Two days later, fifty members of the House, including eighteen from the president's own party, opposed intervention, but they were overwhelmed by 373 in favor. Early on April 6, 1917—Good Friday—Congress approved a joint resolution declaring war on Germany. (Subsequently, the United States declared war on Austria-Hungary, but not on the other two members of the Central Powers: Bulgaria and Turkey.)

"There is but one response possible for us," the president announced. "Force, Force to the utmost, Force without stint or limit, the righteous and triumphant Force which shall make Right the law of the world and cast every selfish dominion down in the dust." He did not say this until 1918, but it expressed his attitude from the very beginning of the war. Not content with making the United States the quartermaster of the Allies, he insisted on an all-out commitment to mobilizing industry on a scale never before seen and dispatching an American Expeditionary Force of nearly two million men to the battlefields of France. Without seeking congressional approval, Wilson sent thousands more to Vladivostok and Archangel after the October Revolution in Russia. In the nineteen months the war lasted, the Wilson administration spent more than the total sum that had been laid out by the federal government in the entire history of the republic starting with George Washington's presidency.

Wilson asked for almost unlimited power to prosecute the war, and Congress delegated it to him bountifully. In the 1917–18 conflict, as the historian John Chambers has pointed out, "power flowed to the commander-in-chief." The Lever Act authorized him to requisition food and fuel, take over factories and mines, and fix prices of wheat and coal. The Espionage Act vested in him the capacity to ban exports. The Trading with the Enemy Act empowered him to license foreign trade and to censor all communications abroad by radio, mail, or cable. When

Republicans in Congress sniped at him with accusations of inefficiency, Wilson told them he could improve performance if they gave him near-dictatorial power to reshuffle the executive branch, and, in the Overman Act, Congress complied.

Under Wilson, the government invaded the private sector to an extent that few populists or progressives would have imagined possible and that transgressed every principle of the limited government implicit in the New Freedom. The president issued an edict taking over the nation's railroads; the government seized warehouses, as well as telephone and telegraph lines; a War Finance Corporation supervised large securities issues; a War Labor Board, with former president Taft as cochair, put the government behind the right of workers to unionize; a Fuel Administration closed down nonessential factories and introduced daylight savings time; and a superagency, the War Industries Board, under Bernard Baruch, exercised draconian powers. "Laissez faire is dead," exulted one astonished progressive. "Long live social control!" Herbert Hoover, Wilson's exceptionally capable food administrator, mandated meatless and wheatless days, embargoed shipments to Europe that he did not approve, bullied millers and farmers, penalized retailers who disobeyed his orders, and required the licensing of every person in the food industry—a decree that his biographer has called "perhaps the most extraordinary act ever taken by the federal government." In crises, Hoover declared, democracies must show a "willingness to yield to dictatorship."

Though he was called "food czar" and "the autocrat of the breakfast table," Hoover, in common with other Wilsonians, insisted that the war government was based not on coercion but on voluntarism, a delusion that years later was to bedevil his presidency. "There was no power in autocracy equal to the voluntary effort of a free people," he maintained. The reality was revealed disingenuously by the priorities commissioner of the War Industries Board: "We never used any compulsion. Of course, if a man ... didn't want to play with us, he found he couldn't get any fuel or railroad cars or any labor or anything; but we never used any compulsion."

The imperious nature of Wilson's wartime administration also found expression in its attitude toward the sex lives of men in uniform. By the end of 1918, the US government had closed every important red-light district in the country, including Storyville, with its intimate association with New Orleans jazz. Wilson's secretary of war, Newton D. Baker, and his aide, the social worker Raymond Fosdick, found the welfare of soldiers overseas a knottier problem. In France, Premier Georges Clemenceau, in a gracious gesture, offered to share his nation's prostitutes with his American brethren. When Fosdick forwarded this invitation to Baker, the secretary of war cried, "For God's sake, Raymond, don't show this to the president or he'll stop the war."

Wilson bore a large share of the responsibility for the widespread violations of civil liberties in World War I. "Woe be to the man," the president warned, "that seeks to stand in our way in this day of high resolution when every principle we hold dearest is to be vindicated and made secure." He allowed his zealous postmaster general to deny the mails to dissenting publications and his attorney general to prosecute alleged seditionists and to rely on private vigilantes to harass and punish citizens deemed insufficiently patriotic. "If you stopped to collect your thoughts, you could be arrested for illegal assembly," said a Socialist writer. Prosecutions for criticism of the war netted twenty-year prison terms for a Socialist congressman from Wisconsin and for the Socialist presidential candidate, Eugene V. Debs. The president, said the progressive Amos Pinchot, "puts his enemies in office and his friends in jail." Wilson ensured correct popular attitudes toward the war in yet another way by an executive order establishing a Committee on Public Information under the journalist George Creel. A high-powered propaganda agency, it manipulated, and even manufactured, public opinion.

No one of these edicts or statutes began to approach in significance one 1917 law: the Selective Service Act. Believing that "there is a universal obligation to serve," Wilson urged the drafting of young men into the armed services, but, with his characteristic capacity for self-delusion, he maintained, "It is in no sense a conscription of the unwilling," but "rather, selection from a nation which has volunteered in mass." Others, including a number of powerful Democrats, had a more sober view. Stepping down from the Speaker's chair, Champ Clark gave a passionate speech, which concluded, "In the estimation of Missourians there is precious little difference between a conscript and a convict." But his eloquent appeal fell short when in late April both houses voted to impose a draft. It seemed improbable that the government would be able to transport troops across the Atlantic to the trenches of France on the

Western Front before 1918, but in December 1917 the army reported the first fatalities of American soldiers. In the next eleven months, more than one hundred thousand more doughboys would die and be buried in Flanders fields or other alien corn.

Only a cause of transcendental promise, Wilson believed, could justify such sacrifice. To give voice to his aspirations, the president resolved to deliver an uplifting address that would command the attention of the entire world. In response to the Bolsheviks, who charged that the Allies were fighting for nothing save the spoils of empire, he intended to elucidate his conception of the contours of the globe when the bloodshed ceased. Early in 1918, he closeted himself with Colonel House to peruse memoranda prepared by experts on European affairs and to pull his thoughts together. "We actually got down to work at half past ten and finished remaking the map of the world, as we would have it, at half past twelve o'clock," House recorded in his diary. Then Wilson, after setting down his thoughts in shorthand, hammered out a draft on his typewriter.

On January 8, 1918, the president made a dramatic appearance before Congress to reveal his design—an assemblage of fourteen points. He intended his message for a diverse audience: the American people, the subjugated masses on the Continent, the enemy, and, not least, the Allies. The first five points laid out principles that should guide the peacemaking: "open covenants of peace, openly arrived at"; "absolute" freedom of the seas; removal of trade barriers; drastic arms reduction; and adjustment of colonial claims with equal weight given to the interests of the inhabitants of the colonies. The next eight points dealt with territorial arrangements, such as an independent Poland, which were to be based on the right to self-determination. Nothing was closer to his heart than his climactic fourteenth point: an "association of nations...for the purpose of affording mutual guarantees of political independence and territorial integrity to great and small states alike." He concluded with an apocalyptic utterance: "The moral climax of this the culminating and final war for human liberty has come."

Many months later, on October 25, 1918, with questions of how to fashion a new world order based on the Fourteen Points looming as the war wound down, Wilson made an extraordinary appeal. He asked the American people to preserve the Democratic majority in Congress in the November elections, "if you have approved of my leadership and wish me to continue to be your unembarrassed spokesman in affairs at home and abroad." Conflating his role as party leader with that of commander in chief, he declared that "unity of command is as necessary now in civil action as it is upon the field of battle," and, mimicking a prime minister's quest for a vote of confidence, he contended that turning over control of Congress to the Republicans would "certainly be interpreted on the other side of the water as a repudiation of my leadership." His statement was an egregious misstep, especially surprising for a man who had spent a lifetime studying political behavior. A political scientist should have known that the party in power can almost always expect to lose votes in a midterm election and that it would be advisable ahead of time to minimize the significance of the balloting.

Ten days later, voters turned over supremacy in both houses of Congress to the Republicans. Apart from the natural tides of off-year contests, the Democrats lost out primarily because voters in the Great Plains believed that, in imposing price ceilings on wheat but not cotton, the president was showing partiality to his party's following in the Solid South. Wilson's appeal for confidence probably neither lost nor won him votes, but it had colossal consequences. He had all but invited Republicans to regard him as their enemy, and the miscarriage of his challenge meant that he would be bargaining with the great powers in a few weeks having been, by his own reckoning, disowned. Furthermore, any treaty he did negotiate would have to get by the Senate Foreign Relations Committee, whose chairman, as a consequence of the elections, would shortly be his implacable Republican foe Henry Cabot Lodge.

Theodore Roosevelt drove home the inescapable conclusion. He had been saying for a long time that peace should be dictated by "hammering guns" rather than "clicking . . . typewriters." After the 1918 ballots were counted, he declared:

> Our allies and our enemies and Mr. Wilson himself should all understand that Mr. Wilson has no authority whatever to speak for the American people at this time. His leadership has just been emphatically repudiated by them. The newly elected Congress comes far nearer than Mr. Wilson to having a right to speak for the purposes of the American people at this moment. Mr. Wilson and his Fourteen

Points and his four supplementary points and his five complementary points and all his utterances every which way have ceased to have any shadow of right to be accepted as expressive of the will of the American people.

Roosevelt and Lodge did everything they could to undermine Wilson abroad. "In any free country, except the United States, the result of the Congressional elections on November 5th would have meant Mr. Wilson's retirement from office and return to private life," TR told the British foreign secretary, Arthur Balfour. "He demanded a vote of confidence. The people voted a want of confidence." Roosevelt went out of his way to impress upon not only Balfour but also David Lloyd George and Georges Clemenceau that they should ignore Wilson and impose a Carthaginian peace on Germany. In like manner, Lodge urged against incorporating Wilson's "almost hopelessly impossible" dream of a league of nations in the peace treaty.

The Democrats might well have done better if Wilson had been able to close out the war before Election Day instead of six days later, but his success in ending it as quickly and as deftly as he did stands as one of his greatest achievements. He had first been approached by the Germans early in October when, with their armies reeling, they inquired, through Prince Max of Baden, about an armistice based on the Fourteen Points. German generals thought they could lure the president into protracted negotiations that would allow them to rebuild their forces for a new offensive. But Wilson proved a lot tougher and more skillful than they had anticipated. He would not deal, he said, with "military masters and... monarchical autocrats." Any further communication with Germany would entail "not peace negotiations, but surrender." Wilson's firm stand, and his indication that he would look favorably on a republic, helped precipitate the abdication of the Kaiser on November 9, 1918. Two days later, Berlin agreed to Wilson's terms, and, on the eleventh minute of the eleventh hour of the eleventh month, the carnage of the Great War ended. "The hand of God is laid upon the nations," Wilson said. "He will show them favor, I devoutly believe, only if they rise to the clear heights of His own justice and mercy."

On November 18, one week after the armistice, Wilson startled the country by announcing that he had appointed himself head of the American delegation to the peace conference, scheduled to open in Paris in January 1919. No president before had ever absented himself by crossing the ocean. Moreover, save for one ten-day interlude, he was to spend more than half a year away from the White House. Wilson's selections for the other members of the delegation also aroused controversy. In the most recent peace negotiations, McKinley had named three senators to the delegation, one from the minority party, but Wilson chose no senator and, only after a time, a token Republican. In truth, he did not have attractive options, for the most eligible senator was Henry Cabot Lodge, who held him in contempt. He could, though, have chosen William Howard Taft, who was highly sympathetic to his aims, but he wanted total control in Paris and refused to acknowledge that to get the peace treaty ratified he would need bipartisan support.

When the USS *George Washington* docked in France, Wilson found out how deeply affected Europeans were by his utopian messages about a world that would never again know war. At Brest, where he disembarked, he was driven in an open car through streets arched with flowers as Bretons leaned out of windows to cry "Vive Weelson." On the following day in Paris, an American observer reported: "The parade from the station to the Murat house in Rue de Monceau, which is to be his official residence, was accompanied by the most remarkable demonstration of enthusiasm and affection on the part of Parisians that I have ever heard of, let alone seen.... Troops, cavalry and infantry lined the entire route and tens of thousands of people fought for a glimpse. The streets were decorated with flags and banners,...and huge 'Welcome Wilson' and 'Honor to Wilson, The Just' signs stretched across the streets from house to house." H. G. Wells later wrote: "In that brief interval there was a very extraordinary and significant wave of response to him throughout the earth.... All humanity leapt to accept and glorify Wilson.... He was transfigured in the eyes of men. He ceased to be a common statesman; he became a Messiah."

The tumultuous reception reinforced Wilson's conviction that he must seize upon this moment to secure a just and lasting peace. To do so, he had to overcome the skepticism of "the Tiger" of French politics, Georges Clemenceau, who said, "Wilson bores me with his Fourteen

Paris greets Wilson, 1919. Under the huge sign VIVE WILSON, French crowds surge down an avenue to greet the American president whom they viewed as a savior. *Courtesy of the Woodrow Wilson Presidential Library, Staunton, Virginia. Local Accession Number 991*

Points. Why, God Almighty has only ten." After pointing out that America had not experienced the war during the three years when France had lost a million and a half men, he warned: "You seek to do justice to the Germans. Do not believe that they will ever forgive us; they only seek opportunity for revenge." With European leaders deeply skeptical, it required single-minded tenacity for the president to draft the Covenant for the League of Nations and win the other delegates over to incorporating it in the peace treaty.

On February 15, the president sailed home for a brief visit, basking in his success and confident that the treaty would be approved. Prospects seemed promising. Early in 1919, Theodore Roosevelt had died, and the only surviving former Republican president, William Howard Taft, headed an organization advocating a league of nations. Just before leaving France, Wilson told Clemenceau's main rival, Raymond Poincaré, that though a tough struggle lay ahead, it would last only a day.

Upon arriving home, though, he ran into powerful opposition, and in some quarters implacable hostility. When he returned to the White House, Alice Roosevelt Longworth, TR's acid-tongued daughter, made the sign of the evil eye and cried, "A murrain on him, a murrain on him, a murrain on him!" His old nemesis Henry Cabot Lodge, who had earlier told Theodore Roosevelt that he "never expected to hate anyone in politics with the hatred I feel towards Wilson," treated his efforts in Paris with disdain. The phrasing of the League of Nations Covenant, Lodge sneered, "might get by at Princeton, but certainly not at Harvard." He resented Wilson's repute as "the Scholar in Politics," an encomium he claimed for himself. (In fact, Senator Depew was on point in saying that Lodge's mind was like the New England landscape—"naturally barren, but highly cultivated.") These faultfinders, Wilson assured the Democratic National Committee, were "blind and little, provincial people.... They have not even good working imitations of minds." But however parochial Lodge may have been, he was an adroit politician—as Wilson soon found out.

On March 3, 1919, shortly before midnight, Lodge rose on the Senate floor to read a document declaring that "the League of Nations in the form now proposed...should not be accepted by the United States." When challenged, he called out the names of thirty-seven Republican senators who had signed the resolution. Two absent Republicans immediately wired their agreement, and one Democrat was also known to be strongly opposed—a total of forty, considerably more than the thirty-three needed to block ratification, which required a two-thirds vote. This "round robin" totally transformed the controversy. No longer could anyone suppose that the president was sure to succeed.

Wilson breathed defiance. On the very next day, en route from Washington to the New York docks to embark on his return voyage to Europe, he stopped off at the Metropolitan Opera House for a pro-League rally. Arm in arm with former president Taft, he walked onstage to speak to an overflow audience with fifteen thousand more outside the hall. Wilson drew cheers by stating, "When that treaty comes back, gentlemen on this side will find the covenant not only in it, but so many threads of the treaty tied to the covenant that you cannot dissect the covenant from the treaty without destroying the whole vital structure." It seemed inconceivable to him that the United States Senate, in order to avoid membership in the League, would go to the extreme of rejecting the peace treaty altogether.

No matter how badly he wanted to belittle the round robin, though, Wilson returned to Paris knowing that he had to secure amendments to the covenant if he hoped to prevail. He realized that the small corps of "irreconcilables" were beyond reach. Even before Senator William Borah of Idaho glimpsed the draft covenant, he had said, "If the Saviour of mankind should revisit the earth and declare for a League of Nations, I would be opposed to it." Almost all of the Democratic senators were with him, but they fell well short of giving him the two-thirds vote mandated. Republicans such as Lodge who had strong reservations about the treaty were unlikely to budge. His best hope was to detach the "mild reservationists" from Lodge, and to do that he had to obtain modification of the covenant.

That was not going to be easy. If he requested special consideration for the Monroe Doctrine from the other powers, Japan and Italy could be expected to demand acknowledgment of their spheres of influence, which he did not want to happen. After persistent negotiations, however, the president got the concessions he asked for—exemption of the Monroe Doctrine, stipulation that the League could not touch domestic questions in America, and the right of withdrawal. Critics who charge Wilson with inexorable rigidity do not credit him enough for his willingness to humble himself in Paris. But in return for these concessions, the other powers demanded a free hand. Wilson resisted as best he could, once to the point of ordering the *George Washington* to return to Brest so that he could bolt the conference and sail home. He was able to stave off French attempts to dismember Germany and Italian insistence on acquiring territory assigned to the new country of Yugoslavia. Nations carved out of the former Austro-Hungarian empire conformed reasonably faithfully to the Wilsonian principle of self-determination. And he saw to it that the treatment of Germany was not as severe as the British and French wanted. (Or, it should be added, as harsh as would have been meted out to the Allies if the Germans had won.)

But on major features of the settlement, some of them highly unpalatable, he gave in. The treaty required the Germans to admit that they bore sole guilt for bringing on the devastation of war, obligated them to pay astronomical sums in reparations, stripped them of all of their colonies, parceled out pieces of their country to France and Belgium, and gave Poland a corridor to the sea that severed East Prussia from the rest of Germany. Wilson found hardest of all to accept the Japanese grab for the former German sphere in the Chinese province of Shantung. He knew that this violation of Chinese sovereignty made a mockery of the very spirit of the Fourteen Points, but, after losing sleep over it, he caved in, reasoning that enticing Japan into becoming a member of the League of Nations outweighed adherence to principle. China, indignant, refused to sign the treaty, and a number of young US aides resigned in protest at this and other egregious compromises. These ordeals took a lot out of Wilson. The confident, even overweening, leader whom John Singer Sargent had painted eighteen months before had become, in Sir William Orpen's portrait of June 1919, a tense, careworn figure—though one who still showed resolve.

Two days after he returned to the United States in July 1919, Wilson presented the treaty with the League Covenant to the US Senate in the worst speech of his career. Instead of dealing seriously, and respectfully, with the concerns of the legislators about issues such as Shantung and the quest for Irish independence, he delivered a self-indulgent, pretentious sermon. (His supporters, noted a Democratic senator, "wanted raw meat," but instead "he fed them cold turnips.") Wilson said of the Versailles treaty: "Dare we reject it and break the heart of the world? . . . The stage is set, the destiny disclosed. It has come about by no plan of our conceiving, but by the hand of God who led us into this way. . . . The light streams upon the path ahead and nowhere else." When he concluded, only one Republican clapped. A Democratic senator observed that the performance suggested that of a corporation president, who, called upon to account for himself to a board of directors, "tonefully read Longfellow's Psalm of Life."

This false start presaged a grueling spring and summer in which the breach between the president and his Senate opponents never narrowed. All of his painstaking, sometimes humiliating entreaties in Paris for amendments to the covenant had not gained him a single vote. Not even his willingness to subject himself to questioning by the Senate Foreign Relations Committee, a highly unusual concession, yielded anything.

Unable to make headway on Capitol Hill, Wilson decided to go to the country. Knowing how vulnerable the president's constitution was, his doctors advised against such a strenuous journey, but Wilson could not be dissuaded. "I must go," he said. "I promised our soldiers, when I asked them to take up arms, that it was a war to end wars, and if I do not do all in my power to put the Treaty in effect, I will be a slacker and never be able to look those boys in the eye." On September 3, 1919, his train pulled out of Union Station, and over the course of the next three weeks, he taxed himself to the limit and beyond by covering eight thousand miles and delivering more than three dozen addresses to gatherings, ever larger, ever more enthusiastic. His train took him west to Columbus and Indianapolis, across the Mississippi to St. Louis, up the wide Missouri to Omaha and Bismarck, west through Billings, Helena, Coeur d'Alene, and Spokane to Seattle, then southward through Portland all the way to San Diego before turning east toward home.

In delivering his addresses, he assumed the guise not of a political leader but of an Old Testament prophet warning of a wrathful Jehovah. In St. Louis, with an ominous nocturnal threnody, he warned of what rejection of the League would portend:

And the glory of the Armies and Navies of the United States is gone like a dream in the night, and there ensues upon it, in the suitable darkness of the night, the nightmare of dread which lay upon the nations before this war came; and there will come sometime, in the vengeful Providence of God, another struggle in which, not a few hundred thousand fine men from America will have to die, but as many millions as are necessary to accomplish the final freedom of the peoples of the world.

Again and again on his mission, he spelled out in a Manichaean mode what would ensue if the treaty was not ratified. "If America goes back upon mankind, mankind has no other place to turn," he proclaimed. "A great and final choice is upon the people," he declared. "Either we are going to guarantee civilization or we are going to abandon it." Unless the League of Nations could prevent it, he said, "I can predict with absolute certainty that, within another generation, there will be another world war," and the mammoth guns with which the Germans had bombarded Paris would be "toys...compared with what would be used in the next war." On September 19, he spoke to the people of San

Diego about their children: "I know, if by any chance we should not win this great fight for the League of Nations, it would mean their death warrant."

Wilson knew how to pull heartstrings, and his devoted listeners responded. People wept unashamedly as he spoke of the graves of American soldiers in France and said that such tragedies should never be repeated. In "the noblest errand that troops ever went on," American boys had sacrificed their lives, he maintained, not to protect their own country, which had not been attacked, but for "the salvation of mankind." He drew a thunderous ovation by saying, "When this treaty is accepted, men in khaki will not have to cross the seas again. That is the reason I believe in it." In Seattle, the packed arena was standing room only; in Los Angeles, he spoke to a "monster mass meeting"; as many as fifty thousand welcomed him to San Diego. The spirit of these gatherings was described as "akin to fanaticism." So large and so fervent were the rallies that a number of commentators thought he was turning the tide in his favor, though there was no evidence of any shift in Washington, where, in fact, his speeches may have hardened sentiment against him.

Instead of attempting to coax senators to his side, he lashed out at them, and more than once descended to demagoguery. On learning in St. Louis that the Senate Foreign Relations Committee had voted four reservations to the treaty, he condemned his critics as "contemptible quitters." In Los Angeles, he went so far as to charge his opponents with infidelity to fallen doughboys: "Have these gentlemen no hearts? Do they forget the sons that are dead in France?" In Salt Lake City, he accused even mild reservationists of being pro-German. Alluding to groups such as Irish-Americans, who opposed the League out of distrust of the British, he became even shriller: "I want to say—and I can't say it too often—any man who carries a hyphen about with him carries a dagger that he is ready to plunge into the vitals of this republic whenever he gets a chance. If I can catch any man with a hyphen in this great contest, I will know that I have caught an enemy of the republic."

On his homeward journey, after speaking in Cheyenne and Denver, he stopped at Pueblo, Colorado. There, on the state fairgrounds, he once again adopted the mode of a psalmist. Tears welling, he told the large crowd: "There is one thing that the American people always rise and extend their hand to, and that is the truth of justice and of liberty and of peace. We have accepted the truth and we are going to be led by it, and it is going to lead us, and through us the world, out into pastures of quietness and peace such as the world never dreamed of."

That night, badly fatigued by the grueling pace of the tour, Wilson suffered severe head pain; he wakened the next morning with one side of his face fallen. Still determined to soldier on, he required considerable persuasion to agree to cancel the remainder of his schedule. "I seem to have gone to pieces," he said. After overhearing that admission, his physician wrote in a diary: "The President looked out of the window, and he was almost overcome by his emotions. He choked and big tears fell from his eyes as he turned away." Four days after he got back to the White House, he collapsed on the bathroom floor, where Mrs. Wilson found him lying unconscious. A devastating stroke had left him paralyzed on his left side, with his eyesight badly impaired. An invalid in a sickroom, the president was woefully incapacitated. "Wilson's stroke caused the worst crisis of presidential disability in American history," his most recent biographer, John Milton Cooper Jr., has written. "Out of a dynamic, resourceful leader emerged an emotionally unstable, delusional creature." Only sixty-two, he no longer had the energy to function as president; his judgment was erratic; and even when, after several weeks, he showed some improvement, he found it difficult to concentrate.

He could also be vindictive. On learning that Secretary of State Lansing had, not unreasonably, called cabinet meetings at a time when the country was leaderless, he fired him. "It seems the petulant & irritable act of a sick man," said Secretary of War Baker. (Lansing speculated that the "brutal and offensive" phrasing of Wilson's letter to him was "a species of mania. . . . It sounded like a spoiled child crying out in rage at an imaginary wrong.") In his very last days as president, Wilson received a cogent brief urging executive clemency for the imprisoned Eugene Debs from Attorney General A. Mitchell Palmer, no friend of radicals. On it, Wilson scribbled, "Denied. W. W."

His altered appearance shocked those who knew him. "He lived on; but oh, what a wreck of his former self!" said a White House functionary who saw him daily. "There was never a moment during all that time when he was more than a shadow of his former self. He had changed from a giant to a pygmy in every wise." When the foremost Democrat on the Senate Foreign Relations Committee was allowed to come to the White House in November, he "beheld an emaciated old man with a thin white beard which he had permitted to grow." Six months later, a cabinet officer, observing the president's thin voice and drooping jaw, thought to himself, "It was enough to make one weep to look at him."

From October 1919 until the end of his term in March 1921, the United States did not have, in any meaningful sense, a president. For four months, the cabinet did not meet; for the ensuing four months, it met without him. Laws took effect without his signature because he could barely achieve a scrawl. Major events transpired—race riots that claimed more than a hundred lives; the Palmer raids launched by Wilson's attorney general, who ran roughshod over civil liberties during the Red Scare; the thorny reconversion from a war to a peace economy—with no input from the president, or, sometimes, even any recognition that they were happening. "Wilson's" veto of the Volstead Act enforcing prohibition (quickly overridden) was actually prepared by Joe Tumulty and sent up to the Hill bearing the name of the president, who knew nothing about it. With Wilson laid low—he did not see the streets of Washington for five months—the vacuum in decision-making was filled by young Tumulty or, to a much greater extent, the first lady.

Edith Bolling Wilson, whom he had married after the death of his first wife, came to be called "the first woman president" of the United States. "We have petticoat Government!" Senator Albert Fall of New Mexico ranted. "Mrs. Wilson is president!" In fact, she had no agenda nor any desire to shape policy. She cared so little about politics that she had not even known who was running in 1912. Nonetheless, for many months she exerted a powerful influence. By fueling her husband's suspicions of Colonel House and by elbowing Tumulty aside, she became Wilson's chief adviser. At her behest, physicians concealed the alarming state of the president's condition from the public—even from cabinet officials—and she controlled all access to him. She vetted every document that came to the White House, and she alone decided which ones Wilson would get to see. When in January 1920 his doctor persuaded the president to give up the office, as Wilson should have, she prevented the move.

The president's infirmity gave Lodge the field to himself. On October 14, he reported out of the Foreign Relations Committee a set of reservations, fourteen all told, spitefully matching Wilson's Fourteen Points. In addition to withholding American acquiescence on matters such as Shantung, they disclaimed any obligation to comply with Article X of the covenant, committing the United States to defend nations that were members of the League from "external aggression," unless such action was authorized by Congress.

Lodge's reservations infuriated Wilson. Some of them passed muster, he said, but "if the treaty should be returned to me with such a reservation on Article X, I would be obliged to consider it a rejection of the treaty and of the Covenant of the League of Nations. Any reservation seeking to deprive the League of Nations of the virility of Article X cuts at the heart of the Covenant itself." Girded for battle, he told his party's leader in the Senate: "I want the vote of each, Republican and Democrat, recorded, because they will have to answer to the people. I am a sick man, lying in this bed, but I am going to debate this issue with these gentlemen in their respective states whenever they come up for re-election if I have breath enough in my body. . . . I shall do this even if I have to give my life to it. And I will get their political scalps when the truth is known to the people."

On November 18, the president sent out a letter asserting that the Lodge reservations did not "provide for ratification but for nullification," deliberately choosing a word that was a knife thrust, for Republicans prided themselves on having been the party of the Union in the Civil War. To accuse them of "nullification" implied that they had signed up with John C. Calhoun. He also dispatched instructions to Democratic senators, who had been leaderless for weeks: "I sincerely hope that the friends and supporters of the treaty will vote against the Lodge resolution of ratification."

The following day, the Senate voted for the first time on ratification of the Treaty of Versailles. With the Lodge reservations to the covenant, it won the yeas of thirty-nine senators (all but four of them Republican) but was overwhelmed by the opposition of an odd coupling of fifteen irreconcilables and forty Democrats, who followed Wilson's orders. The treaty without the Lodge reservations fared slightly worse, with only thirty-seven Democrats and one Republican in favor. After the roll calls, a Republican senator told Lodge, "We can always depend on Mr. Wilson. He never has failed us."

Through the winter, Senate Democrats attempted to see if some kind of compromise with the Republican mild reservationists could be reached, but, by a single heedless act, Wilson snuffed out any scant hope for success. In an open letter on March 8, 1920, he wrote: "I have been struck by the fact that practically every so-called reservation was in effect a nullification of the terms of the treaty itself. I hear of reservationists and mild reservationists, but I cannot understand the difference between a nullifier and a mild nullifier." Wilson's bombshell alienated Senate moderates, outraged at being branded nullifiers; provoked senators in his own party to break with him; and got a raking over by the Democratic press, including the *New York World*, which titled an editorial "Ratify!" Wilson, stated the *Washington Post*, had become, though from a different polarity, an "irreconcilable."

On March 19, precisely four months after the earlier roll calls, the Senate voted again on the treaty—but with the only test confined to the pact with the Lodge reservations. After six hours of debate, the Senate registered forty-nine in favor, including breakaway Democrats disobeying Wilson's orders, with thirty-five opposed. In sum, a narrow majority favored the treaty with reservations. But that was not enough to meet the two-thirds requirement, as a number of Democrats joined with Republican irreconcilables to kill it. With that roll call, the final opportunity was gone. The United States never did become a member of the League of Nations.

Contemporaries and historians have frequently placed the blame for the debacle on Wilson, often rendering harsh verdicts on him. The British economist John Maynard Keynes called him a "blind and deaf Don Quixote," and the historian Thomas Bailey concluded: "In the final analysis the treaty was slain in the house of its friends rather than in the house of its enemies.... It was not the two-thirds rule, or the 'irreconcilables,' or Lodge, or the 'strong' and 'mild' reservationists, but Wilson and his docile following who delivered the fatal stab.... This was the supreme act of infanticide. With his own sickly hands Wilson slew his own brain child." The most some of the president's defenders have been able to muster on his behalf is to contend that he was undone by the stroke; if he had been well, it is said, he would have worked out a satisfactory agreement to win ratification.

In truth, granted Wilson's flaws, those who favored an American commitment to a system of collective security never had a chance. Lodge and his allies had seen to it that there was no way that the treaty could be approved save with crippling reservations to the covenant. Only a single Republican senator came close to supporting Wilson, leaving him far short of the two-thirds he needed and with no room for meaningful negotiation—something he perceived both before and after the stroke, which did not significantly alter his attitude. The president was attempting to lead the nation into abandoning a deeply entrenched attachment to isolationism, and that proved to be much too long a leap.

———————

Under the delusion that Americans were craving a larger role in the world when in fact their support for international obligations was ebbing, Wilson urged Democrats to turn the 1920 contest into "a great and solemn referendum" on joining the League of Nations—a strategy certain to put the party in jeopardy. He was so mesmerized by the British paradigm and so out of touch with reality that, at about the same time, he aired a truly asinine idea. He called upon fifty-six US senators, identified by name, to abandon their seats and stand for reelection, with the promise that "if . . . a majority of them are re-elected, I will resign the presidency." (Curiously, he singled out five who were wholly or mostly on his side, while bypassing an irreconcilable.)

Despite his affliction, Wilson actively sought renomination for a third term in 1920 and seriously expected that the Democrats would give it to him. He even made notes on the membership of the cabinet he planned to appoint in his forthcoming administration. He had no comprehension of how many Americans despised him or of what an albatross he had become to his party. By 1920, he had been targeted by a wide constellation of faultfinders: opponents of the war, ethnic groups (German Americans who identified with the Central Powers, Irish Americans who thought he was the pawn of the British), businessmen who resented controls, workers who believed he had not done enough for them, blacks who had suffered in race riots, and all those who had soured on the costs of war. The Democratic convention, which never gave a thought to renominating the president, chose instead the unexciting Ohio governor, James Cox, with the ebullient assistant secretary of the navy, Franklin Delano Roosevelt, as his running mate. Wilson could draw satisfaction only from the keynote address. Which countries, Homer Cummings asked, had not joined the League of Nations? He answered: "Revolutionary Mexico, Bolshevist Russia, unspeakable Turkey, and the United States of America."

So strong was disapproval of Wilson and the Democrats in 1920 that Republicans felt comfortable with settling on a third-rater: Warren G. Harding, a senator from Ohio. Harry Daugherty, campaign manager for this unremarkable man, said of his unambitious client, "I found him sunning himself, like a turtle on a log, and I pushed him into the water." When Harding, unsure he had the right stuff, asked his sponsor, "Am I big enough for the race?" Daugherty replied, "Don't make me laugh. The day of giants in the presidential chair is passed." In one of the most famous prognostications in American political history, Daugherty foresaw that at the GOP National Convention the more formidable candidates would kill one another off and that at "about eleven minutes after two o'clock on Friday morning" in "a smoke-filled room" at Chicago's Blackstone Hotel "fifteen or twenty men, somewhat weary" would settle on his protégé. The scenario did not quite play out that way, but close enough. "The Grand Dukes have chosen their weak Tsar in order to increase the power of the Grand Dukes," wrote Walter Lippmann. On learning of his nomination, the poker-playing Harding said, "I feel like a man who goes in with a pair of eights and comes out with aces full." For the vice presidency, the delegates selected the dour governor of Massachusetts, Calvin Coolidge, who, despite having played an inglorious role in a walkout by Boston police, had won a national reputation for resoluteness by saying that there was "no right to strike against the public safety by anybody, anywhere, anytime."

A number of commentators found the choice of Harding less than inspiring. "We must go back to Franklin Pierce if we would see a President who measures down to his political stature," observed the *New York Times*. Harding, said Woodrow Wilson testily, had a "bungalow mind." Scrutiny of his record revealed not a scintilla of distinction or even conscientiousness. As senator, he had missed two-thirds of roll calls. Even intimates questioned whether he would be up to the job of president of the United States. Right after Harding was nominated, his wife told a journalist, "I can see but one word written over the head of my husband if he is elected and that word is tragedy."

During the 1920 campaign, not even Republican leaders had any illusions about their candidate, and he gave them no reason to harbor any. From his deathbed, the Pennsylvania boss, Boies Penrose, recommended: "Keep Warren at home. Don't let him make any speeches. If he goes out on a tour somebody's sure to ask him questions, and Warren's just the sort of damned fool that will try to answer them." His prolix addresses were mind-numbing. In one purple passage that became notorious, Harding had said: "America's present need is not heroics, but healing; not nostrums, but normalcy; . . . not agitation, but adjustment; not surgery but serenity; . . . not experiment, but equipoise; not submergence in internationality, but sustainment in triumphant nationality." (Though Harding did not coin the word "normalcy," as is often said, the usage was so rare that by employing it he unwittingly fastened a label on the age.)

Instead of attempting to demonstrate that Harding would be an outstanding president, Republicans sought, as Wilson had wished, to make the election a referendum—not, though, on the League, but on Wilson himself. Henry Cabot Lodge asserted: "Mr. Wilson and his dynasty, his heirs and assigns, or anybody that is his, anybody who with bended knee has served his purposes, must be driven from all control, from all influence upon the Government of the United States."

The otherwise lackluster 1920 election did have one significant feature: it was the first presidential contest in which women had the right to vote. In 1914, leaders of both parties, including—to the disappointment of his daughters—Woodrow Wilson, had opposed the Susan B. Anthony Amendment for women's suffrage. But during the war attitudes had changed, and in September 1918 the president had come before the Senate to advocate passage. "I tell you plainly that this measure which I urge upon you is vital to winning the war," he had declared. Southern Democrats had blocked it at that time, but in June 1919 the Senate had come up with the two-thirds vote required for approval, and late in the summer of 1920, the thirty-sixth state, Tennessee, had ratified the Nineteenth Amendment. The veteran suffragist Carrie Chapman Catt told a victory rally exultantly, "We are no longer petitioners, we are not wards of the nation, but free and equal citizens."

Election Night in 1920 marked the first time, too, that presidential election returns were broadcast over the radio, and during the evening listeners to KDKA Pittsburgh heard, hour after hour through the static, reports of ever-mounting majorities for Warren Harding that reached historic dimensions. The first man to move directly from the US Senate into the White House, he received more than 60 percent of the ballots—the highest proportion anyone had ever gotten in a contested presidential election. He swept every county on the Pacific Coast, all but one in New England, and every borough of the Democratic fiefdom, New York City. He even broke the Solid South—for the first time in forty-four years—by taking Tennessee. (The Socialist Eugene V. Debs polled nearly a million votes despite being incarcerated in a federal penitentiary in Atlanta for antiwar activities.)

Cox, pundits agreed, could not overcome resentment at eight years of Woodrow Wilson: government controls, overseas ventures, battlefield casualties, misconceived idealism, postwar inflation. A Democratic campaign worker reported from Sioux Falls, South Dakota: "The bitterness toward Wilson is evident everywhere and deeply rooted. He hasn't a friend." Asked by a reporter to explain the causes of the disaster for his party, the Democratic power broker Champ Clark spat out one word venomously, "Wilson!" No one experienced more malicious pleasure in the outcome than Henry Cabot Lodge. "We have torn up Wilsonism by the roots," he said. "I am not slow to take my own share of vindication which I find in majorities."

Wilson lived out the time allotted to him a shattered man. Two weeks after the devastating election, the journalist Ray Stannard Baker was dismayed by what he saw when he paid a call at the White House: "A broken, ruined old man, shuffling along, his left arm inert, the fingers drawn up like a claw, the left side of his face sagging frightfully. His voice is not human: it gurgles in his throat, sounds like that of an automaton." Baker added that "his mind seems as alert as ever," but Wilson's physician reported that the president "easily loses control of himself" and that "when he talks he is likely to break down and weep." The impression of Wilson—once so mighty, now so crippled as he slumped in his wheelchair—left a searing imprint on the memory of another visitor: Franklin Delano Roosevelt.

Then and afterward, Wilson was a deeply divisive figure. Millions of Americans loathed him. In John Dos Passos's *U.S.A.*, he is Satanic. One character in the novel says of him, "A terrifying face, I swear it's a reptile's face." But he also had a legion of disciples who revered him as the evangel of world peace, and over the next three years they would stroll down S Street in the evening to look up at the lighted third-floor bedroom where the former president labored. In later years, after his warnings about the terrible toll another world war would take proved to be awesomely on the mark, they were to celebrate him as a prophet.

When on a chill February night in 1924 word went out that Wilson was sinking fast, large numbers of his admirers knelt in the snow outside his house to pray for him. They did not know that he had already uttered his final sentences: "I am a broken piece of machinery. When the machinery is broken—I am ready." The bulletin announcing the former president's death on the morning of February 3 reduced his followers to sobs, and that evening they made a pilgrimage to S Street to look up at the window from which light no longer shown. Panegyrists, known for overreaching, sought to identify a personage in the past to whom he might be likened. They found willing believers when they reached back two millennia to a figure in Greek mythology: Icarus, who had soared into the sky with wings of wax and feathers. Rashly, he had dared to venture too close to the sun. Its rays melted his wings—plunging him into the sea.

3

Warren Harding, Calvin Coolidge, Herbert Hoover

ON MARCH 4, 1921, H. L. Mencken went down to Washington to witness the inauguration of Warren G. Harding. That night, after he had returned to Baltimore, he wrote Benjamin Franklin's biographer Carl Van Doren: "Harding's speech was the damnedest bosh that even he has perpetrated. It almost brought me to tears. Was it for this that George Washington was frost-bitten and Grant put his feet into that mustard-bath at Appomattox?" He then sat down at his desk and composed the opening words of his assessment of the new president: "No other such complete and dreadful nitwit is to be found in the pages of American history."

Though the Sage of Baltimore was given to hyperbole, he found plenty of company in ridiculing Harding's speaking style, which he likened to a "rhinoceros liberating himself by main strength from a lake of boiling molasses," and the new president's turgid prose. "Beautiful Warren Gamaliel Harding," said the poet e. e. cummings, was

> the only man woman or child who wrote
> a simple declarative sentence with seven grammatical
> errors.

Harding's orations, stated Senator William McAdoo, "leave the impression of an army of pompous phrases moving over the landscape in search of an idea; sometimes these meandering words would actually capture a straggling thought and bear it triumphantly, a prisoner in their midst, until it died of servitude and overwork." Harding himself acknowledged that he loved to "bloviate," employing rhetoric not to communicate ideas but to cover up the reality that he had so little to say. One journalist noted his "ability to make melodic noises and give the impression of passionately and torrentially moving onward and upward while warily standing still."

Harding was pathetically cognizant of his inadequacy. "I am not fit for this office and should never have been here," he confessed. "I am a man of limited talents from a small town. I don't seem to grasp that I am president." At times, the job overwhelmed him. Required to take a position

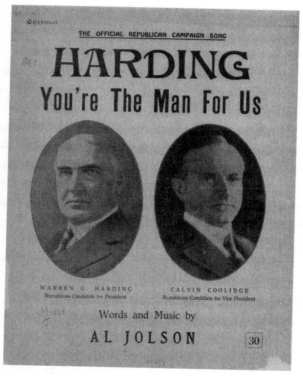

Warren Harding and Calvin Coolidge, the 1920 Republican candidates for president and vice president, are featured on the sheet music for a campaign tune written by the popular entertainer Al Jolson. The lyrics and music have mercifully been forgotten. *"Harding, You're the Man for Us." New York: Al Jolson, 1922. Sheet music. Music Division, Library of Congress (087.00.00) [Digital ID#bhp0087]*

on an issue, he said, "I can't make a damn thing out of this tax problem. I listen to one side and they seem right, and then—God!—I talk to the other side and they seem just as right, and here I am where I started. I know somewhere there is a book that will give me the truth, but hell! I couldn't read the book." Sadly, he acknowledged, "I know how far from greatness I am."

His presidency initiated what the British commentator Harold Laski called "the era of conscious abdication from power." Under Warren Harding, Calvin Coolidge, and (though to a lesser extent) Herbert Hoover, the expansion of the presidency all but ground to a halt. These dozen years formed a hiatus between what had gone before and what was to come. Reflecting on the "temporary eclipse of the presidency," the historian John Morton Blum observed: "No one of Wilson's three successors viewed the office as he and Roosevelt had. No one of them had serious doubts about the benignity of corporations, or a serious interest in the federal promotion of social equity. No one of them achieved a significant command of his party or of Congress. No one of them sought or attained an important stature in the world. In the absence of a strong president, of a powerful leader resolved to lead, federal public policy drifted, as it had in the last several decades of the nineteenth century, and the federal government atrophied." The best the historian most favorably disposed to Harding, Robert K. Murray, has been able to say about him is that he was "certainly the equal of a Franklin Pierce, an Andrew Johnson, a Benjamin Harrison, or even a Calvin Coolidge." More recently, Eugene Trani and David Wilson, in a judicious biography, have concluded that Harding "did little to provide direction in a period of transition" and "failed to sense what was happening to the nation."

In his first State of the Union address, Harding observed, "During the anxieties of war, when necessity seemed compelling, there were excessive grants of authority and an extraordinary concentration of powers in the Chief Executive." He resolved both to defer to Congress and to fetter the government. With millions jobless in a postwar recession, he announced, "I would have little enthusiasm for any proposed relief which seeks either palliation or tonic from the Public Treasury." When progressives advocated continuing government operation of the railroads, they met implacable opposition from Harry Daugherty, whom

Harding had appointed attorney general, though he was a lobbyist of ill repute with no standing at the bar. The recommendation for federal management of railways, Daugherty said, was "a conspiracy worthy of Lenin," portending that "our timetables and freight-rates would be made out in Moscow." Harding also drew back in foreign affairs. America, he said in his inaugural address, wanted "no part in directing the destinies of the Old World," and, in one of his last pronouncements, he stated that the League issue was as "dead as slavery."

Even if Harding had been more aggressive in pushing legislation, it is unlikely that he would have been more successful, for Congress, after years of bridling against Wilsonian usurpation, was in no mood to indulge a strong executive. He did surprise critics by twice appearing before Congress to deliver his annual address, and even called Congress back into special session to urge a subsidy for the merchant marine. But his former colleagues in the Senate denounced his appeals to them as "simply deplorable," a "pitiable, intolerable, and indefensible spectacle." Chastened, Harding did not dare to attempt such interventions again.

When Harding did exercise the powers vested in him as chief executive, he promoted a conservative agenda. "You are not asked to solve the long controverted problems of the social system," he told delegates to a conference on unemployment. "We have built the America of today on the fundamentals of economic, industrial and political life which made us what we are, and the temple requires no remaking now." He nominated William Howard Taft to be chief justice of the United States, and, in filling other vacancies on the Supreme Court, appointed two strict constructionists who would be among the notorious "Four Horsemen" of the 1930s. The Fordney-McCumber Act of 1922, which, said the *New York Commercial*, incorporated "the composite selfishness of the country," entrusted the president with the power to lower or hike tariffs by as much as 50 percent, but Harding almost always employed this discretionary authority to boost duties still higher. He also permitted Attorney General Daugherty to turn the full force of the federal government against striking railway shopmen. Though union leaders had been amenable to a settlement and rail operators recalcitrant, Daugherty obtained what has been called "the most sweeping injunction in American labor history," a ruling so drastic that it forbade workers to speak one word in aid of a strike.

Harding, who had promised to recruit a cabinet of the "best minds," made some impressive choices. For secretary of state, he picked the exceptionally skillful Charles Evans Hughes, who gave a bravura performance at a nine-nation conference on naval disarmament and the Far East and who negotiated the Four-Power Treaty ending the Anglo-Japanese alliance of 1902. Pressed on what his foreign policy would be, Harding replied, "You must ask Mr. Hughes about that." On another occasion he told a Washington correspondent, "I don't know anything about this European stuff." Harding persuaded the multimillionaire aluminum magnate Andrew Mellon, who was very conservative but also very able, to become secretary of the treasury, a post he did not want, and selected for secretary of agriculture the well-regarded Iowa farm journal editor Henry C. Wallace. For secretary of commerce, Harding lit upon Herbert Hoover, a world-famous mining engineer and promoter whose reputation had been burnished by his dedicated service as administrator at home and overseas under Woodrow Wilson. The Republican Old Guard distrusted Hoover, but Harding insisted on him because "he's the smartest gink I know."

This assemblage indicates that there was sometimes more to Harding than Menckenian caricatures of him suggested and that his presidency was not barren of innovation. He recommended antilynching legislation, urged aid to farmers, sought to regulate the radio industry, succeeded in establishing a Veterans Bureau, favored the creation of a department of public welfare, and asked Congress to approve the Sheppard-Towner Act to foster the health of mothers and children. After some waffling, he supported Hoover's demand that U. S. Steel end the inhuman twelve-hour day at blast furnaces. At his twice-weekly press conferences, he created the subterfuge of "White House spokesman" to permit the press to quote him without direct attribution, and in 1922, when he dedicated the Francis Scott Key Memorial at Fort McHenry in Baltimore harbor, he became the first president whose words were heard on radio. He also broke ground by inviting the vice president to attend cabinet meetings, though Calvin Coolidge said nothing.

Unexpectedly, the conservative Harding undid some of the damage the liberal Wilson administration had inflicted on civil liberties by issuing a general amnesty for political prisoners snared in the Red Scare dragnet. He also took under advisement the case of Eugene V. Debs, who had campaigned against him in 1920 from a jail cell after being pros-ecuted by the Wilson administration for obstructing the draft in World War I. Unlike Wilson, who had treated Debs so coldly, Harding not only pardoned Debs but also advanced the date of his freedom to December 24, 1921, "because I want him to eat his Christmas dinner with his wife." He required the longtime Socialist agitator to come to the White House to receive his pardon in person. "Well," said the president as he bounded forward to welcome him, "I have heard so damned much about you, Mister Debs, that I am now very glad to meet you personally."

The Harding years saw, too, the only important institutional change in the executive branch in the 1920s: the establishment of the Bureau of the Budget, placed under the Treasury Department. The Budget and Accounting Act of 1921 centralized control of spending by federal departments in the White House. Until then, the president of the United States had been in the absurd position of having almost no authority to allocate spending by the government of which he was chief executive, and department heads ran their own fiefdoms. The statute called upon the president to pull together estimates of expenditures by segments of the executive branch and to submit to Congress each year a budget and an accompanying message—a stipulation that bound not just Harding but each of his successors. Though Harding never imagined that the Bureau of the Budget would one day be the nerve center of the executive branch, the political scientist Richard Neustadt later wrote that "no other single innovation has so markedly enlarged the practical importance of the Presidency to the whole executive establishment." The 1921 law also created a general accounting office under a comp-troller general who held this post for a fifteen-year term; the president could not remove him without the consent of both houses of Congress. Wilson had vetoed an earlier version of this restriction, but Harding went along with it.

After the frenetic era of Theodore Roosevelt and Woodrow Wilson, the Harding years seemed blissfully tranquil and Washington, DC, a pleasant backwater. Harding played poker once a week and golf twice weekly, honing his game by hitting balls on the White House lawn that his Airedale, Laddie Boy, retrieved. No longer was the executive man-sion the dark fastness it had been during Wilson's reclusion. On the very first day, the Hardings removed guards in order to make the grounds more inviting, and when a maid started to draw curtains to give the presidential couple privacy from gawkers, Florence Harding said, "Let 'em look in if they want. It's *their* White House." Sometimes the first lady surprised out-of-towners by joining them on tours of the mansion. Nothing revealed Harding's laid-back administrative style so well as his casually delegating to his wife the authority to decide which convicts in federal penitentiaries he ought to pardon.

Unhappily, Harding allowed his place in history to be determined by a number of his appointees who fell far below the level of Hughes and Hoover. He named as the first comptroller general an obscure lawyer from his hometown of Marion, Ohio, then compounded his folly by designating the man, who had almost no banking experience, a governor of the Federal Reserve System. Far worse was his reliance on Daugherty, who allowed the Justice Department to become, in the words of one senator, "the Department of Easy Virtue." The nation's chief law officer, Daugherty was the kingpin of an unsavory "Ohio Gang." His sidekick, Jesse Smith, who lived in the attorney general's apartment at the Wardman Park Hotel, exploited his closeness to the president to arrange paroles, sell liquor concessions, and carry out other schemes, while muttering, "My God, how the money rolls in." Harding learned enough about these scams to summon him to the White House and give him a dressing down. The next day, in Daugherty's apartment, Smith put a bullet in his head.

Harding carelessly brought to Washington a number of ne'er-do-wells and thieves. He never discharged a single corrupt subordinate or saw to it that anyone was prosecuted. No thanks to him, his alien property custodian, Thomas Miller, wound up serving eighteen months in prison for taking bribes. When Harding found out that the chance acquaintance he had selected to head the Veterans Bureau, Charles Forbes, was involved on a mammoth scale in shady deals and kickbacks, he covered up for the crook. After an investigation, though, Forbes, who had raked in nearly a quarter of a million dollars by rackets such as condemning carloads of bandages destined for wounded veterans and selling them cut-rate, was sentenced to two years in Leavenworth penitentiary. Forbes's close associate Charles Cramer shot himself to death at Harding's former home, leaving a suicide note addressed to the president, who refused to read it.

By far the greatest scandal of Harding's presidency implicated two members of his cabinet. Two months after Inauguration Day, Secretary of the Interior Albert Fall persuaded Harding to sign an executive order transferring US naval oil reserves from the Department of the Navy to the Department of the Interior. Subsequently, Fall granted drilling rights in the reserves to Edward Doheny at Elk Hills, California, and to Harry Sinclair at a Wyoming site with a dome shaped like a teapot. Under pressure from Senate investigators, Doheny confessed that he had paid Fall, who was Harding's poker buddy, $100,000; Sinclair gave him several hundred thousand more. Fall, convicted of soliciting a huge bribe, became the first cabinet official in the history of the republic to go to prison for misconduct in office. Secretary of the Navy Edwin Denby, who had been duped by Fall, was forced to step down. Years later, at a dedication of a memorial to Harding in Ohio, President Hoover stated: "Warren Harding had a dim realization that he had been betrayed by a few men whom he trusted. . . . It was later proved in the courts of the land that these men had betrayed not alone their staunch and loyal friend, but . . . their country. That was the tragedy of the life of Warren Harding."

Though Harding knew nothing of the seamier aspects of Teapot Dome, he came to realize in his final days that something in his administration was rotten. "My God, this is a hell of a job!" he said before departing on a long journey in the summer of 1923. "I have no trouble with my enemies. . . . But my damn friends, my God-damn friends, . . . they're the ones that keep me walking the floor nights!" On a voyage to Alaska, on which members of his party noted that he seemed edgy and morose, the president called Secretary Hoover into his cabin to inquire, "If you knew of a great scandal in our administration, would you, for the good of the country and the party, expose it publicly or would you bury it?" Asked what the trouble was, Harding mumbled that there was talk of wrongdoing in the Justice Department. Was Attorney General Daugherty implicated? Hoover wanted to know. Harding clammed up.

On the way back from Alaska in August 1923, Harding died suddenly, apparently of a cerebral embolism. (According to a persistent rumor, Mrs. Harding, to spare her husband from finding out more about how badly his administration had been compromised, poisoned him—but there is nothing to the tale.) Upon learning of Harding's death, the nation was plunged into grief. That response seemed odd to later generations who viewed him as one of America's very worst presidents. But the public did not know of Teapot Dome then, and friendly Harding was regarded with affection. Tall, meticulously dressed, handsome, with silver hair and dark eyebrows, he looked the way Americans thought a president should look. One admirer even imagined that Harding had the appearance of a Roman senator, who "needed only a toga to complete the illusion that he had come out of the ancient world." Moreover, he was lauded for having brought serenity to the White House after the turmoil of the Wilson years.

The mourning for Harding reflected these sentiments, but also the shock, sorrow, and sense of abandonment the nation feels whenever any president is struck down before his time. In *The Man in the White House*, the political scientist Wilfred Binkley wrote that he could "never forget how he found his father, just after the news of McKinley's assassination had arrived, weeping as bitterly as if he had lost a child. So it was to others when Lincoln, Garfield, and Harding died in office. The son who protested to his foreign-born mother Harding's lack of merit, when he found her weeping over news of the President's death, got this significant response: 'Ach, aber er ist doch der Präsident.' [Ah, but he is still the President.]" As the funeral train headed east, Californians strewed flowers on the track, children sang his favorite hymns, and farmers in the Great Plains, doffing their hats in respect, stood bareheaded in wheat fields. When the cortege reached Omaha at two in the morning, forty thousand were waiting in the rain. The engineer was instructed to make haste to Washington, but in Chicago three hundred thousand mourners impeded progress. In Pittsburgh, factory workers sobbed.

It did not take long for a very different perception of Harding to settle in. Just three years later, William Allen White, alluding to the president's affair with Nan Britton, was writing, "If ever there was a man who was a he-harlot, it was this same Warren G. Harding." That judgment was underscored when she published an exposé of her liaison, *The President's Daughter*. In *Revelry*, a novel by the former muckraker Samuel Hopkins Adams, an "Ohio Gang," operating out of a "little green house on K Street," victimized a president, "Willis Markham." When the heroine rescues the drunken president from an alley and brings him to his senses, he reflects, "Simp that I was! Boob! Sap! Bonehead!" No reader had any doubt that Markham was Harding. But well before then, greatly to the relief of Republicans, there was a very different figure in the presidency—a man so unlike Harding that White would later title his biography of him *A Puritan in Babylon*.

———

The mise-en-scène could not have been more redolent of the America of Currier and Ives if it had been staged by Frank Capra. Calvin Coolidge first learned of Harding's death when his father awakened him in the middle of the night in his upstairs bedroom at the family homestead in Plymouth Notch, Vermont—a cottage built in 1672 that had neither electricity nor indoor plumbing. Downstairs in the parlor, at 2:47 a.m. on August 3, 1923, John Coolidge, who was a notary public, swore his son into office by the light of a kerosene lamp, while holding the family Bible. The oath-taking was unnecessary—Coolidge had automatically become president on Harding's death—but the nation found reassurance in learning that it had a president from a pastoral idyll who had been raised in a village with a name suggestive of Plymouth Rock and who had been born on the Fourth of July.

Coolidge may well have been the least magnetic personality in the history of the executive office. "He was splendidly null," a friend said of him in his early days, "apparently deficient in red corpuscles, with a peaked, wire-drawn expression." In the White House, he spent a remarkable amount of time in bed, sleeping as much as eleven hours at a stretch. When Groucho Marx onstage spied the president in the theater at one performance, he called out, "Isn't it past your bedtime, Calvin?" He was the first president to be renowned for torpor—"distinguishable from the furniture only when he moved," the Wilsonian George Creel remarked. "His ideal day," quipped Mencken, "is one on which nothing whatever happens."

A number of observers saw calculation in Coolidge's behavior. "Mr. Coolidge's genius for inactivity is developed to a very high point," observed the country's most influential columnist, Walter Lippmann. "It is far from being an indolent inactivity. It is a grim, determined, alert inactivity which keeps Mr. Coolidge occupied constantly." In truth, the president offered little guidance either to Congress or to his cabinet. "I have never felt that it was my duty to attempt to coerce Senators or

Representatives," he once said. As for administrators, "wherever they exercise judicial functions, I always felt that some impropriety might attach to any suggestions from me." His reticence did not much disturb elite opinion makers. When shortly after he took office Coolidge expressed to Chief Justice Taft his concern about the demands on him, Taft told him "to do nothing. I told him that the public were glad to have him in the White House doing nothing." Justice Oliver Wendell Holmes agreed. "While I don't expect anything very astonishing from him," he said, "I don't want anything very astonishing."

Coolidge's inertia dovetailed with his taciturnity, which was legendary. It was rumored that he decided in 1901 to marry his future wife but did not mention it to her until 1905. Coolidge "could be silent in five languages," commentators maintained. It was said that he and the close-mouthed Mellon "conversed almost entirely in pauses." At one point, Coolidge advised another cabinet official how to deal with callers at the White House: "Nine-tenths of them want something they ought not to have. If you keep dead still, they will run down in three or four minutes. If you even cough or smile, they will start up all over again." His reticence confounded the press. "Have you any statement on the campaign?" a reporter asked in 1924. "No," Coolidge snapped. "Can you tell us something about the world situation?" Again, "No." Did he have any information about prohibition? Once more, "No." As the gathering broke up, Coolidge called out, "Now, remember—don't quote me."

Contrary to his sobriquet, "Silent Cal," however, did a lot of talking, while grumbling that "one of the most appalling trials which confront a president is the perpetual clamor for public utterances." (He did, though, continue to maintain a reserve. One analysis of nearly two dozen Coolidge speeches found that he said "I" only once in more than fifty thousand words.) He actually delivered more public addresses than Wilson had, and he held more than five hundred press conferences—convening them more often, proportionately, than Franklin Roosevelt later would. Coolidge, said Frank R. Kent, the White House correspondent of the *Baltimore Sun*, "was communicative almost to the point of garrulousness." Coolidge was also the first president to exploit the new medium of radio. His State of the Union address in 1923, his acceptance speech at the Republican convention in 1924, and his inaugural address in 1925 all went out over the airwaves.

Coolidge proved to be a poor communicator not because he was silent but because he had so little to impart. His meetings with the press were stilted affairs. He required reporters to submit questions in writing in advance, and he forbade them to identify him as a source of information. He had nothing, or virtually nothing, to say about the most compelling features of the decade: the Ku Klux Klan, the Scopes trial, the Sacco-Vanzetti case, the Great Bull Market. His press conferences were laced with responses such as "I am not familiar enough with the exact workings and practice," "I have very little information," and, on some particular subject, "a matter that I wouldn't happen to know anything about." No Washington reporter, Kent said, "can recall a single word from Mr. Coolidge that sparkled or glowed or indicated any force, feeling, grasp or spirit." His replies were "noncommittal, neutral, evasive,...flat and meatless." Similarly, while introducing the practice of breakfasting with congressmen at the White House, he sat at the table wordlessly.

To create a warmer image of Coolidge, the administration hired the foremost public relations man in the country: Sigmund Freud's nephew, Edward Bernays, who worked out ploys like inviting the Broadway star Al Jolson to breakfast at the White House. The advertising man Bruce Barton, borrowing from cosmetics commercials, arranged for "spontaneous" testimonials to Coolidge's humanity from rank-and-file Americans; Republicans sold the president, said one critic, "as though he were a new breakfast food or fountain pen." This campaign to present Coolidge as folksy and genial covered up the reality that he had a mean streak, evident in his behavior toward his wife: the admirable Grace Goodhue Coolidge. He refused to permit her to drive a car, bob her hair, smoke in public, grant an interview, or voice an opinion on national affairs. (At a luncheon for female journalists, the first lady, who had taught at an institute for the deaf, circumvented him. Adhering to his injunction against speaking to the press, she addressed the women for five minutes in sign language.) The men and women staffing the White House detested him. "He was so severe that everyone shunned him when it was possible," an employee recalled. "Many times he was positively unkind."

But the nation came to enjoy him as a figure of fun—riding on his mechanical hobbyhorse like an old buckaroo, donning Indian war bonnets, or making himself ridiculous in ill-fitting cowboy attire. Even

Coolidge's brevity of speech was ennobled as the most exemplary of virtues. In Sinclair Lewis's gently satirical *The Man Who Knew Coolidge,* the central character recalls: "I can remember just's well as if it was yesterday, Cal and me happened to come out of a class together, and I said 'Well, it's going to be a cold winter,' and he came right back, 'Yep.' Didn't waste a lot of time arguing and discussing: He knew!"

Coolidge won plaudits, too, by freeing Washington of the Harding incubus. Alice Roosevelt Longworth said of her first visit to the White House after the Coolidges arrived that "the atmosphere was as different as a New England front parlor is from a back room in a speakeasy." For a while, Coolidge strung along with Harding's pal Harry Daugherty, the holdover attorney general, but when Daugherty refused to allow Senate investigators to inspect the files of the Justice Department, implying there was information that might reflect on either President or Mrs. Harding, he overstepped. Daugherty, Coolidge recognized, was trying to be both the country's highest legal official and his own defense counsel. Stating that "these two positions are incompatible and cannot be reconciled," the president forced Daugherty out. To replace him as attorney general, Coolidge made the outstanding choice of Harlan Fiske Stone, whom he subsequently elevated to the US Supreme Court, and to investigate the sinister allegations about the oil leases, he appointed two special counsels, one of them a Democrat.

By the time the 1924 campaign season rolled around, Coolidge had become a highly popular president, while his opponents were in disarray. The country cherished his pithy sayings and his Yankee whimsy. As the historian George Mayer later remarked, "The shy, parsimonious Coolidge was lionized by his free-spending, pleasure-loving contemporaries in the way that the homespun Ben Franklin had been lionized by the jaded aristocrats of eighteenth-century France." (The nation also empathized with his anguish after his son Calvin Jr., playing tennis on a White House court, developed a blister that became infected, resulting in his death. "When he went," his father said, "the power and glory of the presidency went with him.")

Meantime, the Democrats imploded. Riven by sectional animosities and hampered by the antiquated two-thirds barrier for nomination, delegates to the Madison Square Garden convention required more than one hundred ballots to select a presidential candidate—a lawyer for the House of Morgan. Dissatisfied with the major parties, Progressives put together their own ticket headed by Wisconsin senator Robert La Follette, thereby fracturing opposition to the administration. Running against a divided field, Coolidge, polling considerably more votes than his two rivals put together, carried every state outside the South. His principal opponent, John W. Davis, received under 29 percent of the ballots, the lowest proportion ever for a Democratic presidential nominee.

Fortified by his victory, Coolidge set out in his second term to shrink the government he had been elected to preside over but for which he had little regard. "If the federal government were to go out of existence," he remarked, "the common run of people would not detect the difference." His words mirrored those of many of the publicists of the era. "Are we approaching a millennium," inquired an editorial in *Life*, "in which visible government will not be necessary and in which the job of running the world will slip away from obtrusive politicians and be taken over by men trained in the shop?" Coolidge took advantage of the new resource of the Bureau of the Budget to instill the principle of austerity in government agencies, and he embraced Secretary of the Treasury Mellon's program to wipe out excess profit taxes, grant billions in rebates to corporations, slash estate taxes by half, and reduce the national debt. "The kind of government that he offered the country," observed Mencken, "was government stripped to the buff." As a consequence, conservatives in recent years have hailed Coolidge as a paragon. He was, wrote the financial historian Robert Sobel, in a comment intended as praise, "the last president who believed in a passive executive branch in times of peace and prosperity." The reality, however, concluded Jacob Heilbrunn in a review essay in the *New York Times*, is that Coolidge "was an extraordinarily blinkered and foolish and complacent leader."

Coolidge tailored his policies to benefit businessmen while showing little concern for other interests. The president of the National Association of Manufacturers served notice: "It is unthinkable that a government which thrives chiefly upon its industries will withhold from them for a single unnecessary moment the protection which they so sorely need and deserve." Coolidge was eager to oblige, for, as his biographer Donald McCoy wrote, the president "had the Babbitts' awe of the Dodsworths." He emasculated the tariff agency and transformed the Federal Trade Commission, created to be the people's watchdog, into a lapdog of corporations. "Never before, here or anywhere else," the *Wall Street Journal* maintained, "has a government been so completely fused with business." Coolidge even sought to install the longtime counsel of the Sugar Trust, which had been charged with violating the law, as attorney general. That went too far for the Senate, which rejected the appointee—the first time that a president's nominee for a cabinet post had been turned down since 1868 in the embattled Andrew Johnson era. Usually, however, Coolidge had his way. Twice he vetoed a measure to boost farm prices by dumping crop surpluses abroad, a venture he called "vicious" and "preposterous," and he pocket-vetoed a bill for federal operation of a hydroelectric site at Muscle Shoals that was the forerunner of the Tennessee Valley Authority.

When the Great Mississippi River flood of 1927 devastated communities, Coolidge denounced a proposal for desperately needed federal aid as "the most radical and dangerous bill that has had the countenance of the Congress since I have been president." Abandoned by Coolidge, half a million people left homeless by the worst national disaster in the country's history waded through a vast sea of fetid brown water in desperate search for shelter and food. At least a thousand drowned during 145 levee breaks (the Mounds Landing breach releasing twice the force of Niagara Falls and creating a wall of water as high as thirty feet). Coolidge refused even to permit the prestige of his office to be used to help the Red Cross raise funds for the victims. When the popular wit Will Rogers implored him to "send me a telegram that I can read at our benefit for flood sufferers tomorrow night," the president turned him down. Calvin Coolidge, concluded a Kentucky editor, had either "the coldest heart in America or the dullest imagination, and we are about ready to believe he has both."

In coping with these domestic problems, Coolidge could draw upon his experience as governor of Massachusetts, but nothing in his background equipped him for responsibilities abroad. When he entered the White House, he had never been outside the United States, save for one brief trip to Montreal on his honeymoon. The distinguished former secretary of state Elihu Root said that Coolidge "did not have an international hair in his head." Indifferent to European anxieties, he enjoyed one notable success in Latin America, but only after starting out bludgeoning the banana republics by sending marines into Nicaragua to protect US property interests. (His special envoy, Henry Stimson, who imposed a right-wing government on the country, believed that Latin Americans were "admittedly like children.") Coolidge, however, reversed course by naming his Amherst College classmate Dwight Morrow ambassador to Mexico. An inspired choice, Morrow, a Morgan partner who deplored dollar diplomacy, took the first steps—through his sensitivity, intelligence, and charm—toward what would later be called the Good Neighbor Policy. Coolidge remained, however, what the British scholar Harold Laski called him: "a natural churchwarden in a rural parish who has by accident strayed into great affairs."

Coolidge's influence outlasted his presidency. When in 1928 he refused to run again, Republicans turned to a member of his cabinet, Herbert Hoover. Though he was not one of the president's favorites, Hoover basked in the glow of the good times associated with Coolidge in "the golden twenties." His Democratic opponent, Alfred E. Smith, had been an impressive four-time governor of New York, but, in this era of Republican dominance, Smith never stood a chance. Furthermore, rural Protestant Americans could not tolerate the prospect of a Catholic in the White House, especially a Tammany Hall sachem who was defiantly wet on prohibition and who spoke in the working-class accent and argot of a man born in the shadow of the Brooklyn Bridge. In November, Hoover not only captured traditional GOP strongholds but also moved a number of southern states into the Republican column—for the first time since 1876.

Few presidents have entered office so highly acclaimed as Herbert Hoover. Hailed as the Great Engineer for his global achievements in mining, he had won new honors after entering the public sphere in 1914 as director of relief to German-occupied Belgium, as US food czar during World War I, and as strategist for the Supreme Economic Council in Paris after the armistice. Justice Louis Brandeis called him "the biggest figure injected into Washington by the war," and John Maynard Keynes rated him "the only man who emerged from the ordeal of Paris with an enhanced reputation." In 1920, a prominent Democrat expressed the same view. "He is certainly a wonder, and I wish we could make him President of the United States," said Franklin Delano Roosevelt. "There would not be a better one."

He had gained more approval in the next decade. So wide-ranging were his activities as a cabinet officer under Harding and Coolidge that he was said to be "Secretary of Commerce and Under-Secretary of all other departments." At the same time, he continued to be the Great Almoner. Though he loathed Bolshevism, he saw to it that shipments of food reached famine sufferers in Soviet Russia. "In the past year," Maxim Gorky wrote him, "you have saved from death three and one-half million children, five and one-half million adults.... In the history of practical humanitarianism I know of no accomplishment [to] which in... magnitude and generosity [it] can be compared." When he ran for the presidency in 1928, Jane Addams and other progressives flocked to his standard. His emphatic triumph, establishing him as the first American born west of the Mississippi to enter the White House, punctuated a career of almost uninterrupted success.

The next four years promised to be even better. "We were in the mood for magic," the *New York Times* correspondent Anne O'Hare McCormick later recalled. "We had summoned a great engineer to solve our problems for us; now we sat back...confidently to watch the problems being solved. The modern technical mind was for the first time at the head of a government....Almost with the air of giving genius its chance, we waited for the performance to begin." Hoover himself had said, in an address at Stanford University's football stadium: "Given a chance to go forward with the policies of the last eight years, we shall soon with the help of God be in sight of the day when poverty will be banished from this nation." Soon after, he added, "In no nation are the fruits of accomplishment more secure."

Only a few commentators questioned whether Hoover had the temperament or the mindset, the political sensitivity or the vision, required for national leadership. Though the country admired him, it did not warm to his frosty demeanor or his staid comportment. He parted his hair in the middle, favored a stiff high collar of the Benjamin Harrison era, and when he cast his fishing line in swift-running trout streams wore a double-breasted blue serge suit. Close associates were shocked by his apparent indifference to their feelings and learned to expect from him neither warmth nor compassion. Though he brought aid to millions, he discussed their plight in much the same way that he talked about railway carloadings. One magazine writer even titled an article "Is

Hoover Human?" Should hard times develop, he could not be counted on to rally the nation with good cheer. "If you want to get the gloomiest view of any subject on earth," his wife once said, "ask Bert about it."

Analysts found Hoover's approach to governing as chilling as his persona. "It has been no part of mine to build castles of the future but rather to measure the experiments, the actions, and the progress of men through the cold and uninspiring microscope of fact, statistics, and performance," he stated. *Time* remarked that "in a society of temperate, industrious, unspectacular beavers, such a beaver-man would make an ideal King-beaver," but the nation expected more than that from its president. Furthermore, Hoover carried into the presidency with him a curious misreading of his own experiences. The most prominent bureaucrat of his generation, he insisted that all of his achievements had resulted from private effort by public-spirited volunteers when, in fact, these successes had largely been made possible by the resources of the state. Seeing himself as a dispassionate engineer operating with the precision of a slide rule, he trapped himself in doctrine. His ideas, remarked a leading economist, were "conceived in advance of the evidence, and...held stubbornly after the evidence goes against him."

A chorus of high-pitched hosannas drowned out these naysayers. At the Republican convention, a California delegate had celebrated him as "practical scientist, minister of mercy to the hungry and poor, administrator, executive, statesman, beneficent American," and the press called him "a genius" and "the most useful American citizen now alive." George Washington, observed the *Los Angeles Times*, had been a quite acceptable president, but "he had never had the training or experience of Herbert Hoover." A vote for Hoover, Republicans had claimed during the campaign, was "a vote for ... the party that has wiped out soup-kitchens ... and bread lines from the land," and party activists passed out Hoover Lucky Pocket Pieces inscribed "Good for four years of prosperity."

No one understood better than Hoover the grave risks these lavish encomiums entailed. Early in 1929, not many days before his inauguration, he confided to an editor: "I have no dread of the ordinary work of the presidency. What I do fear is the ... exaggerated idea the people have conceived of me. They have a conviction that I am a sort of superman, that no problem is beyond my capacity.... If some unprecedented calamity should come upon the nation ... I would be sacrificed to the unreasoning disappointment of a people who expected too much."

Only seven months after Hoover took office, the "unprecedented calamity" arrived. On October 24, 1929, the Great Bull Market of the Roaring Twenties self-destructed. That morning, wrote the economist John Kenneth Galbraith later, investors at the New York Stock Exchange on Wall Street succumbed to "a wild, mad scramble to sell," and by noon the market had "surrendered to blind relentless fears." The following week, "Black Tuesday" brought even steeper declines, with some issues in free fall. "Stock prices virtually collapsed yesterday, swept downward with gigantic losses in the most disastrous trading day in the stock market's history," reported the *New York Times*. Not for thirteen years was the country to recover from this Wall Street Crash and the accompanying Great Depression.

Hoover, often caricatured unfairly as a "do-nothing president," moved briskly to cope with the crisis. He summoned businessmen and labor leaders to the White House for the Conference on Continued Industrial Progress, urged employers to maintain wage rates, asked Congress to approve a tax cut and to appropriate funds for public works, and prodded the Federal Reserve Board to expand the money supply. America, said the *Boston Globe*, could rejoice that it had as its leader "a man who believes not in the philosophy of drift, but in the dynamics of mastery."

After this unparalleled intervention, however, Hoover spent almost all of the rest of his term resisting entreaties that he take a more active role in relieving hardship. He was not a weak president; rather, he acted forcefully to circumscribe the federal government. "We cannot... squander ourselves into prosperity," he insisted. When the Senate began to consider measures to stimulate the economy, he appeared in person in the chamber to upbraid the lawmakers. "We cannot legislate ourselves out of a world economic depression," he declared in 1931. To suppose that Congress could enact measures that would speed recovery was equivalent to thinking that one could "exorcise a Caribbean hurricane by statutory law."

He persisted in this course despite graphic evidence that the devastation of the Depression was deepening. The total unemployed—just five hundred thousand in October 1929—multiplied to more than eight million by the end of 1930. In the winter of that year, the North Carolina novelist Thomas Wolfe wrote home from New York City: "I saw half naked wretches sitting on park benches at three in the morning in a freezing rain and sleet: often I saw a man and a woman huddled together with their arms around each other for warmth, and with sodden newspapers, rags, or anything they could find over their shoulders." By the end of 1931, a Philadelphia welfare official was announcing: "We have unemployment in every third house. It is almost like the visitation of death to the households of the Egyptians at the time of the escape of the Jews from Egypt."

Hoover responded to the dreadful suffering by denial. When in June 1930 a delegation that numbered bankers as well as bishops called at the White House out of concern for the mounting misery, Hoover was barely able to suppress his irritation. "Gentlemen," he said, "you have come sixty days too late. The Depression is over." He set up sixty-two fact-finding groups to provide enlightenment on public issues, then refused to believe what the studies revealed. He even ignored the recommendations of his own appointee who told him that voluntarism was not working and that the federal government had to intercede. "Hoover almost always went deep with a problem, but the depth was like a mineshaft, straightly walled by Hoover's presumptions," the historian Alfred Rollins later observed. "Though his views were always well documented, they frequently lacked all understanding of the complex human and social ramifications of the problem. At the moment of their impact on history, Hoover's narrowness betrayed him."

The more hardship spread, the more determined Hoover was to turn a blind eye to it. In his State of the Union address near the end of 1931, he maintained, "Our people are providing against distress in true American fashion by magnificent response to public appeal and by action of the local government." There was no need for federal aid, he maintained, because, thanks to "the sense of social responsibility in the Nation, our people have been protected from hunger and cold." He expressed these convictions at a time when many thousands were famished—some died of starvation—and when families had been reduced to spending winters in mean tarpaper shacks in desolate makeshift aggregations called derisively "Hoovervilles."

In vain, the dispossessed looked to Washington for cheer and solace. Gutzon Borglum, the sculptor of Mount Rushmore, said, "If you put a rose in Hoover's hand, it would wilt." After one meeting at the White House, Secretary of State Henry Stimson recorded in his diary: "The President . . . went through all the blackest surmises. . . . It was like sitting in a bath of ink to sit in his room." On the rare occasions that he took to the airwaves, he droned on with no attempt to reach the hearts and minds of his audience. "To Hoover," one commentator said, "the millions who listened over the radio were just eavesdroppers." When his advisers urged him to rally the nation, he retorted, "You can't make a Teddy Roosevelt out of me."

Hoover created further difficulty for himself by his disregard for the media and for Congress. A columnist who was one of the very few he could tolerate put him down as "the most left-footed President politically the world ever saw." His relations with the press, said a correspondent who had initially been well disposed, had come to "a stage of unpleasantness without parallel in the present century...characterized by mutual dislike, unconcealed suspicion, and downright bitterness." He called Congress "that beer garden up there on the hill," spoke of "those Democratic swine," and said that a certain US senator was "the only verified case of a negative I.Q." Hoover, one commentator remarked, "has never really recognized the House and Senate as desirable factors in our government."

His independence of Congress occasionally had beneficial aspects. When in 1931 the Senate withdrew its approval of three of his nominees to the Federal Power Commission, though the men were already carrying out their duties, he stood up for the prerogatives of the chief executive, and the US Supreme Court sustained him by establishing the principle that the Senate may not withdraw its consent once it has been given. Acting on his own authority, he also registered important gains for conservation. Bypassing Congress with executive orders, he greatly increased the national forest reserve and augmented national parks by an extraordinary three million acres, notably by opening preserves in the Grand Tetons and Carlsbad Caverns. But by refusing to call Congress back into session for months at a time, he brought upon himself all of the onus for everything that went awry.

Though it was beyond the reach of any president to bring about a speedy recovery, Hoover promoted policies that made a terrible situation even worse. Obsessive about balancing the budget, he sought to slash federal spending and raise taxes—exactly the wrong steps to take at a time when the economy was thirsting for more purchasing power. When the Republican Congress enacted the Hawley-Smoot bill raising tariff walls, more than a thousand economists urged him not to sign it. But Hoover, who, preposterously, claimed that "the protective principle" was "the largest encouragement to foreign trade," not only went along with it but flourished six gold pens at the signing ceremony.

Hoover's behavior suggested that he did not give international concerns high priority. When the Japanese rent asunder the Versailles world order by absorbing Manchuria, he would not consider either military or economic sanctions, contenting himself instead with announcing that the United States refused to recognize the acquisition of territory by aggression—a doctrine that became identified with Secretary Stimson. "The president is so absorbed with the domestic situation that he told me frankly that he can't think very much now of foreign affairs," Stimson noted in his diary.

When, however, the collapse of Austria's largest bank, Kredit Anstalt, in 1931 sent shock waves through financial markets on both sides of the Atlantic, Hoover moved boldly. Ignoring warnings that he was encroaching on the authority of Congress, he announced a one-year moratorium on the payment of war debts that European countries owed the United States, with the understanding that they, in turn, would forgo reparations payments from Germany. One of his strongest critics, the *Nation*, called his action "probably . . . the most far-reaching and . . . praiseworthy step taken by an American President since the treaty of peace."

Hoover's initiative, though, failed to stop the hemorrhaging—an outcome with tremendous consequences for his country as well as for Europe. In the month after Britain went off the gold standard in September 1931, more than five hundred American banks folded. When his expectation that the House of Morgan and other big financiers would come to the rescue of the system proved misplaced, Hoover saw no option save to swallow his dislike of government intrusion and create the Reconstruction Finance Corporation, which Congress chartered in January 1932. Modeled on the War Finance Corporation of 1918, it was empowered to lend huge sums to banks and other institutions to stave off a meltdown. Progressives could not understand why Hoover thought it appropriate to provide two billions to Wall Street but not a penny to the jobless at a time when an official of the Mayor's Unemployment Commission of Detroit saw "no possibility of preventing widespread hunger and slow starvation."

Many Americans concluded that Hoover was heartless, an impression he sealed by his behavior toward the "Bonus Army." In 1932, thousands of hard-up veterans marched on Washington in an attempt to persuade Congress to pay immediately bonuses promised them in the future for their service in the Great War. After Congress turned them down, hundreds stayed on—in unoccupied government buildings along Pennsylvania Avenue or in makeshift shanties in Anacostia Flats. With mind-boggling insensitivity, Hoover ordered the encampments cleared and the squatters ousted. Exceeding instructions, General Douglas MacArthur mobilized cavalry, tanks, bayonets, and tear gas to drive out the veterans and their families. Instead of disciplining MacArthur, Hoover joined him in maligning the former doughboys. Press reports and newsreels of the operation provoked outrage across the country. "For sheer stupidity," wrote the *San Francisco Examiner*, "President Hoover's spectacular employment of the military in evicting a mere handful of the derelicts of the World War from their wretched billets in Washington is without parallel in American annals." Unfortunately for Hoover, the incident came at the start of his campaign for reelection.

On seeing photos of the harried veterans against the backdrop of the flaming Anacostia Flats, his Democratic opponent, Franklin Delano Roosevelt, said, "Well, this elects me." Born to the Hudson Valley gentry ("Delano" derived from the Huguenot "de la Noye"), FDR had followed the example of his fifth cousin Theodore in entering politics, but, unlike TR, as a Democrat. In 1921, a year after he had attracted national attention as his party's vice presidential candidate, he had been felled by polio, an affliction that apparently ended any prospect for national office. But with the encouragement of his wife, Eleanor, and of a reporter, Louis Howe, he had reentered the political arena and had twice won election to the governorship of New York, where he pursued programs to aid the unemployed that Hoover had eschewed.

Not until too late did Hoover recognize how formidable a rival Franklin Roosevelt was. The president was not alone in underrating his challenger. A writer in the *New Yorker* characterized him as a shallow "grown-up Boy Scout," and Lippmann called him "a pleasant man who, without any important qualifications for the office, would very much like to be president." But FDR, who as early as 1912 had articulated a Bismarckian conception of the State, fully grasped the grimness of the

Depression and was determined to be a change maker. Over the course of 1932, he spoke for "the forgotten man at the bottom of the economic pyramid"; pressed for "imaginative and purposeful planning"; and declared, "The country needs, and, unless I mistake its temper, the country demands bold, persistent experimentation." At a time when commentators were dismissing him as a lightweight, he quietly assembled a "Brain Trust," primarily of Columbia University professors, to chart a program for recovery.

After overcoming a strong field of Democratic contenders, he flew to Chicago, battling headwinds, to become the first major-party presidential nominee to deliver an acceptance address at a nominating convention. Having quieted doubts about his mobility and his stamina by embarking on the hazardous flight, he told the delegates: "I have started out on the tasks that lie ahead by breaking the absurd tradition that the candidate should remain in professed ignorance of what has happened...until he is formally notified of that event many weeks later.... You have nominated me and I know it, and I am here to thank you for the honor. Let it...be symbolic that in so doing I broke traditions. Let it be from now on the task of our Party to break foolish traditions." Without intending to do so, he fastened a name on his program by concluding, "I pledge you, I pledge myself, to a *new deal* for the American people."

In November, Hoover went down to a crushing defeat, as Roosevelt became the first Democrat in eighty years—since Franklin Pierce in 1852—to enter the White House with a popular majority. The forty states Hoover carried in 1928 had dwindled to six. Save for 1912, when the party divided, it was the greatest defeat a Republican presidential candidate had ever suffered. "The president was not merely rejected," his biographer Richard Norton Smith has written. "He was virtually excommunicated." At his home in Palo Alto, as he took in the magnitude of his loss, he showed himself gaunt and dispirited. A little girl observing him asked, "Mommy, what do they do to a president to make him look like Mister Hoover does?"

Derided as "President Reject," Hoover still had to carry on through the last long interregnum in American history. The Twentieth Amendment, soon to be adopted, moved Inauguration Day to January 20, but it would not take effect until 1937; consequently, under the Constitution at that time, Hoover did not leave office until March 4. Over his final

In 1928, the year he won election by an emphatic margin, Herbert Hoover presents the image of a confident man who has known little save success. By contrast, the expression on the face of the careworn Hoover in 1933, shortly after having been trounced in his bid for reelection, discloses the terrible toll taken by years of attempting to cope with the Great Depression. *Library of Congress, LC-USZ61-296; Associated Press, ID 350901027*

four months, the country—leaderless and anxiety-ridden—foundered. "Now is the winter of our discontent the chilliest," declared the editor of *Nation's Business.* "Fear, bordering on panic, loss of faith in everything, our fellowman, our institutions, private and government. Worst of all, no faith in ourselves, or the future." Another periodical perceived the leitmotif of the period in Shakespeare's lines:

> I find the people strangely fantasied:
> Possess'd with rumours, full of idle dreams;
> Not knowing what they fear, but full of fear.

As Hoover's presidency drew to a close, the sense of crisis quickened. On February 15, 1933, President-elect Roosevelt barely escaped assassination at Bayfront Park in Miami. (The murderer fired five bullets; all five struck, one of them fatally wounding the mayor of Chicago.) This frightening event coincided with an epidemic of bank failures that spread like an out-of-control contagious disease. On the final morning of Hoover's term, with the doors of almost every bank in the country closed, the New York Stock Exchange shut down. "We are at the end of our string," the president said.

Herbert Hoover, who four years earlier had been a national idol, ended his tenure a pariah. A man who, it was rightly said, had "fed more people and saved more lives than any other man in history" had come to be regarded as a malevolent misanthrope—a reputation that would endure. For decades to come, Democrats would invoke Hoover to scare voters away from choosing a Republican, and in the 1977 musical *Annie*, homeless waifs sing mockingly, "We'd like to thank you, Herbert Hoover. You made us what we are today."

He left his successor an unsettled and unsettling legacy. "No cosmic dramatist could possibly devise a better entrance...than that accorded to Franklin Delano Roosevelt," observed the playwright Robert Sherwood. "Herbert Hoover was, in the parlance of vaudeville, 'a good act to follow.'" It was also true, though, that, as the historian Paul Murphy later wrote, "the United States which Franklin D. Roosevelt inherited on a cold March day in 1933 was a nation of confused, disillusioned, pessimistic and often bitter people." Furthermore, Hoover and his immediate predecessors handed down a seriously impaired office. "By 1933," John Blum concluded, "the presidency had lost the stature that Theodore Roosevelt and Wilson had given it," and "to advance his purpose, Franklin Roosevelt had to reverse a dozen years of entropy in Washington." None of FDR's captious critics realized how eager the incoming president was to take on that assignment.

4

Franklin Delano Roosevelt

ON INAUGURATION DAY, MARCH 4, 1933, the outgoing president, Herbert Hoover, and the president-elect, Franklin Delano Roosevelt, traveled by car toward the Capitol past buildings that brought to mind not the thriving showplace Hoover had rejoiced in four years earlier but a shabby seat of government under siege. A Washington correspondent later wrote of that day: "The city had the look of being rundown and neglected. Leafless trees were silhouetted against a dark sky. Most of the great mansions were closed and cheerless. Even the White House showed the effect of the hard times. Its paint was turning yellow and peeling off, the former custom of annual repainting having been suspended as an economy measure. Flags on government buildings... [drooped] gloomily." When inauguration-bound visitors, after arriving at Union Station, got to their hotel, they found a sign on the registration desk: "Due to unsettled banking conditions throughout the country, checks on out-of-town banks cannot be accepted."

Hoover's mood as the entourage slowly made its way down Pennsylvania Avenue matched the bleak circumstances and the leaden skies. "The day was dark and drear," one columnist subsequently recalled. "Clouds hung heavily as if ready at any moment to open their funnels and pour a torrent upon the huge crowd below." President Hoover and Governor Roosevelt each acknowledged the applause of the crowds lining the thoroughfare, but after a time the president, recognizing that the clapping was not for him but for his rival, no longer doffed his top hat. Roosevelt persisted animatedly in trying to strike up a conversation, but Hoover, his face studiedly glum, held himself stiffly as though he could not wait for the ordeal of the presidency to end.

At the Capitol Plaza, surprisingly, the largest inauguration gathering in history—estimated at from a quarter to half a million—awaited them. It seemed especially remarkable that there should be such a turnout at a time of financial distress. People massed there to greet the incoming president in the wistful hope that he might figure out some way to make his theme song, "Happy Days Are Here Again," a reality, and they seized upon any indication that their desires would be fulfilled. "In ancient Rome, the augurs watched the heavens for a sign when a new consul entered his first day of office," noted *Business Week*. "Americans, too, watched for...portents as their new President took office." It seemed auspicious that at the moment the ceremonies began, the sun broke through the clouds.

When a few minutes after one o'clock Governor Roosevelt, steadying himself on the arm of his son James, appeared on a raised platform above the plaza, the crowd let out a chorus of cheers. Bareheaded and without overcoat in the chill, gusty damp, Roosevelt stood erect, or so it seemed, for he concealed the braces that were, in fact, sustaining him. Uncharacteristically grave, he took the oath of office as thirty-second president, his hand resting on the thirteenth chapter of Paul's First Epistle to the Corinthians in the ancient Dutch Bible brought to Nieuw Amsterdam early in the seventeenth century by Claes Maartenszen van Roosevelt. The chief justice of the United States, the august Charles Evans Hughes, read out the oath, and Roosevelt responded, reported the *New York Times*, "in ringing tones which carried a challenge to the intangible enemies of commerce abroad and within our gates," reiterating the chief justice's phrases "word for word, like a bridegroom repeating his marriage vows." He continued to convey stern resolve in delivering his inaugural address. "His large chin was thrust out defiantly as if at some invisible, insidious foe," *Time* reported. "A challenge rang in his clear strong voice. For 20 vibrant minutes he held his audience, seen and unseen, under a strong spell."

"First of all," he declared, "let me assert my firm belief that the only thing we have to fear is fear itself"—words of reassurance that would echo for years to come. Quickly, however, he added the more disturbing thought that this was a "dark hour of our national life." He reminded his listeners: "The withered leaves of industrial enterprise lie on every side; farmers find no markets for their produce; the savings of many years in thousands of families are gone. More important, a host of unemployed citizens face the grim problem of existence, and an equally great number toil with little return. Only a foolish optimist can deny the dark realities of the moment." The new president continued: "Yet our distress comes from no failure of substance. We are stricken by no plague of locusts. . . . Plenty is at our doorstep, but a generous use of it languishes in the very sight of the supply. Primarily this is because rulers of the exchange of mankind's goods have failed, through their own stubbornness and their own incompetence, have admitted their failure, and have abdicated." In these sentences Roosevelt was sounding familiar themes—want in the midst of plenty, the culpability of Wall Street—but in using the word "abdicated" he was going even further by implying that henceforth the people should expect to turn for leadership not to Big Business but to the State.

For some minutes, he scourged "the unscrupulous money changers" who stood "indicted in the court of public opinion, rejected by the hearts and minds of men." He announced: "The money changers have fled from their high seats in the temple of our civilization. We may now restore that temple to the ancient truths." To that end, he cried, "This Nation asks for action, and action now." The crowd, which until that point had been listening quietly, attentively, broke out in applause, for he was understood to be saying that Hoover hesitancy was over, and a new age was at hand.

Americans, he declared, "must move as a trained and loyal army willing to sacrifice for the good of a common discipline." He hoped "that the normal balance of executive and legislative authority may be wholly adequate to meet the unprecedented task before us," but, he vowed, in words that electrified his listeners in the plaza and the much larger audience clustered around radios across the country, if Congress failed to act, "I shall not evade the clear course of duty that will then confront me. I shall ask the Congress for the one remaining instrument to meet the crisis—broad Executive power to wage a war against the emergency, as great as the power that would be given to me if we were in fact invaded by a foreign foe."

The crowd, which might well have been alarmed by this passage, erupted in a boisterous ovation. Afterwards, Eleanor Roosevelt reflected:

> It was very, very solemn, and a little terrifying. The crowds were so tremendous, and you felt that they would do anything—if only some one would tell them what to do.
>
> I felt that particularly because, when Franklin got to that part of his speech in which he said it might become necessary for him to assume powers ordinarily granted to a President in war time, he received his biggest demonstration.

As she peered from a window in the White House toward the Virginia hills beyond the Potomac, she added: "One has a feeling of going it blindly, because we're in a tremendous stream, and none of us knows where we're going to land." Millions of Americans, though, believed they had been going it blindly ever since the Wall Street Crash, and they took heart from the new president's confidence and his unhesitating willingness to assume the burdens of office. His rousing address elicited an astonishing 460,000 letters. (In contrast, President Taft had averaged only 200 letters a *week*.)

Roosevelt quickly showed that he meant what he said in pledging "action now." On March 5, his first full day in office, he issued an edict calling Congress into emergency session at noon on March 9—the earliest possible time, in an era before air travel was customary, that members from the Pacific Coast could reach the capital by train. Unlike Lincoln in 1861, he resolved to act in a crisis not by fiat but by turning to the legislative branch. At 1 a.m. on March 6, he signed a second edict, halting transactions in gold and imposing a weeklong national bank holiday. "No bank," the executive order said, "shall pay out, export, earmark, or permit the withdrawal or transfer in any manner or by any device whatsoever, of any gold or silver coin or bullion or currency." He took these steps under the questionable authority of a World War I statute, the Trading with the Enemy Act. Hoover called FDR's ukase "the American equivalent of the burning of the Reichstag to create 'an emergency,'" and Senator Carter Glass, who had served as secretary of the treasury under

Wilson, said, "The President of the United States has no more valid authority to close or open a bank than has my stable boy."

When the edict took effect, many found it incredible that in the richest nation in the world no bank was functioning. "Every once in a while I'd look out the window and pinch myself," the Brain Truster Adolf Berle later reminisced. "This sort of thing happened in South American countries, but not in the U.S.A." When Margaret Mead, on an anthropological expedition in a remote area of New Guinea, heard from a South Seas trader that back home every bank was closed, she refused to believe him. But for the most part the nation accepted FDR's decree with good humor, in part because "holiday" was an inspired euphemism for a moratorium. FDR's order helped snap tensions by giving presidential sanction to the reality that most of the banks had already closed their doors, and Americans found ingenious ways to make do—sometimes by resorting to barter. In Providence, a madam announced that in exchange for favors she would accept books with fine bindings to improve the decor of her brothel. Only enterprises requiring cash ran into trouble. Pickpockets were unable to ply their craft; the floating crap game disappeared; at the recently opened Radio City Music Hall in New York, *King Kong* played to empty houses.

The bank holiday gave Roosevelt breathing space to prepare legislation to submit to Congress on its return. Instead of moving in new ways, he accepted a plan to salvage the banking system worked out by Hoover's officials in collaboration with Wall Street titans. (Subsequently, a populist congressman said, "The President drove the money-changers out of the Capitol on March 4th—and they were all back on the 9th.") Yet, while pursuing a thoroughly conventional course, Roosevelt demonstrated that he was willing to act as Hoover had not. The wife of Hoover's RFC chairman, Eugene Meyer, had noted in her diary, "Eugene and H spent the night of Mar 3 in one of their usual struggles. Fed. Res. Bd. recommended a nat'l bank holiday to which he replied severely and even nastily that it wasn't necessary." Two days after Roosevelt took office, she commented, "We felt at once how much more quickly and easily he arrives at decisions and . . . that many people have access to him."

Orthodox though the proposed banking bill was, it could be called, in one respect, as the historian William Manchester has written, "a shocking measure," for it validated all acts "heretofore or hereinafter taken" by the president and the secretary of the treasury—an extraordinary license for the executive—and stipulated prison sentences for hoarders. In addition, it empowered the president to determine which banks might reopen and when, and it authorized the Federal Reserve to issue bank notes to cope with the runs that were anticipated once banks reopened.

Roosevelt's advisers roughed out the banking bill at around two in the morning on March 9, and that afternoon it reached the House—on the first day of its extraordinary session—while newly elected members were still trying to locate their seats. At the start of the scheduled debate, there were no copies of the bill, and the House leadership displayed a rolled-up newspaper as a substitute until printed copies arrived—the ink still wet. Henry Steagall, chairman of the Banking and Currency Committee, told the members that the financial system of the United States was "prostrate and in ruins.... The people have summoned a leader whose face is lifted toward the skies. We shall follow that leadership until we again stand in the glorious sunlight of prosperity and happiness." Under normal circumstances, it would have required months, perhaps years, of nurturing to get legislation of this magnitude through Congress. But the House took only thirty-eight minutes to approve the measure without a word changed while, according to one account, "Mrs. Roosevelt sat knitting in the gallery like a benign Madame Defarge, counting votes."

A half hour later the Senate took up the bill, and by 7:30 the upper chamber, too, had approved it. At 8:36 p.m., less than eight hours after the bill had been introduced, Roosevelt, at a room in the White House cluttered with piles of books and pictures of the new tenants, signed the first legislation of the New Deal: the Emergency Banking Act of 1933. The law gave the president such an unbridled grant of authority that the *New York Times* ran its account under the headline ROOSEVELT GETS POWER OF DICTATOR. That very night, the Bureau of Engraving and Printing put hundreds of new workers on the job turning out the $2 billion in Federal Reserve Notes authorized by the law. Working night and day, they made it possible for government-chartered planes carrying sacks of crisp greenbacks to take off first thing Saturday morning, March 11, for the Federal Reserve cities.

To persuade the American people that their savings were secure, Roosevelt scheduled for Sunday night, March 12, a nationwide radio

address: the first of his "fireside chats." He did not, as is commonly supposed, speak by a fireside, but he did eschew the formal manner of
nineteenth-century oratory, which he recognized was inappropriate for
the new medium of radio. He later said that while speaking as though
carrying on a conversation, "I tried to picture a mason at work on a new
building, a girl behind a counter, a farmer in his field." He read his script
almost nonchalantly but in a way that would inspire confidence. "I want
to talk for a few minutes with the people of the United States about
banking," he began breezily. "No sound bank is a dollar worse off than
when it closed its doors last Monday," he assured his listeners. "It is safer
to keep your money in a reopened bank than under the mattress." He
explained the situation so lucidly, said Will Rogers, that even a banker
could understand it.

The first fireside chat had an enormous impact. A New Jersey woman
wrote him, "Even though I have not worked for almost a year, and my
savings are tied up in a closed bank, I, and millions like me, at last... can
hope for the lifting of that terrible depression that had almost broken
the spirit of a good many of us," and a Syracuse judge, who had been

As he relaxes in his car, the familiar cigarette holder in hand, Franklin Delano
Roosevelt on this visit to Hyde Park is altogether comfortable with himself. The
specially fitted Ford enabled him to move around his estate though he had no use
of his legs. To mark the centennial of his birth, this iconic photograph was chosen
for a commemorative postage stamp. © *Bettmann/CORBIS, ID U401087FACME*

listening to the talk in the company of anxiety-ridden friends, reported that after FDR had concluded, "the frantic individuals of a few moments before declared that they would leave their money in the banks and that they were not afraid of the future." Still, everyone anticipated that when banks opened their doors the next morning in the twelve Federal Reserve cities there would be massive demands for cash, since people had been cut off from money for several days.

Instead, in a remarkable testimonial to their trust in the new president, deposits exceeded withdrawals. That day, too, the dollar rose smartly against the franc and the pound. When the gong sounded to resume trading on the New York Stock Exchange, the market registered the biggest single day's gain in more than half a century. At the end of the session, the Dow-Jones ticker clicked out HAPPY DAYS ARE HERE AGAIN. By the conclusion of the month, a billion dollars in currency had been placed in bank vaults, chastened hoarders had returned gold to the Federal Reserve, and there was little occasion to issue new greenbacks. Agnes Meyer jotted in her diary: "The crisis is over. The people trust this admin. as they distrusted the other. This is the secret of the whole situation." Roosevelt, commented the essayist Gerald Johnson, "had given a better demonstration than Schopenhauer ever did of the world as Will and Idea."

The quick-step tempo of the First Hundred Days of 1933 had begun. An hour after the president signed the banking bill into law on March 9, he summoned congressional leaders to the White House to inform them that on the very next day (the second of the special session) he was going to ask Congress for power to slash millions in salaries of federal workers and millions more from the pensions of veterans. "Too often in recent history," Roosevelt declared, "liberal governments have been wrecked on rocks of loose fiscal policy." He encountered considerably more opposition to these recommendations than he had to the banking bill. Many legislators did not dare risk offending the American Legion and the Veterans of Foreign Wars or felt an obligation to the doughboys who had risked their lives in 1917, and a number of liberals objected to reducing purchasing power at such a bleak time and decried capitulation to big-business budget balancers.

Such resistance could not prevail over the instinct to stand by Roosevelt. In the House debate, Representative John McDuffie of Alabama declared, "It is true this bill grants a great deal of power, but this country is in a state of war—not against a foreign enemy but...against economic evils," and Congressman John Young Brown of Kentucky asserted: "I had as soon start a mutiny in the face of a foreign foe as start a mutiny today against the program of the President of the United States [Applause]. And if someone must shoot down, in this hour of battle, the Commander in Chief of our forces, God grant that the assassin's bullet shall not be fired from the Democratic side of the House [Applause]."

Despite the strong objections, a coalition of administration and conservative Democrats joined by Republicans required only two days to put through the second of FDR's measures, cutting federal outlays a record-setting 31 percent. The statute served to bolster Roosevelt's credibility with forces on the right calling for austerity, making it easier for him to embark on spending programs to aid the disadvantaged. Unnoteworthy in itself, the Economy Act, declared *Time*, marked "an historic transfer of fiscal power from the Congress to the Presidency." A Republican member of the House from Tennessee fumed, "I have seen the Congress of the United States absolutely abdicate its authority to the Executive. I have seen a dictatorship spring up which must have made the noses of Herr Hitler, Stalin, Mussolini and Mustapha Kemal of Turkey turn green with envy."

In the First Hundred Days, everything moved at a breathless pace. On Thursday, March 9, Roosevelt presented the banking bill; on Friday and Saturday he whipped through the economy bill; on Sunday, he paused for the Sabbath (but even then gave his fireside chat); and on Monday he came right back with a new proposal: to amend the Volstead Act (the statute enforcing prohibition) to legalize the sale of beer and light wine. In February 1933, the lame-duck Congress had voted to repeal the Eighteenth Amendment, but it would require some months for the Twenty-first Amendment to win ratification, and Roosevelt did not want to wait that long. Congress quickly complied with the president's request, and on April 7 beer and wine were sold legally in America for the first time since 1919.

The beer law had less economic impact than was often claimed for it, apart from helping the pretzel business, but the act did give the country a lift. It touched off a nationwide jubilee celebrating the end of an era of inhibiting government. The historian Charles Trout later wrote: "Boston celebrated as it had not done in years. Massive crowds surrounded the S. S. Pierce and Company warehouse on Brookline Avenue where 'dignified matrons...and gentlemen in Chesterfield coats and derby hats' lugged away cases of ale, and 'hundreds of Harvard and M. I. T. students arrived in sleek roadsters.' Downtown cafes were jammed, and the sounds of Irish tenors reverberated from Charlestown to South Boston."

Exultation over the demise of prohibition gave fresh evidence that FDR's performance was transmuting the national mood. As early as the third week in March, only eight days after Congress convened, the Washington correspondent Raymond Clapper was jotting in his diary: "Tension completely relaxed, papers turning to light news again. Little bank news, nation-wide confidence, Happy Days atmosphere." That same week, the *New Republic* noted, "Every Washington observer reports an electric change in the atmosphere of that city since Mr. Roosevelt took office," and it soon added, "The speed with which the Roosevelt administration continues to propose and act upon new legislation of the most far-reaching importance is the marvel of the world." Even arch-conservatives shared in the good feeling. The head of the prestigious Cravath law firm in New York City wrote Lord Beaverbrook, "Over here we are very much cheered up, and we Republicans rather surprised, by President Roosevelt's courage and dash and his ability to stampede Congress." The *Wall Street Journal*, after noting "an end to three years of a nation's drifting from bad to worse, an end to helpless acceptance of a malign fate," wrote: "For an explanation of the incredible change which has come over the face of things here in the United States in a single week we must look to the fact that the new Administration has superbly arisen to the occasion."

FDR's inaugural address, his fireside chat, and his three legislative successes had a cumulative impact far beyond their intrinsic significance. The veteran White House correspondent Ernest K. Lindley wrote: "In three quick blows, Mr. Roosevelt had broken as many iron bands which were strangling the country, actually or psychologically. He had broken the banking panic and salvaged most of the banking system. He had beaten the most feared lobby in Washington and established control of the federal credit. He had beaten the remains of the once all-powerful dry lobby, and broken the fourteen-year grip of Volsteadism. The country surged with enthusiasm and hope." It had taken FDR only a fortnight, concluded Walter Lippmann, to achieve a resurgence of morale comparable to the "second battle of the Marne in the summer of 1916."

In describing the altered state of mind, a number of commentators used imagery suggestive of the Christian doctrine of resurrection, the Zoroastrian theme of darkness and light, or the pagan response to the change of seasons. On March 15, a State Department economist wrote former Secretary of State Henry Stimson about the new president: "The outside public seems to behave as if Angel Gabriel had come to earth." The previous administration, observed the literary critic Edmund Wilson, "weighed on Washington, as it did on the entire country, like a darkness," and to many the lights that burned all night in the offices of New Deal agencies seemed to have illumined the Hooverian dreariness. Even in modifying the Volstead Act, Roosevelt was perceived to be ending the "long arctic night" of prohibition and breaking the ice jam of the Hoover winters. The Brain Truster Rex Tugwell distilled these impressions in the name he gave to the First Hundred Days: "a renaissance spring."

Nothing Roosevelt had done thus far, though, had offered any meaningful help to the millions unemployed, and no one knew that better than the president. While the country supposed that he was wholly preoccupied with matters such as banking, he was putting the final touches on plans to come to their aid. On the afternoon of March 9, only a few hours after the new Congress met, he talked enthusiastically with officials about his desire to put jobless young men to work in the forests. The boys needed a "break" in these hard times, he said, and the woodlands required attention. At dinner hour, he dismissed the group with instructions to return with draft legislation. That night at 9 p.m. he met with them again. In the brief interim, a bill had been prepared, and for the next hour and a half, pleased with the swift progress, he expounded on his hopes for this cadre of volunteers.

Once again, Roosevelt moved with dazzling speed. On March 15, he aired the idea; on March 21, he asked Congress to establish a Civilian Conservation Corps; on March 29, the House hurrahed the CCC bill through; and two days later, before the month had ended, the president signed it into law. On April 17, near Luray, Virginia, the Civilian Conservation Corps established its first camp, and, by early May, FDR's "tree army" had moved into 141 national forests. When Roosevelt said he wanted a quarter of a million young men in the camps by summer, it seemed an impossible goal, but the CCC surpassed it. The mobilization was completed more swiftly than that of the American Expeditionary Force in World War I. That summer, 275,000 young men, many from noisome slums, bunked down in camps in forty-seven states—the vanguard of two and a half million. Over the next nine years, they would develop eight hundred state parks, clear 125,000 miles of trails, fight forest fires, build picnic shelters, feed wildlife, create fish ponds, and, to the lasting benefit of posterity, plant trees—nearly three billion of them.

In May, when a second Bonus Army descended on Washington, its members were tactfully escorted to Fort Hunt, across the Potomac

President Roosevelt at a Civilian Conservation Corps camp, 1933. At this CCC site, everyone from the young men in his "tree army" to cabinet officers at the wooden table seems determined to match FDR's smile. His aides include Secretary of the Interior Harold Ickes and Secretary of Agriculture Henry Wallace. *Library of Congress, LC-USZ62-93597*

twelve miles from the Capitol, where, on condition that they would disperse at the end of a week, they were given cots, three square meals each day, electric lights, running water for showers, and, on FDR's instructions, coffee. "There's nothing that makes people feel as welcome as a steaming cup of coffee," the president told an aide. Mrs. Roosevelt paid a visit to the camp, where she slogged through ankle-deep mud to shake hands with the men and lead them in singing "Pack Up Your Troubles in Your Old Kit Bag" and "There's a Long, Long Trail A-Winding," a tune written by a doughboy sent overseas in the Great War. The president offered the "army" jobs in the CCC, only to have the leaders refuse. But the mass of the army rebelled against them and enrolled by the hundreds. Eventually, a quarter of a million veterans signed up for the forest corps. After the first lady's appearance, one vet said, "Hoover sent the army. Roosevelt sent his wife." A few days after coming to Washington, the leaders, admitting they were licked, left with a small contingent, never to return.

On the same March day that Roosevelt advocated the CCC, he requested appropriations for a huge relief program to channel federal money through state and local agencies to the unemployed, and Congress readily agreed. To head the newly created Federal Emergency Relief Administration, the president tapped the social worker Harry Hopkins, who had held a similar post in Albany. The United States had no experience with so massive a venture. Getting desperately needed help to people without delay, Hopkins later said, "was almost as if the Aztecs had been asked suddenly to build an aeroplane." But Hopkins was one of a new breed of can-do public servants. Instead of waiting to be assigned an office, he commandeered a desk in a dingy hallway, and in his first two hours as administrator funneled $5 million to distressed states. Over the next two and a half years, he doled out the huge sum of more than $3 billion to care for some twenty million people.

When it became apparent that even this large-scale venture would not tide the jobless over the winter of 1933–34, Roosevelt launched a considerably more massive effort, again under Hopkins, for direct federal intervention to put people to work. No operation of such magnitude had ever been seen in America before. The Civil Works Administration recruited a corps five times the size of the entire workforce of the federal government in 1930—a cohort equivalent to the payrolls of U.S. Steel,

General Motors, and twenty other gigantic corporations combined. So eager were unemployed men and women to seize upon the opportunity offered by the CWA that in Long Island City mounted police were required to herd job seekers behind barriers, and in Chicago seventy thousand gathered before sunrise. The CWA contributed greatly to the public domain, but it was so costly that Roosevelt terminated it in the spring and Hopkins's FERA once more took over. By the end of 1934, more than twenty million Americans—more than one out of every six in the country—were receiving federal assistance.

On March 16, exactly one week after the new session of Congress commenced, Roosevelt, with the banking crisis behind him and the CCC and FERA projects under way, felt free for the first time to address the fundamental problem he confronted—how to achieve recovery from the Great Depression—by sending Congress his recommendations on the farm crisis. He approached this subject in a candidly experimental frame of mind. "My position toward farm legislation," he told newsmen, "is that we ought to try to do something to increase the value of farm products and if the darn thing doesn't work, we can say so quite frankly, but at least try it."

Roosevelt let his secretary of agriculture, Henry A. Wallace, know that he was willing to push just about any program on which the major farm organizations agreed. Industry had written its own tariffs for years. He saw no reason why agriculture should not spell out its requirements, especially given the need to find a way to cope with the enormous glut of crops for which there was no market. To speed aid to the countryside, Wallace (son of Harding's secretary of agriculture), who, as a former editor of *Wallace's Farmer* and an enterprising plant geneticist, had a broad knowledge of the terrain, assented to an omnibus bill embodying a variety of options. As Wallace's biographer put it, "The measure as drawn sought to legalize almost anything anybody could think up." Since Hoover had wasted half a billion dollars by intervening in the market without limiting output, the Roosevelt administration sought to help rural America by paying subsidies to farmers who agreed to take land out of cultivation—in the expectation that restricting supply would boost crop prices.

The farm bill won quick approval in the House, where Roosevelt enjoyed a great Democratic preponderance, but for some weeks it foundered in the Senate, while anger in the countryside mounted. In Le Mars,

Iowa, masked farmers, infuriated by foreclosure litigation that was depriving thousands of their lands, invaded a courtroom, dragged a judge from the bench, put a noose around his neck, and threatened to lynch him. Though radicals on the prairies thought the measure did not go far enough, Senate conservatives were shocked by the proposed federal intervention, which they blamed on FDR's advisers. The Michigan Republican Arthur Vandenberg said, "When we mix Ph.D.'s and RFDs, we are in trouble." Only FDR's tremendous popularity kept the plan alive. "Filled with horrors and hellishness as this bill is, I'm going to support the president," said one congressman. The Agricultural Adjustment Act revolutionized the raising of staple crops in the United States—from 1933 into the twenty-first century. "Our economy is not agricultural any longer," said William Faulkner. "Our economy is the federal government. We no longer farm in Mississippi cotton fields. We farm now in Washington corridors and Congressional committee rooms."

One feature of the Triple A law prodded the president to choose from a number of options to manipulate the value of the dollar, but Roosevelt needed no prompting. He had already taken the historic step of moving the United States off the gold standard—a decision that shook up the world of orthodox finance. "Maybe the country doesn't know it yet," said the Wall Street investor Bernard Baruch, "but I think we may find that we've been in a revolution more drastic than the French Revolution." Instead of being bound by the gold standard's immutable exigencies, the president freed himself to tinker with the money supply as he saw fit. In "off the record" remarks to the press, he confided, "What you are coming to now really is a managed currency." By depreciating the dollar, Roosevelt hoped to ease the burden of debt in a period of punishing deflation. In addition, with his approval, Congress established the Farm Credit Administration, which in its first two years refinanced one-fifth of all farm mortgages in the country, and another alphabet agency, the HOLC (Home Owners' Loan Corporation), which staved off foreclosures in cities and towns.

Soon after taking office, at a moment when the nation was railing at bankers who had been peddling worthless investments, Roosevelt had sent a message to Congress urging that there be added "to the ancient rule of caveat emptor the further doctrine 'let the seller also beware.'" Spotlighting "practices neither ethical nor honest," he explained, "What we seek is a return to a clearer understanding of the ancient truth that those who manage banks, corporations and other agencies handling or using other people's money are trustees acting for others." (The phrase "other people's money" he borrowed from Louis Brandeis.) The Securities Act, adopted in late May, established federal supervision of the issue of new securities and made company directors civilly and criminally liable for misinformation. A year later, Congress extended regulation to the stock exchanges, with both laws assigned to a new agency, the Securities and Exchange Commission (SEC). In addition, the Glass-Steagall Act of 1933 separated commercial from investment banking and created the Federal Deposit Insurance Corporation (FDIC).

This parcel of laws signified a prodigious transfer of power from Wall Street to Washington. The front page of the newspaper—rife with head-lines on FDR's alphabet agencies—became, one writer noted, "more important to the businessman than the market page, and the White House press conference of vaster import than the closing prices of the New York Stock Exchange." As early as 1934, an analyst was reporting: "Financial news no longer originates in Wall Street.... News of a finan-cial nature in Wall Street now is merely an echo of events which take place in Washington.... The pace of the ticker is determined now in Washington not in company boardrooms or in brokerage offices.... In Wall Street it is no longer asked what some big trader is doing, what some important banker thinks, what opinion some eminent lawyer holds about some pressing question of the day. The query in Wall Street has become: 'What's the news from Washington?'"

Roosevelt dazzled not only the country but the world with another creation of the First Hundred Days: the Tennessee Valley Authority. It originated as a proposal by Senator George Norris to complete a World War I dam at Muscle Shoals, Alabama, to provide a source for cheap electricity and fertilizer. Norris, who had been heartbroken by Coolidge's and Hoover's vetoes of this legislation, called FDR's TVA message "the greatest humanitarian document ever to come from the White House." Under the president's guidance, the measure that emerged from Congress authorized not only multipurpose dams but also a 650-mile navigation channel from Knoxville to Paducah and what Roosevelt envisioned as "the widest experiment ever conducted by a government" in regional planning in an area three-fourths the size of England. In 1938, after a visit to the TVA, a prominent Austrian journalist said, "There is nothing quite like it on the planet."

FDR's familiarity with the War Industries Board of 1917–18 brought about the capstone of the First Hundred Days: the National Industrial Recovery Act. The law, which delegated a huge amount of power to the president, allowed trade associations to plan output and set prices without fear of antitrust prosecution, but under the watchful eyes of the government. To balance this concession to business, Section 7(a) stipulated that these agreements must set minimum wages and maximum hours and guaranteed labor the right to collective bargaining. As a stimulus to the economy, the act also provided the unheard-of sum of $3.3 billion for public works. To head the National Recovery Administration, Roosevelt chose the rambunctious Hugh Johnson, a former general who rapidly placed the symbol of the NRA—a blue eagle—on factories, shops, and newspaper mastheads across America.

Never before in peacetime had the federal government intruded so deeply. In signing the measure on June 16, the president said: "Many good men voted this new charter with misgivings. I do not share these doubts. I had part in the great cooperation of 1917 and 1918 and it is my faith that we can count on our industry once more...to lift this new threat and to do it without taking any advantage of the public trust which has this day been reposed without stint in the good faith and high purpose of American business."

Roosevelt spoke these words on the hundredth, and final, day of the emergency session. He had sent fifteen special messages to the Hill, and Congress had adopted all fifteen proposals. As he signed a series of measures—including the Glass-Steagall bill, an ambitious endeavor to consolidate railroads, and the largest peacetime appropriation ever voted—he turned to two visitors and said, "More history is being made today than in [any] one day of our national life." Senator Thomas Gore of Oklahoma replied, "During all time."

Both then and in retrospect, commentators expressed awe at what had been wrought in less than fifteen weeks. "The change is very much as if some Aladdin has rubbed a magic lamp and summoned his genie to repair the wreckage left by inaction and drift," wrote the Tennessee editor George Fort Milton at the time. Subsequently, the French essayist André Maurois concluded:

One cannot help calling to mind, as one writes the history of these three crowded months, the Biblical account of the Creation. The first day, the Brain Trust put an embargo on gold; the second day, it peopled the forests; the third day, it created ... three point two beer; the fourth day, it broke the bonds that tied the dollar to gold; the fifth day, it set the farmers free; the sixth day, it created General Johnson, and then, looking upon what it had made of America, it saw that it was good.

But it could not rest on the seventh day.

With Congress recessed, Roosevelt took off for New England en route to a summer holiday at his country home on Campobello Island in the Canadian province of New Brunswick. As he moved through the crowded streets of Boston on Bunker Hill Day, cheering throngs greeted him, and at the village green of Quincy hard by the homes of John and John Quincy Adams, not even a relentless downpour deterred citizens from shouting their approval. Enthusiasm was no less keen in other sections of the country. In Mississippi, the editor of the state's leading paper counseled his readers, "Stick to him ... until hell freezes over, and then skate ... with him on the ice." The president, said a southern tenant farmer, "is as good a man as ever lived," and a mill worker chimed in, "I do think that Roosevelt is the biggest-hearted man we ever had in the White House." Another millhand was more blunt. "Mr. Roosevelt," he asserted, "is the only man we ever had in the White House who would understand that my boss is a sonofabitch."

Though FDR grew up on an estate and had never experienced anything save the advantages of privilege, he managed to convey the sense that he knew, bone and marrow, what those who were destitute had to endure. An insurance man said that "my mother looks upon the President as someone so immediately concerned with her problems ... that she would not be greatly surprised were he to come to her house some evening and stay to dinner." Similarly, the novelist Martha Gellhorn, who served briefly as a New Deal fieldworker, reported from the Carolinas: "Every house I visited—mill worker or unemployed—had a picture of the President. These ranged from newspaper clippings (in destitute homes) to large colored prints, framed in gilt cardboard.... And the feeling of these people for the President is one of the most remarkable phenomena I have ever met. He is at once God and their intimate friend; he knows them all by name, knows their little town and mill, their little lives and problems. And though everything else fails, he is there, and will not let them down."

Until FDR, few Americans thought of writing the White House because presidents seemed remote from their everyday lives. From McKinley through Hoover, one man sufficed to handle all of the incoming mail. But under Roosevelt, the chief of mails had to hire a staff of fifty to cope with the deluge. He recalled that when Roosevelt "advised millions of listeners in one of his fireside chats to 'tell me your troubles,' most of them believed implicitly that he was speaking to them personally and immediately wrote him a letter. It was months before we managed to swim out of *that* flood of mail."

His fireside chats took the president into living rooms across the land. He had not a single close friend, but when he addressed citizens as "my friends," that salutation convinced them that he was one of their own. "His voice and his facial expression as he spoke were those of an intimate friend," wrote an associate. "As he talked his head would nod and his hands would move in simple, natural comfortable gestures. His face would...light up as though he were actually sitting on the front porch or in the parlor with them. People felt this, and it bound them to him in affection." The journalist David Halberstam later pointed out:

> He was the first great American radio voice. For most Americans of this generation, their first memory of politics would be sitting by a radio and hearing *that* voice, strong, confident, totally at ease. If he was going to speak, the idea of doing something else was unthinkable. If they did not yet have a radio, they walked the requisite several hundred yards to the home of a more fortunate neighbor who did. It was in the most direct sense the government reaching out and touching the citizen, bringing Americans into the political process and focusing their attention on the presidency as the source of good.... Most Americans in the previous 160 years had never even seen a President; now almost all of them were hearing him, *in their own homes*. It was literally and figuratively electrifying.

Newspaper readers found FDR as inescapable as did listeners to the radio. "God, did he make news!" Halberstam wrote. "Every day there were two or three stories coming out of the White House." The United Press sent four times as many dispatches about the federal government over its lines in 1934 than it had in 1930, when news bureaus often assigned a single reporter to the entire executive branch. "We never covered Washington in the twenties," one journalist recalled. "We covered the Senate. You wasted your time downtown." But "downtown"—the White House—became the liveliest beat in the country. Jack Bell, on assignment for the Associated Press, wrote of Roosevelt: "He talked in headline phrases. He acted, he emoted; he was angry, he was smiling. He was persuasive, he was demanding; he was philosophical, he was elemental. He was sensible, he was unreasonable; he was benevolent, he was malicious. He was satirical, he was soothing; he was funny, he was gloomy. He was exciting. He was human. He was copy."

FDR's first press conference on March 8, 1933, the historian of journalism Leo Rosten later said, became "something of a legend in newspaper circles":

> Mr. Roosevelt was introduced to each correspondent. Many of them he already knew and greeted by name—first name. For each he had a handshake and the Roosevelt smile. When the questioning began, the full virtuosity of the new Chief Executive was demonstrated. Cigarette-holder in mouth at a jaunty angle, he met the reporters on their own grounds. His answers were swift, positive, illuminating. He had exact information at his fingertips.... He was lavish in his confidences.... He made no effort to conceal his pleasure in the give and take.

Hoover, like Harding and Coolidge, had insisted on written questions submitted in advance, but FDR announced that day to the astonished and delighted press corps that he was abolishing the requirement, and it could fire away at will. At the end of the meeting, reporters did something they had never done before. They set aside their notebooks and pencils and gave the president a spontaneous round of applause.

Over the course of his presidency, Roosevelt held more than a thousand press conferences. After the first one, when, said a veteran newsman, "the press barely restrained its whoopees," a columnist wrote, "The doubters among us—and I was one of them—predicted that the free and open conference would last a few weeks and then would be abandoned." But week in, week out, the president submitted to the crossfire. He enjoyed the badinage and gave reporters to understand that, since he had once headed the *Harvard Crimson*, he was one of them. He saw to it that every nervous newcomer on his first White House assignment was introduced to him with a handshake, and he demonstrated that members of the Fourth Estate were socially respectable by throwing a spring garden party for them. Many who recalled Hoover's chill disdain found it hard to believe that they were actually dancing in the East Room. If reporters were 60 percent for the New Deal, one of them said, they were 90 percent for Roosevelt.

From press accounts, fireside chats, and newsreels, the president emerged as a sparkling personality and, in a bleak decade, a reassuring presence. FDR, said the silent film star Lillian Gish, seemed "to have been dipped in phosphorus," and his voice, remarked the philosopher T. V. Smith, "knew how to articulate only the everlasting Yea." The essence of his presidency, the political scientist Clinton Rossiter later observed, "was his airy eagerness to meet the age head on. Thanks to his flair for drama, he acted as if never in all history had there been times like our own." A former member of the Brain Trust concluded: "No monarch,...unless it may have been Elizabeth or her magnificent Tudor father, or maybe Alexander or Augustus Caesar, can have given quite that sense of serene presiding, of gathering up into himself, of really representing, a whole people."

Not even the gravest troubles seemed to ruffle him. "No signs of care are visible to his...visitors or at the press conferences," a Washington journalist reported in the crisis year of 1933. Roosevelt "is amiable, urbane and apparently untroubled.... Those who talk with him informally in the evenings report that he busies himself with his stamp collection, discussing in an illuminating fashion the affairs of state while he waves his shears in the air." To account for what *Time* magazine called his "champagne ebullience," the political scientist Richard Neustadt pointed out: "The White House for him was almost a family seat and... he regarded the whole country almost as a family property. Once he became president of the United States that sense of fitness gave him an extraordinary confidence. Roosevelt, almost alone among our presidents, had no conception of the office to live up to; he was it. His image of the office was himself-in-office." One of his associates remarked, "He must have been psychoanalyzed by God."

On the centennial of FDR's birth, the conservative journalist George Will commented: "Anyone who contemplates this century without shivering probably does not understand what is going on. But Franklin Roosevelt was, an aide said, like the fairy-tale prince who did not know how to shiver.... He had a Christian's faith that the universe is well constituted and an American's faith that history is a rising road.... Radiating an infectious zest, he did the most important thing a President can do: he gave the nation a hopeful, and hence creative, stance toward the future."

Though the simplicity of his religious creed would have distressed theologians, Roosevelt's self-assurance owed a great deal to his faith in a benign providence. He was convinced, his biographer Kenneth Davis wrote, that "history, though it had...a tidal ebb and flow, had, in the long run, a surging flow in one direction...away from polar evil toward polar good,...progress that was inevitable because it was God's will." In that context, Eleanor Roosevelt said of her husband: "He believed in God and His guidance. He felt that human beings were given tasks to perform and with these tasks the ability and strength to put them through."

FDR's sangfroid in coping with the desperate predicaments of the Great Depression inspired the country. Reflecting on the president's attributes, Secretary of Labor Frances Perkins, the first woman appointed to a cabinet post, remarked: "Overshadowing them all was his feeling that nothing in human judgment is final. One may courageously take the step that seems right today because it can be modified tomorrow if it does not work well.... Since it is a normal human reaction, most people felt as he did and gladly followed when he said, 'We can do it. At least let's try.'" In one of his fireside chats, Roosevelt told his radio audience:

When Andrew Jackson, "Old Hickory," died, someone asked, "Will he go to Heaven?" and the answer was, "He will if he wants to." If I am asked whether the American people will pull themselves out of the depression, I answer, "They will if they want to."... I have no sympathy with the professional economists who insist that things must run their course and that human agencies can have no influence on economic ills.

Early in his first term, Roosevelt placed the challenges he confronted in a broad historical context:

> The Presidency is not merely an administrative office. That is the least of it. It is pre-eminently a place of moral leadership.
>
> All of our great Presidents were leaders of thought at times when certain historic ideas in the life of the nation had to be clarified. Washington personified the idea of Federal Union. Jefferson practically originated the party system as we now know it....
>
> Two great principles of our government were forever put beyond question by Lincoln.... Theodore Roosevelt and Wilson were both moral leaders,... who used the Presidency as a pulpit....
>
> That is what the office is—a superb opportunity for applying to new conditions the simple rules of human conduct to which we always go back. Without leadership alert and sensitive to change, we... lose our way.

However good his intentions, opponents questioned whether he had the intellectual capacity for leadership, and even some of his admirers found it hard to explain how he dealt with so many intricate ideas. Figuring out FDR's thinking process, said Henry Stimson, was "very much like chasing a vagrant beam of sunshine around an empty room." A longtime political associate said that he "never saw him read a book" or even "a magazine unless a particular portion was called to his attention." Instead, he absorbed information by watching and listening, and somehow managed to acquire a command of a range of subjects from utilities regulation to finance, as even his enemies acknowledged. An anti–New Deal North Carolina senator who called on him to talk about the port of Morehead City recounted, "I was almost stunned when I found that Roosevelt seemed to know more about the harbor, the ocean depth, and all that sort of thing than I did!" Still, the puzzlement remained. On one occasion, a journalist asked Eleanor Roosevelt, "Just how does the President *think*?" She retorted, "My dear Mister Gunther, the President never 'thinks'! He *decides*."

Most Americans lived all through the age of Roosevelt without ever comprehending that the effervescent, energetic president of the United States was a paraplegic. No photograph showing him disabled ever appeared in a newspaper, and cartoonists depicted him not as an invalid but, in the fashion of a popular song of the day, as the daring young man on the flying trapeze. *Time* reported on FDR's first day in office: "At 10:30 p.m. he stood up, yawned, went peacefully to bed." In fact, Roosevelt was incapable of standing up. Even White House correspondents who, twice a week, saw him confined to a wheelchair did not think of him as in any way handicapped, for he conveyed the impression of a locomotive going full throttle. On breaking off an interview, Roosevelt would say, "I have to run now!"

On the day after FDR's inauguration, the *New York Times* ran a front-page story under the headline VICTORY FOR HITLER EXPECTED TODAY, and within hours the Reichstag vested absolute power in the *Führer*. For all the rest of his life, Roosevelt had to cope with the Nazi menace. While he was cheering on the CCC boys making their peaceful rounds in the forests, Hitler was drilling storm troopers. While the president was launching the Tennessee Valley Authority in the spring of 1933, Jews were being mauled in German towns and villages. Roosevelt was called upon to demonstrate that democracy could survive a worldwide breakdown. In both Europe and Asia, despots reigned—not only in Germany under the swastika but in Italy, where Mussolini's Black Shirts had crushed opposition; in Russia, where Stalin imposed a savage tyranny; and in Japan, which was ruled by a martial regime. Some thought democracy doomed and saw totalitarianism as, in Anne Morrow Lindbergh's later phrase, "the wave of the future."

With leaders in Britain and France exhibiting a failure of resolve, antifascists looked apprehensively toward the United States, not knowing what the advent of Franklin Roosevelt would bring. In 1933, in an open letter to the new president, John Maynard Keynes declared: "You have made yourself the trustee for those in every country who seek to mend the evils of our condition by reasoned experiment within the framework of the existing social system. If you fail, rational change will be gravely prejudiced throughout the world, leaving orthodoxy and revolution to fight it out. But, if you succeed, new and bolder methods will be tried elsewhere, and we may date the first chapter of a new economic era from your accession to office." A year later, Winston Churchill wrote of FDR: "All the world watched his valiant effort to solve...problems with an anxiety which is only the shadow of high hope."

Some of Roosevelt's first statements and actions disappointed these expectations. "Our international trade relations, though vastly important, are...secondary to the establishment of a sound national economy," he declared in his inaugural address. "I favor as a practical policy the putting of first things first." Unlike Hoover, he believed that America's hardships in the Great Depression resulted not from a foreign contagion but from the sickness of the domestic economy, which he needed to remedy. Consequently, he embarked upon a course of economic nationalism.

To advance US interests and to give himself maximum flexibility in devising policies, he devalued the dollar and sent a "bombshell message" to the World Economic Conference in London torpedoing plans for international currency stabilization so that he could loosen the grip of deflation in the United States. Sententiously, he scolded the extraordinary gathering of sixty-six nations assembled in London in June 1933 for embracing a "specious fallacy," though his own delegates had been working toward stabilization with the reasonable understanding that they were carrying out his instructions.

A diminutive role in world affairs did not comport for long either with FDR's outlook or his personality, however. A cosmopolite who had traveled extensively in Europe, he had a keen interest in events overseas, and he had every intention of weighing in on important decisions. Schooled in Wilsonian internationalism, he supported Secretary of State Cordell Hull's efforts to negotiate reciprocal trade agreements lowering the barriers erected by the Smoot-Hawley tariff, and, in expiation of his role in blowing up the London conference, he secured an exchange stabilization pact with Britain and France in 1936.

Beyond these modest steps, Congress forbade him to go. He was alarmed by the march of fascism on the Continent and by the rapaciousness of the Japanese, who had walked out of the League of Nations a week before Hitler took over the government of Germany, but he could not even contemplate a deterrent. In 1933, Congress enacted neutrality legislation that denied the president any latitude in distinguishing between aggressors and their victims because it was convinced that the shipment of munitions to the Allies had drawn the United States into an unnecessary and costly war in 1917.

Roosevelt did what he could within these confines. When Italy invaded Ethiopia in 1935, he invoked the Neutrality Act because an arms embargo would strike a blow against Mussolini and might be regarded as a gesture of support for League sanctions. To hamper Il Duce's tourist business, he warned US citizens against booking passage on the belligerent's ocean liners. He also took advantage of his discretionary powers as chief executive—notably toward countries south of the border and toward Soviet Russia. Both initiatives resulted in surprising Supreme Court opinions enormously expanding the authority of a president in foreign relations.

In his inaugural address, Roosevelt had announced, "In the field of world policy I would dedicate this nation to the policy of the good neighbor." That vague sentiment was meant universally, but it became identified solely with Latin America. In 1933 at the Pan-American Conference in Montevideo, the United States repudiated the Roosevelt Corollary that TR had enunciated by voting in favor of a resolution declaring that "no state has the right to intervene in the internal or external affairs of another." A year later, FDR's administration renounced the Platt Amendment of 1901 asserting US hegemony in Cuba, and it ended military occupation of Haiti. When, in 1938, Mexico nationalized its oil industry, Roosevelt resisted demands that he use force on behalf of American corporations.

Latin America provided the venue for the most far-reaching Supreme Court statement ever made with regard to presidential powers in foreign policy. When war broke out between Bolivia and Paraguay over the disputed Chaco region, Roosevelt, under authority granted him by a joint resolution in 1934, banned the sale of arms to either country—an action challenged by an American aircraft corporation as an improper delegation of congressional power to the executive. In *United States v. Curtiss-Wright Export Corp.* (1936), the Supreme Court not only legitimated Congress's conferral on the president of broad discretionary power to determine whether to impose an arms embargo but, in an opinion by Justice George Sutherland, validated the "very delicate, plenary, and exclusive power of the President as the sole organ of the federal government in the field of international relations—a power which does not require as a basis for its exercise an act of Congress."

In what has been called an "extravagant opinion" based on a "bizarre reading of Anglo-American legal history," Sutherland contended that in determining foreign policy, a president is not confined by the Constitution because his powers in that realm, unlike his circumscribed scope in domestic affairs, derive directly from those of the Crown before the thirteen colonies became a nation. With respect to the foreign policy sphere, "the President alone has the power to speak or listen as a representative of the nation," he asserted. "Into the field of negotiation the Senate cannot intrude; and Congress itself is powerless to invade it." Though Roosevelt had acted not in defiance of Congress but in accord with it, presidents for generations since the 1930s have cited Sutherland's dictum as grounds for unilateral interventions overseas.

Another FDR departure led to a further reaffirmation by the Court of presidential powers. In 1933, Roosevelt had, by executive agreement, recognized the USSR, an outcast since Wilson's time. A year after *Curtiss-Wright*, the Court, in *United States v. Belmont*, again speaking through Justice Sutherland, ruled that, in granting recognition to Soviet Russia, Roosevelt had authority to commit the United States without consulting the Senate, for, despite the treaty-making role vested in the Senate by the Constitution, the president, Sutherland reiterated, is "the sole organ" of foreign relations. An executive agreement, reached without any statutory authorization, had the same validity as a treaty ratified by the Senate, he said.

In contrast to the judiciary, Congress permitted Roosevelt no leeway in foreign affairs, as he learned to his sorrow in 1935 when he proposed US membership in the World Court. Endorsed by both major parties, the measure seemed certain to win approval. But the xenophobic "Radio Priest," the Rev. Charles Coughlin, stirred his vast audience to inundate senators with the most telegrams they had ever received on a single issue. In response, one senator cried, "To hell with Europe and the rest of those nations." A majority of the Senate voted in favor of the protocols, but, in a humiliating setback for the president, not the two-thirds required to ratify. "As to the 36 gentlemen who voted against the principle of a World Court," Roosevelt wrote the majority leader, "I am inclined to think that if they ever get to Heaven they will be doing a great deal of apologizing—that is, if God is against war, and I think He is."

———

During FDR's first years, achievements at home more than offset reverses abroad, but analysts predicted that this advantage would end when his huge majorities in Congress eroded. In all but one midterm election over the past century, the party in power had lost seats, and the only question as the 1934 contest approached was how bad for Roosevelt the rout would be. The country's foremost conservative columnist estimated that if Republicans picked up one hundred seats, the president would be a one-termer. More sanguine, Vice President John Nance Garner thought that the losses might be held to fewer than forty seats. The actual outcome was a shocker. Instead of losing seats in the House, Democrats picked up thirteen. Republicans, with a remnant of fewer than one-quarter of the members, were left with the lowest percentage in their history. Even more depressing for them was the score in the Senate, where Democrats, by adding nine—one of them an obscure Missourian, Harry Truman—ran up the biggest majority either party had ever known. Commentators regarded the results not as a summation of hundreds of races but as a verdict the country had delivered on Franklin Roosevelt. The president, a Republican editor concluded, "has been all but crowned by the people."

Buoyed by this vote of confidence, Roosevelt set out in 1935 to give the United States the lineaments of a Welfare State. From Scandinavia to New Zealand, other nations had instituted old-age pensions and other forms of social insurance that Bismarck had introduced in the nineteenth century, but the American government had never even considered them. After the midterm elections, the president told Frances Perkins: "I see no reason why every child, from the day he is born, shouldn't be a member of the social security system. Cradle to the grave, from the cradle to the grave, he ought to be . . . . When he begins to grow up, he should know he will have old-age benefits direct from the insurance system to which he will belong all his life. If he is out of work, he gets a benefit. If he is sick or crippled, he gets a benefit."

When the new Congress convened in January 1935, Roosevelt stunned the members by calling for creation of an unprecedented system of social welfare. This far-reaching measure, which emerged from a committee chaired by Secretary Perkins, appalled conservatives in both parties. "Never in the history of the world has any measure been brought here so insidiously designed...to prevent business recovery, to enslave workers," asserted an upstate New York Republican congressman, and, unaware of the absurdity of his statement, a Republican senator from Delaware said of the proposal, "I fear it may end the progress of a great country and bring its people to the level of the average European." From the other side of the aisle, a Democratic senator from New Jersey protested: "It would take all the romance out of life. We might as well take a child from the nursery, give him a nurse, and protect him from every experience that life affords." Opponents fought the president implacably, but, after a struggle consuming more than half a year, he prevailed.

The Social Security Act of 1935 established America's first national system of old-age pensions, started a federal-state arrangement for unemployment compensation, and authorized grants to the blind, the incapacitated, and dependent children. The president insisted that most of the program be financed by payroll taxes on workers as well as employers. Told that this feature was regressive and would deter recovery, he replied: "I guess you're right on the economics. But those taxes were never a problem of economics. They are politics all the way through. We put those payroll contributions there so as to give the contributors a legal, moral, and political right to collect their pensions and their unemployment benefits. With those taxes in there, no damn politician can ever scrap my social security program."

In the same month that Roosevelt unveiled his plans for a vast social security apparatus, he pushed for a federal jobs program of staggering dimensions. Congress responded with the Emergency Relief Appropriation Act of 1935 to provide employment for millions of jobless. It constituted the largest single appropriation by any government in the history of the world. The budget of the Works Progress Administration exceeded the total spent in peacetime by every US government in any year prior to 1933. The WPA for New York City alone employed more people than the War Department.

Under Harry Hopkins, called "Santa Claus incomparable and privy-builder without peer," the WPA (in tandem with the Public Works Administration born in 1933) changed the face of the land. A visitor to

New York who arrived at La Guardia Airport, crossed to Manhattan over the Triborough (now RFK) Bridge, motored south on what came to be known as the FDR Drive, and left town via the Lincoln Tunnel could thank the New Deal for all four. Countless structures—from the Cape Cod Canal and Miami's Orange Bowl in the Atlantic littoral to the mammoth dams at Bonneville and Grand Coulee and Mount Hood's Timberline Lodge in the Pacific Northwest—carried into the twenty-first century, and in hundreds of communities boys and girls continued to go to one of the thirty-nine thousand schools built by the WPA and the parks and playgrounds it laid out. The Roosevelt administration also—in the course of constructing seventy-eight thousand bridges and improving or laying half a million miles of roads—beribboned the country with scenic highways: the Blue Ridge Parkway, the Skyline Drive, the Pennsylvania Turnpike, the Overseas Highway linking Florida's mainland to Key West, the Natchez Trace, the Oregon Coastal Highway.

The emergency relief act authorized a tremendous shift of power to the president from Congress, which gave Roosevelt a free hand in disbursing the enormous grant. Taking advantage of this latitude, he allotted some of the money to a new agency: the National Youth Administration (NYA), which made it possible for hundreds of thousands of students to stay in high school or work their way through college. In addition, he approved a federal arts program whose branches gave opportunities to thousands of then unknown jobless artists. Just a sampling: Federal Writers' Project (Saul Bellow, John Cheever, Richard Wright); Federal Music Project (Aaron Copland, Howard Hanson); Federal Theatre (Orson Welles, Joseph Cotten, John Huston); Dance (Helen Tamiris, Katherine Dunham). Sometimes, these ventures dovetailed. The NYA employed a University of Michigan undergraduate, Arthur Miller, to feed mice, and the Federal Theatre in Detroit produced the first play of the young man who would go on to write *The Crucible* and *Death of a Salesman*.

Painters and sculptors may have felt the greatest impact of the cultural project. Asked whether provision should be made in the relief program for artists, Roosevelt replied, "Why not? They're human beings. They have to live. I guess the only thing they can do is paint and surely there must be some public place where paintings are wanted." Indeed, there was. Thousands of post offices, schools, and other edifices were brightened by murals, still a source of civic pride today. Some, such as those by Reginald Marsh in the New York Custom House, are of surpassing beauty. The New Deal launched or fostered the careers of an entire generation of painters—from Jacob Lawrence to Jackson Pollock—and of sculptors—from David Smith to Louise Nevelson. "To consider in a time of general distress starving artists as artists and not simply as paupers is unique to the Roosevelt administration," said the English poet W. H. Auden, and the Austrian composer Erich Wolfgang Korngold concluded: "Nowhere in Europe is there anything to compare with it. . . . No country in Europe has anything to equal this."

The legislation of the Second Hundred Days of the summer of 1935 did not match the First Hundred Days of 1933 in quantity or range but eclipsed it in ultimate significance. That summer saw the emergence, in addition to the Social Security Act, of the National Labor Relations Act (Wagner Act), which placed the federal government behind the drive for unionization, and of a Banking Act that gave America its first centralized system. The Wagner Act—by far the most important statute in the annals of the labor movement—owed infinitely more to the New York senator who bears its nickname than to the president, but Roosevelt did overcome doubts to sign it. More conspicuously, he fought doggedly against the Power Trust in order to put through the Public Utility Holding Company Act that leveled holding-company pyramids erected by speculators. Heeding an FDR "soak the rich" message, Congress also made a small stab at redistribution of wealth.

During the Second Hundred Days, as in the spring of 1933, the president demonstrated his effectiveness as chief legislator. Throughout his tenure, he resorted to special messages, summoned the congressional leadership down to the White House to confer on legislation, dispatched agents up to Capitol Hill to cajole and cudgel, appeared before Congress in person, and turned the previously mundane business of bill signing into political theater by initiating the custom of giving pens to congressional sponsors as mementoes. The historian of the SEC Ralph De Bedts has written: "Presidential support . . . of regulatory powers . . . was never forgotten or neglected. Did Senators need a word of explanation on a bill under consideration? They received a 'Dear George' letter earnestly stating the public need for such legislation. Were Congressional chairmen hard put to keep their committees from amending legislation to the point of emasculation? They—and the public press—received sternly polite notes that clearly threw the considerable weight of the Chief Executive on the side of their efforts."

In numerous ways, the president made clear that, though the Constitution vested the legislative power in Congress, he was calling the tune. He directed his appointees in the executive branch to draft bills that were handed to longtime members of Congress to introduce, and he tantalized legislators by intimations of patronage plums that might be coming their way, but without delivering them until they gave him the bills he demanded. (As a consequence, one scholar said, "His relations with Congress were...tinged with a shade of expectancy which is the best part of young love.") He also broke every record in making use of the veto power. By the end of his second term, his vetoes already totaled more than 30 percent of all the measures disallowed by presidents since 1792. He was the first chief executive to read a veto message personally to Congress and even asked aides to keep an eye out for measures he could veto, in order to remind Congress that the Constitution also accords presidents a vital role in lawmaking.

Roosevelt's boldness as chief legislator elicited expressions of awe both from contemporaries and, generations afterward, from historians. At the end of FDR's first term, the columnist Raymond Clapper wrote, "It is scarcely an exaggeration to say that the President, although not a member of Congress, has become almost the equivalent of the prime minister of the British system, because he is both executive and the guiding hand of the legislative branch," and a half century later the political scientist Harold Barger declared: "FDR changed the power ratio between Congress and the White House, publicly taking it upon himself to act as the leader of Congress at a time of deepening crisis in the nation. More than any other president, FDR established the model of the powerful legislative presidency on which the public's expectations still are anchored."

This galaxy of legislation accentuated FDR's expansive view of the role of the national government. Though Hegel and other European theorists had written of *der Staat*, Americans had rarely spoken of the State. "Nobody would have thought of calling the sleepy, rather inconsequential Southern town that Washington was in Calvin Coolidge's day the center of anything very important," a journalist has observed, and an economist has remarked, "Before the New Deal, the only business a citizen had with the government was through the Post Office. No doubt he saw a soldier or a sailor now and then, but the government had nothing to do with the general public." The diplomat George Kennan, recalling his midwestern boyhood, said that in those days "when times were hard, as they often were, groans and lamentations went up to God, but never to Washington." FDR, however, the British writer Harold Laski asserted, was the first American leader "to use the power of the state to subordinate the primary assumptions of that society to certain social purposes." A South Carolina labor leader expressed the same thought more pithily. "Franklin Delano Roosevelt," he explained, "is void of the laissez-faire personality."

On a number of occasions, Roosevelt articulated his vision. In a message to Congress, he affirmed: "Government has a final responsibility for the well-being of its citizenship. If private co-operative endeavor fails to provide work for willing hands and relief for the unfortunate, those suffering hardship from no fault of their own have a right to call upon the Government for aid; and a Government worthy of its name must make fitting response." In his 1936 acceptance address at Philadelphia's Franklin Field, home of University of Pennsylvania football, he declared: "Governments can err, Presidents do make mistakes, but the immortal Dante tells us that Divine Justice weighs the sins of the cold-blooded and the sins of the warm-hearted on a different scale. Better the occasional faults of a government living in the spirit of charity than the consistent omissions of a government frozen in the ice of its own indifference."

With his control of foreign affairs challenged and the wisdom of his domestic policies disputed, a legion of prognosticators predicted that FDR's bid for reelection in 1936 would end in ignominious rejection at the hands of his Republican challenger, Kansas governor Alf Landon. The Democratic National Committee conceded Illinois to Landon, and a veteran Democratic senator reported, "The New England States will be solidly Republican." So poor were the president's prospects he might even lose New York City, a Tammany Hall operative acknowledged. After closely scrutinizing a poll in Michigan, the country's foremost public relations counsel foresaw "Democratic defeat by landslide proportions." The most highly regarded Republican newspaper in the nation, the *New York Herald Tribune,* assured its readers: LANDON TO WIN 33 STATES. Especially ominous was the reckoning of the hitherto always reliable poll of the *Literary Digest.* Roosevelt, it concluded, would not carry a single state in the North.

No one, though, doubted FDR's mastery of his party, which he demonstrated at the national convention in Philadelphia in 1936 by driving through a resolution abolishing a stipulation that for a century had permitted the South to exercise a veto over presidential nominations. At his behest, the convention abruptly ended the tradition of requiring Democratic presidential aspirants to muster the approval of at least two-thirds of the delegates. Both Martin Van Buren in 1844 and Champ Clark in 1912 had gained a majority but, because they could not vault the two-thirds hurdle, had been denied. In 1936, Clark's son, Missouri senator Bennett Champ Clark, had the immense satisfaction of leading the successful fight to expunge the rule. The change revealed that, under Roosevelt, the white South no longer wielded as great a clout in the Democratic Party as multifarious northern cities.

During the 1936 campaign, the president, exploiting the bitter animosity of urban masses toward Wall Street in the Great Depression, calculatedly pitted class against class. Annual messages to Congress usually offer occasions for benign platitudes, but in January 1936 Roosevelt chose instead to lash out at "political puppets of an economic autocracy" who sought to "provide shackles," indeed "enslavement," for "the people" while seizing "power for themselves." That summer, on accepting renomination in Philadelphia, he incited frenzied cheering by likening his opponents to the eighteenth-century Tories who had supported George III and by branding them "economic royalists" as well as "privileged princes." It seemed, said the journalist Marquis Childs, in that crowd of "a hundred thousand or more, stretched away into the darkness at Franklin Field,... as though the roar out of the warm, sticky night came from a single throat." Meantime, the delegates in Philadelphia were adopting a platform whose first draft incorporated a declaration of war on "kidnappers, bandits, and malefactors of great wealth."

Incendiary though these assaults on the rich patrons of the Republican Party were, they did not reach the level of vitriol of the final speech of

FDR's campaign at Madison Square Garden. "Never before in all our history," Roosevelt told the jam-packed arena, had the forces of "organized money" been "so united against one candidate as they stand today. They are unanimous in their hate for me and I welcome their hatred." Those pugnacious words roused the crowd to raucous clapping and stomping. "I should like to have it said of my first administration that in it the forces of selfishness and of lust for power have met their match," he continued, in a sentence that evoked such impassioned shouting that he had to impose quiet before he could go on to add: "I should like to have it said of my second administration that in it their forces met their *master*." Pandemonium ensued.

Roosevelt's speech could well be regarded as demagogic, but it did not so much foment class hostility as register the reality of it. The historian Donald McCoy later observed: "Civil war raged in the United States in 1936, but it was fought within the confines of the electoral system, and with words and paper instead of gunpowder and steel. It was not a case, as it had been in some earlier elections, of one section of the country against other sections, or of country folk against city-dwellers, or even of the young against the old. It was the closest that America had come to class warfare, as labor was arrayed almost solidly against business, as the poor were pitted against the well-fixed, and as the middle class was split against itself."

Numbers of commentators remarked on how class antagonism found expression in support for or hostility to FDR in 1936. One of them reported: "On almost any train leaving Grand Central Station at five o'clock for Westchester County or Connecticut, you would hear Mr. Roosevelt and the New Deal condemned with an intolerance and bitterness that would astonish any reasonable-minded man. If you took a bus to Jersey at the same hour, you would hear fanatical loyalty to the present administration and a blind acceptance of practically all that Mr. Roosevelt was doing." At the World Series between the Giants and the Yankees, fans in the expensive boxes sported sunflowers, Landon's emblem, while the "bleacher bums," on spotting the president in the stadium, cheered fervently. Roosevelt himself told callers at the White House: "I still think that fellow from New Zealand was right who said to me, 'The Pullmans are against you, but the day-coaches are with you.'"

As he approached another ballpark—Forbes Field, home of the Pittsburgh Pirates—he decided to switch his emphasis from the iniquities of his enemies to the virtues of the New Deal, but he first had to dispose of an embarrassment. Since at Forbes Field in 1932 he had denounced Hoover as a profligate spender who had run up intolerable deficits, he asked his speechwriter to turn out a draft that would square that statement with FDR's freehanded spending. Samuel Rosenman later wrote:

> That evening I went in to see the President in his study and said that as long as he insisted on referring to the speech, I had found the only kind of explanation that could be made. He turned to me rather hopefully and, I think with a little surprise, and said, "Fine, what sort of an explanation would you make?"
>
> I replied, "Mr. President, the only thing you can say about that 1932 speech is to deny categorically that you ever made it."

Instead, Roosevelt offered the huge crowd in the stadium a rationale. When he took office, he recalled, some advised him to let Nature take its course. "I rejected that advice because Nature was in an angry mood," he said, then elucidated: "To balance our budget in 1933 or 1934 would have been a crime against the American people. To do so we should either have had to make a capital levy that would have been confiscatory, or we would have had to set our face against human suffering with callous indifference. When Americans suffered, we refused to pass by on the other side. Humanity came first."

As he went on to talk of the gains that had been made in these years, he employed a ballpark analogy:

> Compare the scoreboard which you have in Pittsburgh now with the scoreboard which you had when I stood here at second base in this field four years ago. At that time, as I drove through these great valleys, I could see mile after mile of this greatest mill and factory area in the world a dead panorama of silent black structures and smokeless stacks. I saw idleness and hunger instead of the whirl of machinery. Today as I came north from West Virginia, I saw mines operating, I found bustle and life, and hiss of steam, the ring of steel on steel— the roaring song of industry.

Though there were still eight million jobless, the economy was surging in 1936, and in speeches in Pittsburgh and elsewhere, Roosevelt claimed credit for the improvement. From the rear platform of a train stop in the resort town of Colorado Springs, he remarked: "You know, there has been a good deal of difference in tourists. In 1932, when I came out through here, there were a lot of tourists—but they were riding in box cars. This year there are more of them—and they are riding in Pullmans."

Wherever FDR campaigned, he attracted passionate throngs of admirers. The large crowds, a diplomat set down in his diary, "passed any bounds for enthusiasm—really wild enthusiasm—that I have ever seen in any political gathering." In Detroit's Cadillac Square, he observed "a seething mass of people, standing packed closely together," while "up each street as far as one could see…the crowd was just as thick," so dense that it was almost impossible for the president's cavalcade to make its way forward. FDR's reception in Pittsburgh, a Pennsylvania senator said, could only be described as "ecstatic frenzy." In cities across the land, the president heard people cry out "He saved my home," "He gave me a job," and saw placards reading "Thank God for Roosevelt." On the side of a boxcar in the Denver freight yards, someone had scrawled in chalk a heartfelt message: "Roosevelt Is My Friend."

When at his Hyde Park estate on Election Night Roosevelt, cigarette holder at an angle, received the early returns, he leaned back, blew a smoke ring, and said, "Wow!" They were the first indications of a historic landslide triumph, the greatest ever achieved in a contested election. His twenty-eight million votes set a new mark, and no one before had accumulated his eleven-million plurality. In carrying every state save Maine and Vermont, he rang up the highest proportion of electoral votes (523–8) since James Monroe had run with no opposition. He was the first Democrat to carry Pennsylvania since 1856 when the state had supported its native son, James Buchanan. Michigan, which had given the 1924 Democratic nominee a paltry 152,000 votes, gave FDR a staggering 1,017,000.

Roosevelt prevailed by building a coalition of lower-income ethnic voters in the cities tenuously leagued with whites in the Solid South. As one periodical later put it, "He forged an alliance between the two great blocs of voters who hated the Republicans: white southerners who could not forgive them for winning the Civil War, and northern immigrants

who saw them as a discredited, self-satisfied Protestant business elite."
The returns revealed vividly the class cleavage the president had been
exploiting. The lower a person's income, the more likely he was to vote
Democrat. A recently created confederation of factory workers—the
Committee for Industrial Organization (CIO), headed by the aggressive
John L. Lewis—joined effectively with the venerable American Federation
of Labor (AFL) to get large numbers of union members to the polls.
"The New Deal," said the journalist Samuel Lubell, "appears to have accomplished what the Socialists, the I. W. W. and the Communists never
could approach. It has drawn a class line across the face of American
politics." This transition largely took place in urban concentrations,
with Roosevelt rolling up advantages of 3–1 over Landon in San Francisco
and New York City (where he enjoyed an extraordinary 1,367,000 plurality), 4–1 in Milwaukee, and even higher in southern towns from
Atlanta to Houston.

The president appealed to a diverse electorate because his was the first
administration that was not almost exclusively the domain of white,
Anglo-Saxon, Protestant men. His cabinet included both Catholic and
Jew; his most conspicuous adviser, the Irish Catholic Tommy Corcoran,
paired with Ben Cohen, a Jew. In twelve years, Roosevelt's three Republican
predecessors had chosen eight Catholics for federal judgeships; FDR
appointed fifty-two. Estimates of FDR's share of Catholic ballots ran as
high as 81 percent. "Everybody in California is for Roosevelt," Monsignor
John A. Ryan reported during the campaign. "Especially the nuns." In
1920, the Democratic presidential nominee in Jewish neighborhoods of
Chicago had received only 15 percent of the total. But in 1936 a Jewish
community on the city's West Side gained recognition as "the best
Democratic ward in the country" by going for Roosevelt 24,000 to 700.
"Far away, remote, there was FDR, who, thank God, believed in jobs for
people," a Boston Jew later remembered. "As I grew older, it also turned
out that he was against Hitler, and we enshrined him in our hearts."

Roosevelt accorded women far greater status in the national government than they had ever known before. In addition to naming the first
woman to a cabinet post, he appointed the first female envoy (as minister to Denmark), the first female assistant secretary of the treasury, and
the first woman to the high judicial post on the US Circuit Court of
Appeals. The director of the Women's Bureau, the historian William

Chafe has noted, "recalled that in earlier years women government officials had dined together in a small university club. 'Now,' she said, 'there are so many of them they would need a hall.'"

No other public figure epitomized the magnified impact of women on civic affairs as well as Eleanor Roosevelt. Never had there been so activist a first lady. She was constantly on the go. In the president's first two terms, she traveled more than a quarter of a million miles. No one knew where she would pop up next. In a celebrated cartoon, a begrimed miner digging a coal seam deep in the bowels of the earth cries out in amazement, "For gosh sakes, here comes Mrs. Roosevelt." According to one tale, Admiral Byrd at the South Pole set an extra place at dinner each night "in case Mrs. Roosevelt should drop in." On returning to the White House from these inspection trips, she briefed the president on what she had found. She became, it was said, his "eyes and ears."

But Eleanor Roosevelt also carved out her own space. Often, letters to her were addressed "Mrs. President." She held 348 press conferences and, to encourage female journalists, permitted only women to attend— a stipulation she did not relax until the outbreak of World War II. She also had her own radio program and a syndicated newspaper column, "My Day." Instead of contenting herself with serving tea and issuing vapid statements, she boldly championed the interests of women, young people, artists, and, especially, African Americans. She spoke out in favor of an antilynching law, served as cochair of the National Committee to Abolish the Poll Tax, and pressed New Deal agencies—and, even more determinedly, her husband—to embrace policies of racial equality. (During World War II, a southern commentator said, "Mrs. Franklin D. Roosevelt has become the most hated woman in the South since Harriet Beecher Stowe.") One of the original members of FDR's Brain Trust wrote, "No one who ever saw Eleanor Roosevelt sit down facing her husband, and holding his eyes firmly, say to him 'Franklin, I think you should...or, Franklin surely you will not...' will ever forget the experience." She became, a columnist asserted, "Cabinet Minister without portfolio—the most influential woman of our times."

Highly important though each of the components of the FDR coalition was, none matched in significance the transit of African Americans, who for generations had been Republicans, committed to the party of the Great Emancipator. In 1932, African Americans had voted overwhelmingly for Hoover, despite their disproportionate suffering during his tenure. But in FDR's first term, a powerful black publisher urged: "My friends, go turn Lincoln's picture to the wall. That debt has been paid in full." In 1936, Cincinnati's Ward Sixteen, which had given FDR only 29 percent in 1932, delivered 65 percent for him. The New Deal fell far short of erasing racial discrimination, but the foremost black intellectual, W. E. B. Du Bois, who distrusted bourgeois politicians, concluded that Roosevelt "gave the American Negro a kind of recognition in political life which the Negro had never before received."

In voting for FDR, African Americans were expressing gratitude for the many New Deal programs that sustained them in desperate times. "Folks where I come from," said young Richard Wright, "they're all singing:

> Roosevelt! You're my man!
> When the time come
> I ain't got a cent,
> You buy my groceries
> And pay my rent.
> Mr. Roosevelt, you're my man."

Near the end of the age of Roosevelt, the Swedish scholar Gunnar Myrdal concluded that the New Deal had "changed the whole configuration of the Negro problem. For almost the first time in the history of the nation, the state has done something substantial in a social way without excluding the Negro."

Neither the switch of black voters nor the abrogation of the two-thirds rule lessened the ancestral loyalty of the white South to the Democratic Party. In 1936, the governors of South Carolina and of Mississippi waged a bet on which state would run up the biggest proportion for FDR that year. On Election Night, when the count in his state topped 97 percent, the Mississippi governor rejoiced. But he lost the bet. South Carolina gave the president a spectacular 98.57 percent. In 1928, the Solid South had been seriously breached—for the first time since 1876—but all four times Roosevelt ran he carried every state of the former Confederacy.

When at a rain-soaked ceremony on January 20, 1937, Franklin Delano Roosevelt was sworn in by the chief justice of the United States, Charles Evans Hughes, for a second term, he took the oath of office at the peak of his powers. With even his conservative critics compelled to acknowledge that the unprecedented outpouring of votes in November constituted both a personal affirmation and an endorsement of his policies, he wielded total control of the executive branch. Furthermore, he had swept so many members of Congress in with him that when the next Senate convened, a number of Democrats would have to sit on the Republican side of the aisle because every seat allotted to Democrats was occupied. FDR's inaugural address conveyed his determination to take advantage of this dominance by pressing Congress to approve a vast expansion of the New Deal. "I see one-third of a nation ill-housed, ill-clad, ill-nourished," he declared. He presented that desolate image, he quickly added, not in discouragement but "in hope—because the Nation, seeing and understanding the injustice in it, proposes to paint it out."

The third branch of the national government, however, not only threatened to obstruct new departures but also placed in jeopardy what Roosevelt had already achieved. From the outset, the president had known that four of the Supreme Court justices were dead set against his program. They were called the "Four Horsemen," a term that summoned up the menacing apocalyptic figures in the Book of Revelation who are harbingers of the Last Judgment. From Inauguration Day in 1933, Roosevelt had lived with the apprehension that if even one of the remaining five justices joined them, the New Deal would be destroyed. His attorney general said that arguing a case was like finding that every time you turned out for a round of golf you would wind up on the back nine four holes down with only five holes left to play.

In the spring of 1935 the president had seen his worst fears realized when one of the five, Owen Roberts, voted with the Four Horsemen to invalidate a pension law—a decision that appeared to presage doom for the Social Security Act. Roberts remained in the conservative camp the rest of 1935 and through all of 1936. During those years, the Court struck down far more important federal and state legislation than in any comparable period before or since. Among the debris were the two foundation stones of FDR's program: the NRA and the AAA. In May 1935, the Court shot down the blue eagle by declaring the National Industrial

Recovery Act unconstitutional in an opinion that implied that the president had been overreaching. "Congress," Chief Justice Hughes declared, "is not permitted to abdicate or to transfer to others the essential legislative functions." Seven months later, the Agricultural Adjustment Act met the same fate, but not without a blistering dissent from Justice Harlan Fiske Stone, a Coolidge appointee who disliked the New Deal but believed in judicial restraint. Stone accused Roberts, who wrote the Triple A opinion, of "a tortured construction of the Constitution," adding, "Courts are not the only agency of government that must be assumed to have capacity to govern."

On the same day that the Court killed the blue eagle, it delivered a mean blow to presidential powers in a case that had arisen out of FDR's determination to get rid of a pugnacious reactionary on the Federal Trade Commission. To be certain that he had the authority to fire the man, who was a holdover from the Coolidge era, Roosevelt had sought legal advice. His consultant assured him that this action was unquestionably legitimate because as recently as 1926, in *Myers v. United States*, Chief Justice Taft had gone out of his way to say that the president's removal power extended even to officials of independent regulatory tribunals. In *Humphrey's Executor v. United States*, though, the Court ruled that a president may not discharge a member of an independent regulatory agency and, brushing aside the Taft dictum, reprimanded Roosevelt for willfully violating the Constitution.

The final decision of the term demonstrated how hostile to social reform the Supreme Court had become. Defenders of the justices in the majority contended that they did not disapprove of progressive legislation, so long as it was enacted by the states. In June 1936, however, the Court, by 5–4 (Roberts and the Four Horsemen prevailing), struck down a New York state minimum wage law for women—an action that shocked the country. Even Herbert Hoover expressed dismay. The Court, Roosevelt said, drawing on imagery of World War I, had created a "no-man's-land," in which neither the federal nor the state governments could act to protect the worker. At the close of the historic session, Justice Stone wrote his sons: "We finished the term of Court yesterday, I think in many ways one of the most disastrous in its history."

As he surveyed the scene at the start of his second term, Roosevelt discerned an intolerable prospect. The reasoning of the Court in its opinions eradicating the NRA and the AAA led legal experts to predict that it would shortly rule both the National Labor Relations Act and the Social Security Act unconstitutional. Furthermore, despite FDR's enormous victory, any new legislation the president might persuade Congress to enact would very likely be expunged too. With six justices over seventy, the Court was the most elderly ever—a best seller called its members *The Nine Old Men*. But no vacancy had developed in FDR's first term, and none was in sight. Roosevelt appeared to be stymied. He showed no indication, however, that he was planning any action to get out of this predicament.

On February 5, 1937, the president dropped a bombshell into these placid waters. Only two weeks after his second inauguration, he stunned the country by sending a message to Congress calling for a major overhaul of the federal judiciary. He recommended that when a federal judge waited more than six months after his seventieth birthday to resign or retire, a president be empowered to add a new judge to the bench. Enactment of the law would permit him to appoint as many as six additional justices to the US Supreme Court. Roosevelt claimed that he was making this recommendation with the aim of helping elderly judges to expedite cases more quickly. Aged judges unable to "retain . . . full mental and physical vigor . . . are often unable to perceive their own infirmities," he said. "A constant addition of younger blood will vitalize the courts." The country understood, however, that what the president really wanted was to install personnel who would approve New Deal laws, and his proposal immediately drew the derogatory label it has had ever since: Court-packing, eliciting an intensity of outrage unmatched by any other legislative controversy of the century.

Editorial writers likening FDR to Hitler and Stalin gave the impression that the entire nation was up in arms against the scheme when, in fact, as many people favored the measure as opposed it. Moreover, Roosevelt's party had a staggering 4–1 advantage in the House, and Republicans held only sixteen of the ninety-six seats in the Senate. Toward the end of March, *Time* wrote, "Last week the staunchest foes of the President's Plan were privately conceding that the necessary votes were already in his pockets." Few in Congress felt comfortable with the measure, but most Democrats on the Hill could not justify rejecting it so long as the Supreme Court persisted in striking down vital laws.

Altogether unexpectedly, however, the Court drastically altered the nature of the controversy on March 29 by validating a state minimum wage law essentially the same as the one it had found unacceptable a short time before. Two weeks later, in another 5–4 division, it upheld the Wagner Act, and in May it rejected challenges to the Social Security law. The dramatic shift was brought about through a change of mind by a single justice: Owen Roberts, who abandoned the Four Horsemen to form a new majority. By doing so, he ended any urgent justification for the president's plan. "A switch in time," it was said, "saved nine."

At this juncture, Roosevelt, instead of exulting in his stunning victory over a recalcitrant Court, let hubris get the better of good sense. Despite the set of favorable rulings and the announcement by one of the Four Horsemen of his imminent retirement, the president insisted on going ahead with Court-packing. With an inflated sense of power after his landslide triumph, he was confident that he could ram it through Congress, since the Democrats would not dare to deny him. That July, he got his comeuppance. In an emphatic rebuke, senators from both parties joined to shelve the audacious proposal. Less than nine months after his resounding victory in the 1936 election, he had been humbled.

Roosevelt later claimed, with good reason, that though he had lost the battle, he had won the war. He had brought about a transformation so momentous that it has been called ever since "the Constitutional Revolution of 1937." Before he left office, he was able to appoint eight of the nine justices, and this newly composed tribunal—"the Roosevelt Court," as it was called—validated every New Deal law and every presidential action that came before it. Furthermore, the reach of the commerce power was so broadened that for the rest of the century, the Court did not strike down even one important law regulating the economy.

Disapproval of his tampering with the Court, though, cost FDR dearly. Combined with dismay at the onset of a severe recession, caused by his premature effort to balance the budget, it fostered the emergence of a bipartisan conservative coalition that would dominate American politics for the next generation. Congress did authorize public housing, agree to help tenant farmers, appropriate funds to jump-start the economy, and approve the Fair Labor Standards Act (another Frances Perkins project) to set minimum wages and maximum hours. But much of this legislation was watered down, and Congress balked at any further enhancement of presidential authority, as Roosevelt learned when he attempted to revamp the executive branch.

Toward the end of his first term, Roosevelt had taken an important step toward augmenting his capacity to exert control over the executive branch by appointing three distinguished political scientists to a commission headed by Louis Brownlow, the foremost authority on public administration. "The President's task has become impossible for me or any other man," Roosevelt informed a member of Congress. In 1937, the Brownlow Commission came up with a number of recommendations, most notably integrating into the federal departments the many independent regulatory commissions, which, it said, constituted a "headless fourth branch of government."

Under normal circumstances, many of its proposals would have been regarded as unexceptionable, but the fight over Court-packing had stoked fears of presidential usurpation, even of fascism. Furthermore, congressmen had a stake in maintaining their cozy relations with regulatory agencies. An upstate New York Republican asked, "Why should Congress continue to surrender...its legislative functions to the Chief Executive and leave itself with no more authority than Gandhi has clothing?" When the reorganization bill came to a vote in April 1938, it went down to defeat, 204–196, with 108 Democrats deserting the president—one of the largest defections in history. Roosevelt was stunned. "Jim, I'll tell you that I didn't expect the votes," he told the party chairman. "There wasn't a chance for anyone to become a dictator under that bill."

Irked by his setbacks on Court-packing and executive reorganization, Roosevelt decided in 1938 to intervene in his party's congressional primaries to urge voters to oust conservative Democratic incumbents, some of them legislators with devoted followings in their states. Assuming a greater political role than any of his predecessors had dared to take on, he announced: "As the head of the Democratic Party...charged with the responsibility of carrying out the definitely liberal declaration of principles set forth in the 1936 Democratic platform, I feel that I have every right to speak in those few instances where there may be a clear issue between candidates for a Democratic nomination involving these principles, or involving a clear misuse of my own name."

From the outset, though, he labored under a severe disadvantage, for the press insisted on fastening a headline word on his effort that associated it with bloodbaths in Nazi Germany and Soviet Russia: "purge." He did succeed in eliminating the obstreperous chairman of the House Rules Committee, but every Democratic senator he targeted survived. After hearing that his attempt to remove the reactionary South Carolina senator "Cotton Ed" Smith had failed, he said wearily, "It takes a long, long time to bring the past up to the present." FDR's experience demonstrated that not even a powerful president can impose his will on a decentralized party system.

Despite this series of reverses, Roosevelt, against all odds, managed to salvage the critical feature of the Brownlow report. His opponents thought that his rebuffs on legislation and the purge, capped by big Republican gains in the 1938 midterm elections, had put an end to his attempt to strengthen the presidency. At one point, the cabinet official closest to him, Harold Ickes, said, "He is punch drunk from the punishment that he has suffered recently." But in 1939 Roosevelt rebounded. He issued an order creating the Executive Office of the President, which he staffed with six assistants expected to have a "passion for anonymity." At the same time, he snatched the Bureau of the Budget from the treasury and moved it into the White House. With the revitalized bureau as its most important engine, the Executive Office of the President became "the nerve center of the federal administrative system." One political scientist later called his action a "nearly unnoticed but none the less epoch-making event in the history of American institutions," and another concluded that it "converts the Presidency into an instrument of twentieth-century government; it gives the incumbent a sporting chance...to fulfill his constitutional mandate.... Executive Order 8248 may yet be judged to have saved the Presidency from paralysis."

When, in the midst of his struggles with Congress on domestic policy, Roosevelt looked around at the rest of the world, he found no solace. Hitler, having marched into the Rhineland in 1936, was frightening his neighbors; Mussolini was completing his brutal conquest of Ethiopia; and both tyrants were intervening in a civil war in Spain to ensure a fascist victory. On the other side of the globe, the Japanese, in killing some three hundred thousand Chinese in Nanking, were engaged in a rampage of slaughter and rape with a viciousness toward victims that sickened the president.

But what could he do? With vivid memories of the horrors of the last conflict with Germany only twenty years earlier, the British and French shied away from a confrontation with Hitler, and in these circumstances, America could not be expected to take the lead. Furthermore, in 1937 Congress, with its own bitter recollections of World War I, had tightened travel by Americans on belligerent vessels, continued the embargo on the sale of arms, and required countries at war who bought other goods to carry them away in their own ships. The *New York Herald Tribune* called the 1937 neutrality law "an act to preserve the United States from intervention in the War of 1914–'18."

At this unpromising time, Roosevelt unexpectedly seized the initiative—or so it seemed. In October 1937, he delivered a major address on foreign policy in Chicago, regarded as the capital of the isolationist heartland. He called attention to an "epidemic of world lawlessness" and, with implicit reference to atrocities in Spain and in Nanking, pointed out that "innocent peoples, innocent nations, are being cruelly sacrificed to a greed for power and supremacy." He warned his listeners, "If those things come to pass in other parts of the world, let no one imagine that America will escape, . . . that this Western Hemisphere will not be attacked." Having delineated the problem, he was ready to present a course of action: "When an epidemic of physical disease starts to spread, the community . . . joins in a quarantine of the patients in order to protect the health of the community against the spread of the disease." He did not spell out precisely what he meant by "quarantine," and he stressed his "determination to pursue a policy of peace." But a few days earlier Ickes had recorded in his diary views that the president had expressed to him: "What he has in mind is to cut off all trade" with the "three bandit nations [Japan, Germany, Italy] . . . and thus deny . . . raw materials."

According to the standard account, the country, by rising up in wrath against FDR's attempt to saddle it with responsibilities overseas, compelled him to retreat. "It is a terrible thing," he told an adviser, "to look over your shoulder when you are trying to lead and to find no one there." In fact, though, most of the response was highly approving. Moreover,

Roosevelt backtracked before there was time to gauge the reaction. At a press conference the very day after the Chicago address, when asked by a White House correspondent whether by "quarantine" he meant economic sanctions, the president retorted, "Look, 'sanctions' is a terrible word. They are out the window." Did he mean a conference of foes of fascism? "No. Conferences are out the window. You never get anywhere with a conference." What then did he mean? Commentators could not puzzle out an answer to that question, but it was clear that he feared to get overextended, especially with Congress.

An incident two months later revealed how well founded was Roosevelt's anxiety. On December 12, 1937, Japanese planes bombed and sank the US gunboat *Panay*, as it lay at anchor on the Yangtse fifteen miles above Nanking. Three Standard Oil tankers were also sent to the bottom. Tokyo, while agreeing to an indemnity for loss of life and other casualties, claimed that the assault was a mistake, though Japan had been kept fully informed of the location of the *Panay*, which had two very large American flags painted on its top deck. Furthermore, the Japanese had repeatedly strafed survivors as they headed for shore in sampans and then machine-gunned them as they sought cover.

Instead of crying havoc, Congress spoke out against retaliation. In the Senate, Republican William Borah announced that he was "not prepared to vote to send our boys into the Orient because a boat was sunk that was traveling in a dangerous zone," and his Democratic colleague Pat McCarran declared, "We should have been out of China long ago." In the House, only a day after Americans learned of the *Panay* outrage, an Indiana Democrat gathered enough signatures to get to the floor a proposed constitutional amendment requiring a national referendum before the country could go to war. Roosevelt managed to defeat the measure by stating that it would "cripple any President in his conduct of our foreign relations," but Congress had served warning.

Despite the constraints imposed upon him, Roosevelt found ways to act. In 1938, after 150 planes were made available to Spanish Loyalists in violation of the Neutrality Act, he ordered the State Department's legal officer to look the other way when false papers crossed his desk. He also pushed for rearmament—less to build America's defenses, as army officers wanted, than to put more airplanes at the disposal of Hitler's foes. When a US military plane, equipped with highly sophisticated (and top secret) innovations, crashed and out of the cockpit, unscathed, emerged a French pilot, the misadventure exposed another of FDR's surreptitious actions. The president not only denounced Nazi persecution of Jews in 1938 on *Kristallnacht* but pointedly called home the American ambassador in Berlin. None of these gestures, though, did anything to slow the march of Hitler: Austria, Czechoslovakia (after the capitulation at Munich), and, early in September 1939 following negotiation of a pact with Soviet Russia, Poland—the invasion that precipitated World War II.

Roosevelt's first words to the nation after the outbreak of war acknowledged both the overwhelming desire of the American people to escape being drawn into the European maelstrom and their hope that Germany would be defeated. "Let no man or woman thoughtlessly or falsely talk of America sending its armies to European fields," he urged in a fireside chat. "As long as it remains within my power to prevent, there will be no black-out of peace in the United States." But he also advised them that total isolation was impossible. "When peace has been broken anywhere, the peace of all countries everywhere is in danger.... Passionately though we may desire detachment, we are forced to realize that every word that comes through the air, every ship that sails the sea, every battle that is fought, does affect the American future." In deliberate contrast to Wilson's statement in 1914, he declared: "This nation will remain a neutral nation, but I cannot ask that every American remain neutral in thought as well. Even a neutral has a right to take account of facts. Even a neutral cannot be asked to close his mind or his conscience."

In mid-September, Roosevelt summoned Congress into special session to revise neutrality legislation by repealing the arms embargo, which made no distinction between aggressor nations and the countries they invaded. He denied that this "peace bill" was the first step in leading the country into war. "The simple truth is that no person in any responsible place...has ever suggested...the remotest possibility of sending the boys of American mothers to fight on the battlefields of Europe." Though these words seemed disingenuous, they accurately reflected his views at the time. He instructed the War Department: "Whatever happens, we won't send troops abroad." By downplaying his desire to arm the Allies, the president persuaded Congress to repeal the embargo, though, under "cash and carry," the British and French still had to pay in hard coin, and US vessels could not transport weapons across the Atlantic.

During the ensuing months, Roosevelt still found it hard to persuade his countrymen that they had a stake in the outcome of the war, but a dramatic series of events in the spring of 1940 aroused them. In April, the Germans unleashed a blitzkrieg that overwhelmed Norway, Denmark, and the Low Countries. "The small countries are simply smashed up, one by one, like matchwood," Winston Churchill told the president. The French had felt secure behind the Maginot Line, but the Reichswehr executed a flanking movement that rendered that vast system of fortifications useless. On June 22 in the Compiègne Forest, Hitler accepted the surrender of France in the very railway car in which the Germans had been compelled to capitulate in 1918. Overnight, the mood in America changed. Suddenly, only Britain stood between the Nazis and the United States; given the rapid pace at which Panzer divisions had rolled through western Europe, a swastika might be flying over the houses of Parliament before the year was out, with America facing Hitler naked and alone.

Even before France fell, Roosevelt called on Congress to appropriate a billion dollars for rearmament. The United States had only 2,806 war planes, most of them outmoded, and no aircraft ammunition at all, but the president proposed increasing output to at least 50,000 planes a year. Two weeks later he asked Congress for another billion dollars, and, shortly thereafter an additional five billion. Congress, which had been planning to cut back military spending, gave him all he asked for and more. The president also insisted that a huge proportion of American-made weapons be reserved for the British. In overruling General George Catlett Marshall and Admiral Harold Stark, both of whom wanted to end aid to the United Kingdom, he was taking a big risk. If Germany attacked and the United States was unprepared because it had permitted armaments to be siphoned abroad, a General Staff official warned the White House, "everyone who was a party to the deal might hope to be found hanging from a lamp post."

At the same time that Roosevelt devised military strategy, he placed the country on a quasi-war footing. Bypassing both Congress and the traditional federal departments, he issued edicts creating defense agencies, notably the Office of Emergency Management, all of them under his supervision through the Executive Office of the President. In June, he disconcerted his critics by naming prominent Republicans to the two defense posts in his cabinet. For secretary of war, he chose Hoover's secretary of state, Henry Stimson, and for secretary of the navy, Frank Knox, the GOP vice presidential candidate on the ticket opposing him in 1936. By establishing a crisis government of national unity, he elevated his stature as leader of the nation and enhanced his chances for reelection just as the 1940 campaign was starting to heat up.

Roosevelt very much wanted to remain in office, but he encountered the vexing taboo against a third term, a tradition established unintentionally by George Washington. Both Grant and Wilson had indicated their willingness to serve again, but by 1940 the ban against more than eight years in the White House had become holy writ. At a time when Republicans were hawking the slogan "No Crown for Franklin," he needed to take pains not to seem dangerously ambitious. Consequently, a Roosevelt faction orchestrated a "spontaneous" draft at the 1940 Democratic convention in Chicago, though even with his closest associates the president remained coy.

On July 16, 1940, the charade began when the convention chairman, Senator Alben Barkley, read a communication from the White House stating that "the President has never had, and has not today, any desire... to continue in the office of President" and that "all delegates...are free to vote for any candidate." As the stunned delegates sat riveted to their seats, they heard a voice boom out through an amplified speaker, "WE WANT ROOSEVELT!" From the basement, where he had been stationed by the boss of the Chicago machine, the city's superintendent of sewers continued his chant: "ILLINOIS WANTS ROOSEVELT! NEW YORK WANTS ROOSEVELT! AMERICA WANTS ROOSEVELT! THE WORLD WANTS ROOSEVELT!" Cued by the sloganeering, the delegates, who could not imagine anyone at the head of the ticket but FDR, surged onto the floor crying "ROOSEVELT! ROOSEVELT! ROOSEVELT!" What had begun as artifice became reality. With the tsunami of support, the president won renomination on the first ballot.

Roosevelt had his way, too, with choice of running mate: Secretary of Agriculture Henry Wallace. Delegates broke into open rebellion at the imposition of a former Republican some regarded as ideologically suspect, and Eleanor Roosevelt was rushed into the hall to mollify them.

But the mutiny was not quelled until the delegates got word that if they did not consent to Wallace, the president would withdraw. Conservative Democrats who thought they had taken over after the failure of the purge were forced to acknowledge that Franklin Roosevelt was still master of the party.

In the 1940 campaign, Roosevelt had to deal with quandaries overseas that, if not handled skillfully, could cost him the election. Repeatedly over the course of four months, Churchill had been badgering the president to lend him "forty or fifty of your older destroyers" to ward off U-boat attacks as Hitler readied an invasion of Britain. "Mr. President, with great respect I must tell you that in the long history of the world this is a thing to do *now*," the prime minister said. "The worth of every destroyer that you can spare to us is measured in rubies."

For two reasons, Roosevelt hesitated. If he gave away US naval vessels and, following a quick conquest of the United Kingdom, Germany seized the Royal Navy, he would be severely criticized, might even be impeached, for stripping his country's defenses. (As the historian Frank Freidel later observed, "There were those who expected that Hitler, fresh from parading down the Champs Elysées, would be reviewing troops in Trafalgar Square by August 1.") Furthermore, he informed Churchill, "a step of that kind could not be taken except with the specific authorization of the Congress, and I am not certain that it would be wise for that suggestion to be made to the Congress at this moment." He also confronted another restraint. Only a few months earlier, an act had stipulated that no vessel or equipment could be sold unless the navy affirmed that it was worthless, and naval officers had just testified to the value of the destroyers.

But as the Luftwaffe dropped bombs on British cities, Roosevelt decided that he had to comply with Churchill's request, however questionable his authority, no matter the political cost. Drawing upon Justice Sutherland's statement in *Curtiss-Wright* that the president is "the sole organ of the federal government" in foreign affairs, he resolved to bypass Congress and resort to an executive agreement. On September 3, the White House announced that the United States had traded fifty antiquated destroyers for ninety-nine-year leases on British bases in the Western Hemisphere from Newfoundland to the Caribbean. Critics, including distinguished authorities on constitutional law, contended that the transaction violated not only the 1940 act but also a 1917 law forbidding transfer of US naval vessels to a belligerent. They scoffed at an opinion Roosevelt obtained from Attorney General Robert Jackson validating FDR's action by construing a president's prerogative even more extravagantly than Sutherland had. Isolationists coupled outrage at the president's claim with alarm that this "decidedly unneutral act," in Churchill's words, was drawing the United States closer to war. "Herr Hitler will not like this transfer of destroyers," Churchill told the House of Commons, "and I have no doubt that he will pay the United States out, if he ever gets the chance."

At the same time that Roosevelt was working up a rationale for the destroyers bill, he was dealing gingerly with another potentially troublesome issue: the draft. Momentum for that departure came not from the White House but from Stimson and hawkish lobbies. Although mail to Capitol Hill ran 90 percent against the bill, in mid-September Congress approved selective service, and in the following month Secretary Stimson, blindfolded, reached into a goldfish bowl to pull out the numbers that would determine which young men would be called up in America's first peacetime draft.

FDR's words and deeds gave his Republican opponent, Wendell Willkie, an opening for attack in the presidential campaign that fall. Though Willkie largely agreed with the administration's foreign policy, he said of Roosevelt, "If his promise to keep our boys out of foreign wars is no better than his promise to balance the budget, they're already almost on the transports." In another tirade, Willkie warned, "On the basis of his past performance with pledges to the people, if you re-elect him you may expect war in April, 1941." Stung by these allegations and uneasy about his rival's gains in the polls, Roosevelt, at a rally in Boston—a city of Anglophobic Irish—made a rash, and unprincipled, pledge. "While I am talking to you mothers and fathers, I give you one more assurance," he told the crowd. "I have said this before, but I shall say it again and again and again: Your boys are not going to be sent into foreign wars." He did not even cover himself with the fig leaf "save in case of attack." On hearing the talk on the radio, Willkie said, "That hypocritical son of a bitch! This is going to beat me."

It did. Though Roosevelt won more narrowly than in the previous two elections, he still rolled up a substantial victory: 55 percent of the

Hundreds of joyous supporters turn out to welcome FDR in Poughkeepsie, New York, a few miles from his home in Hyde Park, in 1940. The sign refers to his unprecedented bid for reelection, "Better a 3rd. Termer than a 3rd. Rater!" © *Bettmann/CORBIS, ID BE002961*

popular vote and a 449–82 preponderance in the Electoral College. Objections to a third term had little resonance with voters save for those who opposed the president on other grounds. FDR's Boston speech, by muting the foreign affairs question, made room for his advantage on domestic issues in a year when defense orders were sparking gains in employment. Even as the economy improved, class divisions remained salient. In Pittsburgh wards with high rents, the president got only 40 percent of ballots; in those with lower rents, 75 percent.

As Roosevelt readied himself for an unprecedented third term, a new crisis arose. In December 1940, Churchill informed him that Britain had run out of cash to pay America for the planes, tanks, and arms it so desperately needed. Initially, it seemed that there was nothing the president could do, because the Johnson Act of 1934 forbade a direct loan. But on a Caribbean cruise, after mulling over his dilemma, he came up with an inspired idea—to lend not money but weapons. The president first aired his response at a press conference on December 17 at which he said he would like to get rid of the "silly, foolish old dollar sign," and then spun out an allegory:

> Suppose my neighbor's house catches fire, and I have a length of garden hose four or five hundred feet away. If he can take my garden hose and connect it, . . . I may help him to put out his fire. Now, what do I do? I don't say to him before the operation, "Neighbor, my garden hose cost me $15; you have to pay me $15 for it." . . . I don't want $15—I want my garden hose back after the fire is over. . . . If it goes through the fire . . . without any damage to it, he gives it back to me and thanks me very much. . . . But suppose it gets smashed up—holes in it—during the fire; . . . I say to him ". . . I can't use it any more." . . . He says, "All right, I will replace it." Now, if I get a nice garden hose back, I am in pretty good shape.

Roosevelt presented the idea to the American people cleverly. Though, if enacted, the legislation would make the United States all but a cobelligerent, he insisted that keeping Britain in the war was the best way to avoid sending American troops overseas. "The whole purpose of your President," he declared in a fireside chat at the end of 1940, "is to keep you . . . out of a last-ditch war," adding, "The people who are defending themselves do not ask us to do their fighting." America's role, instead, was to become "the great arsenal of democracy." Calculatedly assigned a patriotic number, HR 1776 bore the designation "An Act to Promote the Defense of the United States."

In his State of the Union address a few days later, the president reiterated these themes but highlighted what were, in essence, war aims, though the country was at peace. "We look forward," he declared, "to a world founded upon four essential freedoms." He then spelled out what were quickly celebrated as "the Four Freedoms":

> The first is freedom of speech and expression—everywhere in the world.
>
> The second is freedom of every person to worship God in his own way—everywhere in the world.
>
> The third is freedom from want—which . . . means economic understandings which will secure to every nation a healthy peacetime life for its inhabitants—everywhere in the world.

The fourth is freedom from fear, which...means a world-wide reduction of armaments to such a point and in such a thorough fashion that no nation will be in a position to commit an act of physical aggression against any neighbor—anywhere in the world.

The president's rhetoric did little to lessen the antagonism of isolationists to his Lend-Lease proposal. "Lending war equipment," said Senator Robert Taft, son of the former president, "is a good deal like lending chewing gum—you certainly don't want it back." Opponents made an impression by presenting as their lead witness at Senate hearings Joseph P. Kennedy, the US ambassador to the Court of St. James's. Kennedy, though out of line with the president, showed more restraint than another Democrat, Senator Burton K. Wheeler of Montana. In a radio broadcast, Senator Wheeler called Lend-Lease "the New Deal's triple A foreign policy; it will plow under every fourth American boy." At his next press conference, Roosevelt told reporters that Wheeler's statement was "the most dastardly, unpatriotic thing that has ever been said. Quote me on that." He added, "That really is the rottenest thing that has been said in public life in my generation." Resistance to Lend-Lease, most of it from Republicans, delayed approval of the bill until March of 1941, and Congress wrote into the law a number of restrictions on the president—including a ban on employing US convoys to safeguard shipments across the Atlantic.

These constraints notwithstanding, the Lend-Lease Act constituted an extraordinary aggrandizement of the executive office. The statute authorized the president to "sell, transfer title to, exchange, lease, lend, or otherwise dispose of" any weapon to "the government of any country whose defense the President deems vital to the defense of the United States." It gave him what amounted to a book of blank checks to disburse billions (eventually forty-eight billion) as he saw fit. No other country received as large a sum as Great Britain, but after Germany invaded Russia in June 1941, the Soviet Union got ten billion to shore up the antifascist phalanx. "No more sweeping delegation of legislative power has ever been made to an American President," the political scientist E. S. Corwin later concluded. "In brief, the act delegated to the President the power to fight wars by deputy."

Two months later, Roosevelt concentrated still more power in the White House by declaring an "unlimited national emergency." That proclamation instantly activated ninety-nine laws further enhancing presidential authority, with no one knowing for certain how wide an additional swath the pronouncement entailed. In an address accompanying this edict, Roosevelt underscored how far he was taking the country from a posture of strict neutrality. "When your enemy comes at you in a tank or bombing plane," he stated, "if you hold your fire until you see the whites of his eyes, you will never know what hit you. Our Bunker Hill of tomorrow may be several thousand miles from Boston." Hence, in accord with "old-fashioned common sense," he revealed, "we have... extended our patrol in North and South Atlantic waters." He was, he acknowledged in a cable to Churchill, going "further than I had thought possible even two weeks ago."

The ink had hardly dried on the national emergency document when Roosevelt seized the North American Aviation plant in Inglewood, California, to break a strike that was paralyzing production of planes. His edict cited no statutory authority for his action. It rested upon Attorney General Jackson's vague but all-encompassing contention that it derived from the "duty constitutionally and inherently resting upon the President to exert his civil and military as well as his moral authority to keep the defense efforts of the United States a going concern."

Roosevelt acted even more boldly overseas in the spring and summer of 1941. In April, he negotiated an agreement with Denmark to station US troops on its possession Greenland, and in July, by executive agreement, he arranged to send thousands of marines into Iceland. He stressed the need "to repel any and all acts... directed against any part of the Western Hemisphere," but by no stretch of the imagination could Iceland—a short hop from Scotland—be regarded as in the "Western" sphere. Admiral Ernest King, commander in chief of the Atlantic Fleet, said of the move into Iceland: "I realize that this is practically an act of war."

By August, Roosevelt, not yet committed to war but edging closer and closer to it, saw the need for a meeting with Churchill, which, to avoid alarming the American people, he wanted to keep secret. He told reporters that he was taking a brief holiday aboard the presidential yacht and that it was not going to be possible to provide an auxiliary vessel so that they could accompany him. The *New York Times* informed its readers:

New London, Connecticut, August 3, 1941. Dropping the cares of official duties for a long-sought rest at sea, President Roosevelt sailed tonight from the New London submarine base for a week's salt-water vacation. The Presidential yacht *Potomac* headed into Long Island Sound in the afterglow of sunset to take the Chief Executive away from the tension of duties which the critical international situation has made unusually wearing.

After boarding the yacht in New London and making sure that he could be seen from shore fishing as the boat headed toward Cape Cod, he transferred under cover of darkness to the US cruiser *Augusta*, off Martha's Vineyard. While, on land, journalists and tourists continued to follow the voyage of the *Potomac* on which an FDR look-alike, cigarette holder angled, had been stationed, the *Augusta* steamed toward Newfoundland where Americans were building a naval base acquired in the destroyers deal. From New England, Roosevelt wrote a confidante: "Even at my ripe old age I feel a thrill in making a get-away—especially from the American press.... Curiously enough the *Potomac* still flies my flag and tonight will be seen by thousands as she passes through the Cape Cod Canal...while in fact the President will be about 250 miles away." In Newfoundland's Argentia harbor, Roosevelt, his ruse undetected, was joined by Churchill, who arrived on the HMS *Prince of Wales*.

British diplomats came to the Atlantic Conference determined to wrest from Roosevelt three commitments—to deliver a joint ultimatum to Japan to halt its conquests in Southeast Asia, to endorse plans for an "effective international organization," and, most important, to enter the war shortly—but the president refused to agree to any of them. An ultimatum, he believed, would only bolster the hotspurs in the Tokyo government. Disappointed in the League of Nations Assembly, he favored a big-power consortium to maintain peace after the war. And he knew that neither the American people not Congress was ready for intervention. As the Newfoundland rendezvous was breaking up, the House of Representatives came within a single vote, 203–202, of refusing to extend a draftee's term of service beyond twelve months. Some of the negative votes came in response to threats of desertion if the original one-year understanding was breached, with draftees scrawling on walls the cryptic message "OHIO" (Over the Hill in October).

The most important product of the conference—the Atlantic Charter—meant more to FDR than to Churchill. With vivid memories of the distress of Americans over the revelation of secret treaties during the Great War, he took satisfaction in Britain's subscribing openly to what could only be thought of as war aims, though the United States was still at peace. The eight-point manifesto echoed both Wilson's Fourteen Points and FDR's Four Freedoms. Roosevelt altered the pledge in the British draft of a postwar structure to an ambiguous "wider and permanent system of general security." Only afterward did Churchill realize that Point Three, affirming "the right of all peoples to choose the form of government under which they will live," could be read by colonial subjects to imply a breakaway from the British Crown.

When Churchill returned to Downing Street, he relayed to the cabinet what he understood to be FDR's state of mind: "He would become more and more provocative.... Everything was to be done to force an 'incident.'... He would look for an 'incident' which would justify him in opening hostilities." These words have been seized upon by revisionist historians as evidence that the president was engaged in a nefarious conspiracy to lead his countrymen into war, but it is doubtful that he ever spoke quite so blatantly. (Apart from any other consideration, his military advisers had sternly cautioned him that the army of green draftees was not ready for combat.) There may never have been a moment when he acknowledged even to himself that the United States must intervene. Still, the president did behave in the autumn of 1941 much in the manner that Churchill reported.

In a fireside chat on September 11, 1941, Roosevelt told the American people that one week earlier a U-boat had attacked the US naval vessel *Greer* while the destroyer was on a "legitimate" errand, delivering mail to Iceland. "In spite of what Hitler's propaganda bureau has invented, and in spite of what any American obstructionist organization may prefer to believe," he went on, "I tell you the blunt fact that the German submarine fired first upon this American destroyer without warning, and with deliberate design to sink her." In rendering this account, the president was deplorably disingenuous. He chose not to reveal that the *Greer*, far from being on a peaceful mission, was collaborating with a belligerent intent on destroying the German vessel and drowning its crew. Alerted by the RAF to the location of its quarry, the *Greer* stalked the

U-boat for hours, radioing its position to British aircraft, which dropped depth charges. Only then did the sub fire a torpedo toward the destroyer.

Though the navy had informed him that there was "no positive evidence that submarine knew nationality of ship at which it was firing," the president, undeterred by this knowledge, told his listeners, "This was piracy—piracy legally and morally." Moreover, "this attack on the *Greer* was no localized military operation.... This was one determined step towards creating a permanent world system based on force, on terror and on murder." (That was an apt characterization of Nazism, but the *Greer* incident did not demonstrate it, because Hitler, heavily engaged on the Russian front and not wanting to precipitate American entrance into the war, had ordered the German navy not to fire on neutral vessels.) "These Nazi submarines and raiders are the rattlesnakes of the Atlantic," Roosevelt went on, and "when you see a rattlesnake poised to strike, you do not wait until he has struck before you crush him." So, he concluded, "let this warning be clear. From now on, if German or Italian vessels of war enter the waters, the protection of which is necessary for American defense, they do so at their own peril." By "the waters" in the US sphere, he meant all of the North Atlantic clear to Iceland. Any U-boat that appeared there would be shot on sight. In short, wholly on his own authority, with no acknowledgment of the powers allotted to Congress by the Constitution, Roosevelt was initiating an undeclared naval war on Germany. Even his friendly biographer Arthur Schlesinger Jr. later stated that FDR's behavior exhibited only "a lurking sensitivity to constitutional issues."

Contrary to expectations, Roosevelt's order did not bring the United States closer to war. In October, a U-boat torpedoed the US destroyer *Kearny*, killing eleven American sailors, and in November, a German sub sank the destroyer *Reuben James* with the loss of 115 lives, including every officer. But neither attack resulted in any increase in interventionist sentiment. The country in the late fall of 1941 appeared to be directionless—drifting toward war but with little inclination to take the final step. In mid-October, Churchill got an earful from his ambassador to the United States. Lord Halifax reported that FDR had said

that his perpetual problem was to steer a course between the two factors represented by:

(1) The wish of 70 percent of Americans to keep out of war;

(2) The wish of 70 percent of Americans to do everything to break Hitler even if it means war.

He said that if he asked for a declaration of war he wouldn't get it, and opinion would swing against him. He therefore intended to go on doing whatever he best could to help us, and declarations of war were, he said, out of fashion.

Neither Roosevelt nor Churchill anticipated that when war did break out, it would come not in the Atlantic but in the Pacific, though the situation in the Far East had grown increasingly ominous since Tokyo joined the Rome-Berlin Axis in November 1940.

Roosevelt moved with great deliberation in fashioning a policy toward the Japanese. Alarmed by the menace they constituted to Western interests in Asia, he believed that their dependence on the United States for raw materials offered him a way to deter them from carrying out their imperial ambitions. But he acted cautiously because he feared that a total embargo would impel the Japanese to grab what they needed by conquest. When Secretary Ickes, in his role as petroleum coordinator for national defense, took it on himself to cut off Japan's entire oil supply from America without checking first with the White House or the State Department, the president promptly fired off what Ickes called "the most peremptory and ungracious communication that I have ever received from him." Subsequently, Roosevelt instructed him: "It is terribly important for the control of the Atlantic for us to help to keep peace in the Pacific. I simply have not got enough Navy to go round—and every little episode in the Pacific means fewer ships in the Atlantic." The president's judgment coincided with that of navy officials, who cautioned, "An embargo would probably result in fairly early attack by Japan on Malaya and the Netherlands East Indies and possibly would involve the United States in an early war in the Pacific."

While rejecting the course favored by his more militant advisers, the president took a series of graduated actions making it more and more difficult for Tokyo to provision its war machine. As Ickes paraphrased FDR's attitude, "It might be better to slip the noose around Japan's neck and give it a jerk now and then." In July, Roosevelt embargoed the export of aviation gasoline to Japan, and in the fall of 1940, responding to the Japanese invasion of French Indochina, he cut off shipments of scrap iron and steel to Japan. He continued, however, to regard an embargo on petroleum shipments as too provocative since Japan counted on US refineries for as much as 80 percent of its oil. He did, though, interdict high grades of gasoline.

Not until July 1941, when the Japanese set out to swallow all of Indonesia and, at an imperial conference, identified numbers of targets southward including the Philippines, did the president agree to more drastic measures. (He had considerable knowledge of Japanese plans because in August 1940 a US army cryptographer had cracked their top-secret code.) In response, Roosevelt put his name to an order drafted by Assistant Secretary of State Dean Acheson freezing all Japanese assets in the United States and, somewhat reluctantly, consented to what quickly became a total embargo on oil. By these actions, his biographer H. W. Brands has written, "the American president, without consulting Congress, had declared economic war on Japan."

Years later, after exploring archives in Tokyo and Washington, numbers of writers roundly criticized FDR's policies in the Far East. His action in late July 1941, several contended, drove the Japanese to war, because he had boxed them into a corner. This charge falls short, for Japan had decided on aggression *before* Roosevelt acted when, at the imperial conference early in July, it had resolved "to commence hostilities" unless the United States and Great Britain acceded to its demands by early October. Furthermore, it is improbable that any American concessions would have satisfied the army firebrands in Tokyo who grasped control of the government. More well-founded is the allegation that Roosevelt, in insisting that the Japanese withdraw from China, was setting an unacceptable requirement under the illusion that it was essential to American national interest to support Chiang Kai-shek, misconceived to be a passionate democrat.

Conspiracy theorists have gone much further in their accusations. For nearly three-quarters of a century, they have charged that Roosevelt, unable to bait Hitler into war in Europe, manipulated the Japanese into attacking and, with full knowledge of their plans from intercepted messages, deliberately withheld the information from military and naval officers in Hawaii. To plunge America into a needless war, they maintain,

Roosevelt cold-bloodedly sacrificed a large portion of the American fleet and the lives of more than two thousand sailors. The indictment is baseless. Not one dispatch that Roosevelt read indicated that Hawaii was a target. Unable to imagine that Japan was capable of carrying off an attack at a site so far distant as Hawaii, American strategists anticipated a strike in Southeast Asia. Admiral Stark alerted US fleet officers that the Japanese offensive would most likely come "against... the Philippines, Thai or Krai or Kra Peninsula or perhaps Borneo."

To the very last, Roosevelt hoped that war in the Far East, if it could not be averted, might at least be delayed until Philippine defenses had been bolstered, though the navy nurtured no such prospect. "Negotiations with Japan appear to be terminated to all practical purposes," Admiral Stark alerted Pacific commands. "An aggressive move is expected by Japan within the next few days." With Japanese diplomats in Washington, innocent of what was transpiring at home in the war ministry, continuing to negotiate in good faith, the president advised Secretary Hull in November, "Let us make no more of ill will. Let us do nothing to precipitate a crisis." As late as December 6, Roosevelt reached out to the emperor with a message urging peace.

On the very next day, at 1:10 on a Sunday afternoon, Roosevelt received a stunning message: "AIR RAID ON PEARL HARBOR. THIS IS NOT DRILL." Two waves of Japanese planes, it was soon learned, had damaged or destroyed eight battleships, seven other vessels, and 188 planes and had inflicted 3,435 casualties. A day later, in an appearance before a joint session of Congress in the House chamber, where he was welcomed with resounding applause, Roosevelt said, "Yesterday, December 7, 1941—a date which will live in infamy—the United States was suddenly and deliberately attacked by the naval and air forces of Japan." He asked Congress to "declare that since the unprovoked and dastardly attack..., a state of war has existed between the United States and the Japanese Empire." Roosevelt might still have had a tough time persuading Congress to go to war with Germany and Italy too, but a few days after Pearl Harbor Hitler and Mussolini solved that problem for him by announcing that their countries were at war with the United States. America's participation in a global war—so long dreaded, so long expected—had begun.

American intervention in World War II cast Franklin Roosevelt in a new role: commander in chief of the US armed forces engaged in a global struggle against fascism. Never before had a president been called upon to guide the nation through a prolonged war of such dimensions, and, given the perils inherent in thermonuclear exchanges, it is unlikely that such a situation will ever arise again. Furthermore, Roosevelt was not only the head of the American juggernaut but also the acknowledged leader of a multistate international coalition. In this conflict, the historian Michael Beschloss has written, "FDR was as near to being a king of the world as any president would ever be."

Roosevelt relished the opportunity the war provided him. "It must be borne in mind that President Franklin D. Roosevelt was the real and not merely a nominal Commander in Chief," observed an official US Army history. "Every President has possessed the Constitutional authority which that title indicates, but few Presidents have shared Mr. Roosevelt's readiness to exercise it in fact and in detail and with such determination." FDR kept the reins firmly in his own hands and let almost no one around him know all that was going on. "Mr. Roosevelt," said a White House correspondent, "made a fetish of his privacy during the war." He boarded trains not at Union Station but at a basement siding under a federal building on Fourteenth Street. He sent messages over army wires and received responses through navy wires.

Though the president left tactical details to generals and admirals, it was he who framed grand strategy. The chief historian of the US Army catalogued twenty-two critical decisions Roosevelt made "against the advice, or over the protests of his military advisers." Roosevelt, another scholar has written, "intervened more often and to better effect in military affairs than did even his battle-worn contemporaries like Churchill or Stalin.... While not needing to represent himself before the public as a strategist in the Churchill mold, he was one nonetheless and, if concentration on essentials is the hallmark of good strategy, the better of the two." In sum, the historian George Herring has concluded, "FDR was in many ways a brilliant commander in chief."

Roosevelt showed himself to particular advantage in his choice of military and naval leaders. Lincoln's unfortunate experience of discarding one general after another until he found Grant was not repeated. An ardent partisan, Roosevelt never let political considerations determine the choice of generals. He even indulged the vainglorious right-wing Douglas MacArthur. His record, the Republican Henry Stimson acknowledged, "was unique in American war history for its scrupulous abstention from personal and political pressure."

He assembled an impressive array. Army Chief of Staff George Catlett Marshall earned universal respect. Churchill was later to crown him "organizer of victory." An old salt, Roosevelt drew upon the knowledge gained as assistant secretary of the navy in elevating admirals: Admiral Ernest King as chief of naval operations, Admiral Harold Stark as commander of the Atlantic Fleet, and Admiral Chester Nimitz as his counterpart in the Pacific. In 1942, almost casually, Roosevelt created a new institution: the Joint Chiefs, a four-man body. Generals Marshall and Hap Arnold (head of the air force) participated from the army, with the navy represented by Admiral King and the president's wartime chief of staff, Admiral William Leahy, who, as the senior member, chaired meetings and, conferring each day with the president, served as liaison with the White House. George Elsey, an official in the Map Room of the White House during the war, wrote later of Roosevelt:

> It was accepted by *everyone* that he was the Boss—Stimson, Knox, Marshall, King, Arnold—everyone. *Absolutely!* After all, think how many years he had been President! All those officers had been relatively junior officers, and they had risen with his support and under his command.... What was Marshall? Marshall was a colonel, I guess, when FDR was elected president. What was King? Probably a captain in the Navy. And they'd risen to where they were under FDR. They had no reason to challenge or contradict or believe otherwise than to accept his leadership.

More than two years before Pearl Harbor, Roosevelt, wholly on his own, had taken an initiative with literally earthshaking reverberations. On October 11, 1939, Alexander Sachs, a financier who had befriended Roosevelt, read to him a letter from Albert Einstein expressing concern that the Germans were exploring the "possibility...of the release of a chain-reaction in uranium" that had a devastating military potential. On first hearing this, the president was not persuaded that nuclear physics was an arena for federal action, but at breakfast the next morning, after

Sachs made further overtures, he said, "Alex, what you are after is to see that the Nazis don't blow us up," then told an aide, "This requires action."

Boldly, Roosevelt agreed to spend huge sums and divert scarce materials to a project that might not succeed. The physicist Arthur Holly Compton, chair of a National Academy of Sciences committee on the matter, had never been a Roosevelt admirer, but he later wrote: "As I see it, we were rarely fortunate to have at the helm during these critical years a man of his degree of understanding, courage, and sympathy with men and women. No man of lesser understanding and courage could have made the decision to put so much of the nation's strength into what any man of his experience would recognize as a very long chance indeed." By December 1942, in a squash court under the stands of the University of Chicago's football stadium, Stagg Field, scientists had achieved the first chain reaction, and production of uranium and plutonium isotopes proceeded at sites powered by two New Deal projects, the TVA and Bonneville Dam.

Roosevelt also dominated the Anglo-American cooperation. By the time the United States entered the war, the United Kingdom had been fighting valiantly for more than two years, and British leaders understandably thought that the Yanks needed tutoring from the seasoned veterans in Whitehall, which would continue to be the fulcrum of action. "It has not worked out quite like that," Churchill's confidant Lord Moran noted in his diary. At the climax of a hot-tempered wrangle, the British agreed reluctantly that there would be a committee in the United States as well as one in England. "But this did not suit the President," Lord Moran recorded. "He wanted one committee in Washington, and after what Hopkins calls 'a hell of a row' he got what he wanted." As a consequence, Lord Moran concluded, "The Americans have got their way, and the war will be run from Washington"—which is to say that it would be run from the White House. It was FDR who came up with the name for the coalition, not "Associated Powers" but "the United Nations," and when in 1942 twenty-six nations pledged to wage war and fashion a peace jointly, the compact bore the name the Declaration of *Washington.*

The president did, however, consent to a Combined Chiefs of Staff, and, though there was inevitable friction, the two countries carried out a remarkable collaboration, made easier by the maturing friendship of

FDR and Churchill. In essence, the president entered the United States into an alliance with Great Britain, without seeking approval of the Senate. "No other allies could have done it," German field marshal Erwin Rommel's chief of staff later said of the well-coordinated invasion of the Continent. "You Americans and the British. You learn from each other. There is a special chemistry there."

Roosevelt made his most important contribution to this relationship by holding fast to the commitment to an Atlantic-first strategy he had made early in 1941, months before the United States entered the war. Churchill feared in 1942 that the fury of the American people over Pearl Harbor would force the president to change his mind. But despite polls showing that the country cared more about wreaking revenge on Japan than on defeating Hitler, the president never wavered in his conviction that conquest of Nazi Germany had higher priority. The Pacific arena received only 15 percent of Allied resources. That was not a proportion easy to sustain, for in the early months of 1942 the Japanese conquered so large a swath of Southeast Asia and the Pacific with such alacrity that, FDR's speechwriter Robert Sherwood later said, "pins on the walls of map rooms in Washington and London were usually far out of date."

In a fireside chat in February 1942, Roosevelt did not disguise the difficulties. On announcing his forthcoming address, he had said that he wanted listeners to have maps of the world on hand when they tuned in. (Stores soon reported a run on maps.) On the night of February 22, he told the American people that the struggle in which they were engaged was "a new kind of war." It differed from all previous conflicts "not only in its methods and weapons but also in its geography," a war being fought on "every continent, every island, every sea, every air-lane in the world." He added, "That is the reason why I have asked you to take out and spread before you a map of the whole earth, and to follow me in the references which I shall make to the world-encircling battle lines."

Roosevelt spoke frankly about the reverses the United States had sustained around the globe. "We have most certainly suffered losses—from Hitler's U-Boats in the Atlantic as well as from the Japanese in the Pacific—and we shall suffer more of them before the turn of the tide," he acknowledged. He presented that grim report in a historical context. He had chosen to speak on Washington's birthday—an occasion that permitted him to recall the time "when Washington's little army of ragged, rugged men was retreating across New Jersey, having tasted naught but defeat." That allusion led him to quote from the words that Tom Paine had written on a drumhead by light of campfire: "These are the times that try men's souls." The president reminded his listeners that Washington had every regiment in the Continental Army hear Paine's words: "The summer soldier and the sunshine patriot will, in this crisis, shrink from the service of their country; but he that stands it now, deserves the love and thanks of men and women. Tyranny, like hell, is not easily conquered, yet we have this consolation with us, that the harder the sacrifice, the more glorious the triumph." Roosevelt concluded:

> So spoke Americans in the year 1776.
> So speak Americans today.

In pursuit of a Eurocentric strategy, Roosevelt recognized that almost all of the actual combat with Hitler's armies in 1942 was taking place on the eastern front. Against considerable opposition, he insisted on shipments of Lend-Lease supplies to the Soviet Union. "Nothing would be worse than to have the Russians collapse," he told his secretary of the treasury. "I would rather lose New Zealand, Australia or anything else." Afterward, a German general observed, "Without this massive American support, Russia would scarcely have been able to take the offensive in 1943." Roosevelt, who had never met Stalin, employed the former head of the New Deal relief program, Harry Hopkins, as his surrogate. Even before America entered the war, the president wrote Stalin about a forthcoming visit to Moscow by his envoy: "I ask you to treat Mr. Hopkins with the identical confidence you would feel if you were talking directly to me. He will communicate directly to me the views that you express to him and will tell me what you consider are the most pressing individual problems on which we could be of aid." Twice in 1941, Roosevelt sent Hopkins to Moscow to arrange for shipment to Russia of $3 billion in Lend-Lease materials.

Wracked with the cancer that would take his life, Hopkins moved into the Lincoln Room at the White House. "There he sat," Churchill later reminisced, "slim, frail, ill, but absolutely glowing with refined comprehension of the Cause to the exclusion of all other purposes, loyalties, or aims." Utterly devoted to Roosevelt, he served as the president's most trusted emissary. In some respects, he was the equivalent of Wilson's Colonel House, but, unlike House, he did not have his own agenda. With no previous diplomatic experience, he had a keen capacity to separate wheat from chaff. Churchill called him "Lord Root of the Matter." Republicans had viewed with disdain the WPA chieftain who was a militant Democratic activist, but Stimson noted in his diary, "The more I think of it, the more I think it is a Godsend that he should be at the White House."

Roosevelt and Hopkins both understood that Stalin, though grudgingly grateful for Lend-Lease aid, wanted something else even more: establishment of a western front in 1942. On a mission to Washington, Vyacheslav Molotov, the grim-visaged, blunt-speaking Soviet foreign minister, warned the president that Hitler was readying a "mighty, crushing blow" at the USSR, and that, if the Russians were to hold out, it was essential for the Western powers to draw off forty German divisions. "Could we say to Mister Stalin that we are preparing a second front?" Roosevelt asked Marshall. "Yes," the general answered. With that assurance, the president told Molotov that he could let Stalin know that Allied troops would establish a bridgehead on the Continent in 1942.

Churchill, deeply alarmed, took off for Washington soon after he learned of this promise. With good reason, he told Roosevelt that an invasion in 1942 of an ill-prepared Allied force would meet with disaster. The president, knowing that without British participation a cross-Channel operation would be impossible, yielded. Stalin was going to be incensed, but "Sledgehammer" would have to wait until 1943—or, as it turned out, 1944. Stalin was indeed furious. So, too, were the Joint Chiefs of Staff.

When the British rejected every plan for a cross-Channel offensive in 1942, Marshall and King sent a joint memo to the president stating that unless there was "unswerving adherence" to the invasion plans, they were "definitely of the opinion that we should turn to the Pacific and strike decisively against Japan." To this misguided recommendation that the Atlantic-first strategy be abandoned, the president responded in a handwritten message. "My first impression is that it is exactly what Germany hoped the United States would do after Pearl Harbor. Secondly it does not in fact provide use of American troops in fighting except in a lot of islands whose occupation will not affect the world situation this year or next. Third: it does not help Russia or The Near East. Therefore it is disapproved as of the present." He signed the rebuke "Roosevelt C in C."

The president did, though, want to put US troops into battle before the year was out. Once again, he acted against the wishes of his military advisers, who favored a buildup of American forces in England in preparation for an invasion of the Continent projected for 1942. Over the strenuous objections of Stimson and Marshall, the president decided instead to launch a campaign in North Africa. In November 1942, in the greatest amphibious incursion in history, US forces under the command of General Dwight D. Eisenhower landed on the coasts of Algeria and Morocco.

It took a while for the generals to appreciate the president's acumen. Marshall started out with reservations about FDR's capacity to lead. When, in deciding on the North African venture, Roosevelt reasoned that to generate enthusiasm at home for the war he needed to show the nation that he was in earnest about defeating Hitler, Marshall said snidely, "The leader in a democracy has to keep the people entertained." But when Marshall witnessed, early in the war, Roosevelt's decisiveness, he later reflected, "I immediately discarded everything in my mind I had held to his discredit. . . . I decided he was a great man." At the time, Eisenhower, too, thought that FDR's refusal to sanction an invasion of Europe in 1942 might turn out to be the "blackest day in history," but after the war he concluded that a landing in 1942, even if it had not been repelled, would have resulted in such a fierce counterattack "that the break-through would have been immeasurably more difficult than it proved to be in July, 1944."

North Africa taught Eisenhower a harsh lesson, one that Roosevelt dealt with every day: waging war demands political skills as well as adroit military strategy. In mounting the offensive, the general recognized that he was invading French soil and that when the American troops splashed ashore, 120,000 French soldiers awaited them—a number greater than the entire US force. Consequently, he struck a deal with Admiral François Darlan, the only figure whose orders the French regiments would obey. Darlan agreed to cooperate, but only if he was installed as high commissioner of French North Africa. Eisenhower's acquiescence saved the lives of thousands of his men but infuriated the Free French led by Charles de Gaulle. It also brought down on Ike's head the wrath of American liberals, for Darlan had been the deputy head of the despised Vichy regime, which was collaborating with the Nazis. British Intelligence warned that "Eisenhower had better not trust Darlan further than he can throw a piano."

Roosevelt dealt with the uproar circumspectly. In support of Eisenhower, he recited to the press "a nice old proverb of the Balkans that has, as I understand it, the full sanction of the Orthodox church. . . . It says, 'My children, you are permitted in time of great danger to walk with the devil until you have crossed the bridge.'" At the same time, though, he wrote Eisenhower that he wanted him to bear in mind a few home truths:

1. That we do not trust Darlan.
2. That it is impossible to keep a collaborator of Hitler and one whom we believe to be a fascist in civil power any longer than is absolutely necessary.
3. His movements should be watched carefully and his communications supervised.

On Christmas Eve, Eisenhower and the Americans were relieved of this liability when a young French royalist murdered Darlan.

Two weeks later, Roosevelt flew across the Atlantic to meet Churchill at Casablanca. Never before had an American president traveled abroad during wartime. Never before had one flown while in office. On a knoll graced by palm trees and bougainvillea above the cobalt sea, FDR and Churchill agreed that there would be no cross-Channel operation in 1943, but that Allied forces would venture onto the Continent from the south. After United Nations divisions drove Rommel from North Africa, they were to cross the Mediterranean to attack Mussolini's Italy.

Roosevelt made the biggest news after the conference had disbanded, when he surprised Churchill by some offhand remarks to the press. He recalled that Hitler's rise to power had been made possible in no small part because of the claim that Germany had not been defeated in World War I but had been stabbed in the back by Social Democrats and Jews who conspired with the enemy. "Some of you Britishers know the old story—we had a general called U.S. Grant," he continued. "His name was Ulysses Simpson Grant, but in my, and the prime minister's, early days he was called 'Unconditional Surrender Grant.' The elimination of German, Japanese, and Italian war power means the unconditional surrender by Germany, Italy, or Japan." That stipulation had never been discussed, but Churchill went along with it. After parting with Roosevelt at the Casablanca airfield, Churchill told an acquaintance, "Don't tell me when they take off. It makes me far too nervous." Then he added: "If anything happened to that man, I couldn't stand it. He is the truest friend; he has the farthest vision; he is the greatest man I have ever known."

In November 1943, Roosevelt set out again on the longest journey of his presidency—more than seventeen thousand miles. In Cairo, he met with Churchill and Chiang Kai-shek, for he was determined that China be one of "the Big Four," though the country was torn by civil war, with Chiang's Nationalists challenged by Mao Zedong's Communists. From Egypt, Roosevelt and Churchill traveled on to Tehran for much more important summit sessions—with Stalin, whom FDR was encountering for the first time.

Roosevelt, "with his broad shoulders and fine head," said a British interpreter, seemed the dominating presence. "He beamed on all around the table and looked very much like the kind, rich uncle paying a visit to his poorer relations." The British, though, did not appreciate FDR's efforts to cultivate Stalin by twitting Churchill, especially about the prime minister's attachment to the empire. They liked even less the president's siding with the Soviet leader on grand strategy. At Tehran, Churchill still maintained that United Nations forces should concentrate on the "soft underbelly" of Europe fronting on the Mediterranean, but Stalin insisted that there be a cross-Channel invasion in the spring of 1944, and Roosevelt supported him.

Though Stalin made clear Russian intentions to dominate eastern Europe from Yugoslavia to Poland, he also had more benign moments. He paid friendly calls to FDR's room and at one point said: "I want to tell you, from the Russian point of view, what the President and the United States have done to win the war. . . . The United States has proven that it can turn out from 8,000 to 10,000 airplanes a month. Russia can turn out, at most, 3,000 airplanes a month. . . . The United States . . . is a country of machines. Without the use of those machines, through Lend-Lease, we would lose this war."

With plans for D-Day decided, Roosevelt concentrated on winning Stalin's consent to creation of a postwar United Nations organization. It would include a General Assembly and a much more powerful Security Council, with the main responsibility for enforcing peace in the hands of the Four Policemen: the United States, the United Kingdom, Russia, and China. Stalin also confirmed that three months after victory over Germany, Russia would enter the war against Japan.

More absorbed with the imperative need to create a Western front than with postwar dreams, Stalin asked who the D-Day commander was going to be. For a long time, Roosevelt had assumed it would be Marshall, the most esteemed military figure in the country. No one deserved it more. At one point, Roosevelt reflected that everyone knew names such as Grant and Lee, but almost no one could tell you who was chief of staff in the Civil War. He thought it only fair that Marshall be the one to have his name in the history books. The commander of American forces in World War I, General Pershing, told the president, though, that choosing Marshall would be a "very grave error," for he was indispensable as chief of staff in a global war. Gradually, Roosevelt came to the same conclusion. On breaking the painful news to Marshall, he told him, "I feel I could not sleep at night with you out of the country." Every inch a professional, Marshall acquiesced. At an airport in Tunis, the president confided to General Eisenhower, who was there to meet him, "Well, Ike, you are going to command Overlord."

Roosevelt returned to America from his five-week trip—the longest time he had ever been away from the White House—exhausted but exhilarated. His speechwriter Sam Rosenman later wrote of FDR's first day home in Washington: "I do not remember ever seeing the President look more satisfied and pleased than he did that morning. He believed intensely that he had accomplished what he had set out to do—to bring Russia into cooperation with the Western powers in a formidable organization for the maintenance of peace. . . . He was indeed the 'champ' who had come back with the prize." The president reported to the American people, "Within the past few weeks, history has been made. And it is far better history for the whole human race than any that we have known, or even dared hope for, in these tragic times." He said of the Soviet dictator: "To use an American and somewhat ungrammatical colloquialism, I may say that I 'got along fine' with Marshal Stalin. He is a man who combines a tremendous, relentless determination with a stalwart good humor. I believe he is truly representative of the heart and soul of Russia, and I believe that we are going to get along very well with him and the Russian people—very well indeed." Subsequent convocations at Dumbarton Oaks that created a framework for a postwar United Nations and at Bretton Woods that established a World Bank and an International Monetary Fund further strengthened Roosevelt's conviction that he was succeeding where Wilson had failed.

The president did not act effectively, however, to rescue Jews in the Third Reich. He had been shocked by *Kristallnacht.* "I myself could scarcely believe that such things could occur in a twentieth-century civilization," he told a press conference. But he operated under powerful constraints. At a time of mass unemployment in his second term, more than two-thirds of Americans polled said of European Jews that "with conditions as they are we should try to keep them out." Roosevelt, however, made full use of the quotas set under US immigration laws to admit far more refugees than did other countries: 150,000 between the conquest of Austria and Pearl Harbor. Once war broke out, though, he and most of his advisers reasoned that the best hope for Jews trapped in the Nazi empire lay in speeding victory over the Axis. When he learned during the war of the hideous mass extermination, he refused to acknowledge that, to no small degree, the tardy response by the State Department derived from anti-Semitism in its ranks, but he did take away from the State Department the responsibility for the fate of the Jews and vested it in an independent War Refugee Board. It was never in Roosevelt's power to have had any considerable effect on limiting the horror of the Holocaust. Still, he should have devoted considerably more energy to the effort than he did.

In the late spring of 1944, Roosevelt conveyed inspiriting news of progress in the struggle against the Axis in his first fireside chat of the year. At the late hour of 10 p.m., he informed his millions of listeners, "Yesterday, on June 4, 1944, Rome fell to American and Allied troops." Having overcome Rommel's Afrika Korps, the UN armies had crossed the Mediterranean and, at great cost, had fought their way up the Italian peninsula to capture the ancient capital. He later added, "Our victory comes at an excellent time, while our Allied forces are poised for another strike at Western Europe—and while the armies of other Nazi soldiers nervously await our assault." More than that he would not say, for to do so would have let slip the most closely guarded secret of the war. The president knew as he spoke that at that very moment courageous Allied paratroopers were descending on the fields of Normandy and landing craft were making their way across the English Channel to the beaches of the Continent. D-Day had begun.

On the very next day, the president took to the airwaves again—to inform the country that D-Day had arrived. With a hundred million Americans listening to his words on their radios, he asked them to join him, at "this poignant hour," in a prayer, which he had written himself:

Almighty God: Our sons, pride of our nation this day have set upon a mighty endeavor, a struggle to preserve our Republic, our religion and our civilization, and to set free a suffering humanity. Lead them straight and true; give strength to their arms, stoutness to their hearts, steadfastness in their faith. They will need Thy blessings. Their road will be long and hard for the enemy is strong. He may hurl back our forces. Success may not come with rushing speed, but we shall return again and again: and we know that by Thy grace, and by the right-eousness of our cause, our sons will triumph.

By then, Roosevelt had reached an apogee as the preeminent leader of the free world. In *Christ Stopped at Eboli*, Carlo Levi commented on how the inhabitants of an obscure village in the southern part of Italy—a country at war with the United States—viewed FDR:

What never failed to strike me most of all—and by now I had been in almost every house—were the eyes of two inseparable guardian angels that looked at me from the wall over the bed. On one side was the black, scowling face, with its large, inhuman eyes, of the Madonna of Viggiano; on the other a colored print of the sparkling eyes, behind gleaming glasses, and the hearty grin of President Roosevelt. I never saw other pictures or images than these: not the king nor the Duce, nor even Garibaldi; no famous Italian of any kind, nor any one of the appropriate saints; only Roosevelt and the Madonna of Viggiano never failed to be present. To see them there, one facing the other, in cheap prints, they seemed the two faces of the power that has divided the universe between them. But here their roles were, quite rightly, reversed. The Madonna appeared to be a fierce, pitiless, mysterious earth goddess, the Saturnian mistress of this world; the President a sort of all-powerful Zeus, the benevolent and smiling master of a higher sphere.

———

World War II greatly extended the reach of the White House not only overseas but also at home. "As wartime commander in chief, Roosevelt could exert power over the American economy and society transcending any he had previously wielded, even in the first heady days of the New Deal," his biographer Frank Freidel later observed. "He was indeed, as he boasted in the first week of the war, 'the final arbiter in all departments and agencies of the Government.'" The president issued close to three hundred executive orders, and in the year after Pearl Harbor, his decrees resulted in the creation of more than a hundred agencies. From 1940 to 1945, the number of federal employees multiplied from one million to nearly four million, and during the war the government spent more than the total that had been laid out from 1789 through 1940.

At the same time that he was overseeing military strategy, Roosevelt was supervising an extraordinary economic mobilization to turn out armaments for US troops and for America's allies. To coordinate production, he established an Office of Production Management that was succeeded by a War Production Board, and, to clamp down on inflation, he created an Office of Price Administration that imposed rationing on gasoline and other necessities. In addition, he set up a myriad of bureaus, including a War Labor Board and a War Manpower Commission, eventually imposing upon the entire unwieldy apparatus an Office of Economic Mobilization under former Supreme Court justice James F. Byrnes. Throughout the war, Roosevelt saw to it that control of this vast operation was vested in the Executive Office of the President lodged in the White House.

The president set fantastic production goals, and, after some initial mishaps, factories exceeded them. From 1939 to 1945, output nearly doubled. During these years, the nation manufactured far more airplanes than anyone had thought possible, created a synthetic rubber industry and a magnesium industry, increased machine tool output sevenfold, multiplied the capacity for aluminum production, and fabricated more iron and steel than the whole world had turned out a short time before. The Great Depression ended, and unemployment disappeared. The country even had to grapple with a labor shortage.

Roosevelt ran the mobilization with an iron fist. In a Labor Day message on September 7, 1942, he informed Congress that if it did not repeal a provision of an Emergency Price Control Act promptly, he would, on his own authority, treat it as invalid. He declared:

> I ask the Congress to take... action by the first of October. Inaction on your part by that date will leave me with an inescapable responsibility to the people of this country to see to it that the war effort is no longer imperiled by threat of economic chaos.
>
> In the event that the Congress should fail to act, and act adequately, I shall accept the responsibility, and I will act....
>
> The President has the powers, under the Constitution and under Congressional acts, to take measures necessary to avert a disaster which would interfere with the winning of war....
>
> The American people can be sure that I will use my powers with a full sense of my responsibility to the Constitution and to my country. The American people can also be sure that I shall not hesitate to use every power vested in me to accomplish the defeat of our enemies in any part of the world where our own safety demands such a defeat.

Decades later, scholars expressed shock at this audacious—many thought brazen—message, which has been likened to the "claim... advanced by Locke in the seventeenth century on behalf of royal prerogative." To be sure, Roosevelt did go to Congress, and he did say, "When the war is won, the powers under which I act automatically revert to the people—to whom they belong." But the authors of the leading constitutional history textbook have written: "Here was a presidential claim of a right of executive nullification of a portion of the constitutional statute, solely on the ground that the law in question did not conform with the president's notion of what constituted intelligent national policy. No more extraordinary claim to executive prerogative has ever been advanced in the history of the American constitutional system."

Roosevelt also used the might of his office to suppress disruptive strikes in wartime, though unions were a vital component of the FDR coalition. When three railroad brotherhoods called a strike in 1943, Roosevelt announced: "I cannot wait until the last moment to take action to see that...supplies to our fighting men are not interrupted. I am accordingly obliged to take over at once temporary possession and control of the railroads to insure their continued operation....If any employees of the railroads now strike, they will be striking against the Government of the United States." Faced by these threats, the rail union leaders caved in. When, at the direction of John L. Lewis, half a million miners walked out of the coal pits in 1943, the president lashed out at the union leader. "The continuance and spread of these strikes would have the same effect on the course of the war as a crippling defeat in the field," he said. "Without coal our war industries cannot produce tanks, guns, and ammunition for our armed forces. Without these weapons, our sailors on the high seas, and our armies in the field, will be helpless against our enemies."

Lewis's antics whipped Congress into a frenzy, especially when the United Mine Workers chief, after yielding to the president, called his men out a second time because the War Labor Board would not oblige him with the wage hike he demanded. Congress responded by passing the Smith-Connally bill, which required unions in war industries to file thirty days' notice of intent to strike and prohibited unions from making political contributions in national elections. Roosevelt vetoed the bill as too harsh, while asking for standby authority to draft strikers as non-combatants. Both houses of Congress speedily overrode him by sizeable margins. With respect to labor policy, Congress insisted, it and not the president would set the terms. Yet by enacting the law, Congress greatly enhanced presidential power, for it authorized the president to seize privately owned war plants and operate them when a strike threatened. In 1944, Roosevelt made use of the law to send soldiers into Philadelphia to break a transit strike. In the course of his action, he threatened to conscript into the army any worker who persisted in disobedience.

Corporation tycoons, too, had to submit to coercion. In 1942 alone, the *Federal Register* published more than eleven thousand pages of decrees issued by US agencies, a total far greater than the legislative output of Congress. Twice, the president ordered Sewell Avery, the crusty head of Montgomery Ward, to sign maintenance-of-union-membership contracts. When in 1944 Avery balked at making concessions to his workers to end a strike, Roosevelt ordered seizure of Ward's Chicago plant, though the mail order business was only tangentially connected to the war. A widely circulated photograph of Avery being carted out of his office by battle-helmeted troops incensed conservatives across the country. Mississippi senator James Eastland fumed, "If the President has the power to take over Montgomery Ward, he has the power to take over a grocery store or butcher shop in any hamlet in the U.S." But Attorney General Francis Biddle prevailed when he asserted, "No business or property is immune to a Presidential order. Particularly in time of war the Court should not substitute its judgment for that of the executive."

To ensure equality of sacrifice, Roosevelt intervened directly in the framing of tax legislation. He insisted that there be no swollen fortunes, no Daddy Warbucks, but he also asked all Americans to share some of the burdens of war, partly in order to take away discretionary income that pushed up prices. He hoped to raise income taxes on the wealthy so steeply that no one would receive more than $25,000 a year after taxes, and, though that proposal struck Congress as close to confiscatory, he did get a rate as high as 94 percent, with an excess profits tax that reached 95 percent. The Revenue Act of 1942, which Roosevelt rightly called "the greatest tax bill in history," brought about the most significant redistribution of income in the twentieth century. The share of disposable income of the very rich fell from 26 percent in 1940 to 16 percent in 1944. The law also levied a 5 percent "Victory tax" on every annual income above $624, a stipulation requiring fifty million Americans to file tax returns in contrast to only four million in 1939. The adoption of a withholding tax for the first time in 1942 made tax payments a weekly ritual.

Roosevelt confronted considerably greater resistance to another revenue proposal early in 1944. Instead of providing the president with the more than $10 billion in taxes he deemed necessary to curb inflation, Congress voted only $2 billion and concocted a plum pudding of favors to special interests. Roosevelt struck back with a fiery veto message, which brought to mind Andrew Jackson's rhetoric in his war on the Bank. "It is not a tax bill but a tax-relief bill providing relief not for the needy but for the greedy," he asserted. "The nation will readily understand that it is not the fault of the Treasury Department that the income taxpayers are flooded with forms to fill out which are so complex that even certified public accountants cannot interpret them. No, it is squarely the fault of the Congress of the United States in using language in drafting the law which not even a dictionary or a thesaurus can make clear." As the clerk read out the president's words, they seemed to a reporter in the Senate press gallery to be "Crack! Crack! Crack!—laying open the backs of his opponents."

For years, the Senate majority leader, Alben Barkley, had been sneered at as "Dear Alben," FDR's errand boy, but on this occasion he rose on the Senate floor to deliver a stinging rebuke. Roosevelt's statement, he said, was a "calculated and deliberate assault upon the legislative integrity of every member of Congress. Other members...may do as they please; but, as for me, I do not propose to take this unjustifiable assault lying down." The usually preternaturally good-natured Barkley even delivered a personal jab. Roosevelt took pride in his prowess as a forester, but, the senator said, FDR's operation at Hyde Park had been confined to Christmas trees, and "to compare these little pine bushes with a sturdy oak...would be like comparing a cricket to a stallion." At the conclusion of his harangue, senators gave him a standing ovation, and spectators in the gallery joined in. By huge margins, both houses of Congress overrode Roosevelt's veto; the Senate turned thumbs down, 72–14. Never before had a revenue measure been enacted over a presidential veto.

Though the Roosevelt administration had been more than diligent in seeking to root out subversives in the executive branch, Congress attempted to take over that operation too. From 1940 to 1944, the number of FBI agents increased from 80 to 755. In 1942, the Justice Department started the "Attorney General's list" of organizations regarded as disloyal, and in 1943, Roosevelt set up an interdepartmental committee to investigate the loyalty of federal employees. The president also employed the Smith Act of 1940, which interdicted not only action against the government but advocacy of such action, against Trotskyists as well as alleged Nazis. Liberal commentators thought that these forays were excessive, but they did not go nearly far enough for Congress, more particularly for a committee in the House that had become notorious since its founding in 1938 for questionable, and sometimes outrageous, allegations.

During the war, the House Un-American Activities Committee carried on a vendetta against "crackpot, radical bureaucrats." It initially targeted thirty-nine that it demanded be removed from federal service but had to settle for three. The House of Representatives attached to a bill the provision "No part of any appropriation...of this act...shall be used to pay any part of the salary or other compensation for the personal service of Goodwin B. Watson, William E. Dodd, Jr., and Robert Morss Lovett." Since the funds provided by this Urgent Deficiency Appropriation Act were indispensable, Roosevelt had no option save to sign the bill. But on doing so he attached a signing statement branding the rider as "not only unwise and discriminatory, but unconstitutional," and declaring that since "this rider is an unwarranted encroachment upon the authority of both the executive and judicial branches, it is not, in my judgment, binding upon them." Eventually, the Supreme Court ruled, in *United States v. Lovett* (1946), that the rider was unconstitutional—not, as Roosevelt had maintained, because it infringed upon a president's power of removal but rather because it was a bill of attainder.

Commentators watching FDR vigilantly for any sign that war had changed his political outlook interpreted some off-the-cuff remarks he made to the press at the end of 1943 as evidence that he had surrendered to conservatives. "How did the New Deal come into existence?" he asked, then answered that it was because "there was an awfully sick patient called the United States of America," and it had been necessary to call in a doctor to treat this "grave internal disorder." After some years, the patient was cured. But on December 7, 1941, the patient became very ill again, not as the result of "internal trouble" but because he had been "in a pretty bad smashup—broke his hip, broke his leg in two or three places, broke a wrist and an arm, and some ribs. And they didn't think he would live for a while." Dr. New Deal could not treat him, because he was an internist who knew nothing about surgery. "So he got his partner, who was an orthopedic surgeon, Dr. Win-the-War, to take care of this fellow." Reporters raced out to spread the news: the president, veering to the right, had abandoned liberalism.

Two weeks later, however, Roosevelt confounded these Cassandras by delivering what his biographer James MacGregor Burns has called "the most radical speech of his life." In his State of the Union address of January 1944, he tongue-lashed "pests who swarm through the lobbies of Congress and the cocktail bars of Washington" and derided "the whining demands of selfish pressure groups, who seek to feather their nests while young Americans are dying." The time had come, he stated, to make plans for "the establishment of an American standard of living higher than ever before known" because it was intolerable for any "fraction of our people," no matter how small, to be "ill-fed, ill-clothed, ill-housed, and insecure."

In his peroration, the president set forth his far-reaching thoughts about a new constitutional order:

> This Republic had its beginning, and grew to its present strength, under the protection of certain inalienable political rights–among them the right of free speech, free press, free worship, trial by jury, freedom from unreasonable searches and seizures....
>
> As our Nation has grown in size and stature, however—as our industrial economy expanded—these political rights proved inadequate to assure us equality in the pursuit of happiness.
>
> We have come to a clear realization of the fact that true individual freedom cannot exist without economic security and independence. "Necessitous men are not free men." People who are hungry and out of a job are the stuff of which dictatorships are made.
>
> In our day these economic truths have become accepted as self-evident. We have accepted, so to speak, a second Bill of Rights under which a new basis of security and prosperity can be established for all—regardless of station, race, or creed.
>
> Among these are:
>
> The right to a useful and remunerative job in the industries or shops or farms or mines of the Nation;
>
> The right to earn enough to provide adequate food and clothing and recreation;
>
> The right of every farmer to raise and sell his products at a return which will give him and his family a decent living;
>
> The right of every businessman, large or small, to trade in an atmosphere of freedom from unfair competition and domination by monopolies at home or abroad;
>
> The right of every family to a decent home;
>
> The right to adequate medical care and the opportunity to achieve and enjoy good health;

The right to adequate protection from the economic fears of old
age, sickness, accident, and unemployment;

The right to a good education.

It would take a generation for that program to be adopted, but Congress
moved in its spirit by putting through the Servicemen's Readjustment
Act of 1944. Better known as the GI Bill of Rights, the law provided educational and medical benefits, as well as mortgage guarantees, to ease
the transition of World War II soldiers and sailors to civilian life. In
1943, Roosevelt had called for generous treatment of veterans, but the
legislation owed almost nothing to his initiative. He merely stood out of
the way as this highly popular measure was whooped through.

World War II, which had so many bright aspects at home—the GI
Bill, the end of the Great Depression, unprecedented employment opportunities for women, and significant civil rights gains for African Americans,
including the abolition by the Supreme Court of the white primary—
also had darker features, darkest of all the internment of Japanese
Americans. That shameful action arose out of almost irresistible pressure
on Washington from the West Coast, where 90 percent of residents of
Japanese ancestry lived. Long prejudiced against Asian immigrants and
envious of their achievements, whites in California and other states of
the Pacific Rim were confirmed in their distrust by the "sneak attack" on
Hawaii. Fearful of a "fifth column" in their midst, they demanded that
the government remove these people from their region. The *Los Angeles
Times* stated, "A viper is...a viper wherever the egg is hatched—so a
Japanese-American, born of Japanese parents, grows up to be a Japanese,
not an American," and the Hearst columnist Henry McLemore wrote:
"Herd 'em up, pack 'em off and give 'em the inside room in the badlands." Both California's liberal governor, Culbert Olson, who had given
the state a "New Deal," and its attorney general, Earl Warren, who was
to win fame as chief justice of the United States for his devotion to civil
liberties, fed the flames of racist bigotry.

The West Coast army commander, General John DeWitt, shared this
obsession. "The Japanese race is an enemy race," he declared, and there
was "no ground for assuming that any Japanese...though born in the
U. S. will not turn against the U.S. when the final test of loyalty comes."
DeWitt, after acknowledging the absence of even a single provocation,

said, with stupefying illogic, "The very fact that no sabotage has taken place is a disturbing and confirming indication that such action will be taken."

DeWitt's superior, Secretary of War Stimson, had a harder time coming to that conclusion. At first, he reasoned that "we can not discriminate among our citizens on the ground of racial origin," because doing so would "make a tremendous hole in our constitutional system." But it did not take him long to decide that "their racial characteristics are such that we cannot . . . trust even the citizen Japanese." Hence, mandatory removal was imperative, for a Japanese invasion was "quite within the bounds of possibility" and "the people of the United States have made an enormous mistake in underestimating the Japanese." Accordingly, Stimson prepared an edict for the president to sign, and Roosevelt, who could have countermanded it, apparently never gave a second thought to its iniquity.

On February 19, 1942, the president issued Executive Order 9066 empowering the secretary of war "to prescribe military areas . . . from which any or all persons may be excluded." The ukase did not mention Japanese Americans or the Pacific Coast, but everyone understood that both were implied. "The order's bland language concealed an unprecedented assertion of executive power," the historian Greg Robinson has noted. "Under its provisions, the President imposed military rule on civilians without a declaration of martial law, and he sentenced a segment of the population to internal exile (and ultimately forced incarceration) under armed guard, notwithstanding that the writ of habeas corpus had not been suspended by Congress (to whom such power was reserved by the Constitution.)"

In compliance with this directive, the government snatched 120,000 "Japanese" (two-thirds were US citizens) from their homes, businesses, farms, and schools and deposited them in temporary corrals, most conspicuously the horse stalls of racetracks. At Santa Anita, enveloped in barbed wire and with searchlights patrolling every corridor, the internees, "painfully American," set up PTAs, named a street after the swift thoroughbred Seabiscuit, and organized an American Legion post for World War I veterans. The incarcerated included Dr. Yamato Ichihashi, professor of history and government at Stanford; the "Chrysanthemum King," Ryohitsu Shibuya; and numbers of young men who would later enlist in the army and die fighting for their country. After a brief stay, the internees were transported to tarpaper shack camps in forbidding Western deserts and fetid Arkansas swamplands for the duration of the war.

Later generations expressed remorse at these denials of fundamental rights and sought, much too late, to make amends, but at the time the nation found the transgressions of Roosevelt and his subordinates altogether reasonable, especially when in the following week a Japanese sub shelled the coast of California near Santa Barbara. Congress showed its approval by unanimously adopting a resolution making entry into a proscribed military area a federal offense punishable by imprisonment, and the Supreme Court, in a 9–0 ruling in *Hirabayashi* (1943), legitimated FDR's order. Justice Frank Murphy, though, filed a concurrence that sounded more like a biting dissent. The restriction imposed on US citizens of Japanese ancestry, he said, "bears a melancholy resemblance to the treatment accorded to members of the Jewish race in Germany."

In April 1944, the president of the United States vanished in plain sight. His departure would have been unusual under any circumstances, but it was especially so at a time when the Japanese were mounting a major offensive on American air bases in China, the RAF was sustaining heavy losses in a raid on Nuremberg, and Allied armies were engaged in bloody infantry encounters on the Continent. Roosevelt did not scrutinize the Map Room in the White House for a month.

The administration explained that the president had left town because he needed a vacation, which was true but considerably less than the whole truth, for he was seriously ill. Recent blood pressure readings had reached a frightening 210/120. From his retreat at Hobcaw Barony, the financier Bernard Baruch's plantation on Waccamaw Neck in South Carolina, he wrote his cousin and onetime lover Daisy Suckley, "I am really feeling 'no good'—don't want to do anything & want to sleep all the time." He was reduced to but one goal, he confided on another occasion: "Sleep and sleep. Twelve hours a night, and let the world go hang." The American people had no notion at all that he was failing. Only three reporters—one from each of the wire services—were permitted to be in the vicinity of Hobcaw, and they were told by the Secret

Service to "stay out of the old man's way." Furthermore, FDR's physician sent out a stream of disinformation assuring the country that his patient was in fine fettle. Even if citizens had been told the truth, they would have found it hard to accept, for throughout 1944 FDR's voice on their radios sounded as vibrant as it had in 1933.

Washington insiders, though, knew that Roosevelt was slipping, and that knowledge shaped much of the 1944 campaign. Shortly after the president returned to Washington, he met his speechwriter Robert Sherwood, who had not seen him in months. "I had heard that he had lost a lot of weight, but I was unprepared for the almost ravaged appearance of his face," Sherwood wrote later. "He had his coat off and his shirt collar seemed several sizes too large for his emaciated neck." Years later, a doctor who married FDR's daughter concluded, on reviewing once inaccessible evidence, "On medical grounds alone, he should not have run in 1944."

Apprehension about the president's physical decline sparked an unusual amount of preoccupation with the Democratic vice presidential nomination in 1944. Party bosses surmised that in picking FDR's running mate the convention would very likely, even probably, be selecting the next US president, for the candidate would be called upon to finish a good stretch of Roosevelt's fourth term. They regarded the incumbent, Henry Wallace, "the Iowa Robespierre," as too radical and, especially after revelation of his coded letters to a Russian guru, flaky. Roosevelt, who never asked doctors to tell him what was wrong with him, showed little interest in the matter and was content to turn over the choice to the movers and shakers in the party.

After vetting other possibilities, they settled on Harry S. Truman, but, as a sop to liberals, they halfheartedly tossed in another name: Supreme Court Justice William O. Douglas. The strongest contender was Supreme Court Justice Jimmy Byrnes, on leave as "assistant president" in the war mobilization, but, as a South Carolina racist, a man distrusted by labor, and a renegade Catholic, he was "unavailable." Truman, on the other hand, satisfied every element in the party. Once an obscure backbench senator from Missouri, he had made a name for himself as head of the Truman Committee diligently investigating fraud and inefficiency in military procurement. Son of an ardently pro-Confederate mother, he won favor among southerners, who did not know that, despite his background, he staunchly opposed racial injustice. A liege of the Pendergast machine in Kansas City, he was acceptable to urban bosses. Truman, in short, was "the Second Missouri Compromise."

The final decision still lay with the president, who, though he hardly knew Truman, went along—but in a characteristically oblique manner. He gave the chair of the convention a letter to read to the delegates: "I have been associated with Henry Wallace during his past four years as Vice President, for eight years earlier when he was Secretary of Agriculture, and well before that. I like him and I respect him and he is my personal friend. For these reasons I personally would vote for his renomination if I were a delegate to the convention. At the same time, I do not wish to appear in any way as dictating to the convention. Obviously the convention must do the deciding." Seasoned politicians understood instantly how to translate that communication. His statement that he would vote for Wallace appeared to be an outright endorsement. But his declaration that he would not dictate the choice meant, in effect, that he was backing away from Wallace, since the president had not been at all reluctant to insist upon him four years earlier. Furthermore, he supplied another missive to the party chairman: "You have written me about Harry Truman and Bill Douglas. I should, of course, be very glad to run with either of them and believe that either one of them would bring real strength to the ticket." Since it was understood that the delegates would never accept Douglas, an outspoken liberal, Roosevelt was saying that Truman was going to be the vice presidential nominee.

Awareness of FDR's condition also affected the Republican presidential nomination. For a party that hoped to go to the country as the champion of vigor and youth in contrast to the infirm Roosevelt, it did not make sense to choose as its standard-bearer General MacArthur, who was two years older than the president. The GOP turned instead to New York's governor, thirty-eight-year-old Thomas Dewey, with Ohio governor John Bricker for vice president. Republicans charged that Roosevelt was too old, too weary, too ill to give the country the kind of vigorous leadership it needed in wartime, and would get from Dewey, who had won headlines as a crusading, racket-busting district attorney. Dewey himself alluded to "stubborn men grown old and tired and quarrelsome in office."

Roosevelt, who instead of taking on Landon and Willkie in past races had run against memories of Hoover, ignored Dewey and ran instead in 1944 against Hitler and Tojo. He refused to take to the campaign trail, but contented himself instead with visible displays of his role as commander in chief. He had not even appeared at the Democratic convention in Chicago but, while he was being nominated, reviewed a naval display in San Diego. In July, he boarded a cruiser for Pearl Harbor (the ship zigzagging by day, with no running lights at night) on what was partly an electioneering ploy, partly a mission to plan Pacific strategy with Admiral Leahy, Admiral Nimitz, General MacArthur, and others. On the plane from Australia to Hawaii, MacArthur was fuming. "The humiliation of forcing me to leave my command... for a picture-taking junket!" he grumbled. But FDR won him over by his calm, skillful resolution of differences that resulted in a decision to start the win-the-war offensive against Japan at Leyte in the Philippines. "Roosevelt was at his best as he tactfully steered the discussion from one point to another and narrowed... the area of disagreement between MacArthur and Nimitz," Leahy later said. Having achieved what he set out to do, including identifying himself in the eyes of American voters with General MacArthur, the president then sailed to the Aleutians, a lonely outpost of the conflict with the Japanese empire.

On his southward journey from paying a call on troops in the Aleutians, Roosevelt stopped off at Bremerton, Washington, to talk to shipyard workers at the naval installation there. Uncharacteristically, he spoke haltingly. Ill-fitting braces cutting into his legs caused agonizing pain, and, for the first time ever, he suffered an angina attack. In addition, a stiff wind troubled the pages of his manuscript. He never let on about his suffering, but it was hard to tough it out when he got no response from his audience, which, because of the gusts, could not hear his words. His stumbling, lackluster effort fed rumors that he was ill, and photographs in newspapers and magazines showed him haggard.

A masterful campaigner, Roosevelt came up with a mischievous way to counter that impression. As he approached the late September night when he would speak at a dinner of the powerful Teamsters union, he said, "I expect to have a lot of fun with that one." He began by indignantly assailing his Republican critics for their attacks on him (he accused them of "fraud" and of adopting tactics even worse than those of the Nazi propaganda chief, Goebbels), then shifted into a different mode. To the friendly gathering, he said:

> These Republican leaders have not been content with attacks on me, or my wife, or my sons. No, not content with that, they now include my little dog, Fala. Well, of course, I don't resent attacks, and my family doesn't resent attacks, but Fala does resent them. You know, Fala is Scotch, and being a Scottie, as soon as he learned that the Republican fiction writers in Congress and out had concocted a story that I had left him behind on the Aleutian Islands and had sent a destroyer back to find him—at a cost to the taxpayers of two or three or eight or twenty million dollars—his Scotch soul was furious. He has not been the same dog since. I am accustomed to hearing malicious falsehoods about myself—such as that old, worm-eaten chestnut that I have represented myself as indispensable. But I think I have a right to resent, to object to, libelous statements about my dog.

His audience in the banquet hall was convulsed with laughter, and his radio listeners across the country joined in the merriment.

As the campaign drew to a close, the president staged another memorable scene to demonstrate that he was robust and still the tribune of the people. On a dismally cold, rainy morning in Brooklyn in late October, Roosevelt set out for a ride through four of the far-flung boroughs of New York City. He ordered the top down in his Packard, though he was protected from the relentless downpour only by his navy cape and a battered fedora. His physician had urged him to call off the trip, but he soldiered on for four hours in the deluge, waving cheerily to the some three million spectators who turned out to greet him, their teeth chattering, their clothes sodden.

The fortunes of war also smiled on the president, who had been the target of Republican criticism. Exploiting the country's weariness with a conflict that had dragged on for nearly three years, GOP sloganeers urged: "Win the War Quicker with Dewey and Bricker," and the anti-FDR Hearst press demanded: SEND SHIPS TO M'ARTHUR NOW. The bombs exploding on Pearl Harbor had blown the ground out from under the contention of Roosevelt's prewar critics that there was no foreign threat to America, but isolationists had continued to turn their backs on

Europe by promoting an Asia-first strategy with Douglas MacArthur as their hero. Though Dewey was no isolationist, he picked up this theme by charging that Roosevelt was maliciously denying MacArthur the support he needed. That allegation fell flat when on October 20 MacArthur launched an invasion in Leyte Gulf. A week later, speaking in Philadelphia, the president noted that in the past year UN forces had carried out twenty-seven landings in enemy country from Europe to the Philippines. "And," he went on, "speaking of the glorious operation in the Philippines, I wonder whatever became of the suggestion... that I had failed for political reasons to send enough forces or supplies to General MacArthur?" Furthermore, the Allied armies in western Europe had crossed into Germany and on October 21 had taken Aachen.

In November, Roosevelt won 53.4 percent of the popular vote to Dewey's 45.9 percent, with an emphatic 432–99 advantage in the Electoral College. The president succeeded in overcoming the health and age issues in good part because the uptight Dewey, though almost a generation younger than FDR, did not seem nearly so dynamic. When a photographer requested, "Smile, Governor," Dewey replied, "I thought I was." By gaining an unprecedented fourth term, Roosevelt kept the Democrats in power for four more years, the longest reign in the history of their party.

He lost little time in signaling his intentions for postwar America: to carry further the trail blazed by the New Deal. On Inauguration Day 1945, the president "tossed a lighted firecracker to the Senate," in the words of Frank Freidel, by nominating the beau ideal of the liberals, Henry Wallace, for secretary of commerce and putting him in charge of the government finance agencies run by the Houston banker Jesse Jones, favorite of conservatives. Only grudgingly did the Senate consent to Wallace's nomination, and it refused to vest him with authority over federal loans. It also turned down FDR's choice of the progressive southerner Aubrey Williams to head the Rural Electrification Administration.

Roosevelt created another sensation, only days after delivering his inaugural address, by crossing the Atlantic to confer with Stalin and Churchill in Russia. It was an exceptionally arduous journey, especially for a man in a wheelchair who was ailing. The president not only was required to fly all the way to the Crimea by way of Malta, but after he landed, looking "frail" and "ill" to Churchill's eyes, he had to endure a six-hour motor trip up to the summit of an icy mountain range and down to the Black Sea. He had implored Stalin to meet with him at a more convenient venue—Scotland or perhaps Cyprus—but the Soviet dictator had turned him down.

The president came to Yalta with a number of aspirations, but one above all others—to get Stalin to agree to enter the war against Japan quickly after V-E Day. The fanatical resistance in Saipan and the Philippines demonstrated that the Japanese were prepared to fight to the end, and the deadly kamikaze attacks were taking a terrible toll. As the conferees bartered, American troops were dying in the battle for Manila. Marshall and the Joint Chiefs did not want to invade Japan's home islands until three months after Soviet Russia had entered the war and was diverting Japanese troops, and MacArthur stated that "as many Japanese divisions as possible should first be pinned down on the mainland, principally by Soviet forces." Even with Russian involvement, FDR's military advisers foresaw another eighteen months of bloodshed. Without Soviet engagement, the cost in American casualties was incalculable, perhaps as many as a million.

At Tehran, Stalin had promised to enter the Pacific war, but he had not committed himself to a specific date—and timing was crucial. Just as the Allies had chosen the most advantageous moment for D-Day, the Kremlin might well decide not to enter the war against Japan until after the Americans had invaded Kyushu and were pulling Japanese troops away from the Asian mainland. Roosevelt regarded as the greatest single achievement of the Yalta conference the adoption of a secret codicil that stated, "The leaders of the three Great Powers...have agreed that in two or three months after Germany has surrendered and the war in Europe has terminated, the Soviet Union shall enter into the war against Japan."

Roosevelt realized that Stalin, in turn, expected concessions, and he was willing to grant some, but not nearly so many as the Soviet leader wanted. He consented to the return of the Japanese-held Kurile Islands and the lower half of Sakhalin to the USSR, and he dangled the prospect of a huge postwar loan. But, supported by Churchill, he refused to approve enormous reparations for the USSR as part of a scheme for a deindustrialized Germany. Contrary to the allegations of his critics, the president proved to be a hard bargainer. He resisted Soviet demands for a sphere in Manchuria, and he secured from Stalin approval of US bases

The Big Three at Yalta, February 1945. In this official photograph, Winston Churchill, Franklin Delano Roosevelt, and Joseph Stalin affect an amiability that was not always evident during the negotiations. *Courtesy Franklin D. Roosevelt Presidential Library, ID NPx 48-22:3659(66)*

in Siberia. He also refused to let Stalin modify a Declaration of Liberated Europe, drafted by the US State Department, expressing the intent to "form interim governmental authorities broadly representative of all democratic elements in the population and pledged to the earliest possible establishment through free elections of governments responsive to the will of the people."

The president knew even before the meetings commenced that the toughest negotiations would be over the fate of Poland. After one set of exchanges with Stalin, he became so fatigued and his blood pressure so irregular that his physician banned all morning visitors. The president appreciated that Russia had a far greater national security stake in eastern Europe than did the Western powers, but he also knew that it had been extraordinarily vicious in establishing its dominion. In 1940, the Soviet Union had massacred thousands of Polish officers and soldiers in the Katyn Forest. In 1944, as Soviet forces approached Warsaw, the Polish underground had risen up against the Germans, but the Russian army held back on the outskirts of the city, and even impeded Allied efforts to aid the uprising. Within weeks, the German army had stamped out the resistance, taking close to a quarter of a million lives of Polish men, women, and children. Only then did Soviet troops move into the capital. With native leadership largely eradicated, the USSR rounded up the very few Communists in Poland and installed them as the new regime.

Roosevelt and Churchill opposed Russian ambitions in Poland as far as they dared. The president realized that if he pushed Stalin too far on Poland, the Soviet leader might delay the invasion of Japan—at the cost of thousands of lives of American soldiers. They also feared that he might dynamite plans for a postwar United Nations by boycotting it. Nonetheless, Roosevelt told Stalin bluntly that the United States would not recognize the puppet regime in Lublin, and Churchill, in demanding that Stalin relent, pointed out that Great Britain had, after all, gone to war in defense of the territorial integrity of Poland. They could take some satisfaction from the agreement announced by the conference: "The Provisional Government...in Poland should...be reorganized on a broader democratic basis with the inclusion of democratic leaders from Poland itself and from Poles abroad." It further stated, "This Polish Provisional Government of National Unity shall be pledged to the holding of free and unfettered elections as soon as possible on the basis of universal suffrage and secret ballot."

Stalin, though, had no intention of honoring this commitment. "I want this election in Poland to be...like Caesar's wife," Roosevelt said. "I did not know her but they say she was pure." Stalin, who did not care how the election was conducted so long as it confirmed Soviet domination of Poland, gave a jaundiced response. "They said that about her," he rejoined, "but in fact she had her sins." Churchill left Yalta feeling blue, and after returning to Washington, the most that Roosevelt could muster up to say in confidence to a State Department official was that it was the best he could do. In the postwar era, innumerable right-wing orators and publicists charged that at Yalta a "sick Roosevelt," no longer competent to cope with Stalin's wiles, had lost the peace—most shamefully by giving away Poland. But with Soviet forces in control of Poland, Bulgaria, Romania, and East Prussia, they could not have been dislodged from eastern Europe save by a World War III the American people would never have tolerated.

Critics further alleged that, with the atomic bomb at his disposal, Roosevelt needlessly brought the USSR into the war, sowing endless future trouble in Asia. FDR's military advisers, however, strongly believed that Russian participation was indispensable. Leahy did not think that the bomb would work, and others could not see that it significantly differed from the firebombing that was already being carried out. The biographer Kenneth Davis, often highly critical of FDR, concluded that at Yalta no one "could doubt that he was in full possession of his faculties. Somehow, at whatever expense of inner resources that were no longer renewable, he summoned up a sufficient energy to negotiate diplomatic passages strewn with treacherous shoals, employing . . . far more patience and understanding than many of his hale and hearty colleagues."

On March 1, Roosevelt reported to an extraordinary session of Congress on his Big Three meetings with Churchill and Stalin. "I hope that you will pardon me for this unusual posture of sitting down during the presentation of what I want to say," he began. "But I know that you will realize that it makes it a lot easier for me not to have to carry about ten pounds of steel around on the bottom of my legs; and also because . . . I have just completed a fourteen-thousand-mile trip." Never before had he spoken publicly about his paralysis. Never before had he confessed to weariness.

He characterized the conference as a success, for it had made significant progress on its two principal goals: to defeat Germany speedily and to create a framework for postwar cooperation. To avoid alerting the Tokyo government, he said nothing about the Russian pledge to enter the war against Japan but maintained that the meeting had dealt only with the European theater. Though he knew better, he called the agreement at Yalta for free elections in Poland an "outstanding example of joint action by the three major Allied powers."

Departing from his text, he looked out at the members of Congress, all of them with memories of the League of Nations struggle, and said:

The conference in the Crimea was a turning point, I hope, in our history and therefore in the history of the world. There will soon be presented to the Senate of the United States and to the American people a great decision that will determine the fate of the United States and of the world for generations to come.... For the second time in the lives of most of us, this generation is face to face with the objective of preventing wars.... Twenty-five years ago, American fighting men looked to the statesmen of the world to finish the work of peace for which they fought and suffered. We failed them then. We cannot fail them again.

One month later, the president left Union Station for "the little White House" in Warm Springs, Georgia, for the thirty-ninth time, his hands trembling, his face ashen. For some days, warmed by the southern sun, he revived. But on April 12, 1945, his secretary recorded in his diary: "Today the great and final change. In the quiet beauty of the Georgia spring, like a thief in the night, came the day of the Lord. The immortal spirit no longer supported the failing flesh, and at 3:35 p.m. the President gave up the ghost." After far more years in office than any predecessor or any successor, Franklin Delano Roosevelt had died of a cerebral hemorrhage.

Bulletins announcing the shocking news of the death of Franklin Delano Roosevelt reverberated for thousands of miles beyond the little Georgia village—through the nation and around the globe. Millions of Americans—conspicuously the young men who had crossed the Elbe and were on the road toward the capture of Berlin or who were poised for the perilous assault on Japan's home islands—had never known another president, and the forces of the United Nations felt bereft. Banners on store windows across America displayed the message "Closed out of Reverence," and in London, stunned members of the centuries-old House of Commons convened, then immediately adjourned out of respect. FDR's death, said a newspaper in his adopted state of Georgia, "has cast a pall over the entire universe."

It had become commonplace through the dark years of the Great Depression and in the travail of war to speak of Roosevelt as a father figure, and many Americans truly did feel fatherless. Writing of the "stabbing pain of grief," the *Atlanta Journal* confessed that "we are so stricken and stunned by the loss of our beloved leader that we can hardly imagine what the future will be without him." They also sensed that they had been in the presence of greatness. The *New York Times* declared: "Men will thank God on their knees, a hundred years from now, that Franklin D. Roosevelt was in the White House."

Numbers of Americans did not hold him in such high esteem. Some had long thought of him as a man with neither principles nor ideas. Hoover had called him "a chameleon on plaid," and another critic had charged him with "blathering platitudes like a parson on vacation." Mencken had said that if Roosevelt "became convinced tomorrow that coming out for cannibalism would get him the votes he so sorely needs, he would begin fattening a missionary in the White House backyard come Wednesday." In an address to the Chicago Bar Association, a US senator had even likened FDR to the beast of the Apocalypse, "who set his slimy mark on everything."

Accused of being "a traitor to his class," he had especially aroused the ire of the well-to-do. In 1937, an American who had been vacationing in the Caribbean said, "During all the time I was gone, if anybody asked me if I wanted any news, my reply was always 'there is only one bit of news I want to hear and that is the death of Franklin D. Roosevelt. If he is not dead, you don't need to tell me anything else.'" It has been reported that "J. P. Morgan's family kept newspapers with pictures of Roosevelt out of his sight, and in one Connecticut country club . . . mention of his name was forbidden as a health measure against apoplexy." A few even countenanced violence. "I would shoot him!" a millionaire told a British correspondent stationed in America. The writer asked, Would he really? "Shooting's too good for him," the man answered. "I'd send him to the chair."

Without any of this extreme animus, historians, too, have noted Roosevelt's shortcomings. They have pointed out that the New Deal failed to bring the country out of the Great Depression, though they credit it with a marked improvement in economic conditions and an extraordinarily imaginative response to the plight of the unemployed. He has been faulted as well for sanctioning the internment of Japanese American citizens, and for not doing enough to save European Jews from Hitler's extermination chambers. Troublesome also was FDR's casual attitude toward veracity in the conduct of foreign affairs. In the spring of 1942, he said, "I am perfectly willing to mislead and tell untruths if it will help win the war." Some critics have accused Roosevelt of establishing an unconstrained plebiscitary presidency and have charged that he was much too fond of the prerogatives of office. Never did he relinquish power voluntarily. Only death cut short his reign.

Even scholars who greatly admire Roosevelt have found aspects of his character disturbing. As well-disposed a biographer as Arthur Schlesinger wrote that FDR, "though his better instinct generally won in the end, was a flawed, willful, and, with time, increasingly arbitrary man." Similarly, the historian Robert McElvaine, in a fair-minded and often approving assessment, has said that Roosevelt "did things in his personal and political life that were simply despicable," noting that in the 1940 campaign the president was not above urging that "way, way down the line" his campaign workers noise it about that his Republican opponent, Wendell Willkie, was carrying on an extramarital affair and that they should also spread the rumor that Mrs. Willkie had been paid to pretend that nothing was going on. He set dangerous precedents by installing a primitive taping system in the White House to record conversations and by ordering the FBI to wiretap not only his political opponents but even his own aides, including Harry Hopkins. The historian Patrick Renshaw has written of Roosevelt: "He lacked ... gravitas. Blind to art and deaf to music he was uninterested in literature or philosophy. ... He completely lacked the theological and philosophical dimension of Lincoln." Nonetheless, Renshaw concluded, "he was a model of what presidents should aspire to" and belongs "in the pantheon with Washington and Lincoln."

That is where a consensus of historians places him—among the only three presidents ranked "great," and in recent polls of scholars he has moved past Washington to be excelled only by Lincoln. Stated in another way, he is regarded as the most significant chief executive of the last century and a half. In May 1945, the Oxford don Herbert Nicholas wrote: "When Franklin Roosevelt died on April 12 he concluded a longer period of continuous office than any President of the United States or any British Minister since the Reform Bill. During these twelve crowded years, by political speech and ceremonial proclamation, by executive action and legislative direction, in his three roles of party leader, chief executive and titular head of state, he exercised a cumulative influence on the American public mind which for duration and intensity can hardly be paralleled in the history of modern democracies." Roosevelt, he concluded, "discovered in his office possibilities of leadership which even Lincoln had ignored."

"With Franklin Roosevelt's administration," the political scientist Fred Greenstein has written, "the presidency began to undergo not a shift but rather a metamorphosis." After serving in the White House of Lyndon Johnson, a domineering chief executive, Joseph Califano Jr. reached the same conclusion. "The foundations of the presidency for the final decades of the twentieth century," he asserted, "were set more in the terms of Franklin D. Roosevelt than in the terms of George Washington or any of his intervening successors.... The combination of domestic crisis... and global war focused ever-increasing power in the White House.... The presidency would never be the same again." FDR's "most dazzling successes were domestic and psychological," observed the novelist Saul Bellow. "It is not too much to say that another America was formed under his influence."

Roosevelt and the New Dealers altered the very nature of political discourse in the United States. Instead of debating the tariff, Americans discussed valley authorities, social welfare, and the rights of labor unions. "Mr. Roosevelt may have given the wrong answers to many of his problems," the *Economist* commented. "But he is at least the first President of modern America who has asked the right questions." Early in FDR's second term, the historian Charles Beard, often a caustic critic, wrote: "He has discussed in his messages and addresses more fundamental problems of American life than all other Presidents combined.... President Roosevelt has made a more profound impression upon the political, social, and economic life of America than any or all of his predecessors." At about the same time, a former US Supreme Court justice echoed that view. "Of course you have fallen into some errors—that is human," he wrote FDR, "but you have put a new face upon the social and political life of our country."

Architect of the New Deal, Roosevelt won further renown for his leadership of the antifascist alliance in World War II. "He overcame both his own and the nation's isolationist inclination to bring a united America into the coalition that saved the world from the danger of totalitarian conquest," the historian Robert Divine declared. "His role in insuring the downfall of Adolf Hitler is alone enough to earn him a respected place in history." Winston Churchill told the House of Commons: "Of Roosevelt...it must be said that had he not acted when he did, in the way he did, had he not...resolved to give aid to Britain and to Europe in the supreme crisis through which we have passed, a hideous fate might well have overwhelmed mankind and made its whole future for centuries sink into shame and ruin." For a legion of commentators, FDR's foreign policy melded with his achievements at home in bringing about a more humane social order. Sir Isaiah Berlin concluded: "What the Germans thought Hitler to be, Hitler, in fact, largely was, and what free men in Europe and America and in Asia and in Africa and in Australia, and wherever else the rudiments of political thought stirred at all, what all these felt Roosevelt to be, he in fact was. He was the greatest champion of democracy, the greatest champion of social progress, in the twentieth century."

He came to office at a time when America had turned its back on Europe and mustered an army smaller than that of a minor Balkan state; he left it not only a country about to become a member of the United Nations (with headquarters in Manhattan) but also one that was the locus of the Pentagon and the sole possessor of the atomic bomb. "When FDR died in 1945," the columnist George Will has written, "America was more supreme than Great Britain after Waterloo, than France of Louis XIV—than any power since the Roman Empire. And it had a central government commensurate with that role."

Roosevelt imprinted no less a mark on American politics, for he brought about the only long-lasting realignment of the twentieth century. Thanks to the strength of the FDR coalition, Republicans, in the half century after the Wall Street Crash, managed to win only two congressional elections. A decade after FDR died, a Chicago Democrat said, "Franklin Roosevelt was the greatest precinct captain we ever had. He elected everybody—governors, senators, mayors, sheriffs, aldermen." And he went on electing them. Although the Solid South did not survive FDR, Catholic devotion to the Democrats languished, and union power diminished, the urban–working-class–ethnic nexus of 1936 remained the core of Democratic strength. As late as 1980, a commentator reported that two authorities had "likened the demise of the FDR coalition to the death of theater in New York City. There have been decades of rhetoric about its death, but if you venture into Manhattan's theater district the lights are bright. So it is with the FDR coalition. For 47 months we hear about how it is breaking up, yet, on Election Day, presto, there it is again." Four years later, in its lead editorial on the 1984 election, the *New York Times* stated: "The old New Deal coalition, though 50 years old, remains very much alive. Look at the exit poll data on voter blocs and observe the very few among which Walter Mondale triumphed. He won the black vote, 90 percent to 9 . . . the unemployed, 68–31 . . . Jews, 66–32 . . . Hispanic voters, 65–35 . . . big-city residents, 62–36 . . . union members, 57–41." The chronicler of the Kennedy and Johnson elections Theodore White concluded, "All contemporary national politics descend from Franklin Roosevelt."

Franklin Delano Roosevelt cast a long shadow on the presidents who came after him—through all the rest of the twentieth century and into the twenty-first century. A generation after FDR departed Washington, the *Time-Life* correspondent Hugh Sidey wrote of a gathering to honor him: "You could stand on this Tuesday afternoon of 1967 and look out over the faces in the East Room of the White House and suddenly understand that Franklin Roosevelt still owned Washington. His ideas prevailed. His men endured." From the White House, he added, "you looked on down the Mall and saw the gray Federal buildings that stood there, and they were monuments to that amazing man."

Roosevelt crafted the template for how a modern chief executive was expected to perform. A political scientist duo has written that two centuries of a "tug of war" between conflicting conceptions—"a chief clerk president" and "a chief executive president"—ended with Roosevelt; "after FDR . . . every president was strong whether he was committed to the strong presidency or not." Each who entered the White House from 1945 on knew that on the one hundredth day of his tenure the media would be comparing—or, more likely, contrasting—his record to Roosevelt's, though his circumstances were very different: no domestic crisis approaching that of 1933, no prolonged global conflict remotely like World War II. In the 1980s, a *Sacramento Bee* writer expressed the sentiments of many others in saying, "Saturday will be the 100th birthday of FDR, a fact I am finding it hard to accept, for to me FDR is still The President, much more alive than any of the nine worthies—more or less—who have come after him." Roosevelt left his successors a rich legacy, but he proved an awfully tough act to follow.

5

Harry Truman

AFTER MORE THAN TWELVE YEARS of Franklin Delano Roosevelt in the White House, America found it hard to acknowledge that Harry Truman was president of the United States. When on his first morning in office a messenger sounded the traditional cry, "The President is coming out," and Truman emerged, a secretary, momentarily stunned, burst into tears, then explained, "I thought he meant *the President*—I mean President Roosevelt." Jonathan Daniels, who had worked for FDR, wrote of Truman's early weeks in the White House that, though his predecessor had departed, "it still seemed to be Roosevelt's desk and Roosevelt's room. It seemed to me, indeed, almost Roosevelt's sun which came in the wide south windows and touched Truman's thick glasses."

FDR remained an awesome presence. Five months after taking over, Truman was still writing Eleanor Roosevelt, "I never think of anyone as the President, but Mr. Roosevelt." Like Andrew Johnson, with whom he identified, Truman had the misfortune of following a larger-than-life figure, and, like Johnson too, he was accused, often unfairly, of departing from his predecessor's policies. Throughout his presidency, he heard the repeated plaintive query, "What would Roosevelt do if he were alive?" Truman himself often raised that question, especially at the beginning of his tenure. He started out, two columnists later noted, "by regularly telephoning his predecessor's widow to inquire anxiously 'what *he* would have done' about this or that great problem." The president, they said, "humbly consulted Mrs. Roosevelt as he might have consulted a medium."

Truman had difficulty accepting that he had been catapulted into the White House. "He did not visualize himself in the robes of greatness," said one commentator, "and he approached power with a disbelieving look." Unlike Theodore Roosevelt, he did not greet his elevation to the highest office in the land with exhilaration but regarded it as a cruel trick of fate. "Boys, if you ever pray, pray for me now," he told reporters. "I don't know whether you fellows ever had a load of hay fall on you. But when they told me yesterday what had happened I felt like the moon, the stars, and all the planets had fallen on me." Journalists and even members of his administration found it hard to accept his ascension. "It was difficult, unnatural to address this man as 'Mr. President,'" one correspondent later recalled. "So we skirted around the edges by prefacing our questions with the word 'Sir' or by not using any form of address at all." On the night Truman was sworn in, Secretary of Agriculture Claude Wickard entered in his diary: "I . . . resolved that I would be very careful when I addressed the new President to call him 'Mr. President' . . . but much to my surprise and somewhat to my disgust I shook hands with him and said, 'Harry, we want to help you all we can.'"

Little about this son of a mule swapper impressed the country as being of presidential caliber. A commentator in the *New Yorker* remarked: "You go to a men's shop to buy a pair of pajamas, President Truman waits on you. You go to have a tooth X-rayed, Truman takes the picture. You board a downtown bus, Truman is at the wheel." Similarly, reflecting on attitudes in an East Texas town, a writer observed: "One looked at Truman and saw not a President of Rooseveltian stature, but a man as ordinary as Mr. Bradbury, who ran the men's wear store in Marshall, or Sam Hall, the Harrison County judge. Imaginations would stretch, but not so far as to put either of these men in the White House. So why Truman?" Shriner, Moose, Elk, Lion, Eagle, deacon of the Second Baptist Church, graduate of the Kansas City Business School, failed haberdasher, Harry S. Truman appeared to be a hinterland Mr. Nobody. Symptomatically, his middle initial did not stand for anything. He was, and remained, the only twentieth-century president never to have spent a day in college. As a cog in Kansas City's Pendergast machine, he had been dismissed by the *St. Louis Post-Dispatch* as the "Ambassador . . . of the defunct principality of Pendergastia."

Truman conveyed little of the majesty of the office or of the comportment the nation expected of the head of state. The historian William Manchester later observed that "his customary air was that of an alert shopkeeper," and that his visitors, even the distinguished British foreign secretary, Anthony Eden, the future Earl of Avon, "were always referred to by the President as 'the customers.'" A widely circulated photograph showed him, only days before he became president, banging out a tune while atop the piano perched the sultry young actress Lauren Bacall, showing plenty of leg and more than a hint of thigh. In later years, on his vacations in Key West, cameras snapped him in loud Hawaiian shirts swinging an oversized cane as though strutting at the head of a mummers' parade.

Too frequently, he sounded off in a fashion that made people wince. He lowered himself in one speech by calling the syndicated columnist Drew Pearson an SOB, and when the *Washington Post*'s music critic published a harsh review of his daughter Margaret's debut concert in the capital as a coloratura soprano—saying that "she cannot sing with anything approaching professional finish," was "flat a good deal of the time," and "communicates almost nothing of the music she presents"— the president wrote him that if he ever got his hands on him, the reviewer would require "a new nose, a lot of beef steak for black eyes, and perhaps a supporter below!" (To an inquirer, he later rephrased his message as "If I could get my hands on him, I'd bust him in the jaw and kick his nuts out.") The letter was published, to the acute embarrassment of Truman's friends and family. The president's behavior, said the *Chicago Tribune*, called into question his "mental competence and emotional stability."

Yet this ill-tempered, lackluster provincial was to lead the nation through the treacherous postwar transition, embark upon extraordinary ventures in foreign affairs, write a new chapter in the saga of civil rights, and leave a larger legacy of new institutions in the executive branch than any other president. He also impressed some of the most critical observers with his acumen and his sturdy integrity. Two years after Truman left the White House, the Columbia University history professor Allan Nevins wrote: "What a cocky, decisive person he is, with an instinct for the right act—in major affairs—worth tons of formal education; and what a down-to-earth Missouri farmer outlook he kept through all his ascendancy. A unique figure in our political annals."

———

Truman took office at a precarious moment. In his tellingly titled memoir, *Present at the Creation*, Dean Acheson, who for a time served as secretary of state, was to call the challenge confronting the new president "just a bit less formidable than that described in the first chapter of Genesis." Truman, he said, had to figure out how to preserve freedom in half the world "without blowing the whole to pieces in the process." Though 9th Army tanks had crossed the Elbe and were nearing Berlin, the Chiefs of Staff expected that the war in Europe would go on for another six months. On Okinawa, US forces were engaged in the most terrible bloodletting of the war. Before it ended, the fighting there would cost nearly fifty thousand American casualties with the loss of eight hundred planes and thirty-six ships, a number of them resulting from suicidal attacks by kamikaze pilots. Conquest of Japan, the Joint Chiefs estimated, would require a year and a half more of death and destruction.

European chancelleries found it hard to comprehend why, at such a critical juncture, America was placing its fate in the hands of a man so transparently unqualified. His biographer Alonzo Hamby has written: "When he became president Truman had no experience in diplomacy, little travel abroad, and no record of consistent engagement with diplomatic issues while in the Senate.... Like many Americans, he found it difficult to conceive of foreign issues and leaders in non-American terms; ... Joseph Stalin reminded him of Tom Pendergast." As the sagacious journalist Richard Rovere observed, "It was a cruel time to put inexperience in power."

While vice president, Truman had been kept woefully ill informed. In the eighty-two days he served under Roosevelt, Truman recalled, "I don't think I saw him but twice...except at Cabinet meetings." He told his daughter, "He never did talk to me confidentially about the war, or about foreign affairs or what he had in mind for the peace after the war." During those months, Truman had not set foot in the War Room of the White House. He ascended to the presidency without having met the American ambassador to Russia, Averell Harriman, and did not even know his secretary of state, Edward Stettinius Jr. He had not been privy to the negotiations at Yalta, knew nothing about vexing issues such as the Polish boundaries, and was kept in the dark on the atomic bomb. When, at the close of the first cabinet meeting, Henry Stimson took him aside to inform him that the government had a secret weapon of "almost unbelievable destructive power" that Congress knew nothing about, the secretary of war spoke so guardedly that the new president did not grasp what he was being told. Not until two weeks had gone by did Stimson feel that it was safe to let the president of the United States know about the bomb. Winston Churchill later noted the "deadly hiatus...between the fading of President Roosevelt's strength and the growth of President Truman's grip of world problems." He concluded, "The indispensable political direction was lacking at the moment when it was most needed."

Night after night, Truman sat up all hours poring over State Department documents, badly straining his eyes in the effort to get caught up. Before long, Anthony Eden was expressing pleasure at Truman's "air of quiet confidence in himself," and Ambassador Harriman was finding the new president "astonishingly well prepared." But Truman found what he uncovered in the files disconcerting. Roosevelt, in his last message to Churchill, had said, "I would minimize the general Soviet problem as much as possible," but he had also stressed, "We must be firm," and in his final message to Stalin had spoken of "bitter resentment" of "vile misrepresentations" by the dictator's informants. Truman had started out hoping to nurture the wartime alliance with the USSR, but Harriman returned from Moscow to urge him not to indulge in any illusions. The Russians, he said, were engaged in a "barbarian invasion of Europe."

Only two weeks after becoming president, Truman, in a piece of political theater, made sure that the Russians understood that he was no pushover. When Stalin's chief lieutenant, Foreign Minister Vyacheslav Molotov, paid a courtesy call at the White House, Truman barked at him, even cursed him, on the USSR's failure to live up to its pledges for a freely elected government in Poland. Molotov turned ashen, and when he tried to justify Soviet policy, Truman cut him off curtly and sent him away. According to Truman's probably fanciful account of the exchange, Molotov told him, "I have never been talked to like that in my life," and the president retorted, "Carry out your agreements, and you won't get talked to like that." Those particular words may not have been spoken, but they convey the substance of Truman's castigation. He socked

Molotov with a "straight one-two to the jaw," he informed a former US envoy in Moscow. He then asked, "Did I do right?"

As his plaintive question suggested, Truman had no desire to feud with Moscow. Though most of his advisers urged him to take a tough line on Poland, he had some sympathy with Stimson's view that the Russians "perhaps were being more realistic than we in regard to their own security," and with General Marshall's conviction that Balkan issues should yield to the priority of persuading the USSR to enter the war promptly against Japan. Moreover, he thought it essential that the Soviet Union become a member of the United Nations. "The truth of the matter was that without Russia there would not be much of a world organization," he said. In his dealings with the Russians, Truman, the historian John Gaddis has written, seemed more hostile than he actually was because he departed from "the graceful ambiguities of FDR."

To dissuade Stalin from thinking that "we're ganging up on him," Truman sent Harry Hopkins to Moscow in May to say that America was not greatly concerned about the welfare of countries in the Soviet sphere. He instructed his envoy: "Poland, Rumania, Bulgaria, Czechoslovakia, Austria, Yugo-Slavia, Latvia, Lithuania, Estonia, et al make no difference to US interests." Poland ought to have a "free election," he wanted Stalin to understand, but no freer than the boss of a city machine in America would permit. Moreover, "Uncle Joe should make some sort of gesture—whether he means it or not—to keep it before our public that he intends to keep his word." In short, he was asking Stalin to give him a bit of cover for a policy of conciliation and not to embarrass him or force his hand.

Truman placed much of the hope for the future in the creation of a world organization where countries could iron out differences. His first big decision had been to announce that the founding conference of the United Nations would not be postponed by Roosevelt's death but would meet later that month in San Francisco on schedule. This was a matter he cared deeply about. Ever since high school, he had carried in his wallet handwritten lines from Tennyson's "Locksley Hall":

> Till the war drums throbbed no longer, and the
> battle flags were furled
> In the Parliament of Man, the Federation of the World.

On April 25, 1945, the day that American and Russian troops embraced at the Elbe, the conference opened at San Francisco's elegant Opera House, with the war-wounded in red hospital robes looking down from the balcony. For nine weeks, while the fighting in the Pacific raged on, eight hundred delegates shaped the contours of the world that would emerge from the war. Four days after the meeting convened, Hitler took his life in a subterranean bunker in Berlin; and on May 7, while delegates were meeting, the Third Reich surrendered unconditionally. The United States, which had rejected German overtures for a separate peace that would exclude the Russians, proved equally obliging about the postwar settlement. At Yalta, the Big Three had drawn the boundaries of postwar occupation zones in Germany, but when the war ended, American forces had pushed 125 miles east of its zone. Churchill kept cabling Truman to keep the army there, but in June the president told him that, to signal Moscow his good faith, he was going to adhere to the agreement Roosevelt had signed and withdraw the troops. That same month, he wrote in his diary that the Russians had "always been our friends and I can't see why they shouldn't always be." Furthermore, so powerfully had sentiment in America moved in an internationalist direction that, in sharp contrast to 1919, the United States became the first major power to ratify the charter of the United Nations, which found a permanent home in New York City.

In July, Truman sailed to Europe for a meeting in Potsdam of the Big Three victors at a palatial country retreat that had been the estate of Crown Prince Wilhelm of Hohenzollern. It was a big leap for a onetime Missouri farm boy to be sharing a council table with Joseph Stalin and Winston Churchill (and then Clement Attlee after Labour replaced the Tories), but the president gave a good account of himself. By keeping lines of discussion taut, Truman made a favorable impression on diplomats who had arrived in the German city as doubters. The British foreign secretary, Alexander Cadogan, wrote his wife that, while Churchill was "woolly and verbose," Truman was crisp and decisive. The conference achieved little, but Truman got what he came for. Stalin told the president that he would launch an invasion of Japan in August. "We'll end the war a year sooner now," Truman wrote gleefully to his wife, "and think of the kids who won't be killed! That's the important thing."

Nothing, it seemed, could match that momentous development in significance, but a coded message received in Potsdam dwarfed it. In the predawn hours of July 16 at a remote desert site in Alamogordo, New Mexico, the president learned, awestricken scientists had witnessed the explosion of the world's first atomic bomb, sending a blinding ball of fire into the empyrean, where it climaxed in a mushroom cloud. For the director of the project, Robert Oppenheimer, two passages in the *Bhagavad Gita* came to mind: "If the radiance of a thousand suns were to burst into the sky, that would be the splendor of the Mighty One," and "I am become Death, the shatterer of worlds." On hearing the news in Potsdam, Churchill said, "This is the Second Coming, in wrath." Truman used similar imagery in writing in his diary, "It may be the fire destruction prophesied in the Euphrates Valley era, after Noah and his fabulous ark." He thought the bomb "the most terrible thing ever discovered," and in another entry said: "I hope for some sort of peace—but I fear the machines are ahead of mortals. ... We are only termites on a planet and maybe when we bore too deeply into the planet there'll [be] a reckoning—who knows?"

On July 26, in accordance with Stimson's conviction that Japan be given "a last-chance warning," Truman joined with Churchill and the Chinese president, Chiang Kai-shek, to issue the Potsdam Declaration demanding unconditional surrender. "The alternative for Japan," it declared, "is prompt and utter destruction." The words, though harsh, did not convey the immensity of the atomic bomb. Nor did the declaration offer the inducement of assuring the Japanese that they might retain their emperor. Even if the communication had, it is highly unlikely that the warlords in Tokyo would have capitulated. When they treated the Potsdam Declaration with contempt, Truman gave the go-ahead for dropping atomic bombs on Japanese cities.

No other action of the Truman presidency has drawn so much opprobrium. How, in good conscience, it has been asked, could Harry Truman order the unleashing of bombs that would take the lives of so many innocent people, many of them victims of hideous slow deaths from radiation? It is a question that merits sober consideration, but it should be noted that Truman did not act impulsively. Both an advisory committee that included the president of Harvard and a panel of prominent physicists had recommended that the bomb be "used against Japan as soon as possible," that it target "war plants surrounded by workers' homes," and that "it should be used without warning." But might not its terrible power have been demonstrated to the Japanese by dropping it on an uninhabited island? Oppenheimer told him, "We can propose no technical demonstration likely to bring an end to the war; we see no acceptable alternatives to direct military use." To Truman and to other policymakers, the "ultimate weapon" did not seem materially different from conventional ones. Firebombing of Dresden and Tokyo took more lives than the two atomic bombs were to do. But is it not true that there was no need for an atomic bomb because Japan was badly beaten and ready to admit defeat? Since Americans had broken the Japanese code long before, they could read messages sent by the foreign minister in Tokyo: Japan had no intention to surrender.

One question looms larger than any other: Why, instead of employing the A-bomb, did not Truman simply continue the Pacific war and achieve victory by a blockade or invasion of Japan? Attempting to starve out the Japanese by a blockade would have caused awful suffering and would still not have eliminated the need for an invasion. With the dreadful loss of life caused by the suicidal resistance on Okinawa fresh in mind, Stimson was told that an invasion could cost more than a million American casualties and an incalculable number of Japanese deaths. Given this prospect, Truman's biographer David McCullough has asked, "How could a President...answer to the American people if...after the blood-bath of an invasion of Japan, it became known that a weapon sufficient to end the war had been available by midsummer and was not used?"

On August 6, Truman announced the shocking news: an atomic bomb, "harnessing...the basic power of the universe," had been dropped on Hiroshima. He warned: "We are now prepared to obliterate more rapidly and completely every productive enterprise the Japanese have.... If they do not now accept our terms they may expect a rain of ruin from the air, the like of which has never before been seen on this earth." Hiroshima suffered 140,000 deaths; three days later, a second atomic bomb took 74,000 more lives in Nagasaki.

Even after the bombs fell and the Russians entered the war, Japanese army and navy leaders wanted to go on fighting. It required unprecedented intervention by Emperor Hirohito, the Son of Heaven, to bring them around. The Japanese agreement to surrender carried the proviso that the emperor continue to be their sovereign. Most Americans, viewing the emperor as the symbol of Japanese savagery, overwhelmingly opposed letting him stay (one-third wanted him executed), but Truman went along. On September 2, capitulation ceremonies took place aboard the USS *Missouri*. "We have had our last chance," MacArthur declared from the deck of the ship. "If we do not devise some greater and more equitable system, Armageddon will be at our door."

Truman never sought to duck responsibility for his deeds. "The final decision of where and when to use the atomic bomb was up to me," he said later. "Let there be no mistake about it." A short while after Hiroshima and Nagasaki, he reflected, "It occurred to me that a quarter of a million of the flower of our young manhood were worth a couple of Japanese cities, and I still think they were and are." Churchill shared this view. He regarded the advent of the atomic bomb as "a miracle of deliverance," for it averted "a vast, indefinite butchery." The final word belongs to one of Truman's aides, George Elsey. "It's all well and good to come along later and say the bomb was a horrible thing," he commented subsequently. "The whole goddamn war was a horrible thing."

———————

Harry Truman stepped into the postwar domestic arena at full stride. Only four days after the surrender rituals on the *Missouri*, he fired off a twenty-one-point message to Congress that he had roughed out on the high seas while returning from Potsdam. In June, he had told his wife: "Well, I'm getting organized now. It won't be long until I can sit back and study the whole picture and tell 'em what is to be done in each department. When things come to that stage there'll be no more to this job than there was to running Jackson County and not any more worry." Little did he imagine how intractable the task of managing the country in peacetime was to be. "The storm of the war had passed," commented the journalist Robert Donovan. "But the turbulence in its wake, occasioned by the toils of simultaneously demobilizing the armed forces and reconverting the economy from wartime to peacetime production, all but capsized the Truman administration."

Both abroad and at home, Americans vented their impatience with any prolongation of the crisis atmosphere. At a number of points around the globe, GIs demanding to be discharged rioted. In Manila, more than two thousand soldiers besieged the headquarters of the commanding general, and in Paris, thousands more marched four abreast down the Champs-Élysées chanting, "We want to go home." As he prepared to testify before the House Military Affairs Committee, General Eisenhower was ambushed by angry women from "Bring Back Daddy Clubs," and servicemen's wives inundated congressmen with baby shoes carrying tags pleading to have fathers in uniform sent home right away. "On V-J afternoon and night," noted one journalist, "crowds were shouting, dancing, laughing, and crying in front of the White House. In many of the economic control offices in the slum area, men who had been clamped down at their desks worrying over regulations kissed their secretaries and tore up mimeographed sheets of orders. Thank God, it was all over."

On the day that Americans celebrated the end of the fighting, the federal government canceled one hundred thousand contracts. Before the week was out, Springfield Arsenal had fired every employee. It seemed inconceivable that an economy which only three years earlier had not pulled all the way out of the Great Depression—a downturn lasting thirteen years—was going to be resilient enough to provide work for all those abruptly discharged from war plants, plus twelve million more about to enter the job market from the armed services. No less worrisome was the danger that consumers, their wallets bulging, might create runaway inflation. With assembly lines only beginning to shift to civilian production of automobiles and other products for which buyers were clamoring, many too many dollars pressed on many too few goods.

The country made unreasonable demands on the new president. It required him not only to stoke production but also to hold prices down and to do so while getting rid of government controls. As the historian Barton Bernstein has pointed out, "Whereas the politics of depression... allowed the Roosevelt Administration, by bestowing benefits, to court interest groups and contribute to an economic upturn, the politics of inflation required a responsible government like Truman's to curb wages, prices, and profits and to deny...growing expectations." Furthermore, unlike Roosevelt, he could not appeal for sacrifice to the cause of winning the war. By the end of 1945, Truman was already remarking that in saying war was hell, General Sherman misspoke. "I'm telling you," he said, "I find peace is hell."

Nothing would ease Truman's travail more than the sound of factory whistles calling men and women to work to manufacture products in demand, but organized labor came out of the war determined to secure a fair share of swollen profits, even if it meant shutting down assembly lines in order to coerce management. Truman had long enjoyed good relations with unions, and he did not doubt that they had legitimate aspirations, but there were limits to his empathy. He had a shopkeeper's aversion to labor militancy, and he loathed John L. Lewis. Truman told one of his cabinet officers that Lewis and Molotov were the "principal contenders for top rating as walking images of Satan." He did not want to crack down on unions, which were the most important components of the Democratic coalition, but he had no intention of permitting labor strife to paralyze essential industries.

In the first year after the war, strikes consumed more than one hundred million man-days. In November 1945, autoworkers closed down General Motors, and in January 1946, while the four-month-long GM strike went on, eight hundred thousand steelworkers banked their furnaces. Steel production did not resume for eighty days. The president responded to the multitude of shutdowns by seizing scores of oil refineries and meat-packing plants, the Great Lakes Towing Company, and ninety-one tugboats—all to no effect in slowing the pace of strikes. Furthermore, settling the auto and steel strikes required whopping wage boosts that blew a large hole in the government's dike against inflation, especially after steel companies, to compensate for rising labor costs, were allowed to jack up prices.

Thoroughly exasperated, the president scrawled a memo to himself setting down what he should say to union officials after he summoned them to the White House:

> Tell them that patience is exhausted. Declare an emergency—call out troops. Start industry and put anyone to work who wants to go to work.
> If any leader interferes, court martial him.
> Lewis ought to have been shot in 1942, but Franklin didn't have the guts to do it.

(Plagued by troubles abroad as well, Truman added: "Adjourn Congress and run the country. Get plenty of Atomic Bombs on hand—drop one on Stalin, put the United Nations to work, and eventually set up a free world.")

Lewis put the president's resolve to a stern test when, on April 1, 1946, he led four hundred thousand miners out of the pits. Denied coal, Chrysler and Ford plants closed, and, as fuel supplies dwindled, cities dimmed their lights. On May 21, the president issued an executive order taking over the mines. In tackling Lewis, he was joining combat with a man most Americans regarded as a villain. When he had shut down the mines during World War II, *Stars and Stripes* said, "Speaking for the American soldier—John L. Lewis, damn your coal-black soul." But Truman found that without Lewis's authorization miners would not return, and the president wound up giving the truculent UMW leader most of what he demanded.

At the same moment that he was grappling with Lewis, Truman had to deal with a much graver crisis: the threat of the greatest railroad strike in the country's history. On May 15, he called officials of the twenty railway brotherhoods to his office. All but two said they were willing to settle for the substantial wage rise offered them. The two who held fast to their determination to strike for more, however, were much the most powerful: A. F. Whitney, president of the Brotherhood of Railroad Trainmen, and Alvanley Johnston, who headed the Brotherhood of Locomotive Engineers. Truman owed these two a lot because when he was facing almost certain defeat in his bid for reelection to the Senate in 1940, they had come up with the cash to pull him through. But recognition of that debt did not impede him. Fixing them with an icy stare, he said, "If you think I'm going to sit here and let you tie up the whole country, you're crazy as hell."

The rail strike came close to causing chaos. Trains ground to a halt, even in the middle of a desert. The strike marooned more than ninety thousand passengers, including war brides on their way west and members of the world-renowned Philadelphia Symphony Orchestra en route to San Francisco. Ringling Brothers could not keep its circus engagements; major league baseball clubs had to tear up their schedules; commuters in New York and Chicago could not reach their homes in the suburbs. Twenty-five thousand freight cars, many laden with perishable food, stopped dead on the tracks. In Europe, hundreds of thousands faced starvation when shipments from the American hinterland could not reach Atlantic ports. A blizzard of telegrams to the White House carried messages such as IS THE PRESENT INCUMBENT IMPOTENT IN THE RAILROAD STRIKE? IF SO HE SHOULD RESIGN.

Hopping mad, Truman ordered a government takeover of the railroads, then handed his press secretary, Charlie Ross, the text of what he planned to say in a nationwide radio address that evening. Scribbled on a dozen pages of a lined tablet, it accused Lewis of "sabotage" for calling "two strikes in war time to satisfy his ego . . . that were worse than bullets in the backs of our soldiers." After the war, he went on, "all" the union leaders "lied" to him. Instead of cooperating with him as they had promised, they had created work stoppages, and "a weak-kneed Congress didn't have the intestinal fortitude" to halt them because they were intimidated by "Mr. Murray and his communist friends." (In fact, Philip Murray, who headed the steelworkers' union, was a staunch anti-Communist.) "Every single one of the strikers and their demigog [sic] leaders have been living in luxury, working when they pleased and drawing from four to forty times the pay of a fighting soldier," he charged. In the most inflammatory segment of his jeremiad, he concluded:

> Now I want you men who are my comrades in arms, you men who fought the battles to save the nation just as I did 25 years ago, to come with me and eliminate the Lewises, the Whitneys and the Johnstons; the communist Bridges [head of the longshoremen's union] and the Russian Senators and Representatives and really make this a government of, by and for the people. . . .
> Let's give the country back to the people. Let's put transportation and production back to work, hang a few traitors. . . .
> Come on boys, let's do the job.

Distressed by the lynch-mob implications of the message, Ross, a longtime friend, persuaded the president to revamp the document, but neither he nor anyone else could deter Truman from drastic action. Consulting no one, he informed his cabinet grimly of the course on which he was about to embark—to draft strikers into the army. No president had ever advocated anything so rash before. When his conservative attorney general questioned the constitutionality of the action, Truman retorted, "We'll draft 'em first and think about the law later."

In one of the most dramatic episodes of the century, Truman appeared before a joint session of Congress to ask for a law "to authorize the President to draft into the Armed Forces of the United States all workers who are on strike against their Government." The chamber erupted in raucous approval. At that moment, as if on stage cue, Truman read aloud from a slip of paper he had just been handed, "Word has just been received that the railroad strike has been settled, on terms proposed by the President!" Both sides of the aisle rose to their feet to applaud.

Despite his victory, he asked Congress for standby authority to draft strikers in case of a future emergency. That evening, after less than two hours of discussion, the House whipped the legislation through, 306–13. The Senate, though, raised a roadblock. He would abandon his seat in the Senate before he would vote for such a bill, said the leftish liberal Florida Democrat Claude Pepper. Much more significant was the opposition of Robert Taft. Regarded by unions as their most powerful foe, the Ohio Republican declared that Truman's demand "offends not only the Constitution, but every basic principle for which the American republic was established. Strikes cannot be prohibited without interfering with the basic freedom essential to our form of government." Administration senators were forced to concede that if workers did not return to their jobs, they could be court-martialed, even shot. So the ultimate penalty, a Republican senator pointed out, was "death or penitentiary." The Senate voted down the measure, 70–13.

His labor policies cost Truman support at both ends of the political spectrum. The national secretary of the CIO Political Action Committee took down the photograph of the president and himself from the wall in his office and dropped it into a wastebasket. "Labor," he announced, "is through with Truman." Whitney said he would spend every penny of the $47 million in his brotherhood's treasury to defeat the president in 1948. In a mean shot at Truman's background, he added, "You can't make a president out of a ribbon clerk." At the same time that labor rallies were branding him the nation's "No. 1 Strikebreaker," Truman antagonized business by vetoing a bill restricting unions that was considerably milder than the legislation to draft strikers he had recommended. He did so by making a valid distinction between a temporary measure in an emergency and a permanent one, but his action reinforced the impression that he vacillated.

Five weeks after the railroad melodrama, Truman faced a showdown in his struggle to maintain price ceilings set by one of FDR's wartime agencies, the Office of Price Administration. Consumer discontent with food shortages and rising grocery bills was boiling. "The fight over OPA," reported the *New York Times*, "has reached proportions of bitterness, stridency, and obfuscation which have not been matched in years." In Denver, thwarted housewives hijacked a bread delivery truck. Three days before the OPA's authority was to expire on July 1, 1946, Congress passed a bill ending many price controls and requiring rapid abandonment of others. Truman, refusing to give in, vetoed the measure, although that decision meant that there would be no lid at all. In the next two weeks, prices jumped more than in the previous three years.

On July 25, Truman signed a new bill, only slightly better than the one he had turned down, and in late August the government imposed price ceilings on selected items—notably meat. In retaliation, stockmen held back their cattle. Nine out of ten butcher shops in New York City closed, a pattern repeated across the land. By early October, with midterm elections only a month away, a frenzy over the meat shortage engulfed the country. The press harped on "famine," though people were well fed. The meat shortage resulted from a strike of cattlemen, but it was the president who felt the lash of public resentment. "A housewife who cannot get hamburger," remarked one commentator, "is more dangerous than Medea wronged." The *New York Herald Tribune* chose to report the end of a Caribbean cruise with the headline STELLA POLARIS IN, 106 BID MEAT GLUM FAREWELL, and a *New York Times* headline read QUEENS RESTAURATEUR, WORRIED OVER MEAT, DIVES OFF BROOKLYN BRIDGE.

In mid-October Truman put together a message to the American people that he never sent but that expressed how frustrated and angry he felt:

> You've deserted your president for a mess of pottage, a piece of beef— a side of bacon.... If you the people insist on following Mammon instead of Almighty God—your President can't stop you all by himself....
>
> I can no longer enforce a law you won't support.... You've gone over to the powers of selfishness and greed.

Therefore I am releasing the controls on meat and will proceed to release all other controls.

He wound up: "Tell 'em what will happen and quit."

Truman did not release that screed, but he did run up the white flag. On October 14, realizing that he was licked, he ended price controls on meat. Beef reappeared at the butcher's counter, but at shocking prices. Once again, Truman got the blame. A New York newspaper ran this headline:

PRICES SOAR, BUYERS SORE
STEERS JUMP OVER THE MOON

Truman's approval rating, which had peaked at 87 percent, plunged to 32 percent.

In the midterm campaign that autumn, Republicans took advantage of the president's fall from grace. They jeered at "Horsemeat Harry," circulated the taunt "Don't shoot the piano player—he's doing the best he can," and highlighted the apothegm "To err is Truman." Sound trucks cruised streets near groceries blaring the message "Ladies, if you want meat, vote Republican." So deeply had Truman's reputation sunk that the Democratic national chairman told the president to lie low, and the party dusted off recordings of Roosevelt's voice to inspire the faithful.

No one summed up the outcome more succinctly than Truman's daughter, Margaret, in recounting the November day after the 1946 elections: "My father awoke aboard his special train, en route to Washington, and discovered that he had a bad cold and a Republican Congress." In ending the sixteen-year reign of the Democrats, the Republicans ran up a six-seat advantage in the Senate, where Joseph McCarthy of Wisconsin arrived, and a fifty-eight-seat dominance in the House, including, among the GOP freshmen, Richard Nixon of California. (One of the very few Democratic newcomers was Representative John F. Kennedy of Massachusetts.) In capturing 75 percent of House seats outside the South, the GOP wiped out entire Democratic delegations in Connecticut and Wisconsin. So massive was the Republican rout that when a national poll was taken after the election, only 8 percent of respondents thought that the next president would be a Democrat, with the possibility that Truman might serve another term out of the question.

The Arkansas Democrat Senator J. William Fulbright urged Truman to name a Republican as secretary of state, then resign from office, like a British prime minister who had lost a vote of confidence in a general election. In that fashion, Republicans could take over the White House without delay. (In this period, the secretary of state was next in line of succession when there was no vice president.) That proposition won the endorsement of the liberal *Chicago Sun* and of the foremost Democratic newspaper in the South, the *Atlanta Constitution*. Truman treated it with contempt. Ever thereafter, he referred to its author as "Senator Halfbright." Fulbright, whose proposition derived from his time at Oxford as a Rhodes Scholar, would have benefited from study of the Constitution at a land grant college, the president said. It was a sassy remark, but, in fact, Truman was crushed by the election downfall. "To be president of the United States," he reflected, "is to be lonely, very lonely.... Melancholy goes with the job."

Engrossed in the paroxysms of reconversion, Truman gave only fleeting attention to foreign affairs in the year and a half following V-J Day, and when he did, he sent mixed signals. He said of the Russians that he could see "no reason why we should not welcome their friendship and give ours to them," and when visitors dropped in at the White House, he called to their attention a miniature plow on his desk that replaced the tiny cannon once there. But the boorish behavior of Soviet officials at meetings of foreign ministers and worrisome evidence of their designs on the Dardanelles and the eastern Mediterranean made him more aggressive. At one point, the president, apparently unaware of the contradiction in his thoughts, summed up his approach by stating, "I want peace and I'm willing to fight for it."

Truman had a difficult time impressing his views on his secretary of state. He had appointed his former Senate colleague James F. Byrnes to that position in 1945, despite the South Carolinian's scant experience in and little aptitude for diplomacy. With an inflated sense of his own importance, Byrnes ignored the State Department and refused Truman even the courtesy of reports on meetings abroad with the Russians.

Certain that his role as "Assistant President" during World War II had entitled him to the vice presidential nomination in 1944, he viewed Truman as usurper of his rightful place in the White House. Byrnes, the historian Robert Ferrell has stated, looked upon Truman as "an accident of history and not a very good accident at that." Truman found it necessary to tell Byrnes forcefully in January 1946 that he was not going "to forego the President's prerogative to make the final decision." In his memoirs, Truman set down: "I read him the riot act. A Secretary of State should never have the illusion that he is President of the United States."

Byrnes got a dressing down not only for his arrogance but also because of his performance. Truman could find no evidence of concessions from the Kremlin that Byrnes claimed he had been able to wheedle, and some in the president's circle even regarded the secretary of state as an appeaser. "Unless Russia is faced with an iron fist and strong language another war is in the making," Truman admonished him. "Only one language do they understand, 'How many divisions have you?' I do not think we should play compromise any longer.... I'm tired babying the Soviets."

Secretary Byrnes had especially provoked Truman by failing to push hard on Iran. During World War II, the Allies occupying that oil-rich country had agreed to pull out shortly after the Axis was defeated. The British and the Americans withdrew, but Moscow aroused alarm by refusing to honor its pledge and by setting up pro-Soviet puppet regimes in the northern Iranian provinces of Azerbaijan and Kurdistan. In the first serious confrontation of the postwar era, the United States brought severe pressure on the USSR to evacuate, and the Russians buckled. The retreat may have owed more to adroit maneuvering by the Iranians than to American initiatives, but Truman and his aides concluded that success had been brought about by their "get tough" stance.

Two speeches further polarized the world powers. In February 1946, Stalin gave a major address in Moscow saying that war between capitalism and communism was inevitable. Hence, the Kremlin announced, it intended to triple output of munitions. In the very next month, Winston Churchill struck back—in a talk delivered in Truman's home state. Since he was accompanied by the president, his words appeared to express the sentiments of the United States as well as Great Britain. Speaking in the gymnasium of Westminster College in Fulton, Missouri, the former prime minister declared: "From Stettin in the Baltic to Trieste in the Adriatic, an *iron curtain* has descended across the continent. Behind that line lie all the capitals of the ancient states of central and eastern Europe." To block Soviet expansion, he called for "full military collaboration between Great Britain and the US." Nothing did the Russians admire "so much as strength," he said, "and there is nothing for which they have less respect than...military weakness."

Many Americans found Churchill's approach disturbing. Though irritated by the Russians, they were not yet willing to acknowledge that the wartime alliance with the defenders of Stalingrad had disintegrated and that the world had divided into two irreconcilable halves. "To follow the standard raised by this great but blinded aristocrat," said the *Chicago Sun*, "would be to march to the world's most ghastly war." Truman, after reading the text of the speech, had told Churchill that it would "do nothing but good." But when a storm of criticism descended on Churchill for risking a detonation of World War III, the president denied that he had known what the British leader was going to say. He could not gloss over the reality of polarization, however. "Let us not be deceived," Bernard Baruch declared. "Today we are in the midst of a *cold war*."

This intensification of animosity between the West and the USSR especially disconcerted the one man Truman believed he could least afford to lose: his secretary of commerce, Henry Wallace. Like Byrnes, Wallace thought he should have been FDR's successor—and with better reason, for he had been dislodged from the vice presidency to make way for Truman. The president knew, too, that for liberals, Wallace was the tribune of "the century of the common man." But Wallace became agitated when, on September 6, 1946, in Stuttgart, Byrnes, newly won over to get-tough tactics, issued a stern warning to the Russians to respect Germany's territorial integrity.

Six days later, a left-wing rally at Madison Square Garden featured a speech by Wallace on US behavior in Europe. When, before taking off for New York, he read aloud at the White House the sentence "I am neither anti-British nor pro-British, neither anti-Russian nor pro-Russian," the president burst out, "By God, Henry, that is our foreign policy!" Truman did not read the document carefully, and at a press conference on the afternoon before the event, he dug himself into a hole. Having seen an advance copy of the address, which Wallace claimed Truman endorsed, a reporter asked the president if he approved just the paragraph about Britain or the whole speech. All of it, Truman replied dismissively. Disbelieving, another correspondent inquired whether what Wallace was about to say was in line with Byrnes's remarks in Stuttgart. "They are exactly in line," the president snapped.

That evening, in a blunt attack on Byrnes, Wallace told the raucous Madison Square Garden crowd: "'Getting tough' never brought anything real or lasting—whether for schoolyard bullies or businessmen or world powers." Rebuking Churchill's appeal for an Anglo-American alliance, he declared that the United States could "get co-operation once Russia understands that our primary objective is neither saving the British empire nor purchasing oil in the Near East with the lives of American soldiers." He added, "On our part, we should recognize that we have no more business in the *political* affairs of Eastern Europe than Russia has in the *political* affairs of Latin America." When the partisan crowd booed even mild disagreement with Russian policy, Wallace deleted further references critical of the Soviet Union, while interpolating, "The danger of war is much less from communism than it is from imperialism—whether it be of the United States or England."

Still reluctant to part with the last FDR legatee in his cabinet, Truman hoped to work out a compromise that would silence Wallace for the moment but retain him. Byrnes, though, was implacable. From Paris, he cabled the president, "The world today is in doubt not only as to American foreign policy, but as to *your* foreign policy." Over a course of fifteen months, he said, "we did a fine job convincing the world that it was a permanent policy upon which the world could rely. Wallace destroyed it in a day." He told the president bluntly that "if it is not completely clear in your own mind that Mr. Wallace should be asked to refrain from criticizing the foreign policy of the United States while he is a member of your Cabinet, I must ask you to accept my resignation immediately." The Republican architect of the bipartisan foreign policy, Senator Vandenberg, who was in Paris with Byrnes, announced, "We can only cooperate with one Secretary of State at a time." An unrepentant Wallace sealed his fate by saying, "I shall within the near future speak on this subject again."

That statement drove Truman over the edge. He scrawled a note to Wallace laced with profanity. Shocked, Wallace phoned Charlie Ross to say that the letter was so rabid it should not be lodged in the National Archives. Ross, once again interceding to spare the president, burned it. Its contents may be surmised from an entry about Wallace in Truman's diary:

> He is a pacifist 100 percent. He wants us to disband our armed forces, give Russia our atomic secrets and trust a bunch of adventurers in the Kremlin Politbureau. I do not understand a "dreamer" like that. The German-American Bund under Fritz Kuhn was not half so dangerous. The Reds, phonies and the "parlor pinks" seem to be banded together and are becoming a national danger.
>
> I am afraid they are a sabotage front for Uncle Joe Stalin.

On the morning of September 20, Truman, using less objectionable language, told Wallace that he had been fired.

Truman sensed that he could not have handled the situation more poorly, but he found that hard to admit. He made matters much worse for himself by denying that he had approved the text of Wallace's speech in advance, a statement that *Time* branded "a clumsy lie." He was miserable. When Ross, seeking to console him, said that in discharging Wallace, he had demonstrated that he would rather be right than president, Truman responded, "I would rather be *anything* than president." In a memo to himself, he acknowledged, "Wallace affair is very embarrassing," then added lamely that "there were one or two things" in the speech "which I thought were a little wild but I did not interpret them as contrary to the general policy." Only to his mother would the cocky Truman confess, "Never was there such a mess and it is partly my making." Both abroad and at home in late 1946, Truman gave the impression that he had lost the capacity to lead and would be a pushover for the brassy Republicans when the 80th Congress convened in January.

In the aftermath of the 1946 smashup, Truman resembled no one so much as a Chinese emperor who has lost his mandate from Heaven. Conservatives disdained him, and liberals thought him a sorry comedown from FDR. Not long after the election, a prominent liberal said of Truman: "I look at him, and I say to myself, 'Yes, he is in Roosevelt's chair, yes he is, yes he is.' And then I say, 'Oh, no, no, my God, it's impossible.'" Clearly, it seemed, Truman's days in the White House were numbered. "The President," pontificated *United States News*, "is a one-termer."

Publicists and politicians paid too little heed to how much authority resides in the presidency even in the most adverse circumstances, and they underestimated the resourcefulness of Harry Truman. He retained the prerogative of policy initiatives; he alone made appointments to high office, though with the consent of the Senate; he was, if not as the Supreme Court had stated the sole organ of foreign affairs, the principal architect; and he could make full use of the veto, which during his tenure he did 250 times. Truman knew that the incoming 80th Congress would target him, but he, in turn, could target it. Feistier than ever, he concluded, after a momentary bout of depression, that the election of a Republican Congress was liberating. "I'm doing as I damn please for the next two years," he said, "and to hell with all of them."

Even before the new Congress met, Truman demonstrated that he was not going to sound retreat—by once again taking on John L. Lewis. Capriciously, in repudiation of the highly favorable contract he had extorted in the spring, the United Mine Workers chieftain called his men out again shortly after the November elections when the president refused to cave in to a new demand. With boundless conviction of his indispensability, Lewis had decided to flaunt his power by deliberately picking a fight not with the coal barons but with the US government, which still controlled the mines.

Truman struck back by initiating legal action against Lewis. On December 3, 1946, a federal judge held Lewis and his union in contempt of court. He fined Lewis $10,000 and the UMW the monster sum of $3,500,000 (a figure later reduced), as well as a quarter of a million dollars more each day the walkout continued. Unable to withstand the combined force of the executive branch and the judiciary, Lewis gave in. To avoid depleting the union treasury, he ordered the miners to return to the coalfields. Lewis, the president wrote in his diary, was "as yellow as a dog pound pup." Proud of having "whipped a damned traitor," Truman experienced a surge of confidence in the victory he had won for himself and for the presidency. "I can tell you, there was a big difference in the Old Man from then on," his young aide Clark Clifford later said.

Republicans also improved Truman's chances for a comeback by misreading the election returns. They believed that the American people in November 1946 were ratifying their desire to eradicate the liberal programs of the past two decades. But a poll conducted by the business magazine *Fortune* revealed that, far from signaling a revolt against federal intervention, the "hamburger election" was only a transient tantrum and that those who switched to the Republicans in 1946 were actually more liberal than Democrats who were steadfast. All groups, including traditional Republicans, favored an extension of Social Security. The midterm voting, *Fortune* concluded, did not represent a "swing to the right"; at most, it constituted "a halt to the left."

Insensitive to this reality, the Republican 80th Congress seized the reins like royalists returned from years of exile. One apoplectic critic described the drastic change: "This Congress brought back an atmosphere you had forgotten or never thought possible. At first, even the vested interests themselves couldn't believe it. And then you saw them, the Neanderthal Men, lurching forward on hairy feet—the sugar lobby, the wool lobby, the rail lobby, the real estate lobby, the power trust—tiptoeing back again, fingering things tentatively and then more boldly. Victories fought and won years ago, like the TVA, were suddenly in doubt." Controlling Congress for the first time since 1931, Republicans turned down not only Truman's efforts to extend the New Deal but even Robert Taft's modest proposals to improve housing and education. Though dependent on the votes of farmers, they slashed funds for rural electrification, soil conservation, and crop storage. When the president sent a special message urging that a "substantial number" of Europe's displaced persons be admitted to the United States, Congress responded with a law that, as Truman said, was "flagrantly discriminating." In particular, as Senator Pepper protested, the act exhibited a bias against the "most persecuted, most massacred, most butchered of people—the Jews."

By approving the Twenty-second Amendment stipulating that no president could serve more than two terms, Congress delivered a posthumous reprimand to Franklin D. Roosevelt, and also registered its alarm at the continuing expansion of presidential power under Truman. The amendment served to curb executive power by assuring that any president elected to a second term would immediately become a lame duck, with his opponents no longer needing to fear that he might strike back at them in an ensuing term. The measure, however, had more than one unintended consequence. After ratification, it assured FDR a unique place in the history of the presidency as the only person, past or future, with so long a tenure in the White House. And the first two incumbents restricted turned out to be Republicans, popular enough to have been elected to a third term.

The noisiest fracas in Congress came over Truman's resistance to the determination of Republicans to alter the National Labor Relations Act of 1935. The Taft-Hartley bill outlawed the secondary boycott, jurisdictional strikes, and the closed shop; authorized eighty-day injunctions against stoppages that could jeopardize national safety or health; banned union contributions to candidates in federal elections; and required labor leaders to take a non-Communist oath. Far from being the "slave labor act" of union propaganda, it did embody the demands of the National Association of Manufacturers.

In June 1947, Truman fired off a 5,400-word veto message denouncing this "shocking" assault on the working class. While the clerk was reading it aloud, one Republican leader conspicuously perused the comics. When the ritual ended, there were boos and cries of "Vote! Vote!" In short order, Truman's veto was overridden. The roll call underscored how little respect the president was accorded even by members of his own party. In the Senate, prominent Democrats deserted him. In the House, most of the Democratic members voted to override him. Little notice was taken, however, in the gloating by his opponents, of two other features of the episode. In pushing the legislation, Republicans had enhanced Truman's prospects in 1948 by throwing most of labor back into the president's arms. And, though Republicans asserted that they favored congressional supremacy, the Taft-Hartley Act considerably broadened presidential power over labor relations. Unexpectedly, aggrandizement of the presidency turned out to be the most significant legacy of the 80th Congress.

Truman had a keen sense of the majesty of the presidency. "I mean to pass this office on to my successor unimpaired," he said. He did a great deal more than that. Truman headed a government that carried the

United States from the largely personal administration of Franklin Roosevelt to the institutionalized presidency of the last half of the twentieth century and beyond. He concentrated especially on framing an appropriate response to the transformation being wrought by the Cold War. As the historian Robert Dallek has written, "The old distinction between war and peace simply vanished, and the White House... was expected to be in a continuing state of readiness to respond to any foreign policy predicament that might arise." Yet when Truman took over, one of his aides later pointed out, "There was no vast foreign policy machinery at the White House. There was no vast machinery on *any* subject at the White House." Under Truman, who doubled the budget for White House staff, the American government embarked on creating what has been called "the national security state."

The president scored a huge victory by getting Congress to accept his bold plan for unification of the armed services. The National Security Act of 1947 created a single military establishment under a cabinet official, soon to be called the secretary of defense. It also reduced the secretaries of war and navy to subcabinet status and provided for a secretary of the air force. To centralize authority, it gave statutory status to the Joint Chiefs of Staff—composed of the uniformed leaders of each of the services. Despite the intent of the statute, admirals and generals continued to quarrel, even after General Dwight Eisenhower was brought in to discipline them. At one point, the hero of D-Day said, "I am so weary of this inter-service struggle for position, prestige and power that this morning I practically 'blew my top.' I would hate to have my doctor take my blood pressure." When coordination finally was achieved, the accomplishment was seen as one of Truman's most important contributions.

In addition to establishing the Department of Defense, the law created two other agencies that soon loomed mightily in the conduct of foreign affairs. The National Security Council, which started out as an advisory body with no power, eventually rivaled the State Department in importance. At first, Truman paid little attention to the NSC, but he came to view it as so useful that he scheduled weekly meetings. He also found it advantageous to work with another new organization: the Central Intelligence Agency. The CIA's forerunner was the Office of Strategic Service under "Wild Bill" Donovan in World War II. Truman had scuttled the OSS as inappropriate for a country at peace, but the emergence of the Cold War prompted him to recognize the need for an intelligence-gathering agency independent of the regular departments. The CIA began sending the president reports on the state of the world, including trouble spots, each day—forerunners of their later daily briefs—and before long Truman was authorizing covert operations, one of them to frustrate the Communists in the 1948 Italian elections. Little more than two years after taking office, Truman had brought forth an intricate military apparatus that equipped the United States to fight a cold war for generations.

With Truman's approbation, Congress in July 1947 established a Commission on the Organization of the Executive Branch. To head the panel, Truman turned to Herbert Hoover, who had not been permitted to set foot in the White House in the FDR era. The appointment dismayed liberals but heartened conservatives, who counted on the former president—a bitter critic of Roosevelt's capacious view of federal authority—to be zealous in fulfilling Congress's goal of "limiting executive functions." Hoover confounded both factions by insisting that the power of the presidency be augmented. Though disturbed by how far FDR had reached, he had become convinced that power so diffused that no one could be held accountable was even more troubling. Hence, he sought to establish "the clear line of executive authority that was originally intended under the Constitution." Moreover, in a nuclear age with dangerous enemies abroad, a president, he maintained, needed adequate support. To strengthen the managerial capacity of the chief executive, the commission recommended giving him more money and more staff and granting him greater flexibility. Hoover quoted Hamilton's *Federalist* paper: "An energetic and unified executive is not a threat to a free and responsible people."

The report of the Hoover Commission constituted a milestone in the history of the executive office. Hoover, said one political scientist, "had come out of retirement to legitimate the Rooseveltian concept of the presidency." In like manner, another political scientist concluded that "the last Republican president joined in a celebration of the expansive, modern presidency" and the "central authority required by the majoritarian positive state." Furthermore, the historian Richard Norton Smith has observed, Hoover "built a bridge...over which congressional conservatives could migrate into the camp of a strong presidency." Congress responded to the report in an unconventional manner by authorizing the president to submit proposals to reorganize the executive branch that would take effect unless Congress disapproved. Of the thirty-six plans Truman advanced, all but one made it through.

Truman's experiences in 1945 led him to press for a new procedure on presidential succession. He was distressed to find when he took office, at a time when there was no vice president, that next in line for the White House were cabinet members, none of whom had been elected to their positions by the American people. He did not think it right that, by nominating the secretary of state, he would be designating his own successor, if his tenure ended abruptly. In 1947, Congress provided that succession to the presidency, after the vice president, would begin with the Speaker of the House, followed by the president pro tempore of the Senate, and then the cabinet secretaries—beginning with the secretary of state—in the order that their departments had been created.

The Truman years saw, too, significant accretions to the executive branch in the realm of domestic policy, starting with the creation of the three-member Council of Economic Advisers. The Employment Act of 1946, which established the CEA, added to the duties of a president by requiring him, each January, to transmit an annual economic report to Congress—in the same month as his State of the Union and budget messages. The president treated the CEA gingerly at first, but, after the ardent New Dealer Leon Keyserling took over as chair, the agency gave him the opportunity to pursue an expansionist economic policy.

Truman demonstrated his leadership in a different fashion after asking Congress to create an Atomic Energy Commission. When the War Department drafted a bill bypassing the president and providing for a strong military presence in the new agency, Truman threw his support to an alternative measure, and when the secretaries of war and navy lobbied for the War Department version, he silenced them. The Atomic Energy Act of 1946 provided for military liaison but under civilian control. To seal his victory over promilitary elements, he named the liberal David Lilienthal, who had been the sparkplug of the Tennessee Valley Authority, to chair the new commission. A cabinet officer caught in the midst of the scheming of admirals and generals for dominance said,

"In the person of Harry Truman, I have seen the most rock-like example of civilian control the world has ever witnessed."

———

President Truman made the most significant use of his executive power in the field of civil rights on learning of the extent of racial violence in postwar America. A delegation to the White House told him of what had befallen a black sergeant who had been awarded a battle star in the war. On his way home from fighting in the Pacific to see his wife and child, he had been yanked off a bus by South Carolina policemen who had blackjacked his eyes in a jail cell until he was blinded. The president also learned of hideous cold-blooded murders of other African Americans that had been carried out with impunity elsewhere in the South. His face registering shock and anguish, he resolved to authorize a far-reaching investigation that would provide the basis for vigorous national action. Reminded that a Senate filibuster by Southern Democrats would kill the proposal if he went to Congress, he said, "I'll create it by executive order and pay for it out of the president's contingent fund." He informed an aide, "I am very much in earnest on this, and I'd like very much to have you push it with everything you have."

On December 5, 1946, Truman established a President's Committee on Civil Rights "to make a very broad inquiry" into violations of freedom, especially in the South. To the large blue ribbon panel, he appointed only two southerners, both progressive on race. Truman was accused of intervening in order to solicit black votes, but as Walter White, the longtime leader of the National Association of Colored People, pointed out, "If the President wanted to play politics he would have followed the course of his predecessors of evading... this most explosive of American issues." In his lengthy account of the death of Jim Crow, the historian Richard Kluger concluded, "Franklin Roosevelt may have opened the White House door to Negroes, but Harry S. Truman risked his future tenancy there in their behalf.... No President before or since Lincoln had put his political neck on the chopping block to help the colored people of the nation."

In June 1947, a day before his committee was to decide on its recommendations, Truman went to the Lincoln Memorial to address the NAACP—the first time a president had done so. He chose the occasion to announce a historic advance in thinking about civil rights. "The extension of civil rights today means, not protection of the people *against* the Government, but protection of the people *by* the Government," he declared. "We must make the Federal Government a friendly, vigilant defender of the rights and equalities of all Americans." He drove this point home by adding:

> Many of our people still suffer the indignity of insult, the harrowing fear of intimidation, and, I regret to say, the threat of physical and mob violence.... The conscience of our nation, and the legal machinery which enforces it, have not yet secured to each citizen full freedom from fear.
>
> We cannot wait another decade or another generation to remedy these evils. We must work, as never before, to cure them *now*.

On concluding, he turned to Walter White and said, "I mean every word of it—and I am going to prove that I do mean it." Truman's address, White later reflected, was "the hardest hitting and most uncompromising speech on the subject of race which any American President has ever delivered."

As the task force convened to sum up its findings, its "members, many of whom had listened to the speech on the radio," were "buzzing with excitement about Truman's remarks," the historian William Juhnke has written. They recognized that they could hardly "recommend less than the President's own rhetoric anticipated." In its historic 178-page report, *To Secure These Rights*, the committee declared that the treatment of minorities in America constituted "a kind of moral dry rot which eats away at the emotional and rational bases of democratic beliefs." To remedy gross injustices, it advocated a number of measures, including an antilynching law and a ban on poll taxes. Furthermore, it denounced not only discrimination but also racial segregation.

When the committee came to the White House to hand in its findings, the president greeted its authors by saying, "I have stolen a march on you. I have already read the report and I want you to know that...you have done what I wanted you to." Confident "that it will take its place among the great papers on freedom," he viewed it as "a guide for action." He followed up immediately by authorizing the

Department of Justice to file an amicus brief on behalf of the NAACP's legal challenge to racist, anti-Semitic restrictive covenants in housing—an endeavor rewarded by the Supreme Court's decision in *Shelley v. Kraemer* not many months later. And on February 2, 1948, in a Special Message to Congress on Civil Rights, he advanced a ten-point program to implement many of the committee's proposals, including desegregation of interstate trains and buses.

Democratic leaders in the South reacted with a furious outburst of invective. "Not since the first gun was fired on Fort Sumter, resulting as it did in the greatest fratricidal strife in the history of the world, has any message of any president of these glorious United States... resulted in the driving of a schism in the ranks of our people, as did President Truman's so-called civil rights message," said a Mississippi congressman. "No President, either Democrat or Republican, has ever seen fit heretofore to make such recommendations." Turning one photo of Truman in his congressional office to the wall, and draping a second in black, another Mississippian, John Bell Williams, accused the president of catering to radical organizations, "conceived in hate, whelped in treason and deceit," that were seeking to bring about "mongrelization through a forced amalgamation of the races" while "hiding the rotten stench of their insidious aims." Truman, he charged, "has seen fit to run a political dagger into our backs and now... is trying to drink our blood." In Florida, the State Association of County Commissioners denounced the president's program as "obnoxious, repugnant, odious, detestable, loathsome, repulsive, revolting and humiliating," and a South Carolinian informed Jimmy Byrnes that in "small towns it's fever hot. People are scared. One man told me that he was much more afraid of Truman than of Russia."

Virtually no hope remained that the states of the former Confederacy, which Democrats had been able to take for granted in almost every national election since 1880, would stick with Truman in November. The president, reported the moderate Atlanta editor, Ralph McGill, had "touched off the loudest political pyrotechnics since 1860." Under the front-page banner headline MISSISSIPPI IS THROUGH WITH TRUMAN, the *Jackson Daily News* declared: "Insofar as Mississippi is concerned, Truman is... finished, washed up, blotted out. And we don't mean maybe." Mississippi, the paper's editor said, "has about as much use for him as a bull has for a blue brassiere." At a rally in Jackson, four thousand "wildly cheering and stomping Mississippians," reported the *New York Times*, "three times lustily booed the name of Mr. Truman." The long-time Memphis boss Ed Crump thought he could finger the culprit behind this deviltry. "Eleanor Roosevelt . . . frogging around with her Communist associates . . . has practically been Truman's mentor," he charged. "The time has come for a showdown in the South."

Mindful that he could ill afford to drive the South out of the party, Truman moved cautiously on carrying his civil rights message into action, but he would not recant. At the White House in March, the Democratic national committeewoman from Alabama told him: "I want to take a message back to the South. Can I tell them you're not ramming miscegenation down our throats—that you're not tearing up our social structure—that you're for all the people, not just the North?" The president retorted, "Well, I've got the answer right here for you," whipping out a copy of the Constitution from his coat pocket. He then proceeded to read her the Bill of Rights. Defiantly, he coupled the announcement that he was running for another term with a statement reaffirming his commitment to racial justice. "By refusing to retreat on his civil rights program," said the *Washington Post*, "the President in effect challenged Dixie to do its worst if it wanted to smash the party in November." Truman, said John Bell Williams, should "quit now while he is still just 20 million votes behind."

Stymied by the potent southern bloc in Congress, which could derail any attempt at civil rights legislation, Truman drew upon his authority as president. In July, he jolted his foes by issuing two executive orders. One set up a board to eliminate racial discrimination against federal employees. The other, considerably more consequential, drew upon his prerogatives as commander in chief. It was "the policy of the President," the edict stated, "that there shall be equality of treatment and opportunity for all persons in the armed services, without regard to race, color, religion, or national origin," and Truman pledged "to knock somebody's ears down" if that proved necessary to achieve that goal. The air force, the navy, and the marines all fell in line, but desegregation of the military met stiff resistance from the army brass, conspicuously Omar Bradley. Truman revered almost no one more than the World War II US field commander, but when the general spoke out against integration, the president publicly reprimanded him. "From Tokyo to Heidelberg," Truman told students at Howard, "orders have gone out that will make our fighting forces a more perfect instrument of democratic defense." By the end of the Truman era, black and white troops carried mess kits on the same chow lines, and before long African American sergeants were barking orders at white boys from Mississippi.

As Truman prepared to bid for a second term, no issue caused him so much public disapproval as his stand for civil rights. In April 1948, Gallup reported that only 6 percent of those polled favored his program. Even among whites outside the South, just one out of every five backed it. Seething at Truman's disregard for Jim Crow, southern politicians vowed vengeance. "He ain't going to be re-elected; he ain't going to be renominated," said Senator Olin Johnston. Another South Carolinian, the powerful Congressman Mendel Rivers, his voice trembling with fury, shook his finger as he told his colleagues on the floor of the House, "Harry Truman is already a dead bird. We in the South are going to see to that." Discountenanced by the ferocity of these assaults, the president had the satisfaction of knowing that he had not only opened a dialogue on race at home but also had elevated America's position in the struggle with Russia for the goodwill of African nations.

"Harry, don't you sometimes feel overwhelmed by your job?" a New Hampshire senator asked him. Walking over to a globe and slowly spinning it, Truman replied: "All the world is focusing on this office. The nearest thing to my heart is to do something to keep the world at peace. We must find a way to peace, or else civilization will be destroyed and the world will turn back to the year 900." No matter how compelling civil rights and other domestic concerns might be, the president continued to find, in 1947 and 1948, that foreign affairs—especially relations with Moscow—commanded most of his attention.

Henry Wallace and his leftist supporters identified the president with Byrnes's "get tough" foreign policy, but the day after he got rid of Wallace he wrote another former vice president, John Nance Garner: "There is too much loose talk about the Russian situation. We are not going to have any shooting trouble with them." In January 1947, he replaced Byrnes as secretary of state with the chief of staff of the victorious armed forces in World War II, George Catlett Marshall, who was much less fractious. (Truman said of General Marshall, "The more I see and talk to him the more certain I am he's the great one of the age.") When a federal study recommended that the government ready itself to wage atomic and biological warfare to defend America from Russian aggression, Truman ordered all copies of the report put "under lock and key," for if it got out, the revelation would subvert his wish to avoid hostilities. The Cold War, though, had developed a momentum of its own, and events had a way of playing hob with the best of intentions.

In the history of diplomacy, there may never have been an event to match what transpired late on the afternoon of February 21, 1947. At a time when it was feared that insurgency in Greece might result in a Communist coup, Lord Inverchapel, the British ambassador at Washington, informed the State Department that His Majesty's government could no longer afford to sustain the beleaguered Greek regime. Before the end of March, it was going to withdraw forty thousand troops and halt all economic assistance. The United Kingdom, the "blue paper" added, hoped that America would henceforth assume the burden. In sum, the once-mighty British empire was turning the globe over to the United States.

Truman quickly concluded that America must step in, but he feared that the Republican leadership in the 80th Congress would recoil at the cost. Consequently, he called congressional leaders to the White House, where Assistant Secretary of State Dean Acheson took over. "We are met at Armageddon," Acheson told them. The collapse of Greece, he warned, "would infect Iran and all to the East," and the malady would "spread through Asia Minor and Egypt, and to Europe through Italy and France." Staggered by the melodramatic presentation, Senator Vandenberg told Truman that there was "only one way" to get the action he sought. "That is to make a personal appearance before Congress and scare the hell out of the American people."

On March 12, Truman went up to the Hill to ask for millions in aid to Greece and also to Turkey, which, he said, confronted a frightening threat from Stalin to seize the Dardanelles. If Russia broke through to the Mediterranean, it might extend its empire into Africa and Asia, he warned. "It must be the policy of the United States," he declared, "to support free peoples who are resisting attempted subjugation." The longtime commitment that sentence implied quickly became known as the Truman Doctrine, a grand design encompassing the doctrine of "containment." Analysts associated that conception with the American foreign service officer George Kennan, who, in a "Long Telegram" from the US embassy in Moscow in 1946 and in an article published under the pseudonym "X," maintained that Soviet ambitions had to "be contained by the adroit and vigilant application of counter-force at a series of constantly shifting geographical and political points." Containment rested on the premise that if the Soviet Union could not expand, it would disintegrate because of internal strains or a "gradual mellowing" of the Russian state would ensue. Implied in the doctrine was the imperative for America to prepare itself for a prolonged endurance contest with the Kremlin.

Immensely pleased with himself, Truman wrote his daughter, Margaret, that her "pop" had told off the Russians and "the American Crackpots Association," typified by people such as Henry Wallace "and the actors and actresses in immoral Greenwich Village," but numbers of critics not thought to be crackpots demurred. "A vague global policy which sounds like the tocsin of an ideological crusade has no limits," Walter Lippmann

His face taut as he addresses a joint session of Congress on March 12, 1947, Harry Truman asks for $400 million to safeguard Greece and Turkey from communism—the first step in a program that will come to be known as "the Truman Doctrine." *Courtesy of the Harry S. Truman Library and Museum, Accession number 59-1252-3*

asserted. The administration, other commentators pointed out, over-simplified the nature of the civil war in Greece and exaggerated Soviet intentions. Furthermore, neither the monarchy in Greece nor the autocracy in Turkey corresponded to the rubric of "free people." But Stalinist Russia seemed so menacing and the eastern Mediterranean such a vital area that the Senate approved Greco-Turkish aid 67–23 and the House 284–107. In addition, the United States sent a large naval flotilla, including the aircraft carrier USS *Franklin D. Roosevelt*, through the straits of Gibraltar all the way to the Turkish coast for "routine training maneuvers." The former Republican presidential nominee Alf Landon, who supported Truman's actions, commented: "We are in European power politics up to our necks, and in it to stay."

At the same time that the president was shaping the Truman Doctrine for the eastern Mediterranean, he confronted a far graver crisis in western Europe. In the early months of 1947, Great Britain, France, and other countries blighted by war appeared to be on the verge of prostration. Reuters's financial editor foresaw "the biggest crash since the fall of Constantinople." That winter, blizzards and bitter cold paralyzed transportation and exhausted supplies of coal and wheat on the Continent. In London, the gears of Big Ben froze. Europe, said Winston Churchill, had become "a rubble-heap, a charnel house, a breeding ground of pestilence and hate." US policymakers feared that desperate Europeans would lose faith in capitalism and democracy; France had already admitted a Communist to its cabinet. Racing against time, they fashioned an audacious American response.

In a historic address at Harvard University on June 5, 1947, Secretary Marshall announced the program. He invited Europeans to collaborate on an assessment of their collective needs and a design for invigorating their economies, which the United States was prepared to fund. His country, Marshall pledged, would do "whatever it is able to do to assist in the return of normal economic health in the world" so that "free institutions" could flourish. Eschewing Cold War rhetoric, he declared, "Our policy is directed not against any country or doctrine, but against hunger, poverty, desperation and chaos." Marshall's invitation did not exclude Russia, though it was improbable that Congress would agree to send money to the Soviet Union. Obligingly, the Kremlin, after some hesitation, eliminated that impediment by rejecting the opportunity and ordering its satellites in eastern Europe not to participate. Western and southern European countries, however, leaped at the opportunity. Calling Marshall's address "a lifeline to sinking men," the British prime minister, Ernest Bevin, lost no time in pulling more than a dozen nations together to meet the American stipulations.

Truman had much more trouble getting the Republican 80th Congress to agree to this unprecedentedly expensive venture. In 1946, he had cudgeled Congress into approving a fifty-year loan of $3.75 billion that was supposed to tide Britain over, and, critics pointed out, just one year later, John Bull was back asking for more. The European Recovery Program had the advantage of being familiarly known as the Marshall Plan, even though it had been developed not by Marshall but by advisers appointed by Truman. ("Anything that is sent up to the Senate or House with my name on it will quiver a couple of times and die," the president told an aide.) But not even the prestige of the highly regarded secretary of state sufficed until it was repackaged as an anti-Soviet weapon. That appeal became especially compelling after the Russians seized control of Prague (a brutal takeover occasioning the death of the revered father of the Czechoslovak republic, Tomas Masaryk), and Communists appeared to be on track to capture the Italian government. To act before Italians went to the polls, the House met in night sessions, and in April 1948, Congress finally approved the European Recovery Program. Over the next four years, it made the huge sum of $13 billion available to sixteen European countries—from Iceland to Turkey.

The Marshall Plan proved to be an extraordinary success. By encouraging the countries of Europe to help themselves, it jump-started their economies and prodded them toward the ultimate creation of the Common Market. Churchill called the program "the most unselfish act by any great power in history." In later years, some scholars contended that much of the credit for the resurgence belonged not to Americans but to Europeans and pointed out that US businesses profited greatly from expanded overseas markets. But even skeptics acknowledged that the policies pursued by the Truman administration were infinitely more enlightened than those adopted following World War I. Arthur Krock, senior White House correspondent of the *New York Times*, called the Marshall Plan "the central gem in the cluster of great and fruitful decisions made by President Truman."

No sooner had Congress approved the Marshall Plan than Truman faced a new predicament—in the Middle East. With the British abandoning their mandate in Palestine, Jews sought to establish a state there. The president warmly sympathized with the desire of survivors of the Holocaust to fulfill the Zionist dream of a homeland. Furthermore, he was acutely aware that Jewish voters held the balance of power in New York state and that Democrats were dependent on campaign contributions from Jews. At one point, he told a delegation of US envoys in the Middle East, "I am sorry, gentlemen, but I have to answer to hundreds of thousands who are anxious for the success of Zionism; I do not have hundreds of thousands of Arabs among my constituents."

Truman's affinity for the Jewish cause aroused fierce objections from the diplomatic and national security establishments, with every branch of the State Department hierarchy antagonistic. Foreign affairs advisers admonished him that he could not afford to alienate the Arabs, who possessed oil reserves indispensable to America's factories and to its armed forces. Furthermore, if the Arabs concluded that the United States was unfriendly, they would very likely gravitate to the Russians. The Joint Chiefs of Staff and Secretary of Defense James Forrestal warned him that it would require nearly fifty thousand US troops—the whole ground reserve of the army—to impose a Jewish state on the region.

At a heated showdown conference, Secretary Marshall accused Truman of planning to sacrifice the national interest for political gain. He then jarred the White House gathering by saying, in what one presidential aide called a "righteous goddam Baptist tone," that if Truman carried through on this course, he would vote against him in November. Implied in that statement was the threat that he would issue a public denunciation and resign, which would have been a devastating blow. (After he cooled down, the general—reared to respect chains of command—conceded that the decision was one that the president was empowered to make, though not one he could endorse.)

On May 14, 1948, Jerusalem announced the creation of a new Jewish state, which it called Israel, and eleven minutes later, on Truman's order, the United States announced de facto recognition. American diplomats were dumbstruck. Marshall had to send an aide, Dean Rusk, to New York to prevent the entire US delegation to the United Nations from resigning. Truman viewed his action in valuing the quest of Jews for a home they could call their own above the need for oil not only as morally right but as striking a blow for the authority of the chief executive. He later wrote: "The difficulty with many career officials in government is that they regard themselves as the men who really...run the government. They look upon the elected officials as just temporary occupants.... I wanted to make plain that the President of the United States, and not a second or third echelon in the State Department, is responsible for making policy."

Little more than one month later, on a day when Republicans convened to nominate a candidate to drive the president out of the White House, Truman had to cope with yet another emergency abroad. On June 24, 1948, the USSR clamped a blockade on access to Berlin. After the war, when Germany was divided into four zones, a four-power occupation had been agreed upon for the old capital, but the Western allies had neglected to stipulate a right of access to Berlin, which lay 110 miles deep in the Russian orbit. By its 1948 edict, Soviet authorities were denying the Western powers any entry to the city—by rail, highway, or water. Acting in retaliation to the decision of the United States, Great Britain, and France to merge their three zones in order to foster the creation of a republic in West Germany, Stalin was challenging the West's will to resist—a potentially perilous undertaking. On September 13, Truman entered in his diary: "Forrestal, Bradley, Vandenberg (the Gen., not the Senator!), Symington brief me on bases, bombs, Moscow, Leningrad, etc. I have a terrible feeling afterward that we are very close to war."

The embargo presented Truman with thorny choices. Within a month, stocks of food in West Berlin would run out, and two and a half million people would be on the brink of starvation. No less urgent was the imperative of restocking the dwindling supply of fuel for the bitter northern winter ahead. The American commander in Germany, General Lucius Clay, recommended driving an armed convoy through the Russian sphere. If Truman had accepted that advice, the result might well have been World War III. Other advisers, reasoning that Berlin was indefensible, advocated discreet withdrawal. The president rejected that counsel too. He wrote in his diary, "We'll stay in Berlin—come what may."

Instead, he adopted a nonconfrontational strategy that many thought quixotic—to supply West Berlin by air. It was a daunting task. Sustaining the city on the barest essentials would require four thousand tons of food and other necessities every day for as long as the shutdown lasted. The thought of delivering tons of coal from the sky was mind-boggling. Keeping the city functioning normally would mean that a C-47 would have to take off or land every minute and forty-eight seconds. In England, the *New Statesman and Nation* stated, "Every expert knows that air-craft...cannot be relied upon to provision Berlin in the winter months."

But the Berlin Airlift turned out to be an inspired idea. For 321 days courageous American, British, and French aviators flew 277,804 missions, depositing more than 2.3 million tons of food, fuel, and supplies. In addition, planes dropped thousands of tiny parachutes bearing gifts of candy and toys (including dolls) for the children of the capital. (That initiative came not from the government but from a young American lieutenant, and every penny of the cost of the presents came from the pockets of the flyers.) The operation took the lives of forty-eight airmen, twenty-eight of them American. In May 1949, realizing that he had been outwitted, Stalin retreated, and rail lines and highways to Berlin were reopened. But as the 1948 campaign got under way that triumph lay well in the future. At the time, a happy outcome seemed highly unlikely, the Berlin imbroglio one more mess that Harry Truman did not know how to get out of.

Truman's prospects for election in 1948, already slim, appeared to dissolve when his party began to implode. At the same time that the South was becoming mutinous, the left wing of the Democrats was breaking away. In December 1947, Henry Wallace announced that he planned to run as an independent candidate for president in 1948, and seven months later his supporters nominated him to head a new third party. The Progressives, denouncing both major parties as warmongers, demanded the scrapping of the Truman Doctrine and the Marshall Plan, which they dubbed "the Martial Plan." The choice, announced the keynoter at their convention, "is Wallace or war." Analysts predicted that Wallace would pull several million votes away from Truman—very likely costing the president California and New York, states with a host of leftists and huge blocs of electoral votes.

Certain that Truman would be badly defeated in November, and fearful that he would drag Democratic congressional candidates down with him, liberals sought to dump him as the party's nominee. In its April 5, 1948, issue, the *New Republic* featured on its blue-inked cover the legend TRUMAN SHOULD QUIT. A day earlier, Arthur Krock had stated in the *New York Times*, "At this writing, the President's influence is weaker than any President's has been in modern history." Liberals—among them FDR's two eldest sons—joined big-city bosses in an odd alliance to persuade the immensely popular Dwight Eisenhower to accept the Democratic nomination in 1948, although they had only the haziest notion of the general's political views. Ike turned them down flatly, and, with Truman in firm control of the convention machinery, the movement sputtered out.

On the night of June 3, 1948, the president set off on a 9,500-mile rail journey that was to take him all the way to the Pacific coast. At Washington's Union Station, he told reporters, "If I felt any better, I couldn't stand it." More than once on the trip, he shot off his mouth. The worst moment came in Eugene, Oregon, when he said of Stalin: "I like old Joe! He's a decent fellow." But Truman, who spoke poorly from a script, also showed a flair for homespun populist sermons that had wide appeal. He drew one hundred thousand people in Chicago and Seattle, a million in Los Angeles, where, the press reported, "they clung to the roofs of buildings, jammed windows and fire escapes and crowded five deep along the sidewalk." Small communities were no less enthusiastic. "My goodness!" he exclaimed on seeing the number of welcomers in Dillon, Montana. But none of the enthusiasm meant anything, newspapers told their readers. Summing up the prevailing sentiment, a prominent Republican, Clare Boothe Luce, called the president a "gone goose."

At their national convention, Democrats, smell of defeat in their nostrils, wore buttons saying, "We're Just Mild about Harry," but, altogether unexpectedly, two hours past midnight, Truman delivered an acceptance speech that brought the groggy, morose delegates to their feet applauding. At a moment when Democrats were hearing nothing save portents of defeat, he said jauntily, "Senator Barkley and I will win this election and make these Republicans like it—don't you forget that." The president went on to scourge his opponents by pointing out the divergence between the moderate Republican platform and the performance of the 80th Congress. "The Republican platform urges extending and increasing social security benefits," he noted. "Think of that—and yet when they had the opportunity, they took 750,000 people off our social security rolls. I wonder if they think they can fool the people with such poppycock." Delighted with the "new" Truman, delegates yelled, "Pour it on 'em, Harry."

Drawing upon his constitutional powers, he announced to the startled but gleeful gathering that he was summoning the 80th Congress into special session on July 26—a date capriciously chosen because it was the day that Missouri farmers plant turnips. He elaborated: "I am going to call Congress back and ask them to pass laws to...meet the housing crisis—which they are *saying* they are for in their platform.... I shall ask them to act upon...aid to education, which they *say* they are for...civil rights legislation, which they *say* they are for." Raising his voice to be heard above the roars of approval, he concluded: "Now, my friends, if there is any reality behind the Republican platform, we ought to get some action from a short session of Congress. They can do this job in 15 days, if they want to." A critical liberal wrote in his next column: "It was fun to see the scrappy little cuss come out of his corner fighting...not trying to use big words any longer, but being himself and saying a lot of honest things. Unaccountably, we found ourself on top of a pine bench cheering."

His speech did nothing, however, to halt the further disintegration of his party. To ward off a breakaway of the Solid South, Truman sought to mollify Dixie hotspurs by retaining a moderate civil rights plank in the Democratic platform, but an alliance of liberals would brook no compromise. The irrepressible young mayor of Minneapolis, Hubert Humphrey, declared that "the time has arrived for the Democratic Party to get out of the shadow of states' rights and walk forthrightly into the bright sunshine of human rights." When a majority of the delegates agreed, the stony-faced Mississippi delegation and thirteen of the Alabama delegates marched out of the convention, saying, "We bid you good-bye." Three days later in Birmingham, they joined with other racists to create a new political party, demanding "complete segregation." The States' Rights Democrats, soon to be dubbed "Dixiecrats," named Governor Strom Thurmond of South Carolina as their presidential candidate, with the unabashed white supremacist Governor Fielding Wright of Mississippi as his running mate. Though Thurmond claimed to be motivated only by a desire to preserve state sovereignty, the organization, as Ralph McGill wrote, was "really the anti-Negro party."

Republicans heeded the command that they return to Washington in steamy midsummer in an angry mood. Not since Franklin Pierce in 1856 had a president called Congress back in an election year. GOP senator Styles Bridges of New Hampshire fulminated that "this petulant Ajax from the Ozarks" would find the "maddest Congress you ever saw." As Truman anticipated, the "turnip session" enacted nothing of importance. But the president had achieved his goal: to take the country's attention away from the fairly advanced Republican platform and the moderate-to-liberal ticket of Thomas Dewey, the successful governor of New York, and California's progressive governor, Earl Warren, and focus it on the hard-bitten conservatism of the Republican delegation in Congress.

Early in September, Truman boarded a train in Washington for the first of a series of lengthy campaign tours of major cities, small towns, and whistle-stops. At Union Station to send him off, his running mate, Senator Barkley, urged, "Mow 'em down, Harry," and the president responded, "I'm going to give them hell." Over the next eight weeks, he traveled twenty-two thousand miles—almost enough to circuit the earth—and gave 271 speeches. Never before had so many Americans seen a president in the flesh. Again and again, he blasted that "no-account, do-nothin', good-for-nothin'" 80th Congress and the GOP leadership. "You've got the worst Congress you've ever had," he informed a Spokane audience. The 80th Congress, he charged, was in the grip of a "bunch of old mossbacks still living back in 1890," doing the bidding of "bloodsuckers who have offices in Wall Street." People needed to understand that "these Republican gluttons of privilege are cold men." He told a Detroit audience that "your typical Republican reactionary is a very shrewd man with a calculating machine where his heart ought to be," and in St. Paul he said, "The Republican party either corrupts its liberals or it expels them." So low were the party's finances that in Oklahoma City Democrats had to raise emergency funding to move the train out of the yards, but Truman persevered.

Instead of truckling to voters, he scolded them. "If you send another Republican Congress to Washington," he lectured audiences, "you're a bigger bunch of suckers than I think you are." He chided Iowa farmers, "You stayed at home in 1946 and you got the 80th Congress, and you got just exactly what you deserved." At another campaign stop, he said, "I wonder how many times you have to be hit on the head before you find out who's hitting you." And the revved-up spectators loved it. One hundred thousand greeted him in Oklahoma City, two hundred thousand in San Antonio.

Truman, in his off-the-cuff remarks, hit the high road and the low road. He never acknowledged the cooperation he had received from Republicans in Congress on foreign policy, and he got so carried away at one point that he implied that Tom Dewey was a fascist. The Republican palaver about unity, Truman told an overflow audience in Boston's Mechanics Hall, was "a lot of hooey—and, if that rhymes with anything, it is not my fault." With Dewey, apparently far ahead in the race, content with bromides such as "We need a rudder to our ship of state and...a firm hand at the tiller," Truman jeered that GOP meant Grand Old Platitudes. The White House correspondent Robert Donovan later recapped the cross-country campaign as "sharp speeches fairly criticizing Republican policy and defending New Deal liberalism mixed with sophistry, bunkum piled higher than haystacks, and demagoguery tooting merrily down the tracks."

In spite of all the indications that the president was winning over his listeners, almost no one thought that he had a ghost of a chance. Commenting on the ovations Truman was receiving, the well-regarded journalist Richard Rovere wrote, "Travelling with him you get the feeling that the American people who have seen him and heard him at his best would be willing to give him just about anything he wants except the Presidency." Two months before Election Day, Elmo Roper stopped taking polls. The huge Dewey advantage, he explained, revealed "an almost morbid resemblance to the Roosevelt-Landon figures as of about this time in 1936." In fact, "Mr. Dewey is still so clearly ahead that we might just as well get ready to listen to his Inaugural on Jan. 20, 1949." When *Newsweek* polled fifty top political writers, every one forecast Truman's defeat. Democratic leaders in Washington put their homes on the market, and foreign diplomats in Washington dispatched sealed pouches carrying reports alerting their homelands that there would shortly be a new government in America. On the eve of the election, the high-priced *Kiplinger Washington Letter* informed its readers, "Dewey will be in for eight years, until '57," and below a photograph of Dewey,

Life ran the caption "The Next President Travels by Ferry Boat over the Broad Waters of San Francisco Bay."

On Election Night in November, people settled down beside their radios expecting an early bedtime since Dewey's victory statement could be expected shortly after polls closed. Truman took an early lead, but that, listeners were told, was to be expected; they should "keep waiting for those rural returns." Newsboys hawked an extra of the right-wing *Chicago Tribune* with the headline DEWEY DEFEATS TRUMAN. After hours passed, with Truman still ahead, commentators began to ask the unthinkable: Could Harry pull it off? At Republican headquarters in Manhattan's Roosevelt Hotel, one columnist noted, the mood of "victory" celebrants changed from confidence to surprise, "from surprise to doubt, from doubt to disbelief, and then on to stunned fear and panic." By dawn, the story line centered on which state would give Truman the last electoral votes he needed. A few hours later, Ohio put him over the

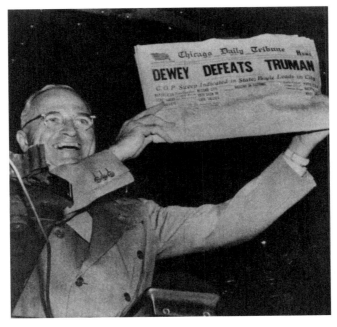

DEWEY DEFEATS TRUMAN. So confident of a Republican triumph in 1948 was the country's most conspicuously conservative newspaper, the *Chicago Tribune*, that it published an inaccurate early edition with the anticipated results. An exultant Truman takes pleasure in displaying it. Dewey, Democrats jeered, had "snatched defeat from the jaws of victory." *Library of Congress, LC-DIG-ppmsca-33570*

top. For spunky Harry Truman, vindication could not have been sweeter. He had survived the loss of both wings of his party, bemused the pollsters, and outfoxed his critics, and he could look forward to four more years in the White House—president of the United States, for the first time, in his own right.

———

No one had more fun at the merry inauguration gala in January 1949 than Harry Truman. Republicans, certain of a Dewey landslide, had appropriated a record sum for the greatest bash in history, and the president spent it jubilantly. He reinstituted the Inaugural Ball and chose his friend the radio comedian Jack Benny as maestro. He saw to it that African Americans were asked to all events, including the ball, and insisted that Washington's segregated hotels accommodate black guests. Some four score and seven years after the Emancipation Proclamation, the 1949 inauguration was the first to be integrated. Truman also invited a rabbi to participate in the ceremonies, another first. More than a million well-wishers crowded the Capitol plaza to witness the oath-taking, and the parade that followed stretched out for seven miles. More people watched the inauguration than had seen all of the previous ceremonies combined, for this was the first to be televised. When a band marched past the reviewing stand, the president danced a jig. At the end of the lengthy procession, a calliope played cheerily, "I'm Just Wild about Harry."

Despite these promising auguries, Truman had a vexed second term. Given a renewed lease on the White House, he could not live in it. When a leg of his daughter's grand piano pierced the floor of her sitting room, it became clear that the deteriorating executive mansion required substantial reconstruction. Before his term had even begun, the president had to move across the street to Blair House, where he was compelled to reside until his final months in office. His situation became considerably more intolerable after two Puerto Rican separatists stormed Blair House on November 1, 1950, intent on murdering him—and nearly succeeded. They were thwarted only because a courageous guard, mortally wounded, managed to fire a final shot that killed one of the assailants. Henceforth, heavily armed Secret Servicemen closely regulated Truman's movements, and he was required to travel the short distance across Pennsylvania Avenue to the White House in a bulletproof car. "It's hell to be president," he said. He was "really a prisoner now." The turmoil and displacement epitomized much of his second term. "Never in my wildest dreams did I ever think or wish for such a position," he confided. He had "succeeded in getting [himself] into more trouble than Pandora ever let loose in the world."

In his first address to the new Congress, Truman asserted that "every segment of our population and every individual has a right to expect from his government a *fair deal*." But, save for the creation of the National Science Foundation, all he could achieve were warmed-over New Deal measures. At Truman's behest, Congress nearly doubled the minimum wage; extended Social Security benefits to another ten million people; expanded soil conservation, rural electrification, and public power projects; closed a loophole in the Clayton Antitrust Act; and started a broad-gauged program for low-income housing and slum clearance. This legislation, however meritorious, did not move the national agenda beyond where it had been in the Great Depression. With good reason did a British periodical call Truman's tenure "Roosevelt's Fifth Term."

The president had considerably more in mind, but Congress would not go along. Although, as a result of the 1948 elections, Democrats controlled both houses, numbers of them, especially from the South, participated in a powerful bipartisan conservative coalition. The liberal Democratic senator Paul Douglas was appalled by the effrontery of the Republican Robert Taft and the Virginia Democrat Harry Byrd, whom he saw sitting together in the Senate chamber "checking the list of Senators and sending out for the absent or few recalcitrants." They met only timid resistance from the Democratic leaders in the Senate, who, Truman said, did "not have the guts of a gnat." Both houses of Congress balked at forward-looking Fair Deal proposals: federal aid to education, civil rights legislation, an innovative approach to farm subsidies, and TVAs in the Missouri and Columbia valleys. The most venturesome plan—to establish national health insurance for the first time in the United States—fell victim to the potent American Medical Association lobby. When in January 1950 he delivered his State of the Union address, congressmen booed him and laughed at him, turning the president's face an angry red.

Many liberals, though, blamed Truman for failing to rally the country as, they were sure, Roosevelt would have. "Alas for Truman," said one commentator, "there is no bugle note in his voice." Even in his second term, Washington correspondents were writing, "When Franklin Roosevelt died in 1945 and Harry Truman took his place, it was as if the star of the show had left and his role had been taken by a spear carrier from the mob scene"; and Elmer Davis, who had headed the Office of War Information under FDR, said, "What I miss about Roosevelt means of course what I miss in Truman—what people will miss this summer in the good major-leaguer who tries to take Joe Di Maggio's place. He will try to do the same things, with considerable success; he will have devotion, industry, talent, everything but the touch of genius." No one who had not gone through the experience of being president could know how great a burden he carried, Truman told his cousin. "It bears down on a country boy." He still nurtured the wistful hope that the midterm elections in 1950 might swell the ranks of his supporters, but unforeseen events abroad, reverberating at home, snuffed out any possibility for enactment of the Fair Deal.

Truman had no reason to anticipate that foreign affairs would cause him so much distress. True, he had not been able to get a grasp on the civil war in China between the Nationalist forces of Chiang Kai-shek and the Communists of Mao Zedong. He had sent George Marshall there to try to forge an agreement—to no avail. As Hamby has written, "Marshall's goal, a coalition government that would include both Chiang and Mao, was about as likely as a collaboration between a scorpion and a tarantula." But Asia was dwarfed in significance by western Europe, where everything was going so well. Marshall Plan aid was sparking a spectacular recovery there, the Reds had been beaten back in the Italian elections, and the Berlin Airlift had ended triumphantly. Secretary Marshall had stepped down for reasons of health, but Truman had been able to replace him with the impressive Dean Acheson, an even more vigorous promoter of administration policies. The United States, Acheson believed, was the "locomotive at the head of mankind," and "the rest of the world is the caboose." As leader of the foremost power, Truman had one other conspicuous advantage: America alone possessed an arsenal of atomic bombs—and the secret formula for how to build them. But he was in for a series of shocks.

In August 1949, the White House issued a disturbing bulletin: China had fallen to the Reds. The Truman administration explained, rightly, that the Communist takeover had come about because the Nationalists were corrupt and Chiang, who had retreated with the remnant of his army to Formosa, had been unable to win the allegiance of the Chinese people. Still, there was no denying that the outcome was galling. After Mao's triumph, maps of the world showed the United States tucked in between Canada and Mexico, with a huge land mass stained red stretching from the Baltic to the China Sea.

The White House revelation brought a storm of abuse down upon Truman and his appointees. "This is the tragic story of China, whose freedom we once fought to preserve," said Democratic congressman John F. Kennedy. "What our young men had saved, our diplomats and our President have frittered away." A conservative columnist said of the debacle in Asia: "The errors which brought on his defeat were not Chiang's; they were Marshall's. They were not China's; they were America's." For a long time, General Marshall was so highly esteemed that no one dared attack him. But after Mao seized power, a Republican senator charged that Marshall had been "eager to play the role of the front man for traitors" and called him "a living lie."

Acheson, the new secretary of state, offered a far more exposed and vulnerable target. Son of an Episcopal bishop who had served in the Queen's Own Rifles, he seemed more at home in Belgravia or Kensington than Terre Haute. With his stiff carriage, arched eyebrows, meticulously waxed mustache evocative of a British guardsman, and Savile Row suits and homburg, he created an image not often seen on American streets. A Republican senator from Nebraska said of him: "I look at that fellow, I watch his smart-aleck manner and his British clothes and that New Dealism, everlasting New Dealism in everything he says and does, and I want to shout, 'Get out! Get out! You stand for everything that has been wrong with the United States for years.'"

Just one month after acknowledging the Communist takeover in China, the White House made a far more alarming announcement. On September 23, Truman's press secretary handed out mimeographed statements that sent awestruck reporters in a pell-mell rush to phones to inform the country of shattering news. The document read, "We have evidence that within recent weeks an atomic explosion occurred in the USSR." In plain English, Russia had the Bomb! And far sooner than anyone had expected. Less than six months before, Truman, in a frank discussion with friendly foreign ministers, had confided that "our best estimate is that we have several years in which we can count on a breathing spell."

Rage became the order of the day. Only four years earlier, right-wing publicists and legislators pointed out, the United States had been a Colossus astride the world, Chiang headed one of the Big Four powers, and the Russians, shattered by the war, confronted a task of reconstruction that, it appeared, would require decades. How could so much have gone so wrong so quickly? There was, they said, only one conceivable explanation: subversion. Officials in the Truman administration, they maintained, had "lost" China, and traitors in Washington had turned over recondite equations to the Kremlin.

These presumptions confounded reality. Chiang could have been saved only by sending a huge US expeditionary force across the Pacific—an action the country would not have tolerated. Moreover, as one of the foremost scholars on Asia, John King Fairbank, pointed out, "The illusion that the United States could have shaped China's destiny assumes that we Americans can really call the tune if we want to, even among 475 million people in the inaccessible rice paddies of a subcontinent 10,000 miles away." And critics who imagined that the USSR could not have constructed a bomb on its own greatly underestimated Soviet capabilities. To be sure, these allegations were not altogether groundless. America's China hands in the Foreign Service sometimes fell short, and there were, indeed, spies in the federal government, though they had little or no effect on policy. A sensational court case, however, made these imputations seem plausible.

Three months before the 1948 election, a *Time* magazine editor, Whittaker Chambers, told the House Committee on Un-American Activities that a former State Department official, Alger Hiss, had been a member of the Communist Party. He offered no convincing proof, and Truman dismissed charges against Hiss and others as a "red herring" drawn across the path of the campaign by irresponsible Republicans. But on a December night in 1948 Chambers, accompanied by two investigators, reached into a pumpkin on his Maryland farm and pulled out microfilm of classified State Department documents that he claimed had been given to him when he was a Soviet agent by a spy ring to which

Hiss belonged. In short, he was no longer accusing Hiss merely of having been a Communist, but of having been a traitor. The evidence was turned over to the young California congressman Richard Nixon, who, at a time when many derided the charges, was convinced of Hiss's misdeeds and pursued him doggedly. Hiss stoutly affirmed his innocence and sued Chambers for libel.

For more than a year, the Hiss case engaged the country in sorting out the evidence—an ancient Woodstock typewriter, the sighting of a prothonotary warbler, a road company performance of *She Stoops to Conquer*—and finding it hard to decide between the frumpy, weird Chambers and the slim, elegant Hiss, who seemed to epitomize the liberal internationalism of the FDR-Truman era. Accordingly, the first trial ended in a hung jury. But at the conclusion of a second trial in January 1950, Hiss was found guilty of perjury. In fact, though the statute of limitations spared him, he was being convicted of treason.

While the outcome raised questions about Truman's judgment in scoffing at the original revelation, the affair appeared to have no relevance to Truman-Acheson foreign policy, for it dealt with behavior in the 1930s. (At Yalta in 1945, Roosevelt never saw Hiss, whose chief contribution was to circulate a memorandum hostile to Soviet ambitions.) But on the very day that a federal judge imposed a sentence of five years in prison, Acheson declared, "I do not intend to turn my back on Alger Hiss." His code of honor, he told reporters, came from the gospel according to St. Matthew. Acheson's statement, his supporters said, bespoke admirable loyalty to a longtime family friend. It also, however, appeared to reflect the determination of eastern patricians to protect their own. Appallingly insensitive to the political reverberations, Acheson had fed raw meat to foes who had been saying that the Truman administration was indifferent to infiltration of the government, even condoned it.

From the pack of senators baying at the Truman circle emerged a hitherto obscure and ill-regarded Wisconsin Republican, Joseph McCarthy, whose name was to brand a period of demagoguery and character assassination. In a Lincoln's Birthday speech in Wheeling, West Virginia, on February 9, 1950, McCarthy announced, "While I cannot take the time to name all of the men in the State Department who have been named as members of the Communist Party and members of a spy ring, I have here in my hand a list of 205 . . . still working and shaping the policy of the State Department." He said of Acheson: "When this pompous diplomat in striped pants, with the phony British accent, proclaimed to the American people that Christ on the Mount endorsed Communism, high treason, and betrayal of a sacred trust, the blasphemy was so great that it awakened the dormant indignation of the American people." Picking up on an earlier theme, McCarthy, a Johnny-come-lately of the Red Scare, charged: "It was Moscow which decreed that the United States should execute its loyal friend, the Republic of China. The executioners were that well-defined group headed by Acheson and George Catlett Marshall." These diatribes produced an avalanche of mail to Acheson so menacing that around-the-clock guards were stationed at his home to shield him from harm. A Senate investigating committee concluded that McCarthy was waging "the most nefarious campaign of half-truths and untruth in the history of the Republic," but he attracted millions of believers.

At the very time that right-wing zealots were assailing Truman and Acheson for failing to combat the Soviet menace, the two men were busily constructing a buffer in Europe against Russian aggression. In Washington in April 1949, envoys from twelve nations—from Iceland to Portugal, from Canada to Italy—signed the North Atlantic Treaty, a mutual defense arrangement presaged by the Rio Pact of 1947 for Latin America. Signatories pledged that if any member of the alliance was attacked, they would retaliate with whatever actions they deemed necessary, "including the use of armed force." In essence, the compact warned the Soviet Union, whose large number of army divisions could readily overwhelm any resistance on the Continent, that an invasion of western Europe might be regarded as an act of war on the United States, with terrible consequences.

The treaty, once and for all, ended the US tradition of isolation. Not since the Convention of 1800 terminated the American tie to France, which had come to the aid of American rebels at Yorktown, had the United States entered into a peacetime alliance outside the Western Hemisphere. Shortly after the 1949 signing ceremony, the creation of the North Atlantic Treaty Organization gave a military dimension to the concordat. When the Senate voted down a proposal requiring congressional approval of any commitment of US forces to NATO, it sanctioned an additional huge expansion of the president's war-making powers.

Another White House bulletin revealed how much more dangerous the world had become in the age of Truman. Less than a week after the sentencing of Hiss, the president announced that he had given his approval to construction of a superbomb using thermonuclear fission. It was a portentous decision. Hydrogen bombs—infinitely more powerful than atomic bombs—raised the specter of the eradication of all human life. Albert Einstein warned, "General annihilation beckons." But once Truman was informed that Russia had the capacity, and no doubt the determination, to build a superbomb, he saw no other course.

Far from being "soft on communism," Truman's foreign policy advisers pushed him toward greatly expanding anti-Soviet operations. In April 1950, the National Security Council handed the president a document— drafted in the State Department under Acheson's direction—that depicted the Russians, mesmerized by a "fanatical faith antithetical to our own," as bent upon world domination. NSC-68 advocated arousing the American people to this peril, Acheson said, by hammering out "Hemingway sentences" to make the danger "clearer than truth." In the core of the report, its authors pressed for more than tripling spending for the military. NSC-68's intent, Acheson later acknowledged, was to "bludgeon" the president into agreement. Hence, the report adopted a tone of "bluntness, almost brutality."

They found Truman a hard sell. He had persuaded Congress in 1948 to reinstitute the draft, but he had clamped down on military spending that he believed would distort the budget. When Congress insisted on appropriating many millions above the president's allocation to the air force, he impounded the money. Truman's determination to discipline the Pentagon was admirable, but in leaving the US army a mere miniature of the Soviet force, he weakened the capacity of the military to carry through on his ambitious foreign policy initiatives. Not even the shrill rhetoric of NSC-68 moved him to endorse a massive buildup. Truman did, however, oblige his anti-Soviet advisers in a different way—by intensifying the hunt for enemies of the state.

In sharp contrast to the attitude of the McCarthyites, historians fault the Truman administration not for harboring subversives but for discharging allegedly radical government employees without following fair procedures. In March 1947, the president had issued an executive order establishing a Federal Employee Loyalty Program. Instead of limiting the investigation to workers in sensitive agencies, he sanctioned background checks even on people hired for menial jobs. Though Roosevelt had authorized discharges of suspect employees in World War II, Truman's dragnet was the first to screen workers in peacetime. In addition, the edict empowered the attorney general to publish a list of subversive organizations. Most if not all were, in fact, Communist fronts, but the register caught up people who had joined innocently. The Truman administration also prosecuted prominent Communists under the Smith Act of 1940 and put all of the party leaders, as well as some in lower ranks, in jail.

Truman hoped to preempt the issue of Communist infiltration of government raised by Republicans, who had been accusing Democratic administrations of laxity ever since a raid in March 1945 on the offices of the magazine *Amerasia* had found a cache of restricted federal documents implicating a Foreign Service officer. Six months later, a Soviet code clerk in Ottawa, Igor Gouzenko, had defected, taking with him damning evidence of an international spy network with agents in the United States. The Red Scare has often been likened to seventeenth-century witch hunts, notably in Arthur Miller's drama *The Crucible*, but, unlike Salem, the nation's capital housed a few actual witches—that is, traitors.

Further revelations had prodded Truman to take an even tougher stand. In January 1950, Klaus Fuchs, a highly placed atomic physicist who had worked at the US facility in Los Alamos, confessed to British authorities that for years he had been passing on secret materials, including designs for the hydrogen bomb, to USSR military intelligence. Information extracted from Fuchs led to the indictment in August 1950 of Julius and Ethel Rosenberg, as well as their accomplices, for engaging in atomic espionage for Moscow. In April, the Rosenbergs were sentenced to death. As Republican cries grew louder, Truman stiffened the program by issuing another executive order: no longer were officials required to prove disloyalty to justify sacking a federal employee; all they needed to demonstrate was that there was "reasonable doubt"—a highly malleable standard. Those being investigated were not permitted to confront their accusers or even allowed to know what the charges against them were.

In January 1951, disturbed by what was happening, Truman set up a committee headed by a hero of the Pacific fighting in World War II, Admiral Chester Nimitz, to explore "how a free people protect their society from subversive attack without at the same time destroying their liberties." He had expressed unease about loyalty investigations from the outset. If he could prevent it, he had written his wife, "there'll be no NKVD [Soviet secret police] or Gestapo in this country." J. Edgar Hoover's FBI, he added, "would make a good start toward a citizen spy system. Not for me." But his attempt at reform came to naught. The powerful Nevada senator Pat McCarran, a conservative Democrat, saw to it that the Nimitz commission never got under way.

However good his intentions, Truman bears a considerable share of the blame for the excesses. The out-of-control investigations demoralized the civil service, with little to show for all the labor. Careful historical analysis has established that Hiss, the Rosenbergs, and others regarded by many at the time as innocent victims were, in fact, guilty, but Truman's program had nothing to do with their apprehension. Agency boards scrutinized the pasts of nearly five million federal employees but, even under a loose definition of disloyalty, found cause by 1953 to discharge or refuse to hire only 560. (In addition, several thousand resigned—perhaps to escape detection, quite possibly for other reasons.) Not one instance of espionage was ever uncovered by these probes. And this drastic operation gained the president no favor from his enemies, who regarded it as an overdue concession to the righteousness of their cause and redoubled their attacks.

To Truman's dismay, the allegation that he and his fellow Democrats catered to the Reds found willing ears in the 1950 midterm elections. In Maryland, Millard Tydings lost his US Senate seat when Republicans flaunted a doctored photograph showing him chatting with Communist Party chief Earl Browder—a man he had never met. In California, Richard Nixon won election to the US Senate by defaming his Democratic opponent, Helen Gahagan Douglas. A highly regarded congresswoman who was outspokenly critical of Communists, she was called by Nixon "the Pink Lady," who was "pink right down to her underwear." Republican gains were unremarkable, but they were interpreted as a direct repudiation of the president and were enough to render the Fair Deal, already moribund, dead on arrival at Capitol Hill. On Election Night, Truman, altogether uncharacteristically, drank himself into oblivion, because he was so disheartened by the obsession with subversion in high places. McCarthyism, however, had less to do with the outcome of the elections than national anguish over Truman's decision to wage war in a part of the world where trouble was least expected—a war that, in November 1950, was going very badly.

———

Most Americans in 1950 gave no thought to Korea, and US policymakers paid it little more. In 1945, the United States had arranged to accept the surrender of Japanese forces south of the 38th parallel in Korea, with the Soviet Union taking charge to the north. That imaginary line was intended to be temporary, but it soon served to demarcate the boundary between two countries: North Korea under the pro-Soviet Kim Il-Sung, and, to the south, the Republic of Korea, headed by the conservative Syngman Rhee—a Princeton graduate who had been a protégé of Woodrow Wilson. Rhee hoped that America would shield his nation from Kim Il-Sung's ambition to consolidate the Asian peninsula into a single Communist state, but in 1949 the United States withdrew its entire garrison, in keeping with Truman's determination to cap military spending. At the National Press Club in January 1950, Secretary Acheson delineated a "perimeter" from the Aleutians to the Philippines that the United States was prepared to defend. Conspicuously, Korea fell outside this protected area. But as late as June 1950, the assistant secretary for Far Eastern affairs, Dean Rusk, assured a congressional committee that, despite the American withdrawal, there was no cause to fear a North Korean assault on its southern neighbor.

On June 24, while visiting his home in Independence, Missouri, Truman received a phone call from Acheson relaying shocking news: North Korea had launched an invasion of the Republic of Korea. Within hours, the president learned that 135,000 troops—accompanied by tanks, heavy artillery, and planes—were marching on the southern capital, Seoul. Truman and other policymakers assumed that the attack had been ordered by the Kremlin, although, in fact, Stalin had repeatedly vetoed it before agreeing halfheartedly. "If you get kicked in the teeth," he told Kim, "I shall not lift a finger." (The Soviet Union did, however, provide some support.) "By God!" Truman cried on returning to Washington, "I am going to let them have it."

The administration quickly swung into action. Even before Truman got back from Missouri, Acheson had taken the initiative with the United

HARRY TRUMAN | 299

Nations. On June 25, the UN Security Council adopted an American resolution calling for a cease-fire, demanding that North Korea retreat behind the 38th parallel, and asking member states to "render every assistance in the execution of this resolution." Truman, impelled by what he regarded as a test of his will, ordered air and naval forces to South Korea and dispatched the 7th Fleet to create a barrier between Formosa and the Chinese mainland. Two days later, in response to a desperate message from General MacArthur, he sent in troops who had been garrisoned in Japan. For the first time in the history of the world, soldiers fought under the banner of an international organization. To most Americans, though, this seemed their country's war, since the United States provided 33 percent of the UN forces, and all other nations, save for South Korea, less than 6 percent. (The bulk of the fighting was carried on by South Koreans, who bore by far the heaviest casualties.) On authorization by the Security Council, Truman designated MacArthur to be supreme commander of the UN legions.

Years later, Truman recalled his ruminations as he flew back to Washington over midwestern farmland on a summer afternoon. He "kept coming back," he said, "to the 1930's—to Manchuria, to Ethiopia, the Rhineland, Austria, and finally Munich." In a correlation that in the 1960s was to be scoffed at as "the Munich analogy," he reflected:

> I remembered how each time that the democracies failed to act it encouraged the aggressors to keep going ahead. . . . If the Communists were permitted to force their way into the Republic of Korea without opposition from the free world, no small nation would have the courage to resist threats and aggression by stronger Communist neighbors. If this was allowed to go unchallenged, it would mean a third world war, just as similar incidents had brought on the second world war.

"Jack," he said to a State Department official on another occasion, "in the final analysis I did this for the United Nations. I believed in the League of Nations. It failed. Lots of people thought it failed because we weren't in it to back it up. Okay, now we started the United Nations. It was our idea, and in this first big test we just couldn't let them down."

Neither Truman nor his circle, in carrying out what appeared to be a textbook lesson derived from the 1930s, had the remotest conception of what was going to ensue. "I don't think you can say that any of us knew, to start, when we went into this thing, what would be involved," General Bradley later testified. "No one believed that the North Koreans were as strong as they turned out to be." The Korean War, Hamby has written, "wholly rearranged the priorities of his administration, consigned the Fair Deal to limbo, left his presidency in tatters, and did grave damage to his morale. At the end of 1950, however, it seemed that he had made the only decision possible."

A wave of enthusiasm, at home and abroad, greeted news of Truman's action. The Norwegian ambassador called on Acheson to say that "he remembered no event which had stirred such unanimous acclaim," and a Washington correspondent wrote: "I have lived and worked in and out of this city for twenty years. Never before in that time have I felt such a sense of relief and unity pass through the city." These same sentiments were voiced beyond the capital. "You may be a whiskey guzzling poker playing old buzzard as some say," a midwestern Republican wrote him, "but, by damn, for the first time since old Teddy left there in March of 1909, the United States has a grass roots *American* in the White House."

Armed with these ringing endorsements, Truman decided not to seek the consent of the Senate. Both Acheson and the chairman of the Senate Foreign Relations Committee, Tom Connally, advised against risking a long battle on the Hill and assured him that he had ample authority as commander in chief. "If a burglar breaks into your house, you can shoot at him without going down to the police station and getting permission," Connally told him. Truman also feared that if he went to Congress he would, in Acheson's words, set a "precedent in derogation of presidential power to send our forces into battle" that would burden his successors. Consequently, he asked approval neither for an act of war nor for intervening under the flag of the United Nations. He also blundered by insisting at a press conference, "We are not at war," and then permitting a reporter to put in his mouth a characterization of the intervention as a "police action." His failure to obtain congressional assent, which would readily have been given, enabled Republicans to indulge freely in criticism of him later, and when casualties mounted, "police action" seemed awkwardly flippant.

Truman's conduct riled a number of legislators. A Missouri senator said: "I notice that in the president's statement he says, 'I have ordered the fleet to prevent any attack on Formosa.' Does that mean he has arrogated to himself the authority of declaring war?" The loudest outcry came from "Mr. Republican," Robert Taft. The Ohio senator denounced Truman's order as "a complete usurpation by the president of authority to use the armed forces of the country. His action unquestionably has brought about a *de facto* war…without consulting Congress and without congressional approval." Unless there was a joint resolution, a measure he would back, Taft declared, "we would have finally terminated for all time the right of Congress to declare war, which is granted to Congress alone by the Constitution."

In the first fervor of nationalistic enthusiasm, though, most of Taft's colleagues joined in the ovation for Truman. When the House of Representatives heard the announcement from the White House, members rose from their seats to applaud, and in the Senate, Republican William Knowland said that the president's action should receive "the overwhelming support of all Americans, regardless of their partisan affiliation." Truman's decision, asserted his recent rival, Governor Dewey, "was necessary to the security of our country and the free world."

Both on Capitol Hill and in the countryside, that initial ardor quickly ebbed when the costs of challenging a greatly underrated foe began to set in. It took North Korean forces only three days to overrun Seoul, causing Syngman Rhee to abandon the capital. Green US soldiers, inadequately trained and poorly equipped, proved no match for enemy armor and troops greatly outnumbering them. Badly battered, the UN contingent had to hole up in the southeastern tip of the peninsula. Accounts of these events in the American press left newspaper readers distraught and irascible. "In heaven's name, what are you doing?" one citizen asked the president. "The blood hasn't dried from World War 2."

To reverse the course of the conflict, General MacArthur proposed an audacious plan: opening a salient behind enemy lines at the port of Inchon. In a heroic mode, he envisioned himself as the British commander James Wolfe, who in 1759 became "The Man Who Won the French and Indian War" by carrying off the seemingly impossible feat of scaling the Plains of Abraham, catching his adversary by surprise. Bradley and the Joint Chiefs hesitated to approve what appeared to be a daft scheme for an amphibious landing of fifty thousand men at a spot that had no beach, with forbidding seawalls and tides topping thirty feet, but Truman insisted that MacArthur be allowed to attack. The maneuver, executed on September 15, succeeded beyond all expectations. Inchon fell the next day; Seoul was recaptured in eleven days; pincer tactics trapped more than half of the North Korean army; and before the month was out, all of South Korea had been liberated. It was an astonishing turnaround, wholly because of MacArthur's brilliant tactic. With the aggressors routed and Syngman Rhee returned to office, Truman had fulfilled the purpose of his intervention, which Acheson had delineated as "solely for... restoring the Republic of Korea to its status prior to the invasion from the North."

At this critical juncture, Truman made a fateful and foolhardy decision. In the euphoria over Inchon, he authorized carrying the fighting into North Korea. In an "eyes only" message, the new Secretary of Defense, General Marshall, wired MacArthur, "We want you to feel unhampered tactically and strategically to proceed north of 38th parallel"—an extraordinary grant of license. No longer was the aim of the intervention to liberate South Korea; instead, it had become "the destruction of the North Korean Armed Forces." Implicit in this goal was the extermination of the North Korean government and the unification of the entire peninsula under Syngman Rhee.

A moment's reflection should have apprised Truman and his counselors that Mao's China could not conceivably accept the destruction of an adjacent Communist state, nor having its security jeopardized by a hostile country emerging abruptly on its border. At the end of September, Zhou Enlai, in an address celebrating the first anniversary of his regime, had served warning that China would not "supinely tolerate the destruction of its neighbor by the imperialist power." Through diplomatic channels, Beijing had let Washington know that if UN forces drove north across the parallel, China would step in militarily. But the State Department—conspicuously Acheson and Dean Rusk at the Far Eastern desk—was sure the Reds were bluffing, and Truman did not question this judgment.

In mid-October, the president took off from Washington for a theatrical rendezvous on Wake Island with Douglas MacArthur, whom he had never met. No affairs of state necessitated this ill-considered mission. Truman might have wanted to fly to a Pacific island in order to explore the possibility of Chinese intervention, but that prospect did not greatly concern him. He appears to have gone for no better reason than to gild his reputation and to boost Democratic chances in the forthcoming elections by being photographed with the hero of Inchon. The conference lasted only an hour, after which Truman turned around and completed his journey, which totaled nearly fifteen thousand miles.

To an interviewer years later, Truman spun out a melodramatic account of how he had given the general a dressing down for insolence toward a president and bragged that MacArthur "kissed my ass at that meeting." Totally untrue. Their rendezvous was cordial, though unproductive. On the tarmac, Truman honored MacArthur with a Distinguished Service Medal for his "vision, judgment, indomitable will, gallantry, and tenacity," and when he got stateside, he delivered an address lauding the general and emphasizing their complete agreement on strategy. Far from bringing MacArthur to heel, he had inflated the general's reputation, for MacArthur had refused to go to America to see the president; the president had humbled himself by flying to Wake.

In the course of their discursive exchange, Truman asked what chance there was that the Chinese would respond militarily to the approach of a hostile force to their border. "Very little," MacArthur replied. If the Chinese did hazard a move down the peninsula, the commander said, "there would be the greatest slaughter." By Thanksgiving, he promised, the war would be over; by Christmas, GIs would be back in Japan; and by New Year's Day, the UN would be holding elections in Korea—united under Western control. In January, he would be able to spare a division for service in Europe. So confident were both men of this scenario that they talked at some length about how to reconstruct Korea after the UN triumph a short time away. Not even a lightning-strike foray by Chinese forces into Korea on November 1 alerted the administration to the perils that lay ahead.

Only hours after MacArthur launched his "boys home for Christmas" offensive on November 24, half a million Chinese troops poured across the border. Wave after wave engulfed UN forces. Disobeying orders to put South Koreans at the head of the UN force, MacArthur had placed US soldiers at the front, where, peering across the frozen Yalu, they had been able to see Manchuria, and the Chinese on the other bank had been able to observe the provocation. Very early on the morning of November 28, General Bradley phoned Truman to report that he had received "a terrible message" from MacArthur. After absorbing the news, the president told his staff, "We've got a terrific situation on our hands." Disconsolate, Truman wrote in his diary: "I've worked for peace for five years and six months and looks like World War III is here."

The United States confronted "an entirely new war," MacArthur reported. "This command...is now faced with conditions beyond...its strength." The bloodied US 8th Division reeled backward in the longest retreat in American history—one that has been likened to Napoleon's from Moscow. GIs spent Christmas not opening presents in warm quarters in Japan but fighting on nasty terrain with the unnerving din of screeching winds in subzero cold. Temperatures as low as −25° cost as many lives as were inflicted by the vastly bigger Chinese army. The radio commentator Walter Winchell told his audience: "If you have a son overseas, write to him. If you have a son in the Second Infantry Division, pray for him."

MacArthur demanded reinforcements of the "greatest magnitude" and urged expansion of the war into China. He wanted to pursue MIGs across the Yalu, blockade the Chinese coast, unleash Chiang's Nationalist army on Formosa to attack the mainland, and bomb mainland China's heavily populated cities. He favored dropping thirty or fifty atomic bombs on China, an operation widely supported in the United States. In Montana, a draft board refused to induct any men until MacArthur was authorized to employ atomic bombs. But neither Truman nor the National Security Council favored earning obloquy by annihilating millions of civilians or getting bogged down in a conflict on the Asian continent, not least because such a course would give Russia a free hand in Europe.

Truman did, however, talk in a way that kindled anxiety. Recognizing that the main liability of the Democrats in the recent elections had been news of the Chinese offensive in Korea, he resolved to take advantage of a press conference to express his determination to win the war. But he stumbled badly. Asked if one of the weapons he might employ was the atomic bomb, Truman, who made a vice of the virtue of directness, replied, "That includes every weapon we have." Furthermore, he said that "the military commander in the field will have charge of the use of the weapons." Thoroughly alarmed at the prospect that MacArthur was being authorized to drop an atomic bomb, if he saw fit, British prime minister Clement Attlee scurried to Washington. The president tried to placate him, but the damage had been done.

Instead of shouldering responsibility for his gross miscalculation, MacArthur foisted all of the blame on spineless politicians. As early as August 1950, he sent a message to the Veterans of Foreign Wars implying that Truman was guilty of "timidity or vacillation." In December, he informed *U.S. News & World Report* that "extraordinary inhibitions... without precedent in military history" were preventing him from carrying the war to the enemy. The Joint Chiefs did nothing to silence MacArthur because they were intimidated by him. Even when McArthur deliberately sabotaged an effort to negotiate a truce, the government temporized. In March 1951, after UN forces under the resourceful General Matthew Ridgway had retaken Seoul and freed all of South Korea, Truman and the United Nations associates resolved to reach a settlement on the basis of status quo antebellum, with both sides accepting a dividing line approximating the 38th parallel. Four days after he was informed of this decision, MacArthur issued a brazen statement preempting his superiors by threatening "an expansion of our military operations to... coastal areas and interior bases," an offensive that "would doom Red China." Acheson regarded MacArthur's "pronunciamento" as "insubordination of the grossest sort," and General Bradley saw it as "unforgivable and irretrievable." Nonetheless, no one did anything about it.

It required one more episode of defiance to impel Truman to move. On April 5, 1951, the Republican minority leader, Congressman Joe Martin, read aloud on the floor of the House a letter he had received from MacArthur: "It seems strangely difficult for some to realize that here in Asia is where the Communist conspirators have elected to make their play for global conquest, and that... here we fight Europe's war with arms while the diplomats there still fight it with words.... As you point out, we must win. There is no substitute for victory." Truman entered in his diary: "This looks like the last straw. Rank insubordination." But, though furious, he still hesitated to fire the immensely popular five-star general who was promising the American people victory while all he could offer was a return to the conditions before all the bloodletting had begun. The president came to recognize, though, that only one course was open to him.

On April 11, 1951, Truman cabled MacArthur, "I deeply regret that it becomes my duty as President and Commander in Chief of the United States military forces to replace you as Supreme Commander, Allied Powers; Commander in Chief, United Nations Command; Commander in Chief, Far East; and Commanding General, US Army." He accompanied this announcement with a press release declaring: "It is fundamental... that military commanders must be governed by the policies and directives issued to them."

Mail to the White House ran 20–1 in opposition to Truman's deed, and from New England to the Pacific Coast flags were lowered to half-staff and the president was burned in effigy. The Los Angeles City Council recessed in "sorrowful contemplation of the political assassination of General MacArthur." Senator McCarthy called the president a "son of a bitch" who was the pawn of a White House cabal addled by "bourbon and benzedrine." Some even insinuated that Truman was a Russian plant. "The country today," said Senator William Jenner of Indiana, "is in the hands of a secret coterie which is directed by agents of the Soviet Union." The *Chicago Tribune* declared: "President Truman must be impeached and convicted. His hasty and vindictive removal of Gen. MacArthur is the culmination of a series of acts which have shown that he is unfit, morally and mentally, for his high office. The American nation has never been in greater danger. It is led by a fool who is surrounded by knaves."

MacArthur, who had not set foot in the United States since 1937, returned to a welcome unparalleled in the country's annals. On his journey east, one hundred thousand people greeted him in Honolulu, a half million in San Francisco. In Manhattan's financial district more ticker tape fluttered down on him than had on Lindbergh or General Eisenhower. And Republicans saw to it that he received a special invitation to come to Washington to deliver a formal oration on Capitol Hill.

In a masterful address to a joint session of Congress, MacArthur denounced Truman's policies as "appeasement" and stated, falsely, that the Joint Chiefs "fully shared" his convictions. In an indictment of limited war, he recounted, "Why, my soldiers asked of me, surrender military advantages to an enemy in the field?" Dropping his voice to a whisper, he said, "I could not answer." He wound up with a peroration that provided the lyrics for a mawkish pop tune. Reminding the spellbound legislators that he was "closing...52 years of military service," he concluded, in the manner of a histrionic Lionel Barrymore:

> The hopes and dreams have long since vanished. But I still remember the refrain of one of the most popular barracks ballads of that day which proclaimed most proudly that "Old soldiers never die. They just fade away." And like the old soldier of the ballad, I now close my military career and just fade away—an old soldier who tried to do his duty as God gave him the light to see that duty.
>
> Goodbye.

During the thirty-four minutes he spoke, applause punctuated his words thirty times. Herbert Hoover saw MacArthur as "a reincarnation of St. Paul into a great General of the Army who came out of the East," and Congressman Dewey Short, who had studied at Harvard, Oxford, and Heidelberg, said that he had been in the presence of "God in the flesh, the voice of God."

The fanatical adulation did not long endure, save among far-right nationalists. Republican insistence on a blue ribbon congressional inquiry backfired when the country learned that, contrary to MacArthur's claim, the Pentagon supported Truman, less because of the general's willful disobedience than because he was a blunderer with faulty conceptions of strategy and tactics. MacArthur's approach, declared General Omar Bradley, chairman of the Joint Chiefs of Staff, "would involve us in the wrong war, at the wrong place, at the wrong time, and with the wrong enemy." Seven weeks of testimony exposed the illogic of MacArthur's approach, for he was maintaining that small casualties in limited engagements were intolerable while huge losses in all-out conflicts were acceptable. The country was informed too that if, after Hiroshima and Nagasaki, the United States once again dropped atomic bombs on Asians, it would never be able to overcome the damage to its standing in the third world. Headstrong and self-infatuated, MacArthur made a poor showing. He did not believe, it became clear, that the president, the Joint Chiefs, the UN Security Council, or anyone else had the right to give orders to a commander. Alarmed by the prospect of a man on horseback, the editor of the *Nation* spoke for others in writing that the president had "ended a very present threat of Bonapartism." Truman's action has come to be seen as the most important blow ever struck for the principle of civilian control of the military and for the prerogatives of a chief executive. "I didn't fire him because he was a dumb son of a bitch, although he was," he later told an interviewer. "I fired him because he wouldn't respect the authority of the president."

MacArthur's comedown did not liberate Truman from the burden of a miserable war in Asia that persisted for all the rest of his days in the White House and beyond. American casualties, totaling more than fifty-seven thousand at the time the UN commander was fired, continued to mount—and for no better reason than to take or hold meaningless terrain: No-Name Ridge, Pork Chop Hill, Heartbreak Ridge. One American soldier said, "It's the war we can't win, we can't lose, we can't quit." On the floor of the House, Joe Martin said, "If we are not in Korea to win, then this Administration should be indicted for the murder of thousands of American boys." By October 1951, 56 percent of respondents to a poll agreed that Korea was a "useless war." From the spring of 1951 to the end of his presidency in 1953, Truman's standing in the polls never rose above 32 percent.

The president, with no hope of ending the war by force of arms, could not get out of it at the negotiating table either, for the United States would not agree to forcible repatriation of Chinese and North Korean prisoners, who, Truman declared, did not want "to return to slavery and almost certain death at the hands of the communists." It appeared that the loss of life would go on forever—brutally, pointlessly. In January 1952, Truman expressed his frustration in another mindless rant in his diary: "It seems to me that the proper approach now would be an ultimatum with a ten day expiration limit, informing Moscow that we intend to blockade the China coast from the Korean border to Indo-China and that we intend to destroy every military base in Manchuria. . . . This means all out war. It means that Moscow, St. Petersburg, Mukden, Vladivostok, Peking, Shanghai, Port Arthur, Dairen, Odessa, Stalingrad and every manufacturing plant in China and the Soviet Union will be eliminated." Four months later, he vented in his diary: "Now do you want an end to hostilities in Korea or do you want China and Siberia destroyed?" He signed that entry "The C. in C."

Truman always regarded his intervention in Korea as his biggest achievement when, in fact, it was his greatest failure. If the United States had displayed credible determination, it is improbable that the invasion, and the ensuing war with so many deaths, would ever have happened. Throughout his first term and well into his second term, Truman proclaimed a large role for America in world affairs at the same time that he insisted on a constrained military budget. When he decided to intercede in Korea, he threw into combat—into slaughter—young draftees unprepared for confrontation with hardened warriors in tank brigades. He followed that up by approving a reckless invasion of North Korea—with an outcome that General Ridgway later likened to Custer's at Little Big Horn—on the fatuous assumption that China would not retaliate, and by tolerating MacArthur's insubordination far longer than he should have.

The Korean War had long-range consequences. When the United States was struggling against Communists in Asia, it seemed unreasonable to deny aid to a NATO ally in French Indochina in putting down an insurrection. Though Truman never considered sending US soldiers, his action was a first step toward the ultimate American involvement in Vietnam. After the French nation had wearied of *"la guerre sale"* (the dirty war), the American government, with an initial investment of more than $2 billion, adopted Southeast Asia as a battleground in the Cold War. By the time Truman left office, the United States was footing 40 percent of the cost of France's struggle against the Communist Vietminh.

In these years, Truman took a long stride toward the imperial presidency. Wilson in 1917 and FDR in 1941 had asked Congress for a declaration of war, but after Truman's unilateral action in Korea, the power vested in Congress alone to declare war became almost a relic. "By insisting that the presidential prerogative alone sufficed to meet the requirements of the Constitution," Arthur Schlesinger Jr. later concluded, "Truman...dramatically and dangerously enlarged the power of future Presidents to take the nation into major war." Truman further expanded executive power by sending four US divisions to Germany in 1951 without requesting congressional assent, an action he justified by his authority as commander in chief. A "Great Debate" ensued, but although senators railed against his bold initiative, they did nothing effective to negate it or to rescind the precedent he had set.

Finally, Truman, who tried so hard for so long to avoid a massive arms buildup, bears a considerable share of the responsibility for the militarization of American society. The Korean War broke down his resistance to NSC-68 so completely that, in a total reversal of his earlier position, he more than quadrupled the defense budget. At its inception, the Marshall Plan set down as a requirement for aid that not a penny could go to armaments. In 1951, the United States stipulated that henceforth every US dollar sent to Europe had to be earmarked for the military.

———

Truman's last months in office brought him little save tribulation. By November 1951, the president's approval rating, which had begun at 87 percent, had descended to 23 percent—the lowest recorded since polling began. On January 1, 1952, he scribbled in his diary: "What a New Year's Day! 1952 is here and so am I—gloomy as can be." He ended his presidency knowing that in the 1952 presidential campaign, he had been regarded as a huge liability. But throughout this period, he continued to battle.

With no expectation of getting liberal legislation through Congress, he resorted to other weapons in the arsenal of a president. He defended the national domain by blocking an attempt to turn "tidelands" oil over to the states, and he vetoed a bill hiking the price of natural gas, though it had the backing of powerful Democratic senators. (On hearing of this courageous act, the liberal Illinois senator Paul Douglas cried, "God bless the president of the United States!") To constrain the excesses of the Red Scare, Truman vetoed two measures sponsored by the McCarthyite Democrat Senator McCarran. In his message condemning an omnibus Internal Security Act providing for the internment of subversives in an emergency, he declared, "In a free country, we punish men for the crimes they commit, but never for the opinions they have." He denounced the McCarran-Walter Immigration Act of 1952 as "worse than the infamous Alien Act of 1798." By large margins, Congress overrode both vetoes.

On behalf of civil rights, the Truman administration made full use of the powers of the executive branch. The Justice Department, following up on its earlier amicus brief in the suit against restrictive covenants in housing, went into court again in two education cases that resulted in decisions shredding the 1896 rationalization of segregation in *Plessy v. Ferguson*. When a lawsuit challenged an Interstate Commerce Commission ruling upholding racially segregated dining cars, the Justice Department, instead of taking the expected course of defending a government agency, pleaded error. "Together" these three interventions, one historian has written, "constituted the most formidable legal assault ever made on Jim Crow." The Truman administration went still further by interceding on behalf of black plaintiffs in the landmark litigation *Brown v. Board,* with a thirty-two-page brief that has been called "a good deal more useful to the Justices than all ten briefs filed...by the litigants."

As a consequence of these actions, a scholar has observed, "the South's hatred of Truman bordered on the fanatical." He had set himself against Gulf states wanting to cash in on the tidelands, gas-and-oil Democrats seeking to exploit their resources, and, most of all, whites throughout the former Confederacy who were determined to perpetuate racial caste. In the hot contest for US senator in South Carolina between Strom Thurmond and Olin Johnston, the candidates, reported the *New York Times,* "gave the impression that their chances for election...rested upon the vehemence with which they could denounce President Truman and his civil rights program." A Sumter newspaper reported: "Who Dislikes Truman Most? It's the Burning Question in South Carolina's Race for Senate." It charged Senator Johnston with being "tainted with Trumanism," the worst accusation that could have been laid upon him. Thurmond himself derided Johnston as "a Trumanite,...a man who wants to break down all separation of the races." To regain momentum, Johnston called that "political mishap" Truman "a blabbermouth."

The president's conduct of the Korean War aroused further ill feeling. On December 15, 1950, he had announced a state of national emergency. Though there was no prospect that either the North Koreans or the Chinese would cross the wide Pacific in pursuit of Americans, he maintained, "Our homes, our Nation, all the things we believe in, are in great danger." To establish order in an overheated economy, he set up an Office of Defense Mobilization and appointed the head of General Electric, Charles E. Wilson, to run it. Despite his unhappy experience with price and wage controls in his first term, he reimposed them. Nonetheless, prices skyrocketed, causing still more resentment.

Truman's attempt to clamp a lid on prices brought about the greatest confrontation between a president and the Supreme Court in the half century following World War II. The conflict began in the fall of 1951 when, with steel corporations raking in huge profits, the United Steelworkers announced that its 650,000 members would walk off their jobs when their contract expired on December 31 if they did not receive a pay boost. After Truman referred their demand to the Wage Stabilization Board, the union consented to postpone the strike until April 8. The board reported in favor of a raise of twenty-six cents an hour, which the union accepted but the steel firms rejected unless they were granted a big price hike. Truman, who balked at the steel firms' terms, accused corporation executives of trying to exploit the emergency. Without a settlement, the steelworkers resumed preparations for a work stoppage that could shut down the mills for a protracted period.

Since Congress would not intervene, Truman decided that he had to act to ward off a strike that would cut off vital supplies in wartime. The president, he reasoned, "must use whatever power the Constitution does not expressly deny him." If Lincoln could suspend the right to habeas corpus in wartime, he could take the much less drastic step of seizing the mills, he believed, for "the President of the United States has very great inherent powers to meet great national emergencies." Having witnessed the Supreme Court's validation of expansive presidential power since the Constitutional Revolution of 1937, he anticipated that his action would be upheld, but, in coming to that expectation, the historian Maeva Marcus has observed, "he did not consider the fine legal line between a congressionally declared war and a presidentially instituted one" and did not bear in mind that his "political base had evaporated." On April 8, hours before the walkout was scheduled to begin, Truman issued an executive order directing his secretary of commerce, Charles Sawyer, "to take possession of and operate the plants and facilities of certain steel companies." The corporations speedily took legal action to quash the decree.

On June 2, 1952, in *Youngstown Sheet and Tube Co. v. Sawyer*, the US Supreme Court, dividing 6–3, ruled Truman's edict unconstitutional. For years, Felix Frankfurter had been feuding with a liberal bloc on the Court led by William O. Douglas and Hugo Black, but on this matter all three agreed. In the majority as well were two of Truman's appointees—one of them Tom Clark, a former attorney general. All six in the majority concluded that Truman had overstepped, but they could not come together on precisely how they thought he had transgressed. Each of the six filed a separate opinion.

Speaking for the Court, Hugo Black enunciated a rigid conception of the separation of powers and of the circumscribed nature of the presidential office: "In the framework of our Constitution, the President's power to see that the laws are faithfully executed refutes the idea that he is to be a lawmaker. The Constitution limits his functions in the lawmaking process to the recommending of laws he thinks wise and the vetoing of laws he thinks bad. And the Constitution is neither silent nor equivocal about who shall make laws which the President is to execute. The first section of the first article says that 'All legislative powers herein granted shall be vested in a Congress of the United States.' "

None of the other justices was willing to go so far in boxing in a president. In his concurrence, Robert Jackson maintained that though the Founding Fathers had divided powers among the three branches, they had also, in the interest of viable government, provided for sharing of power: "separateness but interdependence, autonomy but reciprocity." Yet Jackson too thought that Truman had flouted the will of Congress, which, in the Taft-Hartley Act, had stipulated that property could not be seized to forestall a strike. In finding that Truman had encroached upon the congressional domain, Jackson declared, "I cannot be brought to believe that this country will suffer if the Court refuses further to aggrandize the presidential office, already so potent and so relatively immune from judicial review, at the expense of Congress." Jackson expanded on that assertion by saying, "No doctrine that the Court could promulgate would seem to me more sinister and alarming than that a President whose conduct of foreign affairs is so largely uncontrolled... can vastly enlarge his mastery over the internal affairs of the country." The Constitution, in establishing the president as commander in chief of the army and navy, did not also make him "Commander in Chief of the country, its industries and its inhabitants."

Even in the era of the Cold War, the Court made clear, a president's powers were not limitless. Rexford Tugwell, who had been a member of FDR's Brain Trust, called the ruling "perhaps the most serious setback the presidency has ever suffered," because Truman, attempting to assert the authority of his office, had precipitated a decision that has been a warning light to presidents ever since. Glumly, Truman returned the mills to the owners and, as a long strike got under way, held his tongue, but not without composing another of those letters that he never sent. He wrote Justice Douglas: "I am sorry that I didn't have an opportunity to discuss precedents with you before you came to the conclusion on that crazy decision. I don't see how a Court made up of so-called 'Liberals' could do what that Court did to me."

His knuckles rapped by the Supreme Court, Truman had to endure the further embarrassment of headlines blazoning accusations of corruption in his administration. Though the press overreached in writing of "the Missouri Gang," a term implying a similarity to Harding's notorious Ohio Gang, the allegations did bring to light the president's penchant for unfortunate appointments. On resigning from the cabinet, Harold Ickes had called Truman's choices "a nondescript band of political Lilliputians" and characterized his style as "government by crony." The columnist Joseph Alsop wrote his cousin Eleanor Roosevelt that, in contrast to FDR's time, the White House resembled "the lounge of the Lion's Club of Independence, Missouri, where one is conscious chiefly of the odor of ten-cent cigars and the easy laughter evoked by the new smoking room story." Sometimes, Truman could be shockingly irresponsible. To rid the White House of one of his poker buddies, Naval Aide Jake Vardaman, who had become a nuisance, he elevated him to the Federal Reserve Board.

Investigative journalists insinuated that the White House had become a haven for chiselers. Truman had appointed to his staff, with the rank of major general, an old army chum, Harry Vaughan, who was written off as a "flap-mouthed dunderhead" with the face of "a slack, vacuous St. Bernard," and the president refused to part with him even though the general had accepted gifts of highly valued deep freezers and was associating with a man who was pocketing a 5 percent fee for procuring government contracts—activity that led to the coining of the derogatory term "five percenter." Sleuths also found out that Vaughan had taken advantage of his proximity to the Oval Office to further the interests of the developer of a racetrack. A more inviting target for photographers was a lowly stenographer who turned up for work at the White House on winter mornings flaunting a $9,450 royal pastel mink coat—a present from her husband, a former Reconstruction Finance Corporation loan examiner who, after leaving his government job, had become a big-time fixer with easy access to the executive mansion. Later, he would be sentenced to prison for committing perjury.

A hostile press made these developments seem far more venal than they were. Influence peddling was not illegal, and no connection was ever established between the mink coat and malfeasance by a federal official. No one in the White House orbit was remotely engaged in the kind of criminal activity that disfigured the Harding years. The worst that a critical Washington correspondent could bring himself to say against Vaughan was that he was "a big mud-brained jerk throwing his weight around for small favors." Furthermore, commentators overlooked the many exemplary appointments Truman made: among them, George Catlett Marshall, David Lilienthal, Averell Harriman, and Clark Clifford. Still, there was more than a little that was seamy about Vaughan's associates, and it was imperative for the president, especially as a former machine politician, to make clear that he would not tolerate sleaze.

Instead, he became aggressively defensive—huffy, testy, stonewalling inquirers and giving every indication that not even the most irrefutable proof would impel him to scotch wrongdoing. True to his tutelage in Kansas City politics, he was determined to be loyal to subordinates who he was sure were being falsely arraigned, as they sometimes were. But he showed little awareness of the crass impression he was projecting. When the young Democratic senator from Tennessee Estes Kefauver, as chair of a special committee to investigate organized crime, exposed the unsavory links of Democratic mayors to mobsters, the president expressed outrage not at the betrayal of public trust but at Kefauver for uncovering it. "Truman," as Hamby has written, "had no sense of the number of bullets he was firing through his feet."

The issue mounted in importance after congressional committees fingered not General Vaughan's peccadilloes but an epidemic of malfeasance in the Reconstruction Finance Corporation, the Bureau of Internal Revenue, and the Tax Division of the Department of Justice. Once again, Truman's response was tardy. To his credit, he reorganized the RFC in February 1951 and put a tough administrator in charge. Not until January 1952, however, did he begin to revamp the Bureau of Internal Revenue. When his appointee as attorney general, Howard McGrath, discharged an arrogant special prosecutor for being too zealous in seeking to root out pervasive misconduct, Truman fired the attorney general. But that did not happen until April 1952. In a single year, 166 Internal Revenue officials resigned or were dismissed, a number of them facing indictments and eventual conviction for tax fixing, bribery, extortion, and embezzlement. Repelled by the extent of the corruption, the public found the intricate details of tax collecting harder to grasp than the simpler narratives of General Vaughan and the befurred stenographer. As the 1952 presidential campaign approached, Republicans relished the prospect of making "five percenters," "deep freezers," and "mink coat" stigmata of the indifference of Democrats to moral turpitude.

With Truman in ill repute, Democrats reached into a midwestern state house for their 1952 presidential nominee, Governor Adlai Stevenson of Illinois, and, in a transparent gambit to placate mutinous southerners, chose Senator John Sparkman of Alabama as his running mate. To distance himself from the White House, Stevenson got rid of the Democratic national chairman picked by Truman and set up headquarters not in Washington but in Springfield, Illinois. Implicitly or directly, the Democratic nominees disavowed Truman. Sparkman said that the president had bungled the steel strike, and Stevenson infuriated Truman by vowing to "clean up the mess in Washington." In another of his letters scrawled in a high dudgeon but never mailed, Truman, deliberately misspelling Senator Kefauver's name, wrote Stevenson: "I'm telling you to take your crackpots, your high socialites with their noses in the air, run your campaign and win if you can. Cowfever could not have treated me any more shabbily than have you."

Stevenson had the misfortune to run not against Robert Taft, as the Democrats had initially anticipated, but against the immensely popular Dwight Eisenhower, who bested Taft in a hard-fought contest. The general had not wanted to run. In 1948, he had said that "nothing in the international or domestic situation especially qualifies for the most important office in the world a man whose adult years have been spent in the military services. At least, this is true in my case." Furthermore, he had no objection to Taft's conservative views on domestic policy. But he reluctantly agreed to enter the race because he feared that the Ohioan would undo the international structure he had helped build. To appease the resentful Taft wing of the party, the convention—the first on national television—gave the vice presidential nomination to the young Red-hunting California senator Richard Nixon, in recognition of the voting potential of the Pacific Coast and the power of the Communist issue.

Hardly had the GOP campaign gotten under way when it hit a roadblock. In mid-September, a New York newspaper revealed that Nixon had been the recipient of a secret fund solicited from California businessmen. For a party crusading against corruption, the implication that Nixon's votes on issues had been paid for was extremely awkward. A hostage to self-pity, Nixon always thought that the media were out to get him and that they treated him unfairly. This time he was right. There was very little money in the fund, certainly not enough to buy anyone's vote, and no evidence of misdeeds. But the UPI syndicate circulated the story under the headline NIXON SCANDAL FUND, and the *Sacramento Bee* charged that Nixon was "front man" for "rich southern Californians." The *New York Post* went further: SECRET RICH MEN'S TRUST FUND KEEPS NIXON IN STYLE FAR BEYOND HIS SALARY. As the furor mounted, Eisenhower became agitated. "Of what avail is it," he asked, "for us to carry on this Crusade against this business of what has been going on in Washington if we ourselves aren't as clean as a hound's tooth?" On learning that Nixon was going to appear on a national television network to defend himself, Eisenhower, using Governor Dewey as an intermediary, instructed his running mate to conclude his talk by announcing that he was withdrawing from the ticket. That unsettling message reached Nixon less than two hours before he had to nerve himself for a demanding performance.

On September 23, 1952, the largest audience that had ever watched a television program—sixty million—tuned in to Nixon's half-hour denial of misconduct. Unlike the Truman administration, he said, he was not going to ignore accusations. He spoke of his impoverished childhood and of his war service in the Pacific. ("I guess I'm entitled to a couple of stars...but I was just there when the bombs were falling.") To the embarrassment of his wife, who sat by his side so stony-faced she seemed programmed, he bared the most private details of their financial situation, including the fact that he had no insurance on her and their children: "Pat doesn't have a mink coat," he confided. "But she does have a respectable Republican cloth coat. And I always tell her that she'd look good in anything." He went on:

> One other thing I probably should tell you because if we don't they'll probably be saying this about me too. We did get...a gift after the election.... You know what it was? It was a little cocker spaniel.... Black and white spotted. And our little girl—Tricia, the 6-year-old—named it Checkers. And you know, the kids, like all kids, love the dog

and I just want to say this right now, that regardless of what they say about it, we're gonna keep it.

The "Checkers Speech," as ever after it has been tagged, appalled sophisticates as a mawkish descent into soap opera in which Nixon had humiliated himself, but it was very cleverly contrived and enormously effective. Though, as his biographer Stephen Ambrose later noted, a number of critics viewed the address as "one of the most sickening, disgusting, maudlin performances ever experienced," more than four million letters, wires, and phone calls—running 75–1 in favor of Nixon's remaining on the ticket—inundated Republican headquarters. By cannily making the GOP National Committee the arbiter, the California senator had taken the decision away from Eisenhower and left him no option but to go along. At their next meeting, Ike thrust out his hand and said, "Dick, you're my boy." The impact of the Checkers Speech revealed that, for the first time in a presidential campaign, television had become a significant forum. Since the 1948 election, the number of households with a TV set had soared from 172,000 to 15.3 million, one-third of the country. Taking advantage of this new medium, Eisenhower addressed the electorate in a number of thirty-two-second TV spots. Commentators accused the Republicans of "selling the President like toothpaste," and Adlai Stevenson protested, "The idea that you can merchandise candidates for high office like breakfast cereals—that you can gather votes like box tops—is... the ultimate indignity to the democratic process."

A second controversy arose early in October when Eisenhower's campaign tour took him to Wisconsin, home state of Joe McCarthy, who had accused General Marshall of taking part in "a conspiracy so immense, an infamy so black, as to dwarf any previous such venture in the history of man." Eisenhower knew not only that Marshall was a fine man of unimpeachable loyalty to his country but also that he, more than anyone else, was responsible for Ike's rise in the military to a position of prominence. Reporters received an advance copy of Eisenhower's address, in which he planned to affirm that Marshall had demonstrated the "profoundest patriotism." But, with McCarthy sharing the platform, Eisenhower deleted that statement from his speech. Instead, he gave a talk that could have come from McCarthy. For "two whole decades," he said, alluding to the FDR and Truman years, America had been "poisoned" by indulgence of Communists, with "a government by men whose very brains were confused by the opiate of this deceit." They were responsible, he charged, for the fall of China and, in eastern Europe, for the "surrender of whole nations." Eisenhower added, "We have seen this sort of thing go on and on until my running mate, Dick Nixon, grabbed a police whistle and stopped it." It was the low point of Ike's long career. Incensed by Eisenhower's perfidy, Truman told an Indiana crowd, "I thought he might make a good president, but that was a mistake. In this campaign he has betrayed almost everything I thought he stood for."

Republicans in 1952 encoded their message in a chemical formula: K_1C_2 (Korea, Communism, Corruption). In a vicious assault, Nixon, calling Truman and Acheson "traitors to the high principles in which many of the nation's Democrats believe," charged that Stevenson held a "Ph.D. from Dean Acheson's Cowardly College of Communist Containment." In late October, Eisenhower took hold of the Korea issue with a headline-grabbing declaration. At the climax of a powerful indictment of the Truman administration for bringing about the deaths of thousands of American soldiers by "appalling" conduct that had all but invited an invasion, Ike announced that he planned to bring the bloody conflict in Asia to "an early and honorable end." To accomplish that, he declared, "I shall go to Korea."

Eisenhower's statement provoked both the president and his long-time associates among the Joint Chiefs. Having accepted appointment as supreme commander of NATO, the general had been a member of Truman's inner council on foreign affairs. "Ike was well informed on all aspects of the Korean War and the delicacy of the armistice negotiations," General Bradley later reflected. "He knew very well that he could achieve nothing by going on to Korea." When Eisenhower spelled out his ideas on how to achieve peace, they were vacuous. But by pledging to go to Korea, he had delivered the masterstroke of the 1952 campaign.

In November, Eisenhower scored a smashing victory, running up 442 electoral votes to Stevenson's 89. His followers, sporting "I like Ike" buttons, warmed to his radiant grin and genial manner. "The crowd is with him," reported one correspondent. "Idolatry shows in their solemn, upturned faces." Both arms extended overhead in a victory salute, he

The cold warriors. Secretary of Defense George Marshall, President Truman, and Secretary of State Dean Acheson bid farewell to General Dwight D. Eisenhower, who is heading for Europe to inspect Atlantic Pact forces. He was named supreme allied commander of NATO in December 1950. *Courtesy of the Harry S. Truman Library and Museum, Accession number 2005-16*

projected, too, an image of high competence—of a man with the military experience to bring the American troops home from Korea. In thrashing Stevenson, Eisenhower captured not only four southern states but the president's home state of Missouri. Though Stevenson was the ostensible loser, commentators said that when voters went to the polls they were actually turning thumbs down on the president. They wanted no more of Harry Truman.

The next generation held a very different view of Truman. In the mid-1970s such a tidal wave of adulation swept the country that *Time* labeled it "Trumania." James Whitmore's impersonation, *Give 'Em Hell Harry!*, played to standing room only; Merle Miller's assemblage of interviews with the former president, *Plain Speaking*, became a best seller; a roadside restaurant chain with shops offering customers a choice of plates each bearing the picture of a different president reported that the number-one favorite was Mr. Truman; and the rock group Chicago pumped up audiences with the lyrics:

America needs you, Harry Truman,
Harry, could you please come home?

This national infatuation with Truman derived less from retrospective fondness for his policies than from admiration for his character—a quality, historians came to realize, to which they had given too little attention in appraising presidents. "Trumania," explained the historian John Lukacs, "was the national appreciation for a man of the older American type: outspoken, courageous, loyal to his friends, solidly rooted in his mid-American past, and *real*—a self-crafted piece of solid wood, not a molded plastic piece." The essayist Gerald Johnson, stressing that "government must at all cost be conducted with honesty and courage or it will inevitably blow up," said of Truman: "Croesus couldn't buy nor the devil scare him."

Truman had an instinctive distrust of people he regarded as "counterfeits." His grandfather had taught him that whenever you heard someone praying unnaturally loudly, "you'd better go home and lock your smokehouse." Simple in manner, he was no less straightforward in speech. Richard Nixon, he once said, was "a shifty-eyed goddamn liar." When a woman offended by his using the word "manure" asked his wife, "Bess, couldn't you get the president to say 'fertilizer'?" the first lady replied, "Heavens no. It took me twenty-five years to get him to say 'manure.'" When he mailed personal letters from the White House, he purchased his own stamps and pasted them on himself. His sister, Mary Jane, once gave a capsule summary of their upbringing: "Mamma said just be in the key of B natural, and that's what all of us have always been."

On his desk he had placed a framed manuscript with two sentences that Mark Twain had written out: "Always do right! This will gratify some people and astonish the rest." In his well-worn copy of Marcus Aurelius's *Meditations*, he underlined "If it is not right, do not do it; if it is not true, do not say it." He once ruminated in a memo:

I wonder how far Moses would have gone if he had taken a poll in Egypt?

What would Jesus Christ have preached if He had taken a poll in the land of Israel?

Where would the Reformation have gone if Martin Luther had taken a poll?

It isn't polls or public opinion alone of the moment that counts. It is right and wrong, and leadership—men with fortitude, honesty and a belief in the right that makes epochs in the history of the world.

Instead of exulting in the new lease on power the 1948 election had given him, Truman had worried that Washington, which radiated so much authority, could magnify an officeholder's sense of importance. He told his staff, "Every once in a while I notice it in myself, and try to drag it out in the open." When, at a reunion breakfast on the morning of his inauguration in 1949, World War I buddies addressed him with the respect appropriate to his office, he told them, "We'll have none of that now. When I put on those striped pants and that top hat, you can call me 'Mister President,' but here and at all such reunion occasions you can make it just 'Captain Harry.'" A president "hears a hundred voices telling him that he is the greatest man in the world," Truman remarked. "He must listen carefully indeed to hear the one voice that tells him he is not." He reported home on one of his trips, "People all along the way wanted to see the President—not me!"

Truman had a strong aversion to historical figures with grandiose views of themselves. He resolved not to be one of them. He wrote his daughter: "To be a good President I fear a man ... can't live the Sermon on the Mount. He must be a Machiavelli, Louis XI of France, Caesar, Borgia, Talleyrand, a liar, double-crosser, and an unctious religio (Richelieu), a hero and a what-not to be successful. But I probably won't be, thanks be to God. . . . I'm . . . trying the opposite approach. Maybe it will win." Some time after he left the White House, a reporter asked him whether he had changed. "Not in the slightest," Truman answered. "They are trying to make a statesman out of me but they will never succeed." He meant it. On a visit to Athens in 1964, he refused to look at a life-sized statue of himself not far from his hotel because he thought it improper to erect monuments to living persons.

At his three-hundredth press conference in his last year in office when his reputation was bottoming, he told reporters:

> I have tried my best to give the nation everything I have in me. There are a great many people—I suppose a million in this country—who could have done the job better than I did it. But I had the job and I had to do it.
>
> I always quote an epitaph which is in the cemetery at Tombstone, Arizona. It says: "Here lies Jack Williams. He done his damnedest." I think that is the greatest epitaph a man can have—when he gives everything that is in him to the job he has before him. That is all that you can ask of him and that is what I have tried to do.

Later he reflected, "I wasn't one of the great Presidents, but I had a good time trying to be one, I can tell you that."

Though the concentration on character and temperament is understandable, it distracts attention from the substance of his performance. He made too many lackluster appointments, frequently shot off his mouth, paid insufficient heed to the damage wrought by his loyalty program, and, in Korea, badly overreached. His unsent letters are acutely disturbing. Truman also, though, succeeded in fighting off assaults on the New Deal legacy he inherited and would have achieved much more if he had been able to put through the Fair Deal, especially his proposal for national health insurance. He boldly fortified civilian control of the military, and he expanded the range of the executive office to an extent that has never been adequately recognized.

Even historians steeped in the period find it hard to absorb the totality of the extraordinary range of events in foreign affairs that took place in the Truman years: the birth of the United Nations, the Potsdam Conference, the dropping of the atomic bomb, the occupation of Germany and Japan, the onset of the Cold War, the Truman Doctrine, the containment premise, the Marshall Plan, the Berlin Airlift, the recognition of Israel, the North Atlantic Treaty, NATO, the hydrogen bomb, NSC-68, the Korean War, aid to French Indochina, and the emergence of the Warfare State. Not all of these developments were praiseworthy, but all were significant. "Successes and failures aside," the historian George Herring has written in his overview, "the Truman administration in the

short space of seven years carried out a veritable revolution in US foreign policy. It altered the assumptions behind national security policies,
launched a wide range of global programs and commitments, and built
new institutions to manage the burgeoning international activities."

Aboard the presidential yacht in 1952, Winston Churchill unbur-
dened himself. "The last time you and I sat across the conference table
was at Potsdam, Mr. President," he said. Truman grinned. "I must confess, sir, I held you in very low regard then," the prime minister continued.
"I loathed your taking the place of Franklin Roosevelt." Truman blanched.
But Churchill went on:

> I misjudged you badly. Since that time, you, more than any other
> man, have saved Western civilization. When the British could no
> longer hold out in Greece, you, and you alone, sir, made the decision
> that saved that ancient land from the Communists. You acted in sim-
> ilar fashion . . . when the Soviets tried to take over Iran. Then there was
> your . . . Marshall Plan which rescued Western Europe wallowing in
> the shallows and indeed easy prey to Joseph Stalin's malevolent in-
> tentions. Then you established the North Atlantic Treaty Alliance and
> collective security for those nations against the military machinations of
> the Soviet Union. Then there was your audacious Berlin Airlift. And,
> of course, there was Korea.

In his widely read, Pulitzer Prize–winning biography of Truman, David
McCullough concluded:

> The arc of his life spanned more change in the world than in any prior
> period in history. A man of nineteenth-century background, he had
> had to face many of the most difficult decisions of the unimaginably
> different twentieth century. A son of rural, inland America, raised
> only a generation removed from the frontier . . . he had had to assume
> command of the most powerful industrial nation on earth at the very
> moment when that power, in combination with stunning advances
> in science and technology, had become an unparalleled force in the
> world. The responsibilities he bore were like those of no other presi-
> dent before him, and he more than met the test.

Truman also had a great impact on domestic policy—the transition to a peace economy, the Korean War industrial mobilization, but especially on the movement for greater racial equality. One ardent civil rights activist commented: "Mr. Truman had faults, but his presidency was ennobled because of his stubborn conviction that a problem was something to be faced and a President's job was to make decisions. Here was a Democratic President from a border state, with many personal and political attachments to Southern politicians, facing an election which appeared likely to go against him, harassed by labor problems at home and the most desperate sorts of problems abroad, yet nevertheless deliberately choosing a position bound to antagonize his party's traditional bastion of strength." In marked contrast to Woodrow Wilson's sanctioning of Jim Crow in federal offices, Truman became the first president in the twentieth century to promote civil rights legislation, and the desegregation of the armed forces reverberated in communities across America. His initiatives had a loud echo. As the historian Steven Lawson has written, "His civil rights committee's program—a multifaceted one that challenged both disfranchisement and segregation—would serve as the legislative agenda during the next three administrations."

Above all, Truman cared deeply about the office of the presidency, for which he had a profound respect. A yellow dog Democrat, he embraced a conception of the national interest that rose above partisanship. After hearing his farewell remarks, the judgmental Walter Lippmann wrote, "In the manner of his going Mr. Truman has been every inch the President, conscious of the great office and worthy of it." Truman began his valedictory by saying, "Next Tuesday, General Eisenhower will be inaugurated as President of the United States....I will be on the train going back home to Independence, Missouri," where he would "once again be a plain, private citizen of this great Republic." He went on to say of the inauguration ceremony, which would be his last civic rite: "I am glad to be part of it—glad to wish General Eisenhower all possible success, as he begins his term." Truman was happy, too, that "the whole world will have a chance to see how simply and peacefully our American system transfers the vast power of the Presidency from my hands to his."

Reaching out to the American people, with rising urgency in his voice, he said of the presidency:

There is no job like it on the face of the earth—in the power which is concentrated here at this desk, and in the responsibility and difficulty of the decisions.

I want all of you to realize how big a job it is, how hard a job it is—not for my sake, because I am stepping out of it—but for the sake of my successor. He needs the understanding and the help of every citizen....

Regardless of your politics, whether you are Republican or Democrat, your fate is tied up with what is done here in this room. The President is President of the whole country. We must give him our support as citizens of the United States. He will have mine, and I want you to give him yours.

The incoming president, Dwight David Eisenhower, could not have been given a more gracious welcome.

6

Dwight D. Eisenhower

NO OTHER MAN IN THE twentieth century entered the White House with so lustrous a reputation as Dwight David Eisenhower carried with him to the inauguration ceremony in January 1953. An obscure career army officer at the start of World War II, he had risen swiftly to become supreme commander of the Allied Expeditionary Force in Europe and the overseer of D-Day. Drew Middleton, military correspondent for the *New York Times*, called him "the principal architect of victory in the West, the principal planner and chief executive of the battles which broke the German Army." Hailed as the liberator of Europe from the dark night of fascism, he had ridden down the Champs-Élysées waving to cheering crowds, and as he was driven through London in a landau pulled by white horses, hundreds of thousands waving American flags acclaimed him with "tremendous roars which sent flocks of pigeons fluttering in fright from church belfries." At the bomb-scarred Guildhall, where a British band played "See the Conquering Hero Comes" (from Handel's *Judas Maccabaeus*), he warmed the hearts of English men and women by saying, in a magnificent address: "Had I possessed the military skill of Marlborough, the wisdom of Solomon, the understanding of Lincoln, I still would have been helpless without the loyalty, the vision, the generosity of thousands upon thousands of British and Americans."

In sum, General Eisenhower was, as the historian Robert Burk has said, nothing less than "America's most famous citizen."

Never before in the twentieth century had the American people consented to place a general in the presidency, but nothing about Ike suggested a man on horseback or a martinet. "While MacArthur in the Orient moved around under a heavy load of medals" and Patton brandished "pearl-handled pistols" and wore "boots of burnished leather" that "glistened...brightly in the sun," wrote the journalist Richard Rovere, "Eisenhower, with nothing to glisten but his smile, made a neat and unpretentious appearance before the high and mighty of Europe in the kind of jacket worn here at home by fastidious gas-station attendants." The Eisenhower jacket "became a kind of symbol for democracy fighting its war in simple, tidy, utilitarian, unmartial dress." On being approached about becoming a presidential candidate in 1948, he had declared: "The necessary and wise subordination of the military to civilian power will be best sustained when life-long professional soldiers abstain from seeking high political office."

Considerably more ambitious than he seemed, he nonetheless conveyed a becoming modesty. When a Republican senator put his name forward for the presidential nomination in 1944, he had said, "I can scarcely imagine anyone in the United States less qualified than I for any type of political work." Though he had made his reputation in North Africa and in Europe, he could not have been more authentically American—son of a storekeeper in Abilene, Kansas, whose childhood, the historian Herbert Parmet has written, "could have been created by Willa Cather or O. E. Rölvaag." At whistle-stops during the 1952 campaign, he would say, "It's all a bit overwhelming to me to see a great crowd like this. My memory goes back to a barren Kansas prairie and six little boys running around barefooted in the dust. I never get over my astonishment that you want to know what I think."

Often likened to George Washington, a triumphant commander with a reassuring presence, Eisenhower took office as paterfamilias. His genial manner and infectious grin attracted people across a wide spectrum of opinion. Field Marshal Bernard Montgomery, no admirer of Eisenhower as a military strategist, wrote of him: "He has this power of drawing the hearts of men towards him as a magnet attracts the bits of metal. He has merely to smile at you, and you trust him at once." Senator Paul Douglas,

VOTE for peace
VOTE for prosperity
VOTE for IKE

Smiling broadly, his arm extended, Ike reminds voters that he is the victorious World War II commander in whom they can place their trust. *Library of Congress, LC-DIG-ppss-00450*

a tough-minded liberal Democrat, had proposed that both major parties nominate Ike in 1952. A preelection analysis by the Bureau of Applied Social Research found that only a small minority of people associated Eisenhower with any particular policy. "Because of his sincerity and warmth," it reported, "they expressed *affection and loyalty*, and because of his competence, they expressed a sense of *newfound security*, were he to become president."

This "newfound security" derived from the conviction that Eisenhower was a man of enormous competence who entered the White House with a wealth of experience in running large organizations and making tough decisions—the ideal leader for the United States in a time of grave peril. After his first day in the Oval Office, he wrote in his diary, "Plenty of worries and difficult problems," but his task as president seemed "like a continuation of all" he had been doing "since July 1941—even before that." It could indeed be argued, his biographer Stephen Ambrose wrote, "that no man elected to the Presidency was ever better prepared for the demands of the job than Eisenhower."

Ike's background did have one disquieting aspect, though. Not long after the new administration got under way, the Washington correspondent Joseph Harsch wrote:

> Mr. Eisenhower's...personal emotions were never engaged in the great controversies of the New Deal–Fair Deal period. He had no part in the collective experience of the rest of the American people. It is as though he walked out of the United States when he entered the Army forty years ago, and back into it in June of 1952. He has been as remote from, and as emotionally untouched by, the great American civil conflicts of the past twenty years as William of Orange was remote from the wars between Cavaliers and Roundheads which slid into history when William set sail for England in 1688.

It remained unclear how his posture as father-of-his-country would play out once he became embroiled with Congress in domestic policy squabbles or, even more, how the country would respond once his attitude toward the unnerving Cold War became fully revealed.

———

For many Americans, Eisenhower's presidency invokes recollections of "the fifties" as a golden age of tranquility. In fact, though, the decade bracketing Eisenhower and his successor was the most terrifying the country has ever experienced. In March 1955, Eisenhower chilled many of his countrymen and foreign allies by stating that the United States might employ nuclear weapons "as you use a bullet or anything else." He later affirmed his belief "that it would be impossible for the United States to maintain the military commitments which it now sustains around the world (without turning into a garrison state) did we not possess atomic weapons and the will to use them when necessary."

Anguish over the prospect of nuclear annihilation plagued the nation. At 2 a.m. feedings, infants imbibed strontium-90 in their milk, and, at elementary schools across the land, pupils cowered under their desks during air raid drills until sirens sounded. (Years later, they dredged up hideous memories of nuclear bombs exploding in their dreams.) In the disturbingly dire "Eve of Destruction," a pop-tune singer asked:

> Don't you understand what I'm try'n' to say?
> Can't you feel the fear that I'm feelin' today?
> If the button is pushed there's no running away.
> There'll be no one to save with the world in a grave.
> Take a look around you boy,
> It's bound to scare you boy.

In March 1954, Eisenhower approved the dropping of a hydrogen bomb on the Pacific archipelago of Bikini in the Marshall Islands. Just nine years earlier, the explosion of an atomic bomb in Japan had produced not only anguish and recrimination but also acute anxiety about its destructive capacity. The hydrogen bomb vaporizing an atoll of Bikini was 750 times more powerful than the A-bomb that had devastated Hiroshima. On average during the Eisenhower years, the United States added at least two atomic weapons to its nuclear arsenal every day—far more than could conceivably be used even in a doomsday scenario.

Under Dwight Eisenhower, the imperatives of the Cold War—often on the verge of becoming an annihilating hot war—vested greater authority in the White House than ever before. "Any major reduction now in the powers of the President," wrote the political scientist Clinton Rossiter, "would leave us naked to our enemies, to the invisible forces of boom and bust at home and to the visible forces of unrest and aggression abroad." The prerogatives entrusted to the chief executive were awesome. He alone had his finger on the button. Only he could decide whether to expunge millions of lives. "Hanging," Eisenhower declared, "ought to be the fate of any President who failed to act instantly to protect the American people against a sudden attack in this atomic age."

The Cold War in a thermonuclear era affected American society in countless ways. During the Eisenhower years, as a result of the earlier reinstitution of the draft, US armed forces reached a total of 3.5 million—a figure that a short time before would have been inconceivable—and the Pentagon ate up six out of every ten federal dollars, an exceptionally high proportion for a country not engaged in a major war. Critics deplored this imbalance as a drain of resources that might better have gone to building schools for the baby boomers of the postwar generation. But the spending, even though curtailed under Eisenhower, also had benign consequences. It sparked an economic resurgence that gave the nation piping prosperity between 1954 and 1958, lifting millions out of poverty.

During World War II, *Fortune* had pointed out that "a fracas in Detroit has an echo in Aden." In the Cold War, when Eisenhower hoped to persuade third world countries to align themselves not with the Soviet bloc but with the West, blatant racial discrimination in America hampered him. Especially embarrassing were episodes when dark-skinned envoys in Washington were denied service at restaurants or were harassed. Outrages in the South received widespread coverage in the overseas press. After a United Nations committee castigated Russian behavior in eastern Europe, a Soviet bloc newspaper responded that the UN would do better to study Arkansas. These considerations became even more compelling with the emergence of a cluster of new African states—starting in 1957 with Gold Coast, renamed Ghana. Eisenhower displayed insufficient sensitivity to this reality, but eventually the Cold War gave an important impetus to changed attitudes toward civil rights.

Preoccupation with the Cold War also influenced the way Eisenhower ran the executive office, which he organized along lines of a military chain of command. He created the position of chief of staff, naming the frosty former governor of New Hampshire Sherman Adams as the assistant to the president. At the time, this action was seen as the misguided consequence of too many years in the military, but the post of chief of staff came to be regarded as indispensable. Certainly Ike thought so. It became commonplace over ensuing years for petitioners at the White House to hear the same five words from the president: "Take it up with Sherman." Eisenhower made yet another important contribution to the structure of the executive office by appointing a national security adviser. Truman had limited the executive secretary of the National Security Council to paper shuffling, but Eisenhower magnified that position. In the course of his presidency, he attended considerably more NSC sessions (339) than meetings of the cabinet. With the National Security Council battle-ready, the president was fully primed to wage cold war.

Eisenhower seized the reins of power determined to be much more militant than Truman. He named as secretary of state John Foster Dulles, son of a Presbyterian minister and grandson of a Presbyterian missionary, who viewed the struggle with the forces of darkness in the Kremlin as a religious crusade, and to chair the Joint Chiefs of Staff he chose the pugnacious Admiral Arthur Radford. The 1952 Republican platform registered Ike's attitude when it derided "the negative, futile and immoral policy of containment," and he agreed with Dulles when his principal foreign policy adviser reproached Truman and Acheson for "treadmill policies which, at best, might perhaps keep us in the same place until we drop exhausted." Asserting that containment had abandoned "countless human beings to...despotism and Godless terrorism," Dulles advocated the "liberation" of captive peoples behind the Iron Curtain. These words echoed Eisenhower's own views. "The American conscience," Ike said, "can never know peace until these peoples are restored again to being masters of their own fate."

The extraordinarily ambitious goal of liberation did not seem to square with another Eisenhower policy: constraints on Pentagon budgets. The president rejected the assumptions of NSC-68. Mounting deficits caused by excessive spending for national defense, he warned, would result in "a permanent state of mobilization" in which "our whole democratic way of life would be destroyed." To underscore how earnest he was about fiscal discipline, he added the budget director and the secretary of the treasury to the National Security Council. Ignoring howls from the brass, he cut more than $5 billion in defense spending from Truman's projected budget. Over the next six years, he slashed the size of the army by 862,000 soldiers.

Dulles saw no inconsistency in pledging to roll back the Iron Curtain while clamping down on military expansion because he anticipated that the peoples of eastern Europe would be liberated peacefully, simply by the intensity of America's moral indignation. Those who belittled the power of principle, he said, "just do not know what they are talking about." The mere announcement by the United States government "that it wants and expects liberation to occur would change, in an electrifying way, the mood of the captive peoples." One commentator declared, "Never before had the illusion of American omnipotence demanded so much of American diplomacy." Furthermore, while insisting that the rest of the world hailed the United States as the brightest beacon of liberty, Dulles created dismay by willfully undoing all that Eleanor Roosevelt had achieved in her widely acclaimed

334 THE AMERICAN PRESIDENT

role as chair of the UN Human Rights Commission. He had hardly taken office when he announced that the American government would no longer seek adoption of covenants on human rights or ratification of the genocide convention and that it was abandoning a treaty on the rights of women.

Instead of relying upon costly ground forces, Eisenhower gave priority to nuclear weapons and a large air force (allotted 40 percent of the Pentagon budget) to deliver them. Though it was cutting back defense spending, the administration claimed that the United States was achieving greater security by getting "more bang for a buck." In January 1954, Dulles spelled out the implications of the "New Look," as Admiral Radford called it. The United States, he announced—in a sentence written by Eisenhower—was placing greater reliance on "the deterrent of massive retaliatory power," so that Americans could strike back instantly, "by means and at times of our own choosing." The difficulty with massive retaliation, critics objected, was that it escalated every dispute into a possible war of extermination. At worst, it left the government with a choice between surrender and holocaust. Furthermore, it strengthened the position of hard-liners in the Kremlin who were pressing for an arms buildup. "More bang for the buck," it was feared, would lead to "more rubble for the ruble."

The new administration's approach to foreign affairs got its first test in Korea—with ambiguous results. Toward the end of 1952, Eisenhower had gone there as he had promised at the close of the campaign, but the trip yielded nothing. On his return, he acknowledged, "We have no panaceas." When in July 1953 the war ended, no one knew why. Ike's admirers later claimed that he had achieved a truce by threatening to employ nuclear weapons in China, but it is far from certain that Beijing ever received such a message or would have found the warning credible if it had. The president did, though, make a contribution in overruling his secretaries of state and defense, who wanted to continue the fighting, and in taming Syngman Rhee, who tried to dynamite the settlement.

Eisenhower had run on a platform charging the Truman administration with "ignominious bartering with our enemies" and behaving "without the will to victory," but Ike's bartering brought about no semblance of victory. The settlement left the peninsula divided into two countries approximately along the 38th parallel—about where they had been separated at the outbreak of the fighting—with the Republic of South Korea still facing a menacing neighbor to the north. To the American people, none of this mattered. Eisenhower had been faithful to his pledge to go to Korea, and the undeclared war, which had cost more than one hundred thousand American casualties and countless more of Koreans and Chinese, was over.

At the same time that Eisenhower was negotiating a cease-fire in Korea, he was brewing trouble for himself with China. In his first State of the Union message in 1953, he announced that he was canceling Truman's edict neutralizing the Straits of Formosa in order to free Chiang to attack the mainland. With this encouragement, Chiang sent troops from his retreat on Formosa to garrison islands, notably Quemoy, Matsu, and the Dachens, provocatively close to the Chinese coast—"almost," as Eisenhower acknowledged, "within wading distance of the mainland." When the Chinese, as might have been expected, began to shell the islands, the United States came close to being drawn into a war fraught with great peril over islands that Eisenhower and Dulles conceded were worthless. Admiral Radford recommended reinforcing the islands with US troops and using nuclear devices (called, disarmingly, "tactical" but more powerful than those dropped on Japan in 1945). Eisenhower refused both options, but he did send nuclear weapons to Okinawa and dispatched a nuclear-armed naval vessel to Taiwan Strait. The confrontation wound down inconclusively, but not before the president had gotten a blank check from Congress to use military force in the future. Bloodshed was averted only because the Chinese were more sensible than the Americans.

Secretary Dulles created even greater alarm at home and abroad by telling a magazine interviewer:

> You have to take chances for peace, just as you must take chances in war. Some say that we were brought to the verge of war. Of course we were brought to the verge of war. The ability to get to the verge of war without getting into the war is the necessary art. If you cannot master it, you inevitably get into wars. If you try to run away from it, if you are scared to go to the brink, you are lost. We've had to look it square in the face—on the question of enlarging the Korean War, on the

question of getting into the Indo-China war, on the question of Formosa. We walked to the brink and we looked it in the face.

Critics were appalled by the secretary of state's insouciant justification of what quickly became known as "brinkmanship" in an age of nuclear terror. Dulles created further consternation, especially among nonaligned countries that did not want to be entrapped in the Cold War, when he called neutralism "obsolete" and "immoral." (Insufferably self-righteous and humorless, he elicited from Churchill the progression "Dull, Duller, Dulles.")

The allusion to the "Indo-China war" reveals that Eisenhower approached the brink in Southeast Asia too. America's ultimate tragic involvement in the Vietnam War resulted from no single decision but from cumulative commitments that one president after another believed he could not repudiate and must expand. In French Indochina, Eisenhower doubled the investment Truman had made, so that by 1954 the United States was assuming 80 percent of the cost of the conflict France was waging against Communist insurgents led by Ho Chi Minh.

In the spring of 1954, Eisenhower learned that the position of the French had become desperate. If the United States did not go to their aid, he was warned, their last redoubt—the jungle fortress at Dien Bien Phu—would be overwhelmed, and they would be driven out of the country. Eisenhower viewed this prospect with "transcendent" concern, less for its immediate effects—though he was distressed by the impact on the Vietnamese people and by what a Red takeover could mean for the availability of tin, tungsten, and rubber—but for the threat it appeared to raise to the survival of other non-Communist states in the Pacific rim. Spelling out what came to be known as "the domino theory," he told a press conference on April 7, 1954: "You have a row of dominoes set up; you knock over the first one; and what will happen to the last one is the certainty that it will go over very quickly. So you could have a beginning of a disintegration that would have the most profound influences." He was troubled by what the fall of Saigon might portend not only for Indochina's neighbors such as Burma and Thailand but also for a range of nations from Australia and New Zealand all the way to Japan, including the Philippines. "So," he concluded, "the possible consequences of the loss are just incalculable to the free world."

His hawkish advisers pressed for a drastic response. If necessary, Vice President Nixon said, he was for "putting our boys in." Eisenhower, though, knew that the nation would not tolerate another ground war in Asia. To raise the siege of Dien Bien Phu, Admiral Radford advocated an assault with atomic weapons, but on reading an NSC document recommending that action, the president retorted angrily: "You boys must be crazy. We can't use those awful things against Asians for the second time in less than ten years. My God." Eisenhower was more amenable to Radford's proposal for a massive air attack with conventional bombs. He would approve it, however, only if Congress and the British government agreed. When neither did, Dien Bien Phu fell.

Thereafter, the administration followed a curious and unfortunate course. At a conference in Geneva to work out a settlement between the French and the Communist Vietminh, Dulles absented himself from most of the session. Refusing to shake hands with the Chinese foreign minister, Zhou Enlai, he behaved, a biographer has written, like a "puritan in a house of ill-repute." Instead of being able to enjoy the fruits of their victory, the Vietminh, under pressure from the big powers, including China and Russia, reluctantly agreed to a temporary partition of their country, with unification scheduled for 1956 following free elections to determine who would rule. After the meeting had adjourned, the South Vietnamese leader, Ngo Dinh Diem—with American encouragement—refused to take part in a national election, which he knew he would lose. As a consequence of this violation of the Geneva Accords, two countries emerged: a Communist North Vietnam under Ho Chi Minh, and an anti-Communist South Vietnam under Diem—each nation intent on annihilating the other.

To salvage something out of the situation, Dulles put together a Southeast Asia Treaty Organization associating the United States, Great Britain, France, Australia, and New Zealand with Pakistan, the Philippines, and Thailand as a bulwark against the spread of communism in the Far East. Sometimes depicted as a NATO for the Orient, SEATO was only a paper organization. Unlike NATO, it required no commitments from any of the signatories, save to consult in the event of an attack. Commentators dismissed it as an outbreak of a rare nervous disease that afflicted Dulles: pactomania. The secretary of state had Eisenhower's full support, however. "We have got to keep the Pacific an American lake," the president told his advisers.

During all the remaining years of his presidency, Eisenhower obligated the United States to safeguarding Diem from an attack from the north. It was a fateful decision, setting America on track toward a train wreck. From the outset, Diem was a poor choice. A Catholic and an arrogant patrician, he commanded no following among the mass of Buddhist peasants whom he despised. So intent was Eisenhower on supporting Diem, though, that he expended a billion dollars to prop him up and made Saigon the largest US mission in the world. Revisionist historians have called Eisenhower's refusal to go to war in 1954 "his finest hour," for the president rejected the counsel of Admiral Radford, who on three occasions (and two more on Quemoy and Matsu) advocated war, including resorting to atomic weapons. But it was Ike who had appointed Radford and who retained him. Furthermore, even after Dien Bien Phu had capitulated, Eisenhower approved a recommendation by the Joint Chiefs to respond to any Chinese intervention by "employing atomic weapons...against...military targets in China...and...Communist-held offshore islands." Only Chinese restraint and a change of government in France saved him from folly.

Most important, the pledge to Saigon that his successors believed, unwisely, they must honor came from Eisenhower, and to him should be assigned a large share of the blame for the disaster that ensued, though he found no shortage of willing allies. In an eerie foreshadowing of what was to come, Senator John F. Kennedy declared in 1956, "Vietnam represents the cornerstone of the Free World in Southeast Asia." If "the red tide of Communism" engulfed Vietnam, it would threaten a large sector from Japan to India, he contended. "The United States is directly responsible for this experiment.... We cannot afford to permit that experiment to fail.... If we are not the parents of little Vietnam, then surely we are the godparents."

Elsewhere in the world, too, Eisenhower's performance calls into question the judgment that he was an evangel of peace. In Iran, he authorized the CIA to carry out an undercover operation after its prime minister, Mohammad Mossadegh, vexed the United States and Great Britain by nationalizing oil fields. Truman and Acheson had opposed intervention, but, as Anthony Eden reported to Churchill, Eisenhower "seemed obsessed by the fear of a Communist Iran," though there was little reason for such apprehension. The chief CIA operative in Tehran,

Kermit Roosevelt Jr., TR's grandson, dipped into suitcases of cash to buy off army officers and hire street agitators to yammer against the government. By such methods, the CIA, in a coup organized at the US embassy in cahoots with British agents, toppled Mossadegh and put in power Mohammad Reza Shah Pahlavi. Obligingly, the young shah granted a large stake in Iranian oil to British and US companies. The CIA attempted to keep its scheming secret, but the Iranian people knew, and did not forget, which country was responsible for imposing the shah's harsh rule on them. Nearly half a century later, Secretary of State Madeleine Albright acknowledged, "It is easy to see now why many Iranians continue to resent this intervention by America in their internal affairs."

At about the same time, Eisenhower fostered a brazen CIA operation to overturn the democratically elected government of Guatemala, after the Arbenz regime began to expropriate and redistribute lands of the United Fruit Company, which had vast holdings in the banana republic. The American firm enjoyed intimate connections with high-ranking officials in both the White House and the State Department—not least CIA chief Allen Dulles and his brother, John Foster Dulles, who had been a partner in the corporation. The CIA hired mercenaries, bribed Guatemalan army officers, and orchestrated a propaganda campaign with the aim of scaring Arbenz out of his wits. (The operation was run by E. Howard Hunt, who was later to go to prison for his role in the Watergate break-in.) In blatant violation of international law, the US Navy was ordered to conduct a stop-and-search patrol to prevent arms from reaching the legitimate government—the kind of behavior that had led the United States to declare war on Great Britain in 1812. After Arbenz fled, Guatemala was taken over by a far-right military junta that resorted to torture and massacre. Eisenhower had his way, but at the cost of generating immense ill will. "The coup gravely damaged American interests in Latin America," concluded the historians Stephen Schlesinger and Stephen Kinzer. "The gusto with which the United States had ended the Guatemalan revolution embittered many Latins, and strengthened deep-seated anti-Americanism throughout the continent." Moreover, the intervention left a mischievous legacy. So easily did the CIA prevail that it became giddy with the prospect that such clandestine operations would always succeed.

Under Eisenhower, the CIA flourished. Over the course of his presidency, he found the agency useful for carrying out a number of cloak-and-dagger missions—from an attempt to train Tibetans to attack Chinese and an effort to depose the government of Indonesia, both of which failed miserably, to installing a pro-Western regime in Laos, which succeeded. He authorized the CIA to intrude surreptitiously in Japanese affairs by doling out millions to the political party he favored and by digging up dirt on its rival. Indulged by Eisenhower, the CIA became a runaway locomotive. Apparently without the knowledge or consent either of the president or of Congress, it conspired to murder the head of state of the Congo and recruited Mafia mobsters to kill Fidel Castro in Cuba.

While Eisenhower was approving CIA transgressions and endorsing massive retaliation, however, he was also airing proposals to slow down the arms race and reach an accommodation with the Russians. A month after he took office, he said in an address to the American Society of Newspaper Editors: "Every gun that is made, every warship launched, every rocket fired signifies...a theft from those who hunger and are not fed, those who are cold and not clothed....The cost of one modern heavy bomber is...a modern brick school in more than thirty cities....We pay for a single fighter plane with a half-million bushels of wheat. We pay for a single destroyer with new homes that could have housed more than eight thousand people."

In his celebrated 1953 "Atoms for Peace" address to the UN General Assembly, he urged the big powers, including America, to turn over fissionable materials to an international agency for projects to benefit mankind, and at a summit meeting with the new Soviet leader Nikita Khrushchev at the Palais des Nations in Geneva in 1955, he unveiled an unprecedented "open skies" initiative to break the logjam of the Cold War. He called upon the USSR and the United States to "give to each other a complete blueprint of our military establishments...from one end of our countries to the other....Next, to provide within our countries facilities for...aerial reconnaissance, where you can make all the pictures you choose...providing as between ourselves against the possibility of great surprise attack, thus lessening danger and relaxing tension." He added, "What I propose...would be but a beginning." Some historians have dismissed this speech as a propaganda ploy, but Robert

Donovan has observed that "Eisenhower conveyed a sense of decency and dignity which mocked the picture of his country as an immature nation hell-bent for war," and, for a time, the world talked hopefully of "the spirit of Geneva."

Though Eisenhower sometimes explored the option of tactical atomic weapons, he recoiled from the thought of a nuclear exchange. "If you're in the military," he told his press secretary, "and you know about these terrible destructive weapons, it tends to make you more pacifistic than you normally have been." In 1954, he lectured Syngman Rhee, who favored an assault on Russia: "When you say we should deliberately plunge into war, let me tell you that if war comes, it will be horrible. Atomic war will destroy civilization. . . . There will be millions of people dead. War today is unthinkable with the weapons which we have at our command. If the Kremlin and Washington ever lock up in a war, the results are too horrible to contemplate. I can't even imagine them."

Commentators had portrayed the contest for the Republican presidential nomination in 1952 as one between the "moderate" Eisenhower and the "conservative" Taft, but on taking office, Eisenhower announced that he was intent on eradicating "the Left-Wingish, pinkish influence in our life." He had run for the presidency, he had explained earlier, because "the country is going socialistic so rapidly that, unless Republicans can get in immediately and defeat this trend, our country is gone. Four more years of New Dealism and there will be no turning back." The "dangerous drift toward statism," he declared, must be "stopped in its tracks." Thought to be well to the right of the president, Senator Taft favored legislation such as federal aid to education, which, Eisenhower acknowledged, was "far more 'liberal and radical' than anything to which I could ever agree." After Taft died in the summer of 1953, the president noted in his diary, "In some things, I found him extraordinarily leftish." Excessive federal intervention, he declared, would convert "the American Dream into an American nightmare."

Eisenhower shocked observers who had thought of him as a centrist by naming an exceptionally large number of businessmen to his cabinet, most conspicuously Charles E. Wilson, president of General Motors, as secretary of defense. (Confusingly, the head of Truman's civil rights committee, Wilson of GE, had the same name.) The only exception was the secretary of labor, Martin Durkin, who headed the plumbers' union. The cabinet, said the *New Republic*, was comprised of "eight millionaires and a plumber." (Durkin soon got fed up and was replaced by a former personnel manager for Macy's.) In addition to selecting GM's Wilson, he chose for cabinet posts two former General Motors distributors. "The New Dealers," said Stevenson, "have all left Washington to make way for the car dealers." Eisenhower picked the conservative economist Arthur F. Burns to chair the Council of Economic Advisers, which exerted considerably more influence under Eisenhower than it had in the Truman years. These appointments were significant because Eisenhower, who had a textbook conception of government, fully intended to give cabinet meetings greater status than had any of his recent predecessors.

Secretary of the Treasury George Humphrey, president of Mark Hanna's iron ore firm, exercised by far the greatest influence on the president. "In Cabinet meetings," Eisenhower confided, "I always wait for George Humphrey to speak. . . . I know that when he speaks he will say just what I am thinking." On taking office, Humphrey, whose mother insisted on spelling Franklin D. Roosevelt's name with a lowercase *r*, hung Andrew Mellon's portrait behind his desk. Asked if he had read Ernest Hemingway's *The Old Man and the Sea*, he replied, "Why would anybody be interested in some old man who was a failure and never amounted to anything?" Eisenhower not only relied upon Humphrey's counsel in Washington but also spent holidays at the industrialist's Georgia plantation.

Statements and actions by other cabinet officers aggravated concern about single-interest government. One of the former GM distributors, chosen by Eisenhower to be secretary of the interior, stated bluntly, "We're here in the saddle as an administration representing business and industry." Secretary of Commerce Sinclair Weeks demonstrated what that meant by firing the head of the Bureau of Standards (who, he charged, had not shown proper respect for "the business point of view" in refusing to approve a defective battery additive) and by cutting back the Civil Aeronautics Administration so drastically that air safety was imperiled. After Secretary Wilson invited derision by saying that "what was good for our country was good for General Motors, and vice versa" and by likening the jobless to "kennel-fed dogs," a story made the rounds that the onetime GM executive had devised the automatic transmission so that he would have one foot free to put in his mouth. So loud was the outcry when a cabinet official thwarted free distribution to needy children of a new vaccine against polio developed by Dr. Jonas Salk that she was compelled to resign.

The president took several steps to free the country of "pinkish influence." He abruptly ended price and wage controls, vetoed a school construction bill, supported a drastic reduction of federal aid to public housing, and abolished the Reconstruction Finance Corporation. He got rid of the price supports for farmers enacted in the FDR-Truman era, and substituted a program more geared to the market that proved to be an expensive failure. Unlike Truman, who had twice vetoed bills to turn oil-rich "tidelands" over to seaboard states, he signed a Submerged Lands Act that surrendered federal rights. At the end of his first year, he boasted that he had "instituted what amounts almost to a revolution" in the federal government by "finding things it can stop doing rather than new things for it do."

Eisenhower did everything in his power to hobble the Tennessee Valley Authority, the legacy of FDR's presidency he most loathed. He cited the expansion of the agency as a deplorable example of the "creeping socialism" he vowed to halt. In the summer of 1953, he told his cabinet, "By God, if ever we could do it, before we leave here, I'd like to see us *sell* the whole thing, but I suppose we can't go that far." His desire to dismantle the authority got him into hot water when, with his encouragement, the Atomic Energy Commission negotiated a fat contract with a private utilities syndicate headed by Edgar Dixon and Eugene Yates to provide power for the Memphis area in TVA country. In July 1955, after a congressional committee exposed collusion, Eisenhower had to cancel the contract. When Dixon-Yates sued to recoup its loses, the president was embarrassed by having his Department of Justice claim that the contract, in which he had taken so much pride, had been illegal and "contrary to the public interest" from the outset.

Conservative though his predilections were, however, Eisenhower had not undergone the visceral experience of members of the Republican Old Guard who had seethed for a generation as a minority in a liberal era, and that difference permitted a degree of flexibility in his approach. In November 1954, Eisenhower pithily expressed his conception of public policy in a letter to a brother: "Now it is true that I believe this country is following a dangerous trend when it permits too great a degree of centralization of governmental functions. I oppose this—in some instances the fight is a rather desperate one. But to attain any success it is quite clear that the Federal government cannot avoid...responsibilities which the mass of the people firmly believe should be undertaken by it.... Should any political party attempt to abolish social security, unemployment insurance, and eliminate labor laws and farm programs, you would not hear of that party again in our political history." He added: "There is a tiny splinter group, of course, that believes you can do these things. Among them are...a few...Texas oil millionaires and an occasional politician or businessman from other areas. Their number is negligible and they are stupid."

Eisenhower did not take readily to the role of party leader, but in December 1953 he assembled Republican congressmen for a three-day retreat at the White House where he won their consent to a modest program of social legislation. Congress enacted the greatest expansion of the Social Security system that had ever been undertaken, drawing the self-employed under its umbrella and extending unemployment compensation to four million more workers. By revamping New Deal agencies, it created the Department of Health, Education, and Welfare. The young conservative William F. Buckley Jr. deplored Eisenhower's "measured socialism," and Senator Barry Goldwater of Arizona dismissed his performance as a "dime-store New Deal." In addition, the president authorized cooperation with Canada to construct the St. Lawrence Seaway, linking the Great Lakes and the Atlantic Ocean so that Duluth and Chicago became ocean ports, and in 1956 he put through the biggest outlay for a domestic project in history: the Federal Highway Act, which appropriated $25 billion to lay down forty-one thousand miles of concrete. Taking advantage of the opportunity presented by the fixation on the Cold War, he justified the expenditure as a "National System of Defense" that would increase mobility of the armed forces in case of enemy attack.

The president also disappointed right-wingers by his appointments to the Supreme Court. To fulfill a campaign commitment, he named California's popular governor, Earl Warren, to be chief justice, and he chose for another vacancy William Brennan, a New Jersey Democrat who was the son of an Irish American labor organizer. Eisenhower later called his elevation of Warren "the biggest damfool mistake I ever made," and when Brennan unexpectedly turned out to be an advanced civil libertarian, Ike was nonplussed. More in keeping with the president's outlook were his nominations of two moderates: John Marshall Harlan and Potter Stewart, each a highly respected legal craftsman. A fifth selection, Charles Whittaker, is universally perceived to have been a disaster, but overall, Eisenhower's record with regard to the judiciary is highly creditable.

Irrespective of ideological disposition, political considerations that he had not anticipated pushed Eisenhower toward moderation. He had come to office anticipating a collegial relationship with Congress, especially with the Republican majority in the Senate. In the 1952 campaign, he had emphasized the need to "restore the Congress to its rightful place in the Government." FDR, he believed, had "usurped" legislative authority. After suggesting a bill, he would leave the members of Congress free to "vote their own consciences." To improve relations on the Hill, he became the first president to establish a White House congressional liaison office.

His conciliatory attitude toward Congress did not work out as he had hoped. Later, he recorded: "There was not a single Republican in the Senate, when I came in, who had ever served under a Republican President.... They were raised in this tradition of antagonism between the Executive and the Legislature, and it was very, very difficult for Republican Senators, at first, to remember that their job was now to cooperate with the President.... On the contrary, they felt that they had to cut him down.... It was instinctive." At the time, Eisenhower entered in his diary an observation about the Republican leader in the Senate: "In his case there seems to be no final answer to the question 'How stupid can you get?'" To enact legislation, the president needed to turn to the more liberal, more internationalist Democrats, who, in turn, required him to meet them partway on their priorities.

Democratic backing became indispensable to the conduct of foreign relations, particularly when Eisenhower's prerogatives as chief executive were in jeopardy. The president received less support from Republicans than from Democrats on legislation for foreign aid, a program he esteemed. "We must stop talking about 'giveaways,'" he said. "We must understand that our foreign expenditures are investments in America's future." He especially had to rely on Democrats when almost every Republican senator, as well as numerous Democrats, lined up to cosponsor a constitutional amendment introduced by GOP senator John Bricker to limit the impact of international agreements on domestic matters. Eisenhower, who believed the measure would "cripple the Executive power" and leave him "helpless in world affairs," confided to a press secretary, "If it's true that when you die the things that bothered you most are engraved on your skull, I'm sure I'll have there the mud and dirt of France during [the] invasion and the name of Senator Bricker."

By failing to take a strong stand against Bricker at the outset, Eisenhower permitted support to reach such momentum that it was almost impossible for him to halt it, but when, belatedly, he recognized that Bricker had "gotten almost psychopathic on the subject," he worked adroitly to wean senators away from nationalist Republicans. Instead of joining issue with Bricker, Eisenhower said that all he sought was a bit of alteration in the wording, though, in fact, he intended to drain the resolution of all meaning. "By converting the issue to one of semantics," the political scientist Fred Greenstein has noted, "he gave sponsors of the amendment a face-saving way to change their votes." On the critical roll call on the Bricker amendment, he prevailed by a single vote, thanks largely to his alliance with the minority leader, Lyndon Johnson. In November 1954, the Democrats regained control of both houses of Congress, and for all the rest of his time in the White House, Eisenhower found it necessary to come to terms with the opposition.

In electing Dwight Eisenhower in 1952, voters expected that he would end the acrimony poisoning the country, but one unwelcome result of his victory was that it catapulted Joseph McCarthy into the chairmanship of a US Senate committee. For the next two years, the Wisconsin mountebank, hurling one false charge after another, rampaged through federal agencies, gravely impairing morale in the Foreign Service and the Voice of America. Eisenhower never figured out how to contain him, and for a long time did not even try.

McCarthy made trouble for Eisenhower from the first days of his presidency. He noisily opposed confirmation of the president's appointment of a career diplomat to be ambassador to Russia, even demanding that the man take a lie detector test to disprove allegations of disloyalty, and raised strident objections to other Eisenhower choices. Worse still, he devastated the State Department's International Information Agency by sending two callow, pathetically inept aides, Roy Cohn and G. David Schine, through Europe on an inspection tour. McCarthy instructed them to target the IIA's 187 overseas libraries, though these institutions promoted America's interests in the Cold War by demonstrating to skeptical Europeans that the United States was not a cultural wasteland but had a rich literary tradition.

Senator McCarthy's operatives careened through seven countries, ransacking card catalogues, yanking off shelves books by authors they regarded as subversive (one was Ralph Waldo Emerson), and bullying librarians. A writer for the US Army newspaper, *Stars and Stripes*, later recalled how, in his office in Darmstadt, Germany, "the appearance of these two young gumshoes... struck fear and loathing in... government clerks and officials," to the extent that the colonel in charge of his unit "had us gather scores of books and hide them in the cellar in case Schine and Cohn visited us." In the brief time they were in Europe, they left the program a shambles and the Eisenhower administration an object of ridicule abroad.

Instead of seeking to repair the damage by coming to the defense of his agency, Dulles issued a directive ordering the removal of books and works of art of "any Communists, fellow travelers, et cetera" from US information centers. In a mortifying echo of the Nazis' *Walpurgisnachten*, some books were actually burned, including works written by "et ceteras." Among those that went up in flames were a memoir by Whittaker Chambers and a volume by the altogether noncontroversial historian Foster Rhea Dulles, cousin of the secretary of state. In the course of what, in the words of the *New York Times*, "many Administration officials... concede was a spectacle of Executive retreat before Congressional interference," Eisenhower permitted IIA employees to be hauled into McCarthy's committee room and then fired as security risks because they had dared to find fault with the antics of Cohn and Schine.

Advisers, including his brother Milton, urged Eisenhower to speak out against McCarthy and the Red Scare, but he refused to do so. He reasoned that if he did, he would only be giving the senator more public attention. In addition, he thought it unseemly, for it would jeopardize his role as chief of state. "I will not get into a pissing contest with that skunk," he told his brother. He was also mindful of how many Republican senators were McCarthy followers, and he did not want to alienate

"Have A Care, Sir"

HERBLOCK
© 1959 THE WASHINGTON POST CO.

"Have a care, sir." This devastating cartoon by Herbert Block ("Herblock") harpoons President Eisenhower for his failure to combat the Wisconsin scandalmonger Senator Joe McCarthy. *The Herb Block Foundation*

them. He rationalized his inactivity by claiming that if he ignored McCarthy, he would neutralize him. His inactivity, though, had the opposite effect. Some construed his silence as indicating approval of the senator's methods. More frequently, it was seen as a sign that McCarthy had so much power that he intimidated even the wartime commander, who was afraid to cross him. The president's abstention did nothing to diminish McCarthy's capacity to grab headlines, and during Eisenhower's first year in the White House, the senator's public support markedly increased.

Too often, Eisenhower coped with Republicans in the McCarthy wing of the party by indulging them. On the very day he was sworn in, Aaron Copland's "A Lincoln Portrait" was excised from the inaugural program because a Republican congressman questioned the composer's political affiliations, though anyone familiar with Copland's work knew what a love of country his music conveyed. When a McCarthyite zealot was appointed to the key position of security officer in the State

Department, Eisenhower refused to fire him even after he learned that the man had leaked to McCarthy the personnel file of a diplomat the president had nominated to a highly important post. Called upon for a rejoinder to McCarthy's vendetta against the International Information Administration, Eisenhower stated, "I don't believe it is really a proper thing for me to be discussing publicly a coordinate branch of government." For some months, McCarthy was even permitted to control the policies of the IIA. After instructing Dartmouth undergraduates, "Don't join the bookburners," the president vitiated his message by telling the press that there was no right to disseminate "any document or other kind of thing that attempts to persuade...Americans into Communism."

To demonstrate to McCarthy and his followers that there was no possibility of subversives holding federal jobs, Eisenhower, only three months into his presidency, issued Executive Order 10450 stipulating that federal employees could be fired not only for disloyalty but even for lack of "suitability." Furthermore, his edict denied the right of a government worker to a hearing or an appeal. Even the hard-nosed chair of the Loyalty Review Board acknowledged that this was "just not the American way of doing things."

Not until McCarthy overreached did the president begin to take hold. Even after McCarthy told General Ralph W. Zwicker, a hero of D-Day, that he had "the brains of a five-year-old child" and was "a disgrace to the uniform" he wore, Eisenhower's response was measured. But when McCarthy humiliated Secretary of the Army Robert Stevens, he left the president no wiggle room. "I have declined to get into this mess even when I have been needled by the press," he told the Republican leader in the Senate, "but this is one thing I will fight with all my power—I will not have my men subpoenaed." (Only a former general would speak of high-ranking federal officers as "my men.") In tandem with Secretary Stevens's order to Zwicker not to testify further, Eisenhower stated, "Officials in the executive branch of government will have my unqualified support in insisting that employees in the executive branch who appear before any kind of executive and congressional investigation body will be treated fairly."

To forestall McCarthy, the Eisenhower administration added a new term to the lexicon: "executive privilege." It was "essential to efficient and effective administration that employees of the Executive Branch be completely candid in advising each other on official matters," Eisenhower maintained. Hence, it was "not in the public interest that any of their conversations or communications, or any document or reproductions, concerning such advice be disclosed." Eisenhower claimed not merely, as previous presidents had, that discussions at cabinet meetings were confidential but that every official in the entire executive branch was immune from the legislature's inquiry. "Congress has absolutely no right to ask them to testify in any way, shape or form about the advice that they are giving to me at any time on any subject," he declared. (Arthur Schlesinger Jr., a historian long identified with FDR and other powerful presidents, later disapproved Eisenhower's position as the "most absolute assertion of presidential right to withhold information from Congress ever uttered to that day in American history.") Eisenhower added a stern warning: "Any man who testifies as to the advice he gave me won't be working for me that night."

Numbers of writers have asserted that McCarthy's downfall in 1954, after the Senate rebuked him, resulted from Eisenhower's shrewd decision to avoid a confrontation with the senator while giving him enough rope to hang himself and by maneuvering behind the scenes against him, but hardly a scintilla of evidence supports that contention. In the scenario of McCarthy's demise, as the historian Stuart Gerry Brown concluded, "Eisenhower appeared as little more than a bystander." Giving McCarthy "enough rope," the historian Richard Fried has pointed out, enabled the senator "to hang others first before hanging himself." During "the desperate...eighteen months McCarthy ran wild...many government small fry were served up as *hors d'oeuvres.*"

Eisenhower did more to sustain "the great fear" than to quell it. At no point did he express even mild regret for what had befallen the victims of McCarthyism or for the federal inquisition. When a speechwriter gave him the draft of a letter to a civil liberties gathering, Eisenhower scissored out the sentence "Seldom in our history has the preservation of civil liberties been more clearly important." Subsequently, his friendly biographer Stephen Ambrose concluded, "The darker side of Eisenhower's refusal to condemn McCarthy was that Ike himself agreed with the senator on the nature, if not the extent, of the problem," for "he was rigid and dogmatic in his anti-communism." But as the president's term entered its final months, what mattered to the millions of Americans who abhorred McCarthy was that the senator's juggernaut had been derailed and that it had been sidetracked on Eisenhower's watch. McCarthy's fall from grace seemed one more indication that Ike had brought tranquility to the land.

Republicans, who had not won two national elections in a row since 1928, approached the 1956 contest brimming with confidence. In August 1955, Eisenhower's approval rating soared to a sky-high 79 percent. Despite shortfalls and mishaps, his first term received high marks. In his *The American Presidency* (1956), Clinton Rossiter concluded that Eisenhower "already stands above Polk and Cleveland, and he has a reasonable chance to move up to Jefferson and Theodore Roosevelt." So popular was he that 60 percent of Democrats said they wanted him to head their own ticket. With the securing of an armistice in Korea, no American boy was at risk on a battlefield anywhere in the world, and after an early recession ended, the country was enjoying good times. The GOP boasted, "Everything's booming but the guns."

Eisenhower's style resonated with a nation that, having endured the deprivation of the Great Depression and the Spartan rationing of the 1940s, luxuriated in consumer comforts. Cultural arbiters might frown on the president's middlebrow tastes—Zane Grey westerns, bridge games, rounds of golf—and at First Lady Mamie's addiction to soap operas and canasta and her choice of Lawrence Welk to perform his insipid music at the White House. But suburbanites raising baby-boom children in ranch houses saw nothing wrong with Mamie's serving supper on TV trays or Ike's cultivation of the evangelist Billy Graham, who persuaded him to place on US coins the legend "In God We Trust."

Americans also perceived Eisenhower to be a man of peace, which they thought to be consonant with his persona. Though Dulles took no important actions save on the president's orders, or with his approval, Eisenhower managed to convey the impression that he was much more benign than his grim-visaged, disputatious secretary of state, just as unpopular domestic policies were identified not with him but with Sherman Adams, "the Abominable NO Man." Only intimates knew of Ike's scarily explosive temper, of what one adviser called his "Bessemer furnace" nature. In public, he projected serenity. The American people were largely unaware of the iniquity in Iran and Guatemala and associated the president instead with the Korean truce and his pacific overtures to the Russians, especially his "Atoms for Peace" address to the United Nations, where he had sought to escape "the hopeless finality of...two atomic colossi...doomed malevolently to eye each other indefinitely across a trembling world." Nothing did more to account for Eisenhower's popularity than his reputation as an opponent of war, which made him an odds-on favorite to win reelection in 1956.

In September 1955, however, Republican leaders received grim news: Ike had suffered a heart attack. There had already been some uneasiness about his advanced age. Eisenhower himself—the last president born in the nineteenth century—had pointed out to a friend, "No man has ever reached his seventieth year in the White House." For many months after his attack, he held no press conferences, and for six weeks he was so incapacitated that the vice president had to serve in his stead. Nixon presided over twenty-six National Security Council sessions and nineteen meetings of the cabinet. The power of the president to issue instructions, though, was entrusted not to the vice president but to Sherman Adams, who set up a surrogate White House at the army base in Denver where Eisenhower was hospitalized.

The country followed anxiously Ike's progress toward recovery, apprehensive that he would be limited to a single term. In contrast to earlier cover-ups of disability, Eisenhower insisted on full disclosure, which his outstanding press secretary, James Hagerty, implemented so conscientiously that the most intimate details of body functioning were published each day. After a month, newspapers ran a cheery story highlighted by a front-page photo of the president in red pajamas bearing the words "Much Better, Thanks." Not even a second emergency operation in June—for ileitis, a painful intestinal inflammation—deterred him from seeking reelection.

Eisenhower did not want to run on the same ticket as in 1952, though. Richard Nixon had proven himself to be a loyal servant, but Ike had never liked him and did not hold him in high regard. "Well, the fact is...I've watched Dick a long time, and he just hasn't grown," Eisenhower told a speechwriter. "So I just haven't been able to believe that he *is* presidential timber." Eisenhower went so far as to offer the second spot to a former secretary of the navy, who turned him down. He then pinned his hopes on a dump-Nixon movement within the party, but since he could never bring himself to tell the vice president that he wanted to get rid of him, he was stuck with him. As late as August, the most he could bring himself to say was that Nixon was "perfectly acceptable." Polls revealed that Nixon was something of a drag on the slate, but they also showed Eisenhower running well ahead of Stevenson in a rematch of their 1952 contest, with Republican politicians trumpeting the administration's successes abroad.

Two days before the country was to vote in the November election, however, the administration's foreign policy came apart. In a January 1955 radio broadcast, Dulles had told the people of eastern Europe that if they revolted against Soviet oppression, they could count on America. With such expectations, and with the aid of CIA operatives, Hungarians had rebelled during the last week of October in 1956. For a short time, it seemed that they were going to succeed. But on November 4, the Kremlin sent in two hundred thousand troops and thousands of tanks to subdue insurgents equipped only with pathetically primitive weapons. Eisenhower did nothing. He well knew that intervention would mean igniting World War III. Moreover, it was not feasible. Hungary, he later said, was "as inaccessible to us as Tibet." While the United States stood idly by, Russia crushed the revolt, killing forty thousand courageous freedom fighters and driving more than 150,000 Hungarians into exile.

At the same time that Eisenhower was suffering this humiliating setback in Europe, the Middle East erupted. The crisis began when Dulles, after promising a large loan to the Egyptian strongman Gamal Abdel Nasser for construction of the huge Aswan Dam on the Nile, abruptly reneged because the general had bought large quantities of arms from eastern Europe and had recognized Red China. Nasser retaliated in July 1956 by nationalizing the Suez Canal, which had been run as an Anglo-Gallic venture. His action jeopardized Western access to vital oil fields in the Middle East and dealt a blow to British imperial pride. "The Egyptian has his thumb on our windpipe," said Prime Minister Anthony Eden.

On October 29, as Russian tanks rumbled down the avenues of Budapest, Israel invaded Egypt, and two days later Britain and France dropped bombs and landed paratroops there. Incensed at this recrudescence of nineteenth-century gunboat tactics, and fearful that the actions opened an opportunity for the Soviet Union to present itself as the savior of the Arab world, Eisenhower said angrily, "Foster, you tell 'em Goddamn it, that we're going... to do everything that there is so we can

The apprehension on the face of the president as he talks with his secretary of state, John Foster Dulles, on October 30, 1956, indicates his concern as the Suez Crisis and Soviet repression in Hungary both erupt in the final week of his campaign for reelection. *Courtesy of the Dwight D. Eisenhower Presidential Library & Museum, National Archives ID 594347*

stop this thing." Accordingly, Dulles appeared before the United Nations to demand that Britain, France, and Israel withdraw. Stevenson, Truman, and Eleanor Roosevelt all criticized Eisenhower for not supporting Israel and America's Western allies, but the president reasoned sensibly that Egypt had every right to nationalize the canal, which was wholly in its territory, and he understood that if the United States took a stand against the legitimate aspirations of Muslim countries to rid themselves of imperialism, it could "array the world from Dakar to the Philippine Islands against us." He told Dulles, "I don't care whether I'm re-elected or not. We must make good on our word, otherwise we are a nation without honor."

Americans went to the polls in November 1956 with Eisenhower's foreign policy, which Republicans had been bragging about, in deep trouble. On Election Day, in response to a Russian threat to intervene on behalf of Egypt, the president put US armed forces on worldwide alert and warned Moscow that America was prepared to respond militarily if the USSR moved in. Though the British, French, and Israelis pulled out of Suez, all three were furious at Eisenhower, who had ordered the United

States to vote alongside the Soviet Union at the UN. Meantime, the Hungarian debacle had exposed the rhetoric of liberation as a sham, and Eisenhower and Dulles were accused of inciting Hungarians with empty pledges that had brought about thousands of deaths. These twin events might well have cost Eisenhower dearly. Instead, Republicans, who had been exalting Ike as a harbinger of peace, were able to persuade the country that only the general could be relied upon at a time of peril.

With nearly 58 percent of the ballots, Eisenhower defeated Stevenson even more decisively than he had four years earlier, widening his advantage of 1952 by three million votes. He captured every state in the North and West and made major inroads in the Deep South, winning even Louisiana, where voters wore "J'Aime Ike" buttons. The triumph was one for Eisenhower but not for his party, since the Democrats retained control of both houses of Congress. The 1956 outcome marked the first time since Zachary Taylor's victory in 1848 that a presidential nominee had won without carrying at least one house.

Second terms are rarely kind to American presidents, and Dwight Eisenhower's experience provided no exception. Ike did begin on a high note. "In our nation work and wealth abound," he said in his second inaugural address. "The air rings with the song of our industry, . . . the chorus of America the bountiful." Hardly a murmur of discontent could be heard in the land. The American people, secure from foreign peril, counted their blessings. An extraordinary "secret speech" to the Twentieth Communist Party Congress by Nikita Khrushchev sometime after midnight on February 24, 1956, denouncing Stalin's crimes and the cult of personality had raised hopes for rapprochement with the USSR. Unhappily, by the time the second four years were over, two serious recessions rendering millions of workers jobless had vexed the country; Eisenhower had dispatched an expeditionary force abroad for the only time in his presidency; relations with Russia had become ugly; the civil rights revolution had compelled him to become the first president since Grant to send troops into the South on behalf of black citizens; Soviet triumphs in space had created panic in America; and, from South America to Japan, Uncle Sam had become a pariah.

October 4, 1957, saw the most shocking announcement of the entire Eisenhower presidency: Radio Moscow reported that the USSR had thrust into orbit a satellite named *Sputnik* (traveling companion) that was circling the globe. With this single act, the Kremlin, as one writer asserted, shattered "the illusion of American omnipotence." The United States—wizard of the Industrial Revolution, creator of the first atomic bomb, the land of know-how—had been outpaced in an area where it thought itself unrivaled: technology. Especially frightening was the prospect that Soviet spacemen might soon be looking down on Vermont farmhouses from extraterrestrial military bases. Asked what Americans would find if they ever managed to get to the moon, the fiercely anti-Communist physicist Edward Teller replied, "Russians." The Soviet success indicated to the uncommitted nations which big power was going to prevail and, hence, with whom they had better align themselves. A Bangkok paper headlined the *Sputnik* story RUSSIANS RIP AMERICAN FACE. Its spectacular feat, the USSR said, proved the superiority of its system. "The present generation," it gloated, "will witness how the...labor of the people of the new socialist society turns even the most daring of man's dreams into a reality."

Alarmed Americans, seeking reassurance that their country would quickly catch and then surpass the Russians, found the complacency of the president and his cabinet irritating. Secretary of Defense Wilson's earlier gibe that basic research is "when you don't know what you are doing," and the postmaster general's claim to "progress in rooting out the eggheads," critics said, revealed how much less scientists were esteemed by the Eisenhower administration than by the Kremlin. Sherman Adams jeered at the Russians' "outer space basketball game," Wilson derided the achievement as a "trick," and a White House aide dismissed *Sputnik* as "a silly bauble." Eisenhower himself said that "one small ball in the air" disturbed him "not one iota." Asked whether he was going to appoint a science adviser, the president replied, "I hadn't thought of that."

On November 3, the Soviet Union commanded the attention of the United States government with a considerably more sensational display of its advanced rocketry. *Sputnik II*, weighing more than half a ton (more than six times heavier than the first satellite), carried scientific instruments and a live dog, Laika—a signal that the Russians would soon send men into space. Within a week, the White House announced the creation of a new post: special assistant to the president for science and technology, headed by Eisenhower's choice, the president of MIT.

Congress also got Eisenhower's assent to a National Defense Education Act, providing scholarships and grants to raise the level of education in the country, especially in mathematics, science, engineering, and foreign languages—fields important for improving American skills in the Cold War and, more particularly, in the space race. Not until eight months after the launching of *Sputnik II*, though, did Eisenhower agree to the creation of a National Aeronautics and Space Administration (NASA), and he did so very reluctantly. He wanted the Pentagon to retain power over missile development, but the legislation lodged most of the authority in the new civilian bureau.

At the height of the *Sputnik II* frenzy, a blue-ribbon commission on the state of national security in a nuclear age issued a report aimed directly at the president. Headed by H. Rowan Gaither Jr., of the Ford Foundation, and with a stellar array of members including the author of NSC-68, the panel warned that America was in mortal peril. If attacked by intercontinental missiles, the country would be all but defenseless, it asserted. Consequently, the report urged colossal increases in spending for all kinds of armaments, in addition to massive fallout-shelter construction at another $5 billion a year. Ostensibly superclassified, its contents quickly became known, presumably because commission members leaked them so that the media would raise a cry that Eisenhower could not resist. "The still-top-secret Gaither Report," revealed the *Washington Post*, "portrays a United States in the gravest danger in its history," for the nation was "exposed to an almost immediate threat from the missile-bristling Soviet Union." A few weeks later, the Rockefeller Brothers Fund advanced similarly strident arguments, a number of them from the young political scientist Henry Kissinger.

Eisenhower refused to be stampeded into a crash program to catch up with the Russians. Huge deficits or confiscatory taxation, he believed, could bring down America as surely as would a foreign foe. Moreover, he had been apprised that the USSR did not have the capability to fire a single missile that could reach the United States and that America was far ahead in long-range missile technology and even more in nuclear warheads. But he could not explain the source of his intelligence without letting it be known that he had authorized supersonic spy planes to fly over Russian territory. With high-altitude photography equipment so advanced that viewers could read newspaper headlines ten miles below, these U-2 planes had been bringing back detailed information on Soviet military installations. "Eisenhower's common-sense, deliberate response...may have been his finest gift to the nation," Stephen Ambrose later concluded, but, since the president could not elucidate his reasoning, Senate Majority Leader Lyndon Johnson and other Democrats were able to accuse him of permitting "a missile gap," and editorialists were at liberty to charge him with gross negligence. "Mr. Eisenhower," wrote Walter Lippmann, "is talking like a tired old man who has lost touch with the springs of our national vitality." In the one area where the five-star general could suppose he was least vulnerable to doubters—his capacity to safeguard the nation—he encountered the greatest distrust.

While coping with the fallout from the space orbits, Eisenhower was implanting an American presence in the Levant far more tenaciously than had any of his predecessors. In January 1957, stating that "the existing vacuum in the Middle East must be filled by the United States before it is filled by Russia," he asked Congress to empower him to employ force there to meet "overt armed aggression from any nation controlled by international communism." Senator Wayne Morse foresaw a "chapter written in blood," and his fellow Democrat Herman Talmadge stated that the resolution "amounts to an undated declaration of war—a blank check to be signed by Congress and handed to the Chief Executive to fill in the date as he sees fit." In response to these objections, Congress amended the resolution to provide that "if the President determines the necessity thereof, the United States is prepared to use armed forces" in the Middle East. In that fashion, Congress, while retaining its constitutional war-making authority, joined the president in serving warning to the Kremlin and to Nasser.

The Eisenhower Doctrine came immediately into play. In 1957, in response to an appeal for help from King Hussein of Jordan, whose reign was being challenged, the president ordered the 6th Fleet into the eastern Mediterranean. Rumblings in Lebanon constituted a much more important test. In July 1958, after the country's president, Camille Chamoun, sought US intervention to save his government from insurgents, Eisenhower dispatched fourteen thousand marines, infantrymen, and paratroopers to secure Beirut. When the marines hit the beach, in the biggest amphibious operation since Inchon, they found not Nasser's agents or menacing Reds but bemused vacationers lolling on the sand.

Eisenhower had totally misinterpreted the situation by perceiving internal rivalries as struggles in the Cold War. The unrest reflected not Kremlin machinations but resentment of Muslims and Arab nationalists at Chamoun, a Christian catering to Western powers that indulged Israel. The Eisenhower Doctrine proved to be a blunder because it permitted Nasser, for whom Marxism had no attraction, to represent himself as the champion of Arab nationalism against Western meddlers, and, after a time, the president was compelled to acknowledge a "campaign of hatred against us." He remained, though, as transfixed by the domino analogy in the Middle East as he was in Southeast Asia.

Eisenhower could find no solace in Latin America, where events in 1958 revealed painfully the cost of his neglect of the region and of his solicitude for US investors there. In the decade after 1951, all of the countries of Central and South America together received fewer US dollars than did Taiwan—$3.4 billion of the $80 billion allotted to foreign aid. Moreover, Eisenhower presented the Legion of Merit to the hated dictators of Peru and Venezuela. In April 1958, following the ouster of both autocrats, the vice president embarked on a goodwill tour of Latin America. In Peru, mobs cried, "Get out, Nixon!" and at the four-centuries-old University of San Marcos, students stoned him. Venezuela was far worse. In Caracas, the vice president and his wife were spat upon by demonstrators who viewed Nixon as a surrogate for Eisenhower. Violent protesters trapped them in their limousine and hurled huge rocks that shattered the car's windows. "The crowd was rocking the car back and forth—slower and higher each time," Nixon later recalled. "At that moment, . . . each of us in the car realized we might actually be killed." The tour had to be called off, its violent demise, said Lippmann, constituting "a diplomatic Pearl Harbor."

In the late summer of 1958, as the American expeditionary force carried on its bootless mission in Lebanon, the dangerously silly game of chicken between Mao and Eisenhower resumed when mainland China once again started shelling Quemoy and Matsu, where, provocatively, Chiang had landed a hundred thousand troops. Considerably more ardently than four years earlier, Eisenhower believed that the islands must be defended. Mao, he said, was challenging "Western unity and resolve" by testing whether the president would flinch. Despite the judgment of the Joint Chiefs that the islands were of no strategic value, Dulles, insisting that they constituted a "vital interest" of the United States, pressed for an atomic strike on airfields on the mainland. For a time, US convoys escorted Chiang's transports, and the 7th Fleet, armed with nuclear weapons, plied the Formosa Strait.

On September 11, Eisenhower addressed the American people about the clash of wills. He assured them that "there is not going to be any appeasement," only to find that they had a very different concern: the prospect that the lives of their sons might be sacrificed for a ridiculous cause. Mail to the White House ran 4–1 against the president. Within NATO, Prime Minister Harold Macmillan, who thought that America's China policy was "almost childish," let Ike know that the British public would not support a war for Quemoy and Matsu. Eisenhower was forced to recognize that "as much as two-thirds of the world, and 50 percent of US opinion, opposes the course which we have been following."

At the end of September, after many anxious days, the United States reversed direction. Chiang, said Dulles, had been "rather foolish," and America had "no commitment to help Chiang back to the mainland." Any prospect that the Nationalists on Taiwan might regain China, he added, was "highly hypothetical." Eisenhower went further. Chiang, he declared, was "a thorn in the side of peace." Three weeks later, under strong pressure from Dulles, Chiang told the world that he was renouncing any use of force to win back the mainland. In what Eisenhower later called a "Gilbert and Sullivan war," Mao shelled only on even-numbered days, and Chiang replenished the islands only on odd-numbered days of the month. After a time, Taiwan scaled down its military presence on the islands, though not, Eisenhower later wrote, "to the extent I thought desirable." Chiang, in short, had been "released," and guff about "liberation" quieted to a whisper.

Less than two weeks before the *Sputnik* scare, the civil rights revolution exploded on Eisenhower. It was a movement for which he had little empathy. In his many years in army posts in the South, he had been altogether comfortable with the mores of white supremacy; he enjoyed telling "darky" stories; and he had dragged his heels on integration of the armed forces. Though he favored equality of opportunity, he told one of his chief advisers that did not mean "that a Negro should court my daughter."

Arthur Larson, regarded as the theoretician of the administration, concluded, "President Eisenhower, during his presidential tenure, was neither emotionally nor intellectually in favor of combating segregation."

He strongly opposed government intervention on behalf of the constitutional rights of African Americans in the South. Asked how he felt about his secretary of labor's endorsement of a fair employment measure of the sort that Truman had advocated, he replied that he disapproved of "punitive or compulsory federal law." When his attorney general, Herbert Brownell, filed an amicus brief on behalf of the suit launched by a black father, Oliver Brown, and others asking the Supreme Court to overturn the "separate but equal" rationale of segregation imposed by *Plessy v. Ferguson* in 1896, he did so only by overcoming Ike's strenuous objections. At the start of his presidency, Eisenhower had recorded in his diary his conviction that "federal law imposed upon our states in such a way as to bring about a conflict of the police powers of the states and of the nation would set back the cause of progress in race relations for a long, long time." Furthermore, he knew full well that his party had made unprecedented gains in the South in the 1952 election, and he wanted to do nothing to jeopardize future prospects for Republicans in the region.

Eisenhower took office as Oliver Brown's petition on behalf of his young daughter Linda, who had been denied admission to an all-white grade school, was making its way through the courts. If the Supreme Court ruled in his favor, the decision would lay a charge of dynamite under every racist institution in the country, especially in the South, though the *Brown* case actually arose in Kansas. To be sure that the outcome was one he sought, the president invited Chief Justice Warren to a stag dinner so that the attorney for the segregationists, John W. Davis, could bring pressure on him. At the affair, Eisenhower told Warren: "These are not bad people. All they are concerned about is to see that their sweet little girls are not required to sit in school alongside some big overgrown Negroes." Grossly improper, the president's action had no effect. On May 17, 1954, Warren spoke for a unanimous court in *Brown v. Board of Education*. "In the field of public education," he declared, "the doctrine of 'separate but equal' has no place." To segregate schoolchildren "solely because of their race," he declared, "generates a feeling of inferiority...that may affect their hearts and minds in a way unlikely ever to be undone."

Millions of Americans welcomed *Brown* as a milestone in the slow progress toward undoing the legacy of slavery, but Eisenhower thought it a terrible intrusion by the federal government. "I am convinced that the Supreme Court decision *set back* progress in the South *at least fifteen years*," he confided. "The fellow who tries to tell me you can do these things by *force* is just plain *nuts*." With white southerners in positions of power announcing that they would defy the Court by continuing to maintain all-white schools, and with critics decrying the caprice of nine blunderers, White House advisers urged the president to speak out in defense of the legitimacy of the ruling and to request peaceful acceptance, but he refused to do so. When, two days after the ruling was handed down, a reporter inquired whether he had any counsel for the South, he retorted, "Not ... the slightest." Asked that summer whether he had considered calling for legislation to compel compliance, he answered, "The subject has not even been mentioned to me." Two years later, he insisted that a passage endorsing the Supreme Court decision be deleted from the 1956 Republican platform, because it dealt with a matter "charged with emotionalism." Advocates of Jim Crow took heart from Eisenhower's silence, which they understood implied disapproval of *Brown* and constituted an unspoken endorsement of their determination to flout it.

In the narrowly circumscribed area where federal jurisdiction was indisputable, Eisenhower compiled an excellent record. On the very day after *Brown v. Board* was announced, he summoned the District of Columbia commissioners to his office and told them he wanted the capital city, with its large black population, to become a showplace of school integration. In addition, the District integrated parks and swimming pools; a committee headed by Vice President Nixon put an end to Jim Crow in the offices of the Chesapeake and Potomac Telephone Company while advancing job opportunities for black streetcar operators and bus drivers; and the White House brought pressure on Washington hotels, restaurants, and theaters to end racial discrimination. Eisenhower also named to the US Fifth Circuit Court John Minor Wisdom, Elbert Tuttle, and John Brown and as a US District Court judge Frank M. Johnson Jr., all of whom proved to be civil rights stalwarts. Before the Supreme Court acted, the Eisenhower administration had already taken the initiative in desegregating army post schools and naval yards, even in the southern ports of Norfolk and Charleston. To avoid a ruckus, federal maintenance workers slipped into shipyards over a weekend when the facilities were shut; on a Monday morning, workers, after punching in, found that Jim Crow signs on drinking fountains, rest rooms, and cafeterias had been painted over and that they were expected to adapt to a new environment. Beyond these parameters, though, Eisenhower would not step.

"No matter how much law we have, we have a job in education, in getting people to understand what are the issues," he declared, but he would not use his advantageous position and his immense prestige to educate about "the issues." Instead, he contented himself with banalities, as when he told Booker T. Washington's daughter, "I like to feel that where we have to change the hearts of men, we cannot do it by cold lawmaking, but must make these changes by appealing to reason, by prayer, and by constantly working at it though our own efforts." Under Eisenhower, the White House was not a bully pulpit but an empty pulpit.

Not a word would Eisenhower speak against the hideous violence inflicted on law-abiding citizens, not even when in Mississippi an African American encouraging exercise of the constitutional right to vote was murdered. After sniper fire raked recently integrated buses in Montgomery, Alabama, early in 1957, and four black churches were bombed, a meeting of African American leaders in Atlanta sparked by Rev. Martin Luther King Jr. called upon the president to "come immediately" to deliver a "major speech in a major Southern city asking all persons to abide by the Supreme Court's decisions as the law of the land." Asked about the appeal at a press conference, Eisenhower seemed clueless. When a few weeks later, he was once again questioned, he responded that he already had "a pretty good and sizable agenda" and "as you know, I insist on going for a bit of recreation every once in a while."

When, in *Brown II*, the Supreme Court mandated desegregation of the nation's schools, it received no support whatsoever from the president. Instead, he warned against trying to change attitudes "merely by laws" and alluded to southern white resistance to "mongrelization of the race." Given Eisenhower's implicit consent, white supremacists in southern states felt at liberty, even emboldened, to stonewall the US Supreme Court, knowing that the national government would not deter them. After the Court ordered the University of Alabama to admit its first black student, a howling mob forced the young woman, Autherine

Lucy, to flee, and the university expelled her. She narrowly missed being lynched. The president of the United States let it happen. When at the start of the 1956 school year the governor of Texas sent Texas Rangers to bar black students from white schools in Mansfield and Texarkana, Eisenhower feigned ignorance of what was going on and intimated that the federal government could, and should, do nothing. In the summer of 1957, he declared, "I can't imagine any set of circumstances that would ever induce me to send federal troops into any area to enforce the orders of a federal court." He had hardly uttered these words when a blow-up in the capital city of a southern state compelled him to eat them.

The showdown came in an unlikely place: Little Rock, Arkansas, a town with enlightened leadership. Its school board had resolved to make a start on compliance with *Brown II* by admitting nine black students to Central High School at the start of the school year in September 1957. Governor Orval Faubus responded by spewing racist rhetoric and by dispatching the Arkansas National Guard to the city to bar the entry of the black students.

One black student made an indelible impression. Fifteen-year-old Elizabeth Eckford, neatly dressed in a fresh white piqué blouse and pretty pleated white cotton skirt she had trimmed with blue-and-white gingham, walked up to the school—head held high, one arm around a notebook—only to be turned aside by Faubus's soldiers. All alone, she tried to make her way to a bus stop for her sad journey back to her home through a gauntlet of taunting white mothers and girls. She later re-called: "They moved closer and closer.... I tried to see a friendly face somewhere in the crowd—someone who maybe could help. I looked into the face of an old woman and it seemed a kind face, but when I looked at her again, she spat at me." A photographer snapped a picture of her ordeal. Called by the Associated Press one of the hundred most important photographs of the twentieth century, it showed the attrac-tive black teenager being hounded by a mob of howling white women, their faces contorted with hate. Widely circulated overseas, it aroused intense indignation at the United States—an acute embarrassment to Eisenhower in waging cold war.

In Newport, Rhode Island, where he was on a golfing vacation, Eisenhower received a wire from Little Rock's mayor, Woodrow Wilson Mann:

immediate need for federal troops is urgent.... mob is armed and engaging in...acts of violence. situation is out of control and police
cannot disperse the mob. i am pleading to you as president of the
united states in the interest of humanity...to provide the necessary
federal troops within several hours.

Eisenhower could not afford to reject this plea. He was already subject
to biting criticism for dithering while the sinister situation worsened.
The Yale Law School professor Alexander Bickel wrote Justice Felix
Frankfurter that the events in Arkansas "reveal Eisenhower as the most
harmfully ineffective President since James Buchanan."

On September 24, Eisenhower ordered a detachment of the 101st
Airborne Division to Little Rock and federalized the Arkansas National
Guard. In a televised address, he explained: "Whenever normal agencies
prove inadequate to the task and it becomes necessary for the Executive
Branch of the Federal Government to use its powers...to uphold Federal
Courts, the President's responsibility is inescapable." For months thereafter, the nine black students filed into school through a cordon of paratroopers with fixed bayonets. Once inside the building, they had no
protection from vicious verbal abuse and physical assaults. Sherman Adams
later said that, for Ike, his intervention was "the most repugnant to him
of all his acts in his eight years at the White House." Eisenhower wanted
it understood that he had issued the edict only to bolster the authority
of federal courts, "not to enforce or advance any governmental policy
respecting integration." Even after Little Rock, he stated, "I have never
said what I thought about the Supreme Court decision—I have never
told a soul."

When Attorney General Brownell began work on a civil rights measure,
Eisenhower warned him not to become another Charles Sumner, the
zealous antidiscrimination senator of Reconstruction. Brownell put together
a package that, in addition to creating two federal agencies, safeguarded
the right of African Americans to vote—a goal the president did espouse. But Eisenhower threw cold water on another feature of the 1957
bill that sought to expedite school integration. In response to a question
from a reporter, he undercut Brownell and Senate liberals by saying,
"Well, I would not want to answer this in detail because I was reading
part of the bill this morning and...there were certain phrases I didn't

completely understand." Racist members of Congress interpreted that lame remark as license to weaken the measure.

Hailed as the first legislation of this nature since Reconstruction, the eviscerated Civil Rights Act of 1957 did not amount to much. Furthermore, the Eisenhower administration put so little effort into enforcing the statute that two years afterward it was found that not a single voter had been added to the rolls. The law did create two new institutions, but, as Bickel wrote, "the Civil Rights Division of the Department of Justice was organized tardily and poorly, and run without distinction. Its record under Eisenhower was laughable when compared...with that of the same department's Antitrust Division." The act also set up a Civil Rights Commission with investigative powers, but, Bickel concluded, "Eisenhower took an unconscionable time making the necessary appointments to the Commission..., and he pretty much ignored it afterward."

Incredibly, for more than six years the president refused to meet with black leaders. When he did talk to them, in May 1958, he was so infuriatingly condescending that, at the end of the session, he was hissed. The first baseball player to surmount the color barrier in the major leagues, Jackie Robinson, wrote him:

> I was sitting in the audience at the Summit Meeting of Negro Leaders yesterday when you said we must have patience. On hearing you say this, I felt like standing up and saying, "Oh no! Not again." I respectfully remind you, sir, that we have been the most patient of all people....17 million Negroes cannot do as you suggest and wait for the hearts of men to change. We want to enjoy now the rights...we are entitled to as Americans....As the chief executive of our nation, I respectfully suggest that you unwittingly crush the spirit of freedom in Negroes by constantly urging forbearance and give hope to...pro-segregation leaders...who would take from us even those freedoms we now enjoy.

At the end of Eisenhower's two terms, not a single pupil in five Deep South states attended a desegregated school. Despite the authority granted by the 1957 Civil Rights Act and (thanks to Lyndon Johnson's parliamentary legerdemain) a somewhat improved 1960 law, his administration initiated a grand total of only six suits on behalf of expanded suffrage. The thoughtful, soft-spoken leader of the NAACP, Roy Wilkins, concluded: "President Eisenhower was a fine general and a good, decent man, but if he had fought World War II the way he fought for civil rights, we would all be speaking German today."

On the afternoon of November 25, 1957, as he was signing papers, Eisenhower suddenly felt disoriented. "I found that the words . . . seemed literally to run off the top of the page," he recalled. "It was impossible for me to express any coherent thought whatsoever. I began to feel truly helpless." The stroke, his third serious illness in three years, left him with a speech impediment for a time and revived concern about his ability to carry out his responsibilities under the strains of office. Coinciding with the *Sputnik* jitters, his temporary paralysis marked the start of a troublesome twelve months for Eisenhower, culminating in the disastrous midterm elections. The year 1958, he later said, was "the worst of my life."

In 1957, Secretary of the Treasury Humphrey warned that if federal spending was not curbed, "you will have a depression that will curl your hair," but it was the Eisenhower administration's affinity for fiscal restraint and tight money that helped bring on late that year the sharpest downturn since the end of World War II, with joblessness the worst since 1941. (The country was not to see so deep a recession again until 2008.) At a time when the Ford Motor Company was attempting to market the despised Edsel, the automobile industry had its poorest sales year of the postwar era. In Detroit, unemployment reached 20 percent. Eisenhower had taken great pride in balancing the budget, which in 1957 showed a surplus, but in 1958, to his consternation, the government ran the largest peacetime deficit in the history of the country. No longer did Americans talk of "Eisenhower prosperity."

The president received an even more disturbing blow to his expectations. Having gained the White House as a crusader who would clean up the "mess" that soiled the Truman administration, he had been boasting that "not one appointee of this Administration has been involved in scandal or corruption." But in quick time, exposures required the resignation of a number of high-ranking officials: the secretary of the air force, the chairman of the ICC, the General Services administrator, the public buildings administrator, and the head of the Republican National Committee. Distressed by these embarrassing downfalls, Eisenhower took comfort in reckoning that no one could conceivably question the probity of his chief of staff.

Sherman Adams had become Eisenhower's indispensable man. "Adams," said a political scientist in 1957, "is more than a trusted personal adviser; more than an efficient chief of staff; he is in fact the President's alter ego." Ike, she added, "likes best a paper that ends, 'OK, SA'; this he can initial 'DDE': such is his confidence in Adams and his staff." When Queen Elizabeth came to visit, the protocol list placed Adams higher than any senator or governor. Eisenhower, who said that "the only person who really understands what I'm trying to do is Sherman Adams," called his assistant "the boss," and a number of observers thought that there was more than a grain of truth in that jocular remark. In one story that made the rounds in Washington, a Democrat said, "Wouldn't it be terrible if Eisenhower died and Nixon became president?" and another Democrat replied, "Wouldn't it be terrible if Sherman Adams died and Eisenhower became president." When critics complained that Adams wielded too much power, Eisenhower retorted angrily, "The trouble with these people is they don't recognize integrity."

Early in 1958, however, a congressional committee grabbed headlines with a stunning disclosure. Adams, it reported, had interceded with the Federal Trade Commission and the SEC on behalf of a New England textile manufacturer, Bernard Goldfine, who had paid thousands of dollars in hotel bills for Adams and his wife and given the president's chief assistant a vicuña coat. Since Republicans had made "mink coat" a symbol of venality in the Truman presidency, the vicuña coat revelation was disproportionately mortifying. Republican leaders, who had all along resented the imperious Adams, urged Eisenhower to get rid of him, but he refused. "I need him," he said frankly. Not until well into September did Adams resign, late enough to encumber Republicans as the midterm elections approached in November.

With the Adams story still buzzing, and the recession causing countless failures of small businesses and massive job loss, the country went to the polls. Eisenhower had been framing an option for voters: "left-wing government or sensible government." When the returns were counted, he had been slapped hard. Nothing prepared him for the dimensions of the Democratic rout. Not since the FDR landslide of 1936 had a party won so large a share of seats in the House, and in the Senate, Democrats, who had been nursing a one-seat margin, expanded their advantage to almost 2–1, leaving Republicans on the short end of a 62–34 division.

Never before had a party in power sustained three consecutive defeats in congressional elections.

That same year, the Supreme Court dealt Eisenhower—and the institution of the presidency—another setback. Five years earlier, he had asked one Myron Wiener to step down as a member of the War Claims Commission created to compensate individuals injured by the enemy in World War II. When Wiener, a Truman appointee, refused, Eisenhower fired him. Wiener brought suit for the salary he would have received, but the Court of Claims dismissed it since, though Congress had not authorized removal, it also had not forbidden it. In *Wiener v. United States*, the Supreme Court reversed that ruling in a unanimous decision, with Justice Frankfurter stating that Eisenhower had exceeded his power. It thereby buttressed the holding in *Humphrey's Executor* (1935) that a president may not discharge a member of a quasi-judicial agency, even if Congress had not proscribed such action.

Confronted by the largest opposition majority in the twentieth century, Eisenhower fought a rearguard action against Congress. He had no hope of imposing his own program, but, despite their huge advantage, Democrats could not get anything of significance through either. Eisenhower vetoed two public works measures and two public housing bills. In addition, he struck down environmental legislation on the grounds that pollution was a "uniquely local blight." Urged to approve a costly program for a lunar landing, he rejoined, "I'm not about to hock my jewels." The consequence was deadlock—two barren years.

In the final span of his presidency, Eisenhower sought to leave his mark on the history of his country not by ameliorating social ills at home but by greatly easing the tensions of the Cold War. With Sherman Adams gone and John Foster Dulles stepping down in April 1959 because of failing health, he held the reins almost alone. Eisenhower said, "There is no place on this earth to which I would not travel, there is no chore I would not undertake, if I had any faintest hope that, by so doing, I would promote the...cause of world peace." As he reached out to Khrushchev and to the third world, his sincerity was transparent, and for one brief, luminous interval, it appeared that he was succeeding. But his tenure ended with Khrushchev snarling in a fit of rage at a session of the UN in New York City, and America's position abroad under siege in every part of the globe. In his last months, concluded Reinhold Niebuhr, Eisenhower's presidency was in "rather pathetic eclipse."

The dispiriting returns in the 1958 elections had hardly been absorbed when Eisenhower encountered yet another crisis. "West Berlin has become a sort of malignant tumor," Khrushchev declared. "Therefore we have decided to do some surgery." In six months, he warned, he was terminating Western access to the city. That threat became palpable when, for eight hours, Russian soldiers halted, and held, an American convoy in Germany. US military advisers urged the use of force, but Eisenhower, recognizing the peril of a third world war, remained unflappable, and, after a nerve-racking half a year, tranquility returned—for the moment.

In September 1959, Khrushchev arrived in the United States for a tumultuous thirteen-day transcontinental journey that the historian John Gaddis has called "a surreal extravaganza." At the outset—in Washington, at FDR's Hyde Park, and in Hollywood, where he fumed at the exposure of flesh on the set of *Can-Can*—Khrushchev, the first head of the USSR to visit America, behaved boorishly. But by the time he reached Eisenhower's Maryland retreat, Camp David, he had mellowed, and the Soviet premier and the president got on famously. "Let us have more and more use for the short American word O.K.," Khrushchev said. On returning to Moscow, he told commissars that he was impressed by Eisenhower's goodwill and believed that a fruitful relationship could be cultivated. He looked forward to welcoming the president to the Soviet Union and even had a golf course laid out for him. As the world had once spoken of "the spirit of Geneva," it now talked of "the spirit of Camp David." With a summit meeting in the offing to resolve problems over Berlin and nuclear weapons, hopes for global harmony ran higher than at any time since 1945. "At this wondrous moment," said Macmillan, "we seem on the threshold of genuine, practical steps toward peace."

Given the harsh realities of the Cold War, these expectations may have been illusory, but Eisenhower's exertions made them seem achievable. In 1959, the American president traveled thousands upon thousands of miles on a jet plane (a recent innovation) across four continents with a message of amity. In India, where he was greeted with signs proclaiming "Welcome Prince of Peace," he walked a foot deep in flowers that had been showered on him. When the stay in India drew to a close, Prime

Minister Jawaharlal Nehru told the president, "As you go, you take a piece of our heart." The historian Eric Goldman later wrote, "Newsmen with decades of experience agreed that at no time, anywhere, had they seen so rhapsodic a reception of a public figure." Unhappily, by a single decision, Eisenhower put an end to all prospects for détente.

On May 5, 1960, only eleven days before the scheduled summit meeting in Paris so freighted with sanguine expectation, Khrushchev, in a three-and-a-half-hour address to the Supreme Soviet, reported angrily that an American plane had been shot down over Russian territory while on a mission of "aggressive provocation aimed at wrecking the Summit Conference." Instead of holding Eisenhower to blame, he charged that "Pentagon militarists" had ordered the flight. Washington knew that a high-altitude US plane had been missing for several days and assumed that the pilot—taken down at 65,000 feet—had not survived. Hence, NASA felt comfortable in suggesting that a U-2 engaged in weather research in Turkey might have strayed across the USSR border, and the State Department's press officer affirmed, "There was absolutely no—N-O—no deliberate attempt to violate Soviet air space, and there never has been."

The very next day, Khrushchev, having led the Eisenhower administration into outright fabrications, sprang his trap. "Comrades, I must let you in on a secret," he told the Supreme Soviet. "When I made my report two days ago, I deliberately refrained from mentioning that we have the remnants of the plane—and we also have the pilot, who is *quite alive and kicking!*" He further revealed that Francis Gary Powers, who had been shot down near Sverdlovsk—1,300 miles inside Russia—had confessed that he had been on a spy mission that had begun in Pakistan and was to end in Norway. Gleefully, Khrushchev displayed the poison needle that the US government had supplied Powers as a suicide instrument should he be captured (but which he had eschewed) and photos of Soviet airfields extracted from the pilot's camera.

Exposed as barefaced liars, Eisenhower officials—and then the president himself—managed to make an acutely embarrassing situation far worse. Reversing itself, the State Department acknowledged that Powers was on a flight of "surveillance." It further stated that such missions had been going on for several years, ever since the USSR had rejected the president's "open skies" proposal at Geneva. Yet it indicated—in keeping with Khrushchev's willingness to exonerate Eisenhower—that "authorities" had not approved this particular provocation. Hardly had these words been spoken than the government changed its story once more. Since American critics had been saying for some time that Ike had no idea of what was going on in his own administration, he did not dare take up the offer to deny involvement. Instead, he told the press that he kept tabs on every important initiative; he justified the flyovers; and he indicated that the United States was going to continue to spy on the Soviet Union.

Without ever intending to do so, Eisenhower had dealt a series of mean blows to Khrushchev's pride and to his standing in his own country. The Soviet premier had been telling the Russian people, and his sometimes questioning associates in the Kremlin, that he had seen to it that they were invulnerable while, unbeknownst to him, American planes had been peering down at them for years. Moreover, Eisenhower, though he knew the summit with Khrushchev was imminent, had signed off on an espionage probe only days before the meeting was to convene. And, to top off these affronts, the president had called penetration of Russian air space a "vital necessity." With ample reason, Khrushchev headed for the Paris conference mad as a hornet and ready to sting.

In Paris on May 15, Khrushchev—blustering and rude—demanded that spy flights cease, that Eisenhower apologize for "past acts of aggression," and that he punish those responsible. U-2 reconnaissance had already been halted, the president responded, but the premier's other terms were unacceptable. The next day, Khrushchev—perhaps putting on a show for Kremlin skeptics and the Red Chinese—angrily accused Eisenhower of "treachery" and of pursuing a "bandit" operation. The summit, he said, should be postponed for six to eight months—that is, until Eisenhower was no longer in the White House—in the hope that the next American president would "understand the futility of pursuing aggressive policies." In a studied insult, he withdrew his invitation to Eisenhower to pay a reciprocal visit to the USSR. "Conditions have now arisen," he said, "which make us unable to welcome the president with the proper warmth which the Soviet people display toward fond guests." Eisenhower, known for his low boiling point and fierce temper, sat through the tirade in a restrained fury. On the following day, Khrushchev was nowhere to be seen. He had torpedoed the summit.

At an explosive press conference before departing Paris, Khrushchev pounded the table, shouted that the United States was "thief-like" and "cowardly," and called Eisenhower a "fishy" friend. American aggressors, he raged, should be treated the way a boy handled an erring cat: "We would catch such a cat by the tail and bang its head against the wall, and that was the only way it could be taught some sense." Any nation that allowed the United States to use it as a base for U-2 flights, he warned, would invite "devastating" rocket assaults. No longer did anyone speak of "the spirit of Camp David."

With his aspirations for détente gone awry, Eisenhower found satisfaction in knowing that he had a staunch ally in Japan—the anchor of US policy in Asia. To cultivate that relationship, he planned a state visit to the island empire. But when in June 1960—one month after Khrushchev's ranting in Paris—he sent James Hagerty to Tokyo to arrange details of the forthcoming trip, a surging mob, chanting "Go Home Yankee," shook the car in which the press chief and the American ambassador rode. Only intervention by police made it possible for a marine helicopter to lift the Americans to safety. Recognizing that he could not guarantee the security of a US chief executive, the Japanese prime minister told Eisenhower, who had already set out from Washington for Asia, not to come. *Life* called the cancellation "the gravest setback for Eisenhower foreign policy in seven years," and the White House correspondent Richard Rovere wrote, "If there has ever been a moment of national failure and humiliation comparable to the present one, no one in this dazed capital can identify it."

Eisenhower had to cope with a much more dire predicament in Cuba. In January 1959, Americans had rejoiced in the overthrow of the vile Batista regime and had lionized the dynamic leader of the rebellion, Fidel Castro—bearded, cigar chomping, dressed in battle fatigues—as the romantic freedom fighter of the Sierra Maestra. Despite warnings from Nixon and others that the *fidelistas* were covert Communists, the president had offered the rebels economic aid. But within months of taking power, the new Cuban government imprisoned hundreds of Cubans, canceled elections, conducted show trials, and staged public executions. It also expropriated extensive American holdings on the island. Influenced by his adviser Che Guevara, Castro lashed out at the United States as a "vulture" that was "feeding on humanity," announced that he had always been a "Marxist-Leninist," and curried favor with Moscow.

This turn of events greatly alarmed the Eisenhower administration, for by his actions Castro gave Soviet Russia its first foothold in North America. The Monroe Doctrine, Khrushchev boasted, had "died a natural death." Furthermore, Castro's defiance inspired leftists throughout the New World. To snuff out the threat of contagion in Latin America, Eisenhower approved a CIA plot to equip hundreds of anti-Castro Cubans and train them in Guatemala and Florida for an invasion of Cuba in expectation that they would spark an insurrection. At the time he left office, arrangements had not been completed, but Eisenhower bequeathed this foolhardy scheme to his successor.

Despite the many tribulations of his second term, few doubted that if Eisenhower had been a candidate for reelection in 1960, he would have won handily. In his eight-year tenure, he averaged an approval rating of 64 percent, an astonishing figure. Republican leaders rued the day that the GOP 80th Congress had put through the Twenty-second Amendment limiting a president to two terms, not imagining that the first man trapped by it would be one of their own, a sure winner. Instead, they had to settle for nominating Ike's controversial vice president, Richard Nixon.

Though he was promoted as a "new Nixon," a statesman far removed from his role as hatchet man in the 1952 campaign, the vice president continued to breed distrust—less because of his policy stands than because he seemed the hollow man of a consumer culture. He appeared to be constantly manipulating his image to secure an advantage. At one point, he solemnly explained how much preparation was required to be spontaneous or to "seem . . . sincere." The essential question, wrote one editor, was not whether the real Nixon was the new Nixon or the old Nixon but "whether there is anything that might be called the 'real' Nixon, new or old."

In contending that he was better qualified for the presidency than any Democrat, Nixon pointed to his eight years in the national government as the president's second in command, but, at a press conference in August, Eisenhower undermined that claim. Asked for instances when Nixon had made an important contribution to an action, Ike responded that the vice president was "not a part of decision-making." When a reporter persisted, "I just wondered if you could give us an example of a major idea of his that you had adopted," Eisenhower cut him off before he could finish his question with the curt retort, "If you give me a week, I might think of one." For the remainder of the campaign, no opponent hit Nixon with a punch so damaging as that sentence.

Nixon's Democratic rival, John Fitzgerald Kennedy, who wrested the 1960 nomination from Stevenson and two fellow senators—Hubert Humphrey and Lyndon Johnson—also carried liabilities. Liberals shied away from any son of Joseph P. Kennedy, a nouveau-riche financier who, as the US ambassador to Great Britain, had pressed for appeasement of Hitler, who had been a patron of Joe McCarthy, and who had detested FDR. When the nation was plunged in grief by Roosevelt's death in April 1945, Joe Kennedy said that "it was a great thing for the country." They were put off, too, by John F. Kennedy's cool comportment and the absence of emotional commitment to causes they cherished. ("Let me put it this way," one senator said. "If my dear old mother were to fall and break her leg, Hubert Humphrey would cry, but I'm not so sure about Jack.") As congressman, he had been discounted as a "Tuesday-Thursday" member with one of the worst attendance records, and he was not an especially distinguished senator. "It was the goddamnedest thing," Lyndon Johnson said later. "Here was a whippersnapper. . . . He never said a word of importance in the Senate and he never did a thing. . . . His growing hold on the American people was simply a mystery to me." One of Johnson's aides wrote that to the hardworking majority leader, Kennedy "was the enviably attractive nephew who sings an Irish ballad for the company, and then winsomely disappears before the table-clearing and dishwashing begin."

Kennedy's public reputation did not bear close scrutiny. To a considerable extent, it had been fabricated by publicists hired, or influenced, by his well-connected father. Unquestionably, Jack Kennedy had been a brave and incredibly resourceful PT boat commander in the Pacific, but his father saw to it that his performance was blown up to mythical proportions. Joe Kennedy also manipulated a Pulitzer Prize jury to give the prestigious annual award to his son's *Profiles in Courage*, though the book, not a work of original scholarship, had been largely pieced together by an aide, Theodore Sorensen. Furthermore, having failed to stand up to McCarthy, the senator had invited ridicule by putting his name to *Profiles in Courage*. Kennedy, it was said, should have shown less profile and more courage. Advertised as a vibrant young sportsman, he had, in fact, been plagued by scary, baffling illnesses since infancy and required daily medication for a gland malfunction. (In 1947, a British physician told Pamela Churchill, "That young American friend of yours, he hasn't got a year to live.") By far his greatest handicap as a candidate, though, was that he was a Roman Catholic, because it was an axiom of American politics, especially after Al Smith's thrashing in 1928, that no papist could be elected president.

Senator Kennedy, however, also had qualities that voters found attractive. Tall, slim, with a high-wattage smile, he radiated the good looks of a film star, especially on the TV screen. Jack, media commentators said, was "telegenic." Calling him "one of the handsomest men in American political life," a female Washington columnist said of Kennedy: "He is as graceful as a greyhound and can be as beguiling as a sunny day." He also conveyed the patrician equipoise that had drawn many to FDR. Though his nineteenth-century forebear had been a refugee from the potato blight in Ireland, his family had moved up the social scale so quickly that his father had been appointed ambassador to the Court of St. James's and his sister had married the Marquess of Hartington. "Jack," a Massachusetts governor said, "is the first Irish Brahmin." Kennedy left the impression, too, that he was a man of letters. In one brief address at the University of Wisconsin, he quoted Goethe, Swift, Tennyson, Emerson, Faulkner, Lord Asquith, Woodrow Wilson, Artemus Ward, Finley Peter Dunne, and Queen Victoria. By facing down bigots at a ministerial conference in Houston, he appealed to Americans' sense of fair play. "I refuse to believe that I was denied the right to be president on the day I was baptized," he said. After winning the primary in the overwhelmingly Protestant state of West Virginia, he coasted downhill to the Democratic nomination. To improve his prospects in the South, he chose the Texan Lyndon B. Johnson, the Senate majority leader, as his running mate.

In his acceptance speech in Los Angeles, Kennedy declared: "We stand today on the edge of a New Frontier—the frontier of the 1960's—a frontier of unknown opportunities and perils—a frontier of unfulfilled hopes and threats." He added: "Woodrow Wilson's New Freedom promised our nation a new political and economic framework. Franklin

Democratic campaigners in 1960. As they tour Manhattan the day before the election, John F. Kennedy, Eleanor Roosevelt, and Lyndon B. Johnson exhibit confidence, but JFK will win only the narrowest of victories. *Library of Congress, LC-USZ62-70670*

Roosevelt's New Deal promised security and succor to those in need. But the New Frontier of which I speak is not a set of promises—it is a set of challenges. It sums up, not what I intend to offer the American people, but what I intend to ask of them. It appeals to their pride, not their pocketbook—it holds out the promise of more sacrifice instead of more security." The country, he asserted, needed bold new leadership, "after eight years of drugged and fitful sleep."

During the campaign, Kennedy pounded hard on this one theme—that America was stagnating and needed to make tough choices to get moving again. Over the past eight years in a Republican administration, he asserted, America's international standing had deteriorated; Eisenhower had come to power pledging to go to Korea and ended up afraid to go to Japan. "I run for the presidency because I do not want it said that . . . the years when our generation held political power . . . were the years when America began to slip," he declared. "I don't want historians writing in 1970 to say that the balance of power in the Nineteen Fifties and Nineteen Sixties began to turn against the United States and against the cause of Freedom."

Kennedy toured the country not as a liberal critical of the failure of Republicans on issues such as civil rights but as a militant determined to wage the Cold War much more aggressively than Eisenhower had. "I have heard all the excuses, but I believe not in an America that is first 'but,' first 'if,' first 'when,' but first, period," he declared. "The first vehicle in space was called Sputnik, not Vanguard. The first passengers to return safely from outer space were named Strelka and Belka, not Rover or Fido. . . . I want to be known as the president . . . who not only held back the Communist tide but who also advanced the cause of freedom and rebuilt American prestige."

At the start of the campaign, polls showed Kennedy trailing Nixon, who was considerably more experienced. When Nixon agreed to a series of televised debates (the first ever in a presidential contest), he figured on widening his advantage because he had used the medium skillfully in his Checkers Speech and had given a good account of himself in an exchange with Khrushchev in the Soviet Union. With television sets in 88 percent of American households by 1960, as many as seventy million viewers tuned in to the first debate. Neither candidate said anything meaningful, and atmospherics proved to be more important than content. The bronzed, youthful Kennedy came across as self-possessed, while Nixon appeared to be anxious and looked haggard—his five-o'clock shadow making him seem vaguely sinister. The main impact of the four debates was that they erased Nixon's claim to be very much better prepared for the presidency than his rival, because Kennedy's performance, while unremarkable, was good enough to level the field. In the closely contested election in November, four million voters said that they had based their choice on the debates; 72 percent preferred Kennedy. That outcome drove home to politicians the need to gather huge sums in future races to buy television time.

Kennedy won, but by the narrowest popular margin since Cleveland's close call in 1884, after votes were reported from remote Eskimo villages in Alaska (admitted to the union in 1959) and from the outlying islands of Hawaii (which entered later that same year as the fiftieth state). Kennedy had a considerably greater advantage in the Electoral College (303 to Nixon's 219, with 15 southern votes for a Virginia senator). In some states, though, he barely prevailed. A small shift of votes in Texas and Illinois, where ballot manipulation by Democratic bosses was notorious, would have placed Richard Nixon in the White House. But the world does not march in step with might-have-beens. The stark reality for Republicans was that once again, come January, as in the Roosevelt-Truman era, they would be out in the cold watching a Democrat sworn in. Whatever successes he had elsewhere, Eisenhower had fallen short as a party builder. "Eisenhower's victories," concluded the political scientist Hans Morgenthau, were "but accidents without consequence in the history of the Republican party."

Highly popular though Eisenhower was in his lifetime, he has fared even better with posterity than he did with his contemporaries, for during his eight years in the White House, he had often been the butt of ridicule. Journalists depicted him as uninformed and dimwitted. He insisted on brief communications, it was said, so that his lips would not get tired. When Eisenhower spoke to the press, noted the dean of White House correspondents, Arthur Krock, "numbers and genders collide, participles hang helplessly, and syntax is lost forever." So incomprehensible was he at times that Hagerty found it necessary to provide reporters with translations.

The president's mangled diction prompted one wag to imagine how Eisenhower might have given the Gettysburg Address. In his eloquent dedication of the bloodstained battlefield at Gettysburg, Lincoln had begun: "Four score and seven years ago our fathers brought forth on this continent a new nation, conceived in liberty, and dedicated to the proposition that all men are created equal. Now we are engaged in a great civil war, testing whether that nation, or any nation so conceived and so dedicated, can long endure." The journalist Oliver Jensen suggested how Eisenhower might have delivered those two taut sentences:

> I haven't checked these figures but 87 years ago, I think it was, a number of individuals organized a governmental set-up here in this country, I believe it covered certain Eastern areas, with this idea they were following up based on a sort of national independence arrangement and the program that every individual is just as good as every other individual. Well, now, of course, we are dealing with this big difference of opinion, civil disturbance you might say, although I don't like to appear to take sides or name any individuals, and the point is naturally to check up, by actual experience in the field, to see whether any governmental set-up with a basis like the one I was mentioning has any validity and find out whether that dedication by those early individuals will pay off in lasting values and things of that kind.

Critics also found fault with Eisenhower as an administrator. In a hierarchical system, he gave subordinates an exceptional degree of leeway. This delegation of authority provided for orderly governance, but it also made less likely the kind of innovative thinking sparked by FDR's free-wheeling style, and it sometimes insulated him from awareness of significant developments, especially when they were fast-breaking. In the 1950s, the political scientist Marian Irish observed: "The President insists that conflicts be resolved before they reach his desk; he wants only to hear the consensus, not the discussion, of the staff.... He expects communications to him to be in the form of neatly drafted, one-page memos—which is probably one reason why he often shows little insight into the complex issues of the day."

After the kinetic FDR and Truman with their New Deal and Fair Deal initiatives, numbers of commentators found Eisenhower a letdown. They rendered his Whiggish approach as "What shall we refrain from doing today?" One political scientist contended that "no president in history failed more poignantly to use his power," and another called Ike's circumscribed conception of the presidency "the greatest retreat in the national experience since the first battle of Bull Run." In particular, critics belabored Eisenhower for failing to take advantage of his great prestige and enormous popularity to lead the nation through necessary social change. When his aides recommended that he address the country, he replied crossly, "I don't think the people *want* to be listening to a Roosevelt, sounding as if he were one of the Apostles, or the partisan yipping of a Truman." Eisenhower's "chalice of fame had been filled to the brim in 1945 and he was reluctant to spill a drop," wrote the syndicated columnist Marquis Childs. The consequence of this passivity and of Eisenhower's predilection for contracting the role of government, Adlai Stevenson charged, was "private opulence and public squalor."

In an early postpresidential assessment, the eminent political scientist Richard Neustadt wrote: "Eisenhower wanted to be President, but what he wanted from it was a far cry from what F.D.R. had wanted. Roosevelt was a politician seeking personal power; Eisenhower was a hero seeking national unity. He came to crown a reputation not to make one. He wanted to be arbiter, not master. His love was not for power but for duty— and for status. Naturally, the thing he did not seek he did not often find." Similarly, in one of the first memoirs to appear, Ike's speechwriter

Emmet John Hughes observed: "Where Roosevelt had sought and coveted power, Eisenhower distrusted and discounted it: one man's appetite was the other man's distaste. Where Roosevelt had avidly grasped and adroitly manipulated the abundant authorities of the office, Eisenhower fingered them almost hesitantly.... Where Roosevelt had sought to goad and taunt and prod the processes of government toward the new and untried, Eisenhower sought to be both guardian of old values and healer of old wounds." Given these judgments, it is not surprising that when historians were polled in 1962 (one year after Eisenhower left office), they ranked him twenty-second among presidents—in the bottom half of the pecking order.

Since then, however, Eisenhower has risen steadily in esteem. After witnessing the excesses and the misadventures of the 1960s and 1970s, scholars developed a new appreciation for his distrust of Big Government. In the wake of the Vietnam War disaster, the 1950s decade especially commended itself. The Eisenhower years came to be conceived of as the felicitous time before the country imploded in the sixties. Polled in 2008, historians moved Ike all the way up to sixth place in the roster of presidents. His most recent biographer has even stated that, save for FDR, Eisenhower was "the most successful president of the 20th century."

Eisenhower himself touched off the process of reconsideration by delivering a startling farewell address in which he called attention to the "conjunction of an immense military establishment and a large arms industry." He added: "The total influence—economic, political, even spiritual—is felt in every city, every Statehouse, every office of the Federal government.... In the councils of government, we must guard against the acquisition of unwarranted influence, whether sought or unsought, by the military-industrial complex. The potential for the disastrous rise of misplaced power exists and will persist. We must never let the weight of this combination endanger our liberties or democratic processes." Though Eisenhower had been warning against excessive spending on armaments all along, his address was viewed as a departure, and his language appeared to echo that of the left—inviting speculation that there was a lot more to this man than had been surmised.

It had already become commonplace to say that, after the acrimony of the FDR-Truman era, Eisenhower had made an important contribution by fostering domestic harmony. "Even at the time," the historian Douglas

Brinkley has written, "both parties seemed to recognize the Eisenhower years as a frozen moment for politics as usual to take a breather after the rancorous New Deal and World War II era." One of the earliest chroniclers, the historian Walter Johnson, in his book *1600 Pennsylvania Avenue*, observed: "Without Eisenhower as head of the Republican party, the venom that had disgraced democratic politics in the closing years of Truman's presidency would have been rife in the nation. He purged national life of rancor. And by presenting himself... as standing at the moderate and reasonable center..., he was able to tune in on the deepest instincts of the people, who, at this stage in their history, desired pause, comfort and repose; a mood which reflected the spectacular expansion of the middle class base of American life." The historian Herbert Parmet has concluded: "To label him a great or good or even a weak President misses the point. He was merely necessary." That was a rather modest claim for an important place in history, though. Not until the opening of the presidential library in Abilene did a more impressive record emerge.

Drawing upon these archives, Fred Greenstein provided the motif for a more positive assessment of Eisenhower: "the hidden-hand presidency." Scholars have established that, without openly revealing his involvement, Eisenhower, not Dulles, determined foreign policy and that he was actively involved in important decisions on domestic legislation as well. They have also derided the notion that he was slow-witted. In fields such as civil rights Eisenhower was lost, but in spheres where he could draw upon his experience as a commander he impressed observers with his perspicacity. George Kennan, a hard-nosed analyst, recalled that during an exploration of national security issues, Eisenhower "showed his intellectual ascendancy over every man in the room."

Revisionists contended that Eisenhower's muddled statements constituted not incoherence but employment of a clever political tactic—what the essayist Garry Wills has called "calculated obfuscation." When his press secretary told him not to commit himself at a press conference on a fracas in the Formosa Straits, the president replied, "Don't worry, Jim. If that question comes up, I'll just confuse them." Determined to conceal from Senator McCarthy a particular action the White House had taken, he replied to a reporter's question: "Well, I wouldn't answer it in any event because, after all, we do come to a place here where you can't go into detail. But my memory wouldn't serve me anyway. I couldn't remember such a thing.... You can well know, ladies and gentlemen, I cannot stay too close to the details of this argument." Though he appeared to be clueless, he was actually being adroit.

He demonstrated this talent for dissembling as early as the start of his first term, revisionists point out. After closely perusing an address by Robert Taft, and noting at some length in his diary how much he disagreed with the senator, Eisenhower answered a question about it at a press conference by saying: "Well now, I am not going to put words in Senator Taft's mouth because I did not read the speech in detail." He then denied that Taft had said what he very well knew the senator had. After the reporter persisted with a more pointed question, the president rambled on: "There is something confusing here. I don't believe I had better answer it. I don't understand what could be meant by such a thing. Look—suppose all of us here are friends, and we are trying to get somebody out on the street to agree to something and he disagrees, does that mean we all suddenly here become enemies and break up? I don't understand that!" Still trying to penetrate the smoke screen, the reporter then read Taft's precise words, only to have Eisenhower respond, "As I say, there is some idea there that I am not grasping, and I don't think it is fair to ask me to try to comment on it when I don't."

Yet, though a half century of reappraisal has rescued Eisenhower from the crude caricatures of the 1950s, homage to him has often outrun the evidence. He has been unpersuasively portrayed as the man who brought down McCarthy and, because he sent troops to Little Rock, as a champion of civil rights. Even his identification with prosperity and peace requires qualification. The affluence of the decade was marred by three recessions in seven years, and he left office with economic growth in Russia outpacing that in the United States. In conceiving of him as the preserver of peace, it is well to bear in mind that, as Schlesinger wrote, "Eisenhower employed the threat of nuclear war far more than any other American president has done, before or since," and the foremost scholar of the Cold War, John Gaddis, has concluded, "The most startling deficiency of the administration's strategy was its bland self-confidence that it could use nuclear weapons without setting off an all-out nuclear war."

Often depicted as a moderate, even as a progressive, Eisenhower revealed his core beliefs at the end of his memoirs when he wrote that if the country continued in the conservative direction he favored, "then the future would hold encomiums for my Administration as the first great break with the political philosophy of the decade beginning in 1933." Furthermore, his role in bringing about domestic tranquility came at the price of hushing public discourse. A Nebraska professor, distressed by the passivity of his students, remarked, "The vague but comforting symbol of Eisenhower has seeped into the vacuum of this generation's mind," and Garry Wills has alluded to "Ike's kind lobotomy of the electorate." Lippmann concluded, "We talk about ourselves these days as if we were a completed society, one which has no further great business to transact."

Eisenhower, who had rejected "the left-wing theory that the Executive has unlimited powers," made little mark on the office of the presidency or on the course of history. "Never has a popular figure who dominated so completely the national political scene affected so negligibly the essential historic processes of his time," wrote the historian Norman Graebner. When the Supreme Court justices paid their traditional final visit to the White House, one of them asked, "What do you consider your outstanding achievements in the eight years of your presidency?" Taken aback, Eisenhower became defensive, took a while to respond, then answered that his greatest accomplishment was the admission of Hawaii and Alaska.

Years after he had been compelled to resign, Sherman Adams suggested a different response to the question posed by the justices. He told an interviewer: "I'm very distressed at this tendency of academics to look down their noses at the Eisenhower administration. It's a common thing with the intelligentsia.... Look at Mr. Roosevelt. He's a great favorite with the academics, and he's probably a great man. But he lost a lot of battles, didn't he?... Well, we may not have done as much, may not have been as spectacular in terms of our willingness to break with the past, but we didn't lose a lot of battles either. A lot of our most important accomplishments were negative—things we avoided."

Adams's final point is on the mark: Eisenhower's place in history rests not on what he did but on what he did not do. Eisenhower "was never more decisive than when he held to a steely resolve *not* to do something that he sincerely believed wrong in itself or alien to his office," said his aide Emmet Hughes. He did not continue the pointless war in Korea; he did not blunder by sending troops to support the French at Dien Bien

Phu; he did not back the British-French-Israeli action in Suez; he did not intervene in Hungary; he did not panic after *Sputnik*. But it also must be said that he did not confront Joe McCarthy; he did not rally the country behind the Supreme Court's *Brown* decision; and he did not speak out against racial violence. Robert Divine, a historian who was one of his strongest champions, acknowledged, "Eisenhower won't rank among the great presidents, because his accomplishments were essentially negative."

The Eisenhower years have been called "the time of the great postponement." Patrick Anderson of the *Washington Post* has commented: "The misfortune of Eisenhower's presidency is that a man of such immense popularity and good will did not accomplish more. All the domestic problems which confronted the nation in the 1960s—the unrest of the Negro, the decay of the cities, the mediocrity of the schools, the permanence of poverty—were bubbling beneath the surface in the 1950s, but the President never seemed quite sure that they existed or, if they did, that they were problems with which he should concern himself." All of these festering sores, as well as a Cold War warming toward combustion, he dumped on the incoming president, John F. Kennedy.

7

John F. Kennedy

EARLY ON A BRILLIANTLY SUNNY but frigid January afternoon in 1961, John Fitzgerald Kennedy took the oath as the thirty-fifth president. At forty-three, the youngest man ever elected to the highest office, he succeeded the oldest man to occupy the White House. As a biting wind whipped the snow-covered plaza, Eisenhower hunkered down in over-coat and muffler, while Kennedy, coatless and bareheaded, looked vi-brantly youthful. "Kennedy turned a page of American history as we went from the 1950s to the '60s," the CBS television correspondent Bob Schieffer later reflected. "It was like *Wizard of Oz*. Remember how the movie started out in black-and-white, and then Dorothy opens her front door into this vibrant Technicolor? That's how I think of the Kennedy administration."

Kennedy's inaugural address highlighted the divergence of ages. "Let the word go forth from this time and place, to friend and foe alike," he proclaimed, "that the torch has been passed to a new generation of Americans—born in this century, tempered by war, disciplined by a hard and bitter peace, proud of our ancient heritage, and unwilling to witness or permit the slow undoing of those human rights to which this Nation has always been committed." (In the year of Jack Kennedy's birth, Konrad Adenauer had already been elected lord mayor of Cologne, Nikita Khrushchev was marching in the army of the czar, and

On Inauguration Day 1961, President-elect John F. Kennedy, with his wife, Jacqueline, and associates, strides swiftly by the snowy White House grounds. *Photo by Paul Schutzer/The LIFE Picture Collection/Getty Images, ID 53372917*

Eisenhower, born in the nineteenth century, had achieved the rank of captain.)

Commentators marveled at, or were dismayed by, the youthfulness of the new administration. Even before Kennedy took office, young people had begun to appropriate him for their own, and he, in turn, had shown an affinity for them. In the 1960 race for the White House, he had encountered so many cheering, leaping youngsters that at one campaign stop in Ohio, he said, "If we can lower the voting age to nine, we are going to sweep this state." He had no hesitation in appointing startlingly young men to the highest posts in his administration, notably when he named as attorney general his thirty-five-year-old brother Robert. When critics harped on Bobby's transparent lack of qualifications, Kennedy responded, in a characteristic jest, "I don't see what's wrong with giving Bobby a little experience before he goes into law practice."

For key posts, Kennedy recruited young "action intellectuals" thought to be, in a phrase he took from the poet Shelley, "the brightest and the best." To fill the two hundred most important posts in the government, he selected three times as many from the university world as Eisenhower had. He named the brash Harvard College dean McGeorge Bundy as national security adviser, and for secretary of defense chose the systems analysis "whiz kid" Robert McNamara, head of the Ford Motor Company. (Deborah Shapley, the biographer of McNamara, has written of his appointment: "That a young Republican businessman could also be well thought of by labor, be Harvard-trained, support the ACLU, and read Teilhard de Chardin were all bonuses.") Precocious, cocksure, brimming with energy, they were, one commentator said, the junior officers of World War II come to power, eager to take on all comers and confident they would prevail. "The currents of vitality radiated out of the White House, flowed through the government and created a sense of vast possibility," the president's assistant Arthur Schlesinger Jr. later recalled. "Intelligence at last was being applied to public affairs. Euphoria reigned: we thought for a moment that the world was plastic and the future unlimited."

Kennedy concentrated his entire inaugural address on foreign affairs. Though it was written by Ted Sorensen, a committed liberal, the speech gave not one sentence to civil rights or any other feature of the progressive agenda. Briefly, the new president, in alluding to the Soviet bloc, struck an accommodating chord. Neither antagonist, he said, could "take comfort from our present course—both sides overburdened by the cost of modern weapons, both rightly alarmed by the steady spread of the deadly atom." He urged: "So let us begin anew—remembering on both sides that civility is not a sign of weakness. . . . Let us never negotiate out of fear, but let us never fear to negotiate. . . . Let both sides, for the first time, formulate serious and precise proposals for the inspection and control of arms—and bring the absolute power to destroy other nations under the absolute control of all nations." But many of his words were strident, breathing defiance of the Kremlin.

Early in his discourse, Kennedy stated, "Let every nation know, whether it wishes us well or ill, that we shall pay any price, bear any burden, meet any hardship, support any friend, oppose any foe to assure the survival and success of liberty," adding ominously, "This much we pledge—and more." He declared: "In your hands, my fellow citizens, more than mine, will rest the final success or failure of our course. Since this country was founded, each generation of Americans has been summoned to give testimony to its national loyalty. The graves of young Americans who answered the call to service surround the globe." He wound up with a stirring peroration that appeared to be a call to arms:

> In the long history of the world, only a few generations have been granted the role of defending freedom in its hour of maximum danger. I do not shrink from this responsibility—I welcome it. I do not believe that any of us would exchange places with any other people or any other generation. . . .
>
> And so, my fellow Americans, ask not what your country can do for you—ask what you can do for your country.

First and last, foreign policy confrontations dominated his time in office. In his campaign for president, Kennedy, echoing Woodrow Wilson, had said, "Congress is quite obviously not equipped . . . to conduct foreign relations, to speak for the national interest in the way that a President can and must." Moreover, he thought that foreign affairs were all that really mattered. A decade earlier, Kennedy had asked Sorensen which cabinet portfolios he would prefer if offered a choice. "Justice, Labor, and Health-Education-Welfare," his assistant replied. "I wouldn't have *any* interest in any of those," Kennedy returned. "Only Secretary of State or Defense." Events abroad he found engrossing, while civil rights had never grabbed his attention, and concerns such as social injustice bored him. In a conversation at the White House with Richard Nixon, he said, "It really is true that foreign affairs is the only important issue for a president to handle, isn't it? I mean who gives a shit if the minimum wage is $1.15 or $1.25, in comparison to something like this?"

During the campaign, Kennedy had promised a dramatic departure from Eisenhower's foreign policy emphases, and in a number of respects he kept that pledge. Rejecting Dulles's conviction that neutralism was "immoral," he recognized the force of nationalism abroad. In a paraphrase of Woodrow Wilson, he announced that he aimed to create a world safe for diversity. He actively promoted a neutralist solution to the crisis in the Congo by helping fund a UN effort to set up a government that was not a Western puppet but would reject right-wing secessionists as well as Communists. Soon after taking office, Kennedy created, by executive order, the Peace Corps to send volunteers into underdeveloped areas, with his brother-in-law R. Sargent Shriver in charge of the program. He appointed envoys who were sympathetic to the aspirations of emerging nations in the third world, and he established the Agency for International Development to coordinate assistance overseas. Under the South Dakotan George McGovern, Food for Peace drew upon US farm surpluses to provide nourishment for workers building schools and hospitals in the third world; in Kennedy's last year, it was feeding ninety-two million people a day, among them thirty-five million children.

On the morning before Kennedy took office, Eisenhower, pointing to Laos on a map of Southeast Asia, said, "This is one of the problems I'm leaving you that I'm not happy about. We may have to fight." The Joint Chiefs recommended that the new president send sixty thousand troops into "the land of the thousand elephants," promising victory over the Communist Pathet Lao if Kennedy would allow them to use nuclear weapons, and his adviser Walt Rostow backed them. But Kennedy rejected immersion in another land war in Asia, especially on unpromising terrain, and he was disturbed by the nonchalance toward nuclear warfare. Still, he did not want to see a Communist takeover, so he made a number of threatening moves, including sending the 7th Fleet to the South China Sea. This calculated course of "veiled ambiguity" forced the Pathet Lao to negotiate. Recognizing that he could not eliminate the Communists, Kennedy wisely settled for neutralization, though it opened him to the charge of being weak-kneed.

In August 1961, he announced the most far-reaching approach ever directed toward Latin America: the Alliance for Progress, which he claimed was a "vast cooperative effort, unparalleled in magnitude and nobility of purpose." One commentator called the ten-year program pledging billions to promote social democracy south of the border "a monumental commitment which for size and complexity makes the Marshall Plan look puny by comparison." Unhappily, Kennedy and his successors, fearful of the spread of Castroism, turned out to have far less interest in land redistribution than in destabilizing governments with left-wing tendencies. The Alianza Para el Progreso did bring some improvements, notably in Venezuela, and chalked up impressive results in reducing illiteracy, but, as the diplomatic historian Walter LaFeber has pointed out, at the end of 1963 per capita gross national product in Argentina and Brazil was markedly lower than at the beginning of the year. The title of the analysis by Jerome Levinson and Juan de Onis sums up the scholarly consensus: *The Alliance That Lost Its Way.*

Despite entertaining these departures, the president at times sounded like no one so much as John Foster Dulles. "The enemy," Kennedy had said in 1960, "is the Communist system itself—implacable, insatiable, increasing in its drive for world domination.... This is also a struggle for supremacy between two conflicting ideologies: freedom under God versus ruthless, godless tyranny." In his first State of the Union message, delivered shortly after he took the oath of office, he declared:

> I speak today in an hour of national peril.... Before my term has ended, we shall have to test anew whether a nation organized and governed such as ours can endure. The outcome is by no means certain. The answers are by no means clear....
>
> No man entering upon this office... could fail to be staggered upon learning—even in this brief 10-day period—the harsh enormity of the trials through which we must pass in the next four years.... Each day we draw nearer the hour of maximum danger.... I feel I must inform the Congress that our analyses over the last ten days make it clear that—in each of the principal areas of crisis—the tide of events has been running out and time has not been our friend.

Over the course of the next year, he maintained this tone. In his speech to the American Society of Newspaper Editors in April, he "spoke apocalyptically," as his biographer Robert Dallek has pointed out. "The complacent, the self-indulgent, the soft societies," Kennedy warned, "are about to be swept away with the debris of history." In his second State of the Union message, delivered in January 1962, he voiced intimations of Armageddon. "Our Nation is commissioned by history to be either an observer of freedom's failure or the cause of its success," he maintained. Reiterating the country's "good fortune" in being at "its hour of maximum danger," he declared, "While no nation has ever faced such a challenge, no nation has ever been so ready to seize the burden and the glory of freedom."

To put America in a position to win the Cold War, Kennedy undertook a massive military buildup. Though he knew full well that there was no "missile gap," he ordered missiles, each eighty times more potent than the Hiroshima A-bomb, at the same time that he was more than doubling the number of Polaris missile submarines and stepping up the output of nuclear-armed bombers. By such actions, he was challenging the Kremlin to an arms race that overheated the Cold War. He also built up more conventional forces and prepared for paramilitary skirmishes. Deploring Eisenhower's reliance on nuclear weapons, which were useless in brushfire conflicts, Kennedy sought an army skilled in guerrilla combat, and he took particular pride in the Green Berets. "We intend to have a wider choice than humiliation or all-out war," he declared.

Kennedy even signed off on carrying the Cold War into outer space, though at first he treated the idea of a moon shot with considerable skepticism. As senator, he had shared Eisenhower's view that the space program was a costly folly, and on becoming president, he "manifested," in the words of British scholars, "almost bottomless ignorance of the matter." But the resounding success of the USSR in rocketing the cosmonaut Yuri Gagarin into space jolted him. Two days later, Kennedy asked advisers, "Is there any place we can catch them?...Can we go around the moon before them?" Though he was troubled by how many billions a moon venture would cost, he said, "When we know more, I can decide if it's worth it or not. If somebody can just tell me how to catch up. Let's find somebody, anybody. I don't care if it's the janitor over there, if he knows how." His top scientific adviser recommended against a gamble that would drain funds from much more worthwhile efforts, but Kennedy would not be dissuaded. He assigned Vice President Lyndon Johnson to come up with the answers to questions: "Do we have a chance of beating the Soviets by putting a laboratory in space, or by a trip around the moon, or by a rocket to land on the moon, or by a rocket to go to the moon and back with a man?"

On May 25, 1961, Kennedy announced that the United States "should commit itself to achieving the goal, before this decade is out, of landing a man on the moon and returning him safely to earth. No single space project in this period will be more impressive to mankind." By "impressive," he meant not that the Apollo project had scientific merit but that it would show the world that America's technological prowess was superior to Russia's. "I do not think the United States can afford to become second in space," he told a press conference in June 1962, "because...space has too many implications militarily, politically, psychologically.... The United States cannot permit the Soviet Union to become dominant in the sea of space." In his very last month in office, in November 1963, he was still saying, with a confidence he did not always feel, "This nation has tossed its cap over the wall of space, and we have no choice but to follow it. Whatever the difficulties, they will be overcome." (In July 1969, true to Kennedy's pledge, the goal was achieved when Neil Armstrong became the first man to walk on the moon.)

To get the country in fighting trim, he reshaped the government. He dismantled much of the hierarchical structure of the Eisenhower administration with its chain of command, and he abolished weekly cabinet meetings, which he thought "simply useless." He asked, "Why should the Postmaster General sit there and listen to a discussion of the problems of Laos?" The State Department took second place to a reconfigured National Security Council, especially after the NSC was moved into a Situation Room in the basement of the West Wing of the White House. This unfettered style liberated Kennedy from institutional sclerosis,

Tense moment, May 5, 1961. Kennedy watches the televised report of the lift-off of the astronaut Alan Shepard on the first American suborbital flight. With him (left to right) are Vice President Lyndon B. Johnson, Special Assistant Arthur Schlesinger Jr., Admiral Arleigh Burke, and First Lady Jacqueline Kennedy. *Cecil Stoughton. White House Photographs. John F. Kennedy Presidential Library and Museum, Boston, ID JFKWHP-ST-116-9-61*

but it invited the risk that he would embark on ventures that had not been methodically vetted.

Kennedy's team got its first testing with the venture he had inherited from Eisenhower: the undercover CIA scheme to prepare anti-Castro exiles for an invasion of Cuba. With no hard evidence, the CIA had adopted the fatuous assumption that once the Cuban people learned of a landing they would rise up against their government, and it also nurtured the naive belief that US participation could be concealed. A number of the president's top advisers warned him that the conspiracy was both reckless and immoral, and the chair of the Senate Foreign Relations Committee, J. William Fulbright, said, "To give this activity even covert support is of a piece with the hypocrisy and cynicism for which the United States is constantly denouncing the Soviet Union." But it had gathered so much momentum that Kennedy was reluctant to call it off, especially since to do so would mean questioning Eisenhower's military judgment.

On April 17, 1961, a brigade of 1,400 rebels landed at the Bahía de Cochinos (Bay of Pigs) on the coast of Cuba. Kennedy denied American complicity, though the facts were widely known, and he even misled the US ambassador to the United Nations, Adlai Stevenson. "When the invasion came," the historian Carl Brauer has written, "Murphy's Law prevailed. If anything can go wrong, it will." With Kennedy refusing to become more conspicuously involved by providing air cover, the pathetic contingent was swiftly overwhelmed by Castro's army, two hundred thousand strong. Hundreds of the exiles were captured and, to the embarrassment of the United States, had to be ransomed. The Bay of Pigs disaster was, as the historian Theodore Draper later wrote, "one of those rare events in history—a perfect failure."

Overnight, the euphoria of the prideful young administration evaporated, and the air was hot with recrimination. Liberals accused Kennedy of reckless adventurism, and conservatives cried that his refusal to follow through with American air and naval support was spineless. Barry Goldwater later wrote: "I was present in the Oval Office...when President John Kennedy faced the reality of the Bay of Pigs. This charming young man, who put his name on a book entitled *Profiles in Courage*, lost his nerve and conveyed to world communism its first outpost in the Western Hemisphere." General Lyman Lemnitzer, chairman of the Joint Chiefs of Staff, later termed Kennedy's behavior "absolutely reprehensible, almost criminal," and Eisenhower called it a "Profile in Timidity and Indecision." Kennedy himself was devastated. "How could I have been so stupid?" he would burst out as he walked around talking to himself. "He came back over to the White House to his bedroom and started to cry," Jacqueline Kennedy later said, "just put his head in his hands and sort of wept.... And it was so sad, because all his first hundred days and all his dreams, and then this awful thing to happen."

Kennedy managed to rally from the fiasco, but he did not get away unscathed. He regained credibility as president by taking full responsibility, though not without wryly observing, "Victory has a hundred fathers and defeat is an orphan." Two weeks later, 61 percent of the American people polled approved of how he handled the situation in Cuba. His rating as president soared to 83 percent. "Jesus, it's just like Ike," Kennedy said. "The worse you do, the better they like you." His comportment in the Cuban crisis, however, was closely dissected in foreign capitals. In Moscow, Khrushchev asked, "Can he really be that indecisive?"

As a June summit meeting with Khrushchev in Vienna approached, Kennedy knew that he faced a thorny assignment and that he needed to convey American resolve. The American ambassador in Moscow had warned him that the Russian leader was determined to drive the West out of Berlin. Khrushchev, the US envoy cabled the White House, had "so deeply committed his personal prestige and that of the Soviet Union to some action on Berlin" that there was a 50–50 chance of war or "ignominious Western retreat." A triumph in Berlin could solidify the Russian leader's standing in the Kremlin and show nations in the Communist bloc that they should look toward Moscow, not Beijing. Khrushchev headed to Vienna determined to overwhelm any resistance from the callow American president. Noting Kennedy's setbacks in Cuba and in Southeast Asia, the French foreign minister, Couve de Murville, said of Kennedy's situation at the summit: "It's rather like fighting a championship bout after your last two sparring partners have knocked you out."

Khrushchev spent almost the entire meeting in Vienna bludgeoning Kennedy with angry tirades and contemptuous remarks, and the president said little in return. Two of his close friends, looking down from an embassy window as the two leaders walked, saw Khrushchev "snapping at him like a terrier and shaking his finger." The Russian leader told the president bluntly that by the end of the year he would enter into an agreement with the government of East Germany that would result in closing access of the West to Berlin and that he would brook no interference. A few minutes after the exchanges concluded, Kennedy confided to the American correspondent James Reston: "Worst thing in my life. He savaged me." Pale and shaken, the president said, "He treated me like a little boy. Like a little boy." American diplomats were shocked that Kennedy had performed so poorly, and Khrushchev told his aides: "He's very young... too weak." British prime minister Harold Macmillan confided, "I 'feel in my bones' that President Kennedy is going to fail to produce any real leadership."

Their meeting ended with an ominous exchange. After Kennedy declared that the United States was committed to remaining in Berlin and that it would regard denial of American rights there as "a belligerent act," the Soviet leader replied that his decision was "irrevocable" and that "if the US wants war, that's its problem." Kennedy retorted, "Then, Mr. Chairman, there will be war. It will be a cold winter." For months thereafter, one of his cabinet officials said, Kennedy was "imprisoned by Berlin." Determined to prove to the Soviet chief that he was mistaken in thinking he had "no guts," he told the editor of the *New York Post*, "If Khrushchev wants to rub my nose in the dirt, it's all over." To make clear how serious he was about not permitting the USSR to extinguish America's right of access to Berlin, he tripled draft calls and asked for additional huge military appropriations as well as stand-by authority to summon reserves.

The world had never known so traumatizing a season as the summer of 1961. On Kennedy's return from Vienna, his first step was to ask for an estimate of how many Americans might die in a nuclear exchange. Told by his military advisers that his only recourse was the employment of nuclear weapons, Kennedy barked, "God damn it... use your head. What we are talking about is seventy million dead Americans." When McNamara and the Joint Chiefs requested him to authorize the use of tactical nuclear weapons in Germany, he turned them down. His chief adviser on Berlin, Dean Acheson, however, dismissed out of hand any thought that the confrontation could be eased by diplomacy, and the president confided to friends that he believed a nuclear conflict was quite possible.

On July 25, Kennedy delivered a major address aimed at persuading the Kremlin that America was willing to fight in defense of Western rights in Berlin but that he hoped the crisis could be resolved amicably. "West Berlin," he declared, "has become...the great testing place of Western courage and will....An attack upon that city will be regarded as an attack upon us all." He added bluntly, "We do not want to fight, but we have fought before." In a passage taken to be an appeal for a peaceful outcome, he warned, "In the thermonuclear age, any misjudgment on either side about the intentions of the other could rain more devastation in several hours than has been wrought in all the wars of human history." But he also heightened anxiety by calling for a massive federal program to encourage the building of shelters to fend off radioactive fallout—an indication that he was prepared for nuclear war. As numbers of Americans burrowed underground in their backyards that summer, clergymen upheld the right of homeowners to kill neighbors who wanted to crowd into their shelters.

Early in August, Khrushchev responded with fusillades of the most bellicose words he ever uttered. He served notice that in event of war, "Germany will be reduced to dust." On the following day, he declared that in the interest of "defending our security,...not only the orange groves of Italy but also the people who created them and who have exalted Italy's culture and arts...may perish," and he threatened "crushing blows" at Greece, Norway, Denmark, Belgium, Holland, France, and Britain. This rodomontade may have been intended primarily for home consumption, especially to impress his brethren in the Kremlin with his militancy, for at the same time that he was indulging in bombast he was mulling over phraseology Kennedy had used both in Vienna and in his July speech that might offer a way out from this dangerous confrontation. He noted that, unlike his predecessors in the White House, the American president had spoken of US resolve to defend not "Berlin" but "*West* Berlin." Perhaps, then, Kennedy would not challenge action the USSR might take in its own zone of the city.

On August 13, 1961, the East Germans, on orders from Moscow, began building a wall to halt the exodus of many thousands of skilled artisans and professionals to the much more prosperous western sector of the city. Though the move was forceful, it was a confession of the failure of the Communist bloc to provide its citizens with the consumer goods and liberties they craved. Initially a makeshift barbed-wire fence, the Wall soon became a hideous concrete barrier with five hundred watch towers and a death strip that was mined and patrolled by dogs and armed troops ready to shoot down anyone who attempted to flee. Numbers of Americans urged Kennedy to smash it down, but, in the interest of peace, he exercised restraint. America would fight to defend West Berlin, he told an adviser, but "we won't go to war to keep East Germany from bleeding to death." He asked another aide, "Why would Khrushchev put up a wall if he really intended to seize West Berlin?" He added: "This is his way out of a predicament. It's not a very nice solution but a wall is a hell of a lot better than a war."

While acquiescing to the Wall, Kennedy decided that he had to demonstrate that the United States was not yielding an inch on its rights in Germany. Consequently, he ordered a US battle force, accompanied by a token British contingent, to drive down the 110-mile Autobahn through the Communist zone into Berlin. (The Soviet bloc offered no armed resistance to the convoy.) He also sent the former commander of the occupation, General Lucius Clay, and Vice President Johnson to Berlin. Exultant West Berliners, who had been fearful they might be abandoned, chanted "Der Clay, der Clay, der Clay ist hier!" and thronged around Johnson as the tall Texan strolled the avenues passing out ballpoint pens inscribed with his name.

That fall, without ever being resolved, the crisis eased. On September 30, at the Hotel Carlyle in Manhattan, a Soviet agent turned over to Kennedy's press secretary a copy of that day's *New York Times* into which had been placed a twenty-six-page letter from Khrushchev to the president—discursive but conciliatory. Secure in the knowledge that the border of East Germany had been sealed, the Russian leader first postponed his deadline, then stopped talking about it.

Yet as Kennedy's first year in office drew to an end, the world remained a fearfully dangerous place. At one juncture, American tanks eyed Soviet tanks at Berlin's Checkpoint Charlie, and one rash officer on either side might have triggered World War III. Russia exploded fifty nuclear bombs, one of them nearly three thousand times more powerful than the one that had devastated Hiroshima. Two days after that blast, Kennedy announced that the United States was going to resume atmospheric testing. The president, however, was not nearly militant enough for a large sector of far-right publicists in the Sunbelt. At a luncheon in the White House, the editor of the *Dallas Morning News* incensed Kennedy by reading aloud an insulting statement directed at him: "You and your Administration are weak sisters.... We need a man on horseback to lead this nation and many people in Texas and the Southwest think that you are riding Caroline's tricycle."

The Cold War framed Kennedy's policies at home as well as abroad. He frowned on social welfare legislation entailing large-scale spending because he was obsessed with not running a balance of payments deficit. Though he had pledged to "get America moving," he pursued cautious policies in order to halt the flow of gold abroad and rejected calls of liberal economists for stimulus projects to reduce unemployment. In June 1961, Walter Lippmann wrote that Kennedy's aim in the early months of his presidency was "first of all to carry on in all its essentials the Eisenhower economic philosophy.... It's like the Eisenhower Administration 30 years younger."

Under the tutelage of the man he appointed to chair the Council of Economic Advisers, the former University of Minnesota professor Walter Heller, however, Kennedy came to understand that he could best promote growth by embracing post-Keynesianism. In contrast to the Keynesians, who favored government intervention during downturns, the apostles of the New Economics urged deliberately creating deficits at a time of prosperity in order to accelerate improvement. After eighteen months of clinging to orthodox financial doctrine, Kennedy changed direction by advocating a multibillion-dollar tax cut. In the course of this "impressive conversion," the Harvard economist Seymour Harris wrote, Kennedy "had become the most literate of all Presidents in his understanding of modern economics and revealed great courage in his willingness to risk political losses in putting his economics to the test of the market place."

JFK's principal domestic confrontation came out of his determination to keep America's economy strong during his struggle with the Soviet Union by clamping down on inflation. Pleased that the steelworkers' union had consented to a noninflationary wage contract, he was incensed when ten days later steel magnates announced a big price hike.

One of his Massachusetts pals came upon him "livid with rage—white with anger." The president told the country:

> In this serious hour in our nation's history, when we are confronted with grave crises in Berlin and Southeast Asia,... when we are asking reservists to leave their homes and their families for months on end and servicemen to risk their lives—and four were killed in the last two days in Vietnam..., the American people will find it hard, as I do, to accept a situation in which a tiny handful of steel executives whose pursuit of private power and profit exceeds their sense of public responsibility can show such utter contempt for the interests of 185 million Americans.

In private, he was much more forthright: "My father always told me that all businessmen were sons-of-bitches, but I never believed it till now." With no statutory authority to curb the steel magnates, Kennedy made full use of the arsenal of weapons possessed by the executive branch. "They kicked us right in the balls," the president told a close friend. "Are we supposed to sit there and take a cold, deliberate fucking?... They fucked us, and we've got to try to fuck them." The Defense Department announced that it would grant contracts only to firms that did not raise prices; the Federal Trade Commission looked into collusive price-fixing; and the Treasury Department launched a tax probe. In his role as attorney general, Robert Kennedy convened a grand jury to investigate top corporation executives. "I told the FBI to interview them all—march into their offices the next day," he recounted. Cowed by this multipronged assault, the steel barons gave in after only seventy-two hours. When the head of U.S. Steel surrendered, Kennedy was asked what he had said to him. The president, alluding to Grant's words to Lee at Appomattox Court House, replied: "I told him that his men could keep their horses for the spring plowing."

Kennedy pleased liberal Democrats by his forcefulness in this showdown, but he disappointed them by seldom displaying the same resolve on Capitol Hill. They had started out with high hopes, because, with their party in control of the White House for the first time in eight years, they could count a 63–35 predominance in the Senate and a 262–175 advantage in the House. When they wound up with little to show for these huge margins, fingers were pointed at the president, who had failed to rally the country behind measures such as federal aid to education and who had managed to lose some pieces of legislation, such as Medicare, by only a few votes.

His defenders responded that the apparently favorable distribution of seats left an illusory impression, for Congress continued to be dominated by the bipartisan conservative coalition that had been blocking forward-looking proposals ever since 1938. They also pointed out that a contented citizenry saw no urgent need to move in new directions. "The trouble is that hardly anybody in America goes to bed angry at night," said the economist George Stigler. The election that brought Kennedy to power had added twenty-one seats to the Republican delegation in the House. Consequently, the president had little reason to suppose that appeals from the White House would have any resonance. Schlesinger noted JFK's "qualified historical fatalism which led him to doubt whether words, however winged, would by themselves change the world." Kennedy was fond of quoting Owen Glendower's boast in Shakespeare's drama, "I can call spirits from the vasty deep," and Hotspur's retort:

> Why, so can I, or so can any man;
> But will they come when you do call for them?

In truth, Kennedy had minimal skills as chief legislator. He had never earned the respect or affection of his colleagues either in the House or in the Senate, and he did not care to. They regarded him much as a dirt farmer viewed a weekend gentleman farmer, and he thought them to be dimwits not worth his time. "He didn't really know the deck on Capitol Hill," said Reston. "Blarneying with pompous Congressmen bored him and he simply would not take the time to do it." He also feared embarrassing setbacks. "In his relations with Congress," one commentator has observed, "Kennedy suffered from what Søren Kierkegaard once called the 'paralysis of knowledge.' He was temperamentally incapable of leading lost causes, or causes which seemed lost in a rational appraisal of the odds."

The Cold War also had considerable influence on Kennedy's attitude toward civil rights, with the president and his circle expressing less concern about flagrant racial discrimination than about how civil rights protests hurt America's image abroad and created disharmony at home.

They vented their anger privately not at the perpetrators of abuses but at those demonstrating against them. When courageous blacks and whites put their lives at risk by traveling together in interstate buses on Freedom Rides through the South to uphold constitutional rights, Kennedy stormed at the chief civil rights advocate in his administration: "Can't you get your goddamned friends off those buses? Tell them to call it off! Stop them!" On hearing that an African envoy driving US 40, the main artery between Washington and New York, could not even get a glass of water at a Jim Crow roadside restaurant, the president asked the State Department's chief of protocol, "Can't you tell these African ambassadors not to drive on Route 40?" As the historian Harvard Sitkoff has observed, "The Kennedys saw the struggle against racism as a conundrum to be managed, not a cause to be championed."

Jack Kennedy carried into the turbulent sixties a complacency he had developed earlier. As senator, during the era of the Montgomery bus boycott and the emergence of Martin Luther King, he had shared none of the passion of the movement. When he sought the Democratic presidential nomination, he pointed out to southern delegates that on critical roll calls on civil rights he, unlike Hubert Humphrey, had voted with the Dixie bloc. In 1960, Jackie Robinson backed Nixon for president, explaining, "Jack Kennedy said, 'Mr. Robinson, I don't know much about the problems of colored people since I come from New England.' I figured the hell with that. Any man in Congress for fifteen years ought to make it his business to know colored people."

On entering the White House, Kennedy refused to sponsor or endorse any civil rights legislation. He reasoned that if he pushed for a civil rights bill, he would not get it and would alienate southern congressmen whose votes he needed on other measures. When in the spring of 1961 Democrats in both houses of Congress introduced a civil rights bill in accord with what Kennedy had proposed during the campaign, the White House issued a chilling response: "The President has made it clear that he does not think it necessary at this time to enact civil rights legislation." In response, the NAACP leader Roy Wilkins accused him of "offering . . . a cactus bouquet to Negro parents and their children."

The administration claimed that it could make greater progress by relying on executive authority, but it moved hesitantly in that realm too. The Justice Department encouraged activists in the South to abandon marches against Jim Crow and to concentrate instead on registering black voters, but African Americans attempting to pursue that course were beaten, even murdered, and the federal government provided almost no protection for them. In the 1960 campaign, Kennedy had said that discrimination in public housing could be ended by "a stroke of the pen" and that it could be done "tomorrow," but as president, he delayed so long that the White House mail room was inundated with pens. When, after twenty-two months, he did act, his order was weak and ineffective. "If tokenism were our goal," said Martin Luther King, "the administration moves us adroitly toward it."

These deficiencies notwithstanding, the government proved much more responsive to the aspirations of African Americans than it had been during the Eisenhower years. Kennedy appointed a number of blacks to high places, notably the NAACP's general counsel Thurgood Marshall to the US Circuit Court, as well as the first blacks ever to serve on a US district court in the continental United States, the first black US attorneys, and an African American ambassador to Finland. In two years, the proportion of blacks in upper civil service jobs nearly doubled. Not in fulfillment of any congressional mandate but solely on the basis of his powers under Article II of the Constitution, Kennedy issued an order banning discrimination by federal employees and government contractors and created a President's Committee on Equal Employment Opportunity to enforce it.

The president's younger brother Robert seized upon his appointment as attorney general to act aggressively to advance racial equality. At a Law Day address in the heart of Georgia, he said: "You may ask, will we enforce the Civil Rights statutes? The answer is: 'Yes, we will.'" When in the spring of 1961 Alabama mobs mauled and threatened the lives of Freedom Riders and set one of their buses afire, Attorney General Kennedy sent hundreds of federal marshals into the South. The Department of Justice challenged denial of voting rights to blacks in 145 southern counties, a nearly fivefold increase over Eisenhower's performance, and, at the instigation of the Justice Department, the Interstate Commerce Commission ordered companies to desegregate interstate buses and to bypass terminals and restaurants that discriminated. By the fall of 1962, Robert Kennedy could claim that "virtually every airport" in the South had been desegregated, as well as bus and railroad depots.

Jack Kennedy still hoped to avoid alienating white southerners, but civil rights activists created confrontations that induced him to intervene, though reluctantly and tardily. When James Meredith, a black air force veteran, obtained a federal court order compelling the state of Mississippi to admit him to its all-white university, Governor Ross Barnett ordered state police to block him from entering. Three times, Meredith arrived on the Ole Miss campus backed by federal court orders and escorted by representatives the Kennedy administration, including the chief US marshal, but each time, he was turned away by Governor Barnett or his agent and by thousands of jeering white students. "I won't agree to let that boy get to Ole Miss," the Mississippi governor declared in defiance of the courts. "I would rather spend the rest of my life in a penitentiary than do that." When on September 30, 1962, Meredith tried for a fourth time, Kennedy dispatched hundreds of marshals to the Ole Miss campus and made sure that they would have sufficient support by federalizing the Mississippi National Guard and setting up a staging base at the Memphis Naval Air Station. He also delivered a televised appeal to the people of the state that had Cold War overtones. "The eyes of the nation and all the world are upon you and upon us all," he declared. That night, more than two thousand students and other rioters engulfed the US marshals. Two people were killed and nearly four hundred were injured, including 160 marshals, twenty-seven of them with gunshot wounds. Kennedy responded by sending in thousands of troops, among them a unit of armored cavalry, and Meredith was able to register.

With Ole Miss integrated, Alabama became the only state where no black and white students attended the same institution—from kindergarten to medical school. In his inaugural address, Governor George Wallace had announced, "I draw the line in the dust and toss the gauntlet before the feet of tyranny and I say segregation now, segregation tomorrow, segregation forever." He had pledged to voters that he would stand in the doorway to bar any African American from enrolling at the University of Alabama in Tuscaloosa. In June 1963, President Kennedy called his bluff by federalizing the Alabama National Guard, and when Wallace made only a ludicrous show of resistance, Jim Crow had drawn his last breath on an American campus.

That spring in Alabama, racism exposed itself in all its ugliness in the gritty steel town of Birmingham, where television cameras beamed into

American homes images of peaceful young black demonstrators bitten by lunging police dogs, fangs bared, and driven to their knees by merciless high-powered fire hoses. The president's advisers had been telling him that he must instruct the country that the struggles of African Americans for equality constituted a great moral cause, but he seemed more interested in achieving peace than justice. When the Department of Justice prepared a statement, he had objected that it "leaned too much on the side of the Negroes." The viciousness of Birmingham, though, changed him.

On the night of June 11, 1963, Kennedy, unusually solemn, gave the most eloquent televised address of his presidency, some of it improvised. He declared:

> We are confronted primarily with a moral issue. It is as old as the Scriptures and is as clear as the American Constitution. If an American, because his skin is dark, cannot eat lunch in a restaurant open to the public, if he cannot send his children to the best public school available, if he cannot vote for the public officials who represent him, if, in short, he cannot enjoy the full and free life which all of us want, then who among us would be content to have the color of his skin changed and stand in his place? Who among us would then be content with the counsels of patience and delay?
>
> One hundred years of delay have passed since President Lincoln freed the slaves, yet their heirs, their grandsons, are not fully free. They are not yet freed from the bonds of injustice. They are not yet freed from social and economic oppression, and the Nation, for all its hopes and all its boasts, will not be fully free until all its citizens are free.

One week later, the president, declaring that "race has no place in American life or law," called upon Congress to enact far-reaching civil rights legislation. Some of his most influential advisers, including Ted Sorensen and Lyndon Johnson, attempted to persuade him to confine himself to executive action, but Kennedy responded, "There comes a time when a man has to take a stand and history will record that he has to meet these tough situations and ultimately make a decision."

Kennedy's resolve entailed grave political risk. By November 1963, when he called the first strategy meeting for the 1964 campaign, he had lost more than four million votes, almost all in the South and border states because of his stand for civil rights. Nor was disapproval confined to the South. Even after the horrifying news that a racist had placed a bomb in a Birmingham church, killing four little black girls at Sunday school, 50 percent of Americans thought that Kennedy was "pushing integration too fast"; a mere 11 percent responded "not fast enough." Furthermore, the civil rights bill, one of its most ardent proponents said, "was absolutely bogged down."

On November 12, 1963, the *New York Times* reported: "Rarely has there been such a pervasive attitude of discouragement around Capitol Hill and such a feeling of helplessness to deal with it. This has been one of the least productive sessions of Congress within the memory of most of its members." *Time* magazine offered a similar reckoning of how well Kennedy was getting on with Congress:

Tax cuts: Passed by the House, but locked in Conservative Democrat Harry Byrd's Senate Finance Committee, and won't even get to the Senate floor before Dec. 20, at which point the Senate plans to adjourn for the Christmas holidays until Jan. 2.

Civil Rights Bill: Locked in House committees until the first week of December. If it gets to the Senate, it faces a filibuster.

The betting: no tax cuts or civil rights bill this year.

In these circumstances, it was almost a relief for Kennedy to turn to foreign affairs, which, even during the civil rights turmoil of 1962, had remained his overriding concern, though the situation abroad was dismaying.

On October 16, 1962, Kennedy received an alarming report: an American U-2 had located Russian medium-range missiles in place in Cuba, and Soviet technicians were constructing launching pads that could hurl hydrogen warheads as far as Minneapolis. (In his account a generation later, Max Frankel of the *New York Times* characterized the sneaky maneuver as "worthy of the horse at Troy.") The president knew that the USSR had dispatched a sizeable number of troops to the island and that in the summer of 1962 ships displaying the hammer and sickle had been unloading cargoes in Cuban ports. But he had not been troubled because, when challenged, Khrushchev had assured him that there were no offensive weapons. Furthermore, he could not imagine that the Kremlin would do anything so audacious. Republican senators raised such a clamor, however, that he had felt compelled to order the U-2 reconnaissance. The photographs with which the plane returned set off the most unnerving thirteen days in the history of the world.

Kennedy speedily called together an executive committee of the National Security Council to consider what to do. At the outset, virtually every member of this "ExComm," including the president, assumed that the only conceivable response was an air strike delivered without warning to destroy the missiles, followed by an invasion to oust Castro. The most ardent "hawks"—Dean Acheson, McGeorge Bundy, Lyndon Johnson, and the Joint Chiefs—strongly favored that action. (Negotiation was not an option, for Khrushchev had proved himself to be a blatant liar.) An air strike, though, was risky. It might not destroy all of the missiles, and it almost certainly would cause Russian casualties. Khrushchev might well retaliate by launching missiles at the United States. At the very least, he could be expected to move on West Berlin. "They can't let us just take out...their missiles, kill a lot of Russians and not do anything," Kennedy said.

Despite these misgivings, the president returned for a time to the notion of a preemptive air attack, until a "dovish" cadre on the ExComm dissuaded him. Adlai Stevenson, Robert McNamara, and Ted Sorensen all objected. Striking from the air without warning, said Undersecretary of State George Ball, would mean "carrying the mark of Cain on your brow for the rest of your life." The most powerful voice in opposition to an unannounced assault was that of Robert Kennedy. A "Pearl Harbor," he protested, would make his brother "the Tojo of the 1960s."

Overriding the Joint Chiefs, the president opted instead for a blockade. A picket line of US naval vessels was to be arrayed in the western Atlantic, where America had overwhelming dominance, at the same time that an effort would be made to communicate with Khrushchev. Rejection of the Joint Chiefs' insistence on an air strike turned nasty. The snarling Air Force Chief of Staff General Curtis LeMay told the president that his temperate decision was "almost as bad as the appeasement at Munich." Kennedy also encountered dissent on Capitol Hill. After being briefed on the crisis, Senator Russell said that war with the USSR was inevitable, so it might as well start right away, and even Fulbright, regarded as the leader of the Senate doves, thought a blockade too weak a response. But Kennedy persisted. To evade the charge that he was violating international law by interdicting shipments when the United States was not at war, the president called it a "quarantine." It would be a peaceful, though coercive, enterprise, but defiant ships could be fired at, and, if the tactic failed to deter the Russians, air strikes remained an option.

Throughout seven days of debate—a time of unrelieved tension in the White House—the American people had no knowledge of what was transpiring, and Khrushchev was unaware that he had been found out, but on the evening of October 22 the president delivered an electrifying televised address that was heard and seen by one hundred million Americans—the greatest audience ever for a presidential address. Though he was informing the American people of the frightening developments, his words were aimed at least as much at Khrushchev, who, alerted to the quarantine, was called upon to end his "clandestine, reckless, and provocative threat to world peace." In a targeted gloss on the Monroe Doctrine, Kennedy announced: "It shall be the policy of this nation to regard any nuclear missile launched from Cuba against any nation in the Western Hemisphere as an attack by the Soviet Union on the United States requiring a full retaliatory response upon the Soviet Union."

At the time the president spoke, Cuban-bound Soviet ships, having weighed anchor in Russian harbors many days before, were nearing the western Atlantic with their deadly cargoes, and no one could predict what they would do when they were confronted by the US Navy. John F. Kennedy and his aides awaited the first report of an encounter with white knuckles. "These few minutes were the time of greatest worry by the president," Robert Kennedy later reported. "His hand went up to his face & covered his mouth and he closed his fist. His eyes were tense, almost gray, and we just stared at each other across the table." When word reached the ExComm that the vessels were slowing their engines or turning back, a sensation of exultation swept the room. "We're eyeball to eyeball," Secretary of State Dean Rusk said, "and I think the other fella just blinked."

The crisis, though, was far from over. The missiles remained in Cuba, and while the ExComm was deliberating, Soviet technicians were working at a fierce pace to make them operational. They were only a few days away from having their missiles ready to launch at America, and Khrushchev would then be in a position to compel Kennedy to pull out of West Berlin. (There was a further concern: that the US Navy might pursue the Soviet vessels. When McNamara sought to deliver the president's order to avoid confrontation, the admiral who was the navy's representative on the Joint Chiefs retorted that his commanders at sea would make decisions, as they had been doing "ever since the days of John Paul Jones." He concluded: "Now, Mr. Secretary, if you and your deputy will go back to your offices, the navy will run the blockade.")

October 27, 1962, "Black Saturday," has been called by the diplomat Richard Holbrooke "the darkest day of the Cold War," the time when Kennedy and his aides did not know whether they—and millions of others—would wake on the morrow. On that day of dread, a Russian antiaircraft battery in Cuba shot down a U-2, killing the American pilot. The Joint Chiefs, who for the past week had been straining at the leash, and most of the members of the ExComm wanted to retaliate with an avenging air strike. On that day, too, the White House received from Khrushchev, who had earlier sent an encouraging letter, a much harsher message demanding that in return for dismantling the missiles in Cuba, the United States must pledge not to invade Cuba and must take its missiles out of Turkey. Kennedy knew that with US Polaris subs roving the Mediterranean, the missiles in Turkey were of no value, even a burden, but he could not consent to this condition publicly, for it would appear that he had been frightened into a concession.

On the night of Black Saturday, the president delegated his brother to tell the Russian ambassador in Washington that after the Soviet missiles were removed from Cuba, the United States would pull its missiles out of Turkey and Italy, but it would not do so for some months so that there would be no opportunity for Republicans, on the eve of the midterm elections, to accuse the administration of having made a deal—though that, in fact, is what it had done. In addition, the ExComm decided on the adroit strategy of replying to Khrushchev's more moderate first letter and ignoring the second. When, on the following day, the USSR, recognizing the superior might of the United States and having won concessions, announced that it was withdrawing the missiles from Cuba, the president sent a communication intended to spare the

Russian leader public humiliation and American gloating. "I welcome Chairman Khrushchev's statesmanlike decision," he said. "This is an important and constructive contribution to peace." In the ensuing weeks, there were further flare-ups and Castro's regime continued to be a provocation, but never again was there anything so potentially lethal as "the missiles of October." Instead, shaken by the realization of how close their two countries had come to a holocaust, Kennedy and Khrushchev began to explore avenues of accommodation.

Encouraged by promising overtures from Moscow, Kennedy decided to present a major statement of his evolving views on foreign policy in a commencement address at American University in June 1963. "What kind of peace do I mean?" he asked. "Not a Pax Americana enforced on the world by American weapons of war." He went on to say, "History teaches us that enmities between nations, as between individuals, do not last forever," and he urged Americans, "Let us reexamine our attitude toward the Soviet Union" and not "see only a distorted and desperate view of the other side." He continued: "No government or social system is so evil that its people must be considered as lacking in virtue. As Americans, we find communism profoundly repugnant as a negation of personal freedom and dignity. But we can still hail the Russian people for their many achievements—in science and space, in economic and industrial growth, in culture and in acts of courage." Linking the two countries, he added, was "our mutual abhorrence of war. Almost unique among the major world powers, we have never been at war with each other." Near the end of his address, he declared, "In the final analysis, our most basic common link is that we all inhabit this small planet. We all breathe the same air. We all cherish our children's future. And we are all mortal." One commentator wrote in astonishment: "He spoke at times of the cold war as if it hardly existed any longer."

In his American University speech, Kennedy announced that the USSR, the United States, and Great Britain were initiating talks toward a nuclear test ban. Disturbed by the hostility of the Joint Chiefs to any restriction on the US arsenal, the president refused to allow any military officer to take part in the negotiations and kept the Pentagon in ignorance of what was transpiring. In July 1963, the three powers agreed to renounce testing in the atmosphere (which produced radioactive fallout), in space, and under water. The compact did not, however, do much to slow down the arms race; spending on missiles and nuclear-armed bombers continued. But it did contribute to a cleaner environment, and it was, as Kennedy said, a first step toward putting "the genie back into the bottle." The United States and the USSR agreed to creation of a direct teletype link to safeguard against the danger that a nuclear war might be caused by a misunderstanding. (When this "hot line" began operation, the first reply from Moscow read, "Please explain what is meant by a quick brown fox jumping over a lazy dog.")

Kennedy, though, never ceased being a cold warrior. Two weeks after giving his American University address, he struck a very different chord. Speaking to a massive throng outside the Berlin Wall, he delivered a rabble-rousing harangue. "There are some who say communism is the wave of the future," he said. "And there are some who say in Europe and elsewhere we can work with Communists.... And there are even a few who say that it is true that communism is an evil system, but it permits us to make economic progress." He countered: "*Lass' sie nach Berlin kommen* [Let them come to Berlin]." He whipped his audience to a frenzy with his peroration: "All free men, wherever they live, are citizens of Berlin, and, therefore, as a free man, I take pride in the words, '*Ich bin ein Berliner.*'" Though his German was faulty, his listeners understood his message: he would not let the Russians seize their city.

More portentously, Kennedy deepened American involvement in Vietnam, where, from his first year in office, he had sought to demonstrate his toughness in the Cold War. He was warned that the Diem regime in Saigon could not be sustained because it did not have the support of the people of the country, but he could not stomach the thought of withdrawal. Years before he became president, he had bought into the domino theory. In 1956, he had called South Vietnam "the keystone to the arch, the finger in the dike," and stated that if it fell, "our prestige in Asia will sink to a new low." He also thought that he had a personal stake. "There are limits to the number of defeats I can defend in one twelve-month period," Kennedy confided in 1961. "I've had the Bay of Pigs, and pulling out of Laos, and I can't accept a third." An aide later recapitulated the administration's attitude: "It's more than the Cold War. It's saving Kennedy's presidency."

Yet he also harbored doubts. The Korean War had come early in his congressional career, and he had seen the political cost of becoming bogged down in a land conflict in Asia. "They want a force of American troops," he told a high-ranking State Department official at one point. "They say it's necessary to restore confidence and maintain morale. But... the troops will march in; the bands will play; the crowds will cheer; and in four days everyone will have forgotten. Then we will be told we have to send in more troops. It's like taking a drink. The effect wears off, and you have to take another."

To determine what course he should follow, he sent a man he highly esteemed, Maxwell Taylor, to Saigon. The general returned recommending the dispatch of as many as eight thousand US "combat troops" to support the Vietnamese army and stated ominously, "Any troops coming to VN may expect to take casualties." Rusk and McNamara followed up the Taylor Report by warning of the consequences of the collapse of South Vietnam and stating, "The chances are against, probably sharply against, preventing the fall of South Viet-Nam by any measures short of the introduction of U.S. forces on a substantial scale." Another Kennedy adviser, Walt Rostow, who had accompanied Taylor to Vietnam, strongly favored turning loose the Green Berets for aggressive action. "In Knute Rockne's old phrase, we are not saving them for the junior prom," he said. Only a few in the White House circle urged restraint. George Ball warned: "Taylor is wrong. ... Within five years, we'll have three hundred thousand men in the paddies and jungles and never find them again." Kennedy retorted: "George, I always thought you were one of the brightest guys around here. But you're just crazier than hell. That just isn't going to happen."

Kennedy took the fateful step. In doing so, he thought, as his successors often did when they escalated the US commitment, that he was being restrained. He was not quite ready to sign off on combat soldiers, and he refused to sanction bombing of North Vietnam. But he gave the Pentagon almost everything else it wanted. Step by step, he increased the number of American "advisers" in Vietnam from nine hundred when he was inaugurated to nearly seventeen thousand in the fall of 1963. On December 10, 1961, they were authorized for the first time to use weapons—in self-defense. Two days later, the first American died in the jungle. He would not be the last. Kennedy also approved the use of napalm (jellied gasoline) and other defoliants, and in January 1962 he signed off on combat responsibilities for American "advisers" in Vietnam.

Recalling the damage Harry Truman had sustained from being charged with "losing China" and how that allegation contributed to the anti-Communist hysteria, Kennedy resolved not to be the president who lost Vietnam. "If I tried to pull out," he said, "we would have another Joe McCarthy red scare on our hands." In fact, Kennedy totally misconstrued the situation. The country in 1961 exhibited massive indifference to Vietnam. It was only when Kennedy and his successors greatly expanded the US commitment, and casualty lists lengthened, that a large number of Americans came to care about the fate of that distant land.

In 1963, the situation in Vietnam, steadily worsening, reached a critical stage, not because of anything the United States did but because of Diem and his Catholic coterie's relentless repression of the Buddhist majority, which descended even to raiding pagodas and killing monks. When a monk horrified the world by setting himself afire in protest, Diem's sister-in-law Madame Nhu dismissed his suicide as a "barbecue." With the Diem government rapidly losing what little favor it had, Vietnamese generals informed American officials they were planning a coup. Kennedy did not condone it, but neither did he forbid it, and the US envoy in Saigon let the plotters know that the United States would do nothing to hinder them. Early in November 1963, the generals deposed Diem and murdered him and his brother Nhu. On hearing of the killings, Kennedy, said General Taylor, "leaped to his feet and rushed from the room with a look of shock and dismay on his face which I had never seen before." The event made it all the harder for the United States to abandon South Vietnam.

If Kennedy had lived to serve a second term, would he have pulled out of Vietnam? Some commentators think so. In his last days in office, McNamara and Taylor were talking of withdrawing one thousand men and of finishing the mission by the end of 1965. Three days before his death, the president sent an aide to Southeast Asia to "organize an in-depth study of every possible option we've got in Vietnam, including how to get out of there. We have to review this whole thing from the bottom to the top." Furthermore, his admirers reasoned, a man of Kennedy's cool temperament would not have sanctioned the excesses of the Johnson years with hundreds of thousands of US troops in Southeast Asia.

Most of the evidence, though, points in a contrary direction. When McNamara and Taylor contemplated withdrawal, they did so on the assumption of imminent victory, which the National Security Council and others thought was illusory, and there is little reason to suppose that Kennedy would have been any more willing in a second term than in his first to shoulder the blame for defeat. In a September 1963 televised interview, he told Walter Cronkite: "I don't agree with those who say we should withdraw. That would be a great mistake. I know people don't like Americans to be engaged in this kind of an effort. Forty-seven Americans have been killed in combat with the enemy, but this is a very important struggle even though it is far away." A week later, in an interview with the NBC anchormen, Chet Huntley and David Brinkley, he was asked, "Mr. President, have you had any reason to doubt this so-called 'domino theory,' that if South Vietnam falls, the rest of Southeast Asia will go?" He replied: "No, I believe it.... If South Vietnam went, it would... give the impression that the wave of the future in Southeast Asia was China and the Communists. So I believe it." Asked further whether aid to South Vietnam was likely to be reduced, he responded, "I don't think... that would be helpful at this time.... We must be patient, we must persist.... I think we should stay." On the very day of his death, Kennedy intended to give an address in which he boasted that he had "increased our special counterinsurgency forces which are now engaged in South Vietnam by 600 percent." He planned to acknowledge that involvement in the third world could be "painful, risky, and costly." But he also wanted to emphasize his conclusion: "We dare not weary of the test."

Millions of Americans cared less about the president's policy than about his personality. They lavished on Jack Kennedy the kind of adulation usually reserved for movie stars or gridiron heroes. Cameras, it was said, loved him. Flashing a radiant smile, his face perpetually tanned, lithe and rangy, he appeared to be exceptionally virile, often photographed at sea with his hand on the tiller. Kennedy's impact on women, James Reston wrote, was "almost naughty." He conveyed the impression, at the same time, of the perfect family man with two adorable children (John-John and Caroline) and a beautiful wife who became an international icon. She made such a hit with her designer clothes and impeccable French on a state visit to France, where she toured the Jeu de Paume and talked spiritedly to de Gaulle about the Duc d'Angoulême, that the president introduced himself, with characteristic disarming wit, by saying, "I am the man who accompanied Jacqueline Kennedy to Paris." Jackie's pillbox hat became a vogue. So did her bouffant hairstyle, sleeveless sheath dresses, and low-heeled pumps.

The president won a reputation, too, as a man of culture and panache. On JFK's very first day in office, Robert Frost, in appreciation for the invitation of men of letters to the inauguration ceremonies, read a verse tribute to the new government for

> Summoning artists to participate
> In the august occasions of the state.

In contraposition to the Muzak of the Eisenhower era, the White House provided the venue for a recital by the world-renowned cellist Pablo Casals, and at a state dinner for Grand Duchess Charlotte and Prince Jean of Luxembourg, Basil Rathbone recited the St. Crispin's Day speech from Shakespeare's *Henry V.* The first lady also redecorated the White House in the elegant style of early nineteenth-century France, and her guided tour of the refurbished mansion attracted a large television audience. Jack Kennedy was so appealing, said the historian John William Ward, because he thought "the world was...open to change and renewal, if only one had the courage to resist the tyrannous weight of mass conformity."

In truth, opera bored the president, and he dozed off at concerts of classical music. (The only music he truly cared for, Jacqueline Kennedy once said, was "Hail to the Chief.") While his wife feasted on *paté de fois gras* at family picnics, he chowed down peanut butter sandwiches, and he much preferred James Bond thrillers to Kafka or Stendahl. For JFK, the historian Thomas Brown has written, culture was "little more than a *chic* commodity and status symbol, certainly not a genuinely enriching aspect of life." His reputation for droll wit, though, was authentic. When he honored Nobel laureates at a banquet, he hailed them as "the most extraordinary collection of talent, of human knowledge, that has ever been gathered together at the White House, with the possible exception of when Thomas Jefferson dined alone."

At a White House press conference, Kennedy radiates charm and self-confidence as he deftly disposes of questions in a style that no other chief executive has ever been able to match. *Abbie Rowe. White House Photographs. John F. Kennedy Presidential Library and Museum, Boston, ID JFKWHP-AR7595-B*

Kennedy's sallies showed to best advantage at press conferences, which he moved from cramped quarters in the Executive Office Building to a State Department auditorium with room for more than four hundred reporters. Confident in his ability to field questions cleverly, he became the first president to permit the conferences to be televised—and in prime time. In contrast to "Silent Cal" Coolidge, who held more than a hundred news conferences a year, Kennedy conducted them only every other month. But many Americans regarded them as first-rate entertainment as well as a source of information. The first drew seventy-five million viewers. They gave him an opportunity to display his quickness on his feet, his self-mocking wit, his range of knowledge, and his gift for banter.

At the end of the third week of November in 1963, Kennedy took off for a speaking trip in four Texas cities, winding up in Dallas. He decided on the journey primarily to raise money for the 1964 campaign, but also to shore up support in a state with twenty-five electoral votes that had become mutinous both because of his advocacy of civil rights and because he was thought to be weak-kneed on foreign affairs. "We're heading into nut country today," he warned his wife. "But, Jackie, if somebody wants to shoot me from a window with a rifle, nobody can stop it, so why worry about it?" Adlai Stevenson had been spat upon and shoved in Dallas, and a speaker at a National Indignation Convention there had whooped up a crowd at Memorial Auditorium by accusing a fellow right-wing extremist of moderation: "All he wants to do is impeach [Chief Justice] Warren. I'm for hanging him."

So venomous had the atmosphere become that Kennedy had been warned against taking the trip. In the past two years, Texas had been the source of no fewer than thirty-four threats against the life of the president. Kennedy himself had expressed concern about the menace of

Dallas, November 22, 1963. In the morning, John F. Kennedy, accompanied by the first lady, makes his way from Love Field airport to the heart of the city. Kennedy would be assassinated less than an hour later. *Associated Press, ID 795433699224*

mindless violence. In the summer of 1963, he had read to White House visitors the speech of Blanche of Castile from *King John*:

> The sun's o'ercast with blood; fair day, adieu!
> Which is the side that I must go withal?
> I am with both: each army hath a hand;
> And in their rage, I having hold of both,
> They whirl asunder and dismember me.

The president arrived in Dallas on November 22 to find the Big D in an ugly mood. That morning, an ad in the city's leading newspaper posed a series of questions to him typified by "Why have you scrapped the Monroe Doctrine in favor of the spirit of Moscow?" It concluded: "Mr. Kennedy, WE DEMAND answers to these questions and we want them now." But as Kennedy rode in an open convertible in bright sunshine on an eleven-mile drive into downtown, thousands lined the avenues to greet him. "It all began so beautifully," Lady Bird Johnson later entered in her diary, "the children all smiling, placards, confetti, people waving from windows." As the motorcade approached the Texas School Book Depository near the heart of the city at 12:30 p.m., the governor's wife remarked to him, "You can't say Dallas doesn't love you." As he turned toward her to reply, shots rang out. The president slumped over, face down, and Jacqueline Kennedy cried out, "Oh, no!" Picking up speed, the motorcade made a mad dash for Parkland Hospital. There, at 1 p.m., the president was pronounced dead.

Mourners all over the world voiced their anguish at the assassination of John F. Kennedy. Londoners traveled great distances to pay homage at the US embassy in Grosvenor Square, and the British poet W. H. Auden composed an "Elegy for J.F.K." set to Stravinsky's twelve-tone music. Ugandans, on hillsides above Kampala overlooking the residence of the American envoy, held silent vigil. Frequently, encomiums took extraordinary, even extravagant, forms. In Tel Aviv, Deputy Prime Minister Abba Eban declared that "the death of John F. Kennedy is one of the most authentically tragic events in the history of nations"; in Lebanon, the diplomat Charles Malik contended, "It is difficult to find another instance in history of a man whose death was as universally mourned"; and, in West Equatorial Africa, Albert Schweitzer said that Kennedy "could have been the saviour of the world." A writer in the staid *Manchester Guardian Weekly* even stated, "For the first time in my life I think I know how the disciples must have felt when Jesus was crucified."

In an interview with the journalist Theodore White shortly after the president's death, Jacqueline Kennedy elaborated another perception. She reminisced: "At night, before we'd go to sleep, Jack liked to play some records; and the song he loved most came at the very end of this record. The lines he loved to hear were: 'Don't let it be forgot, that once there was a spot, for one brief shining moment that was known as Camelot.'" She went on, "There'll be great Presidents again—and the Johnsons are wonderful, they've been wonderful to me—but there'll never be another Camelot again." Her husband's presidency, she told White, had been "a magic moment in American history, when gallant men danced with beautiful women, when great deeds were done, when artists, writers, and poets met at the White House and the barbarians beyond the walls were held back."

Jack Kennedy's closest friends scoffed at this conceit, but it took hold. Benjamin Bradlee, who had written a book about the slain president's "special grace," remarked, "The legends of Camelot and King Arthur were largely laid upon the land in the 12th Century by one Geoffrey of Monmouth, described...as a 'reckless forger.'" The esteemed historian Samuel Eliot Morison of Harvard, however, concluded his chronicle *The Oxford History of the American People*, published shortly after the end of the Kennedy presidency, with lyrics from the musical: "That once there was a fleeting wisp of glory called Camelot."

The assassination traumatized millions of Americans. In the days after the shattering news from Dallas, 26 percent reported rapid heartbeats, 48 percent insomnia, 68 percent nervous tension. Many comments underscored Kennedy's vibrancy, which made his death so hard to accept. "It was a sense of quality, a shirt stud or a witticism, a strong stand or gracious tribute, which gave his brief era that sense of distinction historians are likely not to see when they assay the accomplishments of President Kennedy," wrote a *Washington Post* editor. "New climates will intervene. His was morning sunshine." Some of the eulogies came from unexpected sources. "What a sense of the abyss that the man is no longer with us, not there to be attacked, not there to be conversed with in the privacy of one's mind," wrote the novelist and acerbic critic

Norman Mailer. "It was the first time in America's history that one could mock the Presidency on so high a level, and we may have to live for half a century before such a witty and promising atmosphere exists again." A survey reported that "a full half" of the adult population in the United States regarded Kennedy as "one of the two or three best Presidents the country ever had."

Even in the first years after Kennedy's untimely death, historians took a more dispassionate view. When they scrutinized the record of his achievements, they were struck by how thin it was. He had some successes, or at least standoffs, abroad. Most scholars agree with the judgment of the journalist Al Hunt, who a half century later wrote that, in the Cuban missiles crisis, "Kennedy's skills may well have saved 20 million to 30 million lives," though some critics castigate him for his willingness to take such a risk. His lone institutional innovation, however, was the Peace Corps. His attainments at home were even more modest: trade expansion, area redevelopment, pollution control. (His only breakthroughs came in conservation with the acquisition of national seashores at Cape Cod, Padre Island, and Point Reyes and the creation of a National Wildlife Refuge at Florida's Merritt Island.) So circumscribed were his economic and social programs that liberals called Kennedy's tenure Eisenhower's third term. He did not resort to civil rights legislation until the level of civic disorder and bloodshed made action inescapable, and at the end of the Kennedy presidency, a mere 1 percent of black pupils in the South attended school with whites. The New Frontier, concluded the English critic Henry Fairlie, was just "a limited exercise in civilizing the status quo" and Kennedy "a Man of Only One Season."

A series of revelations splintered the Kennedy marriage idyll. A compulsive womanizer, the president carried on countless sexual liaisons while married, conspicuously with glamorous Hollywood actresses, and in the White House he hosted naked pool parties with call girls. He modeled himself on Lord Byron, who, anticipating that he would die young, lusted for women. Kennedy's "continual, almost heroic sexual performance," Garry Wills has written, was a "cackling at the gods of bodily disability who plagued him." A Senate committee heard credible testimony that he had sexual encounters in the executive mansion with a woman who was the mistress of the Chicago gangster Sam Giancana, charged by Robert Kennedy with being "the chief gunman for the group that succeeded the Capone mob." Still more disturbing, Giancana was one of the two thugs who had been recruited by the CIA to murder Fidel Castro.

In truth, Kennedy held women in contempt. During his prep school days, he had referred to them as "meat," and he never outgrew that attitude. Unlike FDR and Eisenhower, he named no woman to his cabinet or to any other prominent position in the government. The Washington TV correspondent Nancy Dickerson called him "the complete male chauvinist" who "thought it ridiculous to pay [women] the same as men," and Lady Barbara Ward, a world-respected economist, said that he "had little empathy for the trained, intelligent woman." He has even been called a "sexual outlaw."

The vendetta of the Kennedy brothers against Castro and their engagement in a number of other covert actions raised troubling issues. The *New York Times* columnist Tom Wicker subsequently wrote, "Now it is known that during the splendid Kennedy years the F.B.I. . . . was wiretapping Martin Luther King, the C.I.A. was trying to assassinate Fidel Castro and Patrice Lumumba, and both agencies were systematically overstepping the bounds of law and policy, not to mention decency." In the brief Kennedy reign, Operation Mongoose hatched more than thirty plots to murder the Cuban leader, some of them involving such lurid weapons as a poisoned ballpoint pen and an exploding cigar. No evidence has surfaced linking the Kennedys directly to assassination conspiracies, but the CIA could not unreasonably have assumed that it had their approval. In his careful assessment, the biographer Michael O'Brien concluded that "the Kennedys did in fact authorize the CIA to kill Castro." Furthermore, there is no doubt that Robert Kennedy sanctioned other activities of Operation Mongoose to destabilize the Castro regime and that he arranged for the bugging of Dr. King or that the president made improper use of the Internal Revenue Service to probe the tax returns of his opponents.

"Vigor," the watchword the Kennedy clan laid claim to, also came into question. On the eve of taking office, Kennedy had answered an inquiry from a reporter by saying, "I never had Addison's disease," an ailment regarded as terminal. It was an outright lie. At least four times, he had been administered last rites by a priest. He also misled his own press secretary. "They're saying you take cortisone," Pierre Salinger informed him. "Well, I used to take cortisone, but I don't take it anymore," Kennedy responded. In fact, every day, he medicated himself for the Addison's affliction, and, to cope with back pain, his doctor injected him as often as six times a day with novocaine. The painful treatments, bringing only brief relief, aroused fears that he was on his way to becoming addicted. Warned against an amphetamine ("speed") prescribed by a doctor whom experienced respected physicians regarded as a quack, he answered, "I don't care if it's horse piss. It works." In December 1962, the foremost orthopedist in New York told Kennedy that if he ever heard that JFK had received another shot, he would announce it to the world. "No president with his finger on the red button has any business taking stuff like that," he declared. (One consequence of all the medications was they gave Jack Kennedy the perpetual tan that implied perfect health.) Dallek has reported that the president "was under the care of an allergist, an endocrinologist, a gastroenterologist, an orthopedist, and a urologist," in addition to the two primary White House physicians. "In a lifetime of medical torment," another biographer, Richard Reeves, has written, "Kennedy was more promiscuous with physicians and drugs than he was with women."

While not denying this downside, Kennedy's champions have claimed that in the year of his death he had begun to head the country in new directions, for the JFK of 1963 was not the novice of 1961. In 1963, he had finally taken a strong stand for civil rights; he had embraced the New Economics; and he had delivered the American University address. An unexpected admirer, the Socialist Michael Harrington, told an interviewer:

> Within the context of his political and personal limitations, John F. Kennedy grew enormously. He arrived at the White House a young, and not terribly distinguished, senator from the Eisenhower years with a tiny margin of victory and Dixiecrat-Republican majority against him in the Congress.
>
> The America which inaugurated him in January, 1961 still believed in the verities of the Cold War (as did Kennedy in his speech of that day), in the sanctity of the balanced budget, and it had not begun to come to terms with that great mass movement led by Martin Luther

King. The America which mourned John F. Kennedy in November, 1963 was different. It was not transformed—but it was better. That was Kennedy's modest and magnificent achievement.

If Kennedy had lived, his advocates say, he would have thrashed Goldwater in 1964 and, with much larger Democratic majorities in Congress, put through an ambitious program. In support of that contention, they note that at the time of his death polls showed him leading Goldwater, 55 percent to 39. Kennedy's triumphs, Clinton Rossiter asserted, were "just over the next rise." So "how, then," Ted Sorensen asked, "could it be that he should be taken from us when he stood on the very threshold of the promised land to which he had led us?" The unpersuaded would counter that Kennedy never sought to lead anyone to a promised land. On returning to Columbia University from Washington, where he had supervised the transition from the Eisenhower administration as JFK's agent, the political scientist Richard Neustadt had reported, "The Kennedy presidency will bring many things, but the New Jerusalem won't be one of them." Furthermore, his outlook on foreign affairs, however modulated, never ceased being that of a cold warrior. Kennedy, though, remains for his upholders, as one commentator said, a Prince Hal who died before Agincourt. In sum, James Reston remarked, "the heart of the Kennedy legend is what might have been."

History, however, deals not with what might have been but with what did happen. Though Kennedy served less than three years, few presidencies have had so many moments of high drama. Yet, in part because he was granted so little time, he had a negligible impact on the institution of the executive office. A 1988 poll of seventy-five historians and journalists designated Kennedy "the most overrated public figure in American history." Neustadt concluded: "He will be just a flicker, forever clouded by the record of his successors. I don't think history will have much space for John Kennedy."

All of the critiques of Kennedy churned out by scholars year after year have had no more influence on popular opinion than a melting snowflake. A generation after his death, pollsters were still reporting that the American people rated Kennedy the greatest president of all time. Asked in 1983 which president they would like to have in the White House then, three times as many Americans chose Kennedy than the second most popular: 30 percent to FDR's 10 percent. All others who had served fared worse. Fully 65 percent of those polled asserted that the United States would be "much different" if he had not been slain.

Americans, Kennedy's astute biographer Alan Brinkley has written, "look back nostalgically to an era that seemed to be a time of national confidence and purpose. Kennedy reminds many Americans of an age when it was possible to believe that politics could be harnessed to America's highest aspirations, that it could be rooted in a sense of national community, that it could speak to the country's moral yearnings. And perhaps most of all, Kennedy reminds Americans of a time when the nation's capacities seemed limitless, when its future seemed unbounded, when it was possible to believe that the United States could solve social problems and accomplish great deeds." They presume, as the playwright Tony Kushner has said, that, at the moment the shot was fired in Dallas, "History cracked open."

When scholars attempted the first assessments of the presidency, William Carleton delineated the problem historians would always confront. "With Kennedy, one collides with adoration," he wrote. "The uncritical bias in favor of Kennedy derives from his winsome personality, his style and élan, . . . and the sympathetic spiritual kinship with him felt by historians, political scientists, intellectuals, and writers." Similarly, the essayist Gerald Johnson concluded:

> Logical analysis will certainly be applied to Kennedy's career, and will have about as much effect on his position in history as Mrs. Partington's mop had upon the Atlantic tide. . . . Historians may protest, logicians may rave, but they cannot alter the fact that any kind of man, once touched by romance, is removed from all categories and is comparable only with the legendary. . . . Already it has happened to two of the 35 men who have held the Presidency, rendering them incapable of analysis by the instruments of scholarship; and now Washington, the god-like, and Lincoln, the saintly, have been joined by Kennedy, the young Chevalier.

John Fitzgerald Kennedy will forever be a figure not of chronicle but of myth.

8

Lyndon B. Johnson

ON THE TARMAC OF DALLAS'S Love Field, aboard the plane carrying John F. Kennedy's body back to Washington, Lyndon Baines Johnson took the oath of office as thirty-sixth president of the United States, Jacqueline Kennedy in a blood-soaked suit standing beside him. The contrast with his predecessor was stark. Though Johnson was only nine years older, there seemed to be a generation of difference. Unlike Kennedy, who had been born to great wealth and had gone to Choate and Harvard, Johnson was a self-made man from the hardscrabble Texas Hill Country who had attended the unimposing Southwest Texas State Teachers College in San Marcos. While Jack Kennedy had the sophisticated, understated style of a patrician, Johnson was blunt, loud, often deliberately coarse. Throughout his public career, he had a keen sense of inferiority to the well-bred men around him whom he called "the Harvards."

He could not have taken over in more awful circumstances—as the beneficiary of the slaying in Dallas. "I always felt sorry for Harry Truman and the way he got the presidency," Johnson said shortly after the Dallas tragedy, "but at least his man wasn't murdered." He later told an interviewer, Doris Kearns: "For millions of Americans I was...illegitimate, a naked man with no presidential covering, a pretender to the throne, an illegal usurper. And then there was Texas, my home, the home of both the murder and the murderer of the murderer." In the savage 1967 satire

MacBird, loosely based on *Macbeth*, Johnson is presented as an assassin, conniving with "Lady MacBird" to kill the rightful monarch (Duncan aka Kennedy). On the fortieth anniversary of the assassination, nearly one in five Americans still believed Johnson was implicated in the homicide—a higher proportion than fingered the Kremlin or Fidel Castro. As recently as 2004, the History Channel ran a documentary portraying Johnson as, in the words of one commentator, a "Hill Country Claudius, conspiring to bait the dueling rapier, poison the wine, and do away with America's sweet, brainy prince."

Johnson spent his entire presidency in Kennedy's shadow. He knew that a number of men even in his own administration could not stand the sight of him because he sat in the chair that his predecessor should have been occupying. LBJ's biographer Paul Conkin has written of Johnson: "He was more intimidated by a dead Kennedy, by the soon mythological king of Camelot, than he had been by the living but flawed reality. He had to follow a god. However much he achieved, he could not measure up to such a standard. No one could." To maintain continuity and to demonstrate his loyalty, he implored JFK's staff and cabinet officers to stay on. For a time, they agreed—even Attorney General Robert Kennedy, who despised Johnson and was loath to remain.

Despite the friction, the new president took pains to be deferential to the Kennedy family, especially the fallen leader's widow, and to pick up JFK's standard. Not until December 7 did the Johnsons move into the White House. Johnson not only forwarded Kennedy's inchoate notion of a national cultural program but vastly improved it by coming up with government funds. He also embraced the idea of renaming the project, and, two months after taking office, he signed legislation to create the John F. Kennedy Center (later the Kennedy Center for the Performing Arts). When, in order to get an appropriations bill passed, a Florida senator suggested he withdraw Kennedy's plan for a tax cut, Johnson replied, "No, no, I can't do that.... We can't abandon this fellow's program, because he is a national hero."

Self-effacement did not come easily to a man so colossally egocentric. Johnson was determined to put his brand on the world. His wife was Lady Bird Johnson (LBJ); his daughters Lynda Bird Johnson and Luci Baines Johnson (more LBJs). At the LBJ Ranch, three flags unfurled— Old Glory, the ensign of the Bluebonnet State, and his personal banner:

LBJ lettered in white on a field of blue. He lavished scads of electric toothbrushes bearing his seal on callers so that he would be the first person recipients would think about in the morning and the last person at night. His self-infatuation became the stuff of legend. When he visited the Vatican, the pope gave him a Renaissance painting. In return, Johnson presented His Holiness with a bust of himself. On one occasion at Andrews Field, when a solicitous young officer advised him that he was headed toward a helicopter that was not his, Johnson retorted, "Son, all of them are mine." According to an apocryphal tale, when Chancellor Erhard of Germany said to him, "I understand, Mr. President, you were born in a log cabin," Johnson responded, "No, Mr. Chancellor. You have me confused with Lincoln. I was born in a manger."

Johnson aggrandized himself by establishing dominance over his subordinates, whom he did not hesitate to abuse. "Just you remember this:

Rounding up a Hereford yearling at his ranch in Texas, President Lyndon B. Johnson conveys the energy of a man who was said to "ride herd" on Congress. *Bill Hudson/Associated Press, ID 080826011696*

there's only two kinds at the White House," he lectured a staffer. "There's elephants and there's pissants. And I'm the only elephant." He sometimes made the point more crudely: "I want people around me who would kiss my ass on a hot summer's day and say it smells like roses." Johnson, his former press secretary George Reedy reflected, "as a human being was a miserable person—a bully, sadist, lout, and egoist....His lapses from civilized conduct were deliberate and usually intended to subordinate someone else to do his will. He did disgusting things because he realized that other people had to pretend that they did not mind. It was his method of bending them to his desires." If a man of distinction consented to serve in his administration, his top domestic policy aide observed, the president would "humiliate him in some way to make him totally his man." When it fell to Johnson to pick a running mate who would be the future vice president of the United States, one requirement loomed larger than any other: complete subservience. "Whoever he is," Johnson explained, "I want his pecker...in my pocket."

He brought this same insistence on mastery into public affairs. "The President," said a British observer, "comes into a room slowly and warily, as if he means to smell out the allegiance of everyone in it." He had an instinct for power, said an intimate, "as primordial as a salmon's going upstream to spawn." LBJ, an aide observed, was "quick with the hustle of a man who had much to do in a little time." The Minnesota senator Hubert Humphrey remarked, "Rest for him was controlled frenzy," and a journalist characterized him as "utterly cyclonic." His overwrought conduct in the White House, stated one of his assistants, constituted "a grotesque and very unattractive scene which, at best, resembled the dances in the hall of the Mountain King in *Peer Gynt*."

Those who were closest to him saw his worst qualities but also, as Reedy acknowledged, his commitment to "uplift for the poor and downtrodden." His White House aide Joseph Califano has commented: "The Lyndon Johnson I worked with was brave and brutal, compassionate and cruel, incredibly intelligent and infuriatingly insensitive, with a shrewd and uncanny instinct for the jugular of his allies and adversaries. He could be altruistic and petty, caring and crude, generous and petulant, bluntly honest and calculatingly devious—all within the same few minutes." Reedy summed him up by saying: "He may have been a son of a bitch, but he was a colossal son of a bitch."

Though his comportment elicited stern criticism, a number of commentators thought that LBJ had precisely the qualities of temperament, as well as the social vision, to break the stranglehold that a bipartisan conservative coalition had imposed for more than a quarter of a century and, with his deeply felt commitment to social justice, to push through a passel of progressive legislation for the first time since 1938. The psychologist Robert Coles called Johnson an "extravagantly self-centered, brutishly expansive, manipulative, teasing and sly man," but also one who was "passionately interested in making life easier and more honorable for millions of hard-pressed working-class men and women. His almost manic vitality was purposely, intelligently, compassionately used." No one could doubt that he intended to build an unprecedented record of achievement. He revered his mentor Franklin Delano Roosevelt, but he aimed to accumulate so many accomplishments that he would be rated in history books as having excelled even FDR. Johnson, Conkin concluded, "hated subtraction and division; he loved addition and multiplication."

As chief legislator, Johnson faced a discouraging prospect. From his vantage point on Capitol Hill, he had seen the conservative coalition block almost every attempt to enact new social measures—from Truman's effort to win support for medical insurance to Kennedy's failure to advance a civil rights bill and a tax cut. Two years in the White House had led Kennedy to say, "There are greater limitations upon our ability to bring about a favorable result than I had imagined." Thinking back to FDR's second term, Johnson remarked, "Everything on my desk today was here when I first came to Congress." Many analysts expected him to experience the same frustrations that had bedeviled previous presidents. One of the country's most astute political correspondents, Richard Rovere, wrote that the odds against Johnson's doing anything history-making were "almost unimaginable."

Johnson, however, brought to his quest for innovative legislation nearly a quarter of a century of experience in the halls of Congress. He had served in both houses, and in the Senate had won renown as a majority leader with exceptional tactical skills. "There is but one way for a President to deal with Congress, and that is continuously, incessantly, and without interruption," he later said. "If it's really going to work, the relationship between the President and the Congress has got to be almost incestuous." He instructed one of his chief aides, "You've got to learn to mount the Congress like you mount a woman." On one occasion, he phoned a congressman at four in the morning to press him to vote for a pending measure. "Sorry to be calling you so early in the morning," Johnson began. "Oh, that's all right," the congressman retorted. "I was just lying here hoping you would call."

When he set his mind on getting a bill enacted, he behaved, observed his special counsel, like a "pit-bull terrier." A Washington journalist recounted Humphrey's recollection of how Johnson delivered pep talks: "He'd grab me by the lapels and say, 'Now, Hubert, I want you to do this and that and get going.'" Then the president would kick him hard in the shins. "Look," Humphrey told the reporter, who ended the story by writing, "He pulled up his trouser leg and, sure enough, he had some scars there." Earlier, two columnists had put together the classic account of Johnson's method when majority leader. "He moved in close, his face a scant millimeter from his target, his eyes widening and narrowing, his eyebrows rising and falling. From his pockets poured clippings, memos, statistics. Mimicry, humor, and the genius of analogy made the Treatment an almost hypnotic experience and rendered the target stunned and helpless." One victim of the "Treatment," the editor of the *Washington Post*, said of an encounter with Johnson: "You really felt as if a St. Bernard had licked your face for an hour, had pawed you all over."

Johnson knew that no impression he was ever to make would be as important as the first one when, in late November 1963 in the wake of Kennedy's death, he appeared before Congress. As he spoke, listeners heard, the historian Taylor Branch has written, a "slow Texas twang and Southernism." Afterward, the black writer Louis Lomax commented: "We watched our new President on television and remembered that he comes from a state that has had 47 lynchings since 1920. We could not recall a single time when he had spoken out against these murders of our brothers. As we listened to him talk, the cracker twang in this voice chilled our hearts. For we know that twang, that drawl. We have heard it in the night, threatening; in the day, abusing; from the pulpit, sanctifying segregation; in the market place, denying us opportunity; everywhere, abrogating our human dignity. Yes, we know that twang."

But Johnson startled the members of Congress by saying, "No memorial oration or eulogy could more eloquently honor President Kennedy's memory than the earliest possible passage of the civil rights bill for which he fought." That statement evoked waves of applause, though southern senators were conspicuously still. After waiting for the clapping to subside, he continued: "We have talked long enough in this country about equal rights. We have talked for one hundred years or more. It is time now to write the next chapter—and to write it in the books of law." Johnson's oration, the *Washington Post* told its readers the next morning, could not have been improved "by the alteration of one single sentence or a single sentiment."

While the civil rights bill made its way tortuously through Congress, Johnson had to attend to an issue in foreign policy—a concern that, to his distress, kept intruding throughout his tenure. To buy wheat from the United States, which the president saw as a boon to American farmers, the USSR required a loan, but right-wing Republicans in the Senate raised a challenge to him by forbidding federal agencies to approve credits. "If the legislators had tasted blood" on that issue in December, Johnson later said, "they would have run over us like a steamroller when they returned in January." Consequently, he called on a House-Senate conference committee to report out a bill posthaste. A number of members had already left for the Christmas holiday, but the new president, not many days in office, ordered them back to Washington and sent an airlift of military helicopters and planes to fetch them from their hometowns. When they returned to the capital, fuming, Johnson sweet-talked them and treated them to bourbon-laced eggnog and fruitcake at a White House reception in their honor. On the following morning, the committee, meeting at dawn, gave the president what he was demanding. Liberated to go home for the Christmas season, they departed knowing that henceforth they were going to be dealing with a bull elephant.

On January 8, 1964, in his first State of the Union message, Johnson called upon Congress to do "more for civil rights than the last hundred sessions combined," to put through "the most far-reaching tax cut of our time," to enact "the most effective, efficient foreign aid program ever," and, in addition, "to build more homes, more schools, more libraries, and more hospitals than any single session of Congress in the history of our Republic." He added breezily, "All this and more can and must be done. It can be done by this summer."

One passage in his address especially attracted attention. "Unfortunately," he said, "many Americans live on the outskirts of hope—some because of their poverty, and some because of their color, and all too many because of both. Our task is to help replace their despair with opportunity." He then announced: "This administration today, here and now, declares unconditional war on poverty in America." He wound up with a plea: "I urge this Congress and all Americans to join me in that effort. It will not be a short or easy struggle, no single weapon or strategy will suffice, but we shall not rest until that war is won. The richest Nation on earth can afford to win it. We cannot afford to lose it."

On March 16, Johnson sent a special message to Congress reiterating his call for a "nationwide war on the sources of poverty" and asking for a "total commitment...to pursue victory over the most ancient of mankind's enemies." This ambition, said the *Nation*, rested on "an almost mystical belief in the infinite potentials of American society. Poverty, like polio, will be defeated when the right vaccine is found." In like manner, London's *Sunday Times* remarked that Johnson's "was perhaps the most bellicose program of social reform in history. It was to be a *war* on poverty. Federal funds were to be 'fired in' to pockets of poverty in what was known in Washington as 'the rifle-shot approach.'...He actually spoke of 'throttling want.'"

Johnson went all out to win approval of the legislation. He did not advocate a dole, simply writing checks to the down-and-out. "I don't want to be taking any taxpayers' money and paying it to people just to breed," he said. But though he did not favor a "handout," he was absolutely determined to offer a "hand up." He took to the telephone to bring pressure on members of Congress or to woo them with intimations of future favors. Anyone who supported the bill and corralled others for the cause, the onetime schoolteacher promised, would get a "star in his book."

The Economic Opportunity Act (a title incorporating a cherished traditional American value) authorized a many-pronged attack on destitution. It created a Job Corps to retrain the long-term unemployed. Upward Bound encouraged bright inner-city children to go to college; work-study projects of a Neighborhood Youth Corps enabled them to make their way through. Head Start, established to help disadvantaged preschoolers, soon proved to be such an outstanding success that a very conservative Republican senator from Utah became one of its most enthusiastic champions. VISTA (Volunteers in Service to America) marshaled a domestic peace corps to work in low-income sectors. More controversially, a Community Action Program mandated "maximum feasible participation" by the poor in devising their own solutions. (Adopted with much less fanfare, the Food Stamp Act of 1964 proved in years to come to be a significant boon to low-income families.)

Never before had an American president undertaken to address the persistence of poverty in flush times. The "war," though, was fought with a popgun, for Johnson failed to ask Congress to finance it adequately. Instead of the $11 billion estimated to be needed to lift all Americans above the poverty level, he settled for less than $1 billion. "The War on Poverty," the historian Mark Gelfand has written, "produced a classic instance of the American habit of substituting good intentions for cold, hard cash." Yet, for all their shortcomings, LBJ's programs, including the economic growth he fostered, lowered the proportion of the American people living in poverty from 21 percent in 1959 to 12 percent a decade later.

That achievement owed less to the Economic Opportunity Act than to a tax cut he adroitly maneuvered through Congress. Kennedy's proposal for slashing taxes had bogged down in the Senate Finance Committee chaired by Harry Byrd of Virginia, a zealous opponent of runaway federal spending. Two nights after Kennedy's assassination, Johnson gathered his financial advisers around him to lecture them on holding the budget below the symbolic figure of $100 billion in order to persuade Byrd that the new administration was prudent. In addition, he engaged in symbolic politics by turning out lights in the White House to show that he was cost-conscious. "LBJ," it was said, stood for "Light Bulb Johnson." Won over by such gestures, Byrd freed the bill, and Congress in 1964 enacted an $11.5 billion tax cut. On signing the measure, Johnson called it "the single most important step we have taken to strengthen our economy since World War II."

The tax cut had a phenomenal effect. In 1964, GNP jumped $38 billion. Despite the reduction in rates, the government in the next year took in $7 billion more in tax receipts than it had before. By the end of 1965, a million unemployed had joined the workforce. The success left social scientists giddy. Daniel Patrick Moynihan called the outcome of the tax cut "perhaps the most impressive demonstration that has yet occurred...of the capacity of organized intelligence to forecast and direct events."

On May 22, 1964, Johnson seized upon an invitation to speak to the graduating class of the University of Michigan to elaborate his vision of the future. Since November, he had largely been the caretaker of Kennedy's program, though his predecessor had only adumbrated his thoughts about poverty. Richard Goodwin, however, crafted a commencement address for him that was almost as grandiose as LBJ's gargantuan ambitions. Speaking to ninety thousand people massed in the vast football stadium at Ann Arbor, the president declared: "We have the opportunity to move not only toward the rich society and the powerful society, but upward to the Great Society"—a place "where the city of man serves not only the needs of the body and the demands of commerce but the desire for beauty and the hunger for community,...a place where men are more concerned with the quality of their goals than the quantity of their goods." To Johnson, wrote the columnist Tom Wicker, the Great Society was "a promised land in which there will be no poverty, no illiteracy, no unemployment, no prejudice, no slums, no polluted streams, no delinquency, and few Republicans."

Fascinated by Johnson's excursion into what was called "qualitative liberalism," commentators did not always emphasize that the president had also asserted that "the Great Society...demands an end to...racial injustice, to which we are totally committed in our time" or recognize how intent he was on putting through a powerful civil rights bill that spring. He meant what he had said in his State of the Union message: "As far as the writ of Federal law will run, we must abolish not some, but all racial discrimination." When southern senators staged a filibuster that tied Congress in knots for more than eighty days, Johnson vowed to break it, no matter how much it took out of him. "We'll debate civil rights...around the clock," he told an ally. "That means all night, every night. I'll stay here all night, every night to do it myself." Again he resorted to the phone. If a congressman was not home when he called, he would tell his wife, "Now, honey, I know you won't let your husband let his president down." If a child picked up the phone, he would say, "Now you tell your daddy that the president called, and he'd be very proud to have your daddy on his side."

Not once in the past had the Senate provided the two-thirds vote required to shut down a filibuster on civil rights, but Johnson, though he badly needed the votes of Republicans and of doubtful Democrats, refused to make a single concession. "I'm not going to bend an inch," he told an aide. "Those civil rightsers are going to have to wear sneakers to keep up with me." Resolutely, he refused to abandon the provision for a Fair Employment Practices Commission (FEPC) that was anathema not only to racists but also to many businessmen. "Without those sections," he said, "there's no damn civil rights bill worth a fart in a hailstorm."

Southern senators could not puzzle out what had happened to their good friend Lyndon who during the many years he represented a former Confederate state had been their ally, but he had a ready answer. "Those Harvards think that a politician from Texas doesn't care about Negroes," he said. "In the Senate I did the best I could. But I had to be careful. I couldn't get too far ahead of my voters. Now I represent the whole country, and I have the power. I always vowed that if I ever had the power I'd make sure every Negro had the same chance as every white man. Now I have it. And I'm going to use it." He further remarked, "I'm going to be the best friend the Negro ever had. I've lived in the South a long time, and I know what hatred does to a man." Later he explained that nothing made "a man come to grips more directly with his conscience than the Presidency.... The burden of his responsibility literally opens up his soul.... So it was with me.... I would use every ounce of strength I possessed to gain justice for the black American."

Instead of hogging the limelight, Johnson turned over shepherding of the bill to Hubert Humphrey. For the Minnesota senator, who had been a champion of civil rights ever since he was mayor of Minneapolis, this was the moment he had been waiting for all his life. Johnson told him that the one thing he needed to do if he hoped to get the measure passed was to court Everett Dirksen of Illinois, the Republican leader. Dirksen was so given to mellifluous oratory that he was called "the Wizard of Ooze," and he was a man not averse to flattery. As Humphrey later explained:

I don't think a day went by when I didn't say, "Everett, we can't pass this bill without you." ...And I'd say, "This will go down in history, Everett," and that meant, of course, that he would go down in history, which interested him a great deal.

Oh, I was shameless. But...he liked hearing it all, and I didn't mind saying it.

Humphrey knew he had succeeded when Dirksen, quoting Victor Hugo, announced, "Stronger than all the armies is an idea whose time has come."

With invaluable help from Johnson, Humphrey and Dirksen formed an effective team as they batted down one crippling amendment after another. "I don't think I could even get a denunciation of the Crucifixion in the bill," a North Carolina senator complained. Southerners succeeded in only a single alteration. Representative Howard Smith, a crusty Virginian, introduced a proviso forbidding employers to discriminate on the basis of sex. He calculated that liberals would be compelled to vote for his addition, thereby creating, in his view, a monstrosity that would take the whole bill down to defeat. That scenario seemed so plausible to Representative Edith Green of Oregon, an avid feminist who had sponsored the Equal Pay Act and been a member of Kennedy's Commission on the Status of Women, that she voted against the amendment in order to save the civil rights measure. But, to the surprise of both Smith and Green, Congress adopted the ill-intended interpolation, and that action did not derail the bill.

After eighty-three days of delaying tactics, Johnson felt confident enough to risk a roll call on cloture, though it would be difficult to rally two-thirds of the Senate. So uncertain was the outcome that the senator from California, Clair Engle, who was dying of a brain tumor and could no longer speak, was taken onto the Senate floor in a wheelchair. When the crucial roll call came, on whether to vote "aye" or "nay" on cloture, Engle, unable to use his voice, slowly lifted his hand and pointed to his eye ("aye"). With the filibuster broken, the Senate then went on to approve the bill, and the House concurred.

The Civil Rights Act of 1964 ended the lengthy, malevolent reign of Jim Crow by outlawing discrimination in theaters, restaurants, hotels, soda fountains, sports arenas, and other venues and authorizing the attorney general to ban segregation in libraries, museums, and playgrounds. It stipulated that schools that discriminated would lose federal funds, and it empowered the attorney general to bring suits on behalf of parents whose children's rights were violated. The threat of a cutoff of federal

LBJ signs the Civil Rights Act of 1964 into law. Conspicuous in the group of celebrants is Rev. Martin Luther King Jr., sharing his pleasure as he looks down over
the president's left shoulder. Afterward, Johnson handed Dr. King one of the
signing pens. *Courtesy of the Lyndon B. Johnson Presidential Library, 276-10-WH64*

money proved to have much more impact on southern schools than a
decade of litigation. In addition, the law created an Equal Employment
Opportunity Commission to ensure fairness in hiring. On signing the
bill early in July, the president urged, "Let us close the springs of racial
poison."

One of the most important pieces of legislation in the country's history, the act constituted a monumental achievement that would burnish
Lyndon Johnson's reputation—but with a downside for him. At the end
of the exciting day, Press Secretary Bill Moyers called upon the president
in the White House, expecting to find him elated. Instead, he was de-
spondent. Asked why, Johnson retorted, "I think we have just delivered
the South to the Republican Party for the rest of my life and yours."
With the civil rights struggle ended, Johnson was already looking ahead
to the next challenge: the 1964 campaign, not very far off, sensing that
to remain in office he would have to overcome the loss of a number of
southern states that Democrats had long regarded as theirs.

For their presidential candidate in 1964, Republicans might have chosen New York's ebullient governor, Nelson Rockefeller, but, after a bitter contest that came to an acrid climax in San Francisco, they decided instead upon the senator from Arizona, Barry Goldwater, favorite of the far right. In picking him, delegates were expressing their disdain for party moderates—Landon, Willkie, Dewey, even Nixon—who had embraced many of the social policies of the Democrats and who had gone down to defeat. In contrast to "Me Too" Republicans, Goldwater, his admirers said, offered the country "A Choice, Not an Echo."

By nominating Goldwater, Republicans thought that they could build a coalition of South and West, alienated from the liberal, internationalist East. (Goldwater had once remarked, "Sometimes I think this country would be better off if we could just saw off the Eastern Seaboard and let it float out to sea.") They also believed that the outspoken senator would bring to the polls millions of conservatives who in the past had stayed home on Election Day. Playing on two different connotations of the word "right," GOP campaign buttons conveyed their certainty that Goldwater held the correct views and was an authentic conservative with the message, "In Your Heart, You Know He's Right."

Goldwater appealed to southern Republicans for yet another reason—his attitude on race. He was one of the few senators outside the South to vote against the civil rights bill. Furthermore, he had upheld Governor Barnett's refusal to permit James Meredith to enroll at the University of Mississippi and had said of the "jackassian" opinion in *Brown v. Board*: "I don't necessarily buy the idea that what the Supreme Court says is the law of the land."

Attractive though Goldwater was to the Republican right, he alarmed GOP moderates by saying in his acceptance address in San Francisco, "Extremism in the defense of liberty is no vice," a statement regarded as a covert endorsement of the John Birch Society, which thought that even General Eisenhower was a Soviet agent. In the ensuing campaign, the author of *The Conscience of a Conservative* won applause from his followers by holding fast to his convictions, but at the cost of antagonizing large blocs of voters. In the Tennessee Valley, he attacked the TVA, and in towns that were havens for old folks, he criticized Social Security. He also revealed extraordinary insensitivity to the dread with which Americans regarded the prospect of nuclear annihilation by saying offhandedly that he would like to "drop a low-yield atomic bomb on Chinese supply lines in Vietnam." Capitalizing on the fears aroused by the realization that, once president, the Arizona senator would have his finger on the nuclear button, Democratic slogans read, "In Your Heart, You Know He Might." Goldwater's statements put Johnson in the enviable position of being both the candidate of social change and the candidate of stability, a man who was a safer choice than his opponent.

With Goldwater self-destructing, Johnson had every reason to believe he was on the high road when a problem halfway around the world surfaced. Contrary to critics who have presented him as a power-mad imperialist bent on world domination, he much preferred to concentrate on carrying the Great Society to fulfillment. He said of the faltering South Vietnamese: "I want 'em to get off their butts and get out into those jungles and whip the hell out of some communists. And then I want 'em to leave me alone, because I've got some bigger things to do right here at home." When called upon to deal with problems abroad, he felt very unsure of himself. "Foreigners are not like the folks I'm used to," he said. One of his White House aides, the historian Eric Goldman, remarked that Johnson regarded foreign policy as "something you had, like measles, and got over with as quickly as possible." He eschewed shrill anti-Soviet rhetoric and spoke of moving from "coexistence" to "peaceful engagement" with the USSR. At one point, he even said that his goal was not to "continue the Cold War but to end it." Yet he also feared being thought of as weak. As a consequence, when early in 1964 anti-American riots broke out in Panama, he blustered noisily before reaching an agreement he could have had at the outset. He particularly did not want to give Goldwater an opportunity to depict him as indifferent to national security.

In a telephone conversation with one of his Kennedy legatees on foreign affairs in the spring of 1964, Johnson revealed his befuddlement over the quagmire he had inherited in Southeast Asia. He told McGeorge Bundy: "I just stayed awake last night thinking about this thing. . . . It looks like to me we're getting into another Korea. It just worries the hell out of me. I don't see what we can ever hope to get out of there with once we're committed. . . . It's just the biggest damn mess I ever saw. . . . What the hell is Vietnam worth to me? What is Laos worth to me? . . . It's damned easy to get in a war, but it's going to be awfully hard to ever extricate yourself if you get in." The Joint Chiefs wanted him to endorse bombing above the 17th parallel and even "deployment of U.S. Forces, as necessary, in direct action against North Vietnam." But, he informed Bundy, "we haven't got any Congress that will go with us, and we haven't got any mothers that will go with us in a war." Still, in the course of their phone talk, Johnson also said, "Now, of course, if you start running [from] the communists, they may just chase you right into your own kitchen."

On August 2, 1964, Johnson got word that North Vietnamese torpedo boats had attacked the USS *Maddox*, an American destroyer. Critics, then and later, accused Johnson of manufacturing the incident because he was intent on war, but, in fact, he took the news calmly. It "reminds me of the movies in Texas," he ruminated. "You're sitting next to a pretty girl and you have your hand on her ankle and nothing happens and you move it to her knee and nothing happens. You move it up further and you're thinking about moving a bit more and all of a sudden you get slapped. I think we got slapped." The Joint Chiefs urged him to retaliate, but he refused to order bombing in response to nothing more than a slap—one that the United States, like the guy in the darkened movie house, had provoked. The most he would approve was sending a second destroyer, the *C. Turner Joy*, to accompany the *Maddox*, and warning North Vietnam that any further assaults invited "grave consequences." It seemed that the episode would quickly pass.

Only two nights later, though, the president received a report of a second attack. It emerged subsequently that an edgy sonar operator had misread his screen. On neither night had there been any American casualty or any damage to a US vessel. But since Johnson had been told that the second assault was "probable," he concluded that his only option was to strike back. Within hours, he ordered planes to bomb torpedo bases and oil depots in North Vietnam, and shortly before midnight, he appeared on television to accuse Hanoi of "open aggression on the high seas against the United States of America." He never revealed to the American people that US naval vessels had been colluding with the South Vietnamese in clandestine raids on the North Vietnamese coast.

At Johnson's request, Congress adopted a resolution, drafted by McGeorge Bundy, authorizing the "President as Commander in Chief to take all necessary measures to repel any armed attack against forces of the United States and to prevent further aggression." The House approved it without dissent, and it raced through the Senate with only two votes cast against it. When, in later years, Johnson was challenged about a particular move against North Vietnam, he was able to point to this Tonkin Gulf Resolution. "Like grandma's nightshirt," he said, "it covered everything." Still, in his televised speech after the phantom attack on the US destroyers, he concluded: "Our response, for the present, will be limited and fitting. We Americans know, although others appear to forget, the risk of spreading conflict. We still seek no wider war."

The Tonkin Gulf fracas, which had threatened to derail LBJ's campaign, turned out instead to boost his election prospects. Eighty-five percent of the nation approved of his handling of the situation. Having deprived Goldwater of the national security issue by showing himself off as a Texas Ranger, tall in the saddle with gun at the ready, Johnson reached out to a different spectrum of the electorate by appearing as a man of peace and discretion. In September, he told a crowd in Oklahoma, "We don't want to get involved in a nation with 700 million people and get tied down in a land war in Asia," and in October he said at the University of Akron, "We are not about to send American boys nine or ten thousand miles away from home to do what Asian boys ought to be doing for themselves."

In November, Johnson amassed the biggest popular majority in American history. He captured forty-four states as well as the District of Columbia, which, as a consequence of the Twenty-third Amendment ratified in 1961, voted in a national election for the first time. With more than 60 percent of the popular vote, this candidate from the former Confederacy won all of the Northeast, all of the Midwest, all of the Great Plains, and all of the Pacific Coast, leaving Goldwater only his home state of Arizona and five Deep South states that rewarded him for his stance on civil rights. (The novelist Walker Percy wrote of the "bizarre seven-to-one margin in favor of...Goldwater" in Mississippi: "It would not have mattered if Senator Goldwater had advocated the collectivization of the plantations and open saloons in Jackson; he voted against the Civil Rights Bill and that was that.") By winning, Johnson became the first resident of a southern state to make it to the White House since Zachary Taylor in 1848—well over a century earlier. "It was a night I shall never forget," he told Doris Kearns later. "Millions upon millions of people, each one marking my name on their ballot, each one wanting me as their president.... For the first time in all my life, I truly felt loved by the American people."

Johnson approached the opening of the 89th Congress in January 1965 with high hopes and characteristic zeal. He had carried into office with him so many of his party that he had a preponderance in Congress no chief executive had enjoyed for many years: 68–32 Democratic in the Senate and a whopping 295–140 in the House. But he also was apprehensive, for he recalled vividly what had befallen FDR after his huge victory in 1936 with the ensuing Court-packing setback. He reminded a congressional liaison team meeting at the White House that he had been elected by an "overwhelming majority," then quickly added: "I just want to tell you that every day while I'm in office, I'm going to lose votes. I'm going to alienate somebody." With eerie prescience, he foresaw that something would arise, "something like the Vietnam War...where I will begin to lose all that I have now." He concluded: "So, I want you guys to get off your asses and do everything possible to get everything in my program passed...before the aura and the halo that surround me disappear. Don't waste a second. Get going *right now*." Galvanized by the president, Congress, over the next several months and, to a lesser extent, the ensuing years, rang up a record that surpassed the Wilson era's and even challenged the New Deal legislatures.

The 89th Congress, which opened in January 1965, signaled the priority it gave to Johnson's ambitious quest for a national health insurance program by designating the legislation H. R. 1 and S. 1 in its respective chambers. The American Medical Association employed two dozen lobbyists and millions of dollars to kill the bill, and Ronald Reagan warned that if it was adopted, Americans would spend their "sunset years telling our children and our children's children what it was like in America when men were free." But by exerting relentless pressure the president overcame the opposition, and, for the first time, the United States gained the health benefits long enjoyed by other nations. An entirely federal operation, "Medicare" paid for hospital stays and physician services for those sixty-five and older, irrespective of income. In later years, Congress expanded coverage, so that by the start of the twenty-first century, Medicare was costing $272 billion annually, 13 percent of the federal budget. For the elderly poor, a second program, Medicaid, funneled federal funds to the states to meet half the expense of caring for destitute families, especially children. Within a generation, Medicaid was proving indispensable in tending to the needs of some forty-six million Americans. (In 1968, Johnson supplemented these programs with a Health Manpower Act to cope with the shortage of health professionals, a National Eye Institute, and a law eliminating hazards to the handicapped in public buildings.)

Throughout 1965, Johnson created a pageant of bill-signing ceremonies, with the Harry S. Truman Library in Independence, Missouri, designated as the site for approving the Medicare bill. Before affixing his signature, he paid tribute to the former president, who had been the first to fight for national health insurance. People loved Truman, Johnson said, "not because he gave them hell—but because he gave them hope." Johnson then handed Truman the first signing pen and gave him and his wife, Bess, the first two application forms for Medicare. "I am glad to have lived this long," Truman responded.

On Palm Sunday 1965, Johnson signed the $1.3 billion Elementary and Secondary Education Act at the one-room, tin-roofed school in Johnson City, Texas, he had attended as a boy. At his side was his childhood teacher, Kate Deadrick Loney. "Come over here, Miss Katie, and sit by me, will you?" the president said. "They tell me, Miss Katie, that I recited my first lessons while sitting on your lap." Eric Goldman summed up the achievement by noting that, prodded by LBJ, Congress had enacted "a billion-dollar law, deeply affecting a fundamental institution of the nation, in a breath-taking eighty-seven days. The House approved it with no amendment that mattered; the Senate had voted it through literally without a comma changed."

Lyndon Johnson, said Hubert Humphrey, believed in education "just like some people believe in miracle drugs." In the Kennedy years, federal aid to education had foundered on a religious issue. Catholic members of Congress would not vote for grants unless parochial schools were included among the recipients, and legislators of other faiths would not approve a breach in the wall separating church and state. Under Johnson, the dilemma was resolved by giving money not to institutions but to pupils, and the president employed all of his legislative skills to drive the measure through in record time. To win over Oregon's prickly Edith

Green, who could not abide the thought of government money going into classrooms taught by nuns, no matter what the formula, he invited her to the White House. There he gave her the ultimate present: an autographed portrait of himself.

Johnson, who wanted to be known as "the Education President," followed up aid to primary and secondary schools with the Higher Education Act of 1965. He had already approved the Higher Education Facilities Act of 1963 that made possible twenty-five to thirty new community colleges every year and a large number of new graduate schools, as well as a Vocational Education Act and a Library Services Act. The 1965 law so greatly expanded college enrollment that a far higher percentage of Americans went beyond secondary school than did students in any other country on the globe. He signed the bill into law on the campus of his alma mater, Southwest Texas State University.

At the ceremony in San Marcos, Johnson reminisced about the days nearly forty years before when he had lived in a cramped room above a garage, had showered and shaved in the gym, and had held a dozen jobs to work his way through. He also recalled his first teaching job, at a Mexican school in Cotulla. "I shall never forget the faces of the boys and girls . . . and the pain of . . . knowing then that college was closed to practically every one of those children because they were too poor," he said. Now, thanks to the new legislation, "all young people" could go to college. "For them and for this entire land of ours," he declared, "it is the most important door that will ever open." Dwelling on all that had been brought about, including creation of a National Teacher Corps, the president asserted that Congress had done "more for the wonderful cause of education in America than all the previous 176 regular sessions of Congress did, put together."

Johnson approached the environment with the same grand expectations that accompanied other aspects of his program. He sought, he said, "more . . . parks, more seashores and open spaces than have been created during any period in our history." He realized these goals—and more—with the help of the outstanding secretary of the interior he inherited, Stewart Udall. In what Udall called "the third wave of conservation," following the earlier movements under TR and FDR, the government added the unprecedented sum of forty-six new areas to the national park system in many different guises: national seashores (Fire Island and

Assateague), national lakeshores (Indiana Dunes), national recreation areas (Delaware Water Gap), and an international park (Roosevelt Campobello).

Under Johnson, Congress enacted more than three hundred environmental laws, including a Wilderness Act, an Endangered Species Act, a Scenic Rivers Act, and a National Trails Act. The country also took some strides toward curbing pollution, though these measures owed less to the president than to Senator Edmund Muskie of Maine. After Johnson pointed out that "every major river is now polluted" and that Lake Erie was almost bereft of oxygen, Congress approved the Water Quality Act of 1965. When he signed the Air Quality Act of 1967, he announced, "Dirty water and black snow pour from the dismal air to...the putrid slush that waits for them below," then explained that, though he was reporting on conditions in American cities that the legislation sought to remedy, he was actually quoting from Dante's *Inferno*. "Either we stop poisoning our air," he warned, "or we become a nation in gas masks, groping our way through the dying cities and a wilderness of ghost towns." Adopted with much fanfare, these laws did not deliver as much as they promised. Johnson's commitment to the environment, though, never flagged. In the very last edict of his presidency, he added another 7.5 million acres to national parks.

LBJ's interest in the environment took an idiosyncratic turn when he put his prestige behind his wife's desire to eliminate the blight of commercial billboards along the nation's roadways. Lady Bird Johnson had already shown that she had the greatest clout of any comparable figure since Eleanor Roosevelt. In 1964, she had been the first wife to hit the campaign trail on behalf of her husband when she gave forty-seven speeches aboard a special train, the Lady Bird Special, as it toured the southern rim states from northern Virginia to Louisiana, and in the White House she had installed a personal staff of thirty in the East Wing. "You know, I love that woman and she wants that highway beauty bill," the president said to his staff. "By God, we're going to get it for her." But Johnson was no match for the highway lobby. "Lady Bird's bill," the Highway Beautification act of 1965, was largely a sham.

Johnson surprised reformers by his ardor in urging an overhaul of the country's immigration system, which in the 1920s had established quotas favoring the admission of Nordic Protestants and grossly discriminating against groups such as Polish Jews and Sicilian Catholics. Liberals who thought of Johnson as a hinterland bigot did not know him. In his first years in Congress, which he entered a year before the *Kristallnacht* terrors, he had helped a number of Jews—one of them the renowned Austrian conductor Erich Leinsdorf—find refuge in America. When the 1964 civil rights bill was enacted, Johnson phoned its chief sponsor in the House, Brooklyn's Emanuel Celler, to offer congratulations, then told him not to stop for a moment to savor his victory but to go all-out right away to push through a bill ending ethnic restrictions on entry into the United States. At the signing ceremony in the shadow of the Statue of Liberty as he looked out at Ellis Island, Johnson praised the Immigration Act of 1965 for getting rid of "a very deep and painful flaw in the fabric of American justice," adding, "The lamp of the grand old lady is brighter today—and the golden door that she guards gleams more brilliantly."

Most of the migrants to America started their new lives in cities, where, to bolster the ongoing war against poverty, Johnson focused his attention. He was especially concerned with redeeming the squalid ghettos. Congress responded with massive public housing and urban renewal appropriations, and Model Cities rent supplements. LBJ's second term also saw the creation of two cabinet-level agencies: the Department of Housing and Urban Development and the Department of Transportation. To serve as first secretary of HUD, Johnson made the daring appointment of Robert Weaver. In thus becoming the first president to name an African American to a cabinet post, Johnson set a pattern he would often follow. He chose the first black governor of the Federal Reserve Board, tapped Carl Rowan to run the US Information Agency, and selected African Americans as ambassadors. By far his most important appointment in this realm came when he chose the NAACP activist who had led the struggle for school desegregation, Thurgood Marshall, to be the first African American justice of the US Supreme Court.

When the 89th Congress first met, Johnson thought that too little time had passed since the bruising fight over the 1964 Civil Rights Act to take up Martin Luther King's latest demand—a voting rights bill—though he had no doubt about the value of such a measure. Once African American men and women could cast ballots freely, he believed, they would have Southern white politicians eating out of their hands. When, on returning from Oslo where he had been awarded the Nobel

Peace Prize, Dr. King said that the federal government needed to act to prevent local officials from denying black citizens their constitutional rights, the president responded, "Martin, you're right about that. I'm going to do it eventually, but I can't get a voting rights bill through this session of Congress."

King, however, had no intention of abiding by Johnson's timetable. Instead, he organized a protest march from Selma, Alabama, to Montgomery, where Governor George Wallace still flew the Confederate flag above the capitol. As the peaceful marchers sought to cross the Pettus Bridge over the Alabama River on their journey toward the capital of their state, they were bloodied by state troopers wielding nightsticks, cattle prods, and chains—a scene of mayhem that, projected on TV screens, shocked the country. Outrage grew even greater after, on a dark street in Selma, four white men beat to death one of Dr. King's supporters, a white Unitarian minister from Boston.

In a confrontation at the White House where he humiliated Wallace, Johnson insisted that the governor order voting rights officials in his state to register African Americans. When the governor claimed that he lacked the authority, the president, towering over him, retorted, "Don't you shit me, George Wallace!" Johnson asked him whether, at the end of his days, he wanted a big marble monument saying, "HE BUILT," or was he prepared to settle for "a little piece of scrawny pine board lying across that harsh caliche soil" reading "GEORGE WALLACE—HE HATED." When this browbeating did not suffice, Johnson, making Wallace irrelevant, federalized the Alabama National Guard and ordered marshals and military police to protect King's followers as they resumed their march.

On March 15, 1965, a week after the violence in Selma, the president addressed a joint session of Congress. "At times history and fate meet at a single time in a single place to shape a turning point in man's unending search for freedom," he declared. "So it was at Lexington and Concord. So it was a century ago at Appomattox. So it was last week in Selma, Alabama. There, long suffering men and women peacefully protested the denial of their rights as Americans. Many of them were brutally assaulted. One good man—a man of God—was killed." He continued: "Rarely in any time does an issue lay bare the secret heart of America itself. Rarely are we met with a challenge, not to our growth or abundance, or our welfare or our security, but rather to the values and the purposes and the meaning of our beloved nation. The issue of equal rights for American Negroes is such an issue. And should we defeat every enemy, and should we double our wealth and conquer the stars, and still be unequal to this issue, we will have failed as a people and as a nation."

After announcing that he would shortly submit legislation to assure every citizen the right to vote, he stated: "We ought not, and we cannot, and we must not wait another eight months before we get a bill. We have already waited 100 years and more and the time for waiting is gone.... From the window where I sit, ... I recognize that from outside this chamber is the outraged conscience of a nation, the grave concern of many nations, and the harsh judgment of history on our acts." He went on:

> Even if we pass this bill, the battle will not be over. What happened in Selma is part of a far larger movement... of American Negroes to secure for themselves the full blessings of American life.
>
> Their cause must be our cause too. Because it is not just Negroes, but really it is all of us, who must overcome the crippling legacy of bigotry and injustice.

"And"—Johnson broke off his sentence for a moment; then, raising his arms, resumed—"we *shall* overcome."

His biographer Robert Dallek has described the response by the members of Congress and the onlookers in the gallery: "A moment of stunned silence followed, as the audience absorbed the fact that the President had embraced the anthem of black protest. And then almost the entire chamber rose in unison.... Tears rolled down the cheeks of senators, congressmen, and observers in the gallery, moved by joy, elation, a sense that the big victor, for a change, was human decency, the highest standards by which the nation was supposed to live." Even the justices of the Supreme Court—all of them—leapt to their feet applauding.

The president had another thought he wanted to impart. "A century has passed, more than 100 years, since the Negro was freed," he continued. "And he is not fully free tonight.... A century has passed, more than 100 years, since equality was promised. And yet the Negro is not equal." He pointed out: "The real hero of this struggle is the American

Negro. His actions and protests, his courage to risk safety and even to risk his life, have awakened the conscience of this nation.... And who among us can say that we would have made the same progress were it not for his persistent bravery, and his faith in American democracy?" Watching on television, Martin Luther King wept.

Johnson concluded on a personal note. Alluding once again to his experience at the Mexican American school in Cotulla, Texas, he said:

> My students... often came to class without breakfast, hungry.... They never seemed to know why people disliked them. But they knew it was so, because I saw it in their eyes. I often walked home late in the afternoon, after the classes were finished, wishing there was more that I could do....
>
> I never thought then, in 1928, that I would be standing here in 1965. It never occurred to me in my fondest dreams that I might have the chance to help the sons and daughters of those students and to help people like them all over the country.

Looking into the eyes of the assembled members of Congress and pointing a finger at them, he ended: "But now I do have that chance—and I'll let you in on a secret—I mean to use it."

As he left the podium, he said to Congressman Celler, chair of the House Judiciary Committee, "Manny, I want you to start hearings tonight." Over the next months, Johnson fought doggedly for the bill. The militant head of the Congress of Racial Equality, James Farmer, reported that Johnson was "cracking the whip. He was cajoling, he was threatening,...whatever tactic was required with that certain individual, he was using." In May, by the narrow margin of three votes, the Senate invoked cloture, and several weeks later the House fell in line. The Voting Rights Act of 1965 established clear criteria for suffrage and, in case of continuing discrimination, authorized the appointment of federal registrars to enroll applicants. After a celebratory ceremony in the Capitol Rotunda, the president signed the bill into law in the room in the capitol where Abraham Lincoln had liberated slaves coerced into military service by the Confederacy. Over the next three years, the proportion of African Americans registered to vote in Mississippi jumped spectacularly—from 6.7 percent to 59.8 percent.

Johnson carried his determination to achieve racial equality a big leap forward by coming out in favor of affirmative action. Speaking to the graduating class at Howard University, he stated, "You do not take a person who, for years, has been hobbled by chains and...bring him up to the starting line...and still believe that you have been completely fair." It was "not enough," he said, "to open the gates of opportunity. All our citizens must have the ability to walk through those gates." America, he concluded, must insist upon equality not in "theory" but in "result."

Even in his final year—in the hostile atmosphere of 1968, when enthusiasm for civil rights had been badly eroded—Johnson still soldiered on by persuading Congress to enact a fair housing bill that outlawed discrimination in sales or rentals of most of the nation's dwellings. The statute did not have the impact that he hoped for because the real estate industry was defiant, and much of the country was unwilling to accept integrated neighborhoods. But it was a tribute to the president's legislative leadership nonetheless. Johnson's top domestic aide, Joseph Califano, later recalled that the president's advocacy of the bill had "prompted some of the most vicious mail LBJ received on any subject." Califano himself, because of his support of open housing, had received a death threat. Yet, at a time when even many northern Democrats were prepared to shelve the measure, Johnson succeeded in getting it passed.

Not even this cornucopia of enactments—from Medicare to civil rights legislation—satiated Johnson. "He adopts programs," said Califano, "the way a child eats chocolate-chip cookies." In September 1965 in the Rose Garden of the White House, with Agnes de Mille, Katherine Anne Porter, and Ben Shahn looking on, the president signed a bill to create a National Foundation on the Arts and Humanities, and in November 1967, he put his name to the Public Broadcasting Act, which fostered the creation of educational television and radio stations across the land. To protect consumers, he drove through a Fair Packaging and Labeling Act, as well as a Truth-in-Lending Act, and when he signed a Wholesome Meat Act updating the law of 1906, he invited the eighty-nine-year-old Upton Sinclair, whose novel *The Jungle* had sparked the initial reform, to join him. Noting that "a raging epidemic of highway death...has killed more of our youth than all...diseases combined," he put his name to a Highway Safety Act and a National Traffic and Motor Vehicle Safety Act— responses to the alarm aroused by Ralph Nader's *Unsafe at Any Speed*.

Johnson also set out to amend the Constitution to provide for the orderly transfer of power in case of presidential disability. The Twenty-fifth Amendment, ratified in 1967, stipulated that when a president could no longer carry out his duties, the vice president assumed his powers, though not title of office, until the president signaled he was ready to return. If a vice president and a majority of the "principal officers of the executive branch" challenged the decision of the president to retake his powers, Congress was authorized to resolve the dispute. When the vice president succeeded to the office of president of the United States, he might, with the consent of Congress, appoint a vice president to fill the vacancy he had created.

Before his tenure ended, Johnson prodded Congress to put scores of additional proposals in the statute books: a Coal Mine Safety Act, a Handicapped Children's Early Education Assistance Act, a freedom of information law, and legislation to promote child nutrition, as well as measures to spend a billion dollars in impoverished Appalachia and to ban the interstate shipment of handguns. After appointing an unprecedented number of women to key posts in his administration, he issued an executive order forbidding gender discrimination in the federal government. And when, in his final year, he heard a cabinet official talk about prospects for another wave of reform in the future, he said, "I got so excited about it, . . . I had to take sleeping pills at night."

This torrent of laws cascaded throughout LBJ's second term, but especially during 1965, when Congress, wrote a Washington journalist, "brought to a harvest a generation's backlog of ideas and social legislation." Speaker John McCormack said, "It is the Congress of accomplished hopes. It is the Congress of realized dreams." The "fabulous 89th Congress" carried to fruition all of the uncompleted agenda of the New Deal and the Fair Deal. Keenly aware that the 89th was being compared to the legislature of the First Hundred Days of 1933, Johnson, who wanted to be thought of as the greatest president ever, greater even than his mentor FDR, asserted, "This session of Congress has enacted more major legislation, met more national needs, disposed of more national issues than any other session of this century or last."

In 1965, surveying what Johnson had achieved, the political scientist James MacGregor Burns wrote: "The Presidency today is at the peak of its prestige. Journalists describe it as the toughest job on earth, the presiding office of the free world, the linchpin of the Western alliance, America's greatest contribution to the art of self-government." He further contended: "Presidential government, far from being a threat to American democracy, has become the major single institution sustaining it—a bulwark for individual liberty, an agency of popular representation, and a magnet for political action and leadership." Yet at the very moment of his greatest triumph, Johnson made a fateful decision on foreign policy that foredoomed his presidency and cost him the honored place in history that he so coveted.

Blinkered by hindsight, numbers of writers have seen the Gulf of Tonkin flare-up as the first calculated step toward large-scale involvement in Southeast Asia, but Johnson viewed the episode more circumspectly. In May 1964, he had told Adlai Stevenson, "I shudder to get too deeply involved there." When General Maxwell Taylor and the Joint Chiefs prodded Johnson to continue bombing North Vietnam, he turned them down. In mid-September, on learning of another attack on US destroyers, he resisted treating it as a crisis, and when McNamara recommended continuing patrols in the Gulf of Tonkin, he responded: "We won't go ahead with it, Bob. Let's put it on the shelf." Again in November after the Viet Cong (the Communist guerrilla force in South Vietnam) assaulted a US air base at Bien Hoa, destroying all but three of its thirty planes and inflicting more than eighty casualties, the Joint Chiefs urged retaliation, but Johnson held off. Even after a Christmas Eve raid in Saigon targeted a billet of American officers, he refused to strike back.

As early as September 1964, however, George Ball was noting, "An unmistakable smell of escalation is in the air." The Kennedy administration hawks Johnson had inherited kept pushing him to further action. Bundy thought the president needed to consider the "more drastic possibility which no one is discussing" of using "substantial U.S. armed forces in operations against the Viet Cong.... Before we let this country go, we should have a hard look at this grim alternative, and I do not at all think that it is a repetition of Korea." When Johnson explored policy with top aides in September, every one told him that he could not even contemplate withdrawing from Vietnam.

Johnson himself had long since swallowed the domino theory. As vice president, he had told Kennedy, "If we don't stop the Reds in South

Vietnam, tomorrow they will be in Hawaii, and next week they will be in San Francisco." He also believed that his predecessors had made commitments to Saigon that he must honor, and he feared that if he pulled out, the electorate would accuse the Democrats of betrayal and take vengeance. Less than a week after entering the White House, he said that he refused to be "the president who saw Southeast Asia go the way China went." He was "simply not...going to be the man who can't hold the Alamo," an official explained. "I knew from the start," Johnson later confided to Doris Kearns, "that I was bound to be crucified either way I moved. If I left the woman I really loved—the Great Society—in order to get involved with that bitch of a war on the other side of the world, then I would lose everything at home....All my dreams to provide education and medical care to the browns and the blacks and the lame and the poor. But if I let...the Communists take over South Vietnam,...there would follow in this country...a mean and destructive debate that would shatter my presidency...and damage our democracy." (In fact, pollsters found that 63 percent of the nation in 1964 was paying no or little heed to Southeast Asia; 25 percent was not aware that anything at all was going on.)

In February 1965, the Viet Cong ratcheted up the conflict by launching an attack on the US base at Pleiku in the highlands that killed several American "advisers" and wounded many more. Bundy, who was in South Vietnam to gather information for the president, promptly phoned him to urge retaliation, and Johnson, already primed for escalation, said he was not going to let any "raggedy-ass little fourth-rate country" push him around. The president used the occasion to authorize "graduated" bombing of the North. "We have kept our gun over the mantle and our shells in the cupboard for a long time now, and what was the result," he said. "I can't ask our American soldiers out there to continue to fight with one hand tied behind their backs." In the *New York Times*, James Reston wrote: "It is time to call a spade a bloody shovel. This country is in an undeclared and unexplained war in Vietnam."

Even after Pleiku, Johnson had a chance to step back. Telegrams to the White House ran nearly 12–1 against bombing North Vietnam. George Ball repeated the warnings he had given Kennedy; Senate Majority Leader Mike Mansfield urged Johnson to enter into negotiations; and, unexpectedly, the CIA expressed dismay at the likely course of events if the president persisted. The wisest counsel came from Hubert Humphrey, who, finding the nation "worried and confused," foresaw that if America became "embroiled deeper in fighting in the next six months," the Great Society and all "socially humane and constructive policies" would be in jeopardy. Given the great proportions of Johnson's victory in 1964, he said, the president could afford to stand up to the hawks.

Johnson, however, was becoming increasingly feisty. In March, he signed off on Operation Rolling Thunder for systematic bombing of the North to "send a message to Ho Chi Minh" and then deployed two battalions of marines at Da Nang. By May, Reston, observing a "startling change" in the focus of the government from the Great Society to war in Asia, was reporting that Johnson was behaving like an "impulsive giant,...fitful and unpredictable." Still, the president harbored doubts. "A man can fight if he can see daylight down the road somewhere," he told Senator Richard Russell. "But there ain't no daylight in Vietnam. There's not a bit." To be sure that he was on the right track, he called together "the Wise Men": the architects of the Cold War through the last three administrations. "I blew my top," Dean Acheson reported to Truman, "& told him...that he had no choice except to press on."

On July 20, 1965, McNamara sent a memorandum to the White House that, once accepted, locked Johnson into an irreversible course. "The situation in South Vietnam," McNamara declared, "is worse than a year ago (when it was worse than the year before that)." The South Vietnamese army was being so badly beaten that it was unlikely that the Saigon government could last a year, he advised. Nor did bombing the North seem to be having any effect. Consequently, the president had three options. One was "cut our losses and withdraw," a course that would be "humiliating...and very damaging to our future effectiveness on the world scene." The second was to "continue at about the present level," but that policy would merely postpone a decision that would better be taken right away.

Those considerations led McNamara to recommend a third course: "expand promptly and substantially the U.S. pressure," though that implied a "considerable cost in casualties." The increase of "U.S. military pressure," he stated, should come in stages, but in large segments, so that during the first half of 1966, American forces would total the staggering figure of six hundred thousand. Only five advisers, one of them McGeorge Bundy, saw this memo, and all five approved it. No one in Congress, not even the chair of the Senate Foreign Relations Committee, knew about it. While signing on to McNamara's third option, Johnson repeatedly reined in the Joint Chiefs, who wanted far greater engagement. LBJ's course invited disaster. "The president committed the United States to fight a limited war against an enemy totally committed to revolutionary war," the political scientist Larry Berman has written. "He had weighed all the costs and then used his great talents to forge a marginal consensus—enough to get the United States into war, but insufficient for war termination."

That summer, Johnson greatly enlarged US combat forces in Vietnam while deliberately deceiving the American people about what he was doing. He also hid the truth that US troops had been authorized to go on the offensive. He had earlier signed a National Security Action Memorandum stating that the sudden sharp increase in ground troops should be carried out in a way to leave the impression that they were "gradual and wholly consistent with existing policy." As the historian David Wise has observed, the document was "not designed to fool Hanoi or the Viet Cong, who would find out quickly enough who was shooting at them; it was designed to conceal the facts from the American electorate."

Johnson had already left journalists the impression that he hailed from Credibility Gap by the palpably false explanations he had offered for why, a short time before, he had sent marines and an airborne division into the Dominican Republic. He claimed that he was doing so in order to protect the lives of US citizens when it was clear that he was intervening because he feared that an uprising led by Juan Bosch against the right-wing government would turn the Caribbean country into a "second Cuba." Johnson confided, "We don't propose to sit here in our rocking chair with our hands folded and let the Communists set up any government in the Western Hemisphere." Not a Communist, Bosch, who was a distinguished literary figure, had been the Dominicans' freely elected president until he was ousted by a military coup, but Johnson kept US forces there until a follower of the former dictator, Rafael Trujillo, was placed in power. The occupation, which drew such a bad press, went on month after month at the same time that the president was trudging into quicksand in Vietnam.

In his State of the Union address of January 1966, Johnson hardened his commitment to the war in Southeast Asia. "We could leave, abandoning

South Vietnam to its attackers and to certain conquest, or we could stay and fight beside the people of South Vietnam," he said. "We stayed." He then pledged: "We will give our fighting men what they must have: every gun and every dollar...whatever the cost...and let me be absolutely clear: The days may become months, and the months may become years, but we will stay as long as aggression commands us to battle." In June, he ordered bombs dropped on fuel storage depots close to the heavily populated cities of Hanoi and Haiphong. Johnson, who micromanaged the war, insisted on picking out each of the targets of the raids across the border. "They can't even bomb an outhouse without my approval," he boasted.

No matter how grim the reports from the Asian jungles, Johnson kept looking for "the light at the end of the tunnel" that would be the first indication of a successful outcome. Defeat was unthinkable. As the journalist Tom Wicker later asked: "How could Lyndon Johnson...doubt that his superbly equipped forces, representing all the technological and industrial genius of America, organized by the incomparable McNamara with his modern administrator's skills, trained and led by...impressive generals and admirals,...that this juggernaut could deal with a few ill-clad guerrillas,...who had to...bring in supplies on bicycles and the backs of old women?"

Yet while agreeing once again to augment US troop strength in Vietnam, Johnson could not still doubts that continued to assail him. "When we add divisions, can't the enemy add divisions?" he asked General Westmoreland. "If so, where does it all end?" He sought to place more of the burden of combat on the South Vietnamese, but Westmoreland told him that he could not rely on native forces and needed more, not fewer, US soldiers. Asked at a meeting in Guam in March 1967 how much time would be required to win the war, Westmoreland replied, "As things now stand, it may take ten years." Johnson blanched.

———

As the war dragged on through 1966 and all of 1967, it took its toll on Johnson. He was convulsed with tears as he signed letters of condolence to the families of young soldiers whose lives had been snuffed out on his watch, and he wakened before dawn to run his eyes over the names on the latest casualty lists. On some nights, he abandoned the White House for a neighborhood Catholic church where he prayed with monks. By 1967, Paul Conkin has written, "he had aged ten years in only two and was now visibly an old man, shaken, ineffective.... Lady Bird had noted in her diary that the glory was now all over, that no joy remained in the White House, that Johnson's presidency was already an endurance contest." In one diary entry, she wrote, "I found myself pushing against the wall of gloom," and in another she said of her husband, "His life sounded more and more like the tribulations of Job."

Despite his anguish, Johnson ceaselessly expanded the war. Granted, neither he nor McNamara would agree to give the military command in Saigon as many additional soldiers as it claimed were required, and the Pentagon came to view the secretary of defense as an adversary. But the president acquiesced to so many demands that the sixteen thousand military advisers at the start of his second term in 1965 multiplied to more than half a million troops. Since most were draftees on one-year tours of duty, more than two million Americans served in Vietnam. And as the casualty lists lengthened, fury at Johnson became almost boundless.

By the tens of thousands in Washington and in other cities, marchers chanted, "Hey, hey, LBJ, how many kids did you kill today?" Since only months before he had pledged that American boys would not be sent to distant battlefields, his dispatch of huge numbers to Asia, from which many would never return, bred bitter distrust that he could never overcome. The "black power" head of SNCC, H. Rap Brown, called him "a white honky," an "outlaw from Texas," and a "mad wild dog." A cover story in a July 1967 issue of *Newsweek* asserted that "not since the 1930s has an American president been subjected to such scurrilous attack as has Lyndon Johnson." Furthermore, Johnson was the first commander in chief who had to cope with "a living room war," where disturbing scenes of violence appeared each night on TV screens. Both doves and hawks assailed him. Senator Fulbright charged that "the Great Society has become a sick society," while right-wingers snarled at him for not carrying on vigorously enough.

Johnson suffered blow after blow to his pride and to his public standing. In January 1967, he was reduced to scheduling his State of the Union address for a night that would not conflict with the sitcoms *Gomer Pyle* or *Petticoat Junction*. (Another popular weekly television

The president shows his scar. This clever 1966 caricature by David Levine takes off from an episode when, at a press conference, LBJ raised his shirt to expose evidence of a recent operation—an action critics thought unseemly behavior by "the Abdominal Showman." Levine reimagines that moment but sketches the scar in the shape of Vietnam, the jagged wound from which Johnson never recovered. *Walter Daran/Time & Life Pictures/Getty Images*

comedy shocked its viewers by featuring a rendition of Pete Seeger's "Waist Deep in the Big Muddy" with the refrain "And the big fool says to push on"; the big fool, everyone understood, was the president of the United States.) A poll revealed that only 23 percent of the country approved of his performance—a new low. Increasingly, Johnson, who had always loved to mingle and "press the flesh," became imprisoned in the White House. He no longer dared appear in crowds but had to confine himself to turning up at well-secured military bases.

The president's headstrong pursuit of victory in Vietnam also spelled trouble for his economic program. At first, he tried to disguise the way that the combination of guns and butter was overheating the economy by engaging in deception. At one point, he even dared to say that the budget would "actually show a surplus." But by 1967, he was compelled to recognize both rising inflation and growing deficits. To curb them, he asked Congress for a temporary surtax, but months went by before he could get the legislation he sought, and then only if he agreed to slash domestic spending. He managed to keep the cuts few enough to preserve most of the Great Society, but any hope of providing adequate funding for the war on poverty was gone.

Economic woes and clamorous antiwar rallies came at the same time that a series of long hot summers seared by bloody race riots beset Johnson, in keeping with the African American writer James Baldwin's warning that "if we do not dare everything, the fulfillment of that prophecy, recreated from the Bible in song by a slave, is upon us: 'God gave Noah the rainbow sign, no more water, the fire next time.'" Five days after the Voting Rights Act of 1965 was signed, the black neighborhood of Watts in Los Angeles erupted in violence that left thirty-four dead and hundreds of homes and stores burned and looted. In 1967, a riot in Newark marked the start of the worst racial violence in American history. An outbreak in Detroit the following week that brought forty-three deaths led Johnson to send federal troops to quell the disorder. He appointed a National Advisory Commission on Civil Disorders headed by Governor Otto Kerner of Illinois to seek out the causes of the mayhem, but the report of the Kerner Commission riled him because he thought it gave him too little credit for his actions on behalf of civil rights and because it recommended massive federal spending at a time when the Vietnam War was emptying the till.

This concatenation of events stirred up a revolt against Johnson within his own party. On the floor of the Senate, LBJ's longtime menace Robert Kennedy, characterizing the war as a "horror," called attention to the alienation of youth from American institutions in a decade when political disaffection merged with the counter culture. Observing that young people were turning from public commitment to "lives of disengagement and despair," he said, "We seem to fulfill the vision of Yeats":

> Things fall apart, the center cannot hold;
> Mere anarchy is loosed upon the world.

Senator Eugene McCarthy of Minnesota went even further. On November 30, 1967, he announced that he was launching a campaign to wrest the Democratic presidential nomination from Lyndon Johnson by entering the New Hampshire primary.

The louder the dissent, the more angrily Johnson shook his fist at protesters. Calling into question the manliness of his critics, he dismissed them as "nervous Nellies" who would "turn on their leaders and on their country and on their own fighting men," and he ordered the FBI to ferret out the "Communists" who were "behind the disturbances" against the war and to infiltrate the peace movement in order to sabotage it. In addition, he assigned the CIA to spy on demonstrators, though the agency's charter forbade it to engage in domestic surveillance. America was divided, he declared, between "patriotic people" and "cut-and-run people." He attributed reports in the press of reverses in Southeast Asia to the hostility of prejudiced journalists. Saying that columnists and reporters made him feel "like a hound bitch in heat in the country," he explained, "If you run, they chew your tail off. If you stand still, they slip it to you."

No longer willing to tolerate even mild questioning from his advisers, Johnson, who had earlier nursed his own reservations about the war, found Robert McNamara's second thoughts especially exasperating. Long regarded as the foremost hawk in the administration, the secretary of defense had so identified himself with the intervention in Southeast Asia that the conflict was called "McNamara's War." But on the eve of another gathering of the Wise Men at the end of October 1967, he handed Johnson a memorandum stating, "Continuation of our present course of action in Southeast Asia would be dangerous, costly in lives, and unsatisfactory to the American people." Given the prospect of a doubling of casualties in 1968 with concomitant loss of support for the war, he urged Johnson to put a lid on the commitment of US ground forces, stop bombing the North, and enter discussions with Hanoi with modest expectations. The recognition that the United States was never going to win the war that he had advocated for so long shook the defense secretary to the depths of his being. At the point that he came to this realization, McNamara, eyes glazed, broke into tears and wailed with grief. "Perhaps everything I . . . have tried to do since 1961," he said, "has been a failure." Johnson never responded to the memorandum in which McNamara had struggled so hard to give an honest assessment. Before a month was out, the president announced that his secretary of defense would be leaving the administration shortly to head the World Bank. A generation later, McNamara said that he still was not sure "whether I quit or was fired."

At a 1968 cabinet meeting, Secretary of State Dean Rusk, President Johnson, and Secretary of Defense Robert McNamara contemplate grim reports from Southeast Asia. *Courtesy of the Lyndon B. Johnson Presidential Library, A5593-25*

Johnson had called the Wise Men together not to seek their counsel but to get their approbation. To make that outcome certain, he withheld any adverse information from them. Predictably, save for George Ball, they obliged him with assurances that he was making the correct decisions. (As the meeting broke up, though, Ball said to Acheson and other establishment figures, "I've been watching across the table. You're like a flock of old buzzards sitting on a fence, sending the young men off to be killed. You ought to be ashamed of yourselves.")

The president narrowed his circle to a very few aides, men he could count on to tell him only what he was willing to hear. Giving a cold shoulder to any adviser who raised an objection, he insisted on total fealty. No one proved to be more sycophantic than Hubert Humphrey. Though heartsick over a war that, he confided to a friend, resulted in "murdering civilians by the thousands and our boys ... dying in rotten jungles," the vice president cabled Johnson from Vietnam, where he was on a brief inspection tour: "We are winning—steady progress is everywhere evident.... More than ever, I am convinced that what we are doing here is right and that we have no choice but to persevere and see it through to success."

As the new year of 1968 opened, Johnson had not a doubt that he was on the right track. Peace groups might rail at him for not heeding the will of the people, but he knew that polls regularly reported that hawks outnumbered doves. The percentage of Americans demanding "total military victory" had actually increased markedly, and the country opposed a halt in the bombing as a step toward peace by 4 to 1. The president was fortified, too, by a series of rulings by high federal tribunals turning aside challenges to his authority to wage war. Gene McCarthy was just a minor irritation. The first polls gave the senator only 8 percent of the ballots in the forthcoming New Hampshire primary, and nationally syndicated columnists predicted "a defeat close to annihilation." Best of all, Johnson believed, the war was going well. On January 17, he pulled together the good news that he could relay to the American people. "The enemy has been defeated in battle after battle," he reported, and "the number of South Vietnamese living in areas under government protection tonight has grown by more than a million since January of last year."

On January 30, 1968, an hour past midnight, seventy thousand Viet Cong and North Vietnamese soldiers launched an offensive that destroyed all of Lyndon Johnson's expectations and effectually put an end to his presidency. Taking advantage of the popular Tet holiday that saw most of South Vietnamese troops on leave, the attackers struck thirty-six of forty-four provincial capitals, all but one of the biggest cities, and scores of district capitals and hamlets. After a time, the White House claimed that enemy forces had sustained a very costly defeat, which, in a sense, they had, for they failed to win a single capital and suffered heavy losses. They also disgraced themselves by devastating the beautiful city of Hue, leaving it a "shattered, stinking hulk," and massacring many of its citizens. But in the course of their operations they blasted a hole in the wall of the US embassy in Saigon and for several hours occupied the compound of this bastion that had been said to be "impregnable."

Upon learning of the invasion of the embassy compound, political leaders and publicists of a range of persuasions found that they could no longer believe that the bloodshed would soon end or that Johnson's reports of progress were credible. At a campaign rally in Manchester,

New Hampshire, Gene McCarthy said: "Only a few months ago we were told sixty-five percent of the population was secure. Now we know that even the American Embassy is not secure." The country's most prominent periodicals and newspapers, including the *Wall Street Journal*, called for a change of course in Southeast Asia. The atmosphere in the White House, one of Johnson's advisers stated, was like that after the Union defeat at the first battle of Bull Run. "This is crazy," Califano said to one of the president's longest-serving advisers. "It really is all over, isn't it?" The aide replied, "You bet it is."

The alarming bulletins from Saigon came at the worst possible moment for Johnson—just one week after North Korean patrol boats captured the USS *Pueblo*, an American intelligence-gathering vessel in the Sea of Japan, and imprisoned its eighty-three-man crew. Johnson vented his outrage and mobilized navy and air force reserves, but, eschewing war, he was helpless. At a time when the United States, for all its might, was unable to prevail over North Vietnam, another small country underscored the limitations of the United States and of the president. It required almost all of 1968 to gain release of the officers and sailors. To do so, the American government had to apologize, and the *Pueblo* was not returned. During this difficult period, Johnson later said, he felt that he "was living in a continuous nightmare." Humbled by two small Asian nations within a week, Johnson seemed to be a Gulliver bound to earth by scoffing Lilliputians.

A cable from General Westmoreland may have disturbed Johnson more than either the Tet offensive or the *Pueblo* incident. The general, as well as the chairman of the Joint Chiefs of Staff, told Johnson that they needed 206,000 more troops, and another general, seeing 1968 as "a critical year in the war," declared, "The losses will be high in men." McNamara, on his last day in office, challenged the notion that a huge increase in soldiers would turn the tide. Realizing that he was at a great divide, Johnson created a task force headed by McNamara's successor, Clark Clifford, who, in turn, called in the former secretary of state Dean Acheson. After hearing of the new demands, Acheson, long one of the most bellicose advisers, broke with the Pentagon. "With all due respect, Mr. President," he said, "the Joint Chiefs of Staff don't know what they're talking about." Clifford, too, had been a hawk, but at a meeting at the White House on March 4, he said: "We seem to have gotten caught in a sinkhole. We put in more, they match it. . . . I see more and more fighting with more and more casualties on the US side, and no end in sight."

While these discussions were going on, the New Hampshire primary contest was heating up, with Eugene McCarthy inspiriting antiwar college student volunteers to canvass the state. "What is happening," reported a Washington columnist, "is that violet-eyed damsels from Smith are pinning McCarthy buttons on tattooed mill-workers, and Ph.D.s from Cornell, shaven and shorn for world peace, are deferentially bowing to middle-aged Manchester housewives and importuning them to consider a change of Commander in Chief." When New Hampshire voters went to the polls on March 12, they astounded forecasters by giving McCarthy 42.4 percent of their ballots. Commentators largely overlooked the reality that Johnson, with 49.5 percent, won the contest, though his name did not appear on the ballot and had to be written in, and that a large proportion of McCarthy's votes came from hawks who thought the president was not waging war aggressively enough. Nonetheless, the sizeable vote that McCarthy ran up constituted a stunning rebuke to an incumbent from a member of his own party. Four days later, Johnson got considerably more troubling news: Robert Kennedy announced that he was entering the race against LBJ "to end the bloodshed in Vietnam and in our cities."

Johnson sustained yet another blow when he reconvened the Wise Men on March 25 and 26. "Mr. President, there has been a very significant shift in most of our positions since we last met," McGeorge Bundy told him. Though some of the members, including Generals Bradley and Taylor and Justice Abe Fortas, favored holding fast, a large number, among them Acheson, Henry Cabot Lodge Jr., and Cyrus Vance, no longer did. "A great many people—even very determined and loyal people—have begun to think that Vietnam really is a bottomless pit," Bundy explained.

In the final week of March, Johnson had to determine what he was going to tell the American people in a television address he had long planned to deliver on March 31. He was inclined to brazen it out. As late as March 20, he had ordered a draftsman to "get 'peace' out of the speech." Walt Rostow, who had succeeded Bundy as national security adviser, pressed him to ignore the Wise Men, order a full call-up of reserves, and rouse the country behind the war. Infuriated by the remarks of the Wise Men, the president said, "The establishment bastards have bailed out." Attributing their turnaround to faulty briefings, he asked, "Who poisoned the well?"

As he contemplated how to instruct his speechwriters, though, he received discouraging political intelligence. In Wisconsin, where thousands of antiwar students from the university in Madison (Dane County) were determined to defeat him, pollsters told him that he would be crushed by McCarthy in the April 2 primary. "We sent a man into Dane County to recruit for Johnson," one of his workers reported, "and all we've heard from him since is a few faint beeps, like the last radio signals from the beach of the Bay of Pigs." Yet, contrary to the subsequent claims of the peace movement, political considerations did not determine Johnson's course. With his control of party machinery, the president figured that he would prevail over any challenger to his renomination. In the last week of March, the *New York Times* estimated that he would win two-thirds of the delegates to the national convention.

Johnson had far greater concern about whether his health would hold up through another term. Having suffered a heart attack at a worrisomely young age, he feared for his life. In 1967 he had ordered an actuarial estimation of his life expectancy, which had concluded (accurately as it turned out) that he would not live beyond sixty-five. In mid-March, Lady Bird Johnson, who for some months had wanted him to step down to save himself, made note in her diary of "one of those terrific, pummeling White House days that can stretch and grind and use you." When on March 26 the journalist Theodore White, who had written best sellers on national campaigns, visited the White House, he was "shocked" by the president's appearance. White reported:

> When I had last spoken to him, during the exuberant campaign of 1964, Lyndon Johnson had bestrode the nation's politics like a bronco-buster. Now he seemed exhausted. His eyes, behind the gold-rimmed eyeglasses, were not only nested in lines and wrinkles, but pouched in sockets blue with a permanent weariness.... The contour of his large body reflected his exhaustion as he slouched in a large rocking chair, his feet lifting to a carpet-covered footstool, his slate-blue suit rumpled, his hand jingling something in the left pocket, nor did he ever stir to those famous gestures that accompany a classic Johnson performance.

On Sunday night, March 31, millions of Americans turned on their television sets to watch what was billed as an important address by the president. Johnson had never been able to project his pungent personality on the TV screen, and on this occasion he appeared even grayer and more solemn as he delineated policy toward Vietnam. He pledged to take "the first step to deescalate the conflict" by "reducing—substantially reducing—the present level of hostilities" and doing so unilaterally without requiring any concession from Hanoi. In particular, he announced an end to bombing north of the 19th parallel. Almost no one anticipated the stunning peroration to the speech. Johnson concluded: "With our hopes and the world's hopes for peace in the balance every day, I do not believe that I should devote an hour or a day of my time to any personal partisan causes or to any duties other than the awesome duties of this office—the presidency of your country. Accordingly, I shall not seek, and I will not accept, the nomination of my party for another term as your President." In effect, the president of the United States had abdicated.

Johnson's address has often been seen as a turning point in the Vietnam War when, in fact, it changed nothing. Soon after the president's announcement, Hanoi said it was ready for peace talks, but they dragged on month after month to no purpose. In truth, the antagonists had nothing to negotiate. The United States wanted to retain South Vietnam as an independent nation, and Ho Chi Minh would settle for nothing less than a unified country under Communist rule. Nor did the intensity of the fighting slacken. Forbidden to operate above the 19th parallel, the US Air Force accelerated its bombing of the area of North Vietnam below that line. American planes dropped more bombs on that country than they had in all of the Pacific theater in World War II. And more US soldiers died during 1968 than in any other year of the war.

Despite the conciliatory tone of his March 31 speech, the president continued to be hard-nosed. After Clifford, Harriman, and Vance advised him to agree to a full bombing halt, he dismissed their counsel as "mush" and charged that "the enemy is using my own people as dupes." When Clifford told him that there was no way that bombing raids could prevent North Vietnam from delivering arms to the Viet Cong, that the Saigon government had to be dragged to the negotiating table in Paris, and that American engagement in the fighting should be reduced, Johnson replied, "I don't agree with a word that you have said."

Johnson viewed the 1968 presidential contest from the same vantage point. Though he had withdrawn from contention, he wanted to make sure that his successor maintained his policies toward Vietnam without flinching. For that reason, he favored a Republican, Nelson Rockefeller, until it became clear that New York's governor would not be chosen. No Democrat met his approval, though he took some satisfaction in knowing that there was not a formidable antiwar candidate in his own party. Eugene McCarthy had lost momentum, and Robert Kennedy had been murdered minutes after winning the California primary. Despite his disavowal, Johnson contemplated reentering the race. He sent an agent to the Democratic National Convention to talk to party leaders about organizing a movement to draft him for another term. "No way," his envoy was told.

Numbers of Democrats refused to go along, too, when he resolved to fill the vacancy created in June 1968 by the retirement of Earl Warren by appointing Abe Fortas, who was his close friend (critics used the term "crony"), as chief justice. The Senate would not hear of it. Quite apart from the objections of conservatives to Fortas's liberal views, senators from both parties thought that Fortas's behavior while a Supreme Court justice in giving political advice to the president was improper and that a huge speaking fee he had received raised ethical questions. So fierce was the opposition that Fortas asked Johnson to withdraw his name. The outcome marked the first time that a nomination of a chief justice had been blocked since 1795.

The president demonstrated, however, that he still had plenty of clout by getting the stormy Democratic convention in Chicago to shape the party platform to his liking. The presumptive presidential nominee, Hubert Humphrey, who knew he would have a hard time winning in November unless he could lure back disaffected antiwar Democrats, crafted a plank that made a slight concession to them, only to have Johnson quash it. When Humphrey protested that the document had been approved by LBJ's advisers, the president told him harshly, "It hasn't been cleared with *me*." In its place, the platform committee voted 2–1 in favor of an all-out endorsement of the president's policies toward Vietnam.

Johnson put Humphrey in an impossible position. If the vice president moved in the slightest degree away from LBJ's stance, party regulars would regard him as disloyal and Johnson would undermine him. But if he did not offer some path toward ending the bloodletting in Vietnam, he would forfeit any hope of placating the peace element that was drowning out his speeches with shrieks of "Dump the Hump." Johnson, however, cut him no slack. To be sure that Humphrey did not stray, he ordered the FBI to tap the vice president's phone. Despite, or perhaps because of, the service Humphrey had rendered him, Johnson held him in contempt. Humphrey, he said, was "all heart and no balls."

After weeks of waffling, Humphrey decided to give a speech in Salt Lake City that slightly modified Johnson's posture. Though he couched the statement with so many qualifiers that George Ball accused him of "pettifogging," the press treated it as a significant departure, and antiwar dissenters began to drift back to the Democrats. If the president had hit the campaign trail for him and raised cash for a candidate who was broke, Humphrey might well have overtaken the Republican candidate, Richard Nixon. But Johnson was so annoyed by the Salt Lake City address that he refused to talk to the vice president. "You know that Nixon is following my policies more closely than Humphrey," he told a friend.

Johnson relented only toward the very end of the campaign. He was moved by fury at Nixon, who, he believed, had committed "treason." From wiretaps on the phone of the president of South Vietnam, Nguyen Van Thieu, Johnson had learned that, at a time when it appeared that peace might be imminent, Nixon's agents had connived to sabotage negotiations by telling the Saigon government that it could get a better deal from Nixon after the election. Soon after, Thieu announced that he would not send a delegation to Paris to meet Hanoi's representatives, thus denying Humphrey the benefit of a last-minute peace deal. Even then, the vice president continued to narrow the gap (one poll had him leading Nixon by three points). Johnson could have made a decisive difference if he had intervened expediently. But not until November 3, at the Houston Astrodome, did he appear on a platform with Humphrey—too little, too late. In a contest so close that the outcome was not known until midmorning of the next day, Nixon won with 43.3 percent of ballots to Humphrey's 42.6 and George Wallace's 13.5.

On January 20, 1969, Lyndon Johnson, who, after the sterling achievements of the 89th Congress, had expected to be sworn in for a second term on that day, witnessed Richard Nixon take the oath as president of the United States. Johnson, wrote one correspondent, had been "chased out of the White House like a wounded bear fleeing hounds." A British commentary, reflecting on the way Lady Bird looked at the outgoing president as he sat on the inauguration platform, was reminded of Kent's lines at the end of *King Lear*:

> He hates him much
> That would upon the rack of this tough world
> Stretch him out longer.

"This tormented man from his tormented region who had such large visions of what his country might become," in the words of the historian T. Harry Williams, left the capital where he had spent almost all of his adult life knowing that his own party regarded him as a pariah, that scholars viewed him as a flagrant exemplar of the excesses of the imperial presidency, and—hardest of all to bear—that he was no longer wanted. On the first night down at the LBJ Ranch, his wife told him, "The coach has turned back into a pumpkin, and the mice have all run away." He was not invited to the 1972 Democratic convention, and his picture was nowhere to be seen. Shunned by many liberals, he was despised by racists. "As for LBJ," said George Wallace's right-hand man, "he ought to be tried in the docks as a traitor."

Over the past decade, scholars who have been called upon to rank American presidents have been perplexed by where to place LBJ. In little more than five years, he put through more legislation to aid the disadvantaged than any other chief executive save FDR. Johnson, said the novelist Ralph Ellison, was "the greatest American President for the poor and for the Negroes." But he also bears a large share of the blame for the devastation and loss of life caused by the war in Vietnam, which became such an obsession for the sponsor of the War on Poverty and the Great Society that in 1972 he helped Nixon defeat the progressive George McGovern. After looking down at the former president's coffin in 1973, Senator Vance Hartke of Indiana said, "On balance, Lyndon Johnson will be remembered as a sincere humanitarian in the Franklin Roosevelt mold, but with this caveat: the Vietnam War will be hanging over that judgment. Some of the living will forgive him—the dead, never."

9

Richard Nixon

IN HIS VICTORY SPEECH of November 1968, Richard Nixon, harking back to a moment in the fiercely fought recent contest when a thirteen-year-old girl in a red, white, and blue dress turned up at a Republican rally in a small village, said: "I saw many signs in this campaign, some of them not very friendly, some of them . . . very friendly. But the one that touched me the most was one that I saw in Deshler, Ohio, at the end of a long day of whistle-stopping. A little town. I suppose five times the population was there in the dusk. It was almost impossible to see, but a teenager held up a sign, 'Bring Us Together.' And that will be the great objective of this administration at the outset—to bring the American people together."

Nixon sounded that theme again in his eloquent inaugural address. The nation, he stated, had "endured a long night of the American spirit." Setting himself apart from the heated exchanges of the lacerating Kennedy-Johnson era, he declared: "America has suffered from a fever of words; from inflated rhetoric that promises more than it can deliver; from angry rhetoric that fans discontents into hatreds; from bombastic rhetoric that postures instead of persuading. We cannot learn from one another until we stop shouting at one another—until we speak quietly enough so that our words can be heard as well as our voices."

It required only minutes to demonstrate how difficult it was going to be to fulfill that aspiration. As the inaugural parade made its way down Pennsylvania Avenue, radical antiwar protesters, yelling "Four more years of death" and chanting "Ho, Ho, Ho Chi Minh," detonated smoke bombs and, when the president's car reached 15th Street, bombarded it with bottles, beer cans, and rocks. So long as the war in Southeast Asia dragged on, the new administration could expect prolonged violence.

Never before, in the 180-year history of the republic, had an inaugural procession been disrupted, but so often had the nation experienced outbursts in recent times that the incident seemed almost ordinary. The previous five years had witnessed the murders of President Kennedy and other national leaders; the body bags returning from the jungles of Southeast Asia; campus uprisings that had made "Berkeley" a code word for student takeovers; and, each year since 1964, bloody "long hot summers" of racial conflict in urban ghettoes. So apprehensive had authorities become that when Nixon assumed power, he inherited from the outgoing Johnson administration a set of blank executive orders that only needed to be inscribed to impose martial law on any American metropolis.

Nixon took very seriously warnings from pundits about the need to address social unrest. He noted especially the words of John Gardner, a former cabinet member who early in 1969 opened his Godkin Lectures at Harvard by stating, "These are dark days for the nation, days of controversy, days of violence and hostility," adding, "Every person sees— first of all in himself—the anguish of the American people: the shattering of confidence, the anger, the bewilderment." Nixon's first domestic policy adviser, Daniel Patrick Moynihan, told the president at the outset that he needed "to restore the authority of American institutions," since the belief that the State was legitimate provided "the glue that holds society together."

In his first months in the White House, Nixon had some success in fostering greater serenity. Five consecutive years of race riots came to an abrupt end. The president, who believed he could end the Vietnam War quickly, turned his thoughts toward large-scale withdrawal of American soldiers and announced that he had established a commission to end the draft and "achieve the good of an all-volunteer force." Early in 1971,

Newsweek's Washington bureau chief wrote: "Today, the sirens in the night no longer wail as urgently as they once did. An uneasy but palpable calm has settled over the cities and the campuses. Voices have been lowered and, if the President has not succeeded in bringing us together, at least things are no longer falling apart. The center has held."

The president's performance won approval in some surprising quarters. The Marxist historian Eugene Genovese said, "A quiet voice in the White House is all to the good," and the historian H. Stuart Hughes, who had embraced the slogan, "Better Red than Dead," declared, "The President's... reassuring tone, the way he's tried to de-escalate political passions, is a welcome change over the frenetic style of LBJ." Walter Lippmann encapsulated this sentiment when he told an interviewer: "His role has been that of a man who had to liquidate, defuse, deflate the exaggerations of the romantic period of American imperialism and American inflation. Inflation of promises, inflation of hopes, the Great Society, American supremacy—all that had to be deflated because it was all beyond our power."

Nixon's greatest moment came in the summer of 1969 after Apollo 11 astronauts Neil Armstrong and Edwin Aldrin landed on the moon—at the appropriately named Sea of Tranquility. There they unveiled a plaque signed by the president stating: HERE MEN FROM PLANET EARTH FIRST SET FOOT UPON THE MOON JULY 1969, A.D. WE CAME IN PEACE FOR ALL MANKIND. Shortly after the men set down on the lunar terrain, television screens featured Nixon phoning them from Washington. "As you talk to us from the Sea of Tranquility, it inspires us to redouble our efforts to bring peace and tranquility to Earth," he said. "For one priceless moment in the whole history of man, all the people on this earth are truly one—one in their pride in what you have done and in our prayers that you will return safely to Earth."

No one familiar with Nixon's public career, starting with his first despicable campaign for Congress in 1946, anticipated that the president would be content for long, however, with the role of Grand Unifier. Observing him in the House, the veteran Speaker, Sam Rayburn, had said: "His is the most devious face of all those who have served in Congress all the years I've been here." Nixon had inflicted further damage on his reputation by his conduct in the 1950 Senate race. (In a confession to a British publisher about his actions in that contest, Nixon later said, "I'm sorry about that episode. I was a very young man.") His 1950 opponent, Helen Gahagan Douglas, fastened a moniker on him that he had never been able to shake off: "Tricky Dick." (In Philip Roth's 1971 novel *Our Gang*, the unsavory protagonist is called Trick E. Dixon.) For a generation, cartoonists had regularly depicted Nixon as a menacing figure—hunched over, heavily jowled, unshaven, his brow sweating, his hooded eyes malevolent, looking like a villain from the silent screen. Nixon himself recognized that he was miscast as a harmonizer. In his first week in the White House, he instructed an aide to let it be known that the president had a number of fine qualities, including being "kind to his staff," then explained, "I've got to put on my nice-guy hat...but let me make it clear that's not my nature."

A polarizer, Nixon intended to prevail not by bringing people together but by driving them apart. His experience, one account noted, "had taught him that men who cannot unite on the basis of issues can nevertheless unite on the basis of a common enemy, a shared foe." He said of American voters: "You've got to be a little evil to understand those people out there." Consequently, he sought to craft a coalition of resentment. "It was Nixon's political genius," his biographer Herbert Parmet maintained, "that he put together hostility toward the counterculture, the antiwar movement, and the press, incorporating them all in...[an] alliance of antipathies."

Wherever he looked, Nixon saw enemies. The federal departments were "full of vipers," he asserted. He especially distrusted civil servants who were holdovers from previous administrations. "If we don't get rid of those people," he declared, "they will either sabotage us from within, or they'll just sit...on their well-paid asses and wait for the next election to bring back their old bosses." A vicious anti-Semite, he said at one point, "The Jewish cabal is out to get me." He commanded his personnel chief to count the number of Jews in the Bureau of Labor Statistics because he believed that they had concocted troubling figures on joblessness in order to do him in. The CIA, he maintained, was a den of Ivy Leaguers whose only constituency was the Georgetown Establishment, and he persisted in thinking that campus opposition to the Vietnam War was fomented by Mao or Castro despite FBI studies that found no evidence of foreign intrigue. The president even believed, an aide recorded in his diary, that he confronted a "conspiracy of the White House staff that he feels is out to get him."

The press is the enemy, he drilled into Henry Kissinger, his principal foreign policy adviser. "The press is the enemy. The press is the enemy. Write that 100 times on a blackboard, and don't forget it." Newspapers had been "flagrant" in their mistreatment of him, he said. As he approached the presidency, Nixon related in his memoirs, he was "bored by the charade of trying to romance the majority of the news media.... I was prepared to have to do combat." He was convinced that "the press and TV don't change their attitude and approach unless you hurt them."

Commentators did not hesitate to use the term "paranoid" to characterize Nixon—a judgment that his top aides echoed. His domestic policy adviser, John Ehrlichman, called the president "the mad monk"; his chief of staff, H. R. Haldeman, categorized Nixon as "the weirdest man ever to live in the White House"; and Kissinger thought the leader of the free world was "a basket case." Nixon was most unbalanced when he went on alcohol binges. Kissinger sometimes phoned the White House and then let members of his staff listen in so that they could hear the president's slurred speech. Nixon, concluded the Washington correspondent Elizabeth Drew in her incisive biography, was "insecure, self-pitying, vindictive, suspicious—even literally paranoid—and filled with long-nursed anger and resentments."

Nixon surrounded himself with men who shared his conviction that he must wage war on his foes—by fair means or foul. He placed his greatest reliance on dour John Mitchell, his attorney general, who claimed the right to wiretap without court order and advocated preventive detention of suspects. (Mitchell, observed a British journalist, "looked like Judge Jeffreys, the hanging judge of the Bloody Assizes, and in his case looks were not altogether misleading.") Nixon's chief political operative, Charles Colson, said that to get Nixon reelected he would walk over his grandmother. Colson warned the head of CBS, "We'll bring you to your knees," and told a high-ranking federal official that the army ought to seize the *Washington Post* and see to it that a particular columnist was "beheaded." So much did he hate the *New York Times*, he told Haldeman, that he "would like to be in the first wave of Army shock troops going in ... to tear down their printing presses."

The president revealed his own attitude by telling Colson what he had in mind for his opponents: "One day we will get them—we'll get them on the ground where we want them. And we'll stick our heels in, step on them hard and twist...crush them, show them no mercy." When toward the end of his presidency Haldeman was replaced as chief of staff, Nixon hailed his successor, Alexander Haig Jr., as "the meanest, toughest, most ambitious son of a bitch I ever knew." The president summed up his temperament in an interview with a journalist. "I believe in the battle," he revealed. "I perhaps carry it more than others because that's my way."

While venting his animosities to his staff, Nixon projected a public persona of benign leader, leaving divisive rhetoric to Vice President Spiro Agnew, who assumed the same role that Nixon had taken under Eisenhower: the president's attack dog. The *Washington Post* had called his choice of Agnew as his running mate in 1968 "the most eccentric political appointment since the Roman Emperor Caligula named his horse a consul." A lackluster governor of Maryland, Agnew had taken such a strong stand against "black racists" that he had become a favorite of southern whites. Strom Thurmond later called Agnew "next to John C. Calhoun, the greatest Vice President in the history of America."

In a series of tirades, Agnew lashed out at "an effete corps of impudent snobs who characterize themselves as intellectuals," "ideological eunuchs," "thieves, traitors, and perverts," "hopeless hypochondriacs of history," and "nattering nabobs of negativism." At a time when many Americans were as troubled by the counterculture as by radicalism, he drew the two together at a fund-raiser in Fort Lauderdale by saying of the rebellious young: "They are the children dropped off by their parents at Sunday school to hear the modern gospel from a 'progressive' preacher more interested in fighting pollution than fighting evil—one of those pleasant clergymen who lifts his weekly sermons out of old newsletters from a National Council of Churches that has cast morality and theology aside as 'not relevant' and set as its goal on earth the recognition of Red China and the preservation of the Florida alligator." Only a few days after the antiwar movement drew thousands of young protesters to Washington, Agnew declared, "A paralyzing permissive philosophy pervades every policy they espouse." Liberals derided both Agnew's message and his silly obsession with alliteration and assonance, but numbers of blue-collar workers drove cars flaunting the bumper sticker "Spiro Is My Hero."

Not everyone with access to the White House shared the outlook of Agnew or Colson, and some deplored Nixon's excesses. Alexander Butterfield, deputy assistant to the president, later recorded that he had always thought, "deep down," that Nixon was "the strangest man—a great man in many ways,... but he does have a dark side for sure." Nixon's former law partner Leonard Garment, who served as acting counsel to the president, summed up the attitude of the moderates in the administration. "Part of what fueled" Nixon, he said, "was anger, ambition, and the appetite for revenge—the knowledge that unless you made yourself fearful to your enemies, they would savage you. He had a tendency to pursue these instincts with self-damaging consequences." Regretfully, Garment concluded, "he could be awful at times, so he became... the most hated man in modern politics."

"Richard Milhous Nixon," wrote Elizabeth Drew, "was an improbable president. He didn't particularly like people. He lacked charm or humor or joy. Socially awkward and an introvert, he...was virtually incapable of small talk." Nixon once told an interviewer, "You have no idea how fortunate that makes you, liking people. Being liked. Having that facility. That lightness, that charm. I don't have it. I never did." When his presidency eventually came to an ignominious end because he could not keep control of his resentments, Nixon reflected, "What starts the process are the laughs and snubs and slights that you get when you are a kid."

Yet he managed to be elected to the House of Representatives, to the US Senate, to the vice presidency, and twice to the presidency, the second time in a landslide. Unexpectedly open to innovative departures in domestic affairs, he had a global conception of foreign policy matched only by Woodrow Wilson and the two Roosevelts. Furthermore, a number of people, some of them acerbic critics, found this man, who seemed so colorless, to be magnetic. Drew, while calling Nixon the "most peculiar and haunted of presidents," also judged him to be a "smart, talented man," and the *Time-Life* correspondent Hugh Sidey said: "He is an absolutely sinister human being, but fascinating. I'd rather spend an evening with Richard Nixon than with almost anybody else because he is so bizarre. He has splashes of brilliance. He is obscene at times, his recall is almost total; his acquaintanceship with the world's figures is amazing." When, sometime in the future, historians write about Nixon, Ehrlichman said, they will find him "the strangest paradoxical combination of any man [they've] ever heard of. And they'll be right."

Alone of American presidents, Nixon abandoned the Oval Office. During the day, he secluded himself in a hideaway in the Executive Office Building. At night, he cooped up alone in the Lincoln Sitting Room of the White House. In his EOB retreat, where he spent most of his time, he scribbled notes to himself on a yellow pad for hours. The yellow pad, said Garment, was Nixon's "closest friend."

In truth, Nixon had almost no friends. "I don't believe in letting your hair down," Nixon said. "That's just the way I am. . . . Some people think it's good therapy to . . . reveal their inner psyche. . . . Not me. No way."

Richard Nixon's mechanical gesture illustrates why, throughout his political career, commentators struggled to find the "real" Nixon. The political scientist James David Barber maintained that the president was an "active-negative type" with an "unclear and discontinuous self-image" who was engaged in "continual self-examination and effort to construct a Richard Nixon." *Courtesy of the Richard Nixon Presidential Library and Museum, ID 37-whpo-a0446-p*

His closest companion did not feel free to call Nixon by his first name. A man in his entourage in California could not believe his eyes when he observed Nixon, who had not seen his mother for a long time, walk over to her and, instead of giving her a hug, shake her hand. On vacation, he and his wife slept in separate houses. "Nixon," said the political editor of the *Los Angeles Times*, "was a cold, calculating man who treated Pat like just a piece of furniture." Informed that even near the end of his days, Americans did not believe that they knew him, he responded, "Yeah, it's true. And it's not necessary for them to know."

Even when Nixon was winning affirmation in the polling booth, the nation did not warm to him because he and his family seemed so programmed. Nixon, whose gestures were as rigid as those of a marionette, acknowledged, "I have a fetish about disciplining myself." He was so out of touch with his emotions that he referred to himself as RN. First Lady Pat's wan smile was likened to that of a Stepford wife, and in Gore Vidal's *An Evening with Richard Nixon,* "the two daughters are rolled into view; large cutie-pie dolls on wheels." Since some of the most fetching photos of Jack Kennedy caught him taking his ease on Cape Cod, the president's staff arranged for pictures of Nixon walking on the beach at his Pacific vacation retreat in San Clemente, only to be appalled when the prints showed him striding the sand in black wing-tipped shoes.

Nixon shied away from personal contact. If he had to talk to people, he preferred to use a phone in order to keep them at a distance. He once reached the point of asking an aide to put together a list of prominent people who liked him so that he might from time to time give them a ring. (The names on the list he got back included Ronald Reagan and John Wayne.) For weeks, he did not meet the press. Eisenhower noted disapprovingly that while FDR averaged eighty press conferences a year, Nixon held only four in all of 1970.

In contrast to Lyndon Johnson, who could readily reach sixty people from phones on his desk, Nixon confined himself to only two: Haldeman and Ehrlichman (as well as, on foreign affairs, Kissinger). Playing on their names and their Teutonic appearance and styles (flattop haircuts, perpetual scowls, and imperious behavior), journalists called Haldeman and Ehrlichman "the Germans" and their aides "the Katzenjammer Kids," an allusion to characters in a comic strip created by a German immigrant to America. They were also referred to as "the Berlin Wall," because, the *New York Times* explained, "they were said to shield the re-clusive, occasionally paranoid President from unpleasant news and unpalatable choices." They blocked from access to Nixon not only reporters but also US senators, even cabinet officials. National columnists said that the former UCLA classmates and campus politicians (both of them Eagle Scouts and Christian Scientists) were hard to tell apart, be-cause each was "brusque, high on German efficiency, low on frivolity, new to government and Washington."

Viewed as so indistinguishable that they were dubbed Rosencrantz and Guildenstern, the two men actually differed in important ways. Holding a position not unlike that of Sherman Adams under Eisenhower, Chief of Staff Haldeman was much the more powerful of the duo. Conferring with Haldeman absorbed 70 percent of Nixon's time with his staff. "Haldeman is the lord high executioner," the president in-structed his cabinet. "Don't you come whining to me when he tells you to do something." Haldeman said that he took pride in being "Richard Nixon's son of a bitch." Ehrlichman, who in the fall of 1969 moved from his post as White House counsel to become assistant to the president for domestic policy, could be as pugnacious as Haldeman. At one point, he said of an acting FBI director: "Let him twist slowly, slowly in the wind." On television, a commentator remarked, Ehrlichman looked like "a snarling prune." But Ehrlichman also came to be regarded as a "closet liberal." In Seattle, he had won acclaim as an urban reformer who had blocked construction of an aluminum plant on an island in Puget Sound, and in the Nixon administration he distinguished himself as a champion of Native Americans. Ehrlichman's "shop," said the journalist Theodore White, "was one of the few at the White House where ideas were seriously entertained—good ideas, too, on energy, on land-use policy, on urbanization, on preservation of the American environment."

Richard Nixon and Henry Kissinger constitute history's odd couple. An Eastern Seaboard intellectual, a Harvard professor, a protégé of Nixon's opponent Nelson Rockefeller, a consultant to Democratic presidents, Kissinger, who spoke with a guttural German accent, appeared to repre-sent all that Nixon loathed. Moreover, they frequently disparaged one another. Behind his back, Kissinger called Nixon "our meatball presi-dent," and Nixon referred to his principal foreign affairs adviser as "my Jew-boy." Yet they became a formidable combination in pursuit of the

realpolitik that Kissinger had delineated in his Harvard PhD dissertation on two of the hard-nosed masters of statecraft in the post-Napoleonic
era, Castlereagh and Metternich. Gleaning a line from Goethe, Kissinger
said, "If I had to choose between justice and disorder, on the one hand,
and injustice and order, on the other, I would always choose the latter."
In their total disdain for Nixon, contemporary critics noised it about
that foreign policy was formulated not by the president but by his national security adviser, a notion that Kissinger underscored by calling
himself the Lone Ranger. In fact, as the biographer Melvin Small has
written, Kissinger's role was that of Tonto.

Nixon resolved to step outside the traditional executive departments
and make a powerful National Security Council the main engine of his
foreign policy, with Kissinger installed in the West Wing at close reach.
The president largely ignored the cabinet, although its members appeared
to be his own kind: "a steering committee of the conformist middle class
triumphant," in the view of a British journal. All male, all white, all
Republican, they conveyed "cool competence rather than passion or
brilliance," *Time* reported. "There are no blooded patricians in the lot,
just strivers who have acted out the middle-class dream." In his first year,
Nixon averaged only one meeting a month with the cabinet. Determined
to center foreign affairs in the White House, he also bypassed the State
Department because, he explained, he had no respect for "striped-pants
faggots in Foggy Bottom." Though the secretary of state, William Rogers,
was his former law partner, he reduced him almost to a ceremonial figure.
(In September 1972, Nixon forced Rogers out and replaced him with
Kissinger, who continued to hold his national security adviser portfolio.)
Under Nixon, the NSC nearly doubled, and the money allotted to it
almost tripled.

Through manipulating his subordinates and resorting to intrigue,
Nixon created an atmosphere within his administration that resembled
that of the Borgias. By aggrandizing the National Security Council, he
diminished the importance not only of the State Department but also of
the Joint Chiefs of Staff and of the CIA. He communicated with the
Joint Chiefs without letting the secretary of defense know he was doing
so. The Joint Chiefs in turn felt so isolated from decision-making that
they assigned a yeoman from the navy to steal documents from the White
House in order to keep up with what Nixon and Kissinger were plotting.

Moreover, the president's elevation of the National Security Council did not deter him from having a number of its members wiretapped.

Nixon's reconfiguring of the foreign policy apparatus represented only one phase of his determination to revamp the entire executive branch in order to concentrate power in his hands. He appointed a Council on Executive Reorganization under the head of Litton Industries and, on its recommendation, replaced the Bureau of the Budget with a much more powerful Office of Management and Budget. Before Nixon, the Bureau of the Budget had committed itself to "neutral competence," with a staff devoted to giving the incumbent president expert counsel no matter what his political orientation. Nixon, though, lodged the OMB's director amidst his senior political advisers and favored political appointees over career civil servants. Most of the experts with long experience found that situation intolerable and soon resigned, leaving Nixon without the informed, independent counsel he badly needed.

In his machinations at OMB and by other actions, Nixon sought to create an *imperium in imperio*—a personalized government centered in the White House separate not only from the legislative and judicial branches but from the rest of the executive branch. He commanded his personnel director to purge dozens of high-ranking employees but still was not satisfied. "We've checked and found that 96 percent of the bureaucracy are against us," he said. "They're bastards who are here to screw us." In order to prevail, President Nixon, the political scientist Theodore Lowi has written, "built a bureaucracy to control the bureaucracy."

An admirer of Charles de Gaulle, Nixon sought to vest his office with an aura of majesty. Haldeman noted in his diary that the president wanted his staff to project him as a figure of mythic heroism, for "especially since the death of de Gaulle, we have a real opportunity to build the P as *the* world leader." Nixon arranged to have his arrivals blazoned by ornately uniformed trumpeters with medieval horns adorned in heraldry, and he ordered a designer to fashion uniforms for the White House police with "double-breasted tunics trimmed with gold, gold buttons, and a stiff military hat with a crown and plume." Instead of conveying regal grandeur, they appeared to be costumes from a Sigmund Romberg or Franz Lehar operetta set in an imaginary never-never land. Guffaws from reporters at this "Ruritanian" garb put a quick end to the vainglorious attempt at pomp, but not to Nixon's determination to swell the importance of the White House. The Executive Office staff, which had reached 1,664 under Kennedy, expanded to 5,395 in Nixon's third year.

Nixon displayed the same contempt for Congress that he did for the bureaucracy. The Constitution empowers a president to kill a bill simply by refusing to sign, provided that it reaches him near the end of a session, but Nixon pocket-vetoed a measure approved overwhelmingly by both houses of Congress on the sophistic premise that a brief Christmas recess permitted him to do so. He created even greater consternation by impounding (refusing to spend) billions of dollars appropriated by Congress—close to one-fifth of the sums for environmental, housing, antipoverty, and a hundred other programs. Incensed, Senator Sam J. Ervin Jr. declared, "The power of the purse belongs to Congress, and Congress alone." In the teeth of fierce criticism, Nixon continued to maintain that his right to impound simply because he did not like a law was "absolutely clear"—a contention that even his own assistant attorney general could not endorse. "It seems an anomalous proposition," stated William Rehnquist, "that because the Executive is bound to execute the laws, it is free to decline to execute them."

Richard Nixon advanced the most audacious claims for executive prerogative in the country's history. He contended that "if the President... approves an action because of... national security... the President's decision... enables those who carry it out to carry it out without violating a law." (He later advanced that notion more bluntly: "When the President does it, that means that it is not illegal.") Nixon, the political scientist Aaron Wildavsky concluded, "tried to run a foreign policy without the Senate, an expenditure policy without the House, a national campaign without his Party, a government against the bureaucracy."

―――――

Quick-starting his campaign for reelection even before he took office, Nixon made his subordinates understand that every action over the next four years had to be placed in that context. At one point, Haldeman wrote, "The President feels that... the Worship Services should be used for political opportunities." Nixon's greatest fear was that he would be denied a second term because George Wallace, running as a third-party candidate in 1972, would split the conservative, anti-civil-rights vote, permitting a Democrat to slip in. To make a third party candidacy less likely, he poured $400,000 into the campaign of Wallace's opponent in the 1970 Alabama gubernatorial primary—money jocularly called "Republican revenue-sharing"—and he leaked word to an influential columnist that the Department of Justice was investigating Wallace's brother for bribery. When these efforts did not derail the Alabama governor, Nixon concentrated on luring voters in southern and border states from Wallace to the Republican Party by catering to their hostility to civil rights. Nixon readily identified with that sentiment because he believed that blacks "live[d] like a bunch of dogs" and "were not going to make it for five hundred years." Furthermore, he was incensed by "these little Negro bastards on the welfare rolls."

The president seized upon the happenstance of a Supreme Court vacancy as an opportunity to engage southern sensibilities. He thought he had made a ten-strike when, on the recommendation of John Mitchell, he appointed a federal court judge, Clement F. Haynsworth Jr., from Senator Strom Thurmond's state of South Carolina. Haynsworth was a jurist of considerable stature, but unions and civil rights groups mobilized against him, and opponents turned up a damaging conflict-of-interest allegation. After a heated debate, the Senate rejected Haynsworth, 55–45, with seventeen Republicans breaking with Nixon. Even the GOP minority leader voted against the nomination. After the setback, Mitchell said, "If we'd put up one of the twelve Apostles, it would have been the same." Incensed and combative, Nixon gave marching orders: "Go out this time and find a good federal judge further south and further to the right."

Following those guidelines precisely, Mitchell, on his second try, came up with the name of G. Harrold Carswell of Florida, a southerner who, unlike Haynsworth, had virtually nothing to commend him. His work on the bench was so poor that his rate of reversals was twice that of other federal judges. Furthermore, as a state legislator, Carswell had said, "Segregation of the races is proper and the only practical and correct way of life. . . . I have always so believed and I shall also so act." Committed to "the principles of white supremacy," he had carried that conviction into decision-making. Two hundred former US Supreme Court law clerks, including Justice Brandeis's former aide Dean Acheson, announced that they opposed confirmation, and the dean of Yale Law School told a Senate committee that Carswell "presents more slender credentials than any nominee put forth in this century." The president's congressional liaison said: "They think he's a boob, a dummy. And what counter is there to that? He is." The best that a Republican senator from Nebraska could say in defense of Carswell was that "even if he were mediocre, there are a lot of mediocre judges and people and lawyers. They are entitled to a little representation, aren't they, and a little chance? We can't have all Brandeises and Frankfurters and stuff like that there."

Warned that Carswell could not be confirmed, Nixon plunged ahead toward inevitable defeat, with thirteen Republicans in the majority rejecting his choice. No president since Cleveland had suffered two turndowns in a row of Supreme Court nominees, an outcome Nixon attributed to "the accident of their birth, the fact that they were born in the South." After the Senate refused to confirm, Nixon declared that he had "reluctantly concluded—with the Senate as presently constituted— I cannot successfully nominate to the Supreme Court any Federal appellate judge from the South who believes as I do in the strict construction of the Constitution." Though he had failed to win confirmation for Carswell, whom he characterized as a "distinguished jurist," Nixon had won a victory of a different sort, because he had demonstrated to white southerners that he would stick with them to the last.

For a time, Nixon continued to navigate a stormy course. He did well in choosing Harry Blackmun, a Minnesotan who had been appointed to a circuit court by Eisenhower. A man with an outstanding record, Blackmun was approved by the Senate unanimously. Nixon had earlier picked a federal judge from the same state, Warren Burger, to be chief justice, and he and Blackmun were initially regarded as "the Minnesota Twins." No one questioned the competence of either man, but when two more vacancies opened, Nixon once again stumbled. He contemplated two nominees—one a lawyer who had argued against desegregation, the other a California woman of no distinction. When the American Bar Association stated that both "lacked stature," the president backed off.

After these mishaps, Nixon had greater success, though not as much as he had hoped. He won confirmation for Lewis Powell, a former president of the American Bar Association, and William Rehnquist, who was assistant attorney general. (Rehnquist had been saying that he would never be chosen: "I'm not from the South, I'm not a woman, and I'm not mediocre.") Nixon had anticipated that this cadre of judges would give the Court a decidedly conservative complexion, but it disappointed him on a number of issues—the death penalty, obscenity, and, most particularly, litigation affecting him personally. Far from being a clone of Burger, Justice Blackmun showed an independent streak that Nixon had not expected, notably in writing the opinion in *Roe v. Wade* legalizing abortion. Still, Nixon had achieved his main goal: appeasing the South. Powell, a Virginian, had belonged to a whites-only club, and Rehnquist had opposed the Civil Rights Act. Furthermore, of the 230 appointments Nixon made to lower federal courts, only six were African Americans, in contrast to Lyndon Johnson's seventeen.

Nixon mounted a sectional appeal more directly by adopting Mitchell's "southern strategy." He had hardly taken office when the government went to court to delay integration of school districts in Mississippi. Shocked by this action, almost all of the lawyers in the Civil Rights Division of the Department of Justice bonded together to issue a public protest, and the NAACP asked that the federal government be changed from plaintiff to defendant. "The United States Government," the NAACP asserted, "for the first time has demonstrated that it no longer seeks to represent the rights of Negro children." In October 1969, in a unanimous decision in *Alexander v. Holmes County Board of Education*, the Supreme Court ordered Mississippi school authorities to desegregate. "The obligation of every school district is to terminate dual school systems at once," it announced. All-white and all-black schools were "no longer constitutionally permissible." That ruling, while advancing the cause of civil rights, allowed the president to tell southern senators like Mississippi's powerful James Eastland that Jim Crow schools in the state had been ended not by the Nixon administration but by the obnoxious courts.

To demonstrate that the Nixon administration was a friend of the white South, Mitchell proposed to substitute for the Voting Rights Act of 1965, which had succeeded in enfranchising nearly a million African Americans, a uniform national statute that would no longer target Jim Crow precincts in the South. The provisions of Mitchell's bill, objected a Republican congressman from Ohio, "sweep broadly into those areas where the need is least and retreat from those areas where the need is greatest.... The Administration creates a remedy for which there is no wrong and leaves grievous wrongs without remedy. I ask you, what kind of civil rights bill is that?" When the Senate balked at Mitchell's measure, Congress reenacted the Voting Rights Act of 1965, little changed.

Undeterred by reprimands from the judiciary and from Congress, Nixon and his circle continued to distance themselves from the civil rights movement. In July 1969, Attorney General Mitchell and the secretary of health, education, and welfare (HEW) announced that the government no longer would enforce Title VI of the Civil Rights Act of 1964 requiring that funds be cut off from any school district or other local institution that continued to discriminate. A federal district court and, in a unanimous decision, a US Circuit Court of Appeals ruled that Nixon's appointees must follow the course mandated by Congress. So lax was the administration's enforcement of legislation to benefit minorities, however, that the Civil Rights Commission rebuked it three times in one year, and its highly regarded chairman, Father Theodore Hesburgh of Notre Dame, resigned. When the head of the civil rights division of HEW, Leon Panetta, advocated moving more aggressively, Nixon fired him. In 1971, members of the Congressional Black Caucus boycotted the president's State of the Union address, and the NAACP declared, "For the first time since Woodrow Wilson, we have a national administration that can be rightly characterized as anti-Negro."

In April 1971, the Supreme Court created a new problem for Nixon by ruling unanimously, in *Swann v. Mecklenburg Board of Education*, that cities must bus pupils out of their neighborhoods if that was necessary to achieve desegregation of schools. Public sentiment was overwhelmingly against busing; in Denver and in Pontiac, Michigan, opponents went so far as to bomb school buses. At first, since it was the law of the land, HEW complied by including provision for cross-district busing in its guidelines for cities such as Nashville. In a fury, Nixon called compliance to a halt. "I want you personally to jump" on HEW and the Department of Justice, he told Ehrlichman, "and tell them to *knock off this crap.*"

After George Wallace showed his political potency by winning the Florida primary in March 1972, Nixon took a more combative public stance. He asked Congress for a law imposing a moratorium on all court orders requiring busing, and when he did not get what he wanted, he advocated a constitutional amendment to curb the judiciary. Busing, he contended, was "a bad means to a good end." Subsequently, he hit hard against busing every chance he got in the 1972 campaign.

Nixon, however, could not win reelection if he responded only to a single section, nor could he long ignore members of his own party who deplored the persistence of racism. Asked by a reporter, "What has happened to the party of Lincoln?" a pro-civil-rights Republican congressman retorted acidly, "It has put on a Confederate uniform." Even more compelling were rulings by the judiciary. Nixon thought they were the actions of "clowns" who refused to recognize that "integration has never worked," but he could not nullify them no matter how much his compliance might disappoint white southerners. In *Green v. School Board of New Kent County* in 1968, the Supreme Court had insisted on immediate desegregation of schools, and the Johnson administration had set a September 1969 deadline for abolishing every dual school system. By the time Nixon took office, the movement for racial equality had built tremendous momentum.

Early in February 1969, Nixon told the press: "As far as school segregation is concerned, I support the law of the land." Implicit in that statement was his readiness to bring to an end fifteen years of defiance or stalling on wiping out the color line. The most powerful Republican in Georgia, Bo Callaway, fulminated: "The law...the law, listen here. Nixon promised the South he would change the law, change the Supreme Court, and change this whole integration business. The time has come for Nixon to bite the bullet, with real changes and none of this...bullshit." The president did not satisfy Callaway, but he took pains to avoid being confrontational by maintaining a "low profile" on race. "Our people have got to quit bragging about school desegregation," he said. "We do what the law requires—nothing more." An aide summed up this attitude: "Make-it-happen, but don't make it seem like Appomattox."

Without letting on what he was doing, Nixon approved a budget that boosted the $75 million Lyndon Johnson had allotted to civil rights enforcement in the last year of his presidency to $602 million, much of it to be spent by a greatly expanded Equal Employment Opportunity Commission. Although Johnson had advocated affirmative action, the idea did not take specific form until Nixon sponsored "the Philadelphia Plan" requiring employers and unions in the construction industry with federal contracts to establish goals and timetables for hiring blacks, Asians, Native Americans, and people with Spanish surnames. Started in one city, it evolved into a national program. Despite Nixon's pledge that there would be "no quotas," his administration established what were quotas in all but name that corporations, universities, and other institutions had to meet. Federal set-aside contracts for minority firms grew from $8 million in 1969 to $243 million in 1972.

After his presidency ended, even some of his harshest critics expressed astonished approval of Nixon's civil rights record, for, at the same time that he was seeking to win over the Wallace following, he was presiding over a remarkable trend toward greater equality—a disjuncture no one has been able to explain. Nixon, wrote the journalist John Osborne, took giant strides by "cozening the white South" into believing he was on its side while quietly dismantling its racial institutions. By far the greatest progress in school integration took place not under Kennedy or Johnson but under Nixon. The proportion of African American pupils attending all-black schools in the South fell from 68 percent in 1968 to less than 8 percent in 1972. Though much of the change resulted from action by federal judges and from orders initiated by HEW under Johnson, the Nixon administration also deserves credit for initiatives, as when it filed suit against the state of Georgia to speed school integration. In assessing Nixon, Tom Wicker, a liberal journalist who was an ardent advocate of civil rights, concluded: "The indisputable fact is that he got the job done—the dismantling of dual schools—when no one else had been able to do it."

The Nixon administration also turned in an exemplary performance in its relations with Native Americans, though that owed less to the president than to his lieutenants, notably Ehrlichman and Garment. To demonstrate that he favored self-determination, Nixon appointed a Mohawk as commissioner of Indian affairs. In contrast to his attitude about antiwar protests, which drove him to a frenzy, he responded temperately to a series of takeovers by militant Native Americans—from abandoned Alcatraz Island to the Pine Ridge Sioux Reservation at Wounded Knee. Nixon more than doubled federal spending for Indians, and his aides made a series of concessions to the Taos Pueblo, the Menominees, and Alaskan natives. "The sole reason for helping them is Presidential responsibility," Nixon declared. "There are very few votes involved,...but...a grave injustice has been worked against them...and the nation at large will appreciate our having...concern for their plight."

Nixon's conduct of domestic policy confounded both critics and admirers. He had entered politics as a foe of centralized government, an inclination that he carried with him into the White House and that most of his principal appointees shared. Attorney General Mitchell declared, "This country is going so far right you are not even going to recognize it." As president, Nixon advocated a "New Federalism" that would devolve power from Washington to state and local officials. He was taking this step, he explained, because of the American people's "loss of faith" in the gargantuan national government, which had come to be "increasingly remote," excessively bureaucratized, and "unresponsive as well as inefficient." Furthermore, he vetoed legislation for hospital construction, child care for the impoverished, public works, education, health, and welfare, and he refused to ask for appropriations to expand public housing.

Unexpectedly, though, Nixon's abbreviated presidency saw one of the largest compendiums of liberal legislation in the twentieth century. No one at the 1969 inauguration could possibly have imagined that within the next four years America would have an Environmental Protection Agency and an Occupational Safety and Health Administration or that Nixon would be entertaining a visionary approach to supporting millions of the poor with federal funds. One of Nixon's right-wing advisers confided, "It would curl your hair if you knew what some people around here are proposing."

Even earlier, during the 1968 campaign, a conservative aide had been distressed to find that Nixon had little interest in ideology but was intent on positioning himself "athwart the technically determined 'center' of the electorate." Over the course of the next four years, the president wound up somewhere close to the middle of the road, not by holding to true north but only after lurching from side to side. He so detested the elite of latter-day New Dealers that he ordered Ehrlichman to expunge all liberal Democrats from guest lists to the White House. But after reading Lord Blake's biography of Disraeli, he identified himself for a time with the nineteenth-century British prime minister in the age of Queen Victoria who, though a Conservative, came to be regarded as one of the architects of the Welfare State. "You know very well that it is the Tory men with liberal policies who have enlarged democracy," Nixon said.

Always a political animal, Nixon sought a constituency that would be the core of a winning coalition in 1972. Electoral strategists forecast that the majority of votes in the 1970s would be cast by "the unyoung, un-black, and unpoor," so catering to youth, African Americans, and the impoverished was not the road map to victory. Nor need he concern himself with the counterculture. Asked about the future of the leftish New Politics movement of the 1960s, the pollster Richard Scammon replied: "If there is to be New Politics in America, it's going to be the New Politics of the gray flannel suit. I don't think it'll be the New Politics of the beard and the sandal." Consequently, Nixon shaped his program to the millions in "Middle America." The term, coined by a columnist, suggested an income sector above poverty but below affluence, a vast hinterland uncorrupted by seaboard cynicism, and a state of mind of patriotic, commonsensical Americans wearied of the naysaying of the sixties. In appealing to these real and imagined folk, the president was, in *Newsweek*'s words, "champion of the good, God-fearing burghers of Heartland U.S.A."

Nixon, however, frequently veered into the left lane of the highway, in part because he was the first man newly elected to the presidency to find both houses of Congress controlled by the opposite party since Zachary Taylor in 1848. In the 1970 midterm elections, the Democrats widened their advantage over Republicans by more than three million votes as they added nine more seats in the House. Furthermore, the Senate had an exceptional cadre of ardent liberals—Hubert Humphrey, Ted Kennedy, George McGovern, Edmund Muskie, Eugene McCarthy, Fritz Mondale—with a sizeable parcel of initiatives they were determined to see enacted into law. Nixon knew that he had to make concessions to the Democratic Congress if he hoped to build a legislative record on which he could run for reelection.

His presidency had unexpected progressive features for yet another reason: Nixon cared so little about domestic affairs that his appointees, some of them of a liberal persuasion, had considerable leeway. A year before entering the White House, he had remarked: "I've always thought this country could run itself domestically without a president. All you need is a competent Cabinet to run the country at home. You need a president for foreign policy." His attention quickened only when he saw a political payoff. Hence, he involved himself in issues such as drugs and crime but left areas such as the environment to his aides. He told them that he did not want to be troubled about a huge swath of subjects:

among them, agriculture, labor, and health insurance. "I am only interested when we make a major breakthrough or have a major failure," he said. "Otherwise don't bother me."

At the outset, Nixon himself had a hand in the most ambitious social policy venture of his tenure. In his first week in office, he established an Urban Affairs Council, which he conceived of as equivalent to the National Security Council (though it was never nearly so powerful), and he appointed Daniel Patrick Moynihan to head it. Moynihan was everything Nixon despised—a Democrat, a liberal adviser to Kennedy, a Harvard professor, and an ardent foe of intervention in Vietnam. But they enjoyed swapping yarns, and the president recognized that Pat Moynihan was a fountain of ideas. Moreover, Moynihan had experience in the federal government that was a rare commodity in the new administration. One of the president's assistants called him a "charming Irish rogue" who knew which buttons of power to push at a time when most of Nixon's aides were "almost wholly virgin in the ways of Washington."

At Moynihan's behest, Nixon advocated a Family Assistance Plan to guarantee every family a minimal annual income, supplemented by a substantial food-stamp allotment. Able-bodied recipients were required to take jobs or register for training programs; only mothers of very young children were exempted. Though liberals protested that the level of support was too low, it was more than five times greater than poor families in Mississippi were getting and would have tripled the number of children receiving federal aid. The sociologist Nathan Glazer called it "the most enlightened and thoughtful legislation to have been introduced in the field of welfare in some decades."

The proposal failed to win the approval of Congress because it alienated both ends of the political spectrum. Conservatives such as Spiro Agnew were aghast at a scheme that would add thirteen millions to the welfare rolls, though in the expectation that before long there would be far fewer. Liberals distrusted anything sponsored by Nixon and balked at "workfare." The president's own interest soon waned. He had initially been attracted to FAP because it would replace the system instituted by the New Deal, which he detested, and because Moynihan had assured him that it would diminish the role of bureaucrats, especially social workers. But he had second thoughts. By July 1970, Haldeman was recording in his diary that Nixon "wants to be sure it's killed by Democrats and that we make a big play for it, but don't let it pass, can't afford it."

Though Moynihan soon left the administration, the spirit of his approach survived. Congress in 1972 accepted a part of Nixon's ambitious plan by providing for Supplemental Security Income that went to more than six million elderly, disabled, and blind Americans. It also more than doubled Social Security benefits and indexed them to price levels so that the aged would not be victimized by inflation. In one of his budgets, Nixon allotted 60 percent more to social welfare than Johnson had in 1968. He expanded food-stamp distribution and saw to it that every poor schoolchild in the country could count on a free lunch. Under Nixon, funds for human resources outpaced national defense spending for the first time in the post–World War II era. In addition, Nixon stepped up spending for primary and secondary schools, created a program for community colleges, and established a National Student Loan Association as well as an Office of Child Development.

Inadvertently, Nixon won something of a reputation as a champion of the environment. He started off in a contrary direction, pleasing conservatives and alarming ecologists by choosing as secretary of the interior the millionaire governor of Alaska, Walter Hickel, regarded as a crony of oil tycoons. But Hickel surprised him as well as liberal critics. In short order, Hickel held up the laying of a trans-Alaska oil pipeline that jeopardized the tundra, halted oil drilling in the Santa Barbara Channel following a disastrous blowout, pressed the Justice Department to prosecute Chevron for fouling the Gulf of Mexico, banned billboards on federal lands, and stopped construction of a jetport in the Everglades. Soon after the 1970 election, Nixon fired Hickel, who had not only turned out to be a strong environmentalist but also told the president that he lacked "appropriate concern" for the young who were distressed by the Vietnam War.

Frequently, the president's record owed more to the Democratic Congress than it did to his own initiatives. Nixon vetoed the Clean Water Act of 1970 as too costly, and when Congress overrode him, he impounded the funds. He also rejected a Federal Water Pollution Control Act in 1972 but once again was overridden. He turned down the recommendation of his own council on the environment calling for regulation of detergents fouling the country's waterways, and he opposed a ban on the pesticide DDT but was forced to acquiesce after losing a fight in the courts. Still, after Congress established the Environmental Protection Agency, he named men to head it who were strongly committed to its mission—first William Ruckelshaus, then Russell Train.

When polls revealed that in just four years concern for the environment had risen from 25 percent to 75 percent of the nation, Nixon decided that he had better catch up with the movement, typified by the first celebration of Earth Day in April 1970, before it got away from him. Consequently, he advocated a series of environmental laws, though he dismissed enthusiasts as "clowns" talking "crap." He instructed Ehrlichman, "Just keep me out of trouble on environmental issues," leaving him free to concentrate on foreign affairs save when, as his domestic policy adviser said, he was "taking bows" for achievements on preserving the land. He claimed credit for the creation of the National Oceanic and Atmospheric Administration, the Clean Water Act of 1972, and the Endangered Species Act of 1973—all of them adopted under his watch.

Nixon also surprised critics by becoming a patron of the arts, though, as a modern-day Lorenzo de' Medici, he seemed woefully miscast, for, as one of his speechwriters said, he was "aggressively square." He played Mantovani records, put ketchup on his cottage cheese, and, on one occasion, told Haldeman to make sure that for a White House dinner in honor of Duke Ellington invitations go to "all the jazz greats, like Guy Lombardo." He so loathed modern art that he had an abstract sculpture at the nearby Corcoran Gallery removed so that he would not see it, and he ordered "atrocious" paintings taken down from US embassy walls. But after Leonard Garment persuaded him that there were political dividends in appearing to be a connoisseur, he requested Congress to multiply funding more than sevenfold for the National Endowment of the Arts and for the National Endowment for the Humanities. When Golda Meir was a guest at the White House, Leonard Bernstein and Isaac Stern performed, and at a state banquet in honor of Andrew Wyeth, Rudolf Serkin was soloist. Still, as his first term was drawing to an end, the president said, "We should dump the whole culture business."

The Nixon years saw, too, a remarkable number of achievements that appeared to be in the nature of Great Society measures. The president set up the first Office of Consumer Affairs in the White House and approved a Consumer Product Safety Act, went along with the decision of Congress to create Amtrak, and signed Title IX legislation banning sex discrimination in higher education—a measure that significantly enhanced women's athletics. Despite his fear that young voters would support the Democrats, he agreed to a constitutional amendment granting eighteen-year-olds the right to vote. Even though he was often indifferent or even hostile to new departures, this imposing record made it possible for him to seek a second term in 1972 as a "new Nixon."

His actions dismayed right-wing true believers, however. Three weeks after the inauguration, the conservative columnist James Kilpatrick stated on television, "We have had precious little to smile about." Nixon, he noted, had appointed "only one fullblown" right-winger to a cabinet position, and the one exception had a minor portfolio. "I thought he meant it when he talked about closing down the Great Society," said Howard Phillips, chair of the Conservative Caucus, "but he obviously didn't.... He did not have firm opinions—most of his policies in the domestic area were brokerable." Pat Buchanan reached a similar verdict: "The President is no longer a credible custodian of the conservative political tradition of the GOP." At most, Nixon was "a fellow traveler of the right."

Initially, he gratified libertarians, who believed in a free market and the gold standard, with his economic policies. They recognized that he had to do something to halt spiraling prices in an overheated economy that was a legacy of Johnson's conduct of the Vietnam War, and were pleased that he decided to concentrate on battling inflation by such orthodox measures as cutbacks in federal spending and monetary restraints. A fervent football fan, he announced that his "game plan" consisted of putting the country through "slowing pains." When it was suggested in 1969 that he impose a ceiling on prices, he expostulated, "Controls. Oh my God, no! I was a lawyer for the OPA during the war and I know all about controls. They mean rationing, black markets, inequitable administration. We'll never go for controls."

Unhappily, the tight-money tactic that he encouraged the Federal Reserve to pursue plunged the nation into recession. Interest rates soared to their highest level in a century; stock prices plummeted; the Penn Central Railroad went bankrupt; and millions were thrown out of work. Yet, despite the slowdown, prices rose at their fastest rate since the Korean War. "Nixonomics [the name Walter Heller fastened on the president's policies] means," said the chair of the Democratic National Committee, "that all the things that should go up—the stock market, corporate profits, real spendable income, productivity—go down, and all the things that should go down—unemployment, prices, interest rates—go up."

His game plan a bust, Nixon abandoned tight money and, turning his thoughts to fiscal stimulus, startled reporters at a breakfast interview by stating, "I am now a Keynesian." As one of his listeners commented, that was "a little like a Christian crusader saying, 'All things considered, I think Mohammed was right.'" Despite that declaration, Nixon, while modifying his initial course, still opposed stringent federal intervention. His slight departure worked no better. Both prices and joblessness continued to rise, and in 1971 America ran its first trade deficit since 1893.

On August 15, 1971, to the dismay of conservative Republicans, Nixon announced what he called a New Economic Plan, although that term had long been associated with Lenin's drastic actions in Soviet Russia. Abandoning his opposition to controls, he clamped a temporary freeze on prices, wages, salaries, and rents and laid a surcharge on most imports. In addition, his advisers persuaded him to turn his attention to the unfavorable international balance of payments, though he told them, "I don't give a shit about the lira." He took the bold step of devaluing the dollar, permitting it to float on the world currency market. That action brought to an end the international system that had been in effect since the Bretton Woods monetary conference in World War II.

In November, Nixon ended the freeze and tried a number of makeshift methods that bought him time. While jettisoning rigid controls, he authorized citizen pay boards to issue guidelines on how much prices would be permitted to go up. Though unemployment persisted, the pace of inflation slackened, and the balance of payments deficit shrank markedly. In addition, during the campaign year of 1972, the Federal Reserve adopted expansionist policies that abetted Nixon's bid for reelection. That summer, the administration was able to report cheerily the greatest quarterly gain in GNP in seven years. When voters went to the polls in 1972, most of them concluded that, in very difficult circumstances, Nixon had not done badly.

The ultimate cold warrior, Richard Nixon, who had long wanted nothing more than to roll back the Iron Curtain, had the misfortune of coming to office at the ebb tide of the American empire. The brief hour of US dominion after 1945 had ended. Its monopoly of the atomic bomb had vanished, and its once enormous economic advantage was challenged in both Europe and Asia. No less important, its experiences in Korea and Vietnam had soured the country's appetite for overseas ventures. To his credit, Nixon recognized these changed circumstances—at least some of the time. When he read a summary of a British study stating, "The U.S. has lost 'the desire and ability' to be the dominant power in the world," he alerted Kissinger: "H. K. Very important and accurate."

Save for FDR, no president since Woodrow Wilson had so broad a geopolitical conception. Not content with the traditional State of the Union oration, Nixon also delivered State of the World addresses. He understood that, in contrast to the notion that there was a monolithic Red conspiracy, Russia and China were bitter rivals who distrusted and feared one another. So he sought to reconceptualize American foreign policy. He saw opportunities both for playing off Russia against China and for achieving greater rapport with Moscow and Beijing. "Whatever Americans thought of him personally," wrote the British historian Marcus Cunliffe, "his foreign policy was refreshingly (to some, frighteningly) audacious."

From the outset of his presidency, Nixon confounded liberals and disappointed conservatives by avidly seeking détente with the USSR. In his inaugural address, he said that "after a period of confrontation, we are entering an era of negotiations," a message conveying rejection of Cold War verities. During the 1968 campaign, he had excoriated Humphrey for caving in to the Kremlin by expressing a willingness to accept parity in nuclear arsenals, but in his very first press conference after taking office he announced his goal as "sufficiency, not superiority." To foster progress toward an arms agreement, Kissinger held hundreds of meetings with the Soviet ambassador at Washington, Anatoly Dobrynin, in some periods seeing him daily, and the two men set up a direct phone line connecting the Russian embassy to the White House.

Nixon, who had little interest in arms control, left that important area to Kissinger. Ignoring the Joint Chiefs as well as experts, the national security adviser revealed gaps in his knowledge that, critics said, permitted the Russians to get the better of him. But the two countries did manage to consummate a Strategic Arms Limitation Treaty (SALT I), which froze weapons development for the next five years. A more significant pact, which was of "unlimited duration...and not open to material unilateral revision," confined each nation's deployment of ABMs (antiballistic missile systems).

In the spring of 1972, Nixon became the first American incumbent president to set foot on Soviet soil, where, after bargaining sessions with Leonid Brezhnev, with whom he got on well, he put his name to ten formal agreements with the USSR. Taking advantage of one of these pacts, which liberalized trade, the Russians made the biggest purchase in American history to acquire huge quantities of American wheat at an artificially low price. By cornering the world wheat market, they spiked inflation in the United States and other countries, with the price of grain tripling in one year. Senator Henry Jackson called Nixon's operation "one of the most notorious foulups" the nation had ever experienced, but the president found satisfaction in being able to enter the 1972 campaign not as a cold warrior but as a man who had succeeded in easing tensions with the Kremlin.

Surprising though Nixon's overtures to Russia were, his policies toward Mao's China left America and the world dumbstruck. Nixon had first indicated that he might be contemplating a dramatic departure in a widely noted 1967 *Foreign Affairs* article in which he wrote, "We simply cannot afford to leave China forever outside the family of nations, there to nurture its fantasies, cherish its hates and threaten its neighbors." He had to move cautiously because Republican Party officials had long identified with the anti-Communist regime on Taiwan. Nevertheless, Nixon sent signals to Beijing that he would like to open a conversation. In 1969, he loosened restrictions on trade with and travel to China, withdrew the 7th Fleet from permanently patrolling the Taiwan Straits, and took nuclear weapons out of Okinawa. In 1970, he declared in his State of the Union address, "The Chinese are a great and vital people who should not remain isolated from the international community," and later that year, he became the first president to allude not to "Red China" or "Mainland China" but to "the People's Republic of China."

Over the course of 1971, the pace quickened. That April, in what came to be called "ping-pong diplomacy," the Beijing regime invited

American table tennis players to a competition, and Zhou Enlai, Mao's chief lieutenant, welcomed them. That led to the kind of clandestine diplomacy Nixon savored. On a journey to Pakistan in July, Henry Kissinger abruptly disappeared for forty-eight hours. He had "stomach flu," it was explained. In fact, Nixon had sent his national security adviser on a secret mission to China, with the code title "Polo" (after Marco Polo). Not even the secretary of state knew Kissinger was there. Kissinger and Zhou got on well, but in their discussions Kissinger gave a great deal and received little in return. He pledged that the United States would not support independence for Taiwan, and he even informed the Chinese of where Russian troops were stationed along their borders. Zhou brushed aside Kissinger's plea for help in bringing the Vietnam conflict to an end but did promise he would invite Nixon to Beijing before he asked any Democrat to come.

The announcement that Richard Nixon was going to China stunned the nation. It would have been still more shocked if it had known that he had not even been promised that, after traveling thousands of miles, he would get to see Mao. The president was journeying not as head of state of the world's greatest power but as petitioner. Still, the week he spent in China in February 1972 was a public relations triumph as wire services sent out photographs of Nixon at the Great Wall and the Forbidden City. (Subsequently, it even became the subject of John Adams's opera *Nixon in China.*)

Kissinger and Nixon in China. At this relaxed gathering with Zhou Enlai and other Chinese leaders in Beijing, amiability reigns, but the Americans came away from their negotiations with no concessions on Vietnam. Nixon did, however, create an opening to China—an unexpected move for a man who had built a political reputation as a foe of communism. *Courtesy of the Richard Nixon Presidential Library and Museum, ID NA.A10-024.38.138.1*

America got nothing palpable out of the president's visit, whereas Nixon agreed to the Shanghai Communiqué recognizing Taiwan as part of the Chinese republic. Right-wing ideologues were incensed. "This man had been the principal friend of the Republic of China in the United States for twenty years, and then he turned around with cool precision—a politician without any principles at all," said the conservative publicist William Rusher. "He proceeded to double-cross them—one of the greatest historical double-crosses of all time." Such outbursts, though, were drowned out by the chorus of approval for Nixon's boldness in reconfiguring American foreign policy.

Commentators elevated the president's status, too, by writing of "the Nixon Doctrine," a conceit that both inflated the president's record and distorted it. In contrast to Kennedy's pledge to "bear any burden" in order to "support any friend, oppose any foe," Nixon declared: "America cannot—and will not—conceive all the plans, execute all the decisions, and undertake all the defense of the free nations of the world. We will help where it makes a difference and is in our interests.... Our interest must shape our commitments, rather than the other way around." This sounded like a course of moderation, even of withdrawal, but, in fact, it was, as he told a reporter, an "effort to withstand the present wave of new isolationism ... with a revised policy of involvement." Furthermore, he believed that pursuit of "our interests" mandated favoring strongmen such as Ferdinand Marcos in the Philippines who, though they trampled on the liberties of their own people, stood fast against communism, and, over the objections of the State Department, allowing the shah of Iran to buy huge supplies of American weapons, which he used to suppress dissent.

Nixon demonstrated his partiality toward authoritarian regimes most blatantly in Chile, where the CIA sought to prevent the election to the presidency of a Marxist, Salvador Allende. When that effort failed, Nixon waged covert economic warfare on Allende and encouraged a military overthrow of the democratically elected government. At Nixon's behest, the CIA funneled money to right-wing plotters who kidnapped and murdered a general opposed to displacing Allende by force. Though Nixon and Kissinger were not directly involved in the coup by a military junta that resulted in the death of Allende, they had done all in their power to bring about his downfall, and Nixon had no trouble accepting the government of Allende's successor, General Augusto Pinochet, though Pinochet was a savage despot responsible, in the course of his sixteen-year reign, for the deaths of thousands of Chileans.

None of his other overseas ventures—Russia, China, Chile—absorbed nearly so much of his time as the running sore in Southeast Asia. He had been elected on his pledge to achieve "peace with honor" in Vietnam, and during the campaign he had assured a congressman, "We'll end the war in six months." Similarly, he told Haldeman, "I'm not going to end up like LBJ, holed up in the White House afraid to show my face on the street. I'm going to stop the war. Fast." Nixon had no "secret plan," but he thought he could achieve peace quickly, and on favorable terms, by getting Russia to bring pressure on North Vietnam.

To capture the attention both of the Kremlin and of Hanoi, he sometimes aired what he called "the Madman Theory." While running for president in 1968, he had explained to Haldeman: "Bob, I want the North Vietnamese to believe...I might do *anything....* We'll just slip the word to them that, 'for God's sake, you know Nixon is obsessed with Communism. We can't restrain him when he's angry—and he has his hand on the nuclear button'—and Ho Chi Minh himself will be in Paris in two days begging for peace." In October 1969, Nixon ordered the Strategic Air Command to dispatch planes carrying nuclear bombs to the very borders of the USSR in the vain expectation that they would scare the Russians into coercing Hanoi to make concessions. The American people did not know that this frightening nuclear alert lasted for a month. A short while later, he used the "madman" approach in a different way when he asked a Soviet intermediary to warn the North Vietnamese that he would take "measures of great consequence and force" if they did not yield, but he was only bluffing and Hanoi did not blink.

Nixon also resorted to well-worn approaches, which he sought to fob off as new departures. The ballyhoo about "Vietnamization"—shifting increasing responsibility for the fighting to the South Vietnamese—obscured the reality that the practice had begun under Lyndon Johnson, and when Nixon told the Saigon government sternly that he expected it to send representatives to the bargaining table in Paris, he was doing so at the suggestion of LBJ's adviser Clark Clifford. While these formal peace negotiations were taking place, Nixon authorized Kissinger, in cloak-and-dagger fashion, to meet separately and secretly with a Hanoi envoy without informing either the State Department or the South Vietnamese government. In his characteristically egocentric fashion, Kissinger took pride in this assignment, which carried on from February 1970 to January 1972, but he made no progress whatsoever. Meantime, the bloodshed continued. In Nixon's first six months in office, more Americans died in Vietnam than in all but one similar period in the past.

At a meeting Nixon attended with the Johnson circle during the interregnum, Clifford had counseled the incoming president to begin withdrawing soldiers from Vietnam right away, but Nixon did not start the process until the fall of 1969, and then only because doing so would permit him to go on waging war. As his secretary of state confided to Averell Harriman, "It was essential to reduce American casualties and get some of our troops home in order to retain the support of the American people." On that same rationale, Nixon initiated an exploration of how to terminate selective service. He knew that ending the draft would not only please his libertarian supporters but also would give him a freer hand in military ventures because he would not have to cope with weeping mothers of young draftees.

In contriving a strategy for Southeast Asia, Nixon opted for the worst possible choice: very slow de-escalation over a number of years, interspersed with paroxysms of bombing. Especially hideous was the American treatment of Laos. A half million US bombing missions killed or displaced hundreds of thousands of peaceful Laotians, causing, in the words of a US Senate report, "untold agony." Massive bombing in Southeast Asia did not sway Hanoi, and downsizing US forces diminished the likelihood that Nixon could achieve his goals. Hanoi regarded the idea of two nations, with an independent South Vietnam, as an artificial construct imposed by Westerners at Geneva, and it would not abandon its aspiration to rule over a united country.

The more Nixon withdrew troops, the more the North Vietnamese negotiators in Paris sensed that they only had to wait him out and total success would be theirs, but the president refused to acknowledge that reality. Like every predecessor from Truman through Johnson, he believed that American credibility was at stake in Asia and that he could not withdraw unless the South Vietnamese were able to "determine their own political future." In retrospect, it became clear that the only feasible way to end the war was for the United States to accept what amounted to defeat, but, despite the strength of the peace movement, few Americans favored that course. So the parleys in Paris dragged on, with no resolution on the horizon.

When the first anniversary of the president's tenure came and went with his "six months" forecast for terminating the conflict more and more a mockery, Nixon began to turn his thoughts to an audacious move that would give America a decisive advantage. He did so in good part because he viewed Ho Chi Minh's continued defiance as an affront requiring a demonstration of his capacity for dauntless leadership. Recording Kissinger's views, Haldeman set down: "K. takes whole deal as test of P's [President's] authority and I think would go ahead even if plan is wrong just to prove P can't be challenged." As the moment for decision neared, Nixon became extraordinarily nervous. One day, he phoned Kissinger ten times to bark contradictory orders, then hang up abruptly. "Our peerless leader has flipped out," Kissinger told his staff. To whip himself into taking aggressive action, he watched the film *Patton* over and over and strode the Oval Office puffing on a corncob pipe in the style of General MacArthur.

In a televised address on April 30, 1970, Nixon made a shocking announcement: American and South Vietnamese troops were launching an invasion of Cambodia. In language more appropriate for Armageddon, he declared: "We will not be humiliated. We will not be defeated.... If when the chips are down, the world's most powerful nation...acts like a pitiful, helpless giant, the forces of totalitarianism and anarchy will threaten free nations and free institutions throughout the world." At a time when he was sending young Americans to their death, he sought sympathy for himself. "I would rather be a one-term president and do what I believe was right than to be a two-term president at the cost of seeing America become a second-rate power," he said. He also contended that "for five years, neither the United States nor South Vietnam has moved against these enemy sanctuaries because we did not wish to violate the territory of a neutral nation." That assertion was an outright lie. Since taking office, Nixon had approved more than three thousand bombing missions in Cambodia (with Pentagon officials falsifying documents about these actions), and the US Army had crossed the border more than six hundred times. On the following day, Nixon surprised military officials by turning up at the Pentagon. Hurling obscenities, he shouted, "You have to electrify people with bold decisions.

Bold decisions make history, like Teddy Roosevelt charging up San Juan Hill." So, he cried, "let's go blow the hell out of them."

On the morning after Nixon's nighttime speech, the country exploded. For good reason, Americans had thought that the war was winding down. Only ten days earlier, the president had announced that he was withdrawing another 150,000 US troops because there had been so much progress. The invasion of Cambodia, however, appeared to signal an abrupt, scary widening of the conflict. From coast to coast, cities erupted in protest. Within the president's own administration, Secretary of State Rogers, who had been kept in the dark, expressed consternation, and Walter Hickel, who first learned of the incursion at a cabinet meeting, said later, "I was literally screaming inside."

Protests against his Vietnam policies had harried Nixon from the onset of his presidency. Call for a "moratorium" on the war in mid-October 1969 had resulted in the most massive turnout in the country's history. More than two million people had marched in two hundred cities, with an astonishing one hundred thousand participants on Boston Common. Precisely one month later, in a nationwide "mobilization" against the president's bellicosity in Asia, an antiwar rally in the rain at San Francisco's Golden Gate Park had drawn the largest crowd in the city's history, and Washington had been overrun by huge numbers of demonstrators. (One placard read simply MY FRIEND JIMMY SILVERSTEIN IS DEAD: AUG. 16, 1969 VIETNAM WAR.)

Nixon had responded by turning his back on the protesters and by seeking to enlist prowar Americans against them. When peace advocates assembled in Washington, the White House let it be known that the president was engaged in watching the Ohio State–Purdue game on television. Nixon recognized that most of the opponents of his policies were pacific, but that there was a fringe—long-haired, foul-mouthed, waving Viet Cong flags, bent on violence—who might be exploited to buttress his appeal to Middle America. On the eve of a demonstration in the nation's capital, Nixon instructed his top aide: "Be sure police are hurt tomorrow." In addition, with the president's implicit consent, Spiro Agnew let loose another verbal attack to ostracize critics. True Americans, he said, should "separate" the organizers of the Moratorium "from our society—with no more regret than we should feel over discarding rotten apples from a barrel."

Even peace advocates came to recognize that Nixon had outwitted them. On November 3, 1969, in what he regarded as the most important speech he had ever given, the president appealed to "the great silent majority" to back their commander in chief. He had "initiated a plan of action," he announced, for "the complete withdrawal of all U.S. combat forces, and their replacement by South Vietnamese forces on an orderly scheduled timetable," but it was vital for the nation to support him as he carried it out. "North Vietnam cannot defeat or humiliate the United States," he declared. "Only Americans can do that." On the next day, he called reporters to his office to show them stacks of telegrams from thousands of citizens saying "we silent Americans are behind you." More powerful than any words were his troop withdrawals, which took the wind out of the antiwar movement. In mid-April 1970, the Vietnam Moratorium Committee announced that it was shutting down its Washington office and disbanding. "We've got those liberal bastards on the run now, and we're going to keep them on the run," Nixon said.

In deciding to invade Cambodia only a few days later, Nixon miscalculated. Having defanged his opponents, he did not anticipate that his decision would detonate a far greater explosion, especially in college towns, than any he had encountered before. For two nights after the president's announcement, Kent State University students smashed store windows, and they burned the ROTC building to the ground. When the National Guard appeared on campus during the day to restore order, students stoned them. Guardsmen opened fire, killing four undergraduates. The four included two young women on their way to class and a young man who ranked second in his ROTC corps.

Enraged by the expansion of the war and by the slayings at Kent State as well as of two African American protesters at Jackson State eleven days later, campuses across the country erupted. In what the president of Columbia University called "the most disastrous month of May in the history of American education," riots at the University of Maryland injured scores, University of South Carolina students trashed the treasurer's office, and a half-million-dollar fire scorched Colorado State. Four hundred and forty-eight institutions closed down for the remainder of the semester. Nixon was advised not to go to his daughter

Julie's graduation from Smith College because antiwar elements in Northampton, Massachusetts, might endanger him. Abroad as well as at home, fury reverberated. Thousands of marchers descended on the US embassy in London; a mob with gasoline bombs moved on the American cultural center in Berlin; two high school students died at a protest rally in Caracas; two hundred thousand demonstrators turned out to denounce Nixon in Australian cities; and, in Calcutta, the library of the American Center was sacked.

So disturbed by the reaction that he could not sleep, Nixon got out of bed before dawn on May 9 and ordered a limousine to drive him to the Lincoln Memorial, where students were conducting a vigil. "I know you think we are a bunch of sons-of-bitches," he told them, but he too, he said, sought peace. His attempt to be conciliatory, however, miscarried because he did not begin to know how to communicate with the young. When he spoke to students who had traveled three thousand miles from California to protest against a war that could cost them their lives, he asked how they liked surfing, and when he approached undergraduates from Syracuse, closed down by a strike, he inquired how they thought the Orange would fare on the gridiron that fall. He recommended that they see the world—Prague, Warsaw—and, he later recounted, "the place that I felt that they would particularly enjoy visiting would be Asia." After an hour of a rambling monologue that left students bewildered, he went up to the Capitol, where he told a cleaning woman, "My mother was a saint."

His propitiatory mood did not last long. On hearing that 250 Foreign Service officers had signed a protest against the Cambodian incursion, Nixon phoned the State Department to say, "This is the president. I want you to make sure all those sons-of-bitches are fired first thing in the morning." (His order was ignored.) Nixon showed his true colors after hundreds of "hardhats"—helmeted construction workers—crying "All the way USA" and "Love it or leave it," battered peaceful antiwar demonstrators, primarily high school and college students, in New York's financial district. Nixon made a newsworthy event of welcoming the leader of the construction union to the White House, where, in a ceremonial display for photographers of what Elizabeth Drew called the president's "thuggish side," he donned a hardhat.

Over the course of the next year, Nixon took an even more confrontational stance. When, in October 1970, antiwar activists encircled an auditorium where he had a speaking engagement in San Jose, California, shouting, "One, two, three, four—We don't want your fuckin' war," Nixon taunted them: leaving the building, he leaped onto the hood of his limousine and flashed the "V" sign, goading demonstrators to hurl rocks at the motorcade. (Nixon's speechwriter William Safire called the episode "a mob attack upon a U.S. President—unique in our history.") On hearing in the spring of 1971 that Charles Colson was planning to hire hoodlums to assault peace activists, Nixon responded, "Go in and knock their heads off." (Pugnacious though his attitude was, some hawks wanted him to be much more aggressive in Asia. The governor of California, Ronald Reagan, urged the Nixon administration "to level Vietnam, pave it, paint stripes on it, and make a parking lot out of it.")

Unhappy with both Nixon's comportment and his policies, the US Senate resolved to rein him in and to reclaim its own authority over foreign affairs. In 1970, it adopted a resolution sponsored by the Kentucky Republican John Sherman Cooper and the Idaho Democrat Frank Church cutting off funds for the Cambodian operation after June 30. That roll call marked the first time that a president's powers as commander in chief had ever been limited during wartime. Among those voting for the curb were sixteen Republican senators. Though the House refused to go along, the Senate's action demonstrated how swiftly antiwar sentiment was building. In addition, the Senate that year repealed the Gulf of Tonkin Resolution by an emphatic 81 to 10. It continued in 1971 to vote more than a dozen times to fetter the president's authority to wage war in Asia.

The administration treated these efforts with contempt. Nixon insisted that his authority to send men into battle derived not from the Gulf of Tonkin Resolution but from his inherent powers as commander in chief. When a 1971 military procurement law required him to announce a cease-fire and negotiate with Hanoi, he dismissed the measure as "without force or effect" and refused to obey. Spiro Agnew was even more disrespectful. He accused Senators Fulbright, Kennedy, and McGovern of having "developed a psychological addiction to an American defeat," and he characterized other skeptics of the war—Clark Clifford, Averell Harriman, and Cyrus Vance, all figures of distinction—as men "history has branded as failures." The president and vice president displayed this arrogance with no recognition that they ceased to have a majority, silent or vocal, behind them. By the summer of 1971, the proportion of the country concluding that the United States had made a mistake by intervening in Vietnam had risen to 71 percent, and fully 58 percent thought that the American cause was "immoral." Giddy with power, neither man had any premonition of how quickly that power could erode.

On Sunday morning, June 13, 1971, the *New York Times* began printing excerpts from a highly classified account of the course of the war in Southeast Asia that had been prepared by the Defense Department at the behest of Robert McNamara in the LBJ era. Titled *History of U.S. Decision-making in Vietnam, 1945–1968*, the volumes came to be called, more simply, "the Pentagon Papers." Stamped "Top Secret–Sensitive," the document had nevertheless found its way into the press. The report did not immediately affect the president, because it stopped short of his tenure and severely censured his Democratic predecessors for deceit. But Kissinger and other aides pointed out that if the *Times* got away with publishing these papers, it would not be long before the world would learn of the illicit behavior of the current administration. On contemplating that prospect, Nixon became livid. He was already over-wrought about leaks to the media because in his first four months in office the *New York Times* had published nineteen stories on what had transpired in closed-door National Security Council meetings. Furthermore, the chronicle had dangerous implications. Haldeman underscored for Nixon the subversive theme of the Pentagon Papers: "You can't rely on ... the implicit infallibility of presidents, which has been an accepted thing in America," for the study revealed "that people do things the President wants ... even though it's wrong."

With Nixon's approval, Attorney General Mitchell not only warned the *New York Times* that it would be prosecuted under a 1917 espionage law if it continued to publish installments but obtained a restraining order from a federal court. The *Times* halted publication briefly but resumed when the *Washington Post,* the *Boston Globe*, and the Associated Press all picked up on the revelations. Determined to stifle this defiance, Nixon and Mitchell placed their hopes for a total shutdown of the series on the willingness of the US Supreme Court to convert the temporary order into a permanent injunction. But on June 30, the Court, 6–3, ruled against the government. Forbidding publication, Justice Hugo Black said, would constitute "prior restraint," an "indefensible" breach of the First Amendment. That finding led Nixon to resort to other means to deal with his foes. "Although no one suspected it at the time," his biographer Melvin Small has written, "the *Pentagon Papers* case was the beginning of the end for the Nixon administration."

By the time the Court handed down its decision, the country had learned the name of the source of the Pentagon Papers disclosure: Daniel Ellsberg, a summa cum laude graduate of Harvard who had been a marine company commander, had worked in the Pentagon under McNamara, and had spent two years in Vietnam as a civilian expert. Once an ardent hawk, Ellsberg had become so disillusioned about the war that he had handed the tome over to the media. "The Jews are born spies," the president fumed about Ellsberg. "You can't trust the bastards. They turn on you."

Incensed at what they regarded as Ellsberg's perfidy, Nixon and Kissinger launched a vendetta. Calling Ellsberg a "son-of-a-bitch," the president told Mitchell: "Don't worry about his trial. Just get everything out. Try him in the press. Everything, John, that there is on this investigation, get it out, leak it out. We want to destroy him in the press. Is that clear?" The government circulated scurrilous and mendacious rumors about the whistle-blower to sully his reputation, and obtained an indictment of him for theft of federal property and for unauthorized possession of materials vital to national security. If convicted, Ellsberg and his aide could be sentenced to 115 years in prison. The administration acted in part vindictively to punish him, but also to serve as a warning to others of what might befall if they followed his example. Even more important, it sought to silence him or discredit him because Kissinger, especially, feared that he might have still more documents.

Disappointed in the Supreme Court's ruling, Nixon turned to the FBI to hound Ellsberg, but when J. Edgar Hoover refused to tap Ellsberg's phone, Nixon decided to create his own undercover outfit. "If we can't get anyone in this damn government to do something," he told Ehrlichman, "then, by God, we'll do it ourselves. I want you to set up a little group right here in the White House. Have them get off their tails and find out what's going on and figure out how to stop it." In the third week of July, Ehrlichman reported that he had established a White

House Special Investigations Unit. It got a less wordy name when, in opening shop next door to the White House in the Executive Organization Building, it placed a sign on its door, "Plumbers" (to plug leaks).

Ehrlichman put two of his young aides in charge of the Plumbers, and they, in turn, recruited two men with long experience in clandestine operations. A veteran of more than two decades in the CIA, E. Howard Hunt, formerly station chief for US spies in Mexico City, had been involved with the Bay of Pigs, and G. Gordon Liddy had been an FBI bureau supervisor. Both men took literally Nixon's demand that they stop at nothing. Hunt, on Colson's orders, fabricated cables implicating President Kennedy directly in the assassination of South Vietnam's president, Ngo Dinh Diem, and Colson attempted to persuade a journalist to publish the forgeries in *Life*. In August, Ehrlichman approved a plan of the Plumbers to break into the Beverly Hills office of Ellsberg's psychiatrist, Dr. Lewis Fielding, in the expectation that they would come upon data that would prompt questioning of Ellsberg's soundness of mind. On September 3, Hunt, Liddy, and three anti-Castro Cubans with CIA associations entered the office illegally and, using crowbars, smashed open the doctor's file cabinet. They found nothing.

After sanctioning this lawbreaking caper, the methodical Ehrlichman, with his buttoned-down persona, decided that restraint was called for. Hunt, who had written spy novels and hard-boiled fiction under a number of pseudonyms and had a predilection for perilous black bag jobs, was getting out of hand. He had even plotted to murder the widely syndicated columnist Jack Anderson, who had been revealing secret Vietnam operations, but fell short of carrying it off. Ehrlichman found it necessary to constrain Nixon too. When a zealous aide proposed to burglarize the Brookings Institution, the president responded, "I want it done on a thievery basis. Goddammit, go and get those files. Blow the safe and get it." He also approved a harebrained plot to firebomb Brookings, but Ehrlichman quashed the scheme—one of many instances when a subordinate saved Nixon from an infamous action. Disturbed by the excesses, Ehrlichman dissolved the Plumbers, only to have them move over to the president's ad hoc campaign organization.

Almost from the beginning, the president had shown that he had no scruples about employing illicit tactics. As early as April 1969, Ehrlichman, at Nixon's direction, had hired a former New York City detective to carry out undercover investigations, and the president had assigned this private eye and a sidekick to see what dirt they could dig up on senators who had opposed his Supreme Court nominee, with special focus on four Democrats: Ted Kennedy, Ed Muskie, Birch Bayh, and William Proxmire. On another occasion, Nixon told his aides to "destroy" the NBC television anchor Chet Huntley to teach a lesson to other commentators. In July 1969, Haldeman noted in his diary: "RN orders up a 'dirty tricks' team to engage in 'general campaign activity of harassment and needling of opposition, planting spies in their camp, etc.'" Heeding the president's instructions, Haldeman called upon a trio of University of Southern California alumni—Gordon Strachan, Dwight Chapin, and Donald Segretti—to disrupt Democrats.

Segretti, field agent of the "USC Mafia," put together a massive operation—with twenty-eight people in seventeen states bent not simply on gathering political intelligence but on disrupting the Democrats by numerous kinds of foul play. Paid by the president's attorney, Segretti toured the country indulging in mean schemes such as canceling appearances scheduled by Democratic leaders. Colson was even more despicable. In 1970, he circulated false allegations about Democratic senator Joseph Tydings of Maryland. That November, Tydings lost his seat.

In March 1970, Nixon told Haldeman that he wanted "to be sure we are doing an all-out hatchet job on the Democratic leaders, through IRS, etc." He ordered full field audits by the Internal Revenue Service of everyone from Clark Clifford to the CBS correspondent Daniel Schorr to the entire family of the publisher of the *Los Angeles Times*. Noting that the IRS was "full of Jews" and that there were many "big Jewish contributors" to the Democrats, the president asked, "Could we please investigate some of the cocksuckers?" In 1971, John Dean put together an "enemies" list to which Colson and others later added names. It included prominent US senators, college presidents, even the quarterback Joe Namath.

With an eye toward the forthcoming 1972 contest, Nixon targeted potential opponents. He ordered "permanent tails" placed on the most likely Democratic nominees—Ted Kennedy, Edmund Muskie, and Hubert Humphrey—with particular attention to "personal finances, family, and so forth." When Kennedy emerged as the front-runner, the president demanded around-the-clock surveillance of the Massachusetts senator. "Plant two guys on him," Nixon said. "We might just get lucky and catch this son-of-a-bitch. Ruin him for 76. It's going to be fun." E. Howard Hunt, in a red wig, supervised the operation. Nixon was delighted when Colson, who had hired a detective to shadow Kennedy in Paris, obtained photos of the senator with women, which were slipped to reporters.

Nixon also sought to exploit the shooting on May 15, 1972, of George Wallace, who, paralyzed, had to withdraw from the race. Instead of taking satisfaction in the elimination of a formidable opponent, the president directed Colson to send Hunt to the apartment of the man who shot Wallace with instructions to plant there materials of another potential rival, George McGovern, Democratic senator from South Dakota. A summary of a taped conversation reported: "Nixon is energized and excited by what seems to be the ultimate political dirty trick: the FBI and the Milwaukee police will be convinced, and will tell the world, that the attempted assassination of Wallace had its roots in left-wing Democratic politics." The scheme could not be carried out, perhaps because the FBI had quickly sealed off the residence.

With Wallace out of the way, Nixon concentrated on the Democratic senator who had emerged as the front-runner: Ed Muskie of Maine. His party's vice presidential nominee in 1968, Muskie had earned a wide following. In the spring of 1971, a poll showed him leading Nixon, 47 percent to 39 percent. To sabotage Muskie's campaign, the White House sent Segretti to New Hampshire. Even the driver of Muskie's car, as he made his rounds in the state, was a Nixon mole. Faking African American accents, Nixon's operatives awakened New Hampshire voters after midnight to urge them to vote for Muskie. The most devastating action took place after Nixon told Haldeman that Muskie "may have an emotional problem" that they should exploit. The Segretti bunch concocted a letter to the *Manchester Union Leader*, the extremely conservative paper that dominated the state, in which Muskie resorted to the pejorative "Canuck" to refer to French Canadians, a large voting bloc in New Hampshire. It appeared under the headline SENATOR MUSKIE INSULTS FRANCO-AMERICANS. The paper also published a second bogus letter falsely accusing the senator's wife of gross behavior. Provoked by this mean attack on his wife, Muskie gave an emotional speech in front of the *Union Leader* building that permitted the media to characterize him as too unbalanced for the rigors of the presidency.

After that incident, Muskie foundered, particularly following a poor showing in Florida where Nixon's conspirators struck again. Segretti's agents threw stink bombs into the senator's picnics and, once more, awakened voters late at night with calls to support Muskie. To turn the other Democratic contenders against him, they stole Muskie's stationery in order to concoct a letter falsely accusing Humphrey of drunken driving while accompanied by a whore and charging, again falsely, that another Democratic senator had twice been arrested for homosexual conduct. While tearing down Muskie, the rival the president most feared, the Segretti ring boosted McGovern, regarded as the weakest candidate in the race. Haldeman noted in his diary that Nixon had "made the point that the most effective way now for us to build McGovern is to get out some fake polls showing him doing well in trial heats."

The Democrats unwittingly abetted Nixon's designs by adopting changes in nominating procedures that led to the choice of a presidential nominee who, though an admirable public servant, was an ineffective candidate. After the disastrous 1968 convention in Chicago, the party had set up a commission cochaired by Senator McGovern to make the choice of delegates to the national convention more representative of the composition of the electorate. In response to the civil rights movement, the women's liberation movement, and campus insurrections, it set quotas to insure greater participation by African Americans, women, and young people, and it ended the practice of reserving seats for party officials.

Though the reformers aimed at getting an array of delegates approximating the composition of the electorate, the changes resulted in considerable distortion. Nearly 40 percent of the delegates to the 1972 convention had postgraduate degrees, in contrast to 4 percent of the nation. The roster underrepresented people over thirty (who were the most likely to vote); the proportion of delegates under thirty rose from 2.6 percent to 30 percent. It also shortchanged white ethnics, leaving them feeling that they had no home in the Democratic Party and that the Republicans might be offering a safer haven. (In preparing for the 1970 midterm campaign, Nixon had issued an instruction that Haldeman set down: "Mitchell—no prosecutions whatever re Mafia or any Italians until Nov," and at the start of the 1972 campaign, he told Haldeman: "Go for Poles, Italians, Irish...don't go for Jews & Blacks.") Union members, who had proven to be the most reliable Democratic campaigners, also felt left out. "There is too much hair and not enough cigars at this convention," one labor leader groused.

For their presidential nominee, the delegates settled on Senator McGovern. A World War II airman who had been awarded the Distinguished Flying Cross, director of Food for Peace, the "Prairie Populist" was universally viewed as a man of integrity. "George is the most decent man in the Senate," Robert Kennedy once said. "As a matter of fact, he's the only one." But McGovern's proposal to give $1,000 each year to every American "from the poorest migrant workers to the Rockefellers" seemed simplistic, and his choice of vice president, Thomas Eagleton, backfired when the Missouri senator acknowledged that he had twice undergone electric-shock therapy for mental illnesses. McGovern responded to the uproar that followed this embarrassment by saying, "I am 1000 percent for Tom Eagleton and I have no intention of dropping him from the ticket," only to force out his running mate just four days later.

The more McGovern faltered, the better Richard Nixon looked—even to longtime critics. Unapprised of the president's underhanded machinations, Walter Lippmann wrote approvingly of a "new Nixon, a maturer and mellower man who is no longer clawing his way to the top, . . . who has outlived and outgrown the ruthless politics of his earlier days." In this regard, his unsavory reputation helped him. "Everybody is saying that Mr. Nixon is doing better than they expected," James Reston commented, "which proves the success of past failures."

Nixon elicited enthusiastic support from hawkish voters by his aggressive actions in Asia in 1972. In May, with the South Vietnamese army reeling backward, he ordered massive aerial attacks on North Vietnam. "The bastards have never been bombed like they're going to be bombed this time," he said. In addition, to the consternation of some of his advisers, he authorized mining the harbors of Hanoi and Haiphong into which Soviet ships sailed. Ho Chi Minh, he said, "has gone over the brink and so have we. We have the power to destroy his war-making capacity. The only question is whether we have the will to use that power. What distinguishes me from Johnson is that I have the will in spades." The bombing devastated the countryside, left thousands homeless, and killed a hundred thousand North Vietnamese soldiers. Critics likened Nixon's imperious decision for saturation bombing to "Robespierre's claim to personify the general will." But pollsters reported that 60 percent of the American people thought well of Nixon's belligerency, and telegrams approving the mining flooded the White House mailroom.

The president won even more favor by the steps he took to decelerate the war. In his address accepting renomination, he stated: "We have brought over half a million men home. And more will be coming home. We have ended America's ground combat role. No draftees are being sent to Vietnam. We have reduced our casualties by 98 percent. We have gone the extra mile, in fact we have gone tens of thousands of miles trying to seek a negotiated settlement of the war." In August, he announced that the Selective Service System would be dismantled the following summer. That month, the last US ground combat units departed Vietnam. By Election Day, Nixon had scaled down troop levels, which had peaked at 543,000, to 20,000. On October 26, Kissinger announced, "Peace is at hand." That was untrue, but the claim undercut the main source of McGovern's appeal.

Though the nomination of McGovern had all but assured the president's reelection, Nixon fought for every possible vote, because he wanted to win by a margin so great that he could claim a mandate to govern as he pleased in his second term. He entrusted his campaign not to the Republican National Committee but to his own personal vehicle, the Committee to Re-elect the President, which drew the pejorative acronym CREEP. He persuaded John Mitchell to resign as attorney general to head the organization, with Jeb Stuart Magruder as his deputy. CREEP was largely staffed by the White House, just half a block away on Pennsylvania Avenue. Early on, Mitchell welcomed the Plumbers to CREEP and approved a quarter-million-dollar budget for Liddy, who was encouraged to carry on his chicanery.

With Mitchell taking care of campaign tactics, Nixon assigned his personal attorney, Herbert Kalmbach, another member of "the USC Mafia," to the vital task of fund-raising. Kalmbach bled dairymen for hundreds of thousands of dollars of campaign contributions in return for Nixon's backing of higher price supports for milk, and he brassily fixed the sum for how much corporations were required to turn over to the Nixon campaign if they wanted to do business with the federal government. He also tutored them on how to flout the law. Goodyear Tire & Rubber Company, American Airlines, Gulf Oil, and the Minnesota

Mining & Manufacturing Company were among the corporations that subsequently pled guilty to giving Nixon illegal contributions. (To restrict such expenditures, Congress in 1972 adopted a Federal Election Campaign Act, but in *Buckley v. Valeo* [1976] the Supreme Court invalidated a provision of the law regulating outlays for media. Congress did, though, establish a bipartisan Federal Election Commission in 1974 to monitor campaign spending.) One contributor to Nixon's 1972 campaign, the shipping tycoon George Steinbrenner, was later fined for such skullduggery, and the commissioner of baseball barred him from ownership of the New York Yankees for two years. Kalmbach wound up with a harsher punishment: a prison sentence of six to eighteen months for peddling ambassadorships. But these sanctions all lay in the future. In 1972, Kalmbach's legerdemain gave Nixon a huge treasure chest to finance his ambitions.

Only one untoward episode, spread across the pages of the *Washington Post*, raised a threat to Nixon's triumphal march. In the early hours of June 17, the *Post* reported, District of Columbia police, alerted by a vigilant night watchman, had apprehended five men at gunpoint in the Watergate hotel-apartment-commercial complex, where they had broken into the headquarters of the Democratic National Committee. The culprits, wearing surgical gloves, were carrying, in addition to sophisticated eavesdropping devices and tear-gas fountain pens, wads of fresh hundred-dollar bills suspiciously numbered in sequence. Four of the men were Miami-based Cuban exiles who had been in the employ of the CIA; the fifth, James McCord, a former CIA agent, was CREEP's chief of security. The police also arrested two confederates who were running the operation from a room in the Howard Johnson Hotel across the avenue: Gordon Liddy and E. Howard Hunt.

News of the break-in might have cost Nixon dearly, but the administration brazened it out. The president's press secretary, Ron Ziegler, dismissed the occurrence as a "third-rate burglary attempt." When two young reporters on the *Washington Post*, Bob Woodward and Carl Bernstein, turned up evidence of a tie between the burglars and the Nixon circle, the chair of CREEP commented, "The *Post* has maliciously sought to give the appearance of a direct connection between the White House and the Watergate—a charge the *Post* knows—and a half dozen investigations have found—to be false." A week later Ziegler characterized the accounts as "a blatant effort at character assassination that I do not think has been witnessed in the political process in some time."

Nixon positioned himself as a dignified statesman far above such vile affairs. In August, he reported to the press on the results of an investigation by White House Counsel John Dean: "I can state categorically that no one on the White House staff, no one in this administration, presently employed, was involved in this very bizarre incident.... What really hurts is to try to cover up." In fact, the president had never ordered an inquiry, and Dean had not made one. Furthermore, Nixon was deeply enmeshed in a criminal cover-up, and had been for weeks. But the country was unaware. In September, a poll revealed, 48 percent of the American people did not even know that there had been a break-in, and most of the Washington press corps regarded it as a nonevent.

In November, Nixon, with 45.9 million votes to McGovern's 28.4, carried every state from New York to California and swept the South from the Potomac to the Rio Grande. Only Massachusetts and the District of Columbia fell to the Democrats. He received more than fifteen million more votes than he had four years earlier, as he added to the Republican share much of the Wallace vote and numbers of blue-collar, ethnic Democrats. "The Great American Loser," he had twice narrowly missed being dumped by Eisenhower, had gone down to defeat in his 1960 race with Kennedy, had been beaten in the California gubernatorial race in 1962, and had barely won in 1968. But in 1972 he had the best showing of any Republican in the history of the party, outpolling even Ike. As he looked forward to his second term, there was only one note of foreboding. Despite his landslide victory, the Democrats maintained control of both houses of Congress, even picking up a couple of seats in the Senate. That outcome made Nixon the first president in history to start two terms with an opposition Congress.

His lease on the White House renewed for another four years, Nixon stood at the peak of his power. Though the seven Watergate burglars had been indicted, no one had come close to finding the "smoking gun" that would implicate the president. After Nixon's huge success at the polls, Colson called the allegation that the president had ordered the break-in "a work of fiction rivaling only *Gone With the Wind* in circulation and *Portnoy's Complaint* for indecency." On Inauguration Day, the *Washington*

Post published a supplement—"The Nixon Years"—that in the course of twenty-two pages never mentioned Watergate, and a Gallup Poll the following week reported that the proportion of the country applauding Nixon's "handling his job as President" had soared to the highest point in twenty-seven months.

In contemplating the arc of his presidency, Richard Nixon might well have said, with F. Scott Fitzgerald, "There are no second acts in American lives." He began the new term lording it over his more than two hundred million subjects and ended it exiting the capital in disgrace. He sought to impose himself upon the world but was compelled to recognize that Beijing and Moscow did not come to heel when he whistled. He sponsored four successive plans to put ceilings on oil prices, only to find himself at the mercy of desert caliphs.

Nixon started his second term in a nasty mood. On the day after the election triumph, the president, instead of savoring the moment, asked all of his top officials for their resignations while railing against federal bureaucrats. With not a hint of a mellow "new Nixon," he fulminated: "Mitchell was captured by the bureaucracy....Rogers was totally captured....Mel Laird, he didn't change anybody....The people who ran the Pentagon before are still running the goddam Pentagon....HEW, the whole damn bunch....Let's remember the VA—Clean those bastards out....Take that Park Service, they've been screwing us for years. Rog Morton won't get rid of that son-of-a-bitch. But he's got to go." Deploring this attitude, Bryce Harlow, who served as counselor to both Eisenhower and Nixon, later commented that Haldeman, Ehrlichman, and the president "were up there planning the future of the Administration as though they were in Berchtesgaden."

With what he called a "rather massive majority," Nixon sought to carry out a thoroughgoing overhaul of the federal government and, abandoning all claim to being a centrist, veered sharply to the right. In 1972, he had announced his intent to put through "the most comprehensive...reorganization since the executive was first constituted in George Washington's administration 183 years ago." As he began his second term, he set out to eliminate four departments and create four super-secretaries to ride herd on the bureaucracy. He got nowhere with this drastic scheme, but he had greater leeway in his determination to undo the Great Society. He jettisoned community action projects, and he especially targeted the key agency of the War on Poverty: the Office of Economic Opportunity, which he sought to starve to death by providing no funds for it in his budget. To dismantle the OEO, he appointed as its director Howard Phillips, who, the very conservative head of the OMB said, was "an ideologue, not a manager," intent on "tearing apart the agency with unconcealed glee." Phillips claimed that though Congress had established the agency, the president was empowered to eradicate it because his budget message superseded action by Congress—a contention that a federal court dismissed as unconstitutional overreaching by the chief executive.

Nixon had been engaged in a guerrilla war with Congress from the outset, chiefly by impounding funds that had been appropriated for programs he opposed, and in his second term Congress struck back. Impoundment had begun as early as 1803 under Jefferson, but no other president had employed it so frequently as Nixon. The Budget and Impoundment Control Act of 1974 markedly curtailed the practice. It also established a Congressional Budget Office to grapple with the OMB about federal spending. In addition, Nixon had his knuckles rapped by the judiciary. In *Train v. City of New York* (1975), the Supreme Court ruled that a federal official (and presumptively a president) did not have an inherent right to refuse to spend less than Congress had appropriated. When Congress hauled Nixon into court in 1973 for failing to appoint members to a council on education of Native Americans, a judge in *Minnesota Chippewa Tribe v. Carlucci* reminded him that he was obliged to "take care that the laws be faithfully executed."

Exasperated as they were by the president's insolence in domestic affairs, senators found Nixon's conduct of foreign relations far more disturbing. Though the Constitution stipulated that presidents should enter into agreements abroad with "the advice and consent" of the Senate and that Congress alone had the power to declare war, the president, said J. William Fulbright, willfully moved armies around the globe as if they were his chess pieces. "By the early 1970s," wrote Arthur Schlesinger Jr., "the American President had become on issues of war and peace the most absolute monarch (with the possible exception of Mao Tse-tung of China) among the great powers of the world."

To rein in his capability to commit armed forces overseas, Congress, in November 1973, put through the War Powers Act, approved over Nixon's veto. It instructed the president to "consult with Congress" whenever he dispatched troops into danger zones, to report to Congress in writing within forty-eight hours whenever he ordered military forces into action, to "consult regularly with the Congress" while they were engaged, and to withdraw them within ninety days if Congress did not give its explicit consent to keep them there. Furthermore, the law empowered Congress to terminate deployment of soldiers at any time by concurrent resolution, not subject to presidential veto. The act had the unintended consequence of recognizing for the first time the authority of a president to start a war and to wage it, however briefly, despite the provision of the Constitution giving Congress sole power to declare war.

Opponents of the war also challenged Nixon in the courts, but to no avail. In *Massachusetts v. Laird* (1970), the Supreme Court let stand a US Circuit Court ruling that the president, in waging war in Southeast Asia, was not violating the Constitution because he acted with congressional support. A federal district court did hold that Nixon had breached the Constitution by his actions in Cambodia, but it was reversed by higher tribunals, with an appellate court, in *Holtzman v. Schlesinger* (1973), invoking the political questions doctrine. The judiciary, it declared, could not challenge presidential war-making authority.

In framing policy toward Southeast Asia, Nixon paid no heed either to Congress or to the courts. After the 1972 election, the peace Kissinger had announced fell apart. The South Vietnamese would not go along, and Hanoi withdrew from talks. Nixon reacted by ordering the most destructive bombing of the war on Hanoi and Haiphong, starting on December 18 and continuing through the Christmas season until December 30. He told the head of the Joint Chiefs of Staff: "I don't want any more of this crap about the fact that we couldn't hit this target or that one. This is your chance to use military power to win the war, and, if you don't, I'll consider you responsible." The "Christmas bombing" brought worldwide condemnation. Swedish premier Olof Palme likened the United States to Nazi Germany; the pope called the raids "the object of daily grief"; and a *New York Times* correspondent characterized Nixon's action as "shame on earth." The bombing, however, did bring North Vietnam back to the negotiating table.

Early in 1973 in Paris, Kissinger initialed a cease-fire agreement. It permitted 160,000 North Vietnamese troops to remain south of the border while requiring the United States to withdraw all of its soldiers and to dismantle its bases. The American government also acceded to political status for the Viet Cong in governing South Vietnam. Nixon imposed the terms on the South Vietnamese, who accepted them because of secret pledges he made, without notifying Congress, to continue military aid if Hanoi violated the pact—an empty pledge on which he never carried through.

As he unveiled the agreement, Nixon, five times, said that he had achieved a "peace with honor," and for years afterward Kissinger echoed that claim. Many Americans, though, saw no reason to rejoice at a settlement that left the North Vietnamese armies in the south but required the United States to pull out. America got back 591 prisoners of war, but little else. The pact, as the US commander in Southeast Asia, General Creighton Abrams, said, amounted to "slow surrender." The terms were no better than those negotiated the previous October before Nixon unleashed the bombardment that killed so many, or, indeed, those that could have been approved when he first took office. Nixon required longer to end the war than Lincoln did to fight the Civil War, and one-third of the deaths in Vietnam occurred on his watch. Kissinger continued to maintain that the United States had secured South Vietnam's independence, but, as the historian Theodore Draper has written, this conceit was a "pipe dream," for Hanoi soon seized advantage of the opportunity created by the withdrawal of American ground forces, and "the Nixon-Kissinger house of cards collapsed ignominiously." April 30, 1975, saw the fall of Saigon, renamed Ho Chi Minh City. Furthermore, the agreement did not even bring peace. Despite the cease-fire, US planes pounded Cambodia more mercilessly over the next seven months than they had Japan during all of the Second World War. The mayhem ended not by Nixon's volition but only after Congress, in June 1973, cut off appropriations for waging war in Southeast Asia, effective mid-August.

That fall, Nixon shifted his focus from Asia to the Middle East, where the administration had been engaging in bizarre and perplexing intrigue. When, in the hope of forestalling a dangerous war in the region, Secretary of State Rogers formulated a peace plan for a major-powers intervention to require Israeli withdrawal from occupied lands in return for concessions, Kissinger, distrusting both the Russians and the Arabs who would be invited to participate, sabotaged it. The national security adviser sent a message to an aide of Israel's prime minister, Golda Meir, who was heading off for an American cross-country lecture tour: "Tell her wherever she goes, in all her speeches and press conferences, we want her to slam the hell out of Rogers and his plan." Nixon in turn ordered his assistant Leonard Garment to foment protests by Jewish groups in the United States against Rogers. (Kissinger also made clear that he believed that foreign policy ought only to be influenced by the interests of the State. At a meeting with Nixon, he made the appalling observation: "The emigration of Jews from the Soviet Union [to Israel] is not an objective of American foreign policy, and if they put Jews into gas chambers in the Soviet Union, it is not an American concern. Maybe a humanitarian concern.")

In October 1973, as Rogers had foreseen, the smoldering enmities in the Middle East burst into flame when, on the high holy day of Yom Kippur, Egyptian and Syrian forces invaded Israeli-held territory. With no thought of appeasing the oil-rich Arab states, Nixon ordered the most massive military airlift in history on behalf of Israel. The Arab nations retaliated by imposing an oil embargo on the United States and forming the Organization of Petroleum Exporting Countries (OPEC), which raised prices for a barrel of oil nearly 400 percent—a shocking increase. Nixon appointed an "energy czar" and imposed a series of drastic measures, including curtailing flight schedules and shutting down filling stations on Sundays. But skyrocketing oil prices produced long queues at gas pumps and, reverberating through the economy, doubled the rate of what inflation had been when Nixon took office.

The Yom Kippur conflict raised one of the greatest tests of Nixon's years in office, and at the height of it, the president was absent without leave. His gargantuan airlift and the threat of Soviet intervention brought the world the closest to a nuclear confrontation it had been since the 1962 Cuban missiles crisis, but during the sixteen-day war, Nixon did not once attend a White House strategy conference. Left on their own, and acting with excessive zeal, Kissinger and other subordinates made the perilous decision to order a worldwide nuclear alert without informing Nixon until after it was done. Hunkered down, Nixon could not be troubled with events abroad because he was wholly absorbed in coping with a domestic exigency that portended the ruin of his presidency. The Watergate controversy, ostensibly scotched, had become the consuming event of his tenure.

———————

In assuming that he had put the Watergate accusations behind him with his resounding victory in November 1972, Nixon failed to reckon with FBI agents and the chief judge of the US District Court for the District of Columbia, John J. Sirica. It took the FBI only three days to trace the hundred-dollar bills of conspirators to a Miami bank involved in laundering the money, and it quickly found out that one of the burglars had deposited a check signed by Kenneth Dahlberg, Midwest chair of CREEP's finance committee. (Even earlier, DC police had come upon a trail of evidence leading directly to the Nixon administration, including a document with the name of E. Howard Hunt and the identification "W. House.") Nixon had the further misfortune of having the culprits facing trial under Judge Sirica. Known as "Maximum John," Sirica anticipated that the prospect of severe sentences would cause one of those indicted to confess.

Nixon and his associates thought they were invulnerable because of the extraordinary measures they had taken to elude detection. On Ehrlichman's orders, White House staff forced open Hunt's safe at the White House and shredded papers revealing the connection of CREEP to dirty tricks and the Watergate break-in. Dean, Strachan, Magruder, and Colson were among those engaged in this criminal act of destroying evidence. Asked by Dean what he should do with McCord's attaché case found in the safe, Ehrlichman told him to "deep six" it—that is, toss it into the Potomac.

The schemers also took pains to buy the silence of the burglars. The president's attorney, Herbert Kalmbach, told CREEP's financial chief that he was "on a special mission on a White House project and I need all the cash I can get." In a short time, two CREEP officials and Haldeman raised $350,000. Like an evildoer in an overwrought Hollywood spy thriller, Kalmbach got the cash to the burglars by dropping it off at airport lockers and telephone booths. When E. Howard Hunt's wife died in a plane crash in December 1972, she had $10,000 in currency in her purse. Despite these payments of hush money, Dean informed the president on March 21 that the Watergate seven were demanding a million dollars and a promise of clemency as the price of silence. Undaunted, Nixon responded: "I know where it can be gotten.... I mean it's easy, it could be done." A day later, he instructed his top aides not to cooperate with the grand jury. "I don't give a shit what happens," he said. "I want you all to stonewall it, let them plead the Fifth Amendment, cover-up or anything else, if it'll save it—save the plan."

But on the very next day, Sirica opened a gaping hole in the cover-up. On March 23, 1973, the date set for sentencing the burglars, Judge Sirica read in open court a letter he had received from James McCord stating that "political pressure was applied to the defendants...to remain silent," that "perjury occurred during the trial," and that there were "others involved in the Watergate operation" who had not yet been "identified." Sirica followed this up by handing down harsh sentences to the uncooperative felons: thirty-five years for Hunt. In addition, he ordered McCord to testify before a grand jury. More important, he compelled him to speak to a committee probing wrongdoing that the US Senate had established under the chairmanship of Senator Sam Ervin of North Carolina, who, while assuming the guise of a simple country lawyer, proved to be a shrewd interrogator.

It did not take long for counsel of the Ervin Committee to announce that McCord had "named names," and over the course of the next month one after another of Nixon's appointees acknowledged guilt. The "names" that McCord revealed, it turned out, included those of Mitchell, Haldeman, Dean, Magruder, and Colson. On April 3, Dean, sensing that Nixon was prepared to make him the scapegoat, let the Ervin Committee know that he was ready to talk. Eleven days later, Magruder cracked. Seeking the best deal for himself, he told the Ervin Committee that he had earlier perjured himself and that Mitchell, Colson, and Strachan had taken part in illegal transactions. On April 26, the country learned that the acting head of the FBI, L. Patrick Gray, had destroyed two folders from Hunt's White House safe that had been given him by Ehrlichman and Dean. Impervious to how these developments reflected on him, Nixon continued to project himself as a dedicated statesman, declaring, "I condemn any attempt to cover up this case, no matter who is involved." (In fact, he had told Gray, "I gotta have a relationship here where you go out and do something and deny on a stack of Bibles.") The parade of confessions, though, forced Nixon to realize that if he was going to save his presidency, he had to take drastic action. Even the chairman of the Republican National Committee, Senator Robert Dole, was saying, "The credibility of the administration is zilch, zero."

On April 30, Nixon announced that he was accepting the resignations of Haldeman, Ehrlichman, and Mitchell's successor, Attorney General Richard Kleindienst, and that he had fired John Dean. In fact, he had cashiered all four. Less than six months after his landslide triumph in November, he had been compelled to dismantle his White House team. In releasing this information, he affirmed, "There can be no whitewash at the White House," implying that he was innocent and that his most trusted appointees were guilty of wrongdoing. (Four other Nixon associates had already quit the government: John Mitchell, Dwight Chapin, Charles Colson, and Jeb Stuart Magruder. In May, Mitchell was indicted.)

The threatened Republican inner circle closed ranks about Nixon. The dismissals, said House Minority Leader Gerald Ford, were "a necessary first step by the White House in clearing the air....I have the greatest confidence in the President and I am absolutely positive he had nothing to do with this mess." Governor Reagan let the president know, "My heart [is] with you," and when network news commentators raised disturbing questions, Billy Graham phoned Nixon to say, "I felt like slashing their throats."

May brought more bad news for Nixon. Two weeks after he discharged his top advisers, US District Court Judge William Matthew Byrne Jr., a Nixon appointee, dismissed all charges against Daniel Ellsberg because of government misconduct. The trial had exposed the break-in of the office of Ellsberg's psychiatrist as well as a pattern of wiretapping without court order. In addition, Byrne revealed that Haldeman had asked him, while he was presiding over the case, whether he was interested in being appointed by Nixon to head the FBI. He ended the trial when he learned that salient Department of Justice records had never been turned over to Ellsberg's attorneys and, the government claimed, could not be found. "The totality of the circumstances... offend a sense of justice," Judge Byrne declared. "The bizarre events have incurably infected the prosecution of this case."

That same month, to quiet his critics, Nixon named Elliot Richardson, a pillar of the Eastern Establishment with an impeccable reputation, to succeed Kleindienst as attorney general, and said he was cloaking him with "absolute authority." The Senate Judiciary Committee refused to approve Richardson's confirmation unless he pledged to appoint a special prosecutor. Accordingly, Richardson named a Harvard Law School professor, Archibald Cox, who had been solicitor general under President Kennedy. (Cox's great-grandfather William Evarts had defended Andrew Johnson at his impeachment trial.) Nixon did all he could to hamper Cox's investigation. At one point, Cox was told to "stay the hell away" from a fund-raising scandal.

In June, over the course of a week of testimony before the Ervin Committee, John Dean offered riveting allegations of Nixon's participation in the cover-up, but the president brushed them off. A month earlier, Nixon had stated, "I took no part in, nor was I aware of, any subsequent efforts that may have been made to cover up Watergate," then itemized a series of activities such as raising hush money that he avowed he had not been involved in. (Of the seven denials he made, his admirer Alexander Haig later said, six were lies.) In discounting Dean's testimony, however, a Republican senator, Howard Baker, said that the critical question remained unanswered: "What did the President know and when did he know it?" Without providing hard evidence showing that Nixon's hand had held "a smoking gun," Dean had no chance of persuading skeptics of the president's guilt. The Senate committee's counsel, Samuel Dash, later recalled telling Ervin "that we wouldn't be able to draw any real conclusions about the president, nor would an impeachment committee or any prosecuting officer, because the issue was: Do you believe in John Dean or the president of the United States? The answer should be, and has to be, the president of the United States, so the only way Dean's testimony could have impact is if it's corroborated."

Perhaps unintentionally, Dean's testimony did lead to a crucial breakthrough that, many months later, was to yield the smoking gun. When Alexander Butterfield, who had been Haldeman's deputy, was summoned, a lawyer for the Republican minority on the committee asked, "Do you know of any basis for the implications in Dean's testimony that conversations in the President's office are recorded?" Butterfield did not want to be an informer, but neither did he wish to commit perjury. "I said to myself, if they ask a fuzzy question, I'll give a fuzzy answer," he later recalled. "I never in a million years dreamed they would ask about the tapes." He responded, "I hoped you fellows wouldn't ask that question." There was not just one tape, he revealed, but four thousand hours of tapes, recorded in the Oval Office and at other venues, including the Cabinet Room and Camp David. Nixon had installed the system to provide material for his memoirs, but, as a consequence, the president, who had so little regard for the liberties of others, had bugged himself.

Alert to the potential significance of this disclosure, both Senator Ervin and Archibald Cox asked Nixon to release the tapes. He turned them down, saying that there was no point in doing so, for he had listened to them and they were "entirely consistent with what I know to be the truth." Ervin, and Judge Sirica on behalf of Cox, responded with subpoenas for the tapes, making Nixon the only president since 1807 to be subpoenaed. Every member of the Ervin Committee, including all of the Republican senators, supported their chairman in issuing these subpoenas. Nixon, though, would not budge. Invoking executive privilege and the principle of separation of powers, he maintained that "the President is not subject to compulsory process from the courts."

His stonewalling cost him dearly. That summer, pollsters reported that only 32 percent of the country gave him a positive performance rating. No president had ever fallen so far in popular esteem as Nixon had since his second inauguration eight months before. Though right-wingers had hitherto been contending that he was being victimized by liberal media, the country's foremost conservative periodical, William Buckley's *National Review*, not only demanded that Nixon turn over the tapes but also stated that Watergate had "drained his political sinew, his moral authority, and his credibility." In August, Senator Goldwater advised Nixon to "show up some morning at the Ervin Committee and say, 'Here I am, Sam. What do you want to know?'"

As Nixon floundered in this tidal wave of disapproval, he suffered a further embarrassment. A grand jury determined that Spiro Agnew had received more than $100,000 in bribes and kickbacks from contractors while county executive and then governor of Maryland, and that while he was serving as vice president, contractors were still delivering wads of cash. After first blustering that a vice president is immune from criminal prosecution, Agnew, who had been railing against soft judges, plea bargained. On October 10, 1973, he pleaded *nolo contendere* (no contest) to a charge of filing a "false and fraudulent" tax return and resigned.

Never before had anyone so dishonored the second highest office in the land. He got off with a fine in the small amount of $10,000 and a sentence of three years' probation. One consequence of Agnew's downfall was that legislators contemplating the possibility of Nixon's impeachment no longer had to fear that, if he were removed, a corrupt politician would become president of the United States.

To fill the vice presidential office vacated by Agnew, Nixon settled on Gerald Ford, the House minority leader. In making his choice, Nixon took comfort in finding a man who would readily be confirmed. Jerry Ford's colleagues in the House in both parties regarded him as a decent man who worked hard and was easy to get along with. "His success," one journalist observed, "was a triumph of lowest-common-denominator politics, the survival of the man without enemies, the least objectionable alternative." Furthermore, Nixon could count on Ford to be an unquestioning subordinate. The president, a member of the White House inner circle later explained, "knew that Ford was a team player and understood how to work with a wink and a nod." At his confirmation hearings, Ford assured the committee that he had "no intention of seeking any public office in 1976." He also stated, with respect to the Watergate accusations, that the president was "completely innocent."

Before the furor over Agnew's iniquity had begun to die down, Nixon engendered a much more consequential controversy. When a US circuit court ruled that Nixon must surrender the tapes, he temporized by proposing that instead of doing so, he would provide summaries of the recordings that would be authenticated by a Mississippi senator who was a Nixon loyalist. Curiously, Ervin consented to this dubious arrangement. Cox, however, balked. Though Nixon had promised the special prosecutor "complete independence," he ordered Cox "as an employee of the Executive Branch to make no further attempts by judicial process to obtain tapes, notes, or memoranda of Presidential conversations." At a press conference he called, Cox announced that he would persist in his quest, pointing out that the president was not simply attempting to sidetrack his investigation but was defying a federal court decree. (Subsequently, in *Nader v. Bork* [1973], a federal court ruled that Nixon's directive to Cox violated Justice Department procedures.) On Saturday, October 20, Nixon ordered Elliot Richardson to fire Cox. The attorney general refused to do so and resigned. The president then turned to Richardson's deputy, William Ruckelshaus, who also left the government rather than comply. The third man in line, Solicitor General Robert Bork, then consented to discharge Cox. The president followed up by abolishing the Office of the Watergate Special Prosecutor.

In thinking that he could readily rid himself of Cox, Nixon badly mistook the national mood. The public response was nothing less than, in the word of Alexander Haig, a "firestorm." Nearly half a million telegrams of outrage descended on the White House, and Nixon's approval rating fell to 17 percent. A federal prosecutor recalled: "We were stunned, along with the rest of the nation, that this naked use of force would be employed. After all, we were all lawyers; the president himself was a lawyer; we had all been dealing with these matters in lawyerlike ways; and we expected that this would be resolved in the court, not by the president firing Professor Cox without cause—and without obeying court orders.... This was scary; this was not America with a *c*; this was Amerika with a *k*."

Spurred by "the Saturday Night Massacre," antipathy toward the president entered a new, and more ominous, stage. Newspapers that had endorsed Nixon every time he ran turned against him. "It is with regret," said the *Salt Lake Tribune*, "that we now find it necessary, for the good of the country, to call upon Richard M. Nixon to resign." Should he fail to comply, it declared, "Congress should move with alacrity to impeach him." The Democratic leadership in the House launched a preliminary exploration of impeachment, and congressional Republicans warned the White House that, if Nixon did not release the tapes, he was going to be impeached. In a late October cover story, "Richard Nixon Stumbles to the Brink," *Time*, a longtime Nixon supporter, asserted that the Saturday Night Massacre put the president's "survival in the Oval Office in grave doubt," and in mid-November it stated, in the first editorial ever to appear in its pages, "The President Must Resign," for Nixon had "irredeemably lost his moral authority, the confidence of most of the country, and therefore his ability to govern effectively."

Nixon encountered further admonishment by the judiciary. After Judge Sirica ordered him to deliver the tapes, Nixon appealed to the Circuit Court of the District of Columbia, with the claim that Sirica's action "threatened the continued existence of the presidency as a functioning institution." In October in *Nixon v. Sirica*, the circuit court, 5–2, held that, though the president's conversations were "presumptively privileged," the "mere assertion of privilege" to ignore a subpoena "must fail in the face of the uniquely powerful showing made by the special prosecutor." Recognizing that he had to make some concession, Nixon informed Sirica that he was turning over seven tapes to the grand jury. One of the recordings, however, had a suspicious 18½-minute gap. The president's longtime personal secretary blamed herself for inadvertently wiping out that segment, but those who believed that the omission was caused by an accident, said the *National Review*, "could gather for lunch in a phone booth." (A panel of experts later concluded that there might have been as many as nine deliberate erasures.) In addition, the White House confessed that two of the nine tapes Sirica had ordered could not be located.

At this unpropitious moment, the press also raised doubts about the president's financial probity. It revealed that, to gain a big tax advantage, Nixon had backdated a gift of his vice presidential papers to the government. An investigation by the IRS determined that, as the result of his failure to file proper returns and of deceit by his lawyers, he owed nearly half a million dollars in back taxes. In addition, the press reported that the federal government had spent huge sums to improve his San Clemente estate, sticking American taxpayers with bills for items such as den furniture and a swimming pool heater. A new barrage of criticism led Nixon to hold a televised news conference in which he declared: "People have got to know whether or not their president is a crook. Well, I am not a crook." The walls of the Oval Office were closing in on him, and Nixon sensed this. On December 23, 1973, he scrawled, "Last Christmas here?"

Nixon, though, tried to save his hide by bluster. Projecting himself as an innocent victim, he said that he had "never heard or seen such outrageous, vicious, distorted reporting in twenty-seven years of public life." He also insisted that he had "a constitutional responsibility to defend the Office of the Presidency from any encroachment on confidentiality." In his State of the Union address in January 1974, he declared, "I want you to know that I have no intention whatever of ever walking away from the job that the people elected me to do." The country, he said, should turn its attention to more important matters. "One year of Watergate is enough," he maintained.

But the Watergate scandal would not go away. So great had been the outcry against the firing of Cox that Nixon had hastened to appoint a

National-Security Blanket

---from Herblock Special Report (W.W. Norton, 1974)

"National-security Blanket." In late May 1973, at the height of the Watergate revelations, this Herblock cartoon depicts Nixon seeking to hide behind the American flag, but the evidence of his wrongdoing is too overwhelming. He was to be driven from office in the following year. *The Herb Block Foundation*

new special prosecutor: Leon Jaworski, a prominent Houston attorney who had served as president of the American Bar Association. Twice he had voted for Nixon, but he was as dogged as Cox in pursuit of justice. After he had presented evidence, a federal grand jury on March 1, 1974, indicted Ehrlichman, Haldeman, Mitchell, and Colson—the four men who had been closest to Nixon—as well as three other presidential appointees. In April, a jury found Dwight Chapin, Nixon's appointments secretary, guilty of perjury.

Months before the smoking gun showing Nixon's involvement in the cover-up had been located, the grand jury concluded that "beginning no later than March 21, 1973, the President joined an ongoing criminal conspiracy to obstruct justice, obstruct a criminal investigation, and commit perjury (which included payment of cash to Watergate defendants to influence their testimony, making and causing to be made false statements and declarations, making offers of clemency and leniency, and obtaining information from the Justice Department to thwart its investigation) and that the President is also liable for substantive violations of various criminal statutes." Nixon was not arraigned with Mitchell and the others only because Jaworski was uncertain that a grand jury could indict a sitting president. He settled for having Nixon termed "an unindicted co-conspirator" but did not make that designation public.

The struggle over the tapes continued through the spring of 1974, with Nixon attempting to seize high ground. "I have cooperated completely with not only the grand jury but also with other investigative agencies," he told a press conference. "I will not participate in the destruction of the Office of the Presidency of the United States while I am in this office." But both Jaworski (through Sirica) and the House Judiciary Committee subpoenaed Nixon to provide additional tapes. When Nixon refused to heed Sirica's order, Jaworski asked the US Supreme Court to expedite the case. By then, it had become clear that only the highest tribunal could resolve the conflict.

On April 30, 1974, to forestall subpoenas, Nixon released 1,300 pages of edited transcripts of the recordings. "The President has nothing to hide," he declared. The transcripts, he maintained, demonstrated that "I had no knowledge of the cover-up until I was informed of it by John Dean on March 21." Even though the tapes had been bowdlerized, they exposed enough to show that Nixon was, to a considerable extent, implicated in the scandal, and the frequent appearance of the phrase "expletive deleted" impaired his reputation. The tone of conversations in the White House, said the Republican leader in the Senate, was "deplorable, shabby, disgusting, and immoral." Still more newspapers that had long supported Nixon jumped ship. "It's time to hand President Nixon his hat," said the *Topeka Daily Capital*, which reported "a certain heart sickness" on reading the transcripts. One of the very few favorable comments came from Vice President Ford, who said that the transcripts proved Nixon "innocent" and that the word of the president should be preferred to that of John Dean, "an admitted felon." But even Ford acknowledged that he was "a little disappointed."

Through the rest of the spring and into the summer, the country awaited the decision on the disposition of the tapes, and on July 24, in an opinion by Chief Justice Burger in *United States v. Nixon*, the Supreme Court handed down a unanimous ruling. For the first time in its history, the Court recognized the right to executive privilege. That power, Burger said, accepting the principal contention of the president's attorney, "is fundamental to the operation of government and inextricably rooted in the separation of powers under the Constitution." Yet, though there was "presumptive privilege" for the materials of a chief executive, Burger stated, a president did not have "absolutely unqualified privilege." Executive privilege did not extend to withholding information requested for a criminal prosecution, he declared. In such a proceeding, a president, like all other citizens, had to respond to a subpoena. "The generalized assertion of privilege" in a legal action that had no national security aspect "must yield to the demonstrated, specific need for evidence in a pending criminal trial," he concluded. Therefore, the Court ordered the president to surrender sixty-four tapes to Judge Sirica "forthwith."

Nixon did not comply forthwith, partly because the outcome stunned him. He had anticipated that even if the Court ruled against him, there would be a split decision, permitting him to defy it and cite the dissenters as justifying his interpretation of the Constitution. Five of the judges had been named by Republican presidents, three of them—including Chief Justice Burger—by him. But the unanimous ruling left him no "air." Even so, he may still have thought that he had wiggle room. As recently as July 12, Jerry Ford had assured him: "Don't worry, Mr. President, you've got this beat. We have a solid fifty-vote margin in the House."

On July 27, three days after *United States v. Nixon*, the House Judiciary Committee shattered any such illusion. Without even waiting for a smoking gun, it voted three articles of impeachment. Richard Nixon, the committee declared, had "acted in a manner contrary to his trust as President and subversive of constitutional government," causing "manifest injury to the people of the United States." The three articles accused Nixon of obstruction of justice, abuse of power, and contempt of Congress. On each of the roll calls, a number of Republicans joined the Democrats.

Nixon received further discouragement from his inner circle. For two years, he had concealed from his lawyers a particular tape of a meeting on June 23, 1972, but after the Supreme Court's adverse ruling, he asked his chief legal counsel to listen to it. Here, without doubt, was the long-sought smoking gun. The president, Al Haig reported to top White House aides, was "guilty as hell." On hearing Haig's account at that gathering, the journalist David Gergen later recalled, "my feelings raced between devastation and betrayal. How could he possibly...?" Haig told the president: "I just don't see how we can survive this one."

On August 5, Nixon released the tapes, saying, in a classic understatement, "I recognize that this additional material I am now furnishing may further damage my case." It surely did. Nixon had long claimed that he first learned of the transgression in March 1973. But the transcript of the June 23, 1972, meeting in the Oval Office revealed that he knew within a week and was actively engaged from the outset in a cover-up. At that June conference, Haldeman reported that John Mitchell had recommended, and Dean had agreed, that the head of the CIA should call the FBI chief and say, "Stay the hell out of it; this is...business...we don't want you to go any further on." Nixon not only embraced the scheme but fabricated a story that national security was at stake. He could be heard on the tape coaching Haldeman precisely what to say to the CIA chief: "The President's belief is that this is going to open the whole Bay of Pigs thing up again," and the CIA "should call the FBI in and say...don't go any further into this case." Nixon, in sum, had orchestrated a blatant obstruction of justice.

The surrender of the smoking gun tape doomed Nixon's presidency, which survived for only three more days. The *Orlando Sentinel Star* declared, "For those of us who demanded evidence before joining the crowd determined to drive a President from office, we now have it—in spades." All seventeen Republicans on the House Judiciary Committee announced that they would vote to impeach. A California Republican who had been Nixon's staunchest defender on the committee said, brushing back tears, "With great reluctance and deep personal sorrow I am prepared to conclude that the magnificent career of public service of Richard Nixon must be terminated." With Nixon certain to be impeached, the sole remaining question was whether he still had enough support in the Senate to stave off conviction. "There are only so many lies you can take and now there has been one too many," Senator Goldwater said. "Nixon should get his ass out of the White House—today." When, on August 7, a delegation of senior Republicans on the Hill paid a call at the White House, the president asked how many Senate votes he could count on. "Ten at most, maybe less," Goldwater responded. "Some aren't firm."

All that week, insiders found Nixon distraught. He walked the corridors of the White House at night talking to the portraits of past presidents. No one could predict what he would do. Rumors that he would stage a military coup to remain in power were taken seriously enough that the secretary of defense, James Schlesinger, told the Joint Chiefs of Staff to ignore any military order emanating from the White House unless it had the defense secretary's authorization. Nixon's anguish peaked on the night of August 7 after the Senate delegation had pronounced his doom. That night, he alternated sobbing and imbibing liquor. At one point, according to Woodward and Bernstein, he asked Kissinger to kneel with him on the White House floor and pray.

On the night of August 8, 1974, Nixon, flag pin in his lapel, delivered a televised address from the White House. "To leave office before my term is completed is abhorrent to every instinct in my body," he stated. He wanted "to continue to fight through the months ahead for...personal vindication." Though he admitted that some of his judgments were wrong, his use of the word "vindication" implied that he was being unfairly pilloried. He spoke no word of apology, of contrition, for betraying his oath to execute his country's laws faithfully. "I have never been a quitter," he declared, but he "must put the interests of America first." He acknowledged, "I no longer have a strong enough political base in the Congress to remain in office." Hence, he concluded, "I shall resign the presidency effective at noon tomorrow." Next day, as he boarded the helicopter taking him away from the capital that had been his home for most of the past four decades, Nixon, apparently in total denial, grinned glazedly and thrust both hands aloft signaling V for Victory.

When Nixon abandoned the White House to settle into exile in California, millions of Americans viewed him as a pariah, the only president ever to have been driven out of office. Long afterward, many of them—across a broad political spectrum—continued to revile him. "For 25 years," said Bill Moyers, "the man had massaged the baser instincts of politics," and, in his memoirs, the conservative icon Barry

Goldwater wrote: "He was the most dishonest individual I ever met in my life. President Nixon lied to his wife, his family, his friends, longtime colleagues in the US Congress, lifetime members of his own political party, the American people and the world." In 1996, a panel of scholars, asked to rank American presidents, placed Nixon at the very bottom.

In an astonishingly brief time after his downfall, however, reconsideration began, and numbers of writers offered a more positive assessment of his tenure and came to view him, in retirement, as a sage. Nixon had once called the media a "lynch mob," but when he turned up at the annual gathering of the American Society of Newspaper Editors, he received a standing ovation. A member of Parliament, Jonathan Aitken, while acknowledging Nixon's "tyrannical streak," his "mendacity," and the "'dark' side of his nature," maintained that Nixon had been "excessively maligned for his faults and inadequately recognized for his virtues." Even more forthrightly, Nixon's dispassionate biographer Melvin Small has written that "his presidency certainly seems far from a failure. At the least, he can be credited with scores of accomplishments at home and abroad that make those of Democratic contemporaries, Presidents Kennedy and Carter, pale in comparison."

Nixon's rehabilitation rested almost wholly on his conduct of foreign relations. "On the domestic side, Nixon had tried to be bold and innovative,... but without success," his biographer Stephen Ambrose wrote. "In assessing his first term, it must be said that he had no achievement worthy of note." Nixon received much higher grades on foreign policy. His fierce critic Elizabeth Drew wrote: "Nixon's opening diplomatic relations with China and achieving detente with the Soviet Union were his...historic prizes, and they were substantial achievements.... In changing the order of things, Nixon demonstrated imagination and suppleness.... Nixon moved the world away from the Cold War confrontation, with all its dangers, though it would take more time, and a later president, to end it." More surprisingly, his former rival George McGovern said, "President Nixon probably had a more practical approach to the two superpowers, China and the Soviet Union, than any other president since World War II.... With the exception of his inexcusable continuation of the war in Vietnam, Nixon really will get high marks in history."

Though some historians questioned these judgments, Gerald Ford's biographer John Robert Greene asserted:

Few scholars are left who attempt to argue that Richard Nixon's foreign policy was anything less than revolutionary. Nixon was one of the first American leaders of either party to acknowledge that the Vietnam War had limited America's influence throughout the world and also among the first to recognize that the Soviet Union had become similarly restricted on the world stage.... Before the end of his first term of office, Nixon had succeeded in achieving a relaxation in U.S. relations with both the Soviet Union and the People's Republic of China and had succeeded in extricating the United States from Vietnam.... He bequeathed...a foreign policy that had begun a thorough reassessment of America's place in the world.

That widely held view credits him with too much and pays too little attention to his shortcomings. As Elizabeth Drew pointed out, Nixon was "a man who could give long, thoughtful disquisitions and produce lucid conceptualizations about foreign policy, while at the same time his actual policy making was often marked by fits and starts, by rages and impulsiveness, and by major gaps in his attention." Similarly, the historian of diplomacy George Herring concluded: "The administration's focus on Vietnam and detente gave a certain tunnel-vision quality to its foreign policy.... Sometimes,... [Nixon and Kissinger] pursued major goals without regard for the impact on other nations. Often, they viewed events largely in terms of their connection to superpower relations. Thus, in dealing with the rest of the world the administration achieved no better than mixed results."

Nixon focused on Russia and China, and on little else. He gave scant attention to Europe, save for the USSR, where détente had a very short shelf life. Engrossed in realpolitik, he neglected Africa, which did not figure largely in the Cold War. Alluding to Secretary of State William Rogers, Nixon instructed Kissinger: "Let's leave the niggers to Bill." His policies toward South Asia were capricious, in part because he regarded India's prime minister, Indira Gandhi, as a "bitch" and a "witch." In deciding to back Pakistan against India because he could not let an American ally "get screwed," he helped bring about India's resolve to develop nuclear weapons and Pakistan's crushing of Bangladesh. He took a still more cavalier attitude toward Latin America, notoriously in Chile, where he connived to overthrow Allende and gave his support to the vile regime of General Pinochet. Even his one undoubted achievement—the opening to China—came at a cost. The announcement that Nixon was going to China struck Japan with "typhonic force," said the US ambassador in Tokyo—a shock so great that it led to the fall of the Saito government.

Often praised for ending the conflict in Vietnam, Nixon actually pursued a disastrous course in Southeast Asia. He carried on the war in Vietnam senselessly for four more years, and he devastated Laos and Cambodia. As Ambrose noted: "Nearly all the names on the left-hand side of the Vietnam Wall in Washington commemorate men who died in action while Richard Nixon was their commander in chief, and they died after he had decided that the war could not be won." The murderous Khmer Rouge, which had been a negligible faction at the time of the invasion of Cambodia, grew tenfold after it—with awful consequences for the Cambodian people in the killing fields.

Contrary to accepted wisdom, a much stronger case can be made for his domestic policies, even though they commanded little of his attention. To be sure, much of the accomplishment was brought about by his subordinates and by a Democratic Congress. Still, he left an impressive legacy: the Environmental Protection Agency, the Occupational Safety and Health Administration, and the Office of Management and Budget. He also substantially expanded an agency created under Johnson: the Equal Employment Opportunity Commission. Thanks partly to the EEOC, the administration moved toward greater fairness for women, even though, Nixon told an aide, "I'm not for women, frankly, in any job." He added, "I don't want any of them around. Thank God we don't have any in the Cabinet." Representative Bella Abzug called him "the nation's chief resident male chauvinist." Despite his prejudice, he made a somewhat higher percentage of female appointments than had Kennedy or Johnson. "The mark of a leader," Nixon once said, "is whether he gives history a nudge." By leaving behind such institutions as the Environmental Protection Agency, he gave history more than a nudge.

Nixon will go down in the history books, however, not for any achievement in domestic or foreign policy but for the collectivity of misdeeds called "Watergate" that resulted in his being the only president ever to be compelled to resign. More than once, Nixon predicted that Watergate would "become only a footnote" in the chronicles of the times. (His biggest mistake, he said, was not his criminal behavior in the cover-up but not bombing North Vietnam mercilessly soon enough.) Much closer to the final verdict were the *Spectator* in London when it stated that in the course of two centuries America had moved "from George Washington, who could not tell a lie, to Richard Nixon, who cannot tell the truth," and Ambrose in writing: "Nixon wanted to be judged by what he accomplished. What he will be remembered for is the nightmare he put the country through."

No other administration in the two hundred years of the republic has ever committed so many gross transgressions. One account catalogued the crimes of Nixon and his appointees: burglary, forgery, illegal wire-tapping, illegal electronic surveillance, perjury, subornation of perjury, obstruction of justice, destruction of evidence, tampering with witnesses, misprision of felony, bribery, and conspiracy to involve government agencies in illegal action. More than seventy men were convicted or pled guilty—among them cabinet officials, including the country's chief law officer. Mitchell, Ehrlichman, and Haldeman received sentences of two and a half to eight years, later reduced to Dean's punishment of one to four years. Hunt was incarcerated for thirty-three months. Magruder got ten months to four years, Colson one to three years, Liddy six years and eight months to twenty years.

Granted that Nixon was deeply implicated in the cover-up, did he also order the Watergate break-in? A great deal of ink has been spilled in the attempt to solve that conundrum, but the question is irrelevant. He made clear to numbers of subordinates that he wanted a no-holds-barred attack on his opponents. In the context of what he had already approved, the illegal entry into Democratic headquarters was not at all out of the ordinary. One of the president's staunchest friends, Leonard Garment, has acknowledged, "It was Richard Nixon who said: I want information; I'm not going to risk this campaign; it was too close last time; there are people who have information I want. From that point on, everything else was implementation." Philip Lacovara, former counsel to the Watergate prosecutor, who doubted that the president had directly ordered the break-in, stated the responsibility most succinctly, "I relate Nixon to Henry II and the assassination of Thomas à Becket: Will no one give me the head of this meddlesome priest? I believe that this is the way Nixon and his aides related."

Nixon created consternation, too, by his hypertrophied conception of presidential license. "By the time Nixon reached the White House, he had soured on Congress's endless wrangling to the point that he opted to ignore it in favor of the instantly effective executive-order process," the historian Douglas Brinkley has written. The president, bypassing the legislative branch, concentrated power "in a tiny cabal of hand-picked White House aides." Nixon refused to recognize any constitutional restraints on his authority. George Reedy, who had been Lyndon Johnson's press secretary, asserted that the presidency had "taken on all the regalia of monarchy except robes, a scepter, and a crown."

Richard Nixon's aggrandizement, hard on the heels of LBJ's, prompted scholars who had extolled powerful presidents and deplored weak ones to reexamine their assumptions. Political scientists such as Thomas Cronin derided textbook glorification of strong presidents; Nelson Polsby took a stand "Against Presidential Greatness"; and Richard Pious asked, "Is Presidential Power 'Poison'?" Especially noteworthy was the reconsideration by Arthur Schlesinger Jr., who had written celebratory works (*The Age of Jackson, The Age of Roosevelt*) and had served in the Kennedy White House. In *The Imperial Presidency* (1973), a title that quickly became a national catchphrase, he wrote, "Some of us in the past who have been all-out supporters of the presidential prerogative have been forced to think again." In an assessment of the executive office, two political scientists wrote that after Nixon, the image of the president had changed from "Savior" to "Satan."

The disheartening experiences of the past decade moved the country from credulity to cynicism. "Americans certainly sighed with relief when Nixon resigned, but his resignation did not restore the nation's faith in their political institutions," John Robert Greene has written. "A distrust that had begun under Johnson had crystallized under Nixon—the overwhelming majority of Americans no longer believed the word of their president. Thus national self-doubt—not a new domestic and diplomatic steadiness—became Richard Nixon's most important legacy to his nation." In like manner, Alexander Haig reflected: "I wish that Watergate would be a footnote, but Nixon will always be remembered for it because the event had such major historic consequences for the country: a fundamental discrediting of respect for the presidency.... Respect for the institution of the presidency has historically been a vital aspect of the success of this country. We've had scoundrels in that office; we have had saints and mediocre people. But respect for the institution has guaranteed effective government, and, when you destroy that and maul it, it's not a cost-free ride."

Several years after being driven out of the White House, Nixon himself seemed to come to some kind of recognition of what he had wrought. In a televised interview with the British journalist David Frost, he confessed: "I let them down. I let down my friends. I let down my country, and worst of all I let down our system of government, and the dreams of those young people that ought to get into government but now they think, 'Oh, it's all too corrupt.' . . . Yeah. . . . I let the American people down. And I'm gonna have to carry that burden with me for the rest of my life." As he spoke these words, James Reston Jr. noted, his face was "swollen and ravaged by loneliness, self-loathing and defeat." For that fleeting moment, at least, Richard Nixon understood full well what history would say about him.

10

Gerald Ford and Jimmy Carter

IN THE EAST ROOM of the White House a little past noon on August 9, 1974, only minutes after Nixon's helicopter lifted off, Gerald Ford took the oath of office as the thirty-eighth president of the United States. For the first time ever, the country was to be led by a man who had been elected to no national office. His brief inaugural message was appropriately somber. "I assume the Presidency under extraordinary circumstances never before experienced by Americans," he said. "This is an hour of history that troubles our minds and hurts our hearts."

Born Leslie Lynch King Jr., Ford had taken the name of his stepdad after his mother ran away from his abusive father. The Depression years for the Fords, a biographer has written, brought "Dreiserian grimness." Self-reliant, Jerry Ford worked his way through the University of Michigan washing dishes. Star of the Michigan football team, he was chosen to play in the East-West contest at San Francisco and against the Chicago Bears in the College All-Star Game at Soldier Field. Boxing coach and assistant football coach at Yale, he gained admission to Yale Law School, where a prominent professor remembered him as a "decent sort of bird of moderate ability."

He rose steadily in Republican ranks in Congress not through brilliance but by diligence. John Ehrlichman later wrote of his first encounter

Betty and Jerry Ford bid farewell to Pat and Dick Nixon, who are about to board the helicopter that will whisk them away from the White House in disgrace. *Courtesy of the Richard Nixon Presidential Library and Museum, ID E3398-09*

with him: "I came away from his office with the impression that Jerry Ford might have become a pretty good Grand Rapids insurance agent . . . but he wasn't excessively bright." That was a common impression. "Jerry Ford," said Lyndon Johnson, "played too much football with his helmet off." He was "so dumb," Johnson added, "that he can't fart and chew gum at the same time." So dreary were his speeches that it was said that he "had the ability to empty arenas faster than the Chicago Cubs on a bad day." Even his gridiron experience was held against him. Ford, it was said, had played single wing football: put your head down and drive ahead, no imagination. These judgments were less than fair to a man who had finished in the top third of his class at demanding Yale Law School, and no one could deny his stature in the House. In 1961, the American Political Science Association designated him the Congressman's Congressman.

Though the American people had become disenchanted with the presidency as an institution, they wished Jerry Ford well. They understood what a difficult assignment he had, and they appreciated his modest demeanor. "I am acutely aware that you have not elected me as your President by your ballots," he told them. "So I ask you to confirm me as your President with your prayers." He had not "gained office by any secret promises," he declared. (Earlier, he had affirmed that "truth is the glue that holds...together not only our Government but civilization itself.") Pledging an administration of "openness and candor," he announced, "My fellow Americans, our long national nightmare is over."

The country found Ford's down-to-earth manner a welcome relief from the grandiosity of Nixon and LBJ. On his first morning in office, press photographers snapped the president stepping out of his Alexandria home in pajamas, like any suburban husband, to pick up a newspaper, and in his public appearances, he instructed bands to play not "Hail to the Chief" but the University of Michigan fight song. To signal his rejection of executive omnipotence, he ordered the uniformed marine guards removed from their station at the entry to the West Wing. When he was chosen vice president, he had said—in a pun drawing on the automobile culture of his native state of Michigan—"I'm a Ford, not a Lincoln." Committed to greater government transparency, Ford held more press conferences in his short tenure than Nixon had in a much longer one, and he permitted reporters to ask follow-up questions after he had answered their first inquiry. Everything about him suggested "Grand Rapids," the furniture from his hometown that did not have much style but was sturdy and reliable.

Ford sought to bring tranquility to an aggrieved land. "Like President Truman and President Lincoln before him, I found on my desk...the urgent problem of how to bind up the Nation's wounds," he said. "And I intend to do that." He retained all of Nixon's cabinet and almost all of the White House staff, making his mark only by selecting as press secretary the Washington correspondent of the *Detroit News*, Jerald terHorst. In late August, a Gallup Poll registered an approval rating for

Ford of 71 percent; a minuscule 3 percent disapproved. There was, said *Time*, a "mood of good feeling and even exhilaration in Washington that the city had not experienced for many years."

By a single act, Ford shattered this benign quiescence. On September 8, 1974, little less than a month after he took office, he issued a proclamation granting Richard Nixon "a full, free, and absolute" pardon for all federal crimes he had "committed or may have committed or taken part in" during his presidency. Nixon and "his loved ones have suffered enough," he said. "Theirs is an American tragedy in which we all have played a part. It could go on and on, or someone must write 'The End' to it. I have concluded that only I can do that, and if I can, I must." Ford anticipated that his intervention would liberate him and the nation from the Nixon horrors. Instead, his edict served to perpetuate and exacerbate them, as he should have anticipated. Asked during his confirmation hearings to succeed Agnew as vice president if Nixon's successor could forestall a prosecution, he had said, "I do not think the public would stand for it."

The proclamation exploded like a burst of shrapnel. In a fury, the young *Washington Post* reporter who had helped break the scandal, Carl Bernstein, phoned his collaborator Bob Woodward to relay the bulletin: "The son of a bitch pardoned the son of a bitch!" In Pittsburgh the next day, enraged protesters greeted the president with chants of "Jail Ford!" Americans found it galling that Ford's words implied that they shared in Nixon's guilt. Furthermore, though Nixon expressed regret that he had not acted "more forthrightly," he never acknowledged that he had violated any law or had participated in a cover-up. Ford had allowed him to get away scot-free. (In his memoirs, Ford conceded that Nixon "hadn't been as forthcoming as I had hoped. He didn't admit guilt and it was a good deal less than a full confession.")

It was palpably unfair that Nixon's lieutenants who had carried out his orders would spend months in jail cells while the "unindicted co-conspirator" would be sunning himself on a Pacific beach. "All men are created equal," said the Senate majority leader, Mike Mansfield, and "that includes presidents and plumbers." Ford compounded the unfairness eight days later by announcing to a convention of the Veterans of Foreign Wars that he was going to issue a conditional amnesty for the fifty thousand Vietnam deserters and draft evaders. That move, which antagonized right-wingers (Barry Goldwater likened it to "throwing mud in the faces of the millions of men who had served their country"), had a further disadvantage. Clemency would be granted only in return for community service, while Ford had not required Nixon to make any amends.

Numbers of thoughtful commentators have concluded, upon reflection, that Ford acted wisely to avoid the spectacle of a former president in the dock or the possibility that Nixon, visibly depressed, might take his life, but even though "reasonable people can disagree on the wisdom of the pardon," observed the historian Laura Kalman, "the timing of the pardon was poor, its justification ill conceived," and the deal giving Nixon the right to dispose of his papers "unacceptable." Another bewildering aspect of the episode was that Nixon had not been charged with any crime. A letter writer to *Newsweek* asked, "Since Nixon doesn't admit any guilt and as none has been proven since he hasn't been tried, what is it that Ford is pardoning?" The *Washington Post* characterized Ford's deed as "nothing less than the continuation of a cover-up," and the *New York Times* called the pardon "profoundly unwise, divisive and unjust," demolishing the new president's "credibility as a man of judgment, candor and competence." As an act of conscience, his longtime admirer Press Secretary terHorst resigned on the spot. In a moment, Ford's approval rating plunged from 71 to 49 percent.

Indignation at his decree led the president to the extraordinary step of consenting to interrogation in a public hearing before a House Judiciary subcommittee, where he did not acquit himself well. In his testimony, Ford falsified the record, especially by claiming that "at no time after I had been president...was the subject of a pardon raised by...Nixon...or people representing him," when, in fact, there had been intricate negotiations during which Nixon's chief of staff had spelled out for him his options on a pardon. The impact on the nation's faith in its political institutions was devastating. Opinion analysts found that "Ford's pardon of Nixon was more highly correlated with the drop in political trust than were any of the previous events of Watergate." Ford never recovered from his shocking announcement. "In that brief instant," the presidential adviser David Gergen later wrote, "Ford had severed the gossamer thread of trust that ties the people to a presidency."

Though everyone acknowledged that the new president was warm-hearted, he exhibited a social vision far narrower than Nixon's. One of Jerry Ford's assistants viewed him as "the kind of guy who would take his shirt off his back and give it to a poor kid he saw on the street and then walk in and veto the day care program." In his final term in Congress, the liberal Americans for Democratic Action had given him a grade on key issues of zero. A longtime foe of the Great Society, he opposed social welfare bills, and on entering the White House, he told the heads of federal agencies that he wanted a minimum of regulation in the interest of "maximum freedom for private enterprise." So hostile was he to measures such as busing that the Civil Rights Commission accused him of seeking to return America to a Jim Crow society. Nothing revealed his fundamentalist economic views so nakedly as his appointment to chair the Council of Economic Advisers: Alan Greenspan, a confederate of the evangelist for capitalism Ayn Rand.

His convictions soon embroiled him in combat with congressional Democrats. After many years as a leader in the House, he did not share Nixon's contempt for Congress, and he had hoped for "communication, conciliation, compromise, and co-operation." Newly arrived presidents can usually count on a "honeymoon" of a few weeks when they are immune from criticism, but three days after his initial remarks, Ford told Congress, "I don't want a honeymoon with you. I want a good marriage." Unable to reconcile himself to progressive measures, however, he vetoed bills for health care, federal aid to education, public housing, and regulation of strip mining. After assuring his highly regarded secretary of labor that he would sign a measure desired by building trades unions, the president vetoed it in order to appease the Republican right. Shocked by Ford's double cross, the secretary of labor left the government. When Ford struck down school lunch legislation, a congressman excoriated him as "the most veto-prone Republican President in the 20th Century," for in little over a year he had disapproved more bills (thirty-nine) than Hoover had in all of his four-year term.

Ford's ideology also shaped his response to the refractory recession he inherited from Nixon. As the *New York Times* reported, he had fallen heir to "the worst inflation in the country's peacetime history, the highest interest rates in a century, the consequent severe slump in housing, sinking and utterly demoralized securities markets, a stagnant economy with large-scale unemployment in prospect and a worsening international trade and payments position." Bewilderingly, he confronted "stagflation": a conflux of rising unemployment and inflation that both classical economists and Keynesians had said could not happen.

Rising prices bothered him much more than mounting unemployment. Convinced that government intrusions were burdening the market, he sought to slash federal spending even if it meant further loss of jobs. He had hardly taken office when he announced that inflation was "domestic enemy number one," which he proposed to deal with not by instituting controls but by appealing to a spirit of voluntarism, much as Herbert Hoover had done. In October 1974, wearing a "WIN" button in his lapel, Ford announced a new gambit: "Whip Inflation Now." Tens of thousands of citizens signed pledges to keep prices down, and twelve million WIN buttons sprouted, but Ford became a figure of ridicule for supposing that such gimmicks would actually resolve the problem.

Harsh experience taught Ford that if he had any hope of shaping policy, he would have to reach some accommodations. Throughout his presidency, he was saddled with a Democratic Congress, and, three months after he was sworn in, the country punished Republicans for Watergate by enormously increasing the opposition's seats on the Hill. With Democrats determined not to let the president gut liberal programs, Ford saw a higher proportion of his vetoes overridden than had any previous president in the twentieth century. Reluctantly, he put his name to bills far more liberal than he wanted because he thought that to be overridden yet again would make him look feckless. But he continued to believe that it was more important to tamp down prices than to deal with unemployment, and he asked Congress for a temporary tax surcharge to suppress demand.

That fall, however, the economy suddenly went into a tailspin, and Ford found it necessary to execute an about-face. With joblessness approaching the highest rates since 1941, he concluded that the greatest challenge was no longer inflation but recession. Accordingly, he jettisoned his demand for a tax boost and, to stimulate the economy, signed into law a tax cut voted by the Democratic Congress, though it was much larger than the one he had recommended. His flip-flop on taxes reinforced the impression that he was a waffler, but the president took satisfaction in knowing that by 1976 inflation had dropped from 11 percent to under 6 percent. In addition, Ford, after struggling for months to persuade Congress to institute immediate and total decontrol of oil prices, reluctantly agreed to an omnibus energy bill that stretched his power to phase out controls over more than three years.

The president also followed a tortuous course in reacting to a financial crisis gripping New York City. When the metropolis, which had been spending recklessly, asked for a federal bailout, he turned it down. In a stark headline, the *New York Daily News* reported in large type:

FORD TO CITY:
DROP DEAD

But after municipal officials adopted an austerity budget, he consented to more than $2 billion in loans for three successive years.

Overseas, too, Ford quickly learned that the presidency was no longer imperial, for, as he grumbled in his memoirs, "Congress was determined to get its oar deeply into the conduct of foreign affairs." The very first crisis of his presidency abroad revealed how the political culture was changing. To safeguard American strategic interests, Ford sided with Turkey in its dispute with Greece over Cyprus. Congress, however, passed a bill forbidding military aid to the Turks. Ford vetoed it, as well as a second bill imposing an arms embargo. But Congress persisted, and the president capitulated. When Turkey retaliated by closing all US bases in its country, Ford felt helpless. Capitol Hill, not the White House, was calling the shots.

Cyprus set the pattern for what was to follow. To induce Israel to modify its hard-line stance in the Middle East, Ford blocked arms shipments to the country, only to be confronted by a letter from seventy-six US senators pressing him to be "responsive" to Israel's request for military and economic aid. Congress intervened even more bluntly in Africa, where Kissinger, bewitched by the lure of dark intrigue, had hatched a costly misadventure in the former Portuguese colony of Angola. By cutting off funds, Congress compelled Ford and the CIA to end covert guerrilla action there.

When the North Vietnamese violated the Paris Peace Accords of 1973 by launching an invasion in December 1974, Ford asked for a sizeable appropriation, but Congress turned him down. Two Democrats walked out of the chamber as he was speaking, and the Republican Senator Jacob Javits declared that he was willing to vote "large sums for evacuation, but not one nickel for military aid." Ford himself knew that victory in Southeast Asia was a forlorn hope. In April 1975, he told Tulane students packed into a basketball field house: "Today, America can regain the sense of pride that existed before Vietnam. But it cannot be achieved by re-fighting a war that is finished as far as America is concerned." Tardily, he approved a massive evacuation program that reached a galling climax in the final week of April. Over a hair-raising nineteen hours, helicopters spirited away thousands of Americans and South Vietnamese, but, with shells exploding, there was neither time nor equipment to rescue all of them. As television viewers around the world watched on their screens, US personnel used rifle butts to beat the fingers of loyal Vietnamese from a ladder perched on the embassy roof that they clawed to ascend to over-loaded helicopters. This ugly scene spotlighted Ford in the unenviable position of being the man who signed off on American defeat.

The president suffered further mortification when a US Senate committee headed by Frank Church of Idaho revealed that the CIA had been violating its charter by spying on American citizens and had recruited the Mafia for eight attempts to assassinate Fidel Castro during the 1960s. It also published the names of other foreign leaders whom, since the 1950s, the CIA, quite possibly at the direction of the White House, had targeted for murder. Ford responded not with indignation at the miscreants but by doing all he could to suppress damaging evidence. When he learned that Church had been drawing on information about nasty plots provided by CIA Director William Colby, he fired Colby. Senator Church, though, foiled him by establishing congressional oversight over what he called this "rogue elephant"—an agency of the executive branch that hitherto had been regarded as a president's fiefdom. Furthermore, in framing an executive order, Ford was obliged to stipulate that "no employee of the US government shall engage in, or conspire to engage in, political assassinations."

In the wake of Watergate, Congress asserted itself in a number of ways to cleanse politics and to curb the abuse of presidential authority. To circumscribe the wanton resort to executive agreements to elude the constitutional stipulation that treaties required Senate "consent," the Case

Act obligated the secretary of state to notify Congress within six days of any international compact that had been negotiated, and the National Emergencies Act put a time limit on declarations of national emergency and empowered Congress to check a president's action. As a consequence of the Federal Election Campaign Act, which imposed spending limits on presidential candidates, the 1976 contest was the first to be federally funded. Congress made the government more transparent, too, through the Freedom of Information Act of 1974, a measure passed over Ford's veto.

Frustrated by the abridgment of his prerogatives, Ford seized upon the opportunity to demonstrate that he was not a milquetoast when a Cambodian Khmer Rouge patrol boat seized a US merchant vessel, the *Mayaguez*, on the pretext that it had sailed into territorial waters. "Let's look ferocious," Kissinger advised him. The president, ignoring the requirement of the War Powers Act that he consult with Congress, ordered a large air assault to rescue the ship and its crew of thirty-nine. When the crew was safely moved to an American destroyer, Ford was applauded for his militant response. "It was wonderful," said Barry Goldwater. "It shows we've still got balls in this country." Lost in the exultation was the grim reality that the operation had cost more American lives (forty-one) than the crew numbered, as well as bringing about the deaths of many Cambodians. But the American people always rise to the support of a president who shows might even when he has been foolhardy, and his action in the *Mayaguez* affair gave Ford an eleven-point boost in the polls.

The president's most important initiatives came in pursuit of détente with Russia, an earnest commitment that led him to fly to Helsinki for an international conference aimed at improving relations between the Communist sphere and the West. At Helsinki, Ford confronted an increasingly intractable Soviet premier, Leonid Brezhnev, at the same time that he was being berated by raucous critics at home. Even before he left, a *Wall Street Journal* editorial instructed him, JERRY DON'T GO. He would rather see that message, Ford reflected, "than headlines all over Europe saying, UNITED STATES BOYCOTTS PEACE HOPES." The Helsinki Accords legitimated the national boundaries fixed by World War II but also pledged adherence to human rights. Brezhnev anticipated that the agreements would consolidate Russian dominance, but they served instead to encourage dissidents throughout the Eastern bloc. One of Ford's most vehement critics, the editor Norman Podhoretz, decades later conceded that the Accords "put a very powerful weapon in the hands of the dissidents... in their struggle against the Communist regime. Ultimately, Helsinki, instead of ensuring the permanence of the Soviet empire, contributed to its eventual demise."

At the time, though, reaching out to Moscow cost the president dearly. Phyllis Schlafly, a propagandist for conspiracy theorists, and Chester Ward, a retired rear admiral, disseminated an eight-hundred-page screed, *Kissinger on the Couch*, accusing the president of adopting a "suicidal" attitude toward the USSR. California's highly popular governor, Ronald Reagan, wanted to know "why Mr. Ford traveled halfway around the world to sign the Helsinki Pact, putting our stamp of approval on Russia's enslavement of captive nations." So fierce were the objections of leaders of the Republican right to what they regarded as an affirmation of FDR's perfidy at Yalta that, incredibly, the likeable Ford could not even be sure that his party would nominate him for another term.

On September 5, 1975, outside the California state capitol in Sacramento, Lynette "Squeaky" Fromme, a disciple of the mass murderer Charles Manson, pointed a loaded pistol at Ford from a distance of only two feet as he reached out to shake her hand, but the Colt .45 misfired, and a Secret Service agent wrestled it away. Seventeen days later, a forty-five-year-old woman fired a revolver at Ford—again in California, as he was leaving a San Francisco hotel—but a bystander deflected her aim. Though these were isolated incidents, they epitomized the most unexpected feature of the Ford presidency: that good-natured Jerry Ford, who had spent a lifetime as a harmonizer, had become a divisive figure.

As the 1976 campaign season approached, conservative Republicans sought to expel the presumptive head of their party from the White House. His trip to Helsinki was only one of their grievances. They especially disliked his appointments, which they thought neither partisan enough nor appropriately doctrinally rigid. He had depoliticized the Justice Department, which had been deeply compromised under Nixon, by choosing as attorney general the president of the University of Chicago, the esteemed legal scholar Edward Levi, and had elevated to the US

Supreme Court John Paul Stevens, a highly respected jurist who frequently sided with the liberal wing on the bench. Worse still in their eyes had been his selection for the vice presidential vacancy of Nelson Rockefeller, the very embodiment of the internationalist seaboard elite that Main Street distrusted. Above all, they viewed Ford as a closet moderate who embraced unorthodox causes, notably the Equal Rights Amendment for women—the result, it was surmised, of pillow talk with his wife.

The first lady gave the Moral Majority fits. In contrast to her husband, who projected the comfortable style of a middle-American small towner, Betty Ford, a divorcée, had worked as a Powers model and had performed in Carnegie Hall with the Martha Graham modern dance company. On a presidential visit to Beijing, she shucked her shoes and traipsed barefoot with a Chinese ballet troupe. When she talked to truckers on CB radio, they dubbed her "First Mama." In an interview with CBS's *60 Minutes*, she celebrated *Roe v. Wade* as "the best thing in the world...a great, great decision." She "wouldn't be surprised," she remarked, to learn that her daughter had been sexually active, since the teenager was "a perfectly normal human being like all young girls." Furthermore, she assumed that her kids had tried marijuana; in fact, if she were their age, she would be smoking a joint herself. Though it was not until after she left the White House that she acknowledged her addiction to alcohol and her chemical dependency, she made an enormous contribution to open discussion of breast cancer by speaking freely of her mastectomy. "When she spoke," one commentary has observed, "the seldom-sniffed scent of honesty was in the air."

To get combat-ready for the campaign, Ford revamped his administration. In what the press called "the Hallowe'en Massacre," he stripped Secretary of State Kissinger of his portfolio as national security adviser and ridded himself of other Nixon holdovers. In their places, he picked men who would play significant roles in Republican administrations for many years to come: Dick Cheney as chief of staff, Donald Rumsfeld as secretary of defense, and George H. W. Bush as CIA director. Confronted by a formidable challenge from Governor Reagan for the Republican presidential nomination, he decided that Nelson Rockefeller constituted too great a liability if he hoped to win over the party faithful, and in the fall of 1975 coerced him into removing his name from the 1976 ticket in favor of the conservative Kansas senator Robert Dole. (The vice

President Ford and First Lady Betty Ford. This photograph of the first couple in their living quarters in the White House projects an intimacy that helps explain why both of them were so likeable. *Library of Congress, LC-DIG-ppmsca-08475*

president did so graciously, leading Ford to write later, "I was angry with myself for showing cowardice in not saying to the ultraconservatives, 'It's going to be Ford and Rockefeller, whatever the consequences.'") In addition, the president mobilized a public relations battalion, fifty strong. He even placed a joke writer on the White House payroll.

Reagan mounted a strong challenge to Ford—especially after capturing the GOP primary in North Carolina, where Senator Jesse Helms said, "Ultra-liberals in this country hate Ronald Reagan like the devil hates holy water." The California governor attracted a conservative following not only because of his nationalistic statements on foreign affairs but also because he had taken a stern stance toward student uprisings at Berkeley. At one point, he had said, "If there has to be a bloodbath, let's get it over with." Ford prevailed because he was able to wield the powers available to an incumbent and because many still regarded Reagan not as a statesman but as a second-rate actor. Ford hit home when he said, "Ronald Reagan and I have one thing in common—we both played football. I played for Michigan. He played for Warner Brothers." But it was a near thing. So far had the Republican Party swung to the right in 1976 that the president came within a few votes at the party's national convention of becoming the first incumbent since Chester Arthur to be denied renomination. Furthermore, in a rude rebuke to the president, the delegates encumbered him with a platform criticizing the Helsinki Accords. Reagan, said the essayist Garry Wills, had "humiliated Ford without defeating him."

In seeking to remain in the White House, Ford faced all but impossible odds. Contemplating the revulsion against Republicans in the aftermath of Nixon's transgressions, a prominent Democrat said, "We could run an aardvark this year and win." Burdened by Watergate, Ford had the added handicap of being covered by journalists who had started treating public figures with a disrespect that sometimes reached savagery. Though the president had been an outstanding athlete, TV evening news programs dwelled on his stumbles—from an airplane ramp in Salzburg, where cameras caught the American president on his hands and knees while deplaning, to a ski slope in Vail, where he had an embarrassing tumble. On the golf course his erratic shots put caddies in peril—misadventures that led Ford to call himself "the Jinx of the Links" and to say that the Secret Service men who accompanied him "qualify for combat pay." Gerald Ford, observed the columnist John Osborne, was perceived as "a loser, a bumbler, a misfit President...prone to slip on airplane ramps, bump his head on helicopter entrances, entangle himself in the leashes of his family dogs, and fall from skis in front of television cameras that showed him asprawl in the snow." Wits circulated the rumor that at his former home in Grand Rapids, a sign read, "Gerald Ford Slipped Here," and on *Saturday Night Live* Chevy Chase won a large and appreciative audience for his impersonation of Ford as a klutz forever on the verge of the next pratfall.

The media presented Ford as not only clumsy but dimwitted. Despite his performance at Yale Law School, he was called "Lennie," an allusion to the mentally retarded character in John Steinbeck's *Of Mice and Men*. A 1974 magazine cover of *New York* showed him as Bozo the Clown, and in New Hampshire the right-wing *Manchester Union Leader* made a practice of calling the president of the United States "Jerry the Jerk." A 1976 poll found that, by an emphatic margin, people thought that Ford was "a nice guy" but "not...very smart about the issues the country is facing."

Democrats did not pick an aardvark, but they settled on someone almost as obscure: a former governor of Georgia, Jimmy Carter, who began his quest with a name recognition in the country of only 2 percent. When he told his mother that he was planning to run for president, she retorted, "President of *what*?" The Speaker of the House, Tip O'Neill, later remembered, "The idea that this Georgia peanut farmer, a complete unknown, saw himself as a serious candidate for the highest office in the world struck me as pretty farfetched." But, shrewdly turning his lack of national experience into an asset, Carter presented himself as an outsider untarnished by Beltway corruption at a time when the main lesson drawn from Watergate, concluded the historian Stanley Kutler, was that "virtue mattered, that some ethical standard applied in political life." With many Americans believing that a president's character meant more than his policies, Carter said, "If I'm at the end of four years or eight years I hope people say, 'You know, Jimmy Carter made a lot of mistakes, but he never told a lie.'" He assured voters that they deserved a government as "decent, honest, truthful, fair, compassionate, and as filled with love as our people are." Ford later reflected: "Carter was running on 'I'll never tell a lie.' I had the albatross of having pardoned Nixon, a known liar." An acceptance address in which Carter pronounced Italian as "Eye-talian" grated on listeners' ears but did not lessen his advantage. In August, he led the president by more than thirty points.

In the final months of the campaign, however, Ford greatly narrowed the gap, aided immeasurably by an inexplicable gaffe. After *Playboy*, a soft-porn magazine notorious for its salacious photos of nude women, published an interview with Carter in which the born-again Christian used words such as "screws" and confessed that he had "looked upon a lot of women with lust" and in his heart had "committed adultery . . . many times," his lead shrank to twelve points. (Bumper sticks announced: "In His Heart He Knows Your Wife.") In a separate interview, Carter made use of a term for sexual intercourse that, the novelist Norman Mailer remarked, was "a word that the *Times* has refused to print for 125 years." Suddenly, the country, realizing that it did not really know very much about this Sunday school teacher who claimed to hold letters patent on virtue, resolved to watch closely three televised presidential debates (the first since 1960) to decide which candidate should run their government.

By performing reasonably well in the first debate, Ford reduced Carter's lead to eight points.

But during interrogation in the second debate—on foreign affairs, an area where the president had infinitely more experience than his opponent—Ford fell apart. In response to a question from Max Frankel of the *New York Times*, he said, "There is no Soviet domination of Eastern Europe." Bewildered, Frankel gave Ford a chance to extricate himself from that preposterous assertion, but the president made matters worse by insisting that Yugoslavia, Rumania, and Poland were all "autonomous." (The conservative journalist William Buckley called that gaffe "the ultimate Polish joke.") The blunders made Ford seem not merely clueless on foreign policy but also, despite his long-standing preoccupation with the Cold War, soft on communism. In addition, it reinforced the false assumption that he was "dumb."

The string of events from his pardon edict to his stumble in the debate cost Ford the confidence of the American people. He later stated that he wanted to be remembered as "a nice person, who worked at the job, and who left the White House in better shape than when I took it over." Even his critics had to grant him that. (He earned plaudits, too, by acting to provide a haven in America for 130,000 South Vietnamese refugees fleeing Communist retribution.) But, though he had some accomplishments to his credit, detractors concluded that he was neither a Ford nor a Lincoln but an Edsel. Despite his quarter of a century on Capitol Hill, where he had been elected minority leader of the House of Representatives, and his many months in the White House, only 5 percent of the electorate thought he was "experienced." In November, faced with a choice between "fear of the unknown and fear of the known," the nation decided to take its chances on the unknown, and Ford went down to defeat, making him the first president since Herbert Hoover to be ousted from office by voters. Carter, however, only narrowly prevailed—297–240 in the Electoral College, with a mere 2 percent advantage in the popular vote. (Seven percent of respondents to exit polls said that they had rejected Ford because of his pardon of Nixon.)

Instead of sending Carter to Washington with a mandate, though, the 1976 election registered widespread popular disaffection with the political process and with the executive branch. Turnout was the lowest since World War II, because four-fifths of American voters did not think that either candidate was "presidential." In explaining why he did not plan to go to the polls, one man said, "I'm a three-time loser. In 1964 I voted for the peace candidate—Johnson—and got war. In '68 I voted for the law-and-order candidate—Nixon—and got crime. In '72 I voted for Nixon again, and we got Watergate." The proportion of US citizens who said they could "trust the federal government" fell from some 75 percent in the mid-1960s (the era of the Vietnam war and race riots) to 25 percent in the late 1970s. It would never come close to reaching 50 percent for the rest of the century.

As Gerald Ford sat on the platform on Inauguration Day 1977, witnessing the final act of his expulsion from office, a gracious statement from the incoming president took him by surprise. "I want to thank my predecessor," Jimmy Carter said, "for all he has done to heal our land." Many years later, Ford took pride in that judgment as he recalled his feelings on the bicentennial Fourth of July 1976. "I can still hear the Liberty Bell toll, echoed by church bells across this beautiful land," Ford said. "It was a long day, and just before my head hit the pillow that night, I said to myself, 'Well, Jerry, I guess we've healed America.'"

A number of commentators, though, found that sentiment too saccharine. The most poignant aspect of the bicentennial, they concluded, was that, two centuries after the Declaration of Independence, the country was being governed by a president and a vice president neither of whom had been chosen by the American people. In his State of the Union message a year earlier, President Ford himself had confessed, "The state of the union is not good." Moreover, so little of consequence took place in Ford's brief reign that it left only the faintest footprint. In John Updike's 1992 novel *Memories of the Ford Administration,* his narrator ruminates: "For that matter, was there ever a Ford Administration? Evidence for its existence seems to be scanty."

James Earl Carter Jr., known to all the world as Jimmy, began his presidency a sworn foe of the government he had been elected to head. He had run as an "outsider" because "we know from bitter experience that we are not going to get the changes we need by simply shifting around the same group of Washington insiders." The federal government, he had declared during the campaign, was a "horrible, bloated, confused ... bureaucratic mess." The welfare program, he charged, was a "failure" that stood in "urgent need of a complete overhaul," and America's tax system "a disgrace to the human race."

Carter deliberately dampened expectations that his tenure would transform people's lives. "I have no new dream to set forth today," he said in his inaugural address of January 1977. Unlike each of his Democratic predecessors in the twentieth century, he did not identify himself with a rubric such as New Freedom, New Deal, Fair Deal, New Frontier, or Great Society. Altogether cut off from that past, he went out of his way to say that he had "never met a Democratic president," almost as though it were a point of pride. His inaugural address exposed a modest conception of what he expected to accomplish. "We have learned that 'more' is not necessarily 'better,' that even our great nation has its recognized limits," he stated. This view reflected a conviction that resources are finite, that the long era of growth was reaching a climacteric, and that the short happy life of the US empire was drawing to a close. Widely accepted by elites, especially readers of a gloomy report by the Club of Rome, this notion was never embraced by the people.

In his memoir, Carter remarked that his assertion "was to prove painfully prescient and politically unpopular," for "Americans were not accustomed to limits—on natural resources or on the power of our country to . . . control international events." He added: "Watching the sea of approving faces on Inauguration Day, I wondered how few of the happy celebrants would agree with my words if they analyzed them closely. At the time, it was not possible even for me to imagine the limits we would have to face. In some ways, dealing with limits would become the subliminal theme of the next four years, and affect the outcome of the 1980 election."

Carter and his Atlanta cadre, dubbed "the Georgia Mafia," arrived in Washington with the heady conceit that, just as they had overcome the party elders in seizing the nomination and winning the presidency, they would show Washington how a country ought to be governed. This presumptuousness did not sit well either with the media or with Congress. "Carter was smarter than most reporters and clearly knew it," his press secretary, Jody Powell—a native of rural Vienna, Georgia—said later. "They do not take kindly to being looked down upon by any politician, particularly not a peanut farmer from some piddly-ass little gnat-hole in south Georgia." Carter showed no more regard for veteran legislators. "Congress is disgusting on this . . . subject," he entered in his diary at one low point. "Having run deliberately and profitably as one who had never been part of the Washington scene, I was not . . . eager to change my attitude after becoming president," Carter later reflected. "This proved to be a mistake."

Critics of the president also had distorted mindsets. They perceived him as, in the words of the humorist Roy Blount, "a Southern Baptist simple-talking peanut-warehousing grit-eating 'Eyetalian'-saying Cracker." His frequent avowals of his commitment to Christianity, noted the political scientist James David Barber, compelled bemused reporters "to cram fast on this strange religion, as if it were some ethnological eccentricity brought back from Pago Pago by Margaret Mead." To many northern liberals, he appeared to be, in the paraphrase by one of his advisers, "a sort of fluke, an ambassador from Dogpatch, at least that's what my old Kennedy friends say." Annapolis graduate, nuclear engineer, a devotee of Reinhold Niebuhr and a fan of Bob Dylan, Carter was, in fact, more sophisticated that his down-home persona suggested.

No one ever arrived in the White House with better intentions than Jimmy Carter, and few have had so little notion of how to carry them out. "Carter," an aide observed, "often seemed more concerned with taking the correct position than with learning how to turn that position into results." Naively, the new president believed that policy ought to be separated from politics and that he did not have to accommodate the need of members of Congress to be responsive to their constituents. "Carter's got the coldest political nose of any politician I ever met," said Vice President Walter Mondale. "Carter thought politics was sinful," he added. "The worst thing you could say to Carter if you wanted to do something was that it was politically the best thing to do." Carter himself later acknowledged ruefully, "We had an overly optimistic impression that I could present a bill to Congress that seemed patently in the best interests of the country and the Congress would take it and pretty well pass it. I have been disabused of that expectation."

Having emerged on the scene at a time of revulsion against the excesses of Richard Nixon and Lyndon Johnson, Carter had good reason to think that he was fulfilling the national will by deconstructing the imperial presidency. On Inauguration Day, he took the oath of office wearing not the traditional top hat and cutaway but a plain business suit, and he asked that he be sworn in not as James but as Jimmy. Afterward, forgoing the customary armored limousine ride from Capitol Hill, he strolled down Pennsylvania Avenue hand in hand with his wife, Rosalynn, smiling and waving at the milling throngs, as his nine-year-old daughter, Amy, skipped along by his side—for sixteen blocks in frigid weather all the way to the White House. He followed up this piece of political theater a few days later by appearing on television in a simple beige cardigan. He lugged his clothes bag on and off Air Force One and sent his daughter to public school in the District of Columbia. To "depomp" the presidency, he spent nights in the homes of rank-and-file Americans, held town meetings, and even accepted random phone calls from citizens—a unique televised happening monitored by Walter Cronkite. He got rid of the presidential yacht, slashed the White House staff by one-third, took government luxury cars away from cabinet members, and insisted that all federal officials fly coach.

Instead of elevating his public reputation, however, these deeds of self-effacement lowered it. Critics accused him of depriving the White House of the aura of majesty, with *Newsweek* scoffing at "corn bread-and-cardigan atmospherics." The country, which initially had welcomed the Carters' unpretentiousness, came to regret their lack of high style. When Rosalynn Carter asked the White House chef whether he could prepare some of the Carter family's favorite meals, he replied, "Yes, ma'am. We've been fixing that kind of food for the servants for a long time." Toward the end of 1977, the columnist Russell Baker commented that Carter had fulfilled his pledge "to dismantle the imperial Presidency… and to restore the Presidency to the arid, nuts-and-bolts business of governing under republican forms," only to find the American people, who said that this was what they wanted, discontent. "Of course, it is dull, terribly dull," Baker remarked. "If the Carter Administration were a television show, it would have been canceled months ago."

In a widely noted article in *Atlantic Monthly*, James Fallows, who had been the president's chief speechwriter, called Carter's tenure a "Passionless Presidency" that was "drained of zeal," and a host of commentators agreed. Senator Eugene McCarthy, a fine poet, dismissed Carter as an

President Jimmy Carter, with nine-year-old daughter Amy and First Lady Rosalynn Carter, waves to the crowd as he breaks precedent by strolling down Pennsylvania Avenue on Inauguration Day, January 20, 1977. *Courtesy of the Jimmy Carter Library and Museum*

"oratorical mortician" who "inters his words and ideas beneath piles of syntactical mush," and the critic I. F. Stone wrote, "There's no music in him." When Carter gave a fireside chat, critics alleged, even the fire fell asleep. "I like Mr. Carter, I respect him," said the executive director of the NAACP. "But, in all honesty, when he walks into a room, it doesn't light up." The historian Eric Goldman, who had once worked in the White House, concluded: "Carterism may be totally lacking in the scourging of a Theodore Roosevelt, the cathedral summoning of a Woodrow Wilson, the rollicking iconoclasm of an FDR. Carterism does not march and it does not sing; it is cautious, muted, grayish, at times even crabbed."

As the second year in office drew to a close, a *Washington Post* writer said of Jimmy Carter:

He did not promise to excite us or entertain us or even "lead" us in the fashion of a Franklin D. Roosevelt, John F. Kennedy or Lyndon

B. Johnson. He promised only to manage our affairs sensibly and with a degree of charity. We in turn responded, and so elected the country's first national city manager.

Is that enough? Along with all the other variables that go into such a close election, it certainly was enough in 1976. But times, and the temper of the American electorate, change. And Carter, having failed to establish much of an emotional bond with the American people,... seems particularly vulnerable to a change in the national temper.

Week in, week out, for four years, Carter encountered relentless, bitter opposition from Republican conservatives, but at the conclusion of his presidency he made a startling observation: "My main problem was with the so-called liberal wing of the Democratic party." In more than one respect, that comment is counterintuitive because Carter achieved a number of the goals on the liberals' wish list. On his first full day in office, he granted unconditional pardons to hundreds of thousands of Vietnam War draft evaders, an act that Barry Goldwater called "the craziest damn thing" he had ever seen. He elevated the status of the vice presidency by installing Mondale, who came out of the Farmer-Labor hotbed of Minnesota, in the West Wing and giving him more responsibilities than any vice president had ever exercised. He expanded the realm of the executive branch by adding both a Department of Education and a Department of Energy. He persuaded Congress to enact an ethics-in-government law that, in addition to creating the Office of the Independent Counsel to investigate misbehavior by federal officials, imposed strict requirements for divestiture of assets and financial disclosure on government employees who became influence peddlers. He pushed through a bill to limit strip-mining that Ford had vetoed and, echoing Franklin Roosevelt's CCC and NYA, sponsored a Comprehensive Employment Training Act. By the fall of 1978, enrollment in CETA had reached 725,000. Most eye-catching was his outstanding record on appointments.

With a recruitment policy that emphasized diversity, Carter named more women to high positions than had any predecessor, at the same time that he advocated extending the time limit for ratification of the Equal Rights Amendment. He picked three women for his cabinet and sent six female ambassadors abroad. Even more remarkable was the role he assigned to Rosalynn Carter. She was the first president's wife to sit in at cabinet meetings, grabbing any available chair even if it was the vice president's, though she did not participate in discussion. To benefit from her counsel, Carter scheduled a working lunch with her in the Oval Office every week. The soft spoken but strong-willed "Steel Magnolia" testified on legislation before Congress, and the president sent her on a mission to discuss trade policy and defense with leaders of seven Latin American and Caribbean nations. No first lady had ever represented the United States abroad before in this manner.

Carter's nominations of African Americans for high office went well beyond tokenism. He selected a black woman for his cabinet; chose six black ambassadors, including the envoy to West Germany; appointed both the first black secretary of the army and a black solicitor general; and tapped thirty-eight blacks for judgeships. To the prestigious post of US ambassador to the United Nations, he named Andrew Young, who had been an intimate of Martin Luther King. Carter, said the historian

At Ebenezer Baptist Church in Atlanta, the president and first lady join civil rights leaders in a hymn. With them are Rev. Martin Luther King Sr., Ambassador to the United Nations Andrew Young, and Coretta Scott King. *Courtesy of the Jimmy Carter Library and Museum, National Archives ID 183007*

John Hope Franklin, "was about as straight on the race question as we've ever seen in this country."

Jimmy Carter also established himself as one of America's greatest presidents on the environment. He installed solar panels on the White House roof and, after creating a Solar Energy Research Institute, appointed the cofounder of Earth Day to head it. His most significant accomplishments came, surprisingly, when the sands were running out on his fourth year and his political clout was minimal. After fighting off gas, mineral, oil, and timber lobbies, he signed a bill in December 1980 safeguarding one-third of Alaska from exploitation. That stroke of the pen doubled the acreage of America's national parks and wildlife refuges. He also established a $1.6 billion Superfund to rid the land and waterways of toxic waste. Liberals had reason to stand up and cheer.

Carter and his circle, though, had a different worldview and dissimilar priorities than the liberals (personified by Mondale), and both groups knew it. The historian Steven Gillon has pointed out that Carter and Mondale, while sharing "a feel for the common man," did not define "the common man" in the same way. "For Carter the average citizen was rural, Protestant, politically independent, financially secure, and fiscally conservative; for Mondale that person was a struggling, urban, blue-collar, union member concerned about a secure job, decent wages, and education for his children." Carter could not relate to the enthusiasms of the Mondale wing of the Democratic Party. When a cabinet officer talked to him about poverty and racism in the slums, he was "frankly pretty bored," an observer noted, but when a staffer displayed an efficiency chart, "the President's eyes lit up."

Whenever anyone spoke of "zero-based budgeting," Carter's pulse quickened. No other president devoted so much time as Carter did to administrative reform. He set three hundred people to work at the OMB on executive reorganization and assigned more than a hundred more to streamlining the bureaucracy. Carter took pride in abolishing the Civil Service Commission and creating an Office of Personnel Management and a Merit System Protection Board, but liberals thought he could better have devoted his energy to addressing critical social problems. In his memoir, Speaker Tip O'Neill expressed his "main complaint" about White House breakfast meetings of congressional leaders with the president: "Carter got wrapped up in foreign policy instead of

GERALD FORD AND JIMMY CARTER | 565

the more pressing domestic issues. Unemployment was rising, inflation was soaring, and interest rates were going crazy, but the president preferred to discuss Angola, Rhodesia, the Middle East, and just about every other place under the sun." (O'Neill, a man of considerable girth, also railed about the meager fare that Carter offered. "I didn't get this way eating sweet rolls," he said. "I want a breakfast, and I'm not coming back until I get a meal!")

Though Carter had campaigned on a pledge to diminish the high rate of joblessness, he quickly concluded, as Ford had, that the main problem he faced was not unemployment but inflation—a judgment that put him on a collision course with liberal Democrats throughout his presidency. Early in his first year, Carter, believing that government deficits fueled price rises, advocated the old Republican remedy of retrenchment, leading George McGovern to say, "It sometimes seems difficult to remember who won last fall." The clash became still sharper in 1978 after Carter announced the first of three "national austerity" budgets scaling back programs that helped the poor. His chief domestic policy adviser, Stuart Eizenstat, noted: "Spent 30 minutes with Mrs. King who says she just can't keep defending him. There is open rebellion from liberals." At a midterm party conference in Memphis, Carter got only a lukewarm response, but when Senator Kennedy urged vigorous resistance to cutting back federal programs, applause rocked the hall.

Carter pursued this course even more insistently in his last two years in office. As the *New York Times* commented, "Instead of satisfying the coalition that has sustained Democratic Presidents since Franklin Roosevelt, he proposes to tame that hungry beast as Republican Presidents since Eisenhower never could." Early in 1979, he recommended taking two billion away from social services and another billion from Social Security and school lunches while boosting spending for the Pentagon, and in March 1980, after sponsoring a large increase in military outlays, he advocated curtailing money for food stamps and programs to safeguard the health of children. "We look heartless," Mondale told Eizenstat. "The reason for Carter's horrible failure in economic policy is plain enough," said Arthur Schlesinger Jr. "He is not a Democrat—at least in anything more recent than the Grover Cleveland sense of the word."

Deregulation of banking and of key industries, which had fateful consequences carrying well into the twenty-first century, began not, as is often supposed, with Reagan but under Carter. In his address accepting renomination in 1980, Carter boasted, "We have slashed government regulation and put free enterprise back into the airline, trucking and financial system of our country, and we are doing the same for the railroads. This is the greatest change in the relationship between business and government since the New Deal." (Deplored by many progressives, deregulation, it should be noted, had the support of Teddy Kennedy and the consumer advocate Ralph Nader, who had concluded that regulators had become agents of the businessmen they were supposed to discipline.) In his second annual address, Carter had spelled out his thinking about both budget restraint and deregulation. "Government cannot solve our problems," he declared. "It cannot eliminate poverty, or provide a bountiful economy, or reduce inflation, or save our cities, or cure illiteracy, or provide energy."

Liberals found these sentiments heretical. If FDR had held such a view, Schlesinger commented, "we would still be in the Great Depression." Mondale told Carter that instead of bleating about what government could not do, he should be reminding the country of "the historic role of government in getting people on their feet." But the president paid him no heed. During a press conference in the fall of 1979 at which he spelled out his differences with Teddy Kennedy, Carter said that the senator was "much more inclined toward the old philosophy of pouring out new programs and new money to meet a social need," while he, as president, stood for "much stronger defense commitments" and was "much more inclined to... start up new programs only when it's absolutely necessary."

———

Carter alienated both conservatives and liberals by his eager and, in many respects, far-sighted efforts to cope with the energy crisis he had inherited. From 1973 to 1976, gasoline prices had nearly doubled, but instead of responding sensibly by reducing consumption and lessening their dependence on foreign reserves, Americans stepped up their demand, requiring imports of oil at an alarming rate. In a televised address in April 1977, Carter berated the citizenry. "Ours is the most wasteful nation on earth," he said. The need to substitute sacrifice for self-indulgence, he asserted, would "test the character of the American people," whom he called upon, in a phrase of William James's, to wage "the moral equivalent of war" if they hoped to avert a "national catastrophe." Borrowing a line from Chicken Little, he warned, "The sky is falling." But the nation yawned. Half of the country did not believe that there was any kind of energy problem. It took Carter a year and a half of dogged persistence to win approval for a National Energy Act (it survived in the House by only one vote), and many of his recommendations were scrapped.

By the summer of 1979, cutbacks in Middle Eastern oil output had reached a crisis stage, for which, unfairly, Carter got much of the blame. Irate motorists fumed over sky-high prices, while shortages caused queues at gas pumps stretching for blocks. At times, drivers waited on line for three hours to fill up, only to find that when their turn came, tanks had run dry. As the Fourth of July weekend approached, with New Yorkers looking forward to a trip to the beach, 90 percent of stations in the metropolitan area were closed. On June 30, the president, anticipating a well-earned vacation stay in Hawaii, received a message as he flew over the Pacific urging him to return to Washington posthaste to respond to a national temper tantrum. "You have no idea of how bad it is here," his pollster Patrick Caddell told him.

The White House alerted television networks to allot time for Carter's fifth national sermon on energy, only to have the president cancel the talk twenty-four hours before he was to appear on TV screens. When one of his aides objected that never before had a scheduled presidential event been called off, Carter replied, "I just don't want to bullshit the American people." Later, Rosalynn Carter explained, "Jimmy had made several speeches on energy," and they "just seemed to be going nowhere with the public." He had given four major addresses on behalf of his energy program—and after each talk, confidence had fallen further. "We're irrelevant and people don't listen to us," he told his advisers. The withdrawal stirred rumors that the president was critically ill or that he had fled the country, and with the United States apparently leaderless, the dollar nose-dived. He then added to the air of mystery by summoning 150 heavy thinkers from government, the clergy, universities, and other realms to a domestic summit at Camp David.

For eleven days, Carter dug in at the retreat in the Maryland mountains as he mulled over what to say to the country. Seated on the floor making notes, he listened attentively even to those, such as the young Arkansas governor Bill Clinton, who rapped his knuckles. One historian has called the proceeding "the most remarkable exercise in presidential navel-gazing in American history." Carter found especially congenial the approach of the historian Christopher Lasch, author of *The Culture of Narcissism*. The president had been persuaded by Caddell that, because of fifteen years of trauma from assassinations, race riots, jungle warfare, and Watergate, the nation was experiencing a "malaise," and much to the distress of his vice president, Carter decided to make this notion the theme of his postponed address. (Impatient with what he regarded as psychobabble, Mondale, believing that to win public support one needed to solve problems, observed, "If, having gotten elected on the grounds that we needed a government as good as the people, we now were heard to argue that we needed a people as good as the government,... we would be destroyed.")

Upon descending from the mountain, Carter told the American people that they were undergoing a "crisis of confidence" that "strikes at the very heart and soul and spirit of our national will." His face on the television screen deadly serious, he declared: "In a nation that was proud of hard work, strong families, close-knit communities and our faith in God, too many of us now tend to worship self-indulgence and consumption. Human identity is no longer defined by what one does but by what one owns." Solving the energy crisis, he said, could "help us to conquer the crisis of the spirit in our country." To cope with the energy predicament, he advocated a far-reaching program that included stricter emission standards on cars, higher taxes on oil and natural gas, and the development of new sources of power. The "malaise" speech, as the press called it (though Carter never used the word), is usually remembered as a disaster, but, in fact, it won wide acclaim, and the president's ratings shot up.

Only two days after this singular triumph, Carter self-destructed. Shockingly, he demanded the resignations of every member of his cabinet. Foreign chancelleries, familiar with parliamentary custom, feared that the US government was collapsing, and his constituents at home concluded that this man had taken leave of his senses. Carter wound up dropping five cabinet officials and bringing in replacements. Even more consequential than the massive cabinet shakeup was his appointment of a Wall Street favorite to head the Federal Reserve Board. Carter counted on Paul Volcker to combat inflation by imposing a tight money regimen, but Volcker plunged the country into a severe recession that increased unemployment without significantly lowering prices. A man of Spartan sensibility, Carter was dismayed that a regimen of limits was proving so painful and was so badly eroding his standing in Congress. "He hasn't a single friend up here," confided a Democratic senator on Capitol Hill. "Not one soul."

Determined to be a Christian of the deed, not a Pharisee, this church deacon sought a moral compass for his foreign policy too. "A strong nation, like a strong person," he said, "can afford to be gentle." To slow down the arms race, he put off development of a neutron bomb, withdrew all US nuclear weapons from South Korea, and, in June 1979, flew to Vienna to sign a SALT II treaty with Russia restricting the building and deployment of strategic missiles. To deal with tragedies such as the missing persons in Argentina and to further the cause of Soviet dissidents, Carter appointed the civil rights activist Patricia Derian as assistant secretary of state for human rights and humanitarian affairs. The first president to visit sub-Saharan Africa, he worked against the white supremacist regime in Rhodesia.

Never averse to taking unpopular stands, Carter moved boldly to dispel the impression in Latin America that the United States was an overbearing Goliath. To defuse the danger of a nasty conflict with Panamanian nationalists, he signed treaties turning over control of the Panama Canal to the republic of Panama after 1999, while preserving the canal's accessibility. Spread-eagle senators were outraged. "The canal is ours; we bought and we paid for it; and we should keep it," Strom Thurmond declared, and the GOP senator from California, S. I. Hayakawa, jested, "We stole it fair and square." But Carter showed unexpected dexterity as a legislative tactician. Early in 1978, against stiff odds, he won ratification of the agreements after amendment, though by just a one-vote margin in the Senate.

Hoping to bring peace to the Middle East—a goal no predecessor had achieved—Carter invited the president of Egypt, Anwar Sadat, and the prime minister of Israel, Menachem Begin, to America. He was taking a big risk in bringing together two sworn enemies for an encounter that was likely to end in awkward failure. At Camp David, they refused even to be in the same room. But Carter was tenacious. For nearly two weeks, he scurried back and forth between their cabins in an attempt to broker an agreement. Prime Minister Begin was often truculent, and at one point Sadat packed his bags to return to Cairo. Carter persuaded him to stay, and, on September 17, 1978, the president's selfless efforts were rewarded with the signing of the Camp David Accords, ending thirty years of hostilities. When the agreement unraveled, and it appeared that all hope was gone, Carter flew to the Middle East to knit it together again. The Israeli-Eygptian treaty was an extraordinary accomplishment. On his return from Cairo, thousands of Americans waited for hours in the dark to cheer him when his plane touched down, and on March 26, 1979, as the two adversaries shook hands on the White House lawn, he grinned ear to ear.

In his first months in office, Carter had also reached out to the Kremlin in the hope of thawing the Cold War, but Soviet intransigence later caused him to change direction. Incensed by the Russian invasion of Afghanistan in December 1979, he urged resumption of registration

Jimmy Carter with Anwar Sadat and Menachem Begin. The president, who had labored mightily at Camp David to bring the two longtime enemies together, beams as the Egyptian president and the Israeli prime minister shake hands on the South Lawn of the White House, signaling their agreement to a peace treaty ending a state of war that had lasted more than thirty years. *Associated Press, ID 790326030*

for the draft, withdrew the pact limiting nuclear arsenals he had negotiated with Brezhnev, imposed an embargo on grain shipments and the export of high-level technology to the USSR, and announced a US boycott of the Olympics scheduled for 1980 in Moscow. He warned against Soviet aggression by enunciating what became known as the Carter Doctrine: "Any attempt by any outside force to gain control of the Persian Gulf region will be regarded as an assault on the vital interests of the United States of America and such an assault will be repelled by any means necessary, including military force." He also spent large sums on new warheads, cruise missiles, the nuclear-powered Trident submarine, and the MX—an awesome missile system lodged in a maze of underground tunnels. In addition, he resumed support for building the controversial neutron bomb. No longer did he turn the other cheek.

At the same time that he was devising a response to the Afghanistan incursion, Carter had to confront a much more acute crisis in Iran, where he had brought the greatest disaster of his presidency down upon himself. In November 1977, he welcomed the shah of Iran to the White House, and on New Year's Eve in Tehran, raising his glass, he toasted the ruler. Though the shah was sustained in power by a vicious secret police force, Carter praised him as a champion of "the cause of human rights" who had earned "the admiration and love" of the Iranian people. Little more than a year later, his subjects, no longer willing to be governed by a monarch imposed on them by the CIA, drove the shah into exile. Critically ill, he sought medical treatment in the United States. Secretary of State Cyrus Vance warned that admitting him could have repercussions in Iran, and Carter hesitated. But under pressure from David Rockefeller, Henry Kissinger, and the head of the National Security Council, Zbigniew Brzezinski, he caved in.

Shortly after the deposed shah entered the Mayo Clinic, three thousand Islamic militants stormed the US embassy compound in Tehran and seized more than fifty diplomats and soldiers. They paraded blindfolded US Marine guards, hands tied behind their backs, through the streets of Tehran while mobs chanted, "Death to Carter, Death to the Shah," as they spat upon the American flag and burned effigies of the president—scenes recorded on camera that Americans found painful to witness. Carter struck back by closing the Iranian embassy and consulates in the United States, declaring Iranian diplomats persona non grata, expelling Iranian students, forbidding the import of oil from Iran, and freezing $8 billion of Iranian assets in the United States. Once again, the adage that the American people rally to a president in a crisis, even if he is at fault, proved true. Over the next months, Carter's approval rating rocketed from 30 percent to 61 percent—the swiftest climb in the history of polling, even faster than FDR's after Pearl Harbor. "Attacks on Carter personally by Iranian leaders, prominently reported via TV to Americans at home, gave the President a stature he had failed to achieve in three years in office," wrote the *Washington Post*'s Haynes Johnson. "Carter became the personification of the nation, the symbol of American resolve, the rallying point for Americans at home to respond to insults from abroad."

But as weeks of captivity of the hostages in Tehran lengthened into months, then to more than a year—eventually to 444 days—public attitudes soured. Carter pursued every possible avenue of negotiation—at one time sending abroad his chief aide, Hamilton Jordan, disguised in false mustache and wig—but his patience was seen as impotence. Carter,

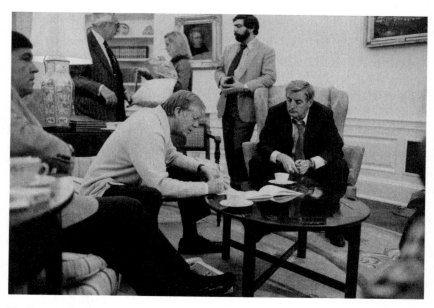

The Iranian hostage crisis. This photograph registers the acute anxiety of administration leaders as, in the foreground, presidential aide Hamilton Jordan, Jimmy Carter, and Vice President Walter Mondale gather in the Oval Office. *Courtesy of the Jimmy Carter Library and Museum*

too, became frustrated. In April 1980, flouting the consultation provisions of the War Powers Resolution, he ordered a secret commando raid. It ended in disaster, taking the lives of eight Americans when a helicopter collided with a transport plane in the Iranian desert. Secretary of State Cyrus Vance, who regarded the operation as foolhardy, resigned in protest, and the botched rescue attempt reinforced the impression that Carter, like Ford, was a bumbler, clueless about how to govern. Eventually, Carter's painstaking procedures succeeded, but, spitefully, the Iranians did not release the captives until a few minutes after the president's term ended.

Unexpectedly, the negotiations resulted in a ruling that sustained presidential power. To ransom the Americans, Carter not only released the billions of Iranian assets in the United States but also suspended claims of private parties against Iran, though no act of Congress authorized that step. The Supreme Court's unanimous, though cautious, decision in *Dames & Moore v. Regan* (1981) validating the president's action was seen by some critics as nothing less than a reversal of the reasoning in the Steel Seizure opinion of 1952 that rebuked Truman. But this vindication did not come until Carter was out of office. Meantime, on *CBS Evening News*, Walter Cronkite ended each program by intoning how many days the hostages had been held—a nightly observance of America's mortification and Carter's helplessness.

So poor were Carter's chances when the 1980 campaign began that he could only hope that somehow his opponent would falter. Carter sought reelection, as the journalist Lou Cannon pointed out, "dogged by the captivity of hostages he could not free" and beset by "an economy he could not seem to improve." Volcker's clamp on the money supply had driven prime rates of borrowing from 5 percent up to a staggering 18.5 percent—an all-time high that snuffed out the mortgage market—at the same time that the nation was enduring its second year of double-digit inflation, mounting unemployment, a greatly increased tax burden, and a decline in real wages. By August, with the election only three months away, Carter's approval rating had sunk to the lowest point that had ever been recorded, even below Nixon's on the eve of his resignation.

For their presidential nominee, the Republicans settled on Ronald Reagan, with his chief rival, George H. W. Bush, as running mate.

A number of Democrats thought Reagan, a movie and TV performer lacking in gravitas, would be a pushover, forgetting that he had been twice elected governor of California. Taking full advantage of popular resentment of the downturn, he said, "A recession is when your neighbor loses his job. A depression is when you lose yours. And recovery is when Jimmy Carter loses his." Reagan also benefited from an unanticipated consequence of the well-intentioned post-Watergate campaign finance legislation: the emergence of political action committees to evade spending limits imposed by reformers. In particular, PACs spawned by Christian evangelicals buttressed the Republicans.

Reagan, however, made a series of outlandish gaffes that prompted voters to reconsider whether the star of *Bedtime for Bonzo*, in which he was paired with a chimpanzee, was qualified to lead the nation. At a county fair near Philadelphia, Mississippi, where three civil rights volunteers had been savagely murdered, he opened his campaign by saying, "I believe in states' rights." That coded message, critics said, signaled to white racists that he was on their side—an impression that was reinforced when, during the campaign, he referred to "welfare queens" and a "strapping young buck" who were cheating on welfare. At a gathering of Christian fundamentalists, he raised no objection when a speaker with whom he shared a platform said that "God doesn't hear the prayers of a Jew." Air pollution, he insisted, was caused not by car exhausts or the chemicals spewed from factory chimneys but by trees. (At Claremont College, where he had a speaking engagement, students hung placards on trees reading "Chop me down before I kill again.") As Election Day neared, Carter, who had started out so far behind, held a slight lead.

But, as Carter's biographer Julian Zelizer has written, "The last week of the campaign went horribly for the administration." Caddell, the president recorded in his diary, "was getting some very disturbing... results, showing a massive slippage as people realized that the hostages were not coming home." Carter experienced the misfortune of having the first anniversary of the Tehran captivity coincide almost precisely with Election Day, a "strong reminder," as his pollster said, "that these people were still over there and Jimmy Carter hasn't been able to do anything about it."

A final televised debate one week before the election also powerfully affected the outcome. A seasoned actor, Reagan was wholly at ease, tossing off bright quips. At one point, he put Carter down with a smile, a shrug, and a nonchalant "There you go again." Carter, on the other hand, made himself seem foolish by indicating that he turned to his young daughter, Amy, for advice on nuclear weapons policy. The critical moment in the debate came when Reagan, peering into the camera lens, urged viewers to ask when they entered the voting booth: "Are you better off than you were four years ago? Is it easier for you to go and buy things in the stores than it was four years ago? . . . Is America respected around the world as it was?" When he posed those questions, he knew that millions of Americans, in a year of so many bleak tidings at home and overseas, would not find it possible to give the answer Carter needed.

With the broad shift of allegiances in the final days of the campaign, Reagan gave Carter a thrashing. Though Reagan polled less than 51 percent of the ballots, that was enough to provide him a decisive win, for, with 8 percent going to minor-party candidates, the president, receiving a lowly 41 percent, wound up with just 49 electoral votes to Reagan's 489. Commentators likened the 1980 contest to that of 1932 when the electorate had been less interested in elevating Franklin Roosevelt than in punishing Herbert Hoover. No one could doubt Carter's dedication: he went without sleep for two nights in a row in order to complete arrangements for bringing the Tehran captives home. But he could not overcome the dual handicaps of the hostage crisis and the woeful economy.

Nor did the country want to hear any more from the village scold about the need to sacrifice and accept limits, though someday he may be regarded as a prophet before his time. Carter, said Governor Bill Clinton, seemed more like a "17th Century New England Puritan than a 20th century Southern Baptist." As Carter's term was nearing an end, a Georgia journalist wrote: "We thought we wanted to be preached to, . . . cleansed, comforted. But Jimmy Carter was a mere Sunday School teacher, not a skillful preacher. More often than not, his homilies came off as self-serving rather than illuminating. There were the fireside chats on television . . . , tendentious, platitudinous embarrassments. Even Walter Cronkite could not jazz up the innate drabness of those telephone calls. They were of the same type that any night city editor gets on a Saturday evening when the moon is full."

Commentators often linked "Jimmy Hoover" to the earlier president who, trained as an engineer, approached human problems with a slide rule mentality. Highly intelligent, exceptionally well informed, dedicated, the two men were bewildered when they found that these sterling qualities did not suffice. Like Herbert Hoover, "Carter was a moralistic progressive with an engineer's fixation on detail and an inability to inspire the electorate," the historian Robert Dallek has observed. A policy wonk, Carter too often became submerged in micromanagement, so obsessed with detail that he even concerned himself with allotting times of play on the White House tennis court. "Jimmy," concluded his friend Attorney General Griffin Bell, "was about as good a president as an engineer could be."

"As he left office after four years in a strange land," one commentator wrote, "Jimmy Carter remained a stranger in a strange land." With no relationship to national politics before he entered the White House, he had none after he departed. "He is like the Cheshire cat in Alice in Wonderland," said a prominent Democrat. "He is disappearing into the trees, and there is nothing left but the smile." Carter did not even attend the 1984 national convention, and Democratic candidates distanced themselves from what was regarded as a failed presidency. Unlike most other presidencies, however, Carter's had an afterlife—one altogether in keeping with his Niebuhrian belief that moral man must act responsibly in an immoral world.

In retirement, Carter became the most effective ex-president since John Quincy Adams. Humbly, as a volunteer for Habitat for Humanity, he and his wife turned up with hammer and saw to build homes for the poor. In Atlanta in 1982, he established the Carter Center, an organization to promote democracy and peace abroad and to eradicate diseases such as river blindness. The center scored a dramatic success in reducing the outbreak of debilitating Guinea worm disease from 3.5 million cases to fewer than ten thousand. In these same years, Carter monitored elections and mediated conflicts in more than two dozen countries—from Paraguay to Mozambique, from Nicaragua to Somalia. He forestalled a US invasion of Haiti by persuading its leader to step down, negotiated an arrangement with Kim Il-Sung to permit inspection of North Korea's nuclear facilities, and played a large part in securing the Nairobi Agreement between Uganda and Sudan. In 2002, Jimmy Carter, who had hoped as president to beat swords into plowshares, was awarded the Nobel Peace Prize.

More than one writer has likened Carter to the Wizard of Oz, who Dorothy discovers is a dissembler. "You are a very bad man!" she cries. "No, I am a very good man," he replies. "I'm just a very bad Wizard." Jimmy Carter was, and is, a very good man. But, sadly, like the Wizard, he was just not very good at his craft.

In the final year of the Carter presidency, Gerald Ford asserted, "We have not an imperial presidency but an imperiled presidency." The White House appeared to have declined so greatly under Ford and Carter that, as Schlesinger wrote, "pundits confidently predicted an age of one-term Presidents." With barely concealed skepticism toward this vagary, he added: "The impression arose... of a beleaguered and pathetic fellow sitting forlornly in the Oval Office, assailed by unprecedentedly intractable problems, paralyzed by the constitutional separation of powers, hemmed in by congressional and bureaucratic constraints, pushed one way and another by exigent interest groups, seduced, betrayed, and abandoned by the mass media." Schlesinger's scoffing tone was appropriate because worriers greatly exaggerated the "crisis." So unexceptional was a one-term presidency that of the twenty-five occupants of the White House between Jackson and Eisenhower only three served eight consecutive years. But the conviction that the institution was at risk informed much of the public perception as Carter's successor readied himself for what was thought to be a Sisyphean assignment.

By the start of 1981, concern about the Oval Office had been building for years. Commemoration of the bicentennial of American independence in 1976 had capped more than a decade of disjunctures. The president chosen in 1960 had been murdered; his successor had not dared to run for another term; and the third man in line had fled Washington in disgrace. "The American presidency has become conspicuously problematic, devouring its incumbents with appalling regularity," observed the political scientist Fred Greenstein. "Kennedy's one thousand days... initiated a period of ephemeral presidencies. Increasingly, the chief executive has become a bird of passage." In his important synthesis, *The American Presidency* (1979), Richard Pious predicted that in the foreseeable future, "the White House will remain in a state of siege." On the eve of Ronald Reagan's inauguration, a British journalist summed up the prevailing view: "My own hunch is that the presidency will never again be at the center of the national consciousness in quite the way it was between 1933 and 1973."

Only a half-dozen years after recoiling at Watergate, however, Americans showed signs of yearning for a powerful president. They dismissed Gerald Ford as "a clerk, not a leader," and Jimmy Carter as a busybody who, said one reporter, "jumps around like a water spider on a June afternoon." They hungered for a president who, in his conduct of foreign affairs, rode tall in the saddle and who, in his messages to the nation, did not chide them on the need to abandon their profligate ways but radiated cheer and faith in the future. They sought, too, a man with panache. Hollywood had never handed Ronald Reagan so choice a role.

I I

Ronald Reagan

ON INAUGURATION DAY IN JANUARY 1981, Americans gave thanks that jaunty Ronald Reagan had replaced gloomy Jimmy Carter. In his speech accepting the presidential nomination, Reagan had shown how adroitly he could pull the country's heartstrings. "They say that the United States has had its day in the sun; that our nation has passed its zenith," he said. "My fellow citizens, I utterly reject that view. The American people, the most generous on earth, who created the highest standard of living, are not going to accept the notion that we can make a better world for others by moving backward ourselves." He wound up by offering his version of John Winthrop's "Citty upon a Hill"—the beguiling image in the sermon delivered after the Puritans set out on the *Arabella* for the New World: "Can we doubt that only a Divine Providence placed this land, this island of freedom, here as a refuge for all those people in the world who yearn to breathe freely?"

Sworn in two weeks before his seventieth birthday, the oldest man ever to take over the presidency, Reagan conveyed the bright spirits of a younger America. In his inaugural address, he declared: "We're not, as some would have us believe, doomed to an inevitable decline.... We have every right to dream heroic dreams." A longtime artisan in Hollywood's "dream factory," Reagan had an extraordinary capacity for putting a smiling face on governance. Assuring the nation that "America's best days are yet to come," he stated, "We see an America where every day is Independence Day, the Fourth of July." In sum, Reagan, said a *Newsweek* writer, was "an aging warrior offering a springtime of hope."

Critics accused him of debasing the currency of public discourse, but, after the darkness of the years from Kennedy's assassination through Carter's dispensations of dreariness, millions of Americans found Reagan a generator of good feeling. "For all his negativity about government," the historian Laura Kalman has written, Reagan "seemed one of the most optimistic, ebullient, and hopeful politicians since Franklin Roosevelt. He was self-assured, he looked like a leader, and he possessed FDR's sense of theatricality."

The president's statements carried conviction because he believed what he said. Every travail, he had convinced himself, has a happy outcome. Reagan, who, as the journalist Haynes Johnson wrote, came out of "a family background of pain, privation, and humiliation, living on the margin," insisted that his childhood had been "as sweet and idyllic as it could be"—indeed, as he said in his autobiography, "one of those rare Tom Sawyer–Huck Finn idylls." Ronnie's father, a failed salesman in the mold of Willy Loman, had been given to drunken stupors. During one awful holiday season of the future president's childhood, his father was fired on Christmas Eve, but Reagan in his high school yearbook dispensed a message of cheer: life was "just one grand sweet song, so start the music."

Early in his Hollywood career, he had fought hard to win the part of the gridiron hero George Gipp in a film being made about the legendary Notre Dame football coach Knute Rockne. Most actors would have regarded this as a tragic role, for, at a very young age, only two weeks after having been elected Notre Dame's first All-American, Gipp had died of strep throat and pneumonia. Reagan, though, savored the opportunity because it permitted him to be associated with an inspirational tale. As every football fan knew, Rockne in 1928, with his underdog eleven trailing undefeated Army at halftime, rallied his team to victory with a locker room speech urging his players to heed the alleged deathbed words of his former star: "Win just one for the Gipper." Ever after, Reagan beamed whenever anyone referred to him as "the Gipper."

The country came to view Reagan not only as an inspirational messenger but as a talisman. At a congressional luncheon following the inaugural ceremony, he gleefully announced glad tidings: after 444 days of captivity, the American hostages in Iran had been freed and were heading home. Though Reagan had nothing at all to do with their liberation, "the news," reported the *New York Times*, "seemed to turn the inauguration celebration...into an event of unbridled joy for Mr. Reagan and his supporters." The Empire State Building sparkled in red, white, and blue, and, in New York harbor, the Statue of Liberty was luminescent.

Throughout his presidency, Reagan conveyed an unquestioning belief in his country's exceptionalism. "He is a Prospero of American memories, a magician who carries a bright, ideal America like a holograph in his mind and projects its image in the air," stated an essayist in *Time*. The country found his sentiments highly congenial, for, as *Newsweek* said, he had internalized "America as it imagined itself to be." Not long after taking office, Reagan said, "What I'd really like to do is go down in history as the president who made Americans believe in themselves again." He was fond of quoting Lincoln's assertion that the United States was the earth's "last best hope," and on one occasion he told Congress: "The poet Carl Sandburg wrote, 'The republic is a dream. Nothing happens unless first a dream.' And that's what makes us Americans different. We've always reached for a new spirit and aimed at a higher goal.... Who among us wants to be first to say we no longer have those qualities, that we must limp along, doing the same things that have brought us our present misery?"

From the very first day of his presidency, Reagan turned his back on Carter austerity. On the night of his inauguration, hundreds of elegantly dressed men and women took to the dance floor at an outlandishly expensive Inaugural Ball, an extravaganza one critic called "a bacchanalia of the haves." With Reagan determined to restore the magisterial aura of the presidency, trumpeters once again sounded "Hail to the Chief," and employees turned up for work at the White House not in sport shirt and blue jeans but in jacket and tie. When he sketched out his views on the economy, Reagan emphasized neither the fiscal probity that had been a staple of Republican policies in the past—what was called "root canal economics"—nor Kennedy's requirement that the American people pay any price, bear any burden. Instead, he preached a message of joy at the same time that he denied that he was abandoning the traditional GOP litany on the need for a balanced budget.

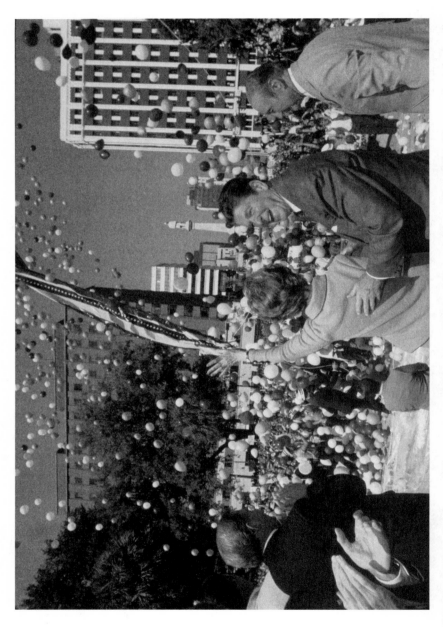

Ronald Reagan with Nancy Reagan. This 1980 campaign scene anticipated his presidency, when White House aides calculatedly arranged to have Reagan pictured against patriotic backdrops. *Courtesy of the Ronald Reagan Library, ID 32-1*

Members of his staff took full advantage of Reagan's ability to identify himself with a fabled past and a boundless future. They perceived that exegesis of Reagan's doctrines held less promise than visual imagery— "photo ops"—of the former Hollywood actor in legendary venues such as the island home of the Statue of Liberty. In a decade when daily newspaper readership fell from 73 to 50 percent (for young people, it dropped to 29 percent) and television news programs strove to be entertaining, Reagan's handlers relied increasingly not on print media but on projections of a radiant president on nightly TV screens.

After CBS showed a television segment by Lesley Stahl critical of Reagan, she was startled to be thanked by a top White House official, Richard Darman, for the "great piece," which he called a "five-minute commercial" for the president. Bewildered, Stahl asked, "Didn't you hear what I said?" Darman replied: "Nobody heard what you said. They just saw five minutes of beautiful pictures of Ronald Reagan. They saw balloons. They saw flags. They saw the red-white-and-blue. Haven't you people figured out yet that the picture always overrides what you say?"

Facing westward as he delivered his inaugural address, President Reagan had offered his countrymen a homily. He began by calling attention to the monuments to Washington, Jefferson, and Lincoln, and "beyond those monuments... the Potomac River, and on the far shore the sloping hills of Arlington National Cemetery with its row upon row of simple white markers." He went on:

> Under one such marker lies a young man, Martin Treptow, who left his job in a small town barbershop in 1917 to go to France with the famed Rainbow Division. There, on the western front, he was killed trying to carry a message between battalions under heavy artillery fire. We're told that on his body was found a diary. On the flyleaf under the heading, "My Pledge," he had written these words: "America must win this war. Therefore I will... fight cheerfully and do my utmost, as if... the whole struggle depended on me alone."

In truth, Martin Treptow was buried not in Arlington Cemetery but more than a thousand miles away in a Wisconsin graveyard. The president's aides had alerted him to that fact, but Reagan persisted in elaborating a falsehood. Remarkably, he found it hard to fathom why truth should be privileged over make-believe. His attitude is explicable only if one bears in mind that he was America's first consumer culture president: TV pitchman for Borax (a product that meant nothing to him), and actor in countless motion pictures in which he mouthed the words of others.

Over the course of the next four years, Reagan spun one narrative after another that was palpably untrue. In 1985, he recalled his horror at his first encounter with Nazi death camps as a Signal Corps photographer in Europe during World War II, though he had never left the United States at any time during the war. More than once, he told the story of a heroic wartime pilot who, instead of bailing out and leaving a wounded crewman to his fate, said, "Never mind, son, we'll ride it down together." Even when it was pointed out to him that there was no way to know what one man said to another as they plunged to their deaths, he would not be dissuaded. Reagan's tale, it turned out, derived from the movie *A Wing and a Prayer*, starring Dana Andrews.

Witnesses to his whoppers realized that Reagan was not lying but had persuaded himself of the validity of his tales. "He finds it next to impossible to say anything that is not in some crucial way untrue," wrote the journalist Jack Beatty. "It's not a credibility gap, for there is no evidence of cynical or even conscious duplicity. The President is so far out of touch that it amounts to a reality gap." Still, listeners were often dumbfounded. His daughter Patti said, "He has the ability to make statements that are so far outside the parameters of logic that they leave you speechless." John Sloan, author of *The Reagan Effect*, has written: "In Reagan's mind, unpleasant facts could be avoided; contradictions could be denied; anecdotes could overcome facts; movie illusions could substitute for history; unpleasant realities could be blamed on a hostile press."

His fictions mattered little, though, for after a generation of assassination and scoundrelry the media decided—consciously or unconsciously—to feature his presidency as a success story and to brush aside inconvenient particulars. "Ronald Reagan," observed the political scientist James David Barber, "is the first modern President whose contempt for the facts is treated as a charming idiosyncrasy." In London, a writer in the *Observer* commented: "His errors glide past unchallenged. At one point...he alleged that almost half the population gets a free meal from the government each day. No one told him he was crazy. The general message of the American press is that, yes, while it is perfectly true that the emperor has no clothes, nudity is actually very acceptable this year."

As a consequence, few Americans comprehended that the new president was not what he seemed to be. A man who identified himself with the nuclear family, he was America's first divorced president and was estranged from his children. An advocate of "Christian values," he rarely could be found in a church pew on Sunday morning. He presented himself as someone who readily empathized with the working class ("We didn't live on the wrong side of the tracks, but we lived so close to them we could hear the whistle real loud"), yet he hung out with super-rich West Coast buddies and despised the less fortunate. He had sought the governorship of California, he explained, in order to harry "welfare bums."

With his ready grin and easygoing manner, Reagan gave the impression that he was a bighearted guy who loved nothing better than to mingle with folks when, in fact, he was chillingly insular. In her memoir, *My Turn*, Nancy Reagan said of her husband: "Although he loves people, he often seems remote, and he doesn't let anybody get too close. There's a wall around him.... There are times when even I feel that barrier." Even more strikingly, his son Michael, in a set of recollections that he subtitled *On the Outside Looking In*, wrote that his father was frequently "completely oblivious" to others. "He can give his heart to the country," his son said, "but he just finds it difficult to hug his own children." At Michael's high school graduation, the future president came up to him and said in all seriousness, "My name is Ronald Reagan. What's yours?"

Those who worked with him found him curiously elusive. On encountering one of his top appointees, the only black member of his cabinet, Reagan greeted him by saying, "How are you, Mister Mayor? How are things in your city?" Some of his associates thought of him as an apparition who would appear, then dissolve. His talented speechwriter Peggy Noonan once remarked, "I never remember hearing his footsteps." (Similarly, Patti Reagan said of her father, "It was like he came in smoke, and disappeared in smoke.") When in 1994 it was revealed that Reagan was afflicted with Alzheimer's disease, the announcement strengthened earlier supposition that his strange behavior in his presidential years had a pathological cause, but that hypothesis remains speculative.

Altogether unreflective, he showed no more curiosity about himself than about others. One woman acquaintance said that he "lived life on the surface where the small waves are, not deep down where the heavy currents tug." Edmund Morris, invited to be Reagan's authorized biographer, found his new subject "shatteringly banal." He elaborated: "I couldn't conceive of writing more than a paragraph about him. . . . When you asked him a question about himself, it was like dropping a stone into a well and not hearing a splash." In John Updike's *Rabbit at Rest*, his protagonist ruminates: "Reagan . . . had that dream distance; the powerful thing about him as President was that you never knew how much he knew, nothing or everything, he was like God that way, you had to do a lot of it yourself."

No one had ever entered the White House so grossly ill informed. At presidential news conferences, especially in his first year, Reagan embarrassed himself. On one occasion, asked why he advocated putting missiles in vulnerable places, he responded, his face registering bewilderment, "I don't know but what maybe you haven't gotten into the area that I'm going to turn over to the secretary of defense." Frequently, he knew nothing about events that had been headlined in the morning newspaper. In 1984, when asked a question he should have fielded easily, Reagan looked befuddled, and his wife had to step in to rescue him. "Doing everything we can," she whispered. "Doing everything we can," the president echoed. To be sure, his detractors sometimes exaggerated his ignorance. The publication of his radio addresses of the 1950s revealed a considerable command of facts, though in a narrow range. But nothing suggested profundity. "You could walk through Ronald Reagan's deepest thoughts," a California legislator said, "and not get your ankles wet."

In all fields of public affairs—from diplomacy to the economy—the president stunned Washington policymakers by how little basic information he commanded. His mind, said the well-disposed Peggy Noonan, was "barren terrain." Speaking of one far-ranging discussion on the MX missile, the Indiana congressman Lee Hamilton, an authority on national defense, reported, "Reagan's only contribution throughout the entire hour and a half was to interrupt somewhere at midpoint to tell us he'd watched a movie the night before, and he gave us the plot from *War Games*." The president "cut ribbons and made speeches. He did these things beautifully," Congressman Jim Wright of Texas acknowledged. "But he never knew frijoles from pralines about the substantive facts of issues." Some thought him to be not only ignorant but, in the word of a former CIA director, "stupid." Clark Clifford called the president an "amiable dunce," and the usually restrained columnist David Broder wrote, "The task of watering the arid desert between Reagan's ears is a challenging one for his aides."

No Democratic adversary would ever constitute as great a peril to the president's political future, his advisers concluded, as Reagan did himself. Therefore, they protected him by severely restricting situations where he might blurt out a fantasy. His staff, one study reported, wrapped him "in excelsior," while "keeping the press at shouting distance or beyond." In his first year as president, he held only six news conferences—fewest ever in the modern era. Aides also prepared scores of cue cards, so that he would know how to greet visitors and respond to interviewers. His secretary of the treasury and later chief of staff said of the president: "Every moment of every public appearance was scheduled, every word scripted, every place where Reagan was expected to stand was chalked with toe marks." Those manipulations, he added, seemed customary to Reagan, for "he had been learning his lines, composing his facial expressions, hitting his toe marks for half a century." Each night, before turning in, he took comfort in a shooting schedule for the next day's television-focused events that was laid out for him at his bedside, just as it had been in Hollywood.

His White House staff found it difficult, often impossible, to get him to stir himself to follow even this rudimentary routine. When he was expected to read briefing papers, he lazed on a couch watching old movies. On the day before a summit meeting with world leaders about the future of the economy, he was given a briefing book. The next morning, his chief of staff asked him why he had not even opened it. "Well, Jim," the president explained, "*The Sound of Music* was on last night."

"Reagan," his principal biographer, Lou Cannon, has written, "may have been the one president in the history of the republic who saw his election as a chance to get some rest." (He spent nearly a full year of his tenure not in the White House but at his Rancho del Cielo in the hills above Santa Barbara.) Cabinet officials had to accommodate themselves to Reagan's slumbering during discussions of pressing issues, and on a multination European trip, he nodded off so often at meetings with heads of state, among them French president François Mitterand, that reporters, borrowing the title of a film noir, designated the journey "The Big Sleep." He even dozed during a televised audience at the Vatican while the pope was speaking to him. A satirist lampooned Reagan by transmuting Dolly Parton's "Workin' 9 to 5" into "Workin' 9 to 10," and TV's Johnny Carson quipped, "There are only two reasons you wake President Reagan: World War III and if *Hellcats of the Navy* is on the Late Show." Reagan tossed off criticism of his napping on the job with drollery. He told the White House press corps, "I am concerned about what is happening in government—and it's caused me many a sleepless afternoon," and he jested that posterity would place a marker on his chair in the Cabinet Room: "Reagan Slept Here."

His team devised ingenious ways to get him to pay attention. Aware that he was obsessed with movies, his national security adviser had the CIA put together a film on world leaders the president was scheduled to encounter. His defense secretary stooped lower. He got Reagan to sign off on production of the MX missile by showing him a cartoon. Once again, the president made a joke of his lack of involvement: "It's true that hard work never killed anybody, but why take a chance?" Cannon, who had observed him closely for years and with considerable admiration, took his lapses more seriously. "Seen either in military or economic terms," he concluded, "the nation paid a high price for a president who skimped on preparation, avoided complexities and news conferences and depended far too heavily on anecdotes, charts, graphics and cartoons."

Subordinates also found Reagan to be an exasperatingly disengaged administrator. "Trying to forge policy," said George Shultz, his longest-serving secretary of state, was "like walking through a swamp." Donald Regan recalled: "In the four years that I served as secretary of the treasury, I never saw President Reagan alone and never discussed economic philosophy.... I had to figure these things out like any other American, by studying his speeches and reading the newspapers.... After I accepted the job, he simply hung up and vanished." One of his national security advisers, General Colin Powell, recalled that "the President's passive management style placed a tremendous burden on us," and another national security adviser, Frank Carlucci, observed: "The Great Communicator wasn't always the greatest communicator in the private sessions; you didn't always get clean and crisp decisions. You assumed a lot.... You had to."

Numbers of observers contended that Reagan conducted himself not as a ruler but as a ceremonial monarch. In the midst of heated exchanges, a diplomat noted, Reagan behaved like a "remote sort of king...just not there." After taking in the president's performance during a discussion of the budget in 1981, one of his top aides remarked that Reagan looked like "a king...who had assembled his subalterns to listen to what they had to say and to preside, sort of," and another said, "He made decisions like an ancient king or a Turkish pasha, passively letting his subjects serve him, selecting only those morsels of public policy that were especially tasty. Rarely did he ask searching questions and demand to know why someone had or had not done something." As a consequence, a Republican senator went so far as to say: "With Ronald Reagan, no one is there. The sad fact is that we don't have a president."

Instead of designating one person as his top aide, as Eisenhower had with Sherman Adams, Reagan set up a "troika": James A. Baker III as chief of staff, Edwin Meese as counselor, and Michael Deaver as deputy chief of staff in charge of public relations—an arrangement that, for a time, left other appointees perplexed. The Reagan White House, said his first secretary of state, Alexander M. Haig Jr., was "as mysterious as a ghost ship; you heard the creak of the rigging and the groan of the timbers and sometimes even glimpsed the crew on deck. But which of the crew had the helm? Was it Meese, was it Baker, was it someone else? It was impossible to know for sure." Similarly, Peggy Noonan ruminated: "Who's in charge here? I could never understand where power was in that White House; it kept moving. I'd see men in suits huddled in a hall twenty paces from the Oval Office, and I'd think, there it is, that's where they're making the decisions. But the next day they were gone and the hall was empty."

The first lady made her own contribution to the diffusion of authority. No one of his appointees, not even his chief of staff, exercised so much power. The *New York Times*, discussing Nancy Reagan, even wrote of an "Associate Presidency." She understood her husband's limitations and did all she could to make sure that he was well served. Their son Michael said, "Dad looks at half a glass of water and says: Look at this! It's half full! Nancy is always trying to figure out: Who stole the other half from my husband?" She sometimes influenced Reagan's policies, notably when she pushed for arms control, and she was thought to have been responsible for the removal of two cabinet officials and of the president's latter-day chief of staff. During his tenure, she dismissed accounts of her impact, but in her memoir, she acknowledged: "For eight years I was sleeping with the president, and if that doesn't give you special access, I don't know what does."

Reagan's staff found especially exasperating the need to clear the president's schedule with a first lady who placed so much reliance upon a West Coast astrologer, Joan Quigley. That had been true since the beginning in Sacramento when Reagan was inaugurated as governor at midnight because, it was reported, that was the hour this woman set after perusing the zodiac. On a number of occasions, Deaver would spend days working out an intricate itinerary for the president's travels down to the last detail only to be told that he had to scrap everything because the astrologer had determined that the stars were not properly aligned. Horoscopes fixed the day and hour of such major events as presidential debates and summit meetings with Soviet leaders. The president's most important aide said, "We were paralyzed by this craziness."

In these unpropitious circumstances, the troika managed much better than anticipated. Public administration theorists likened this three-headed makeshift to the mock definition of a camel: a horse put together by a committee. But Baker proved to be a highly effective chief of staff and Deaver a masterful maestro of staged events. Secretary Haig later remarked, "You couldn't serve in this administration without knowing that Reagan was a cipher and that these men were running the government." That judgment, however, failed to credit Reagan's perspicacity. In setting up his team, he succeeded in taking to Washington two men who had served him faithfully in Sacramento—Meese and Deaver—while acknowledging that, since they and he had no experience inside the Beltway, he needed to salt his inner corps with a veteran of the Ford era. In choosing Baker, moreover, Reagan, stereotyped as a rigid ideologue, showed unexpected flexibility. Baker, a moderate, had been floor manager for Ford's effort to deny Reagan the 1976 presidential nomination, and in 1980 he had run George Bush's campaign against Governor Reagan.

From the start of his political career, commentators, especially liberals, had been underestimating Reagan. When he announced that he was planning to run for governor of California, he encountered ridicule. At a time when Robert Cummings was a prominent film star, the Hollywood mogul Jack Warner responded, "No, Bob Cummings for governor, Ronald Reagan as his best friend." Yet Reagan easily defeated the former mayor of San Francisco to win the Republican nomination, then stunned Democrats by prevailing over the incumbent governor, Pat Brown, by nearly a million votes. Furthermore, he went on to gain reelection to a second term.

Reagan's performance in Sacramento surprised both adversaries and followers. While continuing to proclaim his undying hostility to government intervention, he stepped up taxes on banks and corporations, increased benefits to welfare recipients, more than doubled funds for higher education, and safeguarded "wild and scenic rivers" from exploitation. A vocal advocate of "the right to life," he nevertheless signed a bill in 1967 that resulted in a rise in legal abortions in the state from 518 in that year to nearly 100,000 in 1980. He was able to forge agreements with Democrats in the capital because he had the advantage, as a veteran of Screen Actors Guild battles, of being an experienced negotiator. (In later years, he said of his haggling with Mikhail Gorbachev: "It was easier than dealing with Jack Warner.") His chief Democratic opponent in the legislature, who started out viewing Reagan with contempt, wound up concluding that he had been a pretty good governor, "better than Pat Brown, miles and planets and universes better than Jerry Brown"—the two most conspicuous Democratic leaders of the period.

Scrutiny of his record, however, also raised disquieting features. Months after he took office as governor, a reporter asked him about his priorities. Disconcerted, Reagan turned toward an assistant and said, "I could take some coaching from the sidelines, if anyone can recall my legislative program." Expected to decide between conflicting views on the abortion issue, "Reagan," Cannon noted, "behaved as if lost at sea." His aides often found it difficult to get him to concentrate. On one occasion, in the midst of a vital discussion about the budget, he wandered off: "Do you know how hard it is to mispronounce 'psychiatric' once you know how to pronounce it right? I had to do it in *Kings Row* and at first I couldn't do it." He especially alarmed members of his staff by flying into a rage if the press reported that he had changed his position on an issue, even when he undoubtedly had. All of his disabilities—gross misperceptions and knowledge gaps—he carried into the White House. Yet he was to leave office regarded as a consequential president, and a number of scholars were even to write of an "Age of Reagan."

———

With a thespian's sense of political theater, Reagan bolted the postinauguration ceremonies on January 20, 1981, headed up to the Hill, and put his name to a document imposing a hiring freeze on the entire federal workforce. In that manner, he let the country know that he meant every word he had spoken earlier that day. "Government is not the solution to our problems. Government *is* the problem," he had declared. Later in his oration, he added, "Our present troubles...are proportionate to the...intrusion in our lives that results from unnecessary and excessive growth of government." He underscored his convictions by another symbolic act: he ordered the portrait of Harry Truman taken down from its honored place in the Cabinet Room and substituted that of the most anti-statist president of the twentieth century, Calvin Coolidge.

Those who had known the president in his earlier years found it hard to comprehend his fierce animus toward government. He had cast his first vote in 1932 for Franklin Delano Roosevelt and, as "a very emotional New Dealer," wound up marking his ballot for FDR all four times he ran. Reagan had been not just a "bleeding heart liberal" but, in his own words, a "hemophilic liberal." In 1948, he had headed the Labor League of Hollywood Voters for Truman and, in a radio address supporting the senatorial candidacy of Hubert Humphrey, had denounced Wall Street and oil profiteers. He had also castigated Republicans for enacting the "vicious" Taft-Hartley law that "handcuffed" labor unions. Two years later, he taped a number of radio spots for Helen Gahagan Douglas in her contest with Richard Nixon. When the Douglas campaign managers removed his name from their campaign letterheads, they did so because they thought his reputation was too left-wing.

In 1952, Reagan began a transition toward conservatism that rapidly hardened. He never offered a remotely plausible explanation for his abrupt change, but a critical consideration was his resentment at the steep income taxes he had to pay as a highly salaried movie star. A maestro of the weekly *General Electric Theater* on television, he increasingly expressed notions that were not merely reactionary but antediluvian. "Our graduated income tax," he said, "was created by Karl Marx." So extreme were some of his statements that they embarrassed General Electric, which, to get rid of him, canceled the show. That experience did nothing to temper Reagan's rhetoric. In an address to the Republican National Convention in 1964 that the right wing hallowed as "the Speech," he cautioned Americans that if they cast their ballots for Lyndon Johnson in November, they would be taking "the first step into a thousand years of darkness."

By the 1960s, his words often revealed a nasty sensibility. "Unemployment insurance," he declared, "is a pre-paid vacation for freeloaders," and Medicaid recipients constituted "a faceless mass, waiting for handouts." In 1964, he played to the prejudices of his audience by saying: "We were told four years ago that 17 million people went to bed hungry every night. Well, that was probably true. They were all on a diet." That same year, in a televised interview, he observed: "What we have found in this country, and maybe we're more aware of it now, is one problem that we've had, even in the best of times, and that is the people who are sleeping on the grates, the homeless who are homeless, you might say, by choice."

He carried these coldhearted convictions into the presidency. Again and again, he told false or embroidered tales about people on welfare who were mulcting the taxpayer. He informed a US senator: "You know, a young man went into a grocery store, and he had an orange in one hand and a bottle of vodka in the other, and he paid for the orange with food stamps and he took the change and paid for the vodka. That's what's wrong." (Reagan's Department of Agriculture found it necessary to issue a statement denying that there was any truth in his yarn.)

At a time when millions were jobless, he maintained that the only reason for their grim circumstances was that they were unwilling to work. Even in his second term, he was reciting: "I'm told about the fellow on welfare who makes phone calls looking for work. On the third call they offer him a job, and he hangs up. These people don't want to work." Exasperated by having to listen to this blather, Speaker Tip O'Neill retorted: "Don't give me that crap. The guy in Youngstown, Ohio, who's been laid off at the steel mill and has to make his mortgage payments—don't tell me he doesn't want to work. These stories may work on your rich friends, but they don't work on the rest of us. I'm sick and tired of your attitude, Mr. President. I thought you would have grown in the five years you've been in office, but you're still repeating those same simplistic explanations."

In the White House, Reagan welcomed the opportunity to put his pre-dilections into practice. For years, he had been saying, "Government does not solve problems, it subsidizes them." As chief executive, he sought to impress that maxim on the members of his staff. If he ever heard them referring to the government as "we" rather than "they," he said, he would know that they had been on the job too long. To fetter Washington's domain, he proposed to amputate $40 billion from the federal budget.

To carry that off, he appointed as budget director a precocious Michigan congressman, David Stockman. The thirty-four-year-old Stockman, who had earlier been a radical, represented a new generation of tough-minded tories. Pat Moynihan, at a talk in March 1981 to the Gridiron Club with Stockman in the room, said of the young budget director who had once been his live-in babysitter: "I have never known a man capable of such sustained self-hypnotic ideological fervor. One day he arrives at Harvard preaching the infallibility of Ho Chi Minh. Next thing you know, he turns up in Washington proclaiming the immutability of the Laffer Curve [a conception of conservative economists]." Stockman showed total disrespect for the separation of powers embedded in the US Constitution. His strategy for dealing with members of Congress, he later explained, was "to bring all the power of the Great Communicator to bear...and shove our budget cuts down their throats." He later stated unapologetically his bold expectations: "The constitutional prerogatives of the legislative branch would have to be, in effect, suspended. Enacting the Reagan Admin-istration's economic program meant rubber stamp approval, nothing less. The world's so-called greatest deliberative body would have to be reduced to the status of a ministerial arm of the White House."

Acting with the president's approval, Stockman wielded a machete on the Great Society programs he detested. He pursued a strategy, he said, of "abruptly severing the umbilical cords of dependency that ran from Washington to every nook and cranny of the nation" through "the ruth-less dispensations of short-run pain in the name of long-run gain." He sought to wipe out "forty years' worth of promises, subventions, entitle-ments, and safety nets issued to...every...stratum of society." Con-ceiving of himself as a warrior engaged in "mortal political combat with all the mass constituencies of Washington's largesse," he took nearly $2 billion away from food stamps, stripped $1 billion from Medicaid, and ended altogether public service jobs of the War on Poverty. To conform with the scaleback of funds for child nutrition, the Reagan government provoked a national outcry by authorizing schools to shrivel meal sizes for pupils and allowing them to count ketchup as a vegetable. Stockman (with Reagan's blessing) also slashed money for a huge array of other government operations: unemployment compensation, mass transit, public housing, disability payments, grants to the arts and humanities, Aid to Families with Dependent Children, and a natal care program that had succeeded in lowering the rate of infant mortality. The budget director was fond of quoting Plutarch: "The real destroyer of the liberties of the people is he who spreads among them bounties, donations and benefits."

The new president accompanied this effort to shrink the size of the national government with a drastic change in revenue-raising. In his February 1981 State of the Union message, he called for a 30 percent reduction in individual and corporate tax rates over the ensuing three years, as well as cuts in levies on unearned income. A number of writers contended that Reagan was seeking to return the country to the era of Coolidge's treasury secretary, Andrew Mellon, the *Washington Post* characterizing his outlook as "A Vision Frozen in Time." Reagan's recommendation, however, owed less to the past than to an economic theory that had only recently evolved. Originally called "supply side," it soon bore a new name: "Reaganomics."

In 1974, a little-known economist, Arthur Laffer, had sketched on a restaurant napkin a graph to demonstrate the principles of supply side. He insisted that the main obstacle to economic growth was burdensome taxation, which limited the amount of capital available for investment. Laffer predicted that if tax rates on the very wealthy and on corporations were reduced, the economy would flourish and, with a much larger pool of income, so much money would flow into the treasury that it would wipe out deficits. He and those who shared his views contended that the chief agent of prosperity was not, as the Keynesians asserted, consumer demand but supply (production). Mainstream economists dismissed these assumptions as charlatanry and, in his bid for the Republican nomination in 1980, George Bush had derided such notions as "voodoo economics." But Reagan had become a true believer. At briefing sessions during his presidential campaign, Laffer, it was said, "thoroughly hosed him down with supply-side doctrine."

At the same time that Reagan advocated a huge tax cut, he pushed for a colossal increase in military spending to create "a capacity to fight nuclear wars that range from a limited strike through a protracted conflict to an all-out exchange." During the 1980 campaign, he had said, alluding to the Russians, that "only by mustering a superiority...can we stop the thunder of hobnailed boots on their march to world empire." As president, in proposing a huge military budget, he resorted to statements about Russian military superiority that were as inaccurate as they were alarming. Furthermore, he charged opponents of massive outlays with "really carrying the propaganda ball for the Soviet Union."

Reagan was asking Congress for an awful lot—a budget with controversial slashes in social spending, a far-reaching tax measure, and the greatest military authorization in the country's history—and it was not clear, more than eight weeks into his term as the month of March drew toward a close, that he was going to get it. He had no experience in Washington, and his detached style of governing was not geared to winning over skeptical legislators. Though the 1980 election had given the Republicans a majority in the Senate for the first time in more than a quarter of a century, Democrats still held most of the seats in the House, where Speaker O'Neill and a sizeable band of liberals were determined to kill the president's program.

On March 30, 1981, as Reagan emerged from the Washington Hilton, a delusionary young man, who thought that killing the president would impress the film actress Jodie Foster, fired six shots from a revolver he had bought in a Dallas pawnshop. The explosive bullets penetrated Press Secretary James Brady's brain, leaving him partially paralyzed, and wounded a Secret Service officer and a policeman. No bullet hit the president directly, but one ricocheted off his limousine and struck him under his armpit, puncturing his lung and lodging within an inch of his heart. He was sped to George Washington University Medical Center, where he acquitted himself with admirable courage and aplomb. Grievously wounded, he buttoned his suit jacket smartly and insisted on walking the twenty feet into the emergency room. Once he got through the doors, he collapsed.

His staunch behavior permitted the White House to issue reassuring bulletins, but, in fact, the president's condition was critical. He had suffered a massive loss of blood, and seepage between his lung and ribs made it difficult for him to breathe. His deputy press secretary, witnessing the three-hour operation to remove the bullet, scribbled: "Doctors believe bleeding to death. Think we're going to lose him." A nurse, taking his pulse, said, "I don't hear anything." Only the skillful work of GW surgeons saved his life. If he had arrived at the hospital five minutes later, they could not have done anything. As his son Michael said, "He came very close to dying. It was the difference from the car making a left turn, to the White House, or a right turn, to the hospital."

The president's grace under pressure, relayed to the American people by the media, immediately became the core of legend. To reassure his wife as he was wheeled into the operating room, he smiled and told her, "Honey, I forgot to duck." Making light of his trauma, he quipped, "On the whole, I'd rather be in Philadelphia." The first one-liner came from Jack Dempsey after he had been floored by Gene Tunney, and the second was the inscription the actor W. C. Fields jested he would like to have on his gravestone. But, though recycled, Reagan's banter showed his quickness of wit and his pluck. Other jests were original. As the surgeons readied their knives, he pleaded, "Please tell me you're all Republicans." When he realized that a nurse was holding his hand, he asked, "Does Nancy know about us?"

The shooting left the country without a president. Morphine and other drugs to relieve his acute pain rendered Reagan disoriented. At one point, he scrawled on a pad, "Where am I?" Bulletins assured the nation that its president was recovering so rapidly that he was "wolfing down" food, but his physicians knew that he had trouble eating anything, had developed an infection, and was running a fever. Top White House officials spoke the dread words "Woodrow Wilson," expressing the fear that if Reagan survived, he, like his World War I–era predecessor, would leave the hospital a helpless invalid for all the rest of his term in office.

Terrified by how close the assassination attempt had come to succeeding, Nancy Reagan, fearful for her husband, once again got in touch with her astrologer, who recalled:

> I did some pretty hard thinking. I knew that Ronald Reagan had been elected in a year ending in zero, and that every president since William Henry Harrison (in 1840) who had been elected in a year ending in

zero—and also every Aquarian president—had died in office.... It had to do with the Jupiter star in conjunction; it's called the Great Mutation. At the time Reagan was elected, it fell in Libra. While I felt it was dangerous—and Reagan's own chart showed danger to that type of thing, rather like Lincoln's—I thought...that if I really concentrated, I could keep him safe.

With George Bush away, Secretary of State Haig took over. Self-important, jittery, he told the press: "Constitutionally, gentlemen, you have the president, the vice president, and the secretary of state in that order. As of now, I am in control here in the White House, pending the return of the vice president." Journalists pointed out that he misread the law (he was third in succession, not first, after the vice president), and a high-ranking federal official, observing his agitated performance on television, asked, "Is he mad?" In contrast, the vice president conducted himself with exemplary discretion. Advised by the Secret Service that when he got back to Washington, he should land his helicopter on the White House lawn, Bush replied, "Only the president lands on the White House lawn." At the first cabinet meeting, he made a point of not seating himself in the president's vacant chair. A member of the Reagan circle commented, "George Bush is too much of a gentleman to be reminded how to behave at a time like that."

During the ensuing week, the country rejoiced in the president's recuperation. The attempt on his life was the latest of a series—the Kennedy brothers, Martin Luther King, Medgar Evers, even the home-grown Nazi George Lincoln Rockwell—but, of these, only Reagan had survived. His escape from death was seen as a happy omen that two decades of misfortune were ending and America was taking a turn for the better. Reports of the president's gallantry augmented the good feeling. Instantaneously, his approval rating shot up almost 20 percent, with 64 percent of Democrats telling pollsters they thought well of him.

Washington insiders saw the episode as, in the words of the journalist and White House adviser David Gergen, "the defining moment" of Reagan's presidency. The dean of the capital's press corps, David Broder, wrote in his column: "The gunfire that shattered the stillness of a rainy Washington Monday afternoon...created a new hero in Reagan, the chipper 'Gipper' who took a .22-caliber slug in his chest but walked into the emergency room on his own power and joked with the anxious doctors on his way into surgery.... As long as people remember the hospitalized President joshing his doctors and nurses—and they will remember—no critic will be able to portray Reagan as a cruel or callow or heartless man."

On the night of April 28, only twenty-nine days after he was shot, Reagan appeared before a joint session of Congress. He received a passionate welcome-back, with dozens of Democrats joining Republicans on their feet cheering. Taking advantage of this dramatic moment, he asked for enactment of the tax and spending cuts he favored from a Congress with little will to turn down a man who had rallied so splendidly. That night, the Democratic majority leader in the House, Jim Wright, recorded in his diary: "We've just been outflanked and outgunned. The aura of heroism which has attended him since his wounding, deserved in large part by his demeanor under the extreme duress of his physical ordeal, assured a tumultuous welcome. It was a very deceptive, extremely partisan and probably very effective presentation. Tip and I are embattled, trying to stem the flow of conservative sands through the sieve." Speaker Tip, for his part, knew that the outcome was foreordained. Though he balked at Reagan's proposals, he said: "We can't argue with a man as popular as he is. I've been in politics a long time and I know when to fight and when not to fight."

Reagan still confronted, however, the demanding task of getting enough Democrats in the House to cross over, and, to the surprise of his aides who were experiencing his diffidence as an administrator, he carried out that responsibility assiduously over the next three months. Even before he had recovered from his bullet wound, he was phoning ten members of Congress a day to solicit their votes. During his first hundred days, he conferred sixty-nine times with 467 of them. In that short stretch, legislators said, they had been paid more attention than Carter had given them in all his four years. On a single day in June, Reagan met with 239, including thirty-eight Democrats, at a White House breakfast. On another day, from airports in Texas and California as he flew west, he phoned more than a score of House members, primarily Democrats. In July, he secured the backing of eleven hesitant congressmen by inviting them to a barbecue at Camp David. Regarded as a stringent dogmatist, he demonstrated considerable suppleness. In courting the powerful

Louisiana Democrat John Breaux, he promised to end his opposition to expensive subsidies for sugar. (Asked if his vote could be purchased, Breaux retorted, "No, but it can be rented.") To gain the support of "boll weevils"—conservative Democrats primarily from the South—he pledged that if they came over to his side on pending bills, he would not campaign for Republican nominees running against them in next year's midterm elections. By such tactics, he added nearly fifty members to his ranks in the House.

Over the course of that spring and into early summer, Reagan chalked up a number of major victories, including acceptance of a budget that was anathema to liberals. In May, the House approved the initial version, 253–176, with sixty-three Democrats in his coalition, and the Senate went along even more emphatically, 78–20. In June, the president asked for an additional curtailment of more than $5 billion, and he got that through too. "Step 1 of the Reagan revolution in government economic and social policy," *Time* told its readers, "was just accomplished." Stipulating scalebacks of more than $35 billion, the Omnibus Reconciliation Act of July 1981 slashed funds for health, housing, the environment, the arts, and two hundred other federal programs; denied food stamps to a million recipients; and took Aid to Dependent Children benefits away from four hundred thousand. "We just don't accept the assumption that the Federal Government has a responsibility to supplement the income of the working poor," Stockman said. The House, with most Democrats in rebellion against these drastic decreases, passed the measure by the very thin margin of six votes. Reagan's wooing of the boll weevils proved to be decisive.

That same month, Congress met the president's goal for a significant cut in tax rates, though it settled not for the president's 30 percent but for a slightly more modest, but still substantial, 25 percent. Roll calls once again revealed the effect of Reagan's persuasiveness. In the House, forty-eight Democrats voted for the measure. The law constituted a massive redistribution of wealth upward. It lowered levies on income of the rich by 50 percent, of poorer folk by 3 percent. The legislation also slashed corporation and capital gains levies; bestowed tax breaks on large investors, recipients of unearned income, and the oil industry; and added hundreds of thousands of dollars to the amount that the wealthy could pass on to their heirs tax-free.

Congress also obliged Reagan by agreeing to a huge arms buildup, for legislators did not want to risk giving opponents in the next campaign the opportunity to charge them with being "soft on defense." The military authorization act gave the Pentagon $136 billion, the start of unprecedented increases that by 1985 were to reach more than $300 billion. The law funded the B-1 intercontinental bomber (which Carter had canceled), the MX (Missile Experimental) project, the B-2 stealth bomber, Trident submarine missiles, and a host of other weaponry. The next six years were to see a 50 percent jump in funds for armaments. During his presidency, Reagan wound up spending $1.5 trillion on the military while lowering taxes.

Only when Reagan embraced a Stockman plan to reduce a category of Social Security benefits did he come a cropper. Tip O'Neill called the proposal "despicable," and at a Republican breakfast conference a very right-wing South Carolina congressman "lit into me like a junkyard dog," Stockman said. Even more tellingly, the conservative and highly influential GOP senator Robert Dole let the White House know that Republicans would not go along with their president. Peremptorily, the Senate slapped Reagan down by voting, 96–0, in favor of a resolution stating, "The Congress shall not precipitously and unfairly punish early retirees."

Save for that one misstep, Reagan had rolled up an impressive record as chief legislator—far better than that of Ford or Carter—and had won widespread popular approval for the way that he had performed. Under the headline IT'S RIGHTWARD ON, *Time* reported the findings of a national poll: "Majorities ranging from 71 . . . to 52 percent agreed . . . that Reagan had lived up to his campaign promises in six key areas: working effectively with Congress, providing strong leadership in government, providing moral leadership, keeping US defenses strong, getting rid of waste in government and making Americans feel good again." Even Democrats who regretted the move to the right paid tribute to him. Jim Wright concluded in his diary: "His philosophical approach is superficial, overly simplistic and one-dimensional. What he preaches is pure economic pap, glossed over with uplifting homilies and inspirational chatter. Yet so far the guy is making it work. Appalled by what seems to me lack of depth, I stand in awe nevertheless of his political skill. I am not sure that I have seen its equal."

The president received still more acclaim over his response to the audacious demands of the Professional Air Traffic Controllers Organization for enormous increases in wages and benefits. PATCO felt secure in calling an illegal strike in August 1981, in large part because it thought its members were irreplaceable since air traffic would collapse without them, but also because it was one of only three unions that had endorsed Reagan in 1980. It utterly failed to anticipate the response of the White House. "I respect the right of workers in the private sector to strike," Reagan said. "Indeed, as president of my own union, I led the first strike ever called by the union." But PATCO, he declared, was striking against the government, and hence was guilty of "desertion in the face of duty." He gave members of the union forty-eight hours to return to their posts, and when more than eleven thousand did not, he fired all of them and blacklisted them from federal employment for the rest of their lives. Within weeks, PATCO dissolved. At long last, most Americans decided, the United States had a president who could command, though some were surprised by his solicitude for the government that he usually disparaged.

Reagan had already shown that he was dead set on slackening federal regulation, and he calculatedly made appointments with that goal in mind. In a 1981 *New York Times* article, Howell Raines, noting a "revolution" in attitudes about high level staffing in the federal government, wrote that Reagan had been selecting officials "who in previous administrations might have been ruled out by concern over possible lack of qualifications or conflict of interest or open hostility to the mission of the agencies they now lead." He chose a Wall Street insider to run the SEC, picked a foe of regulation to chair the Federal Communications Commission, and gave an important post in OSHA, charged with safeguarding workers on the job, to a man whose business had been penalized for forty-eight instances of safety violations. To preside over the National Labor Relations Board, he named a notorious union-buster who made it easier for corporations to hire scabs and to break contracts with their employees. Reagan's choice for secretary of commerce, a manufacturer, set out to end restrictions on the emission of carcinogens. By 1986, Reagan had eliminated nearly forty thousand federal regulations—close to half of all those on the books when he took over. Officials also used the rubric of "reductions in force" to get rid of civil servants who were committed to national programs. In the Department of Labor, everyone in the Employment and Training Administration was dismissed.

It took no time for Reagan to demonstrate that he was going to be the very worst president on the environment that the country had ever known. In an era when numbers of Republicans as well as Democrats were seeking alternative sources of energy, he ordered removal of the solar panels Carter had installed in the White House roof and fired nearly half the staff of the Solar Energy Research Institute. The Council on Environmental Quality created in the Nixon administration experienced a 72 percent reduction of its budget, with its staff diminished from forty-nine to fifteen. To head the Bureau of Land Management, he appointed a rancher who had been cited for grazing his livestock illegally on federal lands. In addition, Reagan jettisoned an agreement Carter had reached with the Canadian prime minister to curb emissions from smokestacks and even questioned whether industrial discharges caused acid rain.

Reagan, who as governor had appointed outstanding environmental officials, knowingly made a dreadful choice in naming James Watt secretary of the interior. Formerly legal counsel to the US Chamber of Commerce and spokesman for timber and mining corporations, Watt made clear that he intended to use his authority on behalf of unrestrained exploitation of natural resources. "We will mine more, drill more, cut more timber," he announced. Watt invited concessionaires to set up shop in national parks, proposed to permit oil drilling in a billion acres of offshore land, and advocated phasing out controls of strip mining. But he did himself in by a number of offensive statements. Early on, he denominated two opposing groups: "liberals and Americans." After he created outrage by mocking affirmative action in his statement about the composition of a panel he was compelled to establish in his department ("I have a black, I have a woman, two Jews, and a cripple"), Congress, in September 1983, forced him out. No longer sympathetic to ecological concerns as he had been in Sacramento, Reagan concluded about Watt, "I have to say, if you look back and analyze point by point the things that were done, he was damn good."

The president made just as unfortunate a choice in putting in charge of the US Environmental Protection Agency a woman who had spent her days in the Colorado legislature denouncing efforts to safeguard the environment. Anne Gorsuch cut the EPA budget in half, urged drastic weakening of the Clean Air Act, and refused to enforce most regulations Congress had enacted. (At the same time, Reagan's Department of

Transportation postponed, eviscerated, or wiped out a number of requirements: that cars be tested on assembly lines for toxic emissions; that new vehicles meet fuel economy standards; and that bumpers be capable of absorbing the impact of a collision at five miles an hour.) Asked about criticism of this conduct, Reagan told the press: "There is environmental extremism. I don't think they'll be happy until the White House looks like a bird's nest."

Gorsuch called on another foe of environmental regulations, Rita Lavelle, to monitor the Superfund created under Carter to rid the countryside of hazardous wastes. Of the 378,000 toxic waste sites in the country that required cleaning, the EPA in Reagan's first term got to only six, and botched the operations on them. Lavelle, who had been a public relations executive for a flagrant polluter, negotiated sweetheart deals with corporations that conspired to profit from the Superfund. After lying about these arrangements and defying Congress, she was sentenced to prison for perjury and obstruction of justice. (Years later, convicted of deceiving the FBI and committing wire fraud, she was incarcerated for another fifteen months in a federal penitentiary.)

Reagan did little better on race relations. He sought to weaken the Voting Rights Act, which he called "humiliating to the South," and became the first president to veto a civil rights bill. In contrast to Carter, who had allotted 12 percent of appointments for high government posts to African Americans, Reagan gave little more than 4 percent. The Justice Department asked the Supreme Court to end penalties against southern schools that discriminated, only to be rebuked by the Court in an 8–1 decision. Though the head of the Equal Employment Opportunity Commission, Clarence Thomas, ignored thousands of job bias complaints, Reagan believed that Thomas, "my man on Equal Opp. board," was doing a "h—l of a good job." Later in his presidency, Reagan vetoed sanctions on the racist regime of South Africa, which he valued as an ally against Russia, but the Senate overrode him, with thirty-one Republicans joining Democrats. In 1980, he had received the smallest proportion of votes from African Americans any presidential candidate had ever drawn. In 1984, he fared even worse.

Yet just when Reagan was giving every reason to be written off as hopelessly regressive, especially after halving the female presence on the White House staff, he pulled a surprise. To the delight of liberals and the discomfort of conservatives, he appointed to the US Supreme Court an Arizona state judge, Sandra Day O'Connor—the first woman in the nearly two centuries of the highest tribunal. His action horrified the Moral Majority because she regarded *Roe v. Wade* as the law of the land. Riled by her views on abortion, the Reverend Jerry Falwell called upon all "good Christians" to coalesce against the nomination. (O'Connor's fellow Arizonan Barry Goldwater responded, "Every good Christian ought to kick Falwell right in the ass.") In contrast to the fundamentalists, most Americans were pleased. Tip O'Neill, a constant gadfly, said, "This is the best thing he's done since he was inaugurated." Another liberal Democrat, Congressman Morris Udall, summed up the prevailing sentiment: "The appointment of O'Connor is a master stroke. . . . It shows a political savvy on the part of the president that I had assumed was not there." When, despite the hostility of fundamentalist preachers, O'Connor won easy confirmation, college students sported buttons: "The Moral Majority Is Neither."

Reagan's first year, which had seen success after success, took on a more troubled aspect in the last weeks of 1981. The most unexpected jolt came in November when the *Atlantic* published a fifty-page article by the *Washington Post* editor William Greider, "The Education of David Stockman"—a piece drawing upon eighteen interviews with a stunningly indiscreet Stockman that were recorded at Saturday morning breakfasts. To the distress of the White House, Stockman, Greider reported, had confessed that supply-side theory was just a "Trojan horse" to disguise the conviction that making the rich even richer would eventually benefit those less well off. "It's kind of hard to sell 'trickle-down,' so the supply-side formula was the only way to get a tax policy that really was 'trickle down,'" he explained. "Supply-side is 'trickle-down' theory." Stockman also acknowledged that he could not abide the assumptions of Reaganomics. "I've never believed that just cutting taxes alone will cause output and employment to expand," he stated. Furthermore, he confessed, "None of us understands what's really going on with all these numbers." To nurture Reagan's illusions, he told Greider, he had monkeyed with the data. When the fallacies of the president's policies, which were certain to result in a staggering deficit, became apparent, Stockman had simply "changed the economic assumptions fed into the computer model."

Greider's article hit especially hard because it came out at a time when, contrary to what Reagan had been promising, the country had fallen into a serious recession. Nine million Americans were unemployed—the most since the Great Depression—and the steep increase in bankrupt small businesses was the greatest in decades. Instead of climbing, as supply-siders had prophesied, capital spending was contracting, and the prime interest rate was riveted at a discouraging 16.5 percent. The downturn also spooked the stock market, for investors recognized, even if the president did not, that huge deficits loomed. Economists were forecasting a shortfall approaching half a trillion dollars. In this context, the Greider article led readers to doubt whether the president had any idea of what he was doing.

"Dave, how do you explain this?" Reagan asked. "You have hurt me. Why?" Stockman could offer no plausible justification for his imprudence, but the president decided to retain him as head of OMB anyway. Stockman, the president convinced himself, was the "victim of sabotage by the press," though every quotation in the article could be verified on tape. More important, Reagan showed no interest in examining what his budget director had admitted were spurious premises on which his economic program was based. Instead, he behaved as though nothing had happened.

Reagan had a special reason for his obduracy. After Stockman warned him that "we're headed for a crash landing on the budget" that could only be avoided if the president slowed the pace of the gargantuan arms buildup, Reagan shut him off. "There must be no perception by anyone in the world that we're backing down an inch on the defense budget," he declared. The Russians were "squealing like they're sitting on a sharp nail," he said, "simply because we are now showing...that we are not going to let them get to the point of dominance where they can someday issue to the free world an ultimatum of 'Surrender or die.'" No worry about the economy, no domestic concern of any kind, was going to deter Reagan from achieving his principal ambition: winning the arms race against the Soviet Union.

On one occasion, while readying himself to deliver a radio address, Reagan, not realizing that the microphone was live, said: "My fellow Americans, I am pleased to tell you I just signed legislation outlawing Russia forever. The bombing begins in five minutes." He was only being playful (albeit in a morbid fashion), but his words did approach his longtime attitude toward the fate of the USSR. Two decades earlier, he had declared:

> Today we are engaged in a great war to determine whether the world can exist half-slave and half-free. There are those who challenge the statement that war is now at hand. True, we do not hear the rattle of musketry or smell the burning cordite—that is, unless the wind is too strong from Budapest, Tibet or Havana. Whether we admit it or not, we are in a war. This war was declared a century ago by Karl Marx and re-affirmed by Lenin when he said that Communism and Capitalism cannot exist side-by-side.

On being told, four years before becoming president, that he needed to devise a comprehensive strategy toward the Soviet Union, Reagan had replied, "I do have a strategy: We win, they lose!" In a commencement address to the 1981 graduating class at Notre Dame, he asserted: "The West won't contain communism, it will...dismiss it as some bizarre chapter in human history, whose last pages are even now being written." In London a year later, Reagan, the first American president to address a joint session of Parliament, announced that he had a plan of breath-taking scope: to encourage a "march of freedom and democracy which will leave Marxist-Leninism on the ash heap of history." That bold statement thrilled the Tory MPs (most of the Labour members boycotted his presentation), but it deeply alarmed leaders in European capitals.

The president, departing abruptly from the policy of détente pursued at different times by Nixon and Ford, caused the greatest consternation by a speech he gave in Orlando to the National Association of Evangelicals. Urged to express his innermost convictions with no need to dissemble, Reagan asserted: "There is sin and evil in the world. And we are enjoined by Scripture and the Lord Jesus to oppose it with all our might.... Yes, let us pray for the salvation of all of those who live in...totalitarian darkness—pray that they will discover the joy of knowing God. But until they do, let us be aware that while they preach the supremacy of the state, declare its omnipotence over individual man, and predict its eventual domination of all peoples on earth, they are the focus of evil in the modern world." He wound up by offering a solemn warning against "the aggressive impulses of an evil empire," an epithet he pinned on the USSR. The esteemed historian Henry Steele Commager reflected a widespread response in calling the address "the worst presidential speech in American history." Most of the criticism of Reagan, though, was ill founded. "Evil" was not too strong a word for a regime that had murdered a million of its citizens in the purge, had consigned countless more to forced labor in vile Gulags, and had inflicted so much cruelty on the peoples of Warsaw and Prague. But as Richard Nixon cautioned, "You don't humiliate your opponent in public like that."

Reagan vented again, under extreme provocation, when, on September 1, 1983, a Soviet fighter plane shot down a Korean airliner, KAL 007, with 269 passengers aboard, sixty-one of them Americans, including a fiercely anti-Communist congressman. This "monstrous" display of "savagery," the president declared, was "an act of barbarism, born of a society which wantonly disregards individual rights and the value of human life." Reagan's deeds, though, did not match his words. "We've got to protect against overreaction," he told his national security adviser. "Vengeance isn't the name of the game." That attitude enraged the far right, especially when he refused to end grain sales to Russia. The *Manchester Union Leader*, the New Hampshire newspaper that had brought down Ed Muskie, fulminated: "If someone had told us, three years ago, that the Russians could blow a civilian airliner out of the skies—and not face one whit of retaliation from a Ronald Reagan administration, we would have called that crazy. It is crazy. It is insane."

Though Reagan had some nutty notions about the Soviet Union, he had one insight on a matter of the utmost significance that eluded liberal sophisticates and almost everyone else: the USSR was on the verge of collapse. "President Reagan just had an innate sense that the Soviet Union would not, or could not, survive," observed a future secretary of state. In the address to Parliament, the president stated:

> The Soviet Union . . . is in deep economic difficulty. The rate of growth in the national product has been steadily declining since the fifties and is less than half of what it was then. The dimensions of this failure are astounding. A country which employs one-fifth of its population in agriculture is unable to feed its own people. . . . Overcentralized, with little or no incentives, year after year the Soviet system pours its best resources into the making of instruments of destruction. The

constant shrinkage of economic growth combined with the growth of military production is putting a heavy strain on the Soviet people. What we see here is a political structure that no longer corresponds to its economic base, a society where productive forces are hampered by political ones.

As a result of this predisposition, Reagan had little interest in seeking accommodation with the Kremlin. As early as 1976 when he made his first bid for the presidential nomination, Reagan had explained why he sought the office:

> I was looking forward to negotiating the SALT Treaty with Brezhnev.... It seems that every time we get into negotiations, the Soviets are telling us what we are going to have to give up in order for us to get along with them, and we forget who we are. I wanted to become president of the United States so I could sit down with Brezhnev. I was going to let him pick out the size of the table, and I was going to listen to him tell me, the American president, what we were going to have to give up. And I was going to listen to him for maybe twenty minutes, and then I was going to get up from my side of the table, walk around to the other side, and lean over and whisper in his ear, "Nyet." It's been a long time since they've heard that "nyet" from an American president.

The intensely anti-Soviet Richard Perle, who was assistant secretary of defense, later remarked: "It was tremendously exhilarating to have a president whose view of the US-Soviet relationship was not in the direction of finding as many cooperative ways of dealing with them as possible, but one of someone who was able to resist the idea that the Soviet Union was a permanent fixture."

Reagan concentrated instead on a stupendous weapons mobilization to intimidate the Russians. When he decided to build a neutron bomb, the White House made a point of saying that it was "designed to kill as many people as a regular hydrogen bomb ten times its size." Not content with armaments that were more than enough to defend the United States, he sought to make America so daunting that the Soviet Union would crave an agreement to reduce the nuclear arsenal—an "arm to parley" strategy. "I think there's every indication and every reason to believe that the Soviet Union cannot increase its production of arms," Reagan had said even before taking office. "Right now we're hearing of strikes and labor disputes because people aren't getting enough to eat."

The president struck more directly at Soviet ambitions by throwing American weight against the USSR in its ongoing conflict in Afghanistan. He gave substantial support to the mujahideen fighting to liberate their country from Russian troops, even though the Afghans were Islamic fundamentalists who looked to Iran's Ayatollah Khomeini. In what Hollywood was to call "Charlie Wilson's War," named for a militant congressman, the CIA trained the Afghans and provided them with antiaircraft missiles to offset USSR power in the skies. Before Reagan left office, he had the satisfaction of seeing Soviet forces pull out of Afghanistan, an admission of defeat that dealt a severe blow to Russian pride.

Reagan had signaled a shift to a sterner foreign policy by appointing as secretary of state the brusque Alexander Haig, who had been the supreme commander of NATO. Arrogant and imperious, Haig expected other cabinet officers to pay him the same kind of homage that corporals had accorded him when he was a general, and he badly frightened the Reagan circle by saying of Cuba: "Give me the word and I'll make that island a fucking parking lot." Haig, said Michael Deaver, "scared the shit out of me." A high-ranking staff member of the National Security Council noted that at cabinet meetings Haig was a "cobra... with his lips spread, looking for somebody to bite." Conceiving of himself as foreign affairs "vicar," he announced decisions that the president alone was empowered to take. By his snarling truculence and his self-promotion, Haig wore out his welcome. Early in the summer of 1982, Reagan fired Haig, ironically at a time when he thought his secretary of state was not taking a tough enough stance toward the Soviet Union. The president, though, continued to have trouble getting a grip on foreign policy. He ran through six national security advisers, and during most of his tenure, his top officials carried on a damaging feud, with Reagan doing nothing at all to impose order. Chief of Staff Baker recalled, "You never had a day when the secretary of state and the secretary of defense weren't at each other's throats."

The president replaced Haig with George Shultz, a corporation executive who, considerably more low-keyed than his predecessor but just as much a cold warrior, instigated the most disastrous event of Reagan's early years in the White House. At Shultz's urging, Reagan sent eight hundred marines as a component of a multinational peacekeeping force to Lebanon, a country roiled by civil war and foreign intervention. The very next month, the president-elect of Lebanon was assassinated, and his militia, linked to Israel, reacted by slaughtering hundreds of Palestinians, many of them women and young children. In addition, Israeli troops, violating an agreement, invaded Lebanon. Instead of seeing these episodes as warning signs of the unlikelihood of success in an anarchic situation, Reagan redoubled his effort. General John W. Vessey, chairman of the Joint Chiefs of Staff, told the president that it would "be very unwise for the U.S. to find itself where it had to put its forces between the Israelis and the Arabs," but Reagan ignored him. As Vessey had foreseen, the intervention incensed Muslims, who regarded America as a participant in a US-Israel conspiracy to keep a Christian minority in power in Lebanon. Trapped in a poorly defined mission, the beleaguered marines, with no ammunition in their weapons, were required to hole up for more than a year at the Beirut airport, nakedly vulnerable targets for sniper fire.

In April 1983, a cadre of Muslim suicide saboteurs assaulted the US embassy in Beirut, killing sixty-two, seventeen of them Americans. Reagan rejected Defense Secretary Caspar Weinberger's counsel that he withdraw; instead, over the course of several months, he stepped up US involvement. On ordering the USS *New Jersey*, the last remaining battleship in the world, to the eastern Mediterranean, he said, "I've had the strange feeling that I'm back on the set filming *Hellcats of the Navy*." Provocatively, he authorized the navy to shell Muslim bastions. No longer on a benign peacekeeping venture, the United States had become a combatant—in the eyes of Muslims, "the enemy." Reagan, though, contented himself with strutting. "As a nation, we've closed the books on a long, dark period of failure and self-doubt and set a new course," he stated. "Our military forces are back on their feet and standing tall."

Early on a Sunday morning in October 1983, Hezbollah suicide bombers crashed through barriers of the US Marine barracks in Beirut and detonated the greatest non-nuclear explosion ever recorded, killing 181 Americans, as well as 58 French paratroopers—a shocking disaster that subjected Reagan to vehement criticism. Senator Ernest Hollings said that the tragedy demonstrated the "stupidity of the original decision" to send the marines into Lebanon, declaring, "If they were put there to fight, there are too few. If they were put there to die, there are too many." Another

Democratic senator protested, "We have a trigger-happy president with a simplistic and paranoid world view, leading the nation toward a nuclear collision that could end us all," and Barry Goldwater chimed in that "the president ought to bring everybody in Lebanon who is in American uniform back, and do it now, because we're headed for war." Reagan, however, said that he was not going to "cut and run," because retaining the marines in Lebanon was "central to our credibility on a global scale."

Only a few days later—in February 1984—Reagan ordered US forces evacuated from Lebanon, while refusing to acknowledge what he was doing. The marines, he insisted, were not pulling out but were engaged in "redeployment." He acted only after his White House pollster informed him that outrage over the deaths of the marines had caused his approval rating to drop precipitously. For the first time, Reagan found himself having to justify his policies, a circumstance that galled him but did nothing to strengthen his grip on reality. At a press conference, one reporter gibed, "You...said you weren't going to cut and run," and another asked, "Can you say to those parents, now that you've withdrawn the Marines to the ships, why more than 260 young men died there?" In an angry response, Reagan retorted, "We're not bugging out; we're just going to a little more defensive position." He carried on his retreat with ill grace, accusing Congress of encouraging terrorists and Tip O'Neill of advocating "surrender." Reagan, the speaker rejoined, was displaying "the qualms of a guilty conscience."

His reputation at lowest ebb, Reagan had the good luck to have an altogether fortuitous event rescue him. In response to a coup by pro-Castro elements on the minuscule volcanic isle of Grenada, the president sent in marines and Navy SEALs, as well as hundreds of Army Rangers who parachuted out of the Caribbean sky. They landed ostensibly to safeguard a thousand American medical students from being seized as hostages by what Reagan called a "brutal gang of thugs," though no threat had been made against them. Speaker O'Neill charged that the president had launched the invasion to divert attention from his failure in Lebanon, but the operation, which had been decided on before the disaster in Beirut, was motivated instead by Reagan's alarm at the seizure of power by a faction that gravitated toward Havana and Moscow.

World opinion condemned America's reversion to gunboat diplomacy, which, in defiance of the War Powers Act, Reagan undertook without consulting Congress. Though he pointed out that he intervened at the request of the Organization of Eastern Caribbean States, he was charged with violating both the protocol of the Organization of American States and the UN Charter. The UN General Assembly voted 122–9 (with 27 abstentions) to "deplore" the incursion, and even his ally and admirer Margaret Thatcher chewed him out for invading a member of the British Commonwealth. On Capitol Hill, a number of members of Congress expressed resentment at being "informed but not consulted."

The American people, though, hailed Reagan as a national hero. Since it took only two days for US forces to overwhelm resistance, the Grenada operation, coming immediately after the tragedy in the marine barracks in Beirut, turned attention away from the president's bungling and focused instead on his victory. So hungry was the nation for jubilation—after the run of setbacks from the *Pueblo* capture to defeat in Vietnam to the pullout in Lebanon—that it treated this trivial success, in an engagement where the small American contingent of fewer than two thousand had 10–1 predominance, as though it were the Battle of Yorktown.

The administration cultivated this perception by indulging in overwrought rhetoric. On the day Reagan announced the start of this small skirmish, given the ridiculous rubric "Operation Urgent Fury," he declared: "History will record that one of our turning points came on a small island in the Caribbean where America went to take care of her own and to rescue a neighboring nation from a growing tyranny." The chair of the Joint Chiefs of Staff was much more temperate. "I hope you don't make Grenada a bigger issue than it really was," he later told interviewers. "Grenada was not central to either the presidency or foreign policy or national security. It was a passing incident." But after television cameras showed the first of the evacuated medical students kissing American soil as soon as he deplaned, Secretary Shultz reflected, "Suddenly I could sense the country's emotions turn around. . . . I knew that we had won a clean sweep on the ground in Grenada and in the hearts of the American people." Instantly, the president's approval ratings surged to the highest point since he was shot, and his advantage over his anticipated Democratic rival in the 1984 presidential contest tripled—from 9 percent to 27 percent.

Reagan carried the same obsession with the Communist menace that had impelled him into Grenada to his treatment of Central American

republics, where he supported anti-Communist elements no matter
how vile. Especially noisome was the man he backed in El Salvador:
Roberto d'Aubuisson, who was held responsible for the slaying in 1980
of the archbishop as he celebrated mass and for the raping and murder
of American churchwomen there. Though a former US ambassador to
the country called members of the nefarious death squads sponsored by
the government "pathological killers," Reagan did not hesitate to send
military advisers to El Salvador to help the regime put down a leftist insurrection. Similarly, he called the vicious ruler of Guatemala, accused
of killing many thousands of Mayans, "a man of great integrity and commitment" who had "been getting a bum rap."

The president concentrated most of his attention south of the border
on Nicaragua, where he championed the right-wing "Contras" (counter-
revolutionaries). Reagan exalted these "freedom fighters" as "the moral
equal of our Founding Fathers and the brave men and women of the
French Resistance," though a Human Rights Watch report charged the
Contras with torture, rape, arson, kidnapping, targeting health care
workers for execution, and murdering children. Disturbed by Reagan's
commitment, Congress passed the Boland Amendment forbidding the
CIA or the Defense Department from arming the Contras "for the purpose of overthrowing the government of Nicaragua."

Reagan evaded this stipulation by acting covertly through a cabal in
the White House headed by Robert "Bud" McFarlane of the National
Security Council and McFarlane's deputy, an obscure marine officer
named Oliver North. The head of the CIA, William Casey, cooperated
closely with them, but neither the State Department nor the Defense
Department was apprised of what they were doing. Together, McFarlane
and North sidestepped the intent of Congress by raising money for the
Contras from sources such as the sultan of Brunei. When the conspirators
persuaded the Saudis to give a million dollars a month to the Nicaraguan
rebels, Reagan, informed of this back-door arrangement, scribbled a
message to McFarlane, "Mum's the word."

A *Wall Street Journal* story in April 1984 blew Reagan's cover. It revealed
that the CIA had mined Nicaraguan harbors and that a Soviet tanker had
collided with one of the mines. The International Court of Justice in The
Hague condemned the mining as illegal, and Senator Goldwater, enraged,
wrote his longtime friend William Casey: "I am pissed off." He went on

to say that he had assured fellow members of a Senate committee that there was nothing to the allegation that Reagan had approved the mining of Nicaraguan harbors, adding:

> I found out the next day that the CIA had, with the written approval of the President, engaged in such mining.…
>
> Bill, this is no way to run a railroad and I find myself in a hell of a quandary. I am forced to apologize to the Members of the Intelligence Committee because I did not know the facts.…
>
> The President has asked us to back his foreign policy. Bill, how can we back his foreign policy when we don't know what the hell he is doing?… Mine the harbors in Nicaragua? This is an act violating international law. It is an act of war. For the life of me, I don't see how we are going to explain it.…
>
> I don't like this. I don't like it one bit from the President or from you.

Congress responded by adopting a much stronger Boland Amendment that the Massachusetts congressman who sponsored it explained "clearly ends U.S. support for the war in Nicaragua," but Reagan refused to abandon his surreptitious arming of the Contras. Though Secretary Shultz warned him that he was engaged in an "impeachable offense" and Chief of Staff Baker expressed anxiety about "the crazies" in the White House basement who might involve him in illegal activities, the president ploughed ahead while, in violation of the law, keeping Congress, as well as the American people, in the dark. If what they were doing ever got out, he told his top advisers, "we'll all be hanging by our thumbs in front of the White House."

Early in 1984, the start of a campaign year that Reagan hoped would see his reelection to a second term, the president's advisers warned him that he needed to appear less pugnacious because voter disapproval of his conduct of foreign affairs was jeopardizing his prospects. Respondents to a Gallup Poll gave bad marks to his actions in Central America (49–28 against) and were even more dismayed by his behavior in Lebanon (59–28 adverse). His own pollster informed him that a worrisome proportion of the electorate believed Reagan was "more likely" than his presumed opponent "to start an unnecessary war."

Reluctantly, Reagan shifted away from his confrontational tone and spoke in favor of "constructive cooperation" with Russia. "Nineteen eighty-four," he declared, "is a year of opportunities for peace." He assured the country: "I am willing to meet and talk anytime. The door is open. We're standing in the doorway, seeing if anyone's coming up the steps." To a degree, he may have been speaking from the heart, for he truly did believe what he said when he declared, "My dream is to see the day when nuclear weapons will be banished from the earth." But it is more likely that he was speaking for effect, because he continued to view Soviet Russia as an iniquitous foe. Besides, he did not think that the 1984 election would turn on foreign policy. He took seriously a statement Richard Nixon had once made: "If we get the *economy* in shape, we're going to be able to do a lot of things. If we don't, we're not going to be able to do anything."

Reagan never again achieved as much success in putting through his domestic program as he had in his first year. Not content with the drastic slashes in social spending that he had obtained in 1981, including sharply curtailing aid to two million students, he demanded another $26 billion retrenchment in 1982, at the same time that he sought to boost defense spending by 13 percent. But Congress rebelled, and he engendered severe criticism, some of it from unexpected quarters. J. Richard Munro, a marine sergeant who had risen to the presidency of Time Incorporated and who was later to create the entertainment behemoth Time Warner, charged that Reagan's "retreat from federal aid for the less fortunate among us" was "doing grave damage to the quality of American life" and was "plain unfair."

No longer could Reagan count on rubber-stamp support from his own party. The Republican-controlled Senate scoffed at the budget he presented, in part because Stockman's projections had lost credibility. Senator Dole warned his fellow Republicans that their party had "already got an image across the country of harpooning the poor" and that a reassessment was in order. Especially striking was the change of heart of a GOP legislator from Pennsylvania who had gone along willingly in 1981 with all of the cutbacks. In 1982, Congressman Marc L. Marks lashed out at "a president and his cronies whose belief in Hooverism has blinded them to the wretchedness and to the suffering they are inflicting...on the sick, the poor, the handicapped, the small business person, the black community,...women of all economic and social backgrounds, . . . in fact anyone and everyone other than those who have been fortunate enough to insulate themselves in a corporate suit of armor."

Reagan responded peevishly to such criticism. "I read that crap about my program," he said. "We haven't thrown anybody out in the snow to die." When Bill Moyers produced a CBS documentary about the hardships people were suffering in the prolonged recession, the president complained: "You can't turn on the evening news without seeing that they're going to interview someone else who has lost his job or they're outside the factory gate that has laid off workers. . . . Is it news that some fellow out in South Succotash has just been laid off?"

Congress took the plight of the unemployed more seriously. It approved $14.2 billion in supplemental appropriations to provide jobs for older workers, aid to the handicapped and children living in poverty, and loans to college students. When Reagan vetoed the legislation as a "budget buster," Congress overrode him, with twenty-one Republican senators and eighty-one Republican representatives in the majority. Delivering a backhand slap at the president, Tip O'Neill said, "One would have to have a glib tongue, an effervescent personality, and a stone heart to vote against this bill." The setback, Reagan let it be known, left him "terribly, terribly hurt."

In the end, the president had to settle for considerably less than half a loaf. Congress gave him only one-third of the cuts in social spending he sought and addressed the problem of the soaring deficit by compelling the president to accept a steep raise in taxes. While denying that he was going back on his pledge to cut taxes, he accepted several "revenue enhancements," such as doubling excises on tobacco, that boosted taxes by nearly $100 billion over the next three years. Subsequently, Congress put through still more tax hikes, including a large jump in Social Security payroll levies that hurt lower-income Americans. But the big change was the Tax Equity and Fiscal Responsibility Act of 1982. In signing what the *New York Times* called "the largest revenue-raising bill ever," Reagan stated: "To . . . refer to this as a tax increase, I think was wrong. It was an adjustment."

Reagan dealt with the ballooning deficit by another sortie into make-believe. He refused to speak clearly to the country about what was transpiring, though he knew very well. "We really are in trouble," he wrote in his diary. "Our one time projections . . . are all out the window and we look at $200 billion deficits if we can't pull some miracles." Instead of accepting responsibility for what he had brought about by creating a combustible compound of tax cuts with runaway military spending, he blamed liberal Democrats for the shortfalls. Even more speciously, while continuing to mount up deficits, he announced a "people's crusade" for a balanced-budget amendment to the Constitution, saying sententiously that the nation needed to wean itself "from the long misery of overtaxing, overspending, and the great myth that our national nanny always knows best." His rhetoric on behalf of the amendment, said a syndicated columnist, was "a classic example of the drunk preaching temperance." Congress never paid the proposal any respect.

The negative response to his "New Federalism"—a plan for shifting to the states three-quarters of domestic programs (notably welfare and food stamps)—also stunned him. He labored under the illusion that local governments were writhing under the thumb of tyrannical Washington and were eager to operate projects themselves, but he met a curt rebuff. A California legislator pointed out that the idea of devolution had a "nice appeal to local home rule and self-determination," but "we are in the red, on the verge of bankruptcy, and there's nothing we could pick up," while the Republican governor of Vermont who chaired the National Governors Association declared that "governors cannot support a plan that fails to provide for the medically needy, discourages adequate state welfare assistance, or ignores differences in state burdens." The country's mayors, who were seeking federal funds to cope with hunger experienced by the rising numbers of jobless, were even more hostile. The conservative Minnesota Republican David Durenberger, whom Reagan expected to steer the New Federalism through the US Senate, called it "baloney" and "about the thinnest dodge I've ever seen." He questioned whether it was anything more than "a smoke screen for a repeal of the New Deal" and "a fig leaf to cover a lack of compassion" for the poor. After a few months, the proposal died quietly, unmourned.

Reagan coped more adroitly with the problem of inflation, though at a cost. He believed that a recession was necessary to bring prices down, but he never said it out loud. Instead, he left that bitter medicine to Paul Volcker, chairman of the Federal Reserve, who continued the tight money discipline he had begun under Carter. William Greider wrote in his *Atlantic* article: "One was shadowy and remote, an ominous figure;

the other, bright and cheerful. Paul Volcker was the stern father who admonished and prophesied.... Ronald Reagan was the generous king who inspired hope, whose rhetoric evoked streaks of sunshine across the darkened sky. Together, they promised redemption—if only the faithful flock would first accept the penitential sacrifice." After many months, this tactic did lower prices, but not before causing misery for millions of jobless to which Reagan was flintily indifferent.

Voters flocked to the polls in midterm elections across the country at a bad moment for Republicans. Some 16 percent of blue-collar workers were out of jobs, and 22 percent of construction laborers. In Milwaukee, twenty thousand people stood in line in subfreezing weather at the gate of a factory that had two hundred openings. The country could not escape the presence of the homeless: 2.5 million Americans spending their days and nights on city sidewalks, under bridge girders, on subway grates, wherever they could find escape from rain, sleet, and snow. In New York City, one of five men in shelters had been to college—stark evidence of how poverty was ravaging the middle class.

Commentators found ready listeners to fierce criticism of the president that would not have been acceptable in his first hundred days in office. (As early as the spring of 1982, Gallup reported that more Americans disapproved than approved Reagan's conduct of his presidency.) The Washington columnist Anthony Lewis charged that Republicans had saddled the country with a "government incompetent to govern, a president frozen in an ideological fantasy-land, and an administration spotted with rogues and fools." So bad was Reagan, said the *Washington Post's* David Broder, that the columnist was becoming "nostalgic" for Richard Nixon. The *New York Times*, noting the tottering economy, the "ill-planned military buildup," and the "huge deficits," concluded, "The stench of failure hangs over Ronald Reagan's White House."

Mistaking the temper of the country, Reagan chose to make the 1982 midterm contests a test of support for his program. Americans, he charged, faced a clear choice: between the Democratic Party, which "puts its faith in pipe dreamers and margin scribblers in Washington," and the Republican, which "believes in the collective wisdom of the people and their commitment to the American dream." He got his rebuke in November, when Republicans, while holding steady in the Senate, lost twenty-six seats in the House. The results, judged by the usual midterm losses for the party in power, were not catastrophic, but they were still substantial. They boosted Tip O'Neill's advantage in the House to 269–166, enough to offset the GOP–boll weevil coalition. Analysts saw the outcome as "a measured but sour response" to the president's performance rather than a devastating blow, but postelection surveys were considerably more alarming. Reagan's standing, they reported, was below that of Jimmy Carter's at a similar juncture. So bleak were the numbers early in 1983 that several Republicans doubted whether the president could be reelected in 1984.

Some of the president's severest critics, though, concluded that he was being passed over too quickly, for he had qualities that were going to permit him to rally and to prevail. In a long *New York Times* article, "Teflon Man," Steven Weisman observed:

> One of the most astonishing features of Ronald Reagan's political success is that, whether or not they agree with him and his policies, Americans *like* him....He has committed untold public bloopers, and been caught in dozens of factual mistakes and misrepresentations. He has presided over the worst recession since the Great Depression. The abortive mission in Beirut cost 265 American lives, and there has been a sharp escalation in United States military involvement in Central America. An extraordinary number of Mr. Reagan's political appointees have come under fire, with many forced to resign, because of ethical or legal conflicts. Yet...nothing sticks to him.

Unexpectedly, liberal commentators agreed. Anthony Lewis, who often wrote columns harshly arraigning the president, maintained: "The United States is conducting a remarkable experiment in modern government. It is testing the effects on a great democracy of a vacuum at the center of a Chief Executive who is scarcely informed on the substance of issues and shows no interest in being informed....At the point of decision-making there...is a President with a seven-minute attention span, a President interested not in reality but in appearance, in slogans." Still, Lewis concluded: "None of this seems to affect Mr. Reagan's political appeal. Indeed, a good part of that appeal may be the way he comes on as a bewildered ordinary guy, vulnerable, blundering at times, but aw shucks." A few days later, the columnist Joseph Kraft added: "With

Ronald Reagan, the blithe spirit entered the White House. He exudes charm, geniality and good feeling. Even the massive inattention to the substance of policy has, with him, a positive side. He walks away from failure…in seeming innocence that anything much has happened."

Another journalist, Hugh Sidey in *Time*, had a somewhat different take. He acknowledged that Reagan had "made many blunders," had been guilty of "press conference fictions," was responsible for "the tragedy in Lebanon," and showed "insensitivity to blacks and women." Yet voters, unlike Washington pundits, Sidey pointed out, gave "much weight…to optimism, good cheer, obvious enjoyment of the job, grace, personal kindness, decisiveness, boldness, individuality and other rather misty elements. They add up to leadership, which…creates a national momentum and vitality."

Invaluable though his sunny persona was to his prospects, Reagan had something more important going for him: an upturn in the economy. In 1983, the dark clouds of recession lifted, and the country rejoiced in the onset of prosperity that would persist for all the rest of the president's years in office. Inflation, which had been harrowing pensioners on fixed incomes, ceased to be a serious problem; it cost businessmen less to borrow money; and though the super-rich reaped the greatest rewards, groups at some lower income levels also did better. Admirers credited Reagan for the improvement because he had held fast with Volcker. Skeptics thought that he had lucked into an abrupt worldwide glut of oil accompanied by the breakdown of the Middle Eastern cartel that halted price rises bedeviling consumers, and had benefited inadvertently when his failure to balance the budget resulted in an elixir of deficit spending that pumped billions into the economy. From a political perspective, it did not matter who was right. All the nation grasped in the election year of 1984 was that bad times were over and Ronald Reagan was the man in the White House.

Reagan began his 1984 bid for a second term in high spirits. He gave no more attention to the details of electioneering than he did to the fine points of governing, but he assembled a savvy public relations team. "Detached from the management of his campaign," the president, said *Newsweek*, "preferred to trust in his fellas and his luck, or, as some of his associates guessed, his destiny." In this passive role, he was not at all un-comfortable with being packaged like a product on a supermarket shelf. Early in the campaign, he popped his head into a planning session of Madison Avenue ad men at the White House to say, "Since you're the ones who are selling the soap, I thought you'd like to see the bar."

Republican strategists circulated a memo encapsulating the theme of the forthcoming campaign: "Paint Ronald Reagan as the personification of all that is right with, or heroized by, America," so that "an attack on Reagan is tantamount to an attack on America's idealized image of itself—*where a vote against Reagan is, in some subliminal sense, a vote against a mythic 'America.'*" No conception could have been better tai-lored to the president's own "mythic" sense of reality or to his feel-good instincts. The GOP National Convention in 1984 provided the ideal venue for delivering this message because it took place in the same month that, with the USSR and the eastern European bloc boycotting the Olympic games in Los Angeles, the United States won the most gold medals ever, as flag-waving crowds chanted, "USA! USA!"

In his acceptance address at the Republican National Convention in Dallas, Reagan declared: "Greatness lies ahead of us. Holding the Olympic games here in the United States began defining the promise of this season. The world will beat a path to our door; and no one will be able to hold America back; and the future will be ours!" He went on to use even fruitier rhetoric: "Miss Liberty's torch. Her heart is full; her door is still golden; her future bright. . . . She will carry on in the eighties, unafraid, unashamed and unsurpassed." Enraptured, the delegates cried out, "USA! USA! USA!"

Both during and after the convention, Reagan and his party ham-mered home the contrast between the situation in 1984 and that at the end of Carter's reign. After years of stalemate, they claimed, the presi-dent had gotten government working again, and, unlike the time of the Iranian captivity, the United States had regained its preeminent place in the family of nations. In one highly effective commercial, an announcer, speaking against a backdrop of bucolic countryside, an attractive wed-ding party, hopeful young faces, and Old Glory, told viewers:

> It's morning again in America. Today, more men and women will go to
> work than ever before in our country's history. With interest rates at

about half the record high of 1980, nearly two thousand families today will buy new homes, more than at any time in the past four years. This afternoon, sixty-five hundred young men and women will be married, and, with inflation at less than half of what it was four years ago, they can look forward with confidence. It's morning again in America. And under the leadership of President Reagan, our country is stronger, and prouder, and better. Why would we ever want to return to where we were less than four short years ago?

To oppose Reagan, the Democrats nominated a man who had compiled a very impressive record but could not match the president's high-wattage personality. In his years as US senator from Minnesota, Fritz Mondale had been an important voice for liberal causes, especially civil rights, and he later added a new dimension to the office of the vice presidency. Furthermore, he made history in 1984 by choosing as his running mate Geraldine Ferraro, the first woman to appear on the national ticket of a major party and the first Italian American to rise so high. But when Mondale tried to focus attention on the downside of Reagan's economic program, with its runaway deficits, the president's supporters dismissed him as a grouch. Vice President Bush said of Mondale that "if somebody sees a silver lining, he finds a big black cloud out there. I mean: right on, whine on, harvest moon!" More pointedly, a columnist wrote that Mondale, though well-positioned to attack Reagan on a number of issues, "has yet to show the humorous, self-deprecating qualities" that could offset "the soft-shoe routines of the old stager in the White House." A mock ad for a make-believe film, "Mondale," carried the message:

Jimmy Carter made him Vice-President.
Now he is back.
And he is more boring than ever.

The first presidential debate, however, threw a scare into the Reagan camp. Mondale came across as crisp and well informed, while the president stumbled badly. Reagan had not even glanced at the briefing book that had been painstakingly prepared for him, and his behavior showed it. At one point, he was so flummoxed that he confessed, "I'm all confused now." His younger son later recalled, "My heart sank as he floundered his way through his responses, fumbling with his notes, uncharacteristically lost for words. He looked tired and bewildered." He also seemed dreadfully old. The *Wall Street Journal*, usually reliably Republican, headlined its account FITNESS ISSUE/NEW QUESTION IN RACE: IS OLDEST U.S. PRESIDENT NOW SHOWING HIS AGE? REAGAN DEBATE PERFORMANCE INVITES OPEN SPECULATION ON HIS ABILITY TO SERVE. After the event wound down, Mondale confided to a friend, "This guy is gone. It's scary. He's really not up to it." When an aide tried to reassure Reagan, the president said, "I was terrible." But, incredibly, he had a ready explanation for his bad performance: overpreparation.

Those who had begun to count Reagan out, however, underestimated his capacity to rebound and the charm with which he could deliver a devastating quip. The telling moment came in an ensuing debate when a *Baltimore Sun* correspondent asked the president bluntly if he was too elderly for the office. Primed for this question, Reagan responded, "I will not make age an issue in this campaign. I am not going to exploit, for political purposes, my opponent's youth and inexperience." Even Mondale grinned at that saucy rejoinder, but it was the smile of a man who sensed that whatever slim chance he had to overtake his rival was gone.

Reagan polled 59 percent of the popular vote (54.4 million to Mondale's 37.6 million), a higher proportion than Eisenhower had ever received. He won even more overwhelmingly in the Electoral College, 525–13. Apart from the predominantly black District of Columbia, Mondale got only his own state of Minnesota, and he came close to losing that. No other Democratic presidential nominee had ever suffered so great an electoral defeat. "For a textile worker to vote for Ronald Reagan is like a chicken voting for Colonel Sanders," a Mondale campaigner had said, but election analysts spotlighted the phenomenon of "the Reagan Democrat," with the president gaining a majority of the ballots cast by workingmen. When the last returns were counted, the president might well have repeated what he had told an aide a long time before: "Politics is just like show business. You have a hell of an opening, coast for a while, and then have a hell of a close."

Reagan did not anticipate after his great victory that his few triumphs in domestic policy henceforth would be almost entirely confined to the judiciary, though some actions by the Court in his first term foreshadowed this success. In 1983, the Supreme Court had struck down a legislative veto on actions of the executive branch because it could be imposed by a single house of Congress (*INS v. Chadha*, 1983). The Court had again sustained executive authority in *Chevron USA, Inc. v. Natural Resources Defense Council* (1984) by ruling that the judiciary must countenance decisions rendered by an administrative agency when the wording of a statute was ambiguous and the agency's interpretation not unreasonable. In his second term, too, the Court defended the presidency, notably after Congress, despairing of its capacity to discipline itself on spending, put through the Gramm-Rudman-Hollings Act, a bipartisan measure that set targets for reducing the deficit and stipulated automatic cuts ("sequesters") if they were not met. Though Reagan supported the principle of this 1985 law, he strongly resented a provision empowering the comptroller general to infringe upon his authority. When he gave formal approval to the legislation, he issued a "signing statement" declaring that provision unconstitutional and then filed suit to have it annulled. Critics objected that a signing statement had no legal authority but was a subterfuge to permit a president to impose a veto while denying Congress its constitutional right to override. In 1986, however, Reagan won an important victory when, in *Bowsher v. Synar*, the Supreme Court invalidated the disputed provision. In the very first footnote in his opinion, Chief Justice Warren Earl Burger cited Reagan's objections, thereby confirming judicial acceptance of a presidential signing statement.

In the most notorious confrontation over the judiciary during his tenure, though, Reagan ran into trouble when he sought to gain confirmation of an appointee who could tilt the Supreme Court markedly to the right. In nominating Robert Bork, he raised the hackles of liberals and moderates because, as an official in Nixon's Justice Department, Bork had carried out the Saturday Night Massacre after two higher-ranking men in the department had resigned rather than abide by Nixon's orders. In another respect, too, he was an odd specimen: a Yale Law School professor who had vigorously opposed the Civil Rights Act of 1964.

For more than three months, liberal organizations mounted a full-powered assault on the nomination. Some of it was mean, conspicuously the perusal of Bork's video-rental history to see if anything damaging could be found in his choice of films to watch. But by far the biggest source of difficulty for the aspirant was Bork himself. His sizeable corpus of publications provided ample exposition of his narrow view of the equal protection clause, and his behavior at committee hearings projected cold arrogance. Furthermore, his statements attacking the reasoning underpinning *Roe v. Wade* suggested that he was lusting for the opportunity to reverse that historic ruling on women's rights. The Senate's 58–42 vote rejecting Bork was the largest negative for a nominee to the Court in the country's history.

Reagan also fell short, ludicrously, in his second attempt to fill the slot intended for Bork. On the advice of Meese, he turned next to Douglas Ginsburg, a judge of the US Court of Appeals for the District of Columbia Circuit. A number of attorneys in the Department of Justice thought this was a poor choice, since Ginsburg's entire judicial experience consisted of one year on the bench. Reagan, though, saw that shortcoming as an advantage because Ginsburg had written so little that he was less vulnerable than Bork. In addition, the president believed that Ginsburg's youth (he was forty-one) made it likely that the judge would be wielding his influence for decades to come. But the nomination had hardly been announced when it began to fall apart. The media revealed that as a member of the Justice Department staff, Ginsburg had pursued litigation vitally affecting the cable television industry while holding a $140,000 investment in a cable corporation in his portfolio.

The loudest objections to the appointee, however, came not from liberals concerned with conflict of interest but from leaders of the Radical Right. Disturbed to learn that Ginsburg had dropped out of college to launch a computer dating business, and that his wife, a doctor, had performed abortions, they were outraged by the revelation that he had smoked marijuana not only as a student but also when a professor on the Harvard Law faculty. That disclosure came at a particularly awkward time because Nancy Reagan had been waging a "Just Say No" campaign against drug addiction. Only nine days after Reagan nominated him, Ginsburg, yielding to intense pressure from conservatives, withdrew his name. The second setback in a row for the president on the Supreme Court, it raised grave doubts about the competence of Meese and his staff. Asked whether they had done their homework by carefully vetting Ginsburg, a White House official retorted, "If they did, they didn't turn it in on time."

Reagan fared much better in winning confirmation of his next selection, but even that choice did not prove altogether satisfactory for the president. Well regarded as a circuit court judge, Anthony Kennedy of Sacramento sailed through the Senate, 97–0. On the Supreme Court, he fulfilled conservative expectations in most cases, but on a number of occasions he and Sandra Day O'Connor aligned themselves with the liberal wing. Hence, Kennedy came to be thought of as a "swing" vote—not what Reagan had intended.

In other appointments throughout his second term, though, the president achieved marked success in shifting the federal judiciary rightward. He raised a storm by choosing William Rehnquist to succeed Warren Burger as chief justice because Rehnquist had been by far the most conservative member of the Burger Court, with fifty-four solo dissents. Senator Kennedy called him "too extreme on race, too extreme on women's rights, too extreme on freedom of speech, too extreme on separation of church and state, too extreme to be Chief Justice." But Reagan's nominee prevailed despite these strong objections, albeit with thirty-three votes (from both parties) cast against him—the most ever opposing the nomination of a chief justice in the twentieth century. Reagan's choice of Antonin Scalia for the Supreme Court, on the other hand, generated no controversy, though Scalia was at least as "extreme" as Rehnquist and considerably more disputatious. Even liberals, who were disturbed by his record on civil liberties, conceded that Scalia was brilliant, and he was confirmed unanimously. The *New York Times* headlined the appointments MORE VIGOR FOR THE RIGHT.

Over the course of eight years, Reagan markedly altered the complexion of the federal judiciary by making the most appointments of any president in history: 78 to US circuit courts, 290 to US district courts. He displeased members of the bar, including Eisenhower's attorney general, by setting up screening panels that probed whether candidates were "right-thinking" on issues such as "family values." Yet he named a higher proportion of judges rated by the American Bar Association as "well qualified" or "exceptionally well qualified" than had his four predecessors from LBJ through Carter. His team especially favored white men of means, the younger the better so that their influence over the bench would be long-lasting. In selecting nearly half of all federal judges, the president, said Ed Meese, managed to "institutionalize the Reagan revolution so it can't be set aside no matter what happens in future presidential elections."

Even when Reagan succeeded in revamping the judiciary, however, he could not always count on it to rule in his favor, as he discovered in 1988 in *Morrison v. Olson*, a case arising out of the suspiciously lax enforcement of the Superfund law by his appointees to the Environmental Protection Agency. When House subcommittees requested the EPA turn over pertinent documents, the president had ordered the agency's administrator to refuse to comply on the highly improbable ground that the papers were "sensitive." An ensuing inquiry led the House Judiciary Committee to ask for an independent counsel to investigate charges against two EPA officials and Assistant Attorney General Theodore Olson, who was accused of lying.

Olson, a skilled constitutional lawyer as well as an ardent Republican, responded by challenging the constitutionality of the section of the 1978 Ethics in Government Act that instituted independent counsels and stipulated that they could not be fired by the attorney general or the president save for serious misbehavior. That provision, Olson contended, transgressed the president's realm and created a "fourth branch" answerable to no one. Independent Counsel Alexia Morrison countered by explicating the indispensability of her office and denying that it breached the principle of separation of powers. Siding with Morrison, the Court, 7–1, in an opinion by Rehnquist, ruled that even an official performing unmistakably executive functions such as prosecution could be safeguarded by Congress from removal by a president. The lone dissenter, Justice Scalia, discussing the power of a judicial panel to appoint prosecutors, asked presciently: "What if they are politically partisan, as judges have been known to be, and select a prosecutor antagonistic to the administration?" Over the next decade, both Democrats and Republicans came to view the anomaly of the independent counsel as intolerable, and in 1999 authorization for it was not renewed.

Save for his middling success in reconfiguring the judiciary, Reagan's second term did not work out at all as he hoped it would. He had every reason to suppose that his enormous electoral triumph would be seen as a mandate for new initiatives. Instead, he spent much of the next four years scrambling to patch together a functioning White House team. Foreign policy wrought most of the damage to his reputation, but in domestic affairs, too, he was often at bay. Against his wishes, resurgent Democrats pushed through substantial increases to fund Medicaid, food stamps, and other social programs. For a considerable time, he retained his popularity—indeed, his approval rating did not peak until the late spring of 1986—but he was rarely able to translate it into effective action. Before his tenure ended, there was serious talk of impeaching him.

He put himself in jeopardy at the very start of his new term by doing nothing to halt the breakup of the troika that had been piloting him through the shoals of misapprehension. Burned out from an entire term of propping up the president, his top advisers could not stomach the thought of four more years. Jim Baker, who had many admirers in Washington for the exceptional work he had done as chief of staff with no thanks from Reagan, leaped at the opportunity to switch jobs with Secretary of the Treasury Don Regan—at great cost to the president. In his second term, always a perilous period, Reagan required guidance and protection from error more than ever, but Regan could provide neither. Counselor Ed Meese abandoned the White House to become attorney general, a switch that was good neither for him nor for the country. Mike Deaver, who had been an important conduit for Nancy Reagan and also a restraint on her, took flight for the private sector. The manipulative first lady was left with no White House confidant in the second term, and she could not abide Regan. The president, who had earned praise for his wisdom in creating the troika, was utterly clueless about the forthcoming disaster he was bringing on by his indifference.

The outcome of the midterm elections further exacerbated his predicament. In the autumn of 1986, Reagan barnstormed the country on behalf of Republican congressional candidates, especially senators—a whirlwind tour of twenty-two states covering twenty-four thousand miles, but in a losing cause. By capturing nine seats while giving up only one, Democrats regained control of the Senate emphatically, 55–45, while retaining their advantage in the House, 258–171. For the rest of his days in office, Reagan was going to have to deal with hostile Democrats on the Hill.

Events took a particularly unwelcome turn for Reagan in 1987 when on a Monday in late October the stock market fell 508 points. In a matter of hours, securities lost nearly 23 percent of their value. The collapse constituted the greatest one-day plunge in the history of the market, with more than $500 billion in investments wiped out. For well over half a century, Americans had been told that Black Tuesday—the hideous time in October 1929 when a stock-market free fall signaled the start of the Great Depression—marked the worst day of financial disaster America ever would experience. Black Monday 1987 was twice as bad.

As newspapers across the country headlined the distressing news, Reagan received a memo: "Stated Reasons for Stock Market Decline"; at the head of the list was "Lack of leadership in Washington." *Time* issued a cover with the blunt question "Who's in Charge?," and in a feature story for the magazine, Walter Isaacson wrote: "What crashed was more than just the market. It was the Reagan Illusion: the idea that there could be a defense buildup and tax cuts without a price, that the country could live beyond its means indefinitely. . . . As he shouted befuddled Hooverisms over the roar of his helicopter last week or doddered precariously through his press conference, Reagan appeared embarrassingly irrelevant to a reality that he could scarcely comprehend." The *New York Times,* in a lengthy front-page article, "Reagan Ability to Lead Nation at a Low," reported: "More than ever he is showing signs of his 76 years, so much so that his memory lapses and rambling discourse are no longer a source of friendly jokes, but one of concern, friends say. . . . At a recent news conference, . . . the President was unable to remember the name of the United Nations Security Council."

Analysts credited Reagan with only a single significant legislative accomplishment in the domestic sphere through all four years of his second term, and he backed into that one. In response to a national outcry against tax loopholes in the first term, Secretary of the Treasury Regan had headed a team that worked for months on fashioning legislation to make the tax schedule fairer and more rational. But when the president looked at it, right after the 1984 contest in which he had demolished his Democratic opponent, he saw no need to risk offending special interests in his party. Regan's move to the White House as chief of staff in the second term, however, made it easier for him to get Reagan's ear, while, over at Treasury, Baker and Darman put together a more politically feasible package. Under pressure from both his chief of staff and his secretary of the treasury, the president yielded, in part because the bill once again lowered the rate on wealthiest taxpayers—this time from 50 percent to 28 percent.

In shaping the measure, lawmakers attempted to achieve balance, partly by reducing the farrago of tax brackets from fourteen to three.

The Tax Reform Act of 1986, sponsored by two Democrats (Bill Bradley and Richard Gephardt), pleased conservatives not only by cutting the rates for wealthy individuals but also by reducing corporate taxes, while delighting liberals by stepping up capital gains levies, wiping out tax shelters, and encompassing two strikingly progressive features: removal of six million lower-income Americans from the tax rolls and expansion of the earned income tax credit—a boon to the less well-off. Most in the Reagan circle strenuously opposed that benefit to the working poor, but one White House adviser hoped that the legislation, which amounted to an apology for the unfairness of the 1981 tax cuts, would "erase the cartoon of our party as defender of the rich and privileged."

Reagan received a bit of applause, too, for the Family Support Act of 1986, though it embodied the thinking less of the president and his advisers than of Pat Moynihan and moderates in both parties, including centrist Democrats such as Arkansas governor Bill Clinton and Tennessee senator Al Gore. "Welfare reform" ranked high on the wish list of conservative think tanks, but a congressional aide informed the White House that the chances that the president could get from the Senate the kind of overhaul he and right-wingers wanted were "slim to none, and slim is packing his bags." The administration insisted that the bill authorize no additional cost, but the final version approved more than $3 billion more for the poor, and though the White House sought to reduce burdens on the states, the law increased them. Conservatives did get a provision for "workfare"—the requirement that able-bodied relief recipients seek employment—but the mandate was not nearly so severe as the Republican right had demanded. As he signed the bill, Reagan might well have said with Pyrrhus, "One more such victory and we are lost."

Democrats also shared responsibility, in a way that did not speak well of them, for an ongoing series of unsavory developments that peaked in the second term, but commentators assigned Reagan most of the blame for the worst scandal of the latter half of the twentieth century. With the president's enthusiastic support, a bipartisan act of Congress had freed savings and loan banks ("thrifts") to invest in junk bonds, speculative real estate, and worthless property. Reagan, who took pride in what he called the "most important legislation for financial institutions in the last fifty years," appointed advocates of deregulation to the Federal Home Loan Bank Board and reduced the number of bank examiners scrutinizing accounts of the S&Ls. The most notorious institution, Lincoln Federal Savings and Loan, was operated by Charles Keating, who targeted "the weak, meek, and ignorant" to defraud and who bought protection for himself by contributing lavishly to the campaigns of US senators. When an unusually conscientious federal regulator sought to constrain the thrift, "the Keating Five" (Republican John McCain and four Democratic senators including the prominent liberal Alan Cranston and the hero astronaut John Glenn) brought pressure on him to exempt Lincoln Federal Savings and Loan. After this S&L crashed, taking the life savings of thousands of elderly depositors, the five senators (all of them beneficiaries of Keating's largesse) were rebuked, and Keating was sent to the penitentiary. The bailout of the thrifts, which were covered by federal deposit insurance, cost taxpayers several times more than the entire Vietnam War. The General Accounting Office estimated the damage at nearly $400 billion—the greatest financial debacle in the history of the world.

The S&L scams took place at the same time that the Reagan administration was shaken by revelations of corruption in its highest ranks. Conflicts of interest caused more than forty of Reagan's appointees to resign their posts. The deputy secretary of defense, accused of insider trading and obstruction of justice, was sentenced to prison; Pentagon officials engaged in what one Republican senator called "rampant bribery"; a congressional investigation concluded that executives in the Department of Housing and Urban Development were guilty of "influence peddling, favoritism, abuse, greed, fraud, embezzlement and theft"; and, after leaving the White House, Michael Deaver was convicted of perjury. Most damaging of all was the investigation of Ed Meese, whom Reagan had long relied upon. A special prosecutor stated that Meese had, in four instances, "probably violated the criminal law," and a Justice Department probe concluded that he bore the blame for "conduct which should not be tolerated of any government employee, especially not the attorney general." Meese found it prudent to resign. Reagan, though, was unrepentant. When Congress enacted legislation to forestall federal officials from exploiting their government connections the minute they entered the private sector, he vetoed the bill. Well before the end of the president's second term, it had become clear that if Ronald Reagan was to leave a legacy of accomplishment beyond reconstituting the judiciary, it was going to have to come in foreign affairs.

———

Less than two months after Reagan took the oath of office for a second term, the Soviet Union installed a new leader: Mikhail Gorbachev. The first general secretary born after the revolution, Gorbachev, a youngster when Stalin died, had not participated in the worst period of repression; moreover, he had traveled widely abroad and brought new attitudes toward foreign relations as well as governance. Not for a while, though, did Reagan recognize the significance of the changeover. Even after Britain's Tory prime minister, Margaret Thatcher, informed him that Gorbachev was "someone we could deal with," the president told a reporter, as he prepared for his first encounter with the Russians, "You know they really *are* an evil empire." Yet Reagan was to wind up signing a historic compact with the USSR, strolling the streets of Moscow, and warming to "Ronnie and Mikhail" camaraderie.

Before that happened, Reagan bungled badly a state visit to Europe in the spring of 1985 by accepting an invitation from German chancellor Helmut Kohl to pay his respects at a cemetery in Bitburg on the fortieth anniversary of the end of World War II. Among the many graves were those of dozens of Hitler's murderous 2nd Waffen-SS Panzer Division that had massacred nearly seven hundred French civilians. Furthermore, the Nazis had awarded an Iron Cross to an SS sergeant in that division for killing ten American troops. US veterans associations expressed opposition to his participation in the ceremony; Jewish groups around the world voiced their dismay; and eighty-two of the one hundred members of the US Senate and 390 in the House of Representatives urged him not to go. Reagan, however, refused to reconsider, and the very worried first lady had to content herself with setting the time of the event on advice of her astrologer. She then twice altered it in accord with the dictates of the zodiac.

Though it was understandable that the president did not want to embarrass Kohl, his political ally, by canceling the event, he showed himself to be altogether insensitive to the significance of the rite he was about to perform. He turned down an invitation to visit a death camp that had claimed many Jewish lives, and he said of the SS butchers that they "were victims, just as surely as the victims in the concentration camps."

Only at Kohl's suggestion did he tack on a visit to the notorious facility at Bergen-Belsen. One of the president's enthusiastic admirers, Assistant Secretary of State Elliott Abrams, has observed, "This is one of those rare cases where Reagan's own inner radar totally failed him and he came out on the wrong side." Incredibly, however, the president wrote in his diary, "I always felt it was the morally right thing to do."

Reagan also alarmed his aides by repeatedly articulating an idiosyncratic worldview. "For the first time ever, everything is in place for the battle of Armageddon and the second coming of Christ," he had informed a California legislator in 1970. During the 1980 campaign, he told the leader of the Moral Majority, Jerry Falwell: "Reverend, sometimes I think that we are approaching Armageddon. The horrible arms buildup and the seemingly hopeless dilemma the nations of the world face today can certainly make one wonder if it can be reversed....I do believe the Bible, and that there will one day be a final war." He carried this conviction into the White House with him. "Until now, has there ever been a time in which so many of the prophecies are coming together?" he asked in 1983. "There have been times in the past when people thought the end of the world was coming, and so forth, but never anything like this." The explosion of a nuclear reactor at Chernobyl in the USSR during his second term led him to recite a passage from Revelation: "A great star fell from heaven, blazing like a torch, and it fell on the third of the rivers and on the fountains of water. The name of the star is Wormwood." He found his speculations confirmed when he learned that "Chernobyl" is Ukrainian for "wormwood."

The president dwelt on this notion, however, not because he yearned to fight a holy war but because he was so horrified by the prospect of Armageddon that he believed a bold new approach must be adopted to avert doomsday. Addressing the UN General Assembly, he said: "In our obsession with antagonisms of the moment, we often forget how much unites all the members of humanity. Perhaps we need some outside, universal threat to make us recognize this common bond. I occasionally think how quickly our differences worldwide would vanish if we were facing an alien threat from outside this world. And yet, I ask you, is not an alien force already among us? What could be more alien to the universal aspirations of our peoples than war and the threat of war?" He derived his phantasm of an invasion of Earth by a hostile planet, it turned out, from a science fiction movie, *The Day the Earth Stood Still*. (He so treasured this scenario of an earthly alliance against aliens that he sprang it on Gorbachev, but got no response, perhaps, Lou Cannon has surmised, because the Soviet leader "did not have at his fingertips the Marxist-Leninist position on the propriety of cooperating with the imperialists against an interplanetary invasion.")

His anxiety about the imminence of annihilation led Reagan to ignore the admonitions of his right-wing supporters, who warned that Gorbachev could not be trusted, and to heed the counsel of his wife, who told him that the time had come to abandon Cold War rhetoric. The foremost conservative periodical, *National Review*, called Gorbachev's behavior "vintage Stalin," but the first lady, conscious that her husband was in his final term, wanted him to go down in the history books as a peacemaker. Her attitude was bolstered when her astrologer sent assurance that Gorbachev's "Aquarian planet is in such harmony with Ronnie's... they'll share a vision." Swallowing his misgivings, the president agreed to a course of action he had never previously undertaken: a summit meeting with the head of the USSR.

Before leaving for Geneva in November 1985, he dictated a five-page memo to himself. He saw the Russian as "highly intelligent," likely to be "a formidable negotiator," and "dependent on the Soviet communist hierarchy." But he added comments that observers hoping for some lessening of hostility would have found encouraging and that those who underrated him would not have expected. "Let there be no talk of winners and losers," he said. "Even if we think we won, to say so would set us back in view of their inherent inferiority complex." And he wound up: "We should set up a process to avoid war and settling our differences in the future" by arranging to meet again.

Both men sought an understanding, but the Geneva meeting foundered on Soviet objections to a daunting Reagan initiative that he refused to abandon. In a paragraph at the end of a speech he delivered in March 1983, Reagan had asked, "Wouldn't it be better to save lives than avenge them? Isn't it possible to find a technology to make nuclear missiles impotent and obsolete?" He did not doubt that a mesh of lasers and satellites in space could be devised that would totally safeguard the United States from enemy attack. The president, General Colin Powell has said, "had undying, Reaganesque faith in the ability of American industries and laboratories to provide him with such a shield."

Almost no one thought that "Reagan's folly" made sense. The media labeled the Strategic Defense Initiative (SDI) "Star Wars," title of a cult movie, implying that his idea was simply a Hollywood chimera. Writers familiar with Reagan's career traced his fantasy to a science fiction movie, *Murder in the Air*, in which, as secret agent Brass Bancroft, he had foiled an attempt by evildoers to steal an "inertia projector." He had announced the SDI plan without consulting his defense secretary, and on learning of the president's scheme, the Joint Chiefs were highly skeptical. Secretary of State Shultz thought it was "lunacy." The fervent cold warrior Richard Perle later concluded: "The president's concept...of a hermetic shield was never technically feasible, and certainly wasn't affordable, even if you could imagine the technology that could put it together."

Star Wars, though, thoroughly frightened the Russians. The only ones who believed the project was practicable, it was said, were Reagan and the commissars in the Kremlin. A Soviet foreign minister later informed an American audience that the announcement of SDI "made us realize we were in a very dangerous spot." Shultz later recalled: "Whenever we got together with the Soviets in the Reagan-Gorbachev meetings, SDI was always on Gorbachev's mind. He seemed almost ready to concede anything if he could only manage to deep-six that program." At Geneva, Gorbachev told the president bluntly, "SDI has got to come to an end." Reagan could not comprehend why there should be any objection. He was acting for the benefit of all mankind, he reasoned, and was even offering to share the results with the Soviet Union.

The president's advisers, however, understood very well how his speech had upset the understanding of decades because the United States was seeking a shield that would, by rendering it invulnerable to attack, put it in the position of being able to launch a surprise assault on the Soviet Union without fear of reprisal. Reagan's national security adviser Robert McFarlane later pointed out: "With SDI we seemed to suggest that the United States wanted to have a first-strike capability. If you protect your own people and don't have to worry about getting hit, it is safe for you to attack them. If it looks that way in the Kremlin, won't they attack you before you get SDI built? So you are making the world a much less stable place."

Colin Powell has recalled the response of foreign policy authorities to Reagan's saying to Gorbachev about SDI, "I'll give it to you!":

Now that used to drive us nuts, because he actually meant it. We would have been shocked to ever have given such sophisticated technology to the Soviets, not knowing how they would ultimately have used it. But Reagan meant it with all his heart, because he wanted them to have as strong a shield as we had, because only then would they be comfortable about getting rid of those horrible missiles.... It was really quite noble and far-reaching conceptually, and it scared the hell out of a lot of people—both on our side and on the Russian side—who couldn't believe that this guy meant it. He was giving them his marker: he would give them the technology to defend themselves against us and therefore we could both then disarm. Gorbachev couldn't believe it.

At Geneva, Gorbachev asked: "Why should I accept your sincerity or your willingness to share SDI research when you don't even share your advanced technology with your allies?"

Despite the impasse on SDI, the Geneva meeting proved to be an important step toward arms control, for it gave the two men an opportunity to move beyond preconceptions. As they walked toward a pool house by a lake to resume their exchanges, Reagan halted to say, "Mr. General Secretary, here we are, two men born in obscure rural hamlets, both poor and from humble beginnings. Now we are leaders of our countries, and probably the only two men who can start World War III, and possibly the only two...who can bring peace to the world." Gorbachev concluded that Reagan "wasn't terribly bright or very knowledgeable" and that "ideologically this man is a dinosaur." Still, he also decided that the president was not the "bogeyman" he had been led to believe and that he detected a "spark of mutual trust" in the course of their very heated exchanges. For the president's closing remarks, Pat Buchanan and Peggy Noonan inserted some slighting words about Gorbachev and the USSR, but Reagan deleted them. "Pat, this has been a good meeting," he told Buchanan. "I think I can work with this guy. I can't just keep poking him in the eye." At the close, Reagan whispered to Gorbachev, "I bet the hard-liners in both our countries are bleeding while we shake hands." After he returned to America, Reagan wrote his fellow Hollywood star/California politico George Murphy: "I must say I enjoyed playing the part and the show did have something of a happy ending."

In October 1986 in Iceland, the two men made another try at an agreement. Reagan's insistence on SDI once more threw up an insurmountable roadblock, but not before Gorbachev had startled the American delegation by advocating the deepest arms reductions the USSR had ever offered to accept. They had hardly settled down in Reykjavik when Gorbachev pulled papers out of his briefcase and proposed a 50 percent reduction in strategic nuclear forces and the elimination of Soviet as well as US intermediate-range missiles. His openness to concessions impressed everyone in the US delegation, even hard-liners, but not the president. At one point, exasperated by the way Reagan was dragging his feet, Gorbachev told him: "There is an American expression, 'It takes two to tango.'... Was the president prepared to dance?" After Reagan parried, Gorbachev went much further, proposing the elimination of all nuclear weapons. To the dismay of his advisers, long accustomed to a strategy of deterrence, the president retorted, "It would be fine with me."

Sir Charles Powell, personal secretary to Prime Minister Thatcher, has expressed the response of the president's advisers and of Western heads of state to those words:

> The trouble is that President Reagan wanted to eliminate nuclear weapons before there was anything to put... in their place. At Reykjavik, he seemed to be on the brink of negotiating that with Gorbachev. And luckily for us, Gorbachev insisted that the Star Wars program be stopped.
>
> Mrs. Thatcher said that she really felt the ground moving under her when she heard the president's position. We raced over to Washington a week or two later, and she got him to issue a joint statement with her, reaffirming his commitment to nuclear deterrence and modernization of the British nuclear deterrent, which was a vital part of her whole political position.

Reagan, despite his unexpected assent to Gorbachev's advance, still would not promise to junk Star Wars. Angrily, he told the Soviet leader, "I've said again and again that SDI wasn't a bargaining chip. I've told you, if we find out that SDI is practical and feasible, we'll make that information known to you and everyone else so that nuclear weapons can be obsolete." When Gorbachev persisted, Reagan called out abruptly,

"This meeting is over." Turning to Secretary Shultz, he said, "Let's go, George.... We're leaving." Gorbachev, disheartened, pleaded with the president to stay for another day, but Reagan, his coat on, snapped, "It's too late." In the end, he would not even look at Gorbachev. Reagan noted in his diary, "I was mad—he tried to be jovial but I acted mad & it showed."

After departing Reykjavik in bad humor, Reagan reverted to a bellicose mode. In June 1987, in an address to a crowd of two hundred thousand at the Brandenburg Gate dividing West and East Berlin, he said: "We hear much from Moscow about a new policy of reform and openness. Are these the beginnings of profound changes in the Soviet state? Or, are they token gestures?... There is one sign the Soviets can make that would be unmistakable, that would advance dramatically the cause of freedom and peace. General Secretary Gorbachev, if you seek peace, if you seek prosperity for the Soviet Union and Eastern Europe, if you seek liberalization: Come here to this gate! Mister Gorbachev, open this gate! Mister Gorbachev, tear down this wall!"

Gorbachev, shrugging off this taunt, refused to be distracted from seeing whether, despite the stormy ending at Reykjavik, an arms agreement might still be salvaged, and it was he, not Reagan, who took the initiative on renewing negotiations. He desperately wanted to lower military costs in order to revive the sagging Russian economy and to carry out his ambition to revamp Soviet society by embracing *perestroika* (restructuring) and *glasnost* (openness). To further these goals, and to signal to the United States his peaceful intent, he pulled out of Afghanistan and unilaterally withdrew half a million troops, as well as a large cache of weapons, from the European continent. Still more important, he no longer insisted that Reagan jettison Star Wars. "Everything has changed since Reykjavik," the Russian deputy foreign minister informed American negotiators. "All the reports we saw indicated SDI was not realistic.... It looked frightening initially, but it wouldn't work.... Gorbachev is not nervous about it now." Refusing to accept the widespread characterization of the Reykjavik summit as a failure, Gorbachev called it a "breakthrough," and Shultz soon adopted the same language. In February 1987, Gorbachev proposed that, instead of trying for an omnibus arms agreement, the two powers focus on ridding Europe of frightening intermediate-range missiles.

Over the course of dozens of meetings, Gorbachev's foreign minister, Eduard Shevardnadze, an admirer of Franklin Roosevelt, and Secretary Shultz got along famously. Together, they forged an arms compact that had eluded Reagan and Gorbachev at Geneva and Reykjavik. The Intermediate-Range Nuclear Force (INF) Treaty mandated the dismantling of 332 US missiles in Europe and 629 Soviet missiles. Some of the intermediate weapons being scrapped had a range of three thousand miles. Though the accord reduced the world's nuclear arsenal only 4 percent, it marked the first time that the two superpowers had ever agreed to destroy missiles.

Gorbachev flew to Washington for the formal signing of the eighty-page INF treaty in the East Room of the White House on December 8, 1987, the day (and hour) once again determined by Nancy Reagan's astrologer. On his first visit to the United States, the Soviet leader unexpectedly overshadowed the Hollywood performer in the White House. At one point, as his limousine was moving down Connecticut Avenue, Gorbachev, to the dismay of the KGB, ordered the car to halt, and he leaped out to shake hands with a delighted crowd of cheering Americans. The capital, said a *Washington Post* columnist, was convulsed by "Gorby fever."

The day of the document signing should have been Reagan's finest hour, but he disgraced himself. Gorbachev led off with an impressive accounting of the achievements of *perestroika*, but the president, instead of responding, seemed disoriented, and only managed to retort by telling a stale anti-Soviet story that his advisers recognized to be brutally offensive. On returning to the White House, Reagan got a scolding. "We can't let this happen again," Baker told him, and Shultz said bluntly, "That was terrible." The president, made to understand how badly he had embarrassed himself and his country, said, "I better go home and do my homework."

Reagan encountered rebukes from right-wingers, too. The *Detroit News* highlighted his signing immediately after the anniversary of the Pearl Harbor disaster as "A Day That Will Live in INFamy." The conservative publicist Howard Phillips called Reagan "a very weak man with a very strong wife" who was "a useful idiot for Kremlin propaganda," while the president reminded the *Washington Times* of Neville Chamberlain cowed by Hitler at Munich. In sum, pontificated George Will, "December 8 will be remembered as the day the Cold War was lost."

Reagan and Gorbachev. "Ronnie" is all smiles on December 8, 1977, as he and "Mikhail" sign the INF treaty gradually eliminating medium- and short-range missiles on the European continent. © *CORBIS, ID IH038851*

The biting criticism failed to shake Reagan. He knew he was on the correct track when, after putting his name on the INF agreement, his approval rating shot above 60 percent for the first time in months. He signaled his determination to persist in his changed approach to foreign policy by flying to Moscow in the spring of 1988 to pay a call on Gorbachev, whom he called "my friend." Asked by a reporter in the Soviet capital whether he still termed the USSR an "evil empire," he responded, "I was speaking of another time, another era."

In a nationally televised address from the Oval Office in June 1985, Ronald Reagan had assured the American people: "The United States gives terrorists no rewards and no guarantees. We make no concessions. We make no deals." That message had earlier threaded his 1980 campaign for the presidency. Unlike Jimmy Carter in responding fecklessly to the seizure and detention of American hostages in Tehran, he pledged that he would deal with Iran implacably. In 1986, he affirmed, "Every nickel-and-dime dictator the world over knows that if he tangles with the United States of America, he will pay a price."

Reagan convinced the country of his resolve when in April 1986 he moved beyond words to authorize an air assault on Libya. In retaliation for the bombing of a West Berlin discotheque frequented by American soldiers (a deed believed to have been masterminded by the Libyan Mu'ammar Muhammad al-Gaddafi), US planes rained bombs on two Libyan cities. In an attempt to murder the despot, whom Reagan called a "mad dog," the aircraft targeted his tent compound. Gaddafi escaped unharmed, but the US bombs took a number of lives, including that of the dictator's two-year-old daughter. The president, having bypassed the War Powers Act in sending armed forces into Lebanon and into Grenada, thumbed his nose at congressional leaders again by not informing them of the bombing mission until after the planes heading for Africa were in the air, but, though some on the Hill were vexed, the nation hailed the assault as a demonstration of his determination to carry the fight against terrorists directly to their homeland. After the Libya bombing, Reagan's popular approval ratings climbed to almost 70 percent, a peak as high as it had been in the afterglow of his recovery from the assassination attempt in 1981. The United States, it seemed, had a leader confronting terrorism who was unflinching.

The Reagan administration appeared to be especially determined to ostracize Iran. It not only embargoed arms sales to the Ayatollah Khomeini regime but brought pressure on other countries, especially its European allies, to cut off the flow of weapons to Tehran. At a time when Iran was embroiled in a costly war with Iraq, it went even further by urging the Iraqi leader, Saddam Hussein, to pound Tehran mercilessly and pledging him US aid, despite warnings that Saddam was a ruthless tyrant. Early in his second term, Reagan denounced Iran (along with four other countries) as "the new international version of Murder, Incorporated" and declared that "the American people are not—I repeat, not—...going to tolerate...attacks from outlaw states run by the strangest collection of misfits, Looney Tunes and squalid criminals since the advent of the Third Reich."

Consequently, Americans reeled in shock when early in November 1986 they read in their morning newspapers that, for well over a year, the United States had been delivering scores of highly sophisticated TOWs (tube-launched, optically tracked, wire-guided antitank missiles) to Tehran in the expectation that the Iranians would arrange for the liberation of US hostages held captive in Lebanon by a Muslim group in Iran's orbit. The allegation of arms shipments first appeared in an obscure Lebanese periodical, *Al-Shiraa*, which further reported that National Security Adviser Bud McFarlane had flown to Tehran bearing gifts including a Bible inscribed by President Reagan and a chocolate cake shaped as a key to symbolize American eagerness for an opening to Iran.

The sordid saga of "Irangate" had begun early in Reagan's second term when a shady Iranian exile, Manucher Ghorbanifar, claimed that there were "moderate" elements in Tehran who, in return for the privilege of buying technologically advanced Western armaments, would persuade pro-Iranian terrorists in Lebanon to release seven American hostages, including CIA station chief William Buckley. In 1984, the CIA had circulated an unusual alert to federal officials that Ghorbanifar "should be regarded as an intelligence fabricator and a nuisance" after he failed three lie detector tests. But despite that powerful warning, both McFarlane and the CIA's William Casey took the bait. They endorsed a scheme authorizing Israel, which sought better relations with Iran, to sell a large quantity of arms from its arsenal that, surreptitiously, the United States would replenish.

In July 1985, from his bed in the Bethesda Naval Hospital where he was recovering from surgery, Reagan, anticipating a meeting with his national security adviser, wrote in his diary: "Some strange soundings are coming from the Iranians. Bud M. will be here tomorrow to talk about it. It could be a breakthrough on getting our 7 kidnap victims back." Though he would later claim that his only interest in an approach to Tehran was concern that Iran might fall into the Soviet sphere, he made no mention of that motive. In reality, the president was solely intent on rescuing the hostages. When he met with McFarlane the next day, he gave him the go-ahead on exploring back channels to Iran, but he was not yet ready to commit himself to an arms deal.

The matter came to a head at a top-level gathering on August 6 when McFarlane reported that the Israelis had assured him that an arms shipment to Iran would result in the liberation of a number of American hostages. Both the secretary of state and the secretary of defense vehemently opposed the deal. Shultz asked how the United States could justify arming a country that the Reagan administration had officially designated a State Sponsor of Terrorism, and he foresaw that if hostages were freed, the Hezbollah would only seize other Americans. Weinberger thought the proposal "almost too absurd to comment on," but he voiced his opposition anyway, very angrily. He regarded the transaction as "insanity," asking, "How could you send arms to the Ayatollah when he has sworn to destroy us?" Nonetheless, a few days later the president gave McFarlane his approval, and, on August 20, Israel sent Iran ninety-five TOWs, which the United States replaced. The ayatollah responded to the transfer by demanding hundreds more missiles, and in September Israel complied. Only a single hostage was freed. In November, Reagan, uncritically sanguine, entered in his diary, "We have an undercover thing going by way of an Iranian, which could get [the hostages] sprung momentarily."

At private quarters upstairs in the White House early in December, his top advisers upbraided the president. In his diary, Weinberger recorded: "President wants to free hostages—thinks [arms] would only go to 'Moderate Elements in Army' + would help overthrow Iranian gov't." The defense secretary continued: "I argued strongly that we have an Embargo that Makes Arms Sales to Iran illegal + President couldn't violate it + that 'washing' transaction thru Israel wouldn't make it legal." Weinberger further predicted that the scheme would leave the United States alone in the world because America was demonstrating its unreliability by "at the same time asking other countries not to make sales of weapons to Iran." Shultz, who once again objected that the conspiracy would "negate the whole policy" of not indulging in "deals with terrorists," cautioned that the plot could not be kept secret and that moderate elements in the Arab world would feel betrayed. Casey's deputy at the CIA chimed in by saying, "I was unaware of any moderates in Iran, that most of the moderates had been slaughtered by Khomeini, that whatever arms we give to these so-called moderates... will end up supporting the Khomeini regime." Reagan, though, would not be deterred, even after McFarlane's successor as national security adviser, Admiral John Poindexter, together with his flamboyant aide, Oliver North, reconfigured the arrangement to eliminate the Israelis and provide for direct American delivery of arms to the Iranian military.

In the spring of 1986, McFarlane, who, despite having resigned, remained Reagan's agent, flew to Tehran, where North had told him he was to meet with Khomeini and top Iranian officials. In entering a country that was a bitter enemy of the United States, the president's emissary had no assurance of safe conduct or indeed any guarantee that he would not himself become a hostage and be subjected to savage interrogation, especially since McFarlane knew more classified American secrets than anyone else on earth. An air force major general who had spent years in Tehran later recalled saying, "These people are Persians. You must be nuts; you are going into the heart of darkness." He warned of the risk they were taking: "We can't come and get you; Ronald Reagan can't come and get you." He concluded: "Everybody who went on that mission was crazy. Ollie was nuts for going on it; McFarlane was nuttier—he was the boss." North, who carried on as though he imagined himself to be the hero of a spy thriller, later revealed that they had further endangered themselves by traveling under pseudonyms with fake Irish passports.

Instead of the warm welcome that North had promised, McFarlane got a runaround. For three days, he was isolated at the former Hilton in Tehran and never got to see the ayatollah, the prime minister, or anyone else who mattered. The Iranian underlings he did encounter not only refused to pledge release of the hostages but expressed cold fury at being grossly overcharged for missiles by Ghorbanifar and other intermediaries. They also came up with a whole set of new demands, including the requirement that Israel free large numbers of Muslim prisoners. North wanted these ultimatums considered, but after three days of frustration, McFarlane had heard enough and pulled out. "I was too close to and fond of Ollie then," he later said, "to acknowledge that he had been deceiving Poindexter and the president, and now me." When he got back to Washington, he told Reagan, "You should know, Mr. President, that this is not working." They had started out on the assumption that "we were talking with Iranian politicians said to have a political agenda. It has ended up that we are talking to rug merchants." All communication with Iranians, McFarlane said, should be broken off.

Reagan, though, could not be disenthralled of the delusion that there were moderates in Iran who could be induced to intercede in freeing all of the American captives in Lebanon, and North, who was pursuing his own agenda, pandered to this fantasy. Even when two more US citizens were kidnapped, the president refused to reconsider. Right after they were snatched, North treated an Iranian contact to a private late-evening tour of the White House, including the Oval Office. In October 1986, only a few weeks before *Al-Shiraa* disclosed the operation, Reagan signed off on a new plan—to dispatch another cache of US weapons not to "moderates" but to the Revolutionary Guards, still without even a promise that the remaining hostages would be released. Furthermore, a congressional committee later concluded, North had "divulged to the Iranians classified material of particular sensitivity." After approving the sale of thousands of TOW missiles and hundreds of HAWK spare parts to Tehran, Reagan had wound up with just as many hostages still in captivity and the CIA bureau chief tortured and murdered.

The president responded to newspaper revelations of the chicanery with outright denial. When a battery of reporters fired questions at him, he told them to back off because the accounts had "no foundation." His government, he declared, had absolutely not "trafficked with terrorists" and "swapped...planeloads of American weapons for the return of American hostages." There had been a welter of dispatches about the United States sending arms and parts for combat aircraft to Iran, he said, but "not one of them is true." Furthermore, he maintained, congressional leaders had been kept fully informed of his dealings with Iran. Every one of these statements was fallacious.

He found it hard to contain his indignation. Asked by a CNN correspondent whether, as many were saying, Israel had been in league with the United States to provide Iran with weapons, he replied, "We...have had nothing to do with other countries or their shipment of arms." He angrily accused the media of endangering the lives of hostages by circulating "erroneous reports," stating bluntly: "Our government has a firm policy not to capitulate to terrorist demands. That no-concessions policy remains in force, in spite of the wildly speculative and false stories about arms for hostages and alleged ransom payments. We did not—repeat, did not—trade weapons or anything else for hostages." In a telephone tirade to a *Time* correspondent, Reagan ranted: "There is bitter bile in my throat these days. What is driving me up the wall is that this wasn't a failure until the press got a tip from that rag in Beirut and began to play it up."

On November 19, 1986, Secretary Shultz informed Reagan: "We have been deceived and lied to.... You have to watch out about saying no arms for hostages." Reagan retorted: "You're telling me things I don't know." Shultz replied: "Mister President, if I'm telling you something you don't know—and I don't know very much—something is wrong here.... Our credibility is shot. We've taken refuge in tricky technicalities of language to avoid confronting the reality that we lied to the American people. We have been dealing with some of the sleaziest international characters around." Reagan, though, still thought he could get away with dissembling.

At an ensuing press conference, the president continued to stonewall, even after Helen Thomas, the opening questioner, asked, "How would you assess the credibility of your own administration in the light of the prolonged deception of Congress and the public in...your secret dealings with Iran?" When other reporters echoed her inquiry, Reagan responded: "You've disappointed me....I don't feel I have anything to defend...at all....I don't think a mistake was made." He then told a number of untruths, claiming that everything sent to Tehran could be fitted into a single plane and denying any involvement by Israel. Since Chief of Staff Regan had already implicated Israel, the White House found it necessary that night to provide a bit of cover for the president by admitting that "a third country" had participated. Only when Ed Meese told Reagan that he needed to get his facts straight did Reagan agree to give his attorney general a weekend to sort out what had happened.

With Meese sniffing about and the bloodhounds of the press hot on their trail, Reagan's co-conspirators scurried to destroy and distort evidence. North set his secretary to retyping damaging materials and to inserting false chronologies in his archives. In addition, they engaged in a "shredding party" obliterating so many thousands of pages that they jammed the machine. In the pile were phone logs and a ledger book in which North had recorded payments. (A few days later, the national security chief and the head of the CIA testified falsely to congressional committees, and Admiral Poindexter opened his safe and got rid of its contents.) But North had to move so hastily that one critical document survived, and Meese found it.

On November 25, at a White House press conference, Reagan gave what the historian Sean Wilentz has called "the worst performance of his presidency if not his entire career." Grudgingly, Reagan maintained that "in one aspect" only had "implementation" of his Iranian policy been "seriously flawed." As a consequence of the discovery of this shortcoming, he continued, he had fired Colonel North, Admiral Poindexter had resigned, and he had appointed a three-man commission headed by former Texas senator John Tower to look further into the chain of events. After concluding his recitation from a prepared statement, the president fled the room, leaving Meese all alone to confront reporters. Drawing upon what he had unearthed in North's files, Meese then dropped a bombshell. Yes, he acknowledged, Reagan had dealt arms to Iran. Furthermore, profits from those sales had not been turned over to the US Treasury, as was required by federal statute but, despite the strict prohibition of the Boland amendments, had been diverted to the Contras for their insurrection against the government of Nicaragua.

This announcement touched off a feeding frenzy in the media and on Capitol Hill. The confession that the Reagan government had intervened in Central America was not in itself so startling. Little more than a month before, a Nicaraguan soldier firing a surface-to-air missile had shot down a transport plane carrying rocket grenades, a hundred thousand rounds of ammunition, and other military hardware. Four of the crew died, but the fifth, a cargo handler, refused to go down with the plane as he had been instructed to do and parachuted to safety. Questioned, this American soldier of fortune had revealed that he was on a CIA mission. Reagan, though, had escaped censure. Asked whether there was an association between the United States and the downed plane, he had replied, "Absolutely none.... There is no government connection ... at all." What made the Meese announcement so grievous was the linkage between Iran and Nicaragua. The conjunction, Meese later said, "took two controversial issues and put them together—like putting a match and a stick of dynamite together." At that moment, "Irangate" became "Iran-Contra."

Inquiries by the Tower Commission and a congressional committee exposed vividly Reagan's complicity in dispatching arms to Iran in order to ransom hostages. Investigators found that after a crucial White House conference, Defense Secretary Weinberger had recorded in his diary: "Met with President, Shultz, Poindexter, Bill Casey, Ed Meese, in Oval Office—President decided to go with Israeli-Iranian offer to release our 5 hostages in return for sales of 4000 TOWs to Iran by Israel—George Shultz + I opposed—Bill Casey, Ed Meese + VP [George Bush] favored—as did Poindexter." After deciding it would do no good to resign in protest, Weinberger ordered his chief military aide, Major General Colin Powell, who also thought that paying ransom was a bad idea, to replenish Israel's stock of TOWs from America's arsenal. Furthermore, examination of the archives turned up a "finding" that Reagan had signed in December 1985 retroactively approving three past transfers of weapons to Iran. Titled "Hostage Rescue—Middle East," it left no doubt that he was authorizing a swap of arms for captives. The document stated explicitly: "Because of the extreme sensitivity of these operations, . . . I direct the Director of Central Intelligence not to brief the Congress of the United States, as provided for in Section 501 of the National Security Act of 1947."

No longer could any informed person take seriously the notion that Reagan had approached Tehran solely, or even primarily, with the intent of parrying Russia or that he was unaware of the scheme. Reagan, it turned out, had written tersely in his diary, "I agreed to sell TOW's to Iran." He had further recorded: "Won't even write in this diary what we were up to." But he did not completely cover his tracks, for he referred to "our undercover effort to free our last 5 hostages" and noted, "Only a few in on it." The president, Colin Powell deduced, had a fixation on "almost a Hollywoodesque fading scene—everyone walking, hand in hand, into the sunset."

Evidence of Reagan's guilt in the diversion to the Contras of millions of dollars from the Iranian arms deal profits is less overwhelming. His operatives, though, had every reason to suppose they were carrying out his orders, especially after he instructed North that he wanted him to do whatever it took to maintain the Contras "body and soul." Shultz, while affirming that "the president signed on" to sending arms to Tehran, doubted that he knew about the diversion, but in his autobiography, *Under Fire*, North wrote, "Now, five years later, I am even more convinced *President Reagan knew everything* about the diversion of monies paid by the Iranian government to the Contras," and at his trial, Admiral Poindexter testified that Reagan was fully aware of the Iran-Contra conspiracy and had ordered him to destroy evidence, even though doing so broke the law. (Poindexter was one of nine Reagan officials who, following indictment, were convicted of offenses such as perjury or entered guilty pleas.)

The Tower Commission found it all but impossible to lasso Reagan. His testimony was so incoherent that some commentators wondered again whether he was suffering from early onset of Alzheimer's disease. In his first appearance before the commission, he stunned his aides by saying that he had been fully aware of the shipments of arms to Iran, something that they, to protect him, had been denying. On the eve of his return to testify a second time, they prepared him as though he were a particularly dense pupil. When on one occasion he was asked to clarify an inconsistency, he picked up the briefing memo they had given him and read out: "If the question comes up at the Tower board meeting, you might want to say that you were surprised." The president's White House counsel later wrote of this extraordinary blunder: "I was horrified, just horrified."

Reagan then sent a memo to the Tower Commission that was helpful neither to him nor to the board: "I don't remember, period. . . . I'm trying to recall events that happened eighteen months ago. I'm afraid that I let myself be influenced by others' recollections, not my own. . . . The only honest answer is to state that, try as I might, I cannot recall anything whatsoever about whether I approved an Israeli sale in advance or whether I approved replenishment of Israeli stocks. . . . My answer therefore and the simple truth is, 'I don't remember, period.'"

The commission saw no point in questioning him further. One of its three members, Edmund Muskie, who had been both US senator and secretary of state, remarked, "All the testimony we got from everybody was that the president was preoccupied with this goddamn problem every day. Every day in someone's presence he said, 'What's new on the hostages?'" All of the mountainous information about trading US weapons to Iran "comes to a president who is agonizing over this thing every day," reiterated Muskie, "and yet he can't remember anything about it. My God!" Congress was conducting its own investigation, but Senator William Cohen of Maine, a Republican, decided that it would be a "waste of time" to talk to Reagan because "with Ronald Reagan, no one is there."

As, day after day, the compilation of misdeeds added still more details, Reagan's version of events lost credence, and his denials made him the butt of stand-up comedians. The central question that had been asked about Nixon as the Watergate story unfolded had been "What did he know, and when did he know it?"; of Reagan, the inquiry was "What did he know, and when did he forget it?" A national survey found that only 14 percent of the nation believed that Reagan had not traded arms for hostages. In a feature article on November 25, the *New York Times* wrote that "President Reagan has been grievously damaged by the crisis over secret arms shipments to Iran," and a number of seasoned politicians in both parties "think the damage may be irreparable." It added: "In the

"It Didn't Happen." Herblock's cartoon of May 21, 1987, portrays Reagan as the Hollywood actor he once had been in a series of "takes" with a constantly changing line. Implied in the cartoon is the lack of credibility of the president's claims. *The Herb Block Foundation*

weeks to come, Mr. Reagan seems certain to find his credibility, his competence and his control under stern challenge."

Almost overnight, Reagan's public standing took a nosedive. As early as December 1987, a *New York Times*–CBS poll reported that approval of Reagan, at 80 percent in September, had dropped to 47 percent—the biggest decline in so short a period ever recorded. As the British historian Marcus Cunliffe observed, "President Reagan was...faced with a humiliating either/or. Either he connived at the goings-on, ... or Reagan was not told of their machinations. If he knew, he stood convicted of abominable judgment and perhaps worse. If he did not know, then he was not in control of his own White House." One of the country's most highly respected journalists, William Schneider, titled an article in

National Journal "Reagan Now Viewed as an Irrelevant President." A *New Republic* writer pronounced the "de facto end of the Reagan presidency"; David Broder titled a piece "The Unmaking of a President"; Lou Cannon in the *Washington Post* explained "Why the Band Has Stopped Playing for Ronald Reagan"; and even the country's most widely circulated conservative columnist wrote, "The reality ever more evident...is that the Reagan presidency is dead." Meese and other top officials feared that Reagan faced impeachment.

For three months, with millions of Americans starting each day reading about White House iniquities in their morning newspapers, Reagan spoke not a word to them. "For the first time in my life," he later recalled dumbfounded, "people didn't believe me." Frank Carlucci has related the toll that the ordeal took on Reagan: "When I became national security adviser, I found a very distracted president. It was hard for him to focus; he didn't seem to understand what was happening." Chief of Staff Howard Baker even contemplated invoking the Twenty-fifth Amendment to remove Reagan from office because he was disabled.

Through much of this period, the president refused to acknowledge that he had been arming the enemy, but the Tower Commission compelled him to face up to it. In February, its three members called at the White House and told him firmly that the evidence they had acquired was conclusive: his dealing with Iran was, transparently, an arms-for-hostages barter. Once again, Reagan denied it. But after he was told that at one critical point his agent delayed the flight of a plane from Israel to Iran until he was assured that hostages had been released, Reagan grudgingly said, "Yes, if the plane was waiting there to receive word on the hostages, the arms are loaded up, then it was arms for hostages."

While Reagan was in withdrawal, investigators issued reports. Whatever initiatives might have been taken by subordinates on their own, the Tower Board declared, "the primary responsibility for the formulation and implementation of national security policy falls on the president." Other judgments were considerably more pointed and much more caustic. A joint congressional committee blamed Reagan for encouraging a "cabal of zealots" who carried out an operation "characterized by pervasive dishonesty," and, after gaveling the investigation to a close, Senator Daniel Inouye, a World War II veteran decorated for heroism in battle, said of Iran-Contra: "It is a chilling story of deceit and duplicity and the arrogant disregard of the rule of law. It is a story of how a great nation betrayed the principles that made it great." Investigators were frustrated by being deprived of evidence that North and others had destroyed, by the death of Bill Casey, by the suicide attempt of Bud McFarlane, and by Reagan's befuddled testimony, but the independent counsel appointed by Meese concluded: "President Reagan created the conditions which made possible the crimes committed by others by his secret deviations from announced national policy as to Iran and hostages and by his open determination to keep the Contras together 'body and soul' despite a statutory ban on Contra aid."

Reagan, numbers of observers asserted, had been exposed as a dupe who had witlessly allowed himself to be fleeced by Iranians in a shell game. The United States, Secretary of State Shultz said bluntly, had been "taken to the cleaners." Critics emphasized, too, the deplorable implications of Reagan's gullibility. "The lesson to Iran was unmistakable," stated a congressional report. "All U.S. positions and principles were negotiable." Most important, experts maintained, were the consequences. The world's foremost authority on terrorism, Magnus Ranstorp of Sweden, wrote, "U.S. willingness to engage in concessions with Iran and the Hezbollah not only signaled to its adversaries that hostage-taking was an extremely useful instrument in exacting political and financial concessions from the West but also undermined any credibility of U.S. criticism of other states' deviation from the principles of no-negotiation and no-concession to terrorists and their demands."

On March 4, 1987, prodded by aides who warned him that he could not hide forever, Reagan finally broke his long silence. In a nighttime address from the Oval Office, he acknowledged:

A few months ago, I told the American people I did not trade arms for hostages. My heart and my best intentions still tell me that's true, but the facts and the evidence tell me it is not. As the Tower Board reported, what began as a strategic opening to Iran deteriorated, in its implementation, into trading arms for hostages. This runs counter to my own beliefs, to administration policy, and to the original strategy we had in mind.... It was a mistake.... It's clear from the Board's report ... that I let my personal concern for the hostages spill over into the geopolitical strategy of reaching out to Iran.

In the course of these remarks, he declared, "I take full responsibility for my actions and for those of my administration."

Reagan's acolytes praised this declaration as a statesmanlike assumption of blame, but it requires little parsing of the entirety of his message to recognize that he was foisting the onus on others, for the pivotal words in his speech are "as angry as I may be about activities undertaken without my knowledge" and "as disappointed as I may be in some who served me." In short, he was absolving himself; he had been betrayed by underlings. He was continuing to insist that the deal had been, from the very beginning, not a ransom offer but a "geopolitical strategy." He offered no explanation about the presidential findings he had signed or a word of apology to the members of Congress for persistently deceiving them. His "failure to recollect," he said, was the fault of his appointees to the National Security Council, fine fellows though they were, because "no one kept proper records."

His actions are even more telling. A week before he spoke, he discharged Chief of Staff Donald Regan, who joined Oliver North and Admiral Poindexter in being dumped overboard. "It's as if," said one critic, the president had "rummaged around in the White House and found the old Nixon playbook." Reagan had shown in what deep denial he was mired, though, when, in phoning North to tell him he was being dismissed, he informed the colonel, "You're an American hero" whose "work will make a great movie someday." (On hearing that sentiment, North, standing erect, saluted the telephone.) The most that the president would admit to, said one of his speechwriters, was "I didn't do it, and I'll never do it again." Even when, after his address, his poll numbers climbed, Reagan insisted that "it was as if Americans were forgiving me for something I hadn't done."

Though many analysts thought Iran-Contra a worse transgression than Watergate, Reagan escaped Nixon's fate. The revelation of siphoning funds to the Contras had an odd effect. On top of news of the shipments to Tehran, it should have worsened Reagan's situation. Instead, when the inquiry focused on how much he knew about the diversion, it took attention away from his much more heinous offense: sending arms to an enemy. In addition, centrist Democrats had muddied the waters by approving funding for the Contras in order to show their conservative constituents in the 1986 campaign that they were not soft on communism.

The Democratic leadership feared, too, that, if they succeeded in an impeachment effort, they would invite the accusation of losing two elections by large margins (1972 and 1984) and regaining power not through the expression of popular will at polling booths but by summarily ousting both Republican presidents before they could complete their tenure. Timing also worked in Reagan's favor. Unlike Watergate, which had taken place in Nixon's first term and peaked with most of his second term still left, the Iran-Contra investigation climaxed in the closing frame of Reagan's presidency. Democrats reasoned that Reagan could do little harm in the months left to him and that it was unwise to give their likely opponent in 1988, Vice President George Bush, the advantage of campaigning from the White House.

Important though these circumstances were, Reagan survived primarily because of the idiosyncratic attitude of the nation to his misdeeds. Pollsters found that though two-thirds of the American people thought Reagan was lying about his involvement in Iran-Contra, more than half gave him high marks for his performance as president. Even more curiously, he weathered the storm in good part because less than one-quarter of the American people believed that he was in charge of the government he headed; hence, he could not be blamed. The president prevailed, too, as a result of the country's unexpected response to the grilling of his most conspicuous agent.

Prosecutors reckoned that once they put Oliver North on the witness stand, they would get the goods on Reagan, but that is not how it turned out. Granted immunity, North not only admitted but bragged about lying, shredding documents, deceiving Congress, and falsifying records. He cut such a fine figure in his marine colonel's uniform decorated with two Silver Stars and a Purple Heart, though, and had such a disarming smile that millions of Americans who saw him on TV screens hailed him as a patriot being dogged by politicians. A *Newsweek* correspondent said of North, "He's Rocky, Rambo, Patton and the boy next door all wrapped up in one," and NBC's Tom Brokaw called North's testimony "the most popular soap opera on television." Senate staff had trouble finding room for all the bouquets that arrived for him; crowds outside the Senate chanted, "Ollie, Ollie, Ollie!"

With "Olliemania" sweeping the country, any remaining prospect of impeachment vanished, though a good many Americans continued to deplore Reagan's behavior and to view with scorn the tales that the president and his confederates were spinning. The *New York Daily News*, a mass-circulation tabloid disposed to be conservative, wrote: "People who believe more than 10 consecutive words of what Lt. Col. Oliver North swore to yesterday have a treat in store. Any morning now, they will see the Tooth Fairy leading the Easter Bunny down a garden path, gently, less they disturb the grazing unicorns.... Unless all those unicorns were blocking your view, it's just plain obvious how deeply, broadly, casually North was lying under oath." Nevertheless, at the end of his presidency, Reagan's approval rating was as high as it had been before *Al-Shiraa* published its exposé. It was as though Iran-Contra had never happened. The Teflon had not worn off after all.

To carry on "the Reagan Revolution," Republicans in 1988 picked the vice president, George Bush, who for eight years had been heir apparent. Few other presidential aspirants have ever been able to boast so outstanding a record of public service. The first Republican that Houston ever elected to Congress, he had been appointed ambassador to the United Nations, envoy to China, and director of the Central Intelligence Agency, and he could point out that for eight hours on July 13, 1985, in accordance with provisions of the Twenty-fifth Amendment, he had headed the executive office while Reagan underwent an operation under anesthesia. He had been, indeed, the first person designated acting president of the United States. He also commended himself to delegates at the GOP nominating convention by his fidelity to the party. As chair of the Republican National Committee, he had been one of Nixon's staunchest defenders against the Watergate allegations almost until the very end.

Bush's military record in World War II could not have been more stellar. He enlisted on the day he turned eighteen, only weeks after Pearl Harbor, making him the youngest aviator in the US Navy. He flew fifty-eight missions, completing 1,228 hours in the air. On one sortie, his plane was shot down, and he had to be rescued from the turbulent waters of the Pacific—the only one on the flight to survive. Undaunted, he returned to combat to fly cover over Iwo Jima and other perilous marine landings. At twenty-one, he came out of the conflict, his biographer Timothy

Naftali has written, "with a distinguished flying cross, two gold stars, and the ghosts of the friends he had lost in war."

He had the advantage, too, of a dual sectional background. A Texan who had ventured into the oil fields after the war and emerged a millionaire, he had been born in Connecticut, which sent his father, Prescott Bush, to the US Senate. At Yale, where George Bush was elected to Phi Beta Kappa, he had, as a southpaw first baseman, captained the team that played in the first College World Series. In the 1980s, he continued to vacation at the family compound in Kennebunkport, Maine. In sum, he was, in the words of his biographer Herbert Parmet, "a Lone Star Yankee," who could make a broad North-South appeal.

To extend the regional identity still farther, Bush chose as his running mate the junior senator from Indiana, J. Danforth Quayle. It was anticipated that the handsome midwesterner (one of Bush's advisers thought he looked like Robert Redford) would strengthen the ticket with younger voters, especially women. But it quickly became evident that Bush had made a poor choice. When reporters bludgeoned Quayle with a barrage of questions about why he had avoided combat in Vietnam by joining the Indiana National Guard, he conveyed a "deer in the headlights" response. Even his youthfulness backfired, for Quayle, who had the face of a kid in a high school yearbook photo, "looks twelve," a Republican activist said, and after "he got his hair cut one day...he looked ten." He seemed such a lightweight that in the comic strip *Doonesbury* Garry Trudeau depicted him not as a man but as a feather floating in air. Once the convention hubbub died down, Bush wrote in his diary, "It was my decision, and I blew it, but I'm not about to say that I blew it."

Quayle's callow demeanor contrasted particularly poorly with the gravitas projected by his Democratic counterpart—the self-possessed Texas senator Lloyd Bentsen. In the formal debate between the two vice presidential nominees, Quayle, exasperated by attacks on him as unqualified, said, "I have far more experience than many others that sought the office of vice president of this country. I have as much experience in the Congress as Jack Kennedy did when he sought the presidency." Bentsen countered with a devastating riposte. "Senator," he said to his younger colleague, "I served with Jack Kennedy. Jack Kennedy was a friend of mine. Senator, you are no Jack Kennedy." The audience burst into applause and shouts of approval. (Long afterward, foes guffawed at the apocryphal tale of what Quayle's bride had said to him on their wedding night: "I knew Jack Kennedy. Jack Kennedy was my friend. And, Senator, you're no Jack Kennedy.") In November, nearly 11 percent of voters who turned down Bush reported, on leaving polling booths, that they had cast their ballots for the Democratic nominee because they could not abide the thought that if something befell Bush, Quayle would become president of the United States.

Bush found the accusation that he had picked an associate who was not a real man especially troubling because the same charge was being leveled at him. His determination to be totally loyal to Reagan as vice president had opened him to the allegation that he had neither opinions nor will. A former Republican cabinet official stated, "George's problem is that he is a kind of political moon, who generates no light of his own," merely reflecting Reagan's sun as it brightened or dimmed. The columnist George Will had written that Bush could not emit more than the "tinny 'arf'" of a "lapdog" who was "panting" as he "traipses from one conservative gathering to another," and Doonesbury asked whether Bush had placed his "manhood in a blind trust." At the very start of his campaign, *Newsweek* titled a damaging cover story on Bush FIGHTING THE WIMP FACTOR. The aspersion "wimp" was altogether unfair to a man who had shown such conspicuous bravery as a fighter pilot in World War II, but that did not stop the Texas billionaire Ross Perot from telling Bush, "This world is full of lions and tigers and rabbits. And you're a rabbit."

Detractors merged the insinuation that Bush was a wimp with the contention that he was an elitist who should not be president because he lacked any understanding of the workaday lives of common folk. Son of a wealthy Wall Street investment banker, George Herbert Walker Bush, with a pedigree he could trace to Henry III of England, had been sent to posh Greenwich Country Day and Andover, and at Yale had been tapped by Skull and Bones, the exclusive secret society of bluebloods. Reagan had once called him a "Brooks Brothers Republican." Frequently, Bush's own language inadvertently betrayed him. Attempting to downplay the significance of his weak showing in an Iowa straw poll, he offered the explanation that numbers of his supporters "were at their daughters' coming-out parties," and he talked of someone's being "in deep doo-doo," a euphemism that typed him as prissy. His "white shoe" manner and his malapropisms led the down-home Democratic governor of Texas, Ann

Richards, to say that Bush "was born with a silver foot in his mouth" and one of her populist officials to gibe that Bush "was born on third base and thinks he hit a triple." Texas Democrats also scoffed at Bush's claim to a cross-sectional identity. Speaker Jim Wright said that this Connecticut scion was "the only Texan I know who eats lobster with his chili," and the tart-tongued columnist Molly Ivins wrote that "real Texans do not use summer as a verb . . . and do not wear blue slacks with little green whales all over them."

Bush's lame efforts to overcome these impressions and show that he was a regular guy backfired. He had been at his worst in the vice presidential debate of 1984 when he behaved swinishly toward Representative Geraldine Ferraro, an incident that continued to dog him four years later. He lost face with viewers, especially women, when he said to her condescendingly, "Let me help you with the difference, Mrs. Ferraro, between Iran and the embassy in Lebanon." (She retorted: "I almost resent, Vice President Bush, your patronizing attitude that you have to teach me about foreign policy.") On the New Jersey coast the next day, Bush made matters still worse by bragging to brawny longshoremen that he had "tried to kick a little ass last night." Though Bush had been attempting for decades to erase the impression that he was uppity, nothing seemed to work, not even, as one of his friends remarked, "going out and being a relative roughneck in the oil fields of Odessa." When he chowed down on pork rinds and taco salads or muscled an eighteen-wheeler around a truck stop, he was sneered at for putting on charades. In the late spring of 1988, Bush had the highest percentage of voters with an unfavorable view of him ever recorded for a major party presidential candidate, considerably worse than that in 1972 for George McGovern who had lost so badly.

Seeking to counter the impression that he was a milksop who could not be trusted by the Republican right, Bush, in his acceptance address, delivered lines intended to summon up Clint Eastwood's Dirty Harry snarling, "Make my day." Bush foresaw, he declared, that when he became president "the Congress will push me to raise taxes, and I'll say no. And they'll push, and I'll say no. And they'll push again, and [lifting a finger to his mouth] I'll say to them, 'Read my lips: no new taxes!'" In making this pledge, Bush was inviting future trouble for himself if he was elected, because, given the imperative need to subdue Reagan's

mounting deficits, tax rises were inevitable. Bush also sought to ingra-
tiate himself with right-wingers by endorsing capital punishment, prayer
in schools, and gun rights. To laugh away his critics, he added, "I'll try to
be fair to the other side. Tonight I'll try to hold my charisma in check."

To oppose Bush, Democrats placed their hopes on Michael Dukakis
of Massachusetts, whom the National Governors Association had designated America's most effective governor. He had been so successful
in reviving the economy of his state that journalists spoke of "the
Massachusetts miracle." Son of Greek immigrants from the Ottoman
Empire, he came from a background strikingly different from Bush's.
Observers had come to view him, though, not as a spokesman for newer
Americans but as the ultimate technocrat. At a time when "liberal" had
become a term of derision, his party hoped that this characterization
would blunt the usual Republican charge against a Democratic candidate. But at the Republican convention in New Orleans, Reagan declared: "The masquerade is over. It's time to use the dreaded L-word;
to say the policies of our opposition . . . are liberal, liberal, liberal."
Furthermore, Dukakis found that his reputation as a "functionary" had
the disadvantage of typing him as a colorless, soulless bureaucrat. The
governor, though, could not be tarred with any of the more deplored
features of Bush's vice presidential years: Lebanon, the stock market
crash, the savings and loan scandal, Iran-Contra. When at the Democratic
convention Ted Kennedy ran off a series of mishaps in the Reagan-Bush
administration, the delegates chanted in response, "Where was George?"
Dukakis came out of the convention with a seventeen-point lead.

The Bush team quickly closed that gap by adopting the shopworn
ploy of a vaudevillian whose act is flopping: wave the flag. The keynoter
at the Republican convention, Governor Thomas Kean, usually a man
of restraint, accused Democrats of "pastel patriotism." They "want to
weaken America," he alleged, "but they won't admit it." At the conclusion of his acceptance address, Bush highlighted this theme by asking all
of the delegates to rise and join him in "I pledge allegiance. . . ." On the
campaign trail, the vice president, standing at the gates of a flag factory
in New Jersey, questioned Dukakis's loyalty by denouncing him for
vetoing legislation mandating recital of the Pledge of Allegiance, though
the governor had done so only because he believed that requiring avowals
violated the First Amendment right to free speech. After this histrionic

excess, even one of Bush's closest advisers thought that the Republican nominee had gone "a flag too far," but the tactic was undeniably effective. When Dukakis attempted to counter by being photographed riding in an M-1 tank, he only succeeded in making himself look ridiculous. Dwarfed by his helmet and wearing a goofy smile, he was likened to Charlie Brown's dog, Snoopy.

In one of the very dirtiest campaigns of the twentieth century, Bush, who had been viewed as a laid-back moderate, carried on in a flagrantly mean-spirited way. At the outset, in a demagogic harangue, he fed red meat to five thousand shrieking, foot-stomping Texas Republicans by indicting his opponent for "crimes" and, pinning the wimp label on Dukakis, ascribed what he regarded as the governor's softness on defense to "foreign policy views born in Harvard Yard's boutique." He further accused his foe of being a "card-carrying" member of the American Civil Liberties Union, language insinuating that the governor was a Communist. Determined to take the low road, Bush unleashed his top political operative, Lee Atwater, as his attack dog. Even before Democrats chose their nominee, Atwater had said that "whoever it was, we had to paint him as a frostbelt liberal . . . not in tune with the values of . . . mainstream voters."

With Republicans under fire for Reagan's dreadful performance on the environment, Bush decided that the best defense was to take the offensive, even though that meant distorting the record. Television ads concocted by Atwater featured a photograph of a vile waterway. Not only was the image falsely labeled "Boston Harbor," but Bush blamed the pollution on Dukakis when, in fact, said the leading authority on the subject, the governor was an "unsung hero" for putting together an effective coalition to clean the port. To do so, he had been required to overcome opposition from the Reagan administration, which had fought him without a murmur of protest from the vice president.

Malicious though this disinformation was, it did not begin to match in malevolence the heinous racism that disfigured the Republican quest for the White House. The Bush cadre zeroed in on one William Horton, an incorrigible black felon who had been sentenced to spend the rest of his life in prison for the gruesome murder of a young filling station attendant but had nonetheless been given a weekend pass from a Massachusetts prison. While on leave, he had knifed and savagely beaten a man in Maryland and had mauled and raped the man's fiancée. Atwater said that to undo the "little bastard" Dukakis, he intended to "make Willie Horton his running mate." (Less than three years later, Atwater, stricken by a fatal disease that would cut short his life at an early age, apologized to Dukakis for his "naked cruelty.") While disassociating himself sanctimoniously from supporters who publicized mug shots of Horton that revealed him to be a black fiend, Bush, knowing full well that voters had been apprised of the killer's color, ran ads showing dark-visaged criminals sauntering out of jail through a turnstile thanks to Dukakis's "revolving-door prison policies." The country, he declared, needed "a president who is not going to...furlough a murderer so he can go out and rape and pillage again." Bush never acknowledged that Dukakis had inherited the leave arrangement from a Republican governor or that among the many other states that had instituted weekend passes was Reagan's California.

The critical moment in the campaign came in the last presidential debate when a CNN correspondent, testing Dukakis's commitment to opposing the death penalty, asked, "Governor, if Kitty Dukakis were raped and murdered, would you favor an irrevocable death penalty for the killer?" Instead of responding viscerally to that dreadful prospect, Dukakis delivered an emotionless disquisition, conveying the impression that even buttoned-up George Bush was more likeable. (Furthermore, Dukakis defended the release of a murderer as "rehabilitation," without explaining how a man jailed for life could be a reasonable candidate for "reintegration" into society.) After this episode, the outcome of the contest was no longer in doubt.

With 53.4 percent of the popular vote, Bush carried the Electoral College decisively, 426–111, which made him the first vice president to be elected directly to the presidency since Martin Van Buren in 1836. But the victory was not nearly so impressive as those numbers imply. In the lowest turnout since 1924, millions did not trouble to cast a ballot, and two-thirds of those who did wished they had been offered a choice between two different candidates. Furthermore, Democrats picked up seats in both houses of Congress, strengthening their dominance. The returns also revealed a stark "gender gap" that would continue to plague the Republicans in years to come. (Women voted against Bush, it was said jocularly, because he reminded every woman of her first husband.) For the third election in a row, however, the Democratic nominee had been thrashed, and writers remarked on the Republican "lock" on the Electoral College. Jubilant GOP leaders saw the 1988 victory as yet another affirmation of popular approval for Ronald Reagan, who had told Bush, "George, go out there and win one for the Gipper." Commentators agreed. The smiling prestidigitator in the White House, they concluded, had contrived one final curtain call.

Long before Reagan died in 2004, he had ceased to be a participant in the American political arena, but he remained a powerful presence. In November 1994, he had released a letter to the American people announcing the onset of Alzheimer's disease with the poignant statement, "I now begin the journey that will lead me into the sunset of my life." Yet even as his memory of the eight White House years faded into oblivion, Republicans celebrated him for setting a standard against which each of his successors would be measured, and Democrats confessed to awe of his resilience. Despite Iran-Contra and all the other disasters of his second term, Reagan had left office with the highest public approval of any president since Franklin D. Roosevelt.

In a remarkably short time, he became a revered national icon. As early as 2003, a high peak in New Hampshire's White Mountains had been renamed Mount Reagan. States and cities hastened to put his name on courthouses and schools, and in the Marshall Islands the US Army conducted tests at the Ronald Reagan Missile Defense Site. Poles in the city of Krakow ceased to tell friends to meet them at "Central Square," because it had come to bear the appellation of the American president. When Americans flew into Washington, DC, they no longer landed at "National" Airport but at "Reagan."

Displaying what has been called "selective amnesia," conservatives, forgetting how recently they had denounced him for straying from economic orthodoxy and selling out to the Russians, all but deified him. Reagan, said his biographer Herbert Parmet, "could hike tax rates...and still be praised for opposing taxes. He could increase deficits...and win praise for fiscal responsibility." One right-wing faction launched a campaign to have a sculptor add his head to those of the four statesmen on Mount Rushmore. Even that goal was not great enough for the low-tax zealot Grover Norquist. Reagan, he said, deserved a mountaintop all his own in South Dakota, as well as his portrait on a denomination of US currency. "Reagan was the most successful president of the twentieth century," Norquist maintained. "He took a country that was in economic collapse and militarily in retreat around the globe and turned it completely around."

At the time of Reagan's death, even some liberal Democrats credited the ex-president with enormous achievements in foreign affairs, though some of their encomiums ought to be discounted as obeisance to the ancient maxim *De mortuis nil nisi bonum.* "He will be honored as the president who won the Cold War," said Ted Kennedy, and, in the midst of his presidential campaign, the Democratic senator from Massachusetts John Kerry chimed in: "Free men and women everywhere will forever remember and honor President Reagan's role in ending the Cold War.... Perhaps President Reagan's greatest monument isn't any building or any structure that bears his name, but it is the absence of the Berlin Wall."

Reagan's admirers claimed that he had devised an ingenious foreign policy strategy and had carried it out brilliantly. By a gargantuan acceleration of military spending and by raising the fearsome threat of Star Wars, he had, they contended, lured the Kremlin into a hyperexpensive arms race that had bankrupted the Soviet Union, sped its disintegration, and left it no choice save to capitulate to the West. In her eulogy, Margaret Thatcher said of Reagan:

> Others hoped, at best, for an uneasy cohabitation with the Soviet Union: he won the Cold War—not only without firing a shot, but also by inviting enemies out of their fortress and turning them into friends.... Yes, he did not shrink from denouncing Moscow's "evil empire." But he realized that a man of good will might nonetheless emerge from within its dark corridors. So the President resisted Soviet expansion and pressed down on Soviet weakness at every point until the day came when communism began to collapse beneath the combined weight of these pressures and its own failures. And when a man of good will did emerge from the ruins, President Reagan stepped forward to shake his hand and to offer sincere cooperation.

The president's disciples found it necessary to explain how a man so ill informed could be capable of such an earthshaking achievement. "He knows so little," said a national security adviser, "yet accomplishes so much." The answer to the riddle, concluded a number of writers, was that Reagan had a vision that far better informed political leaders lacked. "Some of Reagan's beliefs were as extravagant as the science fiction that was occasionally their inspiration," observed Lou Cannon, "but he had a sense of the world as it would be and as it might be, not merely of the way it was." Reagan offered his own assessment in his farewell address of January 1989. "We meant to change a nation, and, instead, we changed a world," he claimed. "All in all, not bad, not bad at all."

One striking tribute came from an altogether unexpected source: the former deputy Soviet foreign minister. Alexander Bessmertnykh reported: "Reagan handled negotiations very, very well. He might not have known all the details. He used little cards when he would come to details.... He would try to rush through this formal part, and then he would throw away the cards, and... he would start talking the direct way. I was across the table at all the summits and followed the president for all those years, and I personally admired the man every much.... If it were not for Reagan, I don't think we would have been able to reach the agreements in arms control that we reached... because of his idealism, because he thought we should really do away with nuclear weapons."

Reagan won applause, too, for lifting the economy out of the morass of the Carter period. Sixty months of growth starting in 1983 yielded nearly fifteen million new jobs, with unemployment dropping from more than 7 percent to 5.5 percent. During this upsurge, the gross domestic product rose by nearly one quarter, and the prime interest rate dropped from more than 15 percent to 9.3 percent. Inflation fell from above 12 percent when Carter left office to below 5 percent, with price stability a boon especially to pensioners on fixed incomes.

Historians, however, sharply disputed these highly favorable evaluations. In their first assessment, they ranked Reagan "below average," with 18 percent dismissing him as an outright failure. Eighty-five percent viewed him as, to some degree, racist. Subsequently, he rose several notches in these surveys, but scholars continued to believe that the public greatly overrated him. Analysts scoffed at the notion that Reagan had created an economic miracle. They pointed out that in the six years following the end of the recession in Reagan's first term, the US economy grew 8 percent, far less than it had in a five-year period in the maligned

Ford-Carter era when it had gained 31 percent. They also stressed how much ground was lost in international competition. The United States, which as recently as the mid-1970s had turned out 80 percent of the TV sets in American homes, accounted for only 10 percent when Reagan stepped down. In that same brief period, the US share of the world's steel output fell more than half. In Reagan's final year in office, Japan moved past the United States as the world's greatest industrial power per capita. To the consternation of supply-side theorists, personal savings averaged less in the 1980s than in the allegedly sluggish 1970s, and private investment slumped. Economists acknowledged that inflation had diminished, but they attributed that improvement to Volcker, who had been appointed by Jimmy Carter, and to the virtual collapse of OPEC as the result of a worldwide energy glut. They also demonstrated that Reagan's insistence on scaling down federal supervision had taken a heavy toll, with the lax monitoring of the savings and loans industry costing the American taxpayer hundreds of billions of dollars. "Overall," wrote Cannon, "Reagan left a ruinous regulatory legacy."

On Reagan's watch, too, the United States, the world's largest creditor nation, became the world's biggest debtor. In 1980, at the worst of the Carter downturn, the United States still boasted a decidedly favorable trade balance, but in 1985, Reagan's Department of Commerce announced that the country had become a debtor nation for the first time since 1914 and required transfusions of loans from abroad to keep going. A red-white-and-blue patriot, Reagan never grasped that his policies had turned the United States into a country that depended on the kindness of strangers.

Not a Democratic activist but a former Republican chief executive rendered judgment on another serious shortcoming. In his 1981 inaugural address, Reagan stated: "You and I, as individuals, can, by borrowing, live beyond our means, but only for a limited time. Why, then, should we think that, collectively, as a nation, we're not bound by the same limitation?" However, Gerald Ford later pointed out: "In eight years, President Reagan never submitted a balanced budget—never to the Congress and never to the American people. . . . So the Reagan action on the federal budget does not get high marks. I was personally disappointed in the administration's budgetary record."

Under Reagan, the national debt tripled, reaching the highest point in US history as it rose from some $900 billion in 1980 to nearly $3 trillion in 1989. When his presidency began, the national debt was 33 percent of GDP; when he left, it comprised 53 percent. In eight years, he piled up more debt than had all of his predecessors combined. In 1984, the Congressional Budget Office reported that soaring interest costs from Reagan's deficit exceeded the sum of his cuts in federal spending. At the end of the Reagan era, Americans were stuck with paying $200 billion every year in interest on the national debt. If the tax cuts of 1981 had not been partly revoked, the country would have been drowning in even more red ink. "Reagan," said a writer in the *New Republic*, "did to the government's finances what the iceberg did to the *Titanic*."

Contrary to his pledges, Reagan did not lessen the tax burden, which was as great when he left office as when he began, but he did redistribute income—upward, with an eightfold increase in millionaires. During his presidency, the income of the wealthiest fifth of the nation improved 19 percent, while that of the lowest fifth dropped by nearly 12 percent, as the wages of workers and the income of the middle class stagnated. Though taxes abated for the rich, they rose for lower-income and middle-class Americans. The less advantaged paid more both because of the hike in Social Security obligations and because state and local levies had increased to make up for the gutting of Great Society programs—a brutal action that spurred the columnist David Broder to write of the "moral meanness" of the Reagan administration. Under Reagan, thirty-three million Americans struggled below the poverty line. At the end of his presidency, one out of five children—fully half of all black children—lived in poverty, many thousands more than when he took office. When he stepped down, an American-born child was two to three times more likely to be impoverished than one born in Canada.

Despite these stark manifestations of a shift rightward, however, a number of scholars rejected the "Reagan Revolution" rubric. "Conservatives did not achieve most of their major goals, not even a reduction in the size of government," observed Reagan's biographer William Pemberton, for the two-term presidency left most of FDR's New Deal programs "untouched." The conservative chair of the Council of Economic Advisers under Nixon, Herbert Stein, remarked: "There was ... this difference between the Roosevelt revolution and the Reagan would-be revolution. The Roosevelt revolution was incorporated in statutes, programs and agencies that were not subject to annual reconsideration and that developed constituencies—bureaucracies and beneficiaries—that resisted counterrevolution. The Reagan changes were changes in numbers, mainly budget numbers, that are the subject of redetermination every year. They would not have the lasting effect that the Roosevelt changes had."

Although Reagan had promised to "put federal employment on a diet," the government workforce swelled by two hundred thousand during his reign, growing faster than it had under Carter. He had also pledged to eliminate the Departments of Education and of Energy, but both continued to thrive, and he added another: a Department of Veterans Affairs. Subsidies to agriculture nearly tripled. Indeed, federal spending took a larger bite out of GNP in the Reagan years than under any other president serving in peacetime in the nation's history.

Social conservatives, exultant when Reagan was elected, reaped little benefit. He advocated legislation banning "abortion on demand," which he called a "national tragedy," favored tuition tax credits to enable children to attend private and church schools that frequently buttressed Jim Crow, and promoted a constitutional amendment to reinstitute prayer in public schools. But he did not work effectively to achieve any of those goals. He vowed to overturn *Roe v. Wade*, which he likened to *Dred Scott*, but in 1986, in *Thornburgh v. American College of Obstetricians and Gynecologists*, the Supreme Court reaffirmed it. Republican legislators, who owed a large debt to Christian fundamentalists, introduced twenty-one bills authorizing school prayer and thirty-one limiting abortions, but none was enacted. "Teenagers were urged to remain chaste, ghetto youth to 'just say no to drugs,' and everyone cautioned to be monogamous and heterosexual to avoid disease," noted the historian Michael Schaller. "The result, not surprisingly, was a surge in the teenage pregnancy rate, a drug scourge among poor and minority youth, and the rapid spread of AIDS."

Historians and policymakers also punched holes in Reagan's record on foreign affairs. In particular, they skewered the conceit that Reagan had brought about the disintegration of the Soviet Union by drawing it into an arms race it could not afford. In fact, they demonstrated, Russia had never tried to match the United States on Star Wars; it was spending no more for arms in 1986 than it had in 1980. (Meantime, the United States squandered nearly $26 billion on Star Wars that never came close to being deployed.) Nor, they found, did evidence sustain the claim that Reagan had caused a turnaround in Soviet foreign policy, for the change of mind that led to the end of the Cold War had arisen largely from forces within the USSR. Reagan had far less influence on the Kremlin's reconsiderations than did recoil from the disastrous Afghanistan war and consumer discontent over deprivations because the Russian army was devouring a grossly disproportionate share of resources. In fact, Reagan's blustering, his military buildup, and his obsession with Star Wars made it more difficult for Gorbachev to overcome hard-liners in the Kremlin. When the Berlin Wall fell, a *USA Today* poll found that in Germany, only 2 percent credited Reagan. Even if one did assign a large role to the United States, it was not clear that Reagan, who came at the climax of decades of containment, was primarily responsible. "I feel very strongly," said Gerald Ford, "that our country's policies, starting with Harry Truman and those who followed him—Democratic and Republican presidents and Democratic and Republican Congresses—brought about the collapse of the Soviet Union."

In neither the foreign nor domestic realm has anything proved more devastating to Reagan's reputation than Iran-Contra. His admirers had always said that, however deficient he was in knowledge of details, he was a "big picture" leader. But on Irangate, he wholly failed to comprehend the most basic truth: that a nation does not trade arms for hostages, especially to a country it regards as irredeemable. Worse still, Reagan, knowing full well what he was doing, had fostered a rogue regime within the White House. Over many months of duplicity, he and they violated so many laws, showed such brazen contempt for Congress, and carried out such unconscionable obstruction of justice that the House and Senate would have been fully justified in impeaching the president and removing him from office, as well as jailing his confederates.

Yet even biographers who eschewed the "Reagan Revolution" designation, who refuted the claim that Reagan had ended the Cold War, and who deplored his role in Iran-Contra thought he mattered. "If greatness in a president is measured in terms of affecting the temper of the times, whether you like it or not, Reagan stands second to none among the presidents of the second half of the twentieth century," Cannon maintained.

Reagan, Pemberton agreed, "was a president of consequence. He moved the nation's political center to the right and changed the nature of Washington's 'policy talk' by ushering in an age of diminished expectations in people's attitude toward government."

Toward the end of the president's first term, the *New York Times* correspondent David Rosenbaum wrote: "More than any other President in more than fifty years, Ronald Reagan has changed the terms of the national debate over domestic policy.... The debate over the last four years has been over which Federal aid programs to cut rather than which to expand, over which civil rights rules to limit rather than which to enlarge, and over which natural resources to develop rather than which to protect." Concurring regretfully, the ardent liberal Robert Reich reached a similar judgment. "Reagan has presided over a triumph of ideas," he acknowledged. The Republicans had "shifted the burden of truth onto government." Furthermore, though Reagan did not intend to create huge deficits in order to hamper future presidents, his policies had that effect. A *New York Times* writer concluded: "His Presidency has made it perilous for any politician to propose new programs without specifying how to pay for them."

Washington correspondent David Shribman placed the former president in a world context, observing: "Mr. Reagan's winning the White House in 1980 made him the foremost symbol of the great global shift rightward in the final quarter of the 20th century. Deng Xiaoping moved China toward capitalism. John Paul II reasserted papal authority. Mr. Reagan's friend Margaret Thatcher reinvigorated Britain's Conservative Party. And Mr. Reagan's onetime adversary and eventual friend Mikhail Gorbachev brought glasnost and perestroika to the Soviet Union. But none of them so caught the public imagination, either here or abroad, as Mr. Reagan."

The historian John Gaddis has highlighted "the unexpected Ronald Reagan." Characterized as a right-wing ideologue, Reagan frequently showed surprising adaptability—in agreeing to "revenue enhancements," in appointing an African American and a woman to his cabinet, in nominating Sandra Day O'Connor, in bargaining with congressional Democrats. He especially startled the country and the world by his turnabout on Russian policy. Though he greatly exacerbated relations with Moscow in his first term, he had the good sense, after a time, to recognize that Gorbachev was a man with whom he could negotiate a pact on nuclear weapons. The historian Sean Wilentz, who made a point of announcing that he had voted against Reagan both times, nonetheless asserted: "Reagan deserves posterity's honor...for knowing when to transcend and, finally, reject outdated and counterproductive ideas regarding nuclear warfare and the Soviet Union—...arguably the greatest single presidential achievement since 1945."

Above all, journalists and scholars agreed, the country, thanks to Reagan, no longer thought the office of the presidency imperiled. He had proven by his response to the walkout of the air traffic controllers to be a decisive leader and by his success with getting measures such as the tax cut through Congress to be an effective chief legislator. The columnist Richard Reeves maintained: "Reagan had come into the Oval Office at a time when the man in it...was declaring political bankruptcy and important voices outside it, in the press and the academy, were decrying the end of leadership. They were wrong. The new President made the system work. The leader was an extraordinary man."

One might object that the presidency had never been as endangered as the gloomsayers alleged, but there was no denying that the mood of the 1980s was decidedly more buoyant than it had been. In a 1986 cover story in the *New York Times Magazine*, "The Reagan Legacy," Bernard Weinraub wrote: "His impact, like Franklin D. Roosevelt's, rests in large part on restoring the primacy of the Presidency as an institution after nearly two decades of White House disarray marked by Vietnam, Watergate and the hostages in Iran." The political scientist Richard Neustadt, author of the most influential book on the presidency, recapitulated this consensus. Reagan, he maintained, "restored the public image of the office to a fair...approximation of its Rooseveltian mold: a place of popularity, influence, and initiative, a source of programmatic and symbolic leadership, both pacesetter and tonesetter, the nation's voice to both the world and to us, and—like or hate the policies—a presence many of us loved to see as Chief of State."

No matter how unimpressive in managing the government, Reagan had few peers as head of state. A 2009 poll of historians placed him in the lower depths of presidents as an administrator (in thirtieth place) but in the third spot as a persuader. The historian Chester Pach, a biographer of Dwight Eisenhower, observed: "In many ways, Reagan was far more ordinary than he was exceptional. He possessed only modest intellectual gifts, and he used them indifferently. What impressed more was his smile, sincerity, and soothing rhetoric," talents he brought to Washington from Hollywood. "Whether or not people approved of his policies," concluded the historian Lewis Gould, "they responded to his optimism and unabashed patriotism in a manner that made him seem a Republican counterpart to his own political idol, Franklin D. Roosevelt."

"Ronald Reagan," said *Time* during his presidency, "has a genius for American occasions." During his 1982 State of the Union address, Reagan, standing in the well of the House, pointed up toward a young man he had placed in the balcony, Lenny Skutnik, who had plunged into the frigid Potomac to save a passenger from a jet that had crashed into the river, and ever since, his successors have been looking for "Skutniks" to trot out on the night of the State of the Union. In 1984, he thrilled the nation by his address in France on the fortieth anniversary of D-Day when he told veterans of the invasion—those incredibly brave Rangers who had scaled cliffs under fierce Nazi gunfire— "Gentlemen, I look at you and I think of the words of Stephen Spender's poem. You are men who ... 'left the vivid air signed with your honor.'" Governor Mario Cuomo of New York, a liberal Democrat, said of Reagan: "His personal conduct, when he's shot, when he's told he has cancer, when he goes to Normandy—the way he's comported himself has been a moral instruction to my children."

Reagan's finest hour as a speaker came in response to a horrifying event in January 1986: the explosion shortly after takeoff of the space shuttle *Challenger*, killing all seven aboard—one of them a schoolteacher, Christa McAuliffe—a shocking tragedy that millions of pupils in classrooms witnessed on television screens. That night, from the Oval Office, the president directed his first words to the children: "I know it's hard to understand, but sometimes painful things like this happen. It's all part of the process of exploration and discovery. It's all part of taking a chance and expanding man's horizons. The future doesn't belong to the fainthearted. It belongs to the brave. The *Challenger* crew was pulling us into the future, and we'll continue to follow them." He concluded, addressing all the nation, with an allusion to a poem written by an American pilot who died at nineteen while flying for the Royal Canadian Air Force. He said of the *Challenger* crew: "We will never forget them nor the last time we saw them—this morning—as they prepared for their journey and waved good-bye, and slipped the surly bonds of Earth to touch the face of God."

Americans' response to his eight years in the White House suggests that there is a lot more to being president than policymaking and enforcement of statutes. He contributed nothing at all to the literature of statecraft, offered false reassurance of the sort peddled by patent medicine salesmen, and "too often," as the eminent political scientist Stephen Skowronek remarked, spouted "mawkish truisms." Yet he also knew how to inspirit the nation. In a 1986 address, he affirmed: "In this land of dreams fulfilled where greater dreams may be imagined, nothing is impossible, no victory is beyond our reach, no glory will ever be too great.... The world's hopes rest with America's future.... Our work will pale before the greatness of America's champions in the twenty-first century."

In his farewell address of January 1989, Reagan offered an accounting of his presidency and his legacy. He declared:

> The past few days when I've been at the window upstairs, I've thought a bit of the shining "city upon a hill." ...
>
> And how stands the city on this winter night? More prosperous, more secure and happier than it was eight years ago. But more than that: after 200 years, two centuries, she still stands strong and true on the granite ridge....
>
> My friends, we did it. We...made a difference. We made the city stronger—we made the city freer.

And in his very last message to the American people, informing them that he was drifting into a private exile of forgetfulness, Reagan made sure to add: "I know that for America there will always be a bright dawn ahead."

12

George H. W. Bush

ON TAKING OFFICE IN JANUARY 1989, George Bush faced a number of formidable challenges. By far the most important was demonstrating that he was not a pallid duplication of Ronald Reagan. To establish his own identity, he had both to separate himself from the former president and to articulate his own conception of governance. He also needed to persuade the country that he was not as vicious as he had been in the campaign but was really a good guy. "Having been nasty," the *New Yorker's* Hendrik Hertzberg commented, "Bush now has no choice but to be nice." Finally, he was obliged to reach out to the Democrats, for Bush was only the third president in two centuries to be inaugurated for the first time with both houses of Congress controlled by the opposition party.

Bush did not wait to be sworn in to distinguish himself from his predecessor. Immediately after his victory in November, he announced: "I'm going to be a shake-me and wake-me president. I will personally read the Daily Intelligence Briefing every morning." (It was an extraordinary comment on the character of the Reagan presidency that Bush felt the need to pledge to do something that the American people should have been able to take for granted.) Reagan's admirers bristled at such remarks. The right-wing publicist William Kristol, who was Quayle's chief of staff, expressed resentment that "a lot of Bushies were saying, 'Bush isn't like Reagan. He stays awake in meetings.'" Irritated by "the Bushies," they even rummaged through the new chief executive's vapid rhetoric for evidence of disloyalty. Nancy Reagan was visibly angered when, in his inaugural address, Bush stated that "a new breeze is blowing," pledged "a new engagement in the lives of others," and vowed "new activism."

If the Reaganites sometimes found offense when none may have been given, they did have reason to believe that Bush used symbolic behavior to signal change. In contrast to Reagan, who had appeared at his inauguration in formal attire, including waistcoat, Bush turned up in a plain business suit. To show that he was his own man and to offset the wimp aspersion, he took down the portrait that Reagan had placed in the Cabinet Room of the conservative Calvin Coolidge, who looked like Caspar Milquetoast, and replaced it with one of the virile and much more progressive Theodore Roosevelt. He also made a point of opening the doors of the White House to let thousands of visitors pour through on the first morning of his presidency. He was astonished by the turnout, with "people all over the darn place," who in freezing mid-January had "spent the night . . . literally in the cold, some of them . . . coming through the receiving line with their blankets." Nothing of that sort had been seen in Washington for eighty years. Bush's mode of governing, asserted the *Washington Post* approvingly, was "unscripted . . . a more free-wheeling, self-confident style than the choreographed Reagan."

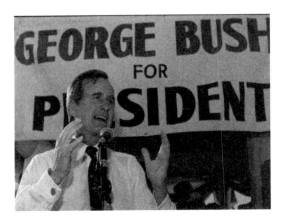

George Bush became widely known as George H. W. Bush only after his son George W. Bush became president, when it was necessary to distinguish the first in line from "Dubya." His casual dress in this campaign shot indicates his desire to be thought a regular guy, but he never shook off his image as a patrician. *Courtesy of the George Bush Presidential Library and Museum, ID HS369*

Not willing to settle for theatrics, Bush took decisive actions to put his stamp on his administration. During the interregnum, he had sent word that every Reagan appointee was to be out of his office, with his desk cleared, by January 20, and it was intimated that if these holdovers did not obey, their tax returns would be audited. He let it be known, too, that he was abandoning the Nicaraguan Contras and that he was ditching Star Wars as too expensive and impractical. Paraphrasing the title of a ballad from an earlier generation, the *New York Times* headed a story on the Bush White House "Reagan Doesn't Work Here Anymore."

In his inaugural address, Bush sought to counter the unsavory reputation he had acquired in the 1988 campaign by setting forth a goal: "to make kinder the face of the nation and gentler the face of the world." By implication, he was advocating a breakaway from Reagan's divisive politics. He drew the loudest applause when he said: "To my friends—and yes, I do mean friends—in the loyal opposition—and yes, I mean loyal: I put out my hand. I am putting out my hand to you, Mister Speaker. I am putting out my hand to you, Mister Majority Leader. This is the age of the offered hand. . . . The American people await action. They didn't send us here to bicker." Save for the prickly Reaganites, no one could find anything objectionable in the oration, but liberal critics responded to it warily. "That was a very nice inaugural address George Bush gave, as nice as nice could be," a *New Republic* columnist wrote sardonically. "It was nice to the Democrats, nice to the Russians, nice to the homeless, nice to kids and old folks. It was just incredibly nice. The new president's new breeze blew in off the West Front of the Capitol in the form of a great howling gale of niceness."

Skepticism and even derision stemmed from the gaping disjuncture in Bush's speech between the bountiful humanitarian sentiments he voiced and the porous remedies he proffered. He called attention to "the homeless, lost and roaming," to "children who have nothing, no love," and to "young women . . . who are about to become mothers of children they can't care for and might not love." But he no sooner expressed this sympathy than he declared: "The old solution, the old way, was to think that public money alone could end these problems. But we have learned that is not so. And in any case, our funds are low. . . . We have more will than wallet." Instead of White House initiatives, he proposed, in an eerie echo of Herbert Hoover, to "turn to the only resource we have that in times of need always grows—the goodness and the courage of the American people." Alluding to a metaphor he had first put forth in his acceptance address, he called for a myriad of community volunteers who would create "a thousand points of light...spread like stars throughout the nation, doing good." That was an attractive image, but, critics said, it did not conceal a blunt reality: George Bush had come to office with no agenda of his own.

The address also exposed how much difficulty Bush had in marshaling his thoughts. Listeners at the inauguration ceremony were hard put to figure out what the new president had in mind when he declared, "I don't seek a window on men's souls." With no strong sense of mission or coherent conception of public policy, Bush was plagued throughout his tenure by his inability to communicate cogently what he called "the mission thing." Sometimes when he nattered, he said the exact opposite of what he intended. He never showed a sign of hostility toward Jews, but his command of language was so poor that, when seeking to express a noble sentiment, he was capable of saying, "I stand for anti-bigotry, anti-Semitism, and anti-racism."

Journalists jeered at his mangled syntax and his fragmented sentences. At one point, he maundered: "You cannot be president of the United States if you don't have faith. Remember Lincoln going to his knees in time of trial and the Civil War and all that stuff. You can't be. So don't feel sorry for—don't cry for me, Argentina." A few weeks after lifting that line from *Evita*, he remarked: "Somebody asked me what's it take to win. I said to them, I can't remember, what does it take to win the Superbowl? Or maybe Steinbrenner, my friend George, will tell us what it takes for the Yankees to win...one run. But I went over to the Strawberry Festival this morning and ate a piece of shortcake over there—able to enjoy it right away, and once I completed it, I didn't have to be approved by Congress—I just went ahead and ate it."

The wit Russell Baker imagined how, if Bush instead of FDR had been elected president in 1932, he would have given the 1933 inaugural address:

So first of all let me assert my firm belief that anybody who thinks we ought to be in a stew about the fear thing—or even the fear-itself thing—has no place in this Administration. You hear about the hundred days, the hundred-days thing.

Well, my friends, there isn't going to be any hundred days, or any two hundred days, or any three hundred days, and I will say it as clearly as I know how: Read my lips—no three hundred days.

Because, my friends, what's the rush? Sure we've had some bad luck with the economy, with the G.N.P., the Depression thing, but we got through eight whole years of Ronald Reagan, and it didn't kill us, not even the Reagan thing, so maybe God, or, you know, the Deity thing, is on our side, so let's just go a little slow.

The president recognized his limitations. "Some wanted me to deliver fireside chats to explain things, as Franklin Roosevelt had done," he wrote later. "I am not good at that."

Bush magnified the confusion by earning an unwelcome reputation as a waffler—a man who had questioned capital punishment, then flipped 180 degrees on that important issue. His biographer Tom Wicker asked: "What's to be said for a man who swung all the way from pro-choice in 1980 to hard-line antiabortion in 1988?" Critics said that he was "elevating irresolution to an art form and inventing new ways of disconnecting political rhetoric from performance."

Nor did the comportment of the first lady suggest that she saw herself as a mover and shaker. When an interviewer awkwardly likened her to Eleanor Roosevelt, she retorted testily, "I wish you wouldn't say Eleanor. I grew up in a household that really detested her. She just irritated my mother." Nor did anyone ever mistake Barbara Bush for svelte Jacqueline Kennedy or Nancy Reagan. A matronly size fourteen, her hair prematurely white, wearing a three-strand necklace of faux pearls, she had no more interest in Paris couturiers than she did in policy wonks. The president, though, found her an asset because, as she said, there were "an awful lot of white haired, wrinkled ladies out there just tickled pink" with her and her ways. Her comical compilation *Millie's Book as Dictated to Barbara Bush*, which matched photographs of the family's springer spaniel with the First Dog's purported commentary, earned close to $800,000, which she turned over to a foundation promoting literacy.

Her benign grandmotherly image camouflaged an astringent personality and an unexpected shrewdness in public relations. She had a biting tongue. In 1984 she had said of the Democratic vice presidential nominee, Geraldine Ferraro, that the right word for her was "I can't say it but it rhymes with rich." Intimates found, too, that she made no attempt to conceal how much she loathed the Reagans. She became the focus of national controversy when Wellesley College invited her to speak at commencement, and students objected that she was an unsuitable role model: she had no avocation, had never held a job, and attracted media attention solely because she was married to an important man. But she won them over by arriving on campus with Raisa Gorbachev in tow and by remarking that "somewhere out in this audience may even be someone who will one day follow in my footsteps and preside over the White House as the president's spouse," adding, after a pause, "I wish *him* well."

Though Bush said he was reaching his hand out to the congressional leadership, he did not extend it very far. He put together a highly skilled team, but its main ambition appeared to be, in one political scientist's words, "to do nothing well." Moreover, he knew that what he did advocate—notably slashing the capital gains tax—formidable Democratic majorities would not even consider. The electorate that had sent him to the White House in 1988 left the Democrats with a 55–45 advantage in the Senate, a 251–183 superiority in the House. After departing office, Bush reflected: "It is a terrible burden to have the opposition party controlling both houses of Congress. . . . The president thinks he's elected to get certain things done his way. Then the reality hits you that every program you send up on domestic policy is declared by a hostile Congress 'dead on arrival,' and so the president is left singing from the other guy's sheet of music, dealing from the other fella's agenda."

His presidency had hardly begun when the Senate slapped him down. Rashly, he announced his choice of the Texan John Tower for the important post of secretary of defense, assuming that, as a former US senator, his nominee would be readily confirmed. In doing so, Bush ignored warning flags, for Tower was known to be a boozer, a boor, and a lecher. At that very moment, Nixon cautioned, Tower, a married man, was shacking up with a Chinese beauty. Furthermore, the president was told, the Democrats were eager for revenge, both because of Bush's demonizing during the campaign and because Tower had manhandled them when he chaired a Senate committee.

Bush persisted in attempting to ram his appointment through even after he was advised that it was doomed. The chairman of the Senate Armed Services Committee, the highly respected Sam Nunn of Georgia, was unimpressed by Tower's claim that though he did drink a lot, he always sobered up by morning. Nothing damaged Tower's chances of approval more than Nunn's statement: "I cannot in good conscience vote to put an individual at the top of the chain of command when his history of excessive drinking is such that he would not be selected to command a missile wing, a bomber squadron, or a Trident missile submarine." By rejecting his choice, the Senate gave Bush a humiliating drubbing, for it had long been taken for granted that a new president has the right to choose his own associates. Never before had a first-term cabinet nomination been turned down. In his *New York Times* column, Wicker concluded: "Bush...had lost political 'face' and some degree of respect for his political muscle and judgment. Every president needs to look strong on taking office and...Bush came near flunking that test."

With his first choice rejected, the president filled the post of secretary of defense with Wyoming's Dick Cheney, who, said Colin Powell, was "tough as nails"—the same characterization applied to White House Chief of Staff John Sununu, a former governor of New Hampshire. Both in his campaigns and in running the government, Bush, while showing the world his genial persona, made sure that his principal aides were men the media called "pit bulls." Sununu made a specialty of showing his contempt for Congress. At a meeting in 1990, he lectured senators and representatives while reading a newspaper, feet hoisted on his desk. "Let me give you a piece of advice," the powerful Appropriations Committee chairman, Senator Robert Byrd, told him in barely controlled fury. "You are [one of] the king's men. Right now the king is riding very high. But six months from now,...when the economy is in a nosedive and unemployment is rocketing, you boys will be back here begging for our help. Don't ever forget that."

Bush's relations with Congress suggested not hands across the aisle but prolonged siege. The president, who, with small ambition and stout Democratic resistance, found it hard to make things happen, often settled for stopping things from happening. Forty-four times he vetoed bills, some of them of considerable significance. He killed measures to raise the minimum wage, to extend unemployment insurance at a time when the ranks of the jobless were growing, and to require corporations to grant unpaid leave to employees who needed to care for newborn or ill children. He drew criticism, too, by vetoing a civil rights measure, which he called a "quota" bill. Just once was he overridden. The result was four years of gridlock, only occasionally mitigated.

Ten of Bush's vetoes halted attempts by Democrats to make abortion more accessible. Since both his father, Senator Prescott Bush, and his wife favored "freedom of choice," and the Bushes had written checks to Planned Parenthood, it was unlikely that the president felt passionate about "right to life." But he knew that he had to convince Republican fundamentalists that he shared their beliefs. Consequently, he even struck down legislation to permit victims of rape or incest to terminate pregnancy.

The president also earned points with the right wing of his party by continuing to exploit flag desecration. He recognized that this was one matter on which he could prevail because, having seen Dukakis mauled for his civil libertarian stance, Democratic lawmakers were not going to be depicted as irreverent toward Old Glory. After the Supreme Court ruled in *Texas v. Johnson* (1989) that flag burning was a protected form of freedom of speech, Democratic senators scurried to join Republicans in adopting the Flag Protection Act of 1989. When the Court invalidated that law as well in *United States v. Eichman* (1990), it permitted Bush to rekindle his campaign, but with no effect.

In the few instances where Bush did associate himself with progressive measures, he fared best when he latched on to a proposal that Democrats had moved far along, as he did with aid to the handicapped. Despite his commitment to reducing the role of government, Bush gave stout backing to adoption of the Americans with Disabilities Act of 1990 over the objections of numbers of fellow Republicans who contended that it burdened small businessmen and represented overreaching by the nanny state. He may have had a personal reason for breaking with the right on this issue because one of his sons was dyslexic and, friends said, had been picked on in school.

He departed from conservatives once again in getting behind the Clean Air Act Amendments of 1990, whose enactment, the historian John Robert Greene has written, "shows George Bush at his policy-making best and was clearly the administration's most significant victory in the domestic sphere." The much-improved Clean Air Act imposed pollution controls on toxic factory emissions and tailpipe exhausts, reduced acid rain by half, and did nearly as well in lowering smog in cities. Infinitely more concerned about the environment than Reagan had been, Bush prosecuted Exxon for the disastrous *Valdez* oil spill, imposed a ten-year moratorium on offshore drilling, added 1.5 million acres to public lands, phased out asbestos, acted to safeguard the Grand Canyon, restored nearly 2 billion acres of wetlands, and created ninety-three wildlife refuges. The president also named the first professional to head the EPA, though the administrator found that he had to fend off repeated attempts by Sununu and Vice President Quayle to sabotage enforcement. Despite their interference, Bush compiled an admirable record in this field.

Bush's approach to policymaking has been encapsulated as "pursuing a relatively conservative agenda while maintaining credibility all the way across the center," but he tilted mostly to the right. On the environment, the president strayed to the liberal segment of the spectrum. But on most issues he settled in the conservative sector. He aspired, he said, to be "an educational president," but the superficial changes he advocated amounted, as Greene concluded, to "reform on the cheap." When his term ended, he had little in the domestic sphere to which he could point with pride.

He left a much deeper imprint on the judiciary than on Capitol Hill. Having lucked into a great many vacancies, he was able to fill one-quarter of the seats on lower federal courts and to make two appointments to the US Supreme Court. He sought nominees of a conservative persuasion, but in one conspicuous instance he failed. At the urging of Sununu, he picked another New Hampshire man, David Souter, for the first opening on the Court, but Souter disappointed right-wingers by proving to be much more moderate than they had anticipated.

To appease conservatives, the president elevated to the Supreme Court a federal judge of very limited experience and extreme views. Not even the most right-wing member of the Rehnquist Court came close to sharing the convictions of Clarence Thomas, who later maintained that more than a half century of jurisprudence ought to be wiped out and the country should return to the deplored heyday of the Four Horsemen. As head of the Equal Employment Opportunity Commission, Thomas, an African American, had demonstrated his hostility to affirmative action for blacks and for women. Though commentators called Thomas a dreadful choice, Bush made himself look foolish by insisting that his nominee was the best-qualified jurist in America. Bush's appointee as attorney general, Richard Thornburgh, later said: "I was there and I kind of did a double take.... It was not a terribly credible statement." Not one lawyer on a fifteen-member American Bar Association committee ranked Thomas as "well qualified"; two rated him "unqualified." The appointment ran into even more serious trouble when a black law professor, Anita Hill, charged Thomas with sexual harassment. After an ugly debate, Thomas won confirmation, but barely, 52–48, with the controversy further alienating women voters from the GOP. Only one satisfaction could Bush conceivably derive from saddling the country with Thomas for decades to come: he might possibly have bought himself a bit of tolerance from conservatives for initiatives in foreign policy he was undertaking that departed from hard-line orthodoxy.

George Bush found international relations infinitely more to his liking than domestic problems. With no stomach for wrangling on Capitol Hill, he noted in his diary: "I must say I hate this dealing with Congress and these budget matters. I much prefer foreign affairs." As a consequence of his years as ambassador to the United Nations, envoy to China, CIA director, and vice president, he knew most of the world's leaders, and each was only a phone call away. After logging well over a million miles on visits to sixty-five nations as vice president, he had accumulated so many friends in foreign chancelleries that he was known as the "Rolodex President." Focusing on developments abroad had one particular advantage: he had much more opportunity to shape the course of events. Irritated by how little attention Bush was giving to domestic policy, one of his cabinet officials chided him: "You majored in economics at Yale. Why don't you take a more active interest?" The president retorted: "Well, I can't get much done with a Democratic Congress. In foreign policy, I can be an activist.... I feel like an executive." On a journey to Rio de Janeiro, he underscored that point. "In foreign affairs, fortunately," he told the press, "I don't need congressional acquiescence every step of the way."

Bush put together a foreign policy cadre that represented the Establishment at its best, but it was not always of one mind. The hawkish secretary of defense, Dick Cheney, and National Security Adviser Brent Scowcroft warned that, despite the flummery of détente at the end of the Reagan era, the Kremlin bear remained frighteningly powerful and untrustworthy. The USSR, they pointed out, still had twelve thousand nuclear warheads that could be launched, as well as nearly four hundred thousand troops in East Germany. Scowcroft later reflected: "I had the sense at the end of the Reagan administration that they had come to the conclusion, *It's all over.* I wasn't at all sure that was the case." Bush's fellow patrician Secretary of State James A. Baker III and the chairman of the Joint Chiefs of Staff, Colin Powell, on the other hand, thought that Gorbachev's pursuit of *glasnost* held promise, and they were considerably warier of resort to arms. The searing memory of Vietnam in his mind, Powell believed that the United States should not commit itself to employing military force unless it had clear objectives and the American people and its representatives in Congress were united behind the action. Powell also differed from other top-ranking generals in concluding that the Soviet Union no longer constituted a threat. "Our bear is now benign," he said.

Though the president leaned toward Baker and Powell, he never shared Reagan's euphoria about *glasnost*, and he was so fearful of Soviet power that he sought to cultivate China as a counterweight to the USSR in Asia. Bush felt convinced enough about the need to offset Kremlin designs that he made his first trip abroad as president not to Moscow but to Beijing. In his inaugural address, he said that "a new breeze" was carrying the "great nations of the world . . . through the door to freedom," but in China he was quickly disabused of any notion that the Beijing government would welcome change. The Chinese leader, Deng Xiaoping, met with him, but authorities refused to allow a dissenter—a famous scientist—to accept a banquet invitation the president had extended. That episode signaled tragedy to come.

During the spring, half a million Chinese citizens marched in Shanghai, and in Tiananmen Square, the principal rialto in Beijing, students erected a Goddess of Democracy modeled on the Statue of Liberty. Americans thrilled at this upsurge in an authoritarian land where it was least expected. But early in June tanks and armored cars rolled across the square, crushing students and their goddess and firing rounds of bullets. Hundreds, more likely thousands, of peaceful demonstrators were slaughtered. The world recoiled in horror, but the president, in his first statement from Washington, warned against "an emotional response."

Bush took some token steps to rebuke the Chinese government, but he never allowed himself to be caught up in the sickened outrage over the massacre that others felt. Neither in China nor elsewhere in the world did he identify with freedom fighters, for he feared instability. He also thought the best hope of ameliorating the harshness of dictatorship lay in quickening consumer appetites, and he valued China as a vast market for American goods. "While he formally protested," the diplomatic historian George Herring has noted, "an elitist president more comfortable with order than with democracy did not feel and therefore could not voice the anger felt throughout the world." When the House of Representatives voted unanimously for stiff sanctions, he vetoed the measure. "At a moment of passion in the story of democracy," wrote a *New York Times* columnist, Bush "has been pale and thin." Though the Beijing government showed no remorse and behaved truculently, Bush continued to cultivate it. He dispatched Scowcroft and the deputy secretary of state to let Deng and his subordinates know that, while he had to appease voters by a show of indignation, he sought to maintain good, and profitable, relations with those whom incensed Americans were calling "the butchers of Beijing." In the spring of 1990, less than a year after the carnage in Tiananmen Square, Washington accorded China most-favored-nation status.

The president acted much more aggressively south of the border in dealing with the second foreign policy crisis of his first year: the long-simmering struggle with the Panamanian strongman Manuel Noriega, which suddenly took a deadly turn. Noriega, who engaged in gunrunning, illicit drug transactions, and money laundering, had been on the payroll of the CIA and, curiously, of the US Drug Enforcement Agency, though he was pushing narcotics for the notorious Medellín cartel. From the 1960s through most of the Reagan years, the United States government had paid him hundreds of thousands of dollars for tasks such as funneling arms to the Contras. "Noriega was always scum," said one US operative, "but you use scum like him." By 1988, however, he had lost his utility as a Cold War operative, and the Justice Department secured indictments of him in Miami and Tampa for drug trafficking. Scowcroft later remarked: "I thought it was a strange way to behave.

I thought that the United States indicting foreign officials, over whom we had no jurisdiction, was really an aberration."

Reagan had been woefully ineffective in coping with Noriega, and at first Bush had no greater success, though he was much less willing to strike a deal. He looked on helplessly as Noriega nullified the results of an election won by a challenger, who was not only denied the office he had won by a large margin but beaten up by the dictator's hoodlums. When, in October 1989, a Panamanian army officer, Moises Giraldi, staged a coup and captured Noriega, the United States failed to come to the officer's aid, and, after a few hours, the government's forces restored Noriega to power and murdered Giraldi. Once again, Bush heard raucous cries of "wimp." His performance, said a prominent Democratic congressman, "makes Jimmy Carter look like a man of resolve." Emboldened by surviving the coup, the puppet Panamanian legislature pronounced Noriega "maximum leader" and declared that a "state of war" with the United States prevailed.

With relations between the United States and Panama at flash point, it did not take much to produce a *casus belli*. In December 1989, Noriega's forces killed a US Marine, brutally beat another American officer, and groped his wife. "That was all the President needed," Scowcroft has said. "I was in sympathy with what he wanted to do and ready to do it, but I was surprised that he would do it on those particular grounds." Declaring that "the will of the people should not be thwarted by this man and his Doberman thugs," the president, acting on his own, ordered a military response. A little past midnight on December 20, in a venture labeled Operation Just Cause, thousands of American troops, including "a sky full of paratroopers," descended on Panama.

US forces quickly overran the country, but Noriega proved to be an elusive quarry. He was finally located in the edifice of the papal nuncio, who had granted him asylum. For some days, the maximum leader refused to come out. But the Americans assaulted him day and night with loudspeakers blasting nerve-shattering sounds—including boisterous hard rock tunes such as "You're No Good," cacophonous music that, as an opera lover, he could not abide. Unable to take it any longer, he gave himself up and was flown to a Miami jail cell. In 1992, he was convicted of money laundering, trafficking in cocaine, and racketeering and sentenced to forty years in a Florida prison. Both the United Nations and the

Organization of American States denounced the US invasion, and authorities on international law questioned the right of the United States to try and incarcerate the leader of another country. In response, the Justice Department issued an opinion asserting that an American president has the authority to abduct the head of a foreign state, and the CIA asked the Senate to lift the ban on assassination of the leader of a country. For the moment at least, Bush had escaped the epithet of weakling. "Whatever the other results of this roll of the dice in Panama," wrote a *New York Times* correspondent, "it has shown him as a man capable of bold action."

With Noriega on his way to the hoosegow, Bush could concentrate on a far more important problem: US policy toward the Soviet Union, which was to absorb the better part of his presidency. He approached Moscow with the same commitment to maintaining order that he had displayed in Beijing. Though he never developed a relationship with the Soviet leader that matched the Russian's joviality with "Ronny," he was convinced that only Gorbachev could provide stability in an explosive area of the world. He did not want to encourage independence movements in the USSR that might induce Kremlin hard-liners to seize the reins and might put control of nuclear weapons in shaky secessionist republics. Gorbachev, for his part, hoped that his policy of *perestroika* would hold the loyalty not only of the constituent states but also of the Warsaw Pact countries.

Neither Gorbachev nor the president, though, could keep up with the pell-mell march of events. During Bush's first year in office, one after another of the satellites—Bulgaria, Czechoslovakia, East Germany, Hungary, Poland—toppled Communist regimes or adopted reforms. In the past, Russian tanks had crushed the Hungarian Revolution of 1956 and the Prague Spring of 1968. But Gorbachev, dispensing with this Brezhnev Doctrine of suppression, refused to employ force. Nowhere were the consequences so graphic as in East Germany.

When on a November day in 1989, the East German government conceded that it could no longer halt the outflow of its citizens who were fleeing by the tens of thousands, it triggered a people's assault on the infamous Berlin Wall. *Time* reported what ensued "at the stroke of midnight":

Thousands...let out a roar and started going through, as well as up and over. West Berliners pulled East Berliners to the top of the barrier along which in years past many an East German had been killed while trying to escape; at times, the Wall almost disappeared beneath waves of humanity. They tooted trumpets and danced on the top. They brought out hammers and chisels and whacked away at the hated symbol of imprisonment, knocking loose chunks of concrete and waving them triumphantly before television cameras. They spilled out into the streets of West Berlin for a champagne-spraying, horn-honking bash that continued well past dawn into the following day and then another dawn.

During the darkest years of the Cold War, few Americans dared imagine that they would ever see such an enthralling occasion for rejoicing, but Bush seemed phlegmatic. At a press conference in the Oval Office, a CBS reporter, puzzled by the president's demeanor, said to him, "You don't seem elated." Bush replied, "I am not an emotional kind of guy." He refused to beat his chest and dance on the Wall, he added. One of the most powerful congressional Democrats, Dick Gephardt of Missouri, commented: "Even as the walls of the modern Jericho come tumbling down, we have a president who is inadequate to the moment." More reasonably, however, Robert Gates, who was to become head of the CIA, said of Bush: "He did not gloat.... He did not threaten or glower.... As the Communist bloc was disintegrating, it was George Bush's skilled, yet quiet, statecraft that made a revolutionary time seem so much less dangerous than it actually was."

Little more than three weeks after the momentous event in Berlin, the president met Gorbachev aboard ship off the island of Malta in the midst of a howling Mediterranean gale that rocked the vessel with twenty-foot waves. "I hope you've noticed," said Bush, "that as change accelerated in Eastern Europe recently, we haven't responded with flamboyance or arrogance so as to make your situation more difficult. They say 'Bush is too timid, too cautious.' I *am* cautious, but not timid. I've tried to conduct myself in a way so as not to complicate your difficulties." In turn, the Russian leader avowed that the Soviet Union was prepared "no longer to regard the United States as an adversary." After Bush proclaimed, "We stand at the threshold of a brand new era of US-Soviet relations," Gorbachev retorted, "The world leaves one epoch of cold war, and enters another epoch." He elaborated: "The characteristics of the cold war should be abandoned. The arms race, mistrust, psychological and ideological struggle, all those should be things of the past." As a consequence of these declarations, historians have come to view December 3, 1989, as dating the end of the decades-long Cold War. Malta, the chief of the Soviet Foreign Ministry Information Department later reflected, was "where Gorbachev and Bush buried the cold war in the bottom of the Mediterranean."

Areas of difficulty remained, however, not least the Kremlin's relationship to the Baltic states. In the summer of 1989, some two million people in the three Baltic countries of Estonia, Latvia, and Lithuania had linked hands to form a Chain of Freedom spanning 370 miles across their lands. That December, the very month of the Malta conference, Lithuanians alarmed Gorbachev by severing their ties to the Soviet Communist Party. When he visited the country to stifle the revolt, a quarter of a million people turned out for an independence rally in the capital, Vilnius. Gorbachev could tolerate the transformation of East Germany but not that of any of the Baltic states, because when Russia seized them in 1940, they had become constituent members of the USSR. If he permitted Lithuania to break away, he would be abetting the secession of Ukraine and other members of the Soviet Union.

At Malta, Bush, sympathetic to Gorbachev's problems, had secretly agreed that he would not publicly criticize Russian actions in the Baltic arena, and Gorbachev had secretly pledged that he would exercise as much restraint as he could, though, as it turned out, his moderation was not limitless. In April 1990, he imposed a crippling embargo on Lithuania, denying it vital supplies. In response, the Lithuanian Parliament issued an "Appeal to the Nations of the World," and the president of Lithuania declared, "The Soviets are strangling our nation like a boa constrictor." When Bush did nothing, critics at home and abroad likened him to Chamberlain at Munich. On January 11, 1991, Gorbachev denounced the breakaway republic for seeking to replace Communist rule with a bourgeois society and threatened reprisals. Two days later, Russian soldiers in tanks and a KGB unit encircled a TV tower in Vilnius and opened fire, killing fourteen unarmed people. Still, Bush held to his policy of "prudence," his favorite word. George Herring, while praising Bush for refusing "to interfere or to gloat" as Gorbachev suffered one setback after another, also observed that the president "at times seemed curiously out of touch with the spirit of human freedom that swept the world during his first years in office."

Journalists, a number of his advisers, and both Republicans and Democrats in Congress condemned Bush for not allying himself with liberation movements and for not rebuking Gorbachev. The president's behavior, said George Will, had made him an "embarrassment." In a *Newsweek* opinion piece, Will charged that "Bushism is Reaganism minus the passion for freedom." When, in a speech in Kiev, Bush damped down the expectations of insurgents in eastern Europe, critics in America sneered at his attitude as "Chicken Kiev." Bush, however, hoping to win Gorbachev's acquiescence to arms control and to reunification of Germany, placed his trust in quiet negotiation, and at a summit in Washington in June 1990, Gorbachev, in return for US economic aid he desperately needed, agreed privately to lift the embargo. After a time, the Kremlin accepted the inevitable, and Lithuania gained its independence.

Bush had much tougher sledding in winning approval for the unification of Germany, especially because he was insisting that the country, which for nearly half a century had been bifurcated by the Iron Curtain, enter the community of nations as a member of NATO. To gain assent, he had to persuade not only Gorbachev but also France's president, François Mitterrand, who had bitter memories of three Teutonic assaults, starting with the Franco-Prussian War, and Prime Minister Thatcher, who feared that a colossus on the Continent might upset the balance of power. She had even implored Gorbachev to maintain the Berlin Wall. Still more alarmed, Gorbachev said that the twenty-seven million Russians killed during World War II gave the Soviet Union a "moral right" to assurances that a unified Germany would not "spell new perils." But, by dint of persistent telephone diplomacy, Bush cajoled Mitterrand and Thatcher into going along, and after returning from the Washington summit with a trade pact from the United States in hand, Gorbachev startled Western officials, and very likely his colleagues in the Politburo, by saying that he no longer objected to German unification. Out of negotiations called "Two-plus-Four" (the two Germanies and the World War II occupying powers: US, USSR, Britain, France) came an agreement permitting the new united Germany to join NATO but with no NATO troops in the former East Germany and with Russia given a few years to withdraw its forces from there.

Not long after the breach of the Wall, the two Germanies merged in a new democratic republic and "East Germany" disappeared from the map of Europe. George Bush, so long dismissed as a wimp, had, said the *New York Times*, managed "a foreign policy coup." Indeed, it concluded, this was "Bush's hour." The unification of Germany, Robert Gates has said, "is a very special achievement of George Bush... because every other leader, East and West, was against it. The French were against it; the British were against it; the Soviets were against it; the Poles were against it; the Czechs were against it; the Hungarians were against it; the Italians were against it. We were totally isolated. And it was... just by sheer force of personality and determination that... Bush finally got all these people on board."

Bush chalked up one more triumph in his relations with Russia. In January 1993, he signed a Strategic Arms Reduction Treaty (START II), a follow-up to two earlier pacts he had negotiated with Gorbachev. Together, these agreements eliminated the dangerous MIRVs (multiple independently targeted reentry vehicles, each carrying more than one warhead) and sharply reduced the number of other missiles. In addition, over a period of four years Russia removed all of its more than half a million troops from Germany—an extraordinary source of satisfaction for Bush.

Neither Gorbachev nor the USSR fared so well. The Soviet leader's brilliant innovations, which he hoped would preserve his huge empire, served instead to loosen the bonds that held his country together. In particular, they unwittingly created space for ethnic animosities and nationalist striving. In the late summer of 1991, starting with Ukraine, then Belarus and Moldova, one after another of the USSR republics seceded—with Kazakhstan, the last of the dozen, departing in December. In August 1991, the month that Ukraine began the departures, a cabal hostile to liberalization placed Gorbachev under house arrest in the Crimea, where he was vacationing, and reimposed authoritarian rule. After three days, the coup collapsed, but Gorbachev's authority to reign had been fatally compromised. In the early morning hours of December 25, 1991, he resigned as president, declaring his office defunct, and on the following day the hammer and sickle was lowered from the Kremlin for the last time. The Soviet Union had become extinct.

For nearly half a century, the American people had been fixated on the Red Menace, but when George Bush led them into war in 1991, he targeted a country that did not identify with the Communist bloc: Iraq, headed by the tyrant Saddam Hussein. Few anticipated this eventuality in the first months of Bush's presidency, for, like Reagan before him, he had valued Iraq as a counterweight to Iran, in keeping with the maxim: "The enemy of my enemy is my friend." During the bloody eight-year war between the two nations in the 1980s, Reagan had covertly favored Iraq, and Bush continued to do so, though Saddam was a vicious despot. When members of Congress sought sanctions on Iraq for human rights violations, Bush opposed them, and when an international conference on chemical weapons in Paris fingered Iraq as a violator, the United States dissented. As late as July 25, 1990, when Saddam was massing troops along the border of his oil-rich neighbor, Kuwait, the US ambassador at Baghdad, April Glaspie, informed him: "We have no opinion on your Arab-Arab conflicts, such as your dispute with Kuwait. Secretary Baker has directed me to emphasize the instruction... that the Kuwait issue is not associated with America."

Nine days later, though, after Iraqi forces invaded Kuwait, Bush denounced this "naked aggression," froze Iraqi and Kuwaiti assets in the United States, and vowed to "take whatever steps necessary" to protect American interests in the region. On August 6, at his behest, the UN Security Council imposed economic sanctions. Still, the president said, "There is little the U.S. can do in a situation like this," and, after meeting with the National Security Council, he told the press, "We're not discussing intervention." Prime Minister Thatcher thought it necessary to scold him: "George, ... this is no time to go wobbly."

The "Iron Lady" misread him. After the mighty Iraqi army took only hours to overrun Kuwait, a country smaller than New Jersey, Bush ordered the first components of Operation Desert Shield—planes and two hundred thousand troops—into Saudi Arabia. The president feared that if Saddam gained control of the huge Saudi oil reserves as well as those of Kuwait, he could dominate the world market, drive up fuel prices, and require Western nations to do his bidding. With 20 percent of the world's oil reserves after swallowing Kuwait, Saddam would have 40 percent if he also conquered Saudi Arabia. The Saudis did not usually welcome an American military presence, but they understood their predicament.

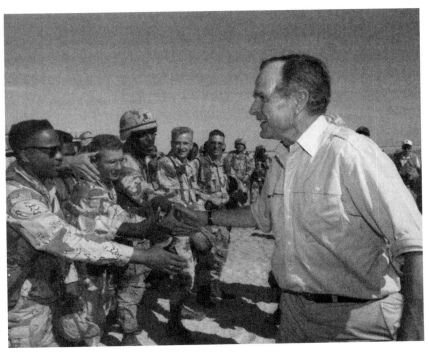

President Bush visits the troops. In late November 1990, at a desert encampment in Saudi Arabia, Bush shared Thanksgiving dinner with US Marines who only a few weeks later would be sent into combat in Kuwait. *Courtesy of the George Bush Presidential Library and Museum, ID P17676-19*

"He who eats Kuwait for breakfast," said Prince Bandar, "is likely to ask for something else for lunch."

Bush won worldwide acclaim for his skill in putting together an international coalition of twenty-nine nations to enforce economic sanctions on Iraq. Working the telephone, he got in touch with dozens of leaders around the globe. He did not even hesitate to phone Mitterrand at three in the morning. In addition to rounding up all of the Western bloc, he won commitments from twelve members of the Arab League. Especially impressive was the behavior of the Kremlin. Russia had been aligned with Iraq for decades, but it agreed to issue a joint declaration with the United States calling for "an international cutoff of all arms supplies to Iraq." That announcement, as Scowcroft observed, "dramatically put the two superpowers on the same side of a major crisis for the first time since the Cold War began." With so many countries in a confederation against Saddam Hussein, economic sanctions had a potent impact. Though he had seized Kuwait's oil, no one would buy it.

But as the weeks went by and, despite the tightening ring around it, Iraq still refused to withdraw from Kuwait, Bush gave increasing consideration to military intervention—a course strongly resisted by some of his own counselors. Both Baker and Powell wanted to give economic sanctions more time. Baker warned the president about "body bags," and Powell told him, "It will be grisly. There will be... reports of dead Americans." Many Americans feared that the Middle East could be a worse death trap than Southeast Asia had been, for Iraq had the fourth largest army in the world, including a Republican Guard of more than a hundred thousand battle-hardened soldiers believed capable of inflicting huge casualties. At a press conference where Bush said that he was willing "to go the extra mile for peace" but that "military action" might be necessary, a woman journalist asked him whether he recognized that he was calling upon "some parents to give up the lives of their children." Not satisfied with his routine response, she persisted, "We all know how important your children are to you. Do you feel that this issue is important enough to you that you could conceive of giving up one of their lives for it?" Since Bush failed to explain convincingly how his longtime favorite, Saddam Hussein, had suddenly become "Hitler revisited," antiwar activists accused the president of being willing to sacrifice young Americans to swell the profits of oil tycoons. In New York's Times Square, a procession of marchers six blocks long chanted, "Hell, No, We Won't Go / We Won't Fight for Texaco."

Bush believed that he had constitutional authority as commander in chief to order troops into action without congressional approval, but as Congress, fortified by strong antiwar sentiment in the country, readied itself for a showdown with the president over the War Powers Act, he sidestepped by asking for its consent. His advisers thought that he was taking a very great risk because Congress might not go along, but Bush wanted to show Saddam that his decision to intervene represented the national will. Furthermore, one of his officials later said, "If it went sour, he wanted Democrats with him." He faced a daunting task in the US Senate, where two of the most respected Democrats—Majority Leader George Mitchell of Maine and Sam Nunn of Georgia, widely thought to be the most knowledgeable member on military matters—had introduced an antiwar resolution. One of the most vocal senators, Ted Kennedy, declared, "There is still time to save the president from himself." The House voted down the antiwar resolution by a considerable margin, though with 183 yeas, but it only narrowly met defeat in the Senate, 52–47, when nine Democrats, conspicuously Al Gore of Tennessee, broke ranks. Years later, in an appearance before the Senate, Bush reflected: "To be honest, for weeks we debated whether to try and push such a resolution in the Senate. I'm glad we did bring it here and pleased that it passed. But...52–47...was the slimmest Senate margin ever to vote for war, and naturally I regret that we couldn't convince more in the majority to help us send a clear and united signal to Saddam, and the world, about our resolve to lead." Sometime after the roll call, Bush said that if Congress had turned him down, he would have gone ahead anyway.

At 3 a.m. Iraqi time on January 17, 1991, five days after Congress authorized use of force, Desert Shield gave way to Desert Storm when, on Bush's orders, US military aircraft began a furious assault on Baghdad from the night skies. For more than a month, Saddam Hussein's capital was pounded relentlessly by bombers as well as Tomahawk missiles launched from destroyers in the Gulf. Americans glued to CNN on their living room screens were captivated by these nocturnal displays of power, which they regarded as a massive fireworks extravaganza providing an occasion for pride in high-tech capabilities that no other nation in the world could match. Only long afterward did the country learn the truth about this "pinpoint, precision" bombing: of the first 167 bombs dropped, 76 failed to hit their targets. Nonetheless, the devastating air attacks, by knocking out Iraqi air defenses and disrupting transportation grids, did soften resistance to the ground warfare that was to come.

Before sending half a million Americans into battle in Kuwait, Bush once again performed impressively in assembling a multinational corps. Taking advantage of a UN Security Council resolution calling for the dislodgment of Saddam Hussein from Kuwait by "all necessary means" (a euphemism for military action), he persuaded thirty-three countries, including twelve members of the Arab League, to join the United States. He got troops not only from Saudi Arabia but also from Egypt, Qatar, Oman, the United Arab Emirates, and Bahrain, as well as from Senegal, Niger, and Bangladesh—a total of more than two hundred thousand.

When, on Bush's orders, Cheney flew into Cairo, he found the president of Egypt, furious that Saddam had lied to him, more than willing to let a US nuclear warship sail through the Suez Canal, and, in Rabat, King Hassan of Morocco was no less obliging. "Diplomacy was easy under those circumstances," Cheney later recalled. "You show up in Morocco and the king is waiting for you. His old buddy, George Bush, has talked to him and, yes, he'll send troops." Bush's "personality, his experience, the fact that he dealt with these guys over the years" meant that "they like[d] him and trusted him." This joint effort, Bush surmised, could lead to "a new world order"—an era "freer from the threat of terror, stronger in the pursuit of justice, and more secure in the quest for peace."

On February 24, not long before dawn, these daunting legions crossed into Kuwait. For months, Saddam had been warning the United States that if it dared to invade, the Revolutionary Guard would decimate its battalions. But the fighting had hardly commenced when Iraqi soldiers began surrendering by the tens of thousands. It took the coalition less than four days to drive them out of Kuwait in full flight back to their homeland. A little before 6 p.m. on February 27, with the enemy routed, Bush decided to halt operations, but, at Sununu's suggestion, he did not announce the cease-fire until midnight so that the conflict would bear the felicitous title of "the Hundred Hours War." ("Hundred hours" took no notice of the five weeks of air bombardment that had preceded the land invasion.)

In later years, critics roundly scolded Bush for forfeiting the opportunity to pursue the retreating Iraqi into Baghdad and topple Saddam Hussein. Even the vice president jawed at Bush for breaking off the fighting too soon. (Bush commented: "It doesn't help Quayle with me, and it doesn't help him at all.") At different times over the past months, Bush himself had believed that getting rid of Saddam was an essential war aim. "I think of the evil that is this man," he had entered in his diary. "We need a surrender—we need Saddam out." But Iraq's cruel dictator remained in power, and, with much of his army intact, he employed helicopters against the Kurds and massacred thousands of Iraqi Shiites.

Bush, though, had sound reasons for not continuing the war. The reputation of the United States in the Muslim world would have been damaged by newsreels of US troops killing fleeing Iraqi soldiers no longer offering resistance on "the Highway of Death." Carrying on a "turkey shoot" of men in full retreat, Bush said, would not be "chivalrous." Furthermore, he recognized that his allies had not committed themselves to regime change, only to clearing the Iraqi invaders out of Kuwait. "The one thing we did know," remembered Robert Gates, "was...that if we did try to move into Iraq...to bring about a change of regime, it would have shattered the coalition instantly and we would have been alone. Possibly the Brits with us, but even that's not entirely sure." Bush later contended that if, just "to show our macho," the United States did oust Saddam, it would "be an occupying power—America in an Arab land— with no allies at our side. It would have been disastrous." He also reasoned that if he removed Iraq as a major power in the Persian Gulf, Iran and Syria would exploit the opportunity to destabilize the region.

On the March evening in 1991 when the members of Congress, each carrying a small American flag, gathered in the House chamber to listen to Bush report to them on the triumphant intervention, no word of criticism could be heard, and when he looked up toward the Kuwaiti ambassador in the gallery and declaimed, "Ambassador Al-Sabah: Tonight Kuwait is free," the chamber erupted in earsplitting applause. In the euphoria over the Gulf War, surveys recorded the highest approval ratings for an American president ever registered. *USA Today* put his numbers at a staggering 91 percent. "The polls, by which we live and die, are up in astronomical heights," Bush noted in his diary. Tom Wicker has summed up the situation a year before the next presidential campaign was to get under way: "Who could believe that a second term for him was not a sure thing? Not George Bush.... It looked as if George Bush, the former wimp, might in 1992 be given a free ride by serious challenges from either party."

The overwhelming victory in the Gulf War and the implosion of the Soviet Union left George Bush the head of the world's lone superpower. "After the end of the Cold War," Herring has written, "the United States enjoyed a degree of world hegemony beyond George Washington's most extravagant dreams." To characterize America's extraordinary dominance, the French felt called upon to add a new term to the lexicon: "hyperpower." A State Department official, Francis Fukuyama, even spoke of "the end of history": democracy triumphant and capitalism never to be challenged again.

Members of the Bush team, though, when they puzzled over how to fashion a foreign policy appropriate to these new circumstances, did not find this position nearly so advantageous as it sounded. "We were suddenly in a unique position," Scowcroft later remembered, "without experience, without precedent, and standing alone at the height of power." Air Force General Merrill McPeak later reflected: "As the glaciers receded from the Cold War, they exposed all the detritus that had been frozen in place.... The new situation of us being an unparalleled single power... meant that when this series of old problems exposed itself, we were the only people capable of handling it. And we weren't ready for it.... Intellectually, conceptually, nobody had prepared for a situation in which we would be calling all the shots, and simultaneously all these... ancient problems would be exposed to the atmosphere for the first time in many years. So we stumbled, badly."

The end of the bipolar equilibrium yielded an upsurge of tribalism as well as resort to terror as a weapon. Furthermore, multinational corporations in an era of globalization regarded themselves as independent sovereigns. Bush sensed the need to formulate a broad-gauged new approach, but the best he could come up with, borrowing a phrase from the State Department's Condoleezza Rice, was "beyond containment." Policy formation had actually been easier when there was an identifiable enemy. "The central paradox of unipolarity," remarked the political scientist Stephen Walt, was that America "enjoys enormous influence but has little idea what to do with its power or even how much effort it should expend."

Though Bush claimed that the dazzling intervention in Kuwait had put an end to "the Vietnam syndrome," characterized by an extreme wariness of foreign imbroglios, the United States continued to think twice, then twice again, before embarking on overseas ventures. When the Serbs slaughtered Muslims and Croats, Bush did nothing to halt the hideous orgy. After returning from the region, Secretary Baker, while acknowledging that Bosnia was a "humanitarian nightmare," said briskly, "We don't have a dog in that fight." In like manner, an official speaking for the State Department asked, "Where is it written that the United States is the military policeman of the world?"

The Bush administration showed little more interest in getting involved in the Caribbean. When the Haitian military overthrew the nation's government, General Powell warned that though US forces could easily make their way into the country, finding an exit would be a lot tougher. In framing policy toward Nicaragua, Bush, who had shared Reagan's conviction that the Contras were freedom fighters, recognized that he fell far short of the votes in Congress he would need to resume military aid. The best he could manage was to strike a deal with the Democrats. In return for their willingness to send medical and other supplies, he embraced a plan devised by Central American leaders, spearheaded by the president of Costa Rica, for free national elections. When the votes were tallied, they spelled doom for the Contras. The president accepted that consequence, leaving North Carolina senator Jesse Helms and his far-right allies with new cause for thinking that George Bush was no Ronald Reagan.

Reluctant though he had become to make commitments abroad, Bush believed that he had no choice save to assume responsibility in Somalia, where famine had claimed more than a quarter million lives—a tragedy graphically displayed on TV screens. For a number of months, America took part in a peaceful United Nations effort to get food to the starving, only to have marauding outlaw bands loot shipments, hijack convoys, and kill humanitarian workers. When in December 1992 Bush resolved to send a US expeditionary force to safeguard supplies, he told the American people: "Imagine 7,000 tons of food aid literally bursting out of a warehouse on a dock in Mogadishu, while Somalis starve less than a kilometer away because relief workers cannot run the gauntlet of armed gangs roving the city."

Bush's Somalian initiative has come to be regarded as a classic instance of America's assuming a disproportionate share of responsibility in the world. Of the thirty-seven thousand in the multinational force, twenty-five thousand came from the United States, with the remainder from twenty-six other members of the UN, including Bangladesh, Botswana, Tunisia, and Zimbabwe. Deputy National Security Adviser Robert Gates later commented: "The Bush administration's intervention in Somalia . . . is probably as good a case study of foreign policy by CNN as I can think of. The public outcry and the pressure from the Congress as a result of the televised pictures of starvation and anarchy in

Somalia,... but above all the starvation just became a huge force to deal with. And... it was in the... same time frame as an election campaign.... I don't think that if it had been a non-election year and if there had been no CNN pictures that we would have ever gone into Somalia." Unhappily, the operation ended in disaster—though not until after Bush had left the White House.

The international endeavor that excited Bush most centered not in Africa or the Levant but in the Western Hemisphere, for nothing quickened his interest more than an opportunity to expand commercial interchange. He cited Macaulay's adage: "Free trade is one of the greatest blessings which a government can confer on a people." He took particular pride in negotiating a trilateral treaty with the prime minister of Canada and the president of Mexico. "The three amigos" hailed the North American Free Trade Agreement (NAFTA), which Bush signed in December 1992, for creating a huge domain liberated from most tariffs extending from the tropical Guatemalan border to the polar bear territory of the frozen Arctic. Others, though, were less enthusiastic, and it was not clear the US Senate would ratify the pact. Environmentalists feared that American corporations would move their factories to Mexico to escape regulation, and unions worried about what the Texan industrialist Ross Perot detected: the "giant sucking sound" of the jobs of American workers drawn south of the border at a time when the US economy was on the skids.

George Bush, who could point to numbers of achievements abroad, did not fare nearly so well at home, largely because of the alarming mountain of debt Reagan had left him. In his first year in office, he held to his "read my lips" rubric of no new taxes, and, as a result, red ink continued to gush. He recognized that he had to stanch the hemorrhaging, and that to do so he might have to consent, however reluctantly, to a tax rise, but he also knew that abandoning his pledge would cost him dearly, especially among Republicans. In May 1990, he wrote in his diary: "Politics is rampant and guts are lacking. We got through the weekend, but we're getting pounded, and the right-wing is the worst, and much more so than the left-wing it seems to me, or maybe its just that when you're attacked by your own, it stings more."

That same month, he invited congressional leaders to the White House. He told them that it was their responsibility to come up with revenues to lower the deficit, but the top Democrats had enough street smarts not to be sucked into an arrangement where all the voters' anger at tax hikes would fall on them. The majority leader, Dick Gephardt, responded acidly, "It's the first time in this century we've seen a president want to give power to Congress." With the Democrats controlling both houses, the president had little leverage, though he did get them to agree to some cutbacks in social spending. On June 26, Bush finally accepted the reality that he had no choice save to abandon his "read my lips" commitment. When the White House released a statement that day of a bipartisan plan to cope with deficits, the media focused on one particular phrase out of several solutions offered: "tax revenue increases," with most of the $134 billion in new levies to come from a gasoline tax. Some of the White House staff thought that the Democrats had scammed the president. The spending cuts lay in the future, while the tax rise would take effect right away.

His fellow Republicans made no effort to contain their wrath at Bush's apostasy, with the minority whip in the House, Newt Gingrich, accusing the president of "betrayal." Unwilling to acknowledge Reagan's advocacy of "revenue enhancements," Republican leaders charged Bush with perfidy to his revered predecessor. Quayle sternly disapproved. He later recalled that he was showering when he heard of the tax rise pact, then reflected that he "probably should have looked at the drain, because that was where the Republican party's best issue—the one that had gotten us elected in 1980, 1984, and 1988,...that had, more than any other, made the Reagan revolution possible—was headed." Rupert Murdoch's *New York Post* headlined READ MY LIPS: I LIED, and a writer in *Time* called Bush "a closet Democrat," a "mole who has burrowed deep behind enemy lines for the sake of the party of the working stiff. It is the only logical explanation for the president's recent political behavior."

Republicans in Congress led by Gingrich precipitated a national crisis by joining with liberal Democrats, unhappy about cuts in welfare and Medicare and about a gasoline tax that burdened low-income consumers, to reject the president's budget. "You are killing us, you're just killing us," Bush told Gingrich. Congress then voted a continuing resolution to keep the government functioning beyond the end of the fiscal year on

October 1, but Bush, in a fit of pique, vetoed it, and the US government shut down. Deprived of essential services, Americans vented almost all their fury at Bush. Calls to the White House ran 6–1 against him. As a result, the closing lasted only through the Columbus Day holiday weekend. Bush, acknowledging that he was beaten, signed a new resolution to keep the government going.

With Republicans in disarray, liberal Democrats took over. They put through a new budget that relied not on a gasoline tax hike but on stepped-up income tax rates on the wealthy. In addition, they cut taxes on the working poor, softened projected reductions of Medicare, and got rid altogether of a tax on home heating oil. Only one out of four Republican members of Congress voted for the measure, but the Democrats massed enough votes. On October 27, Bush signed the Omnibus Budget Reconciliation Act of 1990.

Bush's decision to renege on his pledge never to raise taxes gravely impaired his relations with his party. So discountenanced were right-wingers that the cochair of the Republican National Committee, Ed Rollins, who had been Reagan's political director, urged GOP Congressional candidates to run for office on their own and "not hesitate to oppose... the president." Bush was livid. After the midterm election resulted in a small loss of Republican seats, he got rid of Rollins. A more serious consequence of the budget melodrama was its impact on the president's public standing. Bush's behavior reinforced the impression that the president was a man with no firm convictions or, worse still, that, with his eyes on the 1988 election, he had willfully made a promise that he knew he could not keep.

To the discomfiture both of the president and of his party, the squabble over the budget coincided with a downturn in the economy. In August 1990, the announcement by the Big Three US automakers of losses that were to total $1 billion that year alerted the country that it was entering a recession. By the middle of the next year, joblessness had risen to nearly 8 percent. It was not severe; unemployment had been worse early in the Reagan presidency. But Bush was never able to convey the remotest empathy with the jobless. In his response to the recession, he showed a marked conservative bias, twice preventing Congress from extending unemployment benefits while favoring a reduction in the capital gains tax.

By the start of 1992, Bush's disapproval rating exceeded his approval score. Since polling began, no president had ever suffered so abrupt a loss of support. By the spring of 1992, Bush's numbers had plummeted to the low 40 percent range, the worst of any first-term chief executive in his fourth year in office since Hoover. Asked how to account for his sudden falloff, Bush replied, "Well, I think the answer to why...has been the economy in the doldrums." Bush's approval score, 91 percent at its peak during Desert Storm, bottomed out at 29 percent in the summer of 1992. It was not the most auspicious circumstance for launching a bid for reelection.

Not only Bush's domestic setbacks but also his overseas triumphs profoundly affected the 1992 campaign—often in paradoxical ways. The president's sky-high approval score at the end of the Gulf War made him seem so unbeatable that the Democratic front-runners—Governor Mario Cuomo, Senator Bill Bradley, and Congressman Dick Gephardt— dropped out of the race early, further swelling Bush's advantage. But that development also created an opportunity for the ambitious governor of Arkansas, Bill Clinton, who proved to be a formidable rival. The series of breakthroughs abroad on Bush's watch—the capture of Noriega, the demolition of the Berlin Wall, the dissolution of the Soviet Union, the liberation of Kuwait—had burnished his reputation. But the president's very successes lessened concern over foreign policy, which was his greatest strength, and enabled Clinton to exploit Bush's main source of vulnerability: discontent with the recession. On announcing his candidacy in October 1991 at Little Rock's Old Court House, Clinton declared, "I refuse to be part of a generation that celebrates the death of communism abroad with the loss of the American Dream at home." Clinton's strategist James Carville posted a sign on the wall of campaign headquarters: "It's the economy, stupid," and Democratic speakers alluded scornfully to "George Herbert Hoover Bush." One Democratic bumper sticker even combined criticizing the president's abrupt ending to the Iraq intervention with blaming him for hard times by asking, "Saddam Hussein has a job. Have you?"

Like Gerald Ford, Bill Clinton did not go by his baptismal name. Born William Jefferson Blythe III, he took the surname of his stepfather, though the man was a violent sot who abused Bill's mother, a woman her son adored. A precocious student, Clinton excelled in Arkansas schools, matriculated at Georgetown, won a Rhodes scholarship to Oxford, and enrolled at Yale Law School, where he fell in love with his future wife, Hillary Rodham. From an early age, he was hellbent on a political career—a passion kindled when, as a Boys Nation senator, he met President Kennedy at the White House. At thirty-two, he became the youngest governor in the country, and, after suffering defeat in his first quest for reelection, the "boy governor" of Arkansas won reelection four more times, the final one in a landslide.

In the 1980s Clinton moved on to the national stage. Washington journalists began to make their way to Little Rock when they heard that he was a novel kind of political animal: a "New Democrat" who, while touching the bases of a Great Society liberal, also wanted to get people off welfare. He aligned himself with the Democratic Leadership Council, which sought to turn the party of LBJ in a centrist direction, later serving as its chairman. (Jesse Jackson jeered at the DLC as "Democrats for the Leisure Class" who "comb their hair to the left like Kennedy and move their policies to the right like Reagan.") Impressed by his success in overhauling Arkansas's woeful educational system, his fellow chief executives elected him chairman of the National Governors Association. With his "Third Way" ideology, his record of accomplishment, and his sunny personality, he emerged from the pack of less than outstanding aspirants for the 1992 Democratic presidential nomination. By the time the critical New Hampshire primary campaign got under way, he held a sixteen-point lead.

But just as Clinton was riding high, he struck an obstacle that almost upended his political career. As Election Day approached in New Hampshire, a gossipy supermarket tabloid created a national sensation by alleging that Clinton had carried on a twelve-year extramarital affair with a nightclub singer, an Arkansas woman named Gennifer Flowers. Instead of dismissing the accusation, which, given widespread rumors about his dalliances, many found credible, Clinton took the daring risk of appearing on CBS television right after the Super Bowl on *60 Minutes*, his wife at his side. He had caused "pain" in his marriage, he admitted, without ever specifying how he had done so, but denied that he had ever had a sexual relationship with Gennifer Flowers. (Only years later did

Bill Clinton admit that he had, in fact, gone to bed with her.) The critical moment in the riveting program came when Hillary Clinton said defiantly, "I'm not sitting here because I'm some little woman standing by my man like Tammy Wynette. I'm sitting here because I love and respect him, and I honor what he's been through and what we've been through together. And you know, if that's not enough for people, then heck, don't vote for him." Bill Clinton owed his wife an enormous debt that she could draw upon later at will. To defuse further allegations, she hired private detectives to find out how much was known about nineteen women identified by tabloids as having been in sexual relationships with her husband.

Despite her significant contributions, her husband lost his early lead in New Hampshire and was struggling to make even a respectable showing when he had to defend himself against another, and more serious, charge: that he was a draft dodger unfit to be America's commander in chief. The *Wall Street Journal* published a statement by a colonel who headed the ROTC at the University of Arkansas alleging that Bill Clinton had used political influence and deceit to escape serving his country in the Vietnam War. In support of this accusation, he released a 1969 letter in which Clinton had written him, "I want to thank you... for saving me from the draft," and had gone on to acknowledge that while in Britain he had organized a protest against US foreign policy. The colonel also made the embarrassing revelation that, in his letter, Clinton had explained that he had been motivated by a single consideration: "to maintain my political viability within the system." That account resulted in a "meltdown" that overnight dropped Clinton from 33 to 16 percent.

James Carville later remembered that on reading the *Wall Street Journal* story, he had felt like "a gut-shot Confederate soldier leaning up against a tree ready to die," but Clinton refused to tuck in his tail. On ABC's *Nightline*, less than a week before the New Hampshire voting, he complained, "All I've been asked about by the press is a woman I didn't sleep with and a draft I didn't dodge." He also said to the people of New Hampshire: "I'll tell you what I think the character issue is: Who really cares about you?... I'll be there for you 'til the last dog dies." Early on Election Night, as the returns were being counted, he announced, "New Hampshire tonight has made Bill Clinton the Comeback Kid." In fact, when all the ballots were totaled, his early lead evaporated and he came in second (to the governor of a neighboring state), though well ahead of the rest of the field. Analysts agreed that the Comeback Kid had indeed made an impressive recovery.

Through the rest of that winter and all of the spring of 1992, Clinton rolled up enough victories, especially in southern states, to capture the Democratic presidential nomination, but without gaining the confidence of the electorate. The media came to regard him as "Slick Willie," an operative who was forever copping a plea. Yes, he acknowledged, he had smoked pot, but, he maintained, he had not inhaled. Hillary Clinton, for her part, annoyed housewives by telling a journalist, "I've done the best I can to lead my life. I suppose I could have stayed home and baked cookies and had teas." It rubbed people the wrong way, too, when Clinton promised "far more than Franklin Roosevelt and Eleanor." If he were elected, he said, the country would get "two for the price of one" because his wife would be his co-partner in governing. A poll in 1992 revealed that only 28 percent had a favorable view of Hillary Clinton. Many thought that their marriage was a sham, a cold, calculated arrangement that enabled her to share power with her husband. Nor did insinuations about the governor's sexual misconduct die away. One campaign button bore the legend "If Hillary Can't Trust Him, How Can We?" In June, only four months before the election, well over twice as many potential voters viewed Bill Clinton unfavorably as favorably.

Numbers of Americans disdained Clinton as a Yalie with Oxford airs, but at the Democratic National Convention in July he showed himself in a different light—as a fellow from a country town: Hope, Arkansas. Democrats presented the Man from Hope as an activist looking toward the future, while casting Bush as a feeble remnant of yesterday. In his acceptance address, Clinton declared: "I know how President Lincoln felt when General McClellan wouldn't attack in the Civil War. He asked him, 'If you're not going to use your army, may I borrow it?' And so I say, 'George Bush, if you won't use your power to help America, step aside. I will.'" He wound up his talk by affirming, "I still believe in a place called Hope." As the delegates filed out of the convention hall, the band struck up Fleetwood Mac's "Don't Stop Thinking about Tomorrow." Within days after the highly successful gathering, pollsters were reporting that Bill Clinton was gaining ground.

While the Democrats were rebounding, Republicans were self-destructing, with their national convention in August all but ending the president's prospects. When the delegates gathered in Houston, Bush permitted conservative extremists to take over. The campaign never recovered from what the Republican National Committee chairman later acknowledged was a "flatout mistake" in designating the incendiary right-wing journalist Pat Buchanan to dominate prime time on the widely watched opening night. In asserting that "there is a religious war going on in our country for the soul of America," Buchanan lashed out at Clinton, who, he contended, sought to impose on America "abortion on demand, a litmus test for the Supreme Court, homosexual rights, discrimination against religious schools, women in combat . . . not the kind of change we can tolerate in a nation that we still call God's country." By choosing what he maintained was "the most pro-gay and pro-lesbian ticket in history," Democrats, he charged, were engaged in "the greatest single exhibition of cross-dressing in American political history."

Buchanan's performance, and that of other firebrands in Houston, stunned commentators—at the time and subsequently. The "sulfurous" speeches, wrote Tom Wicker, revealed that Republican strategists "did not understand that such nationally televised oratory was alienating the half—or perhaps more—of the populace that did not feel itself or its neighbors to be in a 'religious' or 'cultural' war, might even be pro-choice, and did not quite see George Bush as a warrior struggling for the nation's soul. They wanted him, or someone, to fight for the nation's pocketbooks." A high-ranking White House aide later asked: "What the hell were they thinking? You take a popular outgoing president, Ronald Reagan, who is one of the more articulate men in our lifetime, and relegate him to a place where no one watches him and you put Pat Buchanan, who still lives in the far right world of Genghis Khan . . . . in prime time. It was outrageous. It was among the worst things we did and it hurt us. . . . It forced the president to run on a platform of extremism and we never quite shook the label and they took advantage of it."

The Quayles exacerbated Bush's difficulties. When, at the convention, Marilyn Quayle, who was presumed to be speaking for the vice president, called upon Republicans to return to a conservative orientation, she appeared to be attacking not Democrats but the moderate George Bush. And there was no limit to the stories that circulated about Dan Quayle—in America and around the world. The *Daily Australian* printed an account of how he was engrossed in the study of Latin because he imagined that when he went to Latin America, he would be able to speak to natives in their own tongue. He became a national butt of ridicule when, monitoring a spelling bee in a New Jersey school, he insisted that "p-o-t-a-t-o-e" was the proper spelling of potato. The twelve-year-old boy he corrected was widely quoted as saying that the incident "showed that the rumors about the vice president are true—that he's an idiot." On another occasion, Quayle said, "I love California; I practically grew up in Phoenix."

Republicans, critics contended, had paired an incoherent vice president with an incoherent president. At one point, Quayle said, "The Holocaust was an obscene period in our history.... No, not our nation's but in World War II. I mean we all lived in this century. I didn't live in this century, but in this century's history." On another occasion, he declared, "I have made good judgments in the past. I have made good judgments in the future." Commenting on the United Negro College fund's well-known slogan, "A mind is a terrible thing to waste," Quayle remarked, "You take the UNCF model that what a waste it is to lose one's mind or not to have a mind is being very wasteful. How true that is!"

While the Republicans were foundering, Clinton and the Democrats were putting together a highly effective campaign that became the subject of the documentary *The War Room*, nominated for an Academy Award. Defying the tradition of geographical balance on a ticket, Clinton chose a running mate from an adjacent state: Senator Al Gore of Tennessee. Gore, who was about the same age, appeared at first glance to add nothing to the ticket. But as a war veteran, he offset Clinton's shortcoming, and as a moderate, he denied GOP tacticians the opportunity to portray the Democratic contenders as northern liberals. Furthermore, Clinton, to demonstrate that he was not "soft on crime," flew to Arkansas to oversee the execution of a murderer, though the man, an African American, was mentally impaired. The contest pitted Bush, the last president who had served in World War II, against Clinton, the first baby boomer to vie for the White House, and the Democrats made the most of the age difference. On the day that Clinton showcased the handsome Gore family to nearly universal applause, he seemed, said the Washington correspondent for an Arkansas newspaper, "to create a spark in the campaign.... Suddenly, it became a campaign not of Bush versus Clinton but New Generation versus Old Generation." With Clinton arousing support from young voters and exhibiting on the campaign trail, as Joe Klein has reported, an "almost carnal" appeal, he moved ahead of Bush in the polls.

The contest, though, took an unexpected turn when a third candidate, the Texas billionaire Ross Perot, entered the race. Perot, who had made a quick fortune by forming Electronic Data Systems, which won a fat government contract, had first caught the nation's attention when he financed a private militia that liberated two of his employees from an Iranian prison and spirited them out of the country—an exploit the best-selling author Ken Follett recounted in *On Wings of Eagles*. In a year when the impact of electronic media attained new heights, he became a candidate not as the choice of convention delegates but simply by announcing his availability on a TV talk show. He then spent chunks of his fortune to buy thirty-minute spots of television time for "infomercials" in which he appeared as the all-wise instructor displaying pie charts on the budget. They were the kinds of programs that, as one critic later said, were "usually associated with the sale of underwater real estate," but they won Perot millions of followers. In the summer of 1992, he took the lead at 39 percent, with Bush trailing at 31 percent, and Clinton bottoming out at 25 percent.

But the quirky Texan's backing rapidly crumbled when reports of his erratic behavior emerged, and Perot abruptly withdrew from the campaign. He later explained that he had done so because, as a true patriot, he did not want to plunge the country into turmoil by throwing the race into the House—an alibi few found credible. *Newsweek*, which featured the headline QUITTER, QUITTER, called Perot "chicken." One publication labeled him "the Yellow Ross of Texas," and another gibed, "You don't realize how short Ross Perot's candidacy was until you consider that Liz Taylor's latest marriage has lasted longer." The gagster Jay Leno said, "A recent survey shows that Ross Perot is still the favorite among young single males. Sure, they can't make a commitment either."

But even after he had ostensibly pulled out, he remained, as he said, an "800-pound gorilla" who kept both parties on edge about whether he might reenter. While remaining coy, he bankrolled a campaign to put his name on the ballot in fifty states. At a press conference on October 1, Perot announced that he was once more a candidate, then got into a shouting brawl with newsmen. He made himself a laughingstock when, in an appearance on *60 Minutes* a week before the election, he said that the "real" reason he had dropped out earlier was that nefarious plotters were planning to circulate bogus lurid photographs of his daughter on the eve of her wedding. One comic said: "Now we know the real reason Perot bowed out of the race last July. He had learned that Martians were planning to jump out of his daughter's wedding cake.... Further dirty tricks included the distribution of a doctored photograph, showing the head of Ross Perot attached to the body of a rational person."

In three televised debates, Bush did not do as well as either of his opponents. He conveyed the impression that he no longer had much interest in being incarcerated for four more years in the White House when he could be golfing on the back nine or skiing the slopes at Vail. In the waning days of the campaign, a journalist conjectured that Bush "wanted to spend his time the way most men do who are sixty-eight and have the money to indulge themselves after a long career." He was "tired of pretending he was happy to be with that governor or this congressional candidate and to have to listen to...the out-of-tune high school marching band." Bush himself said, "I don't seem to have the drive" to plunge into "this political stuff anymore." Yet he also believed that he was entitled to another term, and he appeared to resent having to justify himself to voters and await their verdict. The critical moment in the debates came when a black woman asked how the national debt had affected the contenders personally. Bush, at a total loss, said he did not comprehend the question, but Clinton stepped toward the woman and asked sympathetically, "Tell me how it's affected you." In contrast to this display of empathy, viewers caught Bush glancing at his wristwatch, as though indicating that this nonsense was grating on his patrician sensibility—not an image likely to appeal to the public.

Bush found the last days of the campaign disheartening. Once again, in straining to show himself to be a helluva fella, he struck a false note by referring to his opponents as "bozos." A man who had shown some sensitivity to ecological concerns, he said of Senator Gore: "This guy is so far off on the environment extreme, we'll be up to our neck in owls and out of work for every American. This guy's crazy. He is way out, far out. Far out, man." Four days before voters were to go to the polls, Bush sustained another blow when a prosecutor, in securing an indictment of the former secretary of defense, Caspar Weinberger, revealed that when vice president, Bush, contrary to his claims of innocence, had been very much in the loop on the scheme to swap arms for hostages in the Iran-Contra scandal.

In November, Bill Clinton won election to the presidency. His 43 percent of the popular vote was the lowest for a victor since 1912, below the defeated Dukakis's proportion four years earlier, albeit in a two-way race then. But the Comeback Kid's 370 electoral votes far outpaced Bush's 168. With 19 percent of the ballots, Ross Perot registered the largest protest vote since Theodore Roosevelt in 1912, an expression of discontent with the two major parties, but he scored zero in the Electoral College. Perot drew precisely the same proportion of votes from Clinton that he did from Bush, with a large segment of his support coming from disaffected Americans who, if he had not been on the ballot, would have stayed home.

Analysts saw the outcome not as an expression of approval for Bill Clinton but as a brutal rejection of George Bush, spelling the end of the twelve-year Republican reign and the demise of "the age of Reagan." In the last autumn of Reagan's presidency, 58 percent of the nation thought that America was headed in the right direction. In the same season four years later (Bush's last), that figure had dropped to an abysmal 16 percent. In 1992 Bush, who not long before had enjoyed a phenomenal approval rating of more than 90 percent, received only 37 percent of the ballots. No longer did the victorious Gulf War resonate with voters. When Gallup asked poll respondents to name the most important question facing the country, only 3 percent said "the international situation." (Thirty-seven percent picked the economy.) Bush gained a smaller proportion of the popular vote than the discredited Herbert Hoover in 1932 or the overwhelmed Barry Goldwater in 1964. He even lost 27 percent of registered Republicans, as well as 68 percent of Independents. Bush wrote in his diary: "It's 12:15 in the morning, November 4th. The election is over—it's come and gone. It's hard to describe the emotions of something like this. But it's hurt, hurt, hurt." A week later the president, walking a trail at Camp David with Colin Powell, was still saying quietly, "It hurts. It really hurts to be rejected."

Bush's presidency ended not with a bang but with a whimper. On Christmas Eve 1992, as the sands were running out, the president pardoned six of the participants in the Iran-Contra conspiracy, including Cap Weinberger, who was slated to stand trial in less than two weeks. These men, "whether their actions were right or wrong," were motivated by "patriotism," Bush declared, and the "criminalization of policy differences" was "a profoundly troubling development in the political and legal climate of our country." No one, though, had been prosecuted because of "policy differences." Weinberger, in fact, had been indicted on four felony counts. Critics accused the president of acting in order to prevent Weinberger from giving testimony that might have exposed Bush's lying when he was vice president. "The Iran-Contra cover-up, which has continued for more than six years, has now been completed," the prosecutor charged. Bush was not the only president to tarnish his reputation by late-hour pardons, but the episode brought his single term to a sorry finale. Some of his sadness on Election Night may have derived from intimations of what History would say of him. Forever upstaged by his predecessor, he has been dismissed as "Reagan Lite," and after his successor's tempestuous tenure had passed, George Bush came to be regarded, a friendly observer said, as "the comma between two exclamation points."

13

Bill Clinton

PRESIDENT WILLIAM JEFFERSON CLINTON HIT the ground stumbling. He had promised that he would announce an ambitious economic plan on Day Two of his administration, but when that time came, nothing was in place. A prominent political scientist, Stephen Hess, called it "the worst transition in modern history," while Senator Daniel Patrick Moynihan said simply: "They really weren't ready to govern." Usually, at the start of a president's term, criticism is suspended while the new arrivals in town have a chance to settle in, but "far from enjoying the traditional honeymoon," the journalist John Harris has written, "Clinton and the Washington political class were quarreling like a couple who would have split up years ago except for the kids."

From the moment he took power, Clinton appeared to be snakebit. He had intended to focus on the economy "like a laser beam," but the issue that grabbed headlines in his first week was entirely different, and much more controversial. Carelessly, he told a reporter that he was going to carry out his campaign pledge to permit homosexuals to serve in the military "right away." (He might better have said that he would get to it once he established his economic program.) Outraged, the Joint Chiefs demanded an immediate confrontation with the president. Assailed by fierce objections from the Pentagon and on Capitol Hill, Clinton buckled. Eventually, he acquiesced to "don't ask, don't tell," which required the military not to question recruits about their sexual orientation but permitted it to discharge soldiers who were openly gay. Over the next decade, thousands of men and women in uniform identified as homosexuals were expelled.

The episode brought into question Clinton's capacity as chief executive. Quite possibly because of uneasiness about his evasion of service in Vietnam, he failed to establish his authority over the Joint Chiefs, who veered toward insubordination. No less disconcerting was his lack of political acumen in allowing the question to take such prominence at the very outset. "Awful mistake on the president's part," the US Air Force chief of staff later stated. "To single out the gays-in-the-military thing as the number-one problem on his national security agenda was a misjudgment. He just blew it."

Clinton also drew severe criticism for his undisciplined administrative style. He staffed the White House with his 1992 campaigners, some of them remarkably young, and with fellow Arkansans, none of whom had ever served in such roles before. He named one boyhood pal, Vincent Foster, deputy White House counsel and selected as chief of staff Thomas "Mack" McLarty III, who had been his playmate in Miss Mary's kindergarten in Hope, Arkansas. He counted on "Mack the Nice" not to tell him, or anyone, what to do.

The executive branch often seemed directionless, with energy dissipated by lengthy bull sessions in what a British writer later described as "the Pepsi- and pizza-fueled shambles in the West Wing." David Maraniss, the most important chronicler of Clinton's early career, wrote: "Like many members of his generation, Clinton felt uncomfortable with more traditional lines of authority.... White House meetings dragged on for hours without resolution; young subordinates, from their seats by the wall, tossed out opinions and arguments with the status of frontline policy makers." The *Washington Post*'s Bob Woodward later recorded one aide's conception of the Clinton White House: "The staff was too often like a soccer league of 10-year-olds. No one stuck to his part of the field during a game. The ball—any ball—would come on the field, and everyone would go chasing it." In sum, said a shrewd official, the White House was governed by an "ad hocracy."

Hillary Clinton's unprecedented role exacerbated the disarray. Unlike every previous first lady, she installed herself in the West Wing, close to

President Bill Clinton and First Lady Hillary Clinton on Inauguration Day 1993. During the 1992 campaign, Bill Clinton told voters that he was offering a "twofer": if they voted for him, they would also get his wife. During his presidency, the two were viewed as a tandem—to an extent never before seen in the White House. *Doug Mills/Associated Press, ID 9301200391*

the Oval Office. Only a few days after he was inaugurated, the president, without consulting the secretary of health, education, and welfare, appointed his wife chair of a Task Force on Health Care Reform, and he gave her a veto over all major appointments. Early in March 1993, a story made the rounds about their daughter, Chelsea, a student at a private school in the District of Columbia. When a school official told her that he needed to phone her mother for permission to give her a pill, the young woman replied: "Oh, don't phone my mom. She's too busy. Call my dad."

Altogether insensitive to the reality that the American people had not elected her, she regularly used the word "we" in explaining new departures, with the implication that she and her husband were equals. "Hillary Clinton was at the center of virtually all the controversies that beset the Clinton administration during these first six months," the historian William Chafe has concluded. "She not only confirmed her powerful position as copresident with her husband, but suggested to at least some that she had become the dominant figure in the relationship, highlighting by her example of decisive, if sometimes ill-informed, leadership the more ambiguous and equivocating style of her husband."

Characterized by the celebrated *Washington Post* reporter Carl Bernstein as "America's first Warrior First Lady," Hillary Clinton joined with her husband in combat against the media. The president had hardly begun his term when he issued a flagrantly provocative order closing off the corridor between the press room and the office of his most important aide, communications director George Stephanopoulous—an area where reporters had roamed freely for decades. Veteran journalists felt that they were being infantilized. The Clintons were right in thinking that the media were often unfairly antagonistic, but they did little to mend the breach. To critics who thought he should reach out, Bill Clinton would respond, "I went over there, I kissed their fat asses, and what do I get from it?"

The first lady displayed her influence in a more significant way by insisting that the vital post of attorney general go to a woman. Dutifully, the president named a well-qualified lawyer, only to learn that she had not paid Social Security taxes for illegal Peruvian immigrants she had hired to work in her house. After people phoned talk radio programs to ask how Clinton could choose as the country's principal law officer someone who had flouted the law, he had to back off. Early in February, the White House let it be known that the next appointee for attorney general was a federal district court judge. But she withdrew from consideration after it was revealed that she, too, had hired an illegal alien and had a "nanny tax" problem. He ran into yet a third roadblock when to head the civil rights division of the Department of Justice he chose Lani Guinier, a close friend from Yale Law School days. After perusal of her writings on race led to her being dubbed "the quota queen," though, the president abandoned her with the lame explanation that he had not read her work carefully.

Nearly two months went by before he finally won confirmation of a nominee for attorney general: Dade County state attorney Janet Reno. But she had hardly found her way to her desk when she became implicated in an event that caused the president further distress. She inherited a perilous situation at a compound near Waco, Texas, where the Branch Davidians, a cult led by David Koresh, who claimed to be the Messiah, had holed up for weeks in defiance of federal authorities who were seeking to question him about illegal weapons. The Department of Justice was disturbed not only about the arsenal, which included machine guns, but also about reports of sexual abuse of girls whom Koresh claimed as his consorts, some as young as twelve. A raid on the compound in February had resulted in the deaths of four federal agents. In April Attorney General Reno, resolving to end the prolonged siege, authorized government agents to storm the compound. They sought to carry out their assignment humanely, but a fire burst out that killed eighty-six people, including seventeen children. Reno showed her mettle by taking the blame. Clinton, though he had consented to the operation, was nowhere to be seen.

April 1993 proved to be a month of fiascos, large and small, notoriously one that occurred aboard Air Force One at Los Angeles International Airport, when the president got what was believed to be a $200 haircut from the stylist Cristophe of Beverly Hills, delaying planes on two runways for nearly an hour while passengers fumed. Clinton appeared to have no sense of how this indulgence, widely reported in the media with embellishments, conflicted with the image he sought to convey of a down-home country boy. On his next visit to New Hampshire, he was greeted with a mocking sign: "Nice haircut, Bubba."

This odd series of incidents carried into May, when, at the instigation of Hillary Clinton, all seven career employees of the White House Travel Office were summarily fired. That action might have been regarded as a routine matter, but the administration aroused suspicions by awarding a new travel contract to a Little Rock company run by friends of the Clintons, including a distant cousin of the president. Led by the *New York Times* columnist William Safire, formerly a Nixon aide, the media sounded a tocsin about "Travelgate," a term implying that this minor indiscretion rose to the level of malfeasance in Watergate.

During the campaign, Clinton had promised "an explosive hundred-day action period," but the hundredth day arrived with much that had gone wrong and little to celebrate. The columnist David Gergen reported: "Whoooooosshhhhh...is the air rushing out of Bill Clinton's balloon as he ends his first 100 days in office.... His presidency is losing altitude at an alarming rate." Pollsters recorded approval ratings beneath those of eight of his nine most recent predecessors at the same point. (He did better only than Ford after the Nixon pardon.) And Clinton's scores continued to drop. At the end of May, national surveys showed that his approval rating, all the way down to 36 percent, had plunged faster than that of any other postwar chief executive. *Time* highlighted his descent by running a cover with a photo of a miniaturized Clinton accompanied by the huge legend THE INCREDIBLE SHRINKING PRESIDENT.

———

Despite his affinity for the centrist Democratic Leadership Council, Bill Clinton identified himself with those energetic presidents who had made a difference in people's lives. During his quest for the White House, he had been mocked for saying, "I feel your pain," but he did truly empathize with the afflicted, and he very much wanted the federal government to adopt policies that would help families struggling to make ends meet. No campaign pledge drew more notice than his promise to put through a tax cut for the middle class. In addition, he proposed to foster "investments" for education and retraining of workers so that they could adapt to the demands of a global economy, and to "jump-start" the economy by measures such as "fast-track" spending on public works. He wrapped up a number of these ambitions in a $30 billion stimulus package that he hoped would win early approval from Congress. But that was not to be.

In the weeks before his inauguration, Clinton had received grim advice. The chairman of the Federal Reserve, Alan Greenspan, flew into Little Rock, where he lectured the incoming president on the imperative need to focus not on new departures but on lowering the scary budget imbalance. Clinton's own appointees endorsed Greenspan's contention. Secretary of the Treasury Lloyd Bentsen, Robert Rubin (an investment banker who was leaving Goldman Sachs to head the newly created National Economic Council), and budget director Leon Panetta all counseled him to concentrate on narrowing the deficit in the hope that the Fed and Wall Street would react to his earnest efforts by lowering long-term interest rates. Unless they did so, he was informed, he would not be able to come close to creating the eight million new jobs he had promised. Livid, his face flushed, Clinton responded, "You mean to tell me that the success of the program... hinges on the Federal Reserve and a bunch of fucking bond traders?" Yes, all of his advisers nodded, that was precisely what he was being told.

As a New Democrat, Clinton, though initially incensed, found this line of argument not altogether uncongenial. Moreover, the course of action had a political dimension. To win reelection in 1996, he needed to gain the votes of Ross Perot's followers, with their obsession about taming the deficit. It did not take the president long to embrace the reassessment. Even when he visited Hyde Park, Franklin D. Roosevelt's hometown, less than a month after taking office, he boasted that he had slashed "programs that help a lot of good people but that I don't think we can afford at the present level anymore."

To carry off the strategy he had been persuaded to adopt, Clinton set out to woo the chairman of the Fed, who was a formidable presence. A Republican, Greenspan had been chosen by Reagan, then reappointed by Bush. Since his term ran through March 1996, he would be in charge of interest rates for almost all of the president's term. When Clinton delivered his State of the Union address, he accorded Greenspan the place of honor in the chamber. As the president spoke, TV cameras focused on the Fed chairman, seated in the balcony between Hillary Clinton and Tipper Gore, with the implication that he was embracing the president's economic program. There was a question, though, of who was being co-opted. In fact, Clinton's acceptance of Greenspan's advice had significant implications for the institution of the presidency. It marked a transition from Keynesian fiscal policy engineered from the White House to monetary policy directed not by the president but by the Fed.

On February 17, in his budget message to a joint session of Congress, Clinton divulged the administration's altered plan. He proposed to shrink the deficit by half a trillion dollars over the course of four years. In the next year, he stated, he would make a beginning by slashing $60 billion from Medicare and Medicaid. In addition, as evidence of his commitment to fiscal austerity, he announced that there would be no middle-class tax cut.

Clinton's course dismayed the corps of progressives who had been on his campaign team, including virtually all of his top White House aides. "Why did we run?" asked one of them, pounding a table in frustration. "The presidency has been hijacked." Liberals on the White House staff likened those who were advising Clinton to the alien abductors in the film *Invasion of the Body Snatchers*. The plain-spoken, foul-mouthed James Carville complained: "We've lost our message of hope and optimism. Every time I read a fucking newspaper, I'm hearing about our deficit reduction plan."

Clinton's many concessions, which irked liberals, did not spare him criticism from moderates either, largely because the president continued to indulge in populist rhetoric. Mack McLarty, who had headed a natural gas firm in Arkansas that ranked in the Fortune 500, chided him for failing to be respectful toward men who had accumulated fortunes, and the head of the Democratic Leadership Council (DLC) told the president that "among moderate and conservative Democrats there is a growing feeling that you're just not dancing with the ones who brought you to the dance." As his poll numbers tumbled, Clinton, who was never disposed to blame himself for anything that went wrong, decided that his liberal advisers had led him astray, and he inflicted on Stephanopoulos nasty early-morning temper tantrums.

The president resolved to refashion his image by a move that stunned Washington: an invitation to David Gergen to be White House communications director in place of Stephanopoulos (who was to stay on as senior adviser). When the White House called to say that the president wanted him to come into the administration, Gergen later recalled, "I damn near dropped the phone." The *U.S. News & World Report* editor had been one of Clinton's most outspoken, though respectful, critics. Shortly before the phone call, he had written of the president: "Friends and foe alike think he can be rolled. Sadly, those perceptions are now creeping in about Clinton—one of the most gifted, dedicated men ever to serve in the Oval Office. He has a wonderful head and a big heart, but people are looking for more backbone." Furthermore, Gergen had served under three Republican presidents—Nixon, Ford, and Reagan— and had never been identified with a Democratic administration. But when Clinton asked him if he would "stop jeering, get off the sidelines," Gergen agreed to come aboard. The president told him: "I'm way out of position. I'm way off to the left. I want to get back to the DLC." (On another occasion, he said that he felt bound to the liberal Democrats on the Hill "like Ahab to Moby Dick, with the same results.") After taking over in late May, Gergen brought an unaccustomed crispness to White House operations as well as astute counsel, but, Chafe has noted, "to many staff members, Gergen's appointment seemed like inviting a Republican fox into the Democratic henhouse."

Clinton's turn to the right did not win him any cooperation whatsoever from the Republicans. No matter how greatly he reduced federal spending, they insisted that he slash the budget still more. They even denied his legitimacy. They called him not "President Clinton" but "Mister Clinton." The Republican leader in the Senate, Robert Dole, announced that he would be spokesman for the 57 percent of the electorate who had not voted for Clinton, and, to balk the president, he calculatedly adopted the filibuster as the Republicans' chief weapon—something no party leader had ever done before. Only one remnant remained of Clinton's original program—the $30 billion stimulus package—and Dole employed the filibuster to kill it. Instead of impugning Dole, the media interpreted the event as evidence that Clinton was a failed legislative leader who could not break the stale politics of deadlock, and anointed Dole as his likely successor.

Total Republican intransigence left Clinton wholly dependent on his own party's delegation in Congress to put through his budget. If he lost even a small number of Democrats, he would come to grief. As the day of the showdown roll call on the budget approached in late summer, Clinton found himself ten votes short in the House, with the total in favor stalled at 208. Hunched over spreadsheets showing the disposition of all 435 members, he said, "I just don't see how we get there."

On the night of August 5, the members of the House assembled to vote Clinton's budget up or down. As they scrutinized the scoreboard (green lights for ayes, red for nays—no light for votes withheld), few could be sure of the outcome. At 10:11 p.m., the first tally showed the president trailing, but with eleven Democrats still to cast a ballot. When voting resumed, the count deadlocked, 213–213. After he moved ahead, 216–214, with not a single Republican in favor, he still required another two yeas from the four Democrats who had not yet turned in cards registering their commitments.

The last two Democratic votes he needed came from members in predominantly Republican districts whose seats were in jeopardy in the next election—one of them Marjorie Margolies-Mezvinsky from the posh Main Line neighborhoods outside Philadelphia. With most Democrats cheering lustily as the 218–216 victory was announced, grimacing Republicans cried out, "Bye-bye Marjorie!" When Margolies-Mezvinsky returned to Pennsylvania, her constituents were so angry that she required a police escort to attend town-hall meetings. She did, indeed, go down to defeat in the next election. Her entire congressional career lasted but two years. (The story, though, had an unexpected denouement. Her son married Chelsea Clinton, only child of the president and the first lady.)

With the House on record, the battle shifted to the Senate, where Clinton had been struggling for weeks with recalcitrant Democrats. His first big hurdle was the Senate Finance Committee. With, once again, every Republican in opposition, he needed all eleven Democrats on his side to get his budget reported out. "Eleven votes, Mister President," Chairman Pat Moynihan told him. With them, "you are a strong president." Without them, "you are a weak president." After tedious negotiations, he won the assent of an Oklahoma Democrat tied to the oil industry so that the Finance Committee sent the bill to the Senate floor, 11–9, but only after another $20 billion had been taken away from Medicare. The president faced an even tougher task in seeking to secure a majority of the entire Senate. He could not prevail if he lost more than six Democrats, and his agent on the Hill reported nineteen Democrats in doubt. In overcoming resistance, Clinton performed masterfully. He won one senator by promising him a round of golf, others by invitations to jog with him. But, after all of his devoted effort, he wound up one vote short.

In the end, as though scripted in Hollywood, the resolution of the months of drama lay entirely with one man: Senator Bob Kerrey of Nebraska. He was a very tough sell for the president, who had been his rival for the 1992 Democratic nomination. Clinton's celebrated charm left the Nebraskan cold. Having lost a leg in the Vietnam War, Kerrey found it hard to conceal his contempt for a man who had manipulated the draft to escape serving his country. On the day before the Senate roll call, Kerrey phoned to say, "Mister President, I'm going to vote no."

Though Clinton was powerless to change his mind, other influences moved Kerrey to reconsider. A conference with Bob Dole left him with the realization that he did not feel at home with Republicans. Pat Moynihan and his wife, who had supported Kerrey's presidential candidacy, urged him to fall in line. Even more influential was an Omaha constituent, the country's richest man. Warren Buffett advised him to ignore the bleating of the wealthy, who could well afford to pay taxes. Kerrey's switch produced a 50–50 tie on the bill, and, as presiding officer of the Senate, Vice President Gore cast the deciding vote in favor.

The Omnibus Budget Reconciliation Act of 1993 projected a reduction in the deficit of nearly half a trillion dollars over the next five years, in large part by taking money from programs cherished by liberal Democrats. Furthermore, it stipulated a rise in the gasoline levy, a regressive measure that weighed disproportionately on poorer Americans. But it also cut taxes for fifteen million lower-income Americans while raising them on multimillionaires. The law, flawed though it was, proved to be by far the most important enactment of Bill Clinton's first year in office.

From the north portico of the White House an hour before midnight, Clinton, peering out into the dark, addressed TV cameras. "What we heard tonight at the other end of Pennsylvania Avenue was the sound of gridlock breaking," he declared. "After twelve long years, we can say to the American people tonight we have laid the foundation for the renewal of the American dream. . . . After a long season of denial and drift and decline, we are seizing control of our economic destiny." (At a jubilant gathering, a high-ranking official offered another reason for rejoicing in the outcome: "So the Clinton staff can finish high school.")

Some observers thought the jubilation misconceived. Their misgivings had been presaged earlier that summer by a *New York Times* editorial titled "A Budget Worthy of Mr. Bush," which stated: "Mr. Clinton promised voters more than a rehash. He pledged to end the consumption frenzy of the 1980s by turning the federal budget toward investments in infrastructure, children and training. But Congress is veering in a different direction. Unless it turns around and fast, Mr. Clinton's victory in getting a deficit-reduction package through Congress will be hollow."

Clinton, though, found deep gratification, as well as hope for the future, in his victory. He knew that, whatever the shortcomings of the budget, he had succeeded, by getting it through Congress, in averting a disastrous setback from which his presidency would never have recovered. Furthermore, he had demonstrated that he was a skillful legislative tactician. His triumph led him to believe that new accomplishments might be just over the horizon. "Now," he told his wife, "we can get on with what we really came here to do." Despite their many losses, Chafe has pointed out, "the Clintons found a way to claw their way back." He added: "By early fall, pivotal pieces of Clinton's domestic agenda had fallen into place. Clinton's poll numbers were up, and there was a new sense of possibility in the air."

Even in the fumble-plagued first days of his presidency, Clinton could point to breakthroughs. Barely two weeks after his inauguration,

Congress enacted legislation that he cherished and that Bush had twice vetoed. The Family and Medical Leave Act of 1993 mandated that employees be given up to twelve weeks of leave a year to cope with emergencies—not only illness but also demands such as childbirth. Early on, too, instead of seeking change wholly through Congress, which might obstruct him, Clinton resorted to the power of the pen. He had hardly taken office when he reversed the Reagan-Bush executive orders prohibiting financial support for family planning. He also issued an edict ending the ban on using fetal tissue in medical research. Scientists hailed this action as an important step toward the treatment of diseases such as Parkinson's. In addition, he rescinded a gag order that had forbidden abortion counseling in federally funded clinics.

The president also had more than a little to show from his battles on the Hill. In May, he signed the National Voter Registration Act of 1993, which Congress had been considering, but not passing, since the 1970s. In 1991, the measure had finally made its way through both houses, only to be killed by a Bush veto. The "motor voter" law, as it was popularly called, required states to make it possible for a citizen applying for a driver's license to register to vote at the same time. Advocates expected that, by making voting less difficult, the statute would raise turnout, which was far below that in most other advanced democracies. He took particular pleasure in signing the National and Community Service Trust Act because it authorized one of his pet projects: AmeriCorps, which helped student volunteers to defray costs of a college education. Carrying through from his years in Arkansas when he had been hailed as an "educational governor," Clinton won approval early in 1994 of the Educate America Act, providing federal financing for state programs that developed educational standards.

The president grasped the opportunity to liberalize jurisprudence by appointing Ruth Bader Ginsburg to the US Supreme Court in June 1993. Despite a brilliant law school career, she had been denied a clerkship by Felix Frankfurter solely because of her sex. Undaunted, she had become a cofounder of the Women's Rights Project, general counsel of the American Civil Liberties Union, and the first female tenured professor at Columbia University Law School. She went on to serve for thirteen years as a judge on the prestigious US Court of Appeals for the District of Columbia. Not long after the Senate confirmed her, 96–3,

Clinton filled a second vacancy on the High Court by elevating Stephen Breyer, who had been a professor of law at Harvard and a special Watergate prosecutor before being chosen for the First Circuit Court of Appeals in 1980.

As the year wound down, it brought to a gratifying climax a remarkable rally for the president. A headline in *Congressional Quarterly* highlighted the prevailing perception: CLINTON RECOVERS FROM EARLY STUMBLES, ENDING YEAR IN COMMAND OF CONGRESS. Pollsters found that 63 percent of Americans thought of him as a can-do leader and gave him higher approval ratings than either Congress or the press received. Clinton's revival came as no surprise to those who had followed his career closely from the beginning, for they had witnessed, more than once, that just when he hit bottom he started to climb back. But they had also learned the converse—that when all was going well to expect him to crash. "Clinton's life," remarked the journalist Michael Kelly, "trails him like a peculiarly single-minded mugger, popping out from the shadows every time it seems the President is safe—to whack the staggering victim anew." December 1993, which saw such cheery tidings, also brought omens of troubles that were to plague him for years to come, even threatening to drive him from the White House.

In December 1993, at a time when the president's popularity exceeded that of Reagan's toward the end of the first year in office, a conservative periodical, *American Spectator*, published an article by David Brock alleging that when governor of Arkansas, Bill Clinton had employed state troopers as sexual procurers. In particular, it cited an instance in 1991 when, troopers said, they had lured a young woman identified only as "Paula" to a Little Rock hotel room where the governor had propositioned her. Five months later, Paula Corbin Jones filed suit against Clinton, demanding $700,000 in damages and an apology. She claimed that she had been denied "equal protection of the laws" guaranteed by the US Constitution because Clinton had been guilty of "sexually harassing and assaulting her" and had created "a hostile work environment" for her as a state employee. (A complaint filed by her lawyers stated: "Clinton then approached the sofa and as he sat down he lowered his trousers and underwear exposing his erect penis and asked Jones to 'kiss it.'")

With Washington buzzing over these "Troopergate" accusations, the press detonated another bombshell. As far back as the 1992 campaign, the *New York Times* had intimated that the Clintons might have been involved in skulduggery with regard to Whitewater, a land development corporation in Arkansas. In 1978, they had invested in a resort speculation in the Ozarks with an Arkansas businessman, Jim McDougal, and his wife. The project failed, and McDougal moved on to acquire a savings and loan, Madison Guaranty, for which Hillary Clinton at the Rose Law Firm provided legal services. The collapse of Madison Guaranty triggered an investigation with allegations that the Clintons were implicated in shady dealings. The controversy agitated politicians and pundits inside the Beltway but failed to gain traction in the country until a revelation in December linked it to the fate of the president's deputy White House counsel, Vincent Foster.

Few other Arkansans enjoyed such an intimate association with the Clintons as Vince Foster. He had grown up in Hope a neighbor of Bill Clinton, and as a partner in the Rose Law Firm in Little Rock, he had been the one who had overcome prejudice against women to make possible the hiring of Hillary Clinton. As partners, they were so close that there were even rumors that they were having an affair. Foster, who had long been the personal lawyer for both Clintons, was a man of sterling reputation. He brought to mind, Hillary Clinton said, Gregory Peck playing the noble attorney Atticus Finch.

Foster found Washington a jolting change from Arkansas, where he was so esteemed. Everything he was assigned—from botched nominations to Travelgate—seemed to go wrong, and, a sensitive man who suffered bouts of depression, he took the blame upon himself. Still worse, the *Wall Street Journal* ran mean pieces on its editorial page depicting him as a figure of evil who was masterminding a cover-up of Bill Clinton's nefarious deeds in Arkansas. The conservative Republican senator from Wyoming Alan Simpson later said of these attacks: "They just hounded him. It was ghastly to watch. Ghastly.... The *Wall Street Journal* was after him more than anyone else. But everybody was after him."

On July 20, 1993, the half-year anniversary of Clinton's inauguration, Foster drove to a park in McLean, Virginia, overlooking the Potomac and shot himself. Police came upon his body—a bullet in his head, an ancient Colt revolver at his side, powder burns on his hand. Foster left a torn-up note that, pieced together, read: "I made mistakes from igno-rance, inexperience and overwork.... The public will never believe the innocence of the Clintons and their loyal staff. The WSJ editors lie without consequence. I was not meant for the job or the spotlight of public life in Washington. Here ruining people is considered sport." Every subsequent investigation reached the self-evident conclusion that Foster, depressed, had taken his life, but the right-wing syndicated broadcaster Rush Limbaugh informed his twenty million listeners that Foster had been "murdered in an apartment owned by Hillary Clinton," and rumormongers circulated the story that Foster "knew so much bad stuff about the Clintons that they had him killed."

The mainline press, not beset by paranoia, made no attempt to link Foster's death to possible misbehavior by the Clintons until December 1993, when it headlined a shocking revelation: "Foster's office was secretly searched hours after his body was found," and files labeled "Whitewater" were removed by the White House counsel and turned over to the Clintons on the grounds that, since Foster had been their attorney, these were private documents protected by lawyer-client privilege. It devel-oped that in lifting the papers, he was carrying out Hillary Clinton's orders. The report, as CNN's legal analyst Jeffrey Toobin has noted, fed a "media frenzy." Even when Clinton flew to the former Soviet Union in January, an NBC News correspondent questioned him in Ukraine about the Arkansas land deal.

Journalists found it easy to think the worst of the Clintons because Arkansas was a notoriously corrupt state. His biographer John Harris has written: "Arkansas was a perpetual trapdoor in Clinton's presidency. It was always swinging at unwelcome moments to reveal complicated tales from the past—relationships and rivalries, alleged affairs or murky busi-ness deals, that were always just a bit hard to explain." McDougal was later convicted of eighteen felony counts of fraud and conspiracy, Bill Clinton's successor as governor of Arkansas resigned after he was found guilty of misapplying funds, and the former mayor of Little Rock whom Clinton had appointed associate US attorney general went to prison.

The press, without ever uncovering anything felonious about the Clintons' involvement in Whitewater, ran scare stories day after day im-plying that there was, or might be, something. As Toobin has pointed out, the *New York Times* indulged in vague phrases to insinuate wrongdoing, though "no one could ever say with precision, much less with the spec-ificity required for a criminal case, what Bill and Hillary Clinton had done wrong." Instead, the media hinted darkly at "unanswered questions," creating, as Toobin said, "an almost comic circularity of reasoning, the very existence of inquiries about Whitewater...seen as proof that they were justified."

Even less can be said for Paula Jones's contention that Clinton had denied her equal protection of the laws. A judge was later to dismiss her suit summarily because the plaintiff failed to provide any evidence of job discrimination. She had, in fact, not even troubled to check her employ-ment records. Though she claimed to be acting to safeguard her reputa-tion, she was the one who chose to reveal who "Paula" was, and she wound up posing nude for *Playboy*. No one will ever know for sure what happened in that Little Rock hotel room, but Toobin concluded, "All in all, the record suggests that Clinton and Paula Corbin had a consensual sexual encounter." When it became evident that Jones was concerned not with protecting her honor but with cashing in on her accusation, her lawyers resigned, warning of "a perception of greed and hatred on your part" and of the risk that she would be portrayed as "under the in-fluence of right-wing Clinton-haters," as she undoubtedly was.

Newspapermen sneered at Hillary Clinton when she said that her husband was the target of a "vast right-wing conspiracy," but she was correct, although "vast" overstates the numbers involved. An unsavory ring of enemies of the Clintons in Arkansas connived in a ruthless cam-paign against him financed by the Pittsburgh billionaire Richard Mellon Scaife, who spent millions of the huge fortune he had inherited. No accusation was too ludicrous for Scaife and his associates, who depicted Clinton as a drug kingpin and murderer who "did away with" scores of victims. Paula Jones was able to carry her case all the way to the US Supreme Court because she was bankrolled by far-right outfits. (In his book *Blinded by the Right: The Conscience of an Ex-Conservative*, David Brock, who had broken the original "Paula" story, publicly apologized to Clinton, saying that his article was "bad journalism" and that the troop-ers, who had been paid under the table by the conspirators, "had slimy motives.") The dean of the Washington press corps, Helen Thomas, later said of Clinton: "He never knew a second in the White House when he was not being investigated. The ultraright gave him no quarter. They went after him from the moment he stepped into the White House. Every second, every breathing moment."

Despite the sordid origin of the allegations, the *Washington Post* demanded that the Clintons turn over all the documents relating to Whitewater, which the couple, infuriated by the unconscionable vendetta against them, saw no reason to oblige. "These are my papers," the first lady said. "They belong to me. I could throw them all in the Potomac River if I wanted to." Turning over records to their accusers, the Clintons believed, would only fuel a wildfire that could not be quelled. They had strong grounds for anticipating that outcome, but their reluctance to comply opened them to the insinuation that they, like Nixon, were stonewalling. "There is one strong argument in favor of the Clintons' approach: the unfairness of their enemies," David Gergen has written. "Zealous accusers have been inventing outrageous stories about them and seeking their destruction." He added, though, that this understandable response drew them unwisely into saying "Hell, no!" not just to the "villainous" but to the press, members of Congress, and other legitimate inquirers.

Two days before Christmas, they relented, only to face immediately a new problem that consumed the rest of the holiday season: Should the president agree to the appointment of a special prosecutor to investigate Whitewater, even though it meant that, in essence, he would be encouraging an exploration of whether he had been guilty of a criminal offense before taking office? Gergen and Clinton's other political advisers favored that course as the best way to quiet the furor and win vindication. Only the White House counsel dissented. "They will broaden the investigation to areas we haven't even contemplated," he warned presciently. "They will chase you, your family and friends through the presidency and beyond."

On January 12, 1994, Clinton announced that he wanted the attorney general to name a special prosecutor. "It was the worst presidential decision I ever made," he later said, "wrong on the facts, wrong on the law, wrong on the politics, wrong for the presidency and the Constitution." But at the time he had concluded that the uproar had become too raucous to ignore. Not only Republican lawmakers but also a number of Democratic senators—among them Pat Moynihan and Bob Kerrey—were insisting upon a searching inquiry. Noting the impact of the recent Vince Foster revelations, National Public Radio's legal affairs correspondent Nina Totenberg explained: "Whitewater was complicated. It was a land deal. It was a subject that was obscure, to say the least, not easy to explain. But the idea that somebody who's very close to the president, a boyhood friend, suddenly kills himself out of nowhere, and he's the central contact point on Whitewater, is something everybody can understand, and people wonder if something's being hidden. It became the reason a special prosecutor had to be appointed."

Precisely one year after Clinton's inauguration, Attorney General Reno named as special prosecutor Robert Fiske, a highly regarded lawyer who had been chosen by President Ford to be a US attorney in New York. A Republican, Fiske had compiled such an unassailable record that Jimmy Carter had kept him on. Though Democrats might have been uneasy at the choice of a Republican to assess the president's past in an era of heated partisanship, Fiske proved himself to be impressively fair-minded. In fact, the only outcry against him came from ultrarightists who deplored his conclusion that, contrary to the conspiracy-minded, Vince Foster had not been killed but, as a consequence of untreated depression, had committed suicide. At the same time, the president signed into law a new measure taking the power to appoint an "independent counsel" (no longer called a "special prosecutor") away from the attorney general and vesting it in the federal judiciary.

In August, a three-judge panel picked by Chief Justice Rehnquist and headed by an arch-conservative who was an associate of the right-wing North Carolina senator Jesse Helms turned down Reno's request to reauthorize Fiske and chose instead Kenneth Starr, who had been named a US Court of Appeals judge by Reagan and solicitor general by Bush. Demonized by Clinton admirers, Starr was by no means an ally of the extreme right, though he was unquestionably a committed conservative. More importantly, he had certain liabilities that raised disturbing questions. Nina Totenberg later said of Starr: "He had given advice to the Paula Jones team, and he didn't have any prosecutorial experience.... That's why I thought he was a particularly unfortunate choice." Subsequently, five former presidents of the American Bar Association stated that his relationship to Paula Jones's lawyers disqualified him. Nearly a decade later, Starr told an interviewer that someone else should have been picked.

The prolonged inquiries into Clinton's past seriously compromised the president's capacity to carry out his responsibilities. The Paula Jones allegations, in particular, eroded respect for America's head of state. On

The Tonight Show, Jay Leno remarked: "At a town meeting in Rhode Island, President Clinton said that there were powerful forces threatening to bring down his administration. I think that they are called hormones." Clinton, wrote Elizabeth Drew, confronted "the possibility that the public trust essential to governing was evaporating and might soon be gone, and perhaps irretrievable." In 1994, the proportion of Americans who said they had faith in government hit a new low of 15 percent. This state of disillusion compounded Clinton's difficulties not only in putting through his domestic program but, even more, in gaining the respect of friends and foes heading regimes in other lands.

When pressed to look abroad, Clinton responded, "Foreign policy is not what I came here to do." The president, wrote the essayist Garry Wills, was a "foreign policy minimalist, doing as little as possible as late as possible in place after place," and Elizabeth Drew called him "an absentee landlord on foreign policy." But, as the diplomatic historian George Herring has observed, "Clinton…quickly discovered the painful truth that in foreign policy US presidents do not have to seek trouble, it finds them." Though the Cold War had ended under Bush, Clinton was the first president since FDR nearly half a century earlier to go through his entire presidency with no experience of worldwide conflict with the USSR, and, consequently, both he and most Americans anticipated that he could take a breather from responsibilities overseas. He came to understand, however, that, as he said, he governed in a "new world" that was "more free but less stable." To his and the country's surprise, he was to become not merely a participant in international engagements but a peacemaker who intervened from the Caribbean to the Balkans to the Middle East.

Clinton started out mortifyingly. He inherited a US commitment to a high-risk United Nations effort in Somalia in the Horn of Africa that had begun in December 1992 during Bush's last weeks in office. Early in June 1993, guerrillas controlled by the most aggressive Somali warlord, Mohamed Farah Aidid, killed twenty-four Pakistani soldiers serving the United Nations. On October 3, rocket-propelled grenades brought down two US Black Hawk helicopters in Mogadishu, the Somalian capital. Over the next seventeen hours, Aidid's guerrillas killed eighteen American troops and wounded more than eighty. Television viewers in the United States watched the sickening sight of a mob dragging the body of one slain soldier through the streets and then setting it afire.

The tragedy produced a wave of revulsion in Congress and in the nation—not only at the Somalia mission but for any US involvement in foreign lands where no clear American national interest was at stake. Washington sent out new orders to the field command: "Your first priority is to take no casualties." After a time, Clinton withdrew US forces from Somalia—an ignominious confession of impotence. The ugly encounter, featured in the highly popular film *Black Hawk Down*, left the president extremely wary of ever again approving well-intentioned interventions if they might cost American lives.

Clinton suffered further humiliation in Haiti, where he had already experienced an embarrassing comedown. During the 1992 campaign, he had upbraided Bush for not permitting Haitian refugees to settle in the United States. But when the CIA informed him that, heeding his words, a hundred thousand or more Haitians were building boats with the intention of disembarking in Florida, where they would be unwelcome, Clinton backed off, though he knew that he would be alienating the black caucus in Congress. In 1994, deeply concerned about the blow to democracy delivered by a military coup in Haiti that had displaced the country's elected president, Jean-Bertrand Aristide, he sent an American vessel to the island to facilitate the restoration of Aristide to power. But when, on October 11, the USS *Harlan County* attempted to dock in Port-au-Prince, a ragtag mob of supporters of the junta forced the ship to turn back. With the rioters' mocking chant of "Somalia! Somalia!" in their ears, the peacekeepers slunk home. The mighty United States of America had been vanquished by forty to sixty men, some of them unarmed.

The president revealed himself to be no more effective in the Balkans, where Serbs under Slobodan Milošević were engaged in a bloody orgy of "ethnic cleansing" of Muslims in Bosnia-Herzegovina, which had broken away from Yugoslavia in 1992. During the campaign, he had said he would do "whatever it takes to stop the slaughter," adding, "History has shown us that you can't allow the mass extermination of people and just sit by and watch it happen." In April 1993, he even entertained the possibility of sending an American expeditionary force. But that impulse quickly faded. Secretary of State Warren Christopher characterized Bosnia as "a problem from hell" in a "morass" of ancient enemies. "The

United States," he declared, "simply doesn't have the means to make people in that region...like each other." Clinton, too, was discouraged by reading of centuries of animosity. "I will not let Sarajevo fall," he assured Congress, but added, "Don't take that as an absolute." Congress strongly opposed what might become another Vietnam, General Powell and the Pentagon disapproved of intervention, and European allies wanted no part of it. Given all these objections, Clinton's caution was understandable, but by speaking boldly and then not acting, the president seemed irresolute. With the Western powers immobilized, the mayhem continued: slaughter of men and boys; mass rape of women; and, as Clinton himself said, "innocent people herded into concentration camps, children gunned down by snipers on their way to school, soccer fields and parks turned into cemeteries."

In April 1994, even more hideous ethnic bloodletting erupted in the small African republic of Rwanda, where Hutus massacred eight hundred thousand Tutsis, sometimes by hacking them to death with machetes. To remind the West that it faced another Mogadishu if it tried to halt the killing, the Hutus executed ten Belgian peacekeepers. The United States not only refused to take any action but impeded a UN initiative to send in an African force. Clinton later said that his failure to do anything in Rwanda was the biggest blot on his foreign policy record. "We never even had a staff meeting on it," he confessed. "I blew it."

Clinton faltered in China, too. He had berated Bush for not penalizing the Chinese government after the Tiananmen Square carnage, but as president, he went farther than his predecessor in cozying up to Beijing. He began with a policy of expecting China to improve its behavior on human rights in return for trade concessions, but he soon abandoned that linkage. When decades of economic pressure on the small country of Cuba had brought no moderation, why, he asked, could anyone suppose that the Chinese, comprising one-fifth of the people on the globe, were going to yield? Furthermore, advisers pointed out to him, two hundred thousand Americans were engaged in catering to the vast Chinese market, which absorbed $9 billion annually of US-made goods. Clinton had been in office little more than a year when he renewed China's most-favored-nation privileges, an action that Majority Leader George Mitchell said would "confirm for the regime the success of the policy of repression on human rights and manipulation on trade."

Undeterred by this criticism, Clinton persisted in his unapologetic imitation of George Bush.

After this lackluster beginning, however, Clinton demonstrated a notable capacity to learn on the job. The former governor of Arkansas, who had spent his entire career dealing with provincial matters, entered the White House with no experience and little comprehension of how to handle vexatious problems overseas. Air Force Chief of Staff General Merrill McPeak said of Clinton: "When he came to town, if you asked him a question about health care, you'd better sit down because it's going to be an hour before he's done.... The guy was awesome in his grasp of detail. You asked him about what to do in Bosnia, where Muslims were being slaughtered by the Serbians in large numbers, you got tap dancing." But after months of rough initiation, the young president began to find his footing. McPeak concluded: "I left after Clinton had been there a year and a half. At that point, he was still in the penalty box as far as I was concerned; he hadn't learned enough to be effective internationally. It was after I left that I thought he did a number of things that were pretty smart.... President Clinton was inept at the beginning and rather skilled at the end."

In 1993, the president held the first of a number of meetings with Boris Yeltsin at the University of British Columbia in Vancouver as the Royal Canadian Mounted Police stood guard. Though he knew that American polls showed strong opposition to foreign aid at a time when Congress was cutting back on funds at home, he arrived with a $1.6 billion package for Yeltsin because he thought it imperative to sustain democratic forces in the former dictatorship and because some of the money would go to dismantling nuclear weapons. Yeltsin, a heavy drinker, was a notoriously prickly character, but Canadian prime minister Brian Mulroney told reporters that the Russian and the American "seem to be getting along like a house afire." Soon they were on "Boris" and "Beel" terms. "They just plain liked each other," said Ambassador-at-Large Strobe Talbott. "Clinton, who was a genius at developing personal relationships, made a point of doing so with Yeltsin."

That same year, Clinton lucked into an opportunity to appear statesmanlike when he was asked to allow the White House to be the venue for the signing of an accord between the Israeli prime minister, Yitzhak Rabin, whom he came to admire immensely, and Yasser Arafat, leader of the

Bill on sax. At this dinner party in Russia, President Boris Yeltsin expresses delight at the American's performance on a saxophone that Yeltsin had given him, but critics in the United States thought that Clinton did not have enough sense of the majesty of his office. *Courtesy of the William J. Clinton Presidential Library, ID P11471_26a*

Palestine Liberation Organization. Though the agreement had been negotiated not by the United States but by Norway, the spotlight focused on the American president as the great reconciler, and at a meeting of the two foes in Washington on September 13, Clinton filled the role impressively.

Two days later in the East Room, at a gathering of notables including three former presidents, Clinton received deserved acclaim for his skill in launching a campaign for approval of the North American Free Trade Agreement, felling tariff barriers among Canada, the United States, and Mexico. He did so knowing that the pact was strenuously opposed by organized labor—a major component of his party—and by prominent Democrats on the Hill. After initially hesitating about championing an accord negotiated by Republicans, Clinton had decided that he must take it on. "I have to be a president beyond the borders," he said. In his address at the White House, the president, noting the stark challenges presented by a global economy, declared: "In a fundamental sense, this debate about NAFTA is...about whether we will embrace...changes and create the jobs of tomorrow, or...resist...changes, hoping we can preserve the economic structures of yesterday." His words could not have pleased Republicans more. Senator Dole said of the talk, "President

Clinton hit it out of the ballpark," and George Bush, alluding to the "very eloquent statement by President Clinton," commented, "Now I understand why he's inside looking out and I'm outside looking in."

Republican support alone, though, could not get the covenant through Congress, and, warned that he was forty votes short in the House, Clinton devoted himself almost exclusively for three weeks that autumn to winning over dubious Democrats. He found it a tough grind. Progressives were distressed that the president's eagerness to gain a larger share of world markets for American businesses was relegating US ambassadors to the role, as *Business Week* wrote, of "unabashed peddlers in pinstripes, vigorously lobbying local officials on behalf of Corporate America." The Sierra Club warned of lax pollution controls in Mexico, and organized labor foresaw a southward outflow of jobs to low-wage firms below the Rio Grande. One congressman, an Ohio Democrat, branded Clinton "the candidate of Wall Street, not Main Street." Despite this fierce opposition, the president, refusing to be disheartened by predictions of failure, won the approval of Congress, though in the House, where he benefited from support by more than three-quarters of the Republicans, only 100 of the 258 Democrats voted in favor.

Subsequently, numbers of Americans viewed the enactment of NAFTA and his outreach to Asia as causes not for celebration but for sorrow. The historian Douglas Brinkley has written that in his home state, Ohio, "the whole industrial infrastructure is crumbling because all the jobs have been outsourced." Clinton, he added, "captured the spirit of the age with his vociferous endorsement of globalization, but some of the shortcomings of globalization are coming home to roost." Similarly, a veteran of legislative wars, Michigan congressman David Bonior, who for more than a decade was Democratic whip, has said: "It was clearly a buy-and-sell operation for the multinational corporate elite that was advanced by Prime Minister Mulroney and President Salinas, and Clinton bought into it hook, line, and sinker. While he may think of this as one of his great achievements, it is one of the great disasters in modern economics. ... NAFTA undermined all the progressive legislation that it took a whole century to put together."

But whatever one thought of NAFTA (and it should be noted that no fewer than fifteen Nobel laureate economists endorsed it), Clinton unquestionably emerged from the controversy with considerably heightened prestige. The test of wills had come at a moment, the historian William Berman has observed, when "he had leaped from ice floe to ice floe and was still standing, but...hadn't become a commanding leader." His willingness to defy both powerful Democratic legislators and union chieftains, however, silenced, at least for a time, the most common criticism of him—that he lacked convictions. "It seemed," Berman has concluded, "that he had grown—inwardly and outwardly—that this was a step in his development as President."

Fortified by his success on NAFTA, Clinton revisited overseas predicaments that he had not handled with distinction earlier, conspicuously in Haiti. When he first contemplated military intervention to oust the right-wing junta, a Pentagon official had cautioned that there was "too much of a Mogadishu possibility." But in September 1994, deciding that boldness was required, the president, with the approval of the UN, ordered an invasion. "Leave now or we will force you from power," he warned the junta. Planes carrying paratroopers had already taken off from Pope Air Force Base in North Carolina on a two-hour flight to the island when they were called back. Clinton postponed the mission at the very last second only because a self-appointed delegation of Jimmy Carter, Colin Powell, and Senator Sam Nunn persuaded the country's strongman to step down. When, in the same year as the Haiti showdown, the president's threat to employ force in Iraq compelled Saddam Hussein to retreat from another move on Kuwait, a New York tabloid ran a headline on its front page: CLINTON 2, BULLIES 0. By these displays of resolve, Clinton wound up his early ventures abroad determined to subdue a more formidable foe than any foreign power: the give-no-quarter Republicans on Capitol Hill, who were poised to kill the most important initiative of his presidency—a plan for universal health care.

———

Commentators have been hard put to account for why, in his very first week in office, Bill Clinton designated his wife to take charge of developing the health care proposal that he expected would be his showpiece—the most formidable assignment ever given to a first lady. One explanation has been especially conspicuous. "In the view of many," William Chafe has noted, "Hillary controlled health care as a *quid pro*

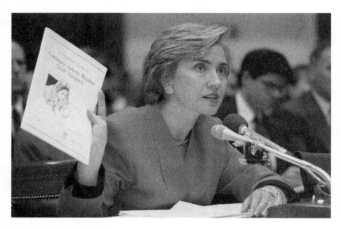

President Clinton was roundly criticized for appointing his wife to head a task force on national health reform, but in several days of testimony before five congressional committees in the fall of 1993, she showed an impressive command of the subject—though to no avail. *Doug Mills/Associated Press, ID 9309280106*

quo for rescuing her husband from the Gennifer Flowers scandal and staying married." David Gergen, while allowing that the president acted in part "because he wanted to promote women as national leaders, which was welcome," and because he "liked to share with his wife, which was generous," added: "But does anyone doubt that he also wanted to placate her? Had it not been for his own past, I doubt he would have placed his presidency so fully in her hands."

Still, as both writers and others have acknowledged, the president had another reason for appointing his wife to chair a task force. "Of all the people I've ever worked with in my life, she's better at organizing and leading people from a complex beginning to a certain end than anybody," he declared. No one questioned her mastery of the subject. In the course of the next year, the *New York Times* reported that she "dazzled" members of congressional committees "in the most impressive testimony . . . anyone could remember."

Brilliant though Hillary Clinton had shown herself to be, the president took an unwarranted risk in agreeing to give her so much authority. Gaining approval for universal health care was going to be difficult under the most propitious of circumstances, and as Gergen, who viewed most of the ensuing struggle from his perch in the White House, has pointed out: "Mrs. Clinton had never been tested in legislative battle in

Washington. She can also have a tin ear politically. To ask that, on her maiden voyage, she take on the most massive social reform in decades, build up a detailed . . . proposal, and guide it through a fractious Congress was simply more than she should have been expected to do."

During that winter and spring, she devised a procedure for piecing together a health care bill so cumbersome that critics derided it as a "Rube Goldberg" monstrosity. The first lady and her staff director, Ira Magaziner (who had arrived in Oxford as a Rhodes Scholar a year after Bill Clinton), set up no fewer than thirty-four working groups, each with a different responsibility, that enlisted the participation of the staggering total of five hundred people. Each of these subcommittees confronted "toll gates" at which their work was criticized by members of the other task forces. So elephantine were a number of the toll-gate sessions that some of the members could not get into the meeting room in the Old Executive Office Building but had to squat in hallways. The discussions often ran on almost interminably—one for twenty-two hours. A veteran adviser said of a critical conference scrutinizing the economic assumptions of the draft plan: "The process was horrible. There were fifty-some people in the room, a very high proportion of them not above kindergarten age."

Indifferent or insensitive to how her behavior might be perceived, Hillary Clinton bulled ahead. Instead of working out a series of principles to be followed, and sending them to the appropriate congressional committees, as members of the president's staff proposed, she resolved to draft her own legislation. She kept congressional leaders, who would have the responsibility of enacting the program, at a distance, and she never seriously consulted the surgeon general, the cabinet secretary in charge of health care, or the secretary of the treasury, who in his years in Congress had become an authority on the subject. She also aroused suspicions by refusing to reveal the names of the five hundred consultants and by conducting meetings behind closed doors.

Her insistence on secrecy had an unexpected long-range outcome in settling the legal status of first ladies. Hostile to the attempt of the government to revamp health care, the Association of American Physicians and Surgeons filed suit for access to the deliberations of the task force, which, it contended, was violating the provisions of a Nixon-era reform law stipulating that only presidential advisory committees wholly composed of federal employees could restrict access. Hillary Clinton, its brief maintained, was an unpaid volunteer who did not qualify for that exemption. In June 1993, however, a federal court ruled that, given the many public functions a president's spouse performed, she was a de facto government official—a holding that gave the office of first lady institutional standing for the first time.

The task force took an inordinately long time to draft a bill, and when it finally did, the measure was a mind-numbing 1,342 pages long—"so heavy," wrote a Scottish journalist, "that you might require surgery for a hernia if you tried to lift it." Even well-disposed Democratic lawmakers found the proposal mystifying—impossible to comprehend or explain. "This ludicrously complex thousand-page document," said one of Hillary Clinton's staffers, "had something in it to piss everybody off. So by the time it goes up to the Hill, it's DOA." Liberals were unhappy that the draft rejected the Canadian single-payer system in favor of relying upon the private insurance industry and market incentives, and conservatives objected that the plan for "managed competition," though it did not mimic the British model, still accorded the federal government too heavy a hand. Clinton's top financial advisers expressed skepticism about Magaziner's claim that in extending health care coverage to every one of the thirty-seven million uninsured in America, the program would save the country billions. CNN's usually temperate Bill Schneider accused the Clintons of "awesome political stupidity" in relying upon a "500-person task force of self-anointed experts, meeting for months in secret" who "came up with a 1,300-page document that could not have been better designed to scare the wits out of Americans."

Despite this widespread criticism, Hillary Clinton refused to entertain any airing of the advisability of her approach and regarded talk of negotiating even a modest compromise as apostasy. If anyone dared to raise a question at a White House conference, said the journalist Joe Klein, "the First Lady would, with cold fury, tell the questioner to stuff it." A number of moderate Republicans, notably Rhode Island senator John Chafee, acknowledged that the country's health delivery system was broken and that federal action was imperative, but, at a Senate Democratic caucus retreat, she squelched all thought of reaching an accommodation with them. Instead, she said, Democrats should "demonize" Republicans who failed to go along. "That was it for me in terms of Hillary Clinton," said Democratic senator Bill Bradley. "The arrogance. The assumption that people with questions are enemies! The disdain!"

The first lady could persist in this course for a single reason: she had total support from her husband, who was the principal driving force behind the demand for universal health care. He refused to allow his chief financial officials to vet the numbers on which she was relying in claiming savings, and when they asked if the plan might better be phased in slowly, he dismissed them as "incrementalists," which became a stinging epithet. Only once did he stray even a little bit. When in a speech in Boston he slackened his absolute stand slightly to accept 95 percent coverage, the irst lady screamed at him on the phone, "What the fuck are you doing up there?" He tried to appease her, but she barked, "You get back here right away!" Tongue-lashed, the president returned to 100 percent.

In September 1993, on behalf of comprehensive health care, Bill Clinton gave the most impressive address of his White House years. As he began to speak to millions of viewers peering at their TV screens, he was shocked to find that the teleprompter was displaying the wrong speech, and, without spectacles, he could not read his script. "Well, I thought," he told an aide afterward, "God, you're testing me." But being compelled to wing it served to enhance the credibility of his words. He took pains to allay suspicion in the medical profession by stating, "We're blessed with the best health care professionals on Earth," and, noting that "my mother is a nurse," added, "I grew up around hospitals. Doctors and nurses were the first professional people I...learned to look up to." But he warned that "millions of Americans are just a pink slip away from losing their health insurance and one serious illness away from losing all their savings." It was essential, he stressed, to guarantee coverage to people who became ill or switched jobs and to stop insurance companies from denying coverage to someone with a preexisting condition or being able to drop a client "for any reason." Congress needed, he asserted, to adopt a measure to "reform the costliest and most wasteful system on the face of the Earth."

During the final minutes, his oration moved to a higher plane. He wound up by telling the country:

> Forty years from now, our grandchildren will...find it unthinkable
> that there was a time in this country when hardworking families lost

their homes, their savings, their businesses, lost everything simply because their children got sick or because they had to change jobs. Our grandchildren will find such things unthinkable tomorrow if we have the courage to change today.

This is our chance. This is our journey. And when our work is done, we will know that we have answered the call of history and met the challenge of our time.

The president took an even more forceful stand on behalf of the plan in January 1994 in his State of the Union address. He announced: "I have no special brief for any specific approach, even in our own bill, except this: If you send me legislation that does not guarantee every American private health insurance that can never be taken away, you will force me to take this pen, [picking up a pen and using it as a weapon to accentuate his final words] veto the legislation, and we'll come right back here and start all over again." As he "waved his pen in the faces of Republicans, he looked like a matador holding up a red cape," Gergen recalled. "It was dramatic," said a US senator from Louisiana. "But when the president threatens to veto things before they're written, Congress doesn't receive it very well." The chief of staff of the Democratic-controlled Senate Finance Committee has remembered: "I was chilled by it. It was not the way you get things done." He added, "By the time Clinton did that... we knew that we were going to have to compromise, but we didn't think we were going to have to do a big compromise." Pointing out that one moderate Republican senator "was at 95 percent coverage," he concluded: "The other guy's at 95, you're at 100, and you can't figure out what compromise is?" Bill Clinton later acknowledged: "It was an unnecessary red flag to my opponents in Congress. Politics is about compromise, and people expect Presidents to win, not posture for them."

Clinton's two speeches rallied his followers but failed to advance his health care bill because opposition to it was so impassioned. A memo by the Republican tactician William Kristol laid down the GOP strategy: wage all-out war on health care reform because, if the legislation was adopted, it "would permanently tie middle-class voters to the Democrats." The health insurance industry and the American Medical Association instigated nearly half a million communications to members of Congress denouncing "Hillarycare," which, it alleged, would deny American families the right to choose their own physician. (That frightening charge, asserted repeatedly, was false, though, under the Clinton proposal, the privilege might have cost a bit more.)

The insurance industry lobby struck the most effective blow against the proposal by paying for a series of television ads in which a worried suburban couple, Harry and Louise, mull anxiously the menaces to their lives that the federal bureaucracy has hidden in the bill. The ads started in September 1993, the month of the president's first speech and two months before the bill was introduced in Congress, and continued for a full year. "The government shouldn't choose our health care plan," Harry tells his wife and millions of viewers. "We should choose our own." (Another canard. In fact, the Clintons were greatly widening the choices available to people.) No matter how grossly Harry and Louise distorted the facts, they seemed highly credible—a couple with whom countless Americans could identify.

Harry and Louise entered the nation's living rooms for the last time in September 1994. That month, Senate Majority Leader George Mitchell, who had been trying to craft an acceptable compromise, announced that there was no longer any hope. Though the Democrats controlled both houses of Congress, the bill never even came to a vote. The millions of Americans denied proper health care would have to do without. The fight had consumed almost all of the first two years of the Clinton presidency, and the defeat was Bill Clinton's single most painful reverse. Years later, Hillary Clinton conceded: "I think that both the process and the plan were flawed. We were trying to do something that was very hard to do, and we made a lot of mistakes," and the president admitted, "We . . . took too long and ended up achieving nothing."

Death notices for the health care plan hit the front pages at the same moment that the campaign season was heating up, with the November 1994 midterm elections only six weeks away. Clinton anticipated that the Democrats would do reasonably well. A keen student of political history, he knew that the party in control of the White House generally loses seats in off-year contests. Democrats held such comfortable margins in both houses, however, that their control of Congress did not seem to be in jeopardy. Political analysts had long relied upon an axiom:

presidential standing correlates with the state of the economy. With unemployment, interest rates, and inflation all declining and consumer confidence rising, Clinton appeared to have good reason not to worry.

Greater vigilance would have alerted him to pending misfortune. "What threatens this President seems to be much larger than mere partisanship," wrote the journalist Michael Kelly. "There is a level of mistrust... that is almost visceral in its intensity." A *U.S. News & World Report* poll found that 20 percent of those questioned said they "hated" Clinton and another 25 percent "disliked" him. One writer observed: "Much of it is intensely personal, fueled by the belief that the president is a libertine and a liar." Expressions of what Joe Klein has called "the pyrotechnic hatred that Clinton inspired" knew no bounds. The Moral Majority's Jerry Falwell found 150,000 customers for a tape alleging that Clinton had ordered murders to cover up his criminal activities as a cocaine smuggler, and a segregationist demagogue in Arkansas called the president "a queer-mongering, whore-hopping adulterer, a baby-killing, draft-dodging, dope-tolerating, lying, two-faced, treasonist." Clinton was especially victimized by talk radio, largely catering to conservatives, which had expanded from two stations in 1960 to 1,130.

One of the most important White House officials, Harold Ickes, son of FDR's secretary of the interior, later said, "There's no question that there's a group of people in the country who hate the Clintons, just fucking hate them, and I don't know why." That puzzlement and the quest for an explanation infuse all of the literature of the Clinton presidency. "Why?" asked the journalist Richard Reeves. "The '60s! It's the 1960s they hate. The passion of the people who hated what was happening then does not seem to have diminished." He added: "The hatred is not because of the great events of his presidency, such as they are, but because of the great events of the recent past, particularly the 1960s—the anti-authoritarianism, the undigested revolutions, the attacks on great institutions from government to education to religion, the overthrow of patriotism and traditional American history. Bill and Hillary Clinton... symbolize the 1960s to many Americans; they symbolize civil rights and feminism, sexual tolerance and abortion. For a lot of people, that's when America went wrong."

A number of observers, however, questioned characterizing Clinton as a creature of the sixties. A moderate Republican congressman said:

"Psychiatrists or psychohistorians would do great trying to figure this out: How the great culture clash of the 1990s was about a guy from the 1950s who was supposed to symbolize the 1960s, but really didn't." Never a disenchanted radical, Bill Clinton sought from his teenage debut in student politics to work within the system. Far from being a child of the counterculture, he had all along been an ambitious careerist, a striver in the mode of a Horatio Alger protagonist. He made himself at home not in Haight-Ashbury but in Georgetown classrooms, where he was a grind who worked hard for high grades. His hero was neither Che Guevara nor Timothy Leary but President Kennedy.

Other analysts, though, rejoined that Bill Clinton did embody certain countercultural behavior patterns. Steven Gillon has written: "Conservatives had successfully made Clinton a metaphor for the 1960s—a decade that produced a generation that rejected mainstream values . . . and was incapable of distinguishing right from wrong. Clinton provided them with plenty of ammunition. It was not just that he avoided the draft, experimented with drugs, and cheated on his wife, but also that he seemed incapable of accepting responsibility for his actions and waffled on the truth. Conservatives did not have to make their case against the 1960s anymore; Bill Clinton was doing it for them." Noting that Clinton was "a Yale Law School wiseguy," Richard Posner, a distinguished federal judge, concluded: "To the moralistic Right he is a carnivalesque roisterer, a scapegrace, a Prince of Disorder, a value-free postmodernist— and . . . an accomplished con artist. To anyone whose sense of morality and decorum assumed its permanent form before 1968 and who thinks the nation has undergone a precipitous moral decline since, this man is a scandal whatever his policies."

More than anything else, the sexual dissonance of the Clinton presidency disturbed angry white males who did not see why someone would want to mess with their hegemony. During the 1992 campaign, Clinton had promised to create "an administration that looks like America," and he followed through by putting together a cabinet in which, for the first time ever, white men were a minority. By promoting the rights of gays in the armed services, issuing his initial executive order on reproductive rights, and insisting that the attorney general be a woman, he threatened the traditional hierarchy. In particular, critics thought it inappropriate for the president to show so much deference to his wife. Her imperious manner and her assumption of co-presidency rankled. "'Bitches like her' is an unpleasant and angry phrase hard to escape whenever Hillary Rodham Clinton is in the news," reported Richard Reeves. Commenting on her experience with hundreds of irate men who shouted at her in Seattle, the first lady said, "I had not seen faces like that since the segregation battles of the sixties. They had such hatred on their faces."

Republicans—conspicuously the House minority whip, Newt Gingrich—fully exploited these sentiments. Gingrich, who took it upon himself to lead his party's bid to win control of Congress, denounced the president as "the enemy of normal Americans," pointing to his choice of an advocate of sex education for surgeon general and of a lesbian for another high federal post. He later called the Clintons "counterculture McGovernicks." When Woody Allen developed an intimate relationship with his adopted daughter, Gingrich maintained that the actor's perverse behavior "fits the Democratic platform." Even more shamelessly, when in the fall of 1994 a South Carolina mother drowned her two young children so that they would not burden her pursuit of her lover, Gingrich asserted that she reflected Democratic Party values.

Gingrich appeared to be ill suited for the role he chose to play as a pillar of morality. He had dumped his cancer-ridden first wife while carrying on an extramarital affair, and then divorced her. In 1993, married a second time, he had begun a liaison with a young staffer. The second marriage, too, ended in divorce. A preacher of ethics in government, he had participated in the check-kiting scandal in the House. Gingrich was no better fitted for his notion of himself as profound thinker. His academic career had been woefully undistinguished. Denied tenure at West Georgia College, he never wrote anything that commanded the attention of scholars. But nothing deterred him from his determination to be regarded as a change maker with a unique perception of the past. Likening himself to the Duke of Wellington in the Napoleonic Wars, Gingrich proclaimed: "I am the most serious systematic revolutionary of modern times." His obsession with bringing about a Republican turnover—first in Congress, then in the White House—led reporters to refer to him as "Robespierre."

Gingrich had an unexpected idol: Franklin Delano Roosevelt, "the greatest leader we ever had." Though he detested the New Deal, he sought to make the forthcoming election the indispensable beginning of an equivalent of the Hundred Days of 1933, when, under FDR, American politics had undergone a sea change. "A Republican victory in November," he trumpeted, would be no ordinary partisan triumph but "the first decisive step back to create a century of freedom for the entire human race."

To set the scene for his rendezvous with history, he alerted the media to be present on a late September day in 1994 when he massed 367 Republican members of Congress or candidates for the House on three tiers of a stage erected on the steps of the Capitol. After a prayer, the nominees—both office holders and aspirants—each holding a small American flag, recited the Pledge of Allegiance while a brass band struck up patriotic music. All 367 then queued up to sign a document that Gingrich had drafted: a "Contract with America" calling for a balanced budget amendment, tax cuts, crime control, and other staples of a ten-point conservative agenda. He left out of the Contract issues such as abortion that he thought too divisive. Despite his demagoguery about moral values, Gingrich, unlike a number of his followers, was not a social conservative. His daughters were prochoice on abortion, his sister was a proud lesbian, and when his fellow Republicans sounded off about Paula Jones, he scolded them for hypocrisy. He intended not a moral awakening but a fundamental restructuring of national economic policy.

Despite Gingrich's fulminations, Clinton continued to believe that Democrats would not fare too badly in November, though he was aware that Democratic members of Congress, fearing that the president's unpopularity would rub off on them, were not inviting him into their districts. A few days before the election, the pollster Dick Morris gave him a wake-up call. "You're going to lose the Senate and the House," he told him. The president responded, "Not the House, no way." Terrier-like, Morris insisted, "*And the House*. And by significant margins." Clinton rejoined: "No way, no way. Not the House, not the House. You're wrong. You really think so? You're wrong."

When the ballots cast in the November elections were counted, however, the president, crestfallen, conceded, "We got the living daylights beat out of us." In a sweeping triumph, Republicans grabbed control of both houses of Congress. They seized the Senate by picking up eight seats (nine when, on the next day, an Alabama senator switched parties), giving them a 53–47 advantage. (The only solace to Democrats in a Senate race came in Virginia, where the Republican challenger, Ollie North, lost.) More startling still was the GOP's capture of the House of

Representatives for the first time in forty years. Republican acquisition of fifty-four seats established a 230–204 division. Among the Democrats who went down to defeat was the Speaker, Tom Foley, a fifteen-term congressman, expelled from his "safe" district in Spokane. Over the course of more than two centuries, no Speaker had ever before suffered that fate. On that day, too, Democratic governors thought to be unbeatable were turned out: in New York, Mario Cuomo; in Texas, Ann Richards, bested by a rising Republican star, George W. Bush, son of Clinton's predecessor.

The country soured on the Democrats for a number of reasons. Voters took umbrage at Clinton's violation of his campaign pledge to lower taxes on the middle class, were vexed by the bungled health plan, and were put off by allegations about Whitewater. Curiously, though, the Democrats may have been damaged less by Bill Clinton's missteps than by his successes—particularly the legislation he managed to get enacted in 1994 during the height of Republican obstructionism. The president realized that he was courting trouble when, in May 1994, he signed the Freedom of Access to Clinic Entrances Act sponsored by Ted Kennedy—a law adopted in response to an alarming rise in the number of violent incidents carried out by antiabortion activists: arson, kidnappings, bombings, death threats, murders. The statute forbade not only assaults and vandalism but a series of other aggressive deeds such as blocking access to a facility or stalking a clinic employee. An Arkansas Baptist, Bill Clinton must have been taken aback when the Southern Baptist Convention fashioned special prayers for churchgoers to bring about his repentance. Incensed by federal intervention to facilitate a woman's right to an abortion and by the president's solicitude for gays, the Christian Coalition marched its members to the polls to wreak vengeance on the Democrats.

Clinton knowingly opened himself to retaliation from another potent lobby by shepherding two gun control measures to passage in defiance of the National Rifle Association. The Brady law of 1993—named in honor of Reagan's press secretary, who had sustained partial paralysis and brain damage in the assassination attempt—required background checks on handgun purchasers, and a 1994 law banned the sale of nineteen types of semiautomatic weapons. At the same time, Clinton sought to dissuade voters from believing that Democrats were "soft on crime" by endorsing the death penalty, advocating putting a hundred thousand more policemen on the streets, and favoring tougher sentencing: "Three strikes and you're out." Clinton's gun control measures, though, enraged militant weapons owners. Of the twenty-four legislators on the National Rifle Association's "hit list" in November, nineteen went down to defeat. The Democratic senator from Pennsylvania, Harris Wofford, attributed his loss primarily to "abortion, and, secondly, guns." (He added, "And the health care failure. If we had succeeded with even a first step, I would have easily won.")

Several Democratic legislators driven out of Congress blamed the president. One of the rejected Democrats, a congressman from Oklahoma, recalled: "I talked about globalization, competitiveness, education.... My opponent talked about 'God, gays, guns, and Clinton.' That was the mantra. Clinton, in his autobiography, mentions 'God, gays, and guns.' But he leaves out the 'and Clinton.'" In fact, the president did confess publicly to his shortcomings. "I had contributed to the demise by allowing my first weeks to be defined by gays in the military; by failing to concentrate on the campaign until it was too late; and by trying to do too much too fast," he said.

Newt Gingrich and Bob Dole, on the other hand, emerged as tomorrow's prospective rulers. The media hailed Gingrich as the architect of victory, who, it was said, had "nationalized" the hundreds of separate contests by his Contract with America, though fewer than one of four Americans had even heard of the Contract. Dole, expected to be his party's candidate to expel Clinton from the White House in 1996, appeared to have even greater reason for rejoicing. On Election Night, he told a large crowd at Republican headquarters in Washington: "I've never known a better night in electoral politics for the Republican Party, and the best is yet to come." The jubilant celebrants shouted back, "96! 96! 96!" Their joy was understandable, but, in counting on an even greater occasion for exultation two years later, Dole and his Republican followers might well have heeded the warning Clinton had given Gingrich not long before: "I am not a pushover. Do you know who I am? I'm the big rubber clown doll you had as a kid, and every time you hit it, it bounces back. That's me—the harder you hit me, the faster I come back up."

For a time, the 1994 election disappointment crushed the Clintons and envenomed them. The president, sullen, felt unappreciated, and the first lady's resentment, said one aide, "took the form of iciness and even anger" toward those around her. For weeks, Bill Clinton appeared to be in a fog. Officials found him impenetrable and inaccessible. He did not even turn up at his office in the White House but hunkered down in family quarters.

When he came to, he summoned Dick Morris for help, though he knew that the White House staff loathed the pollster. In his memoir, George Stephanopoulos described Morris as "a small sausage of a man encased in a green suit with wide lapels, a wide floral tie, and a wide-collared shirt," toting a briefcase that "gave him the look of a B-movie mob lawyer, circa 1975—the kind of guy who gets brained with a baseball bat for double-crossing his boss." When Hillary Clinton mentioned Morris, Harold Ickes retorted, "He's a sleazy son of a bitch." She did not deny that but said, "He understands the underside." Ickes countered, "He *is* the underside." One of the president's top political advisers has said of Morris that he "could advise Hitler or he could advise Mother Teresa—on the same night." Clinton, though, remembering how Morris had once come to his rescue in Arkansas, valued the consultant's street smarts.

At first, Clinton, recognizing Morris's unsavory reputation, had not dared bring the pollster into the White House and hid him from view. Morris took up residence in the Jefferson Hotel, where he adopted the name "Charlie," after the character in the television program *Charlie's Angels* who offered advice as a disembodied voice. John Harris has written of Clinton and Morris: "Their collaboration carried an aroma almost of prostitution—a relationship that was thoroughly transactional, at once intimate and impersonal, driven by mutual need with an overlay of shame." Dick Morris, the historian Michael Takiff concluded, was the president's "evil twin."

Morris told Clinton that to win a second term in 1996, he needed to follow a policy of "triangulation." As a "third force," the president, his consultant said, should separate himself not only from Republicans but from liberals so that he could regain his identity as a New Democrat. Morris abridged his counsel in four words: "Fast-forward the Gingrich agenda." Clinton, he maintained, should deprive the Republicans of planks such as deficit reduction and welfare reform by identifying himself with them, while continuing to resist GOP assaults on Medicare, Medicaid, federal aid to education, and environmental protection—all programs with substantial constituencies. A centrist, Clinton found this advice easy to embrace.

Morris's recommendations, politically canny, had more than one downside. Liberals were appalled that the president thought his path to victory lay in submission to the right. Furthermore, Clinton's willingness to set policy in accord with what Morris's surveys found most popular reinforced the impression that, as was often said, the "poll-driven" president lacked convictions. He appeared to demonstrate the validity of this charge by coming out in favor of a number of puny proposals such as mandatory school uniforms to improve discipline and V-chips to permit parents to block TV programs that might be inappropriate for their children—projects that were a sorry comedown from comprehensive health care. The acid-tongued *New York Times* columnist Maureen Dowd derided him as "President Pothole, a fixer of tiny things." Clinton put so much stock in this approach, however, that for a considerable time Morris was his domestic policy chieftain.

As early as his January 1995 State of the Union address, Clinton showed Morris's influence. To demonstrate that he realized that the 1994 ballots were a rebuke, he twice apologized for "mistakes." To demonstrate that he had learned his lesson and was moving to the center, he stated, "We will have cut a total of more than a quarter of million positions from the federal government, making it the smallest it has been since John Kennedy was president." That allusion was a covert way of saying that he was rolling the government back to where it had been before LBJ's Great Society. In a sanctimonious mode, Clinton acclaimed parents who "teach their children the difference between right and wrong," and he expressed pride that the United States had more "houses of worship than any other country in the world."

The speech ran very long because it was larded with mentions of Republican programs inserted by Morris and willingly accepted by the president. In addition, Morris, who played a central role in drafting the speech, encouraged Clinton to improvise because he was a "verbal guy," and, following this advice, the president interpolated so many times that nearly half of the address was ad lib. The next day the Washington press chewed him out for talking too much, but during the speech the chamber erupted in applause ninety-six times, and overnight polls revealed that people loved it. The newly elected Republican legislators, however, waved their copies of the Contract with America, as though, wrote Elizabeth Drew, they were Mao's Little Red Books but with a drastically contrary text.

Morris's polls, the president was informed, exposed the main source of his unpopularity: Hillary Clinton. The finding prodded the first lady to attempt to refashion her image. No longer did she sit at the head of the table during policy discussions; in the Oval Office, she took a chair toward the wall behind federal officials; never again, she decided, would she assume a position such as running the health care initiative. Instead, she would model herself on Eleanor Roosevelt, who had a powerful impact on the New Deal without holding any government position. She even made a brief sortie at being wifely. "My first responsibility is to whatever my husband would want me to do," she told *Newsweek*, and she acted out a traditional household role by lunching with the *Washington Post*'s food editor. She carried off a more thoughtful leap from the co-presidency by becoming an eloquent champion of the rights of women and children on the international stage at the UN World Summit for Social Development in Copenhagen and at the UN Fourth World Conference on Women in Beijing.

None of these efforts, however, spared the president from being eclipsed by Newt Gingrich. Journalists swooned over him. They wrote not of the "Republican Revolution," or the "Revolution of '94," but of the "Gingrich Revolution." In 1995, *Time* honored the new Speaker as "Man of the Year." He even claimed that the seat of government had moved to Capitol Hill, where he was presiding, and the press behaved as though they thought he was right. The media treated the opening of the new session of Congress with Gingrich in the Speaker's chair like a presidential inauguration. All of the major networks viewed it as a momentous enough event to justify sending their anchormen to Washington. In April 1995, two of the networks granted airtime to Gingrich to speak on the hundredth day of the new Congress—a privilege normally reserved for the president of the United States. In contrast, only one network chose to screen Clinton's prime-time press conference on April 18, 1995.

The interrogation of Clinton by reporters that night marked the nadir of his presidency. At a moment when almost all eyes were focused on Gingrich, a newsman did not hesitate to ask, "Do you worry about making sure your voice is heard in the coming months?" Clinton answered lamely: "The Constitution gives me relevance. The power of our ideas gives me relevance. The record we have built up over the last two years and the things we're trying to do to implement it give it relevance. The president is relevant here." He sounded pathetic.

On the very next morning, a truck packed with two tons of explosives tore apart a federal office building in Oklahoma City, killing 168 people, mostly civil servants but including 19 children, many of them in a child-care facility provided for government employees. Speculation focused on Muslim terrorists, who had been responsible for a blast two years before at the World Trade Center garage in lower Manhattan, but the truck with its lethal cargo was quickly traced to Americans in a paramilitary Michigan militia with ten thousand members. Carried out on the anniversary of the Waco raid, the act of terrorism was the work of two homegrown citizens who detested their own government. Many concluded that the mass killing was the inevitable outcome of antigovernment rants by right-wing Republicans. (A congresswoman from Idaho had gone so far as to welcome a militia leader into her district to testify about black helicopters manned by secret agents of the United Nations bent on surveying terrain for an invasion by "the New World Order" that, she maintained, already controlled America.)

Four days later, at a time of national mourning, Clinton, in his role as head of state, delivered a moving tribute in Oklahoma City to the slain federal workers and their children. He told the bereaved:

This terrible sin took the lives of our American family, innocent children in that building only because their parents were trying to be good parents as well as good workers, citizens in the building ... who served the rest of us, who worked to help the elderly and the disabled, who worked to support our farmers and our veterans, who worked to enforce our laws and to protect us. Let us say clearly, they served us well, and we are grateful....

Realizing that the service was being televised, the president spoke to the entire nation, declaring:

> To all my fellow Americans beyond this hall, I say, one thing we owe those who have sacrificed is the duty to purge ourselves of the dark forces which gave rise to this evil....
>
> Let us let our own children know that we will stand against the forces of fear. When there is talk of hatred, let us stand up and talk against it. When there is talk of violence, let us stand up and talk against it. In the face of death, let us honor life. As St. Paul admonished us, let us not be overcome by evil, but overcome evil with good.

Early the following month, in a rousing commencement address at Michigan State University, he struck a different note. To the thousands gathered in East Lansing, he began: "I say this to the militia and *all others* who believe that the greatest threat to freedom comes from the government instead of from those who would take away your freedom,...you are just plain wrong." His voice revealing barely controlled rage, he asked, "How dare you suggest that we, in the freest nation on earth, live in tyranny?" He concluded: "I say to you, all of you, the members of the class of 1995, there is nothing patriotic about hating your country, or pretending that you can love your country but despise your government."

An NBC News–*Wall Street Journal* poll reported that 84 percent of those surveyed approved of the president's response to the Oklahoma City tragedy. Clinton had not only taken over Reagan's earlier role as national comforter but had exposed the awful consequences of anti-government rhetoric. Henry Cisneros, a cabinet official who had been mayor of San Antonio, later reflected: "I felt a change in the tenor, in the vibrations after Oklahoma City, because all of a sudden the American people saw. First of all, they saw the logical result of the venom and the hatred as it impacts a young man whose mind was so twisted by it that he ended up killing 168 fellow Americans. It was like, 'Enough! Enough, enough, enough! Innocent people are dying. And where's our country going?'"

Unquestionably, many Americans felt precisely the sense of revulsion that Cisneros verbalized, but Oklahoma City did not affect the political culture of Capitol Hill—notably the hostility to the United States government—one whit. Led by Gingrich, and sparked by newly arrived far-right representatives elected in 1994, House Republicans took dead aim on federal programs. Gingrich sought, he said, nothing less than to restore the hegemony of "the bourgeois system which has dominated the country for 200 years." The House Budget Committee proposed to abolish nearly three hundred government agencies, including the Corporation for Public Broadcasting, the National Endowment for the Arts, the National Endowment for the Humanities, and Clinton's national service project, and to eradicate three cabinet-level departments. House Republicans also sought to deny children school lunches, to wipe out nutrition standards, and to cut funding for the widely admired program to help preschool children and impoverished pregnant women. A Republican strategist who deplored these emphases said: "I'm angry.... We're on the side of Grinch and Scrooge."

House Republicans showed conspicuous solicitude for big business. They approved a measure drafted by a lobbyist for the petrochemical industries that not merely imposed a moratorium on future federal regulation but made the ban retroactive to the previous November, when many of them had won election for the first time. They passed legislation to lessen product liability, hamper malpractice litigation, and bar OSHA from safeguarding employees from repetitive stress injuries. Targeting environmental laws, House Republicans proposed to end curbs on hazardous waste and toxic emissions and to abolish the agency enforcing the Endangered Species Act. In addition, a lobbyist for polluters drafted a bill that the House adopted to amend the Clean Water Act of 1972 by removing protection from half of the country's wetlands.

Few of the more extreme measures made their way into the statute books. Republicans who wanted to destroy the Corporation for Public Broadcasting learned that Big Bird had a devoted following ranging far beyond liberal Democrats. (Gingrich himself wound up contributing $2,000 to Atlanta's public TV station.) Some bills failed because the Senate, considerably more moderate, regarded the House firebrands as wild men. Republican senator John Chafee, who chaired the Environment and Public Works Committee, said of the sponsors of this "terrible legislation": "When all the artichoke leaves are peeled away, they are out for the Clean Air Act, the Clean Water Act, the Endangered Species Act; that is what they are gunning for." Still more important was intervention by the president. Clinton, who had not made use of his veto pen a single time in his first two years, wielded it freely in 1995.

For the most part, though, Clinton went along with the Republicans. Oklahoma City had no more changed him than it had his opponents. He continued to follow Dick Morris's advice and to recite reassuring homilies. He recalled that when he was a schoolboy in Arkansas, morning prayers were "as common as apple pie." Willing to tolerate prayer in classrooms, he remarked, "Well, it certainly didn't do any harm. It might have done a little good." In June 1995, he submitted a budget calling for more than a trillion dollars in cuts in federal spending, though one White House official had warned him, "They will go ballistic on the Hill," and Secretary of Labor Robert Reich, a friend of Clinton's since Oxford days, saw his action as the "cave-in that brings us halfway down the slippery slope," adding, "Bill has thrown in the towel."

Clinton's turn to the right elicited contrary responses. Pleased, though not content, Gingrich pointed out: "He agrees that the budget needs balancing, he agrees that Medicare needs change, he agrees there should be tax cuts, he agrees domestic spending should be restrained, he agrees defense has been cut deeply enough. I mean, the president has now conceded that on those major issues we're right." Democrats on the Hill, though, were irate, a Connecticut congresswoman saying that she felt "betrayed." That response delighted Morris, who wanted him to distance himself from liberals.

It took a very long while for Clinton to realize that no amount of concessions would ever satisfy Gingrich. His awakening came after Congress fell so far behind on appropriations for federal departments that it proved necessary to adopt a continuing resolution before the fiscal year expired on October 1 in order to maintain operations. Senator Dole was willing to negotiate further with Clinton, but Gingrich refused to agree to another continuing resolution to keep the national government functioning beyond November 15 unless the president accepted still more savage cuts in federal programs.

At a showdown White House session with the Republican leadership on November 1, Clinton exploded. "I've accepted all your principles—a balanced budget, welfare reform...and you haven't accepted any of ours," he said. "Do you think you're the only ones who have principles?... I worry that hidden behind your Contract...you want to destroy the federal government." Gesturing toward the chair behind his desk, he said, his voice rising, "I don't want to break *my* contract with America," adding that he would let Dole have the chair rather than capitulate. Gingrich replied in kind. "You know, the problem here is you've got a gun to my head," he told the president. "It's called the veto. But...I've got a gun to *your* head, and I'm going to use it. I'm going to shut the government down." And he did.

On November 14, a government shutdown began. With eight hundred thousand federal workers furloughed, there was no one to mail Social Security checks or issue passports. Visitors to Yellowstone, Yosemite, and other national parks could no longer enter. In his diary, Reich wrote: "Desks, files, papers, computers, and coffee mugs are still in place, but the people have vanished. It reminds me of a science fiction story. The heat is off and my office is getting cold." Tourists wandered forlornly past the Washington Monument and other closed sites in the nation's capital that they had traveled long distances to see, angry at being disappointed and knowing whom to blame.

Newt Gingrich had badly misconstrued the country's mood. He had counted on antigovernment sentiment to carry the day for him, only to discover that though Americans might dislike "the government" in the abstract, they cherished any number of federal institutions and services. Surveys found that most people thought Republican demands for still greater budget cuts were unreasonable. Since the reductions in Medicare funds and proposed tax cuts to benefit the wealthy were almost identical sums, Republicans on the Hill exposed themselves to the president's charge that "the Congressional majority appears to be choosing for the first time to use the benefits we provide under Medicare...as a piggybank to fund huge tax cuts to people who don't really need them." Even before the shutdown began, the Gallup Poll announced that Gingrich's approval rating had fallen to 25 percent, while Clinton's numbers were soaring.

Gingrich handed the president a big advantage by telling reporters that he had taken a hard line on the budget because, on an overseas flight, Clinton had refused to let him disembark at the front of the plane. This snub, he told an interviewer, was "part of why you ended up with us sending down a tougher continuing resolution." Gingrich's petulance prompted the large-circulation *New York Daily News* to print the headline CRY BABY, alongside an image of the Speaker in a diaper and holding a rattle. A Republican congressman commented: "He picked the wrong bloody moment to take out a .357 and shoot both kneecaps off."

Yet when, after six days, government doors reopened, the shutdown ended not because Gingrich surrendered but because Clinton did. The president appeared to have the upper hand, but scores of House Democrats, nervous about the next election, feared that they would be punished if they were perceived to be against budget balancing. Hence, the president committed himself for the first time to a goal he had rejected before: a balanced budget in seven years—precisely what Gingrich had been demanding. Reich jotted down: "B. continues to cave. Now he's agreeing to balance the budget in seven years. Of course, Gingrich still isn't satisfied. He wants even deeper cuts in spending, mostly penalizing the poor, and even steeper tax cuts, mostly benefiting the wealthy. B. seems likely to go along."

Budget balancing might appear to be simply an unexceptionable exercise in fiscal probity, but it carried a political agenda. Balancing the budget, Gingrich explained, "changes the whole game.... You cannot sustain the old welfare state inside a balanced budget." When that demand was accompanied by Republican insistence on a tax cut—the "crown jewel" of the Contract with America—the inevitable consequence would be a shortage of money to finance social programs. Medicare, the Speaker anticipated, would "wither on the vine."

Flushed with success, Gingrich grossly overplayed his hand. He put through a new budget that slashed Medicare and deprived the working poor of benefits while giving a huge tax cut to the rich. He was deaf to the rumbling in the country about the blatant unfairness of what he was doing. On December 6, Clinton vetoed the Republican budget, and, with no continuing resolution carrying beyond December 15, Gingrich, egged on by John Boehner and other Republican congressional zealots, closed the federal government once again. Day after day, the shutdown ground on—through all the December holidays and into the new year—and with each passing day, Republican fortunes sank lower. High-ranking congressional Republicans told Gingrich "Newt, this isn't going to work," but he refused to heed. Gingrich might be *Time*'s Man of the Year, said a *Washington Post* columnist, "but he looks like the thug of the week." The Speaker, who had been the toast of Washington, was transmogrified into the "Gingrich who stole Christmas."

Bob Dole looked on in dismay, alarmed that Gingrich was gutting the senator's ambition for the White House in 1996. As he watched TV newscasts, Dole noted that the focus was not on the principled stand Republicans were taking but on "Day X of the shutdown" and the suffering it was causing. One account featured the hardship inflicted on an innkeeper near a national park; another told of a bobsled driver who no longer had any patrons. Especially heartrending were tales of beleaguered federal workers and their families in the Christmas season.

With Senate Republicans led by Dole favoring compromise, the House felt pressure to acquiesce. The more rabid right-wingers wanted to continue to hold out, but, since Americans were blaming the Republicans by 2 to 1, a GOP strategist said, "Republicans can't sustain...this position much longer. We're taking a beating." Dole put through a new continuing resolution in the Senate, and even Gingrich realized that he had to back down after fifty-four Republicans in the House—from districts with national parks or big concentrations of federal workers—voted to resume. "We're going to get the shutdown off the front page," the Speaker said. On January 6, 1996, after what seemed to be an interminable twenty-one days, the government started up again.

This time, the president came out the winner. Gingrich recognized that he could not possibly close down the government a third time. "Most people don't commit suicide twice," said Dick Morris, "but Gingrich did." By showing that he was capable of drawing a line, Clinton greatly strengthened the office of the presidency and his own reputation. He appeared to be strong, sensible, enlightened—in short, statesmanlike. Michael Takiff has written: "If Bill's preaching in Oklahoma City installed him as the nation's comforter-in-chief, it was his battle with Newt Gingrich...that cemented his place as...protector of average Americans against the depredations of a band of extremists." But Takiff concluded: "Yet, for all the credit he accrued among the American people in 1995, he never achieved the standing he'd sought during his first two years in office: as a leader transforming the nation for the better. Rather, he assumed the role of fierce defender of the status quo, admired not for things he did but for things he prevented others from doing."

Bill Clinton entered the presidential campaign year of 1996 riding high. Although more than half of the American people polled did not believe that Clinton had exemplary "personal moral and ethical standards," so many preferred him to Senator Dole that they gave him a sixteen-point lead. He began his bid for reelection with the boost Gingrich had provided him in the prolonged December–January crisis. Dole later said: "Dumbest thing Newt ever did was shut down the government. If there was ever any doubt about Clinton's reelection—probably wasn't much— there wasn't after that. Dumb, dumb, dumb." In his biography of the president, aptly titled *The Survivor*, John Harris wrote: "From the State of the Union until election day 1996, Clinton was never again behind the Republicans in his own polls. In one year, he had gone from being nearly irrelevant to being nearly invincible."

Clinton ran not as the reincarnation of FDR, Truman, or LBJ but as a dedicated centrist with conservative instincts. His views on issues such as welfare and crime, he told the electorate, were not "wildly liberal" and were "different from what, traditionally, people have thought of as Democratic politics." He added, "I know it's convenient for the Republicans to raise the flag of 'Oh, these people would be so liberal if you let them, Clinton will be liberal in his second term,'" but such a contention, he declared, "won't fit with what I'm planning to do in my second term." He continued to pay homage to family values and in 1996, though he did not approve of it, signed into law the Defense of Marriage Act authorizing states to refuse to recognize gay marriages contracted in other states.

He flaunted his New Democrat allegiance in his State of the Union address in January 1996 with one eye-catching sentence: "The era of big government is over." He preceded that disavowal of Great Society–style liberalism by saying: "We know big government does not have all the answers. We know there's not a program for every problem." The *New York Times* wrote of the president, "He has steadily retreated to embrace his rivals' goal of balancing the budget in seven years. This has meant accepting a level of cuts in domestic spending that Mr. Clinton's own advisers had repeatedly denounced as unthinkable." Clinton's words led his fellow Democrat Pat Moynihan to declare: "A pretty large political tradition... is vaporizing before our eyes—the tradition of the Democrats as the party of intelligent government provision."

Gingrich and his fellow Republicans posed the sternest test for Clinton as a Democrat by passing a draconian bill that a London editor reported was "widely viewed as the most drastic assault on the US welfare system since Franklin Roosevelt introduced his New Deal for the poor and unemployed in the 1930s." The legislation set time limits on eligibility for welfare, imposed work requirements, turned social assistance over to the fifty states with no guarantee that they would behave humanely, and eradicated Aid to Families with Dependent Children, established by the Social Security Act of 1935. Only when a Republican congresswoman rebelled did the House agree to modify a chilling lifetime ban on welfare for unwed mothers under eighteen. The measure also deeply cut appropriations for food stamps and denied benefits altogether to legal immigrants during their first five years in America. "The change in welfare reform from an entitlement to a time-limited program," said Gingrich's top aide, "was a huge, huge compromise of everything the progressive Democrats had been for, for at least a generation."

The bill elicited widespread expressions of outrage. One of the many Democrats in the House, including the minority leader, who voted against it, Georgia congressman John Lewis asked: "Where is the compassion? Where is the sense of decency? Where is the heart of this Congress? This bill is mean. It is base. It is downright lowdown." The secretary of health and human services provided Clinton with an analysis demonstrating that the measure would drive more than a million children into poverty. The *Washington Post* called it "a terrible piece of legislation," and the *New York Times* characterized it as "odious."

A deafening chorus of voices urged the president to wield his pen once more to kill this dreadful bill. He had already vetoed two earlier versions, only marginally different. Most of his advisers—among them Secretary of the Treasury Rubin—believed passionately that he should veto it. On the Hill, Pat Moynihan, regarded as the Senate's leading authority on welfare, said that signing the measure "would be the most brutal act of social policy since Reconstruction." But both Vice President Gore, who had thought all along that welfare reform, not health care, should be the administration's centerpiece, and Hillary Clinton, despite her concern with the fate of children, urged him to consent.

Numbers of considerations moved the president in that direction. Unlike the committed liberals, he shared most of the assumptions of the Republicans. He feared, too, that in an election year, if he were to bury a welfare measure for a third time, his opponents would exploit his failure to fulfill his campaign pledge to "end welfare as we know it." Dick

Morris clinched his decision by reporting that his polls showed that signing the legislation would result in a fifteen-point lead for Clinton in his bid for a second term, while vetoing it would put him at a three-point disadvantage. At the end of a tense cabinet session, Reich recorded, "I'm certain B. has decided to sign the welfare bill, and I feel sick to my stomach." On August 22, 1996, acknowledging that the bill had "serious flaws," Clinton put his name to it—with a vow to get rid of its worst features in the next session. The time had come, he stated, "to make welfare what it was meant to be, a second chance and not a way of life."

The president's action brought a torrent of criticism upon his head. "If this administration wishes to go down in history as one that abandoned, eagerly abandoned, the national commitment to dependent children, so be it," said Senator Moynihan. "I would not want to be associated with such an enterprise." Peter Edelman, assistant secretary of health and human services, said afterward: "He did not have to sign the bill. Political advisers—not Dick Morris, but Leon Panetta, Harold Ickes, George Stephanopoulos—all urged him to veto the legislation, or said to him that it would not be fatal to his re-election chances; indeed, it might even help, because of his standing up for a principle." Edelman, a close friend of the Clintons, resigned in protest. The president, one writer concluded, was "a deadbeat dad to the whole country."

But as Dick Morris had foreseen, Clinton's seizure of the center deprived his opponents of space to maneuver. During the State of the Union address in January, GOP legislators, reported a fellow Republican, had "looked as if they had been forced to sit through a long banquet speech—and then had dinner snatched out of their mouths." Clinton, he said, had stolen so many of his party's proposals, such as "beefed-up prison sentences," from their plates that they "were left with little more than the bitter gruel served by Bob Dole in his response."

Neither Republicans nor liberal Democrats paid enough attention, however, to what Clinton had said in the address right after foreswearing big government. "But we cannot go back to the time when our citizens were left to fend for themselves," he affirmed. "Every eight-year-old must be able to read. Every twelve-year-old must be able to log on to the Internet; every eighteen-year-old must be able to go to college; and every adult American must be able to keep learning for a lifetime." During 1996, he persuaded Congress to approve a rise in the minimum wage and to enact the bipartisan Kennedy-Kassebaum portable health insurance bill that preserved benefits when people changed jobs. He no longer sought ambitious legislation, but he had not abandoned the field of battle altogether.

As he strove for another term, Clinton could also point to notable foreign policy successes, achieved by his willingness to brave displeasure at home. Early in 1995, when the Mexican peso fell alarmingly in value after foreign investors lost faith in the viability of the country's economy, he resolved to bail out the Mexicans. It was a bold move at a time when Clinton's prospects for reelection seemed dim. A *Los Angeles Times* poll revealed that 80 percent of the country opposed US intervention. Informed by congressional leaders that his proposal "wasn't going to fly," he employed his executive authority to put together a $20 billion loan package drawing upon the treasury's exchange stabilization fund, and he got $15 billion more from international agencies. "The risks of inaction are greater than the risks of decisive action," he told the nation's governors, because further deterioration would jeopardize American prosperity and have bad repercussions in the third world. "Do I know for sure that the action will solve all the problems? I do not. Do I believe it will? I do. Am I virtually certain that if we do nothing it will get much, much worse in a hurry? I am." The infusion of dollars rescued the peso, and, contrary to the gloomy forecasts of skeptics, Mexico repaid the loan three years ahead of schedule. The United States got all of its money back and half a billion dollars more.

In the former Yugoslavia, too, Clinton embarked upon a bold course, but only after faltering. When, in a speech at the Air Force Academy in Colorado in the spring of 1995, he took a step toward the dispatch of US troops as peacekeepers in Bosnia, he was scolded not just by Republicans in Congress but by his political consultant. "This is terrible!" Dick Morris phoned him. "We've got to walk this back." Warning him not to be a Lyndon Johnson, Morris said, "It's the Democrats' disease to take the same compassion that motivates their domestic policies and let it lure them into heroic but ill-considered foreign wars." As soon as Clinton reached Montana on his western swing, he turned tail in a radio address drafted by Morris, who had no expertise in international affairs.

During July 1995, however, Bosnian Serbs committed atrocities in Srebrenica that caused the president to reappraise. In this town within what the UN had designated as a "safe area," they calculatedly murdered eight thousand men and boys and drove more than twenty thousand women and girls from their homes. For the first time, Clinton took a strong stand and held to it, fully recognizing that, as he told his national security adviser, "I'm risking my presidency." He committed himself to a two-pronged policy: bombing Serb forces into willingness to negotiate and then hosting a conference bringing the bitter antagonists together in the United States. "If we let the moment slip away," the president said, "we're history."

A relentless NATO air assault—with more than 3,500 bombing sorties—broke Milošević's will to resist and drew the warring Slav factions to a conference table in Ohio. Later in the year, the Dayton Accords, negotiated at Wright-Patterson Air Force Base, arranged for peaceful power sharing in Bosnia. Though Congress strongly resisted deploying armed forces abroad, Clinton managed to persuade both houses to approve the dispatch of twenty thousand troops to Bosnia to monitor the Accords. When the president subsequently got word that the military would not back the agreement, he let the Joint Chiefs know that he expected their unstinting cooperation. American soldiers remained there for many years, without a single life lost.

Senator Dole, who, as the challenger, never had the incumbent's opportunity to create a record of achievement, did not match up well with the president. Even the chair of the Republican National Committee conceded that the dour Dole fell far short of the magnetic Clinton. Dole "is not the television personality Bill Clinton is and never will be," he said. "Bill Clinton could sell Fords to Chevrolet dealers." In his acceptance speech to the Republican National Convention in San Diego in August, Dole chose an image that could be turned against him: "Age has its advantages. Let me be the bridge to an America that only the unknowing call myth. Let me be the bridge to a time of tranquility, faith, and confidence in action. And to those who say it was never so, that America has not been better, I say, you're wrong, and I know, because I was there.... And I remember." Later that month, at the Democratic National Convention in Chicago, Clinton responded: "With all respect, we do not need to build a bridge to the past. We need to build a bridge to the future. And that is what I commit to you to do.... Tonight let us resolve to build that bridge to the 21st century."

In those few words, Clinton and the Democrats dismissed Dole as "the candidate of yesterday."

Only the stench of scandal, it appeared, might derail Bill Clinton's victory juggernaut. Just as Clinton was recovering from the ascendancy of Gingrich, the specter of Whitewater had re-emerged. After long maintaining that it had released every document on the finances of the Clintons, the White House confessed that it had held some papers back, including a note that Vince Foster had scrawled calling Whitewater a "can of worms you shouldn't open." Papers surfacing suspiciously late contravened Hillary Clinton's accounts both of her behavior as an attorney in Little Rock and of her involvement in Travelgate. In the *New York Times*, the columnist William Safire wrote that many Americans had been coming to the "sad realization that our First Lady—a woman of undoubted talents who was a role model for many in her generation—is a congenital liar." When Hillary Clinton expressed dissatisfaction that fellow Democrats were not defending her, she was told by a White House staffer: "People are nervous about taking a position that may not hold up.... We can't tell them where these billing records were. We can't tell them why it took two years to find them."

Despite these difficulties, Clinton easily won reelection with a 379–159 rout in the Electoral College. He received better than 49 percent of the popular vote; less than 41 percent went to Dole and 8 percent to Perot, who garnered less than half the proportion he had received as a third-party candidate four years earlier. (The complexion of Congress, though, changed little, with the Republicans maintaining control of both houses.) Afterward, a British journalist observed that Clinton "looks set to be remembered as the Comeback Kid of all time. Two years ago, a second victory for Bill Clinton seemed inconceivable. Yet long before yesterday, it had already become inevitable." The historian William Chafe, a passionate liberal who held Dick Morris in low regard, concluded that "triangulation worked." By advocating a series of petty but popular reforms, he noted, Clinton succeeded in occupying "70 percent of the political spectrum, leaving disgruntled liberals and angry conservatives alone at either end." (Dick Morris was not around on Election Night to receive plaudits, though. Champion of family values, he had been forced to resign when he was found to have been involved with a whore.)

Clinton might well have gotten an absolute majority of the popular vote, save for fund-raising transgressions that led a number of disgusted voters to transfer their allegiance to Perot in protest. In their attempt to overcome the Republican cash advantage, Democrats had gone so far as to publish a brochure with a price list: $25,000 to be in the presence of Al Gore; $50,000 to meet Clinton. And if you forked over $100,000, you got to dine with the president at the Hay-Adams. Fat cats were rewarded with the top prize: invitations to spend the night in the Lincoln Bedroom, which an unseemly number did. Especially alarming was the allegation that the Beijing government was permitted to buy political influence by sending laundered contributions to Clinton's campaign. In return, the president made it easier for big-money contributors to strike deals with China for satellite technology.

Notwithstanding the many blemishes, Clinton ended the year in triumph. It was hard to remember how low he had been a short time before. He appeared to be in fine fettle for a successful second term. "He had stopped acting like a governor," said Secretary of Health and Human Services Donna Shalala, "and he had become the President." He had faced down the Republicans on the budget and, in Bosnia, as Joe Klein wrote, had shown that he "was now more comfortable as commander in chief and...was increasingly confident on the international stage." His popularity echoed Reagan's at a similar point. But, as every Clinton watcher had long ago discerned, whenever Bill Clinton ascended to a peak, he was sure to do or encounter something plunging him into the river bottom at the foot of the mountain.

The president, said to be the most powerful man on earth, found it exasperating, as he entered the new term, that the Paula Jones suit not only would not go away but had even penetrated the chambers of the US Supreme Court, which heard oral arguments one week before his second inauguration. His lawyers claimed, not at all unreasonably, that a president, with his extraordinary responsibilities, should not be distracted by a civil suit that could readily be postponed until after he had left office. Their brief contended: "The demands placed upon the President under Article II are unceasing. A sitting President cannot defend himself against litigation seeking to impose personal financial liability without diverting his energy and attention from the exercise of the 'executive power' of the United States."

In May 1997, in *Clinton v. Jones*, however, the Court decided 9–0 against the president. Speaking for the Court, Justice John Paul Stevens said of the litigation: "It appears to us highly unlikely to occupy any substantial amount of petitioner's time," a statement that has been called possibly "the most boneheaded prediction in the history of jurisprudence." One vocal critic of the president's behavior, the legal expert Jeffrey Toobin, has written: "There is, in retrospect, something almost endearing about the obtuseness of Justice John Paul Stevens's opinion. . . . In a political culture where the 'character issue' was ascendant, the Court failed to recognize that nothing could be more distracting to a president than a sexual harassment lawsuit." Placing *Clinton v. Jones* in an institutional context, Richard Posner, who was not at all well disposed toward Clinton, called the ruling allowing the suit to go forward a "naive . . . and gratuitous body blow to the Presidency."

Fortified by the Court's ruling, Paula Jones's legal team devised a strategy to bolster her weak case by summoning a number of women out of the president's past to demonstrate that Clinton habitually preyed upon female employees. In December 1997, they submitted to the president's lawyer, Robert Bennett, a list of the women they planned to call to the stand. A battle-hardened veteran of Washington courtrooms, Bennett was well aware that rumors of Clinton's extramarital affairs had circulated for years, and as he ran his eyes down the list, he saw the familiar names. But one, altogether unknown to him, caught him by surprise. The following day he asked Clinton whether he had engaged in a sexual liaison with someone called Lewinsky. The president retorted: "Bob, do you think I'm fucking crazy?... The right has been dying for this kind of thing from day one. No, it didn't happen." He added, "I'm retired. I'm retired." It is a truism that a client who lies to his lawyer is a fool. In uttering this denial, though, the president was lying through his teeth.

Clinton's relationship with Monica Lewinsky had begun earlier as a happenstance of his struggles with Newt Gingrich over the budget. With the first 1995 government shutdown leaving the White House short of staff, supervisors moved Lewinsky, an unpaid twenty-two-year-old intern, to a post close to the Oval Office. On Day Two of the closure, November 15, 1995, she chanced to encounter the president. After

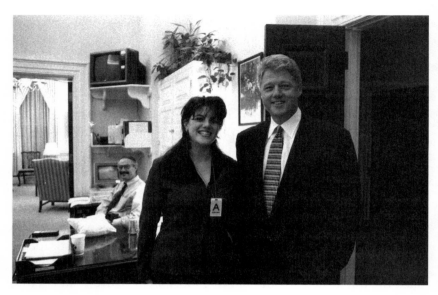

The president poses for an official White House photograph with Monica Lewinsky on November 17, 1995, two days after their first sexual encounter. Independent counsel Kenneth Starr later included this photo in his report rebuking the president's behavior. *Courtesy of the William J. Clinton Presidential Library, P34248_20*

giving him the eye, she lifted her dress and flashed her thong panties. Lewinsky later described this move on Clinton as "subtle," but as John Harris, tongue in cheek, has written, "Somehow, he interpreted this delicate signal as an invitation." That same night, the president met her in an empty office, where she performed oral sex on him while he talked on the phone to a congressman.

With their knowledge of how his skillful conduct during the shutdowns marked the start of the revival of his reputation leading to his reelection, commentators have found it difficult to explain his behavior with Lewinsky. To be sure, he was not guilty, as was often said later, of seducing an innocent girl. Shortly before, Lewinsky had engaged in an affair with another married man, and she had flung herself at the president. But what Clinton did was bad enough, and he was taking a terrible risk. "I was involved in two great struggles at the same time," he later reflected: "a great public struggle over the future of America with the Republican Congress and a private struggle with my old demons."

The historian Taylor Branch explored this issue in a series of frank conversations with the former chief executive, later published as *The*

Clinton Tapes: Wrestling History with the President (2009). In one inter-view, Clinton blurted out, "I cracked; I just cracked." From their talks, Branch surmised that the president had felt "beleaguered, unappreciated, and open to a liaison" after experiencing "the Democrats' loss of Congress in the November 1994 elections, the death of his mother the previous January, and the ongoing Whitewater investigation." The editor of *Newsweek,* Jonathan Alter, has elucidated the consequences. "November 1995 was the beginning of the resurrection, the beginning of the humili-ation. He saved his presidency, and he destroyed it simultaneously."

Far from giving way to impulse just once and then recognizing his folly, Clinton carried on the affair. Over the course of sixteen months, the two got together for sex on ten occasions. Some of these encounters took place when the first lady was upstairs in the family quarters. More than once, Clinton even called Lewinsky at home to summon her to the White House for an assignation. On Easter Sunday, the president, after attending church with his wife, went back to the White House to re-ceive oral sex while he was on the phone with a US senator. In a curious sort of punctilio, Clinton forbade Lewinsky to bring him to climax, apparently reasoning that by denying himself that pleasure, he was not actually engaged in illicit sexual episodes that could be regarded as dis-loyalty to his wife. On one occasion, though, he did not withdraw quickly enough, and semen splashed on her navy blue dress.

Early in April 1996, a White House supervisor, suspecting what might be going on, shunted Lewinsky, now on the federal payroll, to the other side of the Potomac, at the Pentagon—a move that had an unintended outcome. Isolated in that huge congeries in Virginia, Lewinsky found comfort in the friendship of an older woman in her office, and by summer she was confiding to Linda Tripp some startling revelations about the president, often in late-night phone calls. She even told her of the semen-stained dress from the Gap, which Tripp advised her not to clean but to retain as evidence she might need in the future.

Though it took Lewinsky months to discover this, Tripp turned out to be, as the historian James Patterson has written, "a friend from hell." Realizing that she had lucked into a potential best seller, Tripp got in touch with a New York literary agent. She took particular pleasure in the thought of writing an exposé because she was a deep-dyed Clinton-hater. At the agent's suggestion, she began to record telephone conversations without Lewinsky's knowledge or permission. On January 12, 1998, Tripp took the surreptitious recordings to Kenneth Starr, though his jurisdiction at that point was restricted to Whitewater. Her attorney made this recommendation simply because he assumed that Starr, as a fellow conservative, shared her animus against the president. The following day, FBI agents fitted Tripp with a hidden microphone to capture a conversation she expected to have with Lewinsky in a Pentagon City hotel.

On January 15, armed with these tapes, Starr, who in nearly four years of the Whitewater inquiry had turned up no illegal activity by the Clintons, asked Attorney General Reno to broaden his assignment, and, given the information provided by Tripp, she consented. On the very next day, in response to Reno's advocacy, the three-judge federal panel authorized expansion of his mandate. Henceforth, Starr was to examine not only Whitewater but also the Paula Jones proceedings, even though, as Chafe has said, "there was patently no relation between a real estate deal in Arkansas and the president having a sexual affair."

Two days later, Clinton became the first president ever compelled to undergo interrogation in a lawsuit. During six hours of deposition, he was taken aback when Paula Jones's legal team gave only fifteen minutes to the Jones matter and spent all the rest of the time on someone else, asking him bluntly: "Have you ever had sexual relations with Monica Lewinsky?" (The term had been defined as "the person knowingly engages in ... contact with the genitalia, anus, groin, breast, inner thigh, or buttocks of any person with an intent to arouse or gratify ... sexual desire.") Clinton denied outright that he had. Subsequently, Clinton claimed that oral sex did not fit the description stipulated because he had been the recipient, not the giver, but, in truth, he had stroked Lewinsky's breasts and had brought her to orgasm. Starr, for his part, had no doubt that Clinton had perjured himself.

At that point, the American people still knew nothing of the liaison that had begun many months before, but on January 21, the *Washington Post*, as well as the *Los Angeles Times* and ABC News, stunned the country by announcing a shocking allegation: the president had carried on an affair with a White House intern. So overwhelmingly negative was the response that Clinton's presidency appeared to be finished. The columnist George Will pronounced his tenure "dead, deader really than Woodrow Wilson's was after he had a stroke," and Nebraska Democratic senator Bob Kerrey remembered thinking: "Oh, my God, an intern. He's toast." ABC's top White House correspondent, Sam Donaldson, told millions of TV viewers: "Mister Clinton, if he is not telling the truth, and the evidence shows that, will resign, perhaps this week." Donaldson even speculated on the makeup of President Gore's cabinet.

Throughout this period, Clinton continued to prevaricate. He did so despite Bennett's warning: "The only thing you have to worry about is if you lie to them. The crazies will come after you. They will try to impeach you if you lie." He not only lied to his attorney, but to everyone else close to him, and he had no compunction about roping in distinguished cabinet officials and his most trusted advisers to participate unwittingly in his duplicity. "I want you to know that I did not have sexual relations with this woman Monica Lewinsky," he told his White House chief of staff. "And when the facts come out, you'll understand." Yes, he told his wife, he had seen this Lewinsky a few times, but only because he wanted to help the troubled young woman. That falsehood put the first lady, who believed him, in the exposed position of lashing out at conspirators who were treating her husband so unfairly.

On January 21, the president went public with these declarations of innocence. In an interview on the *PBS NewsHour*, Jim Lehrer asked him directly, "You had no sexual relationship with this young woman?" and Clinton replied, "There is not a sexual relationship—that is accurate." (Only close listeners detected that Clinton had fudged by shifting to the present tense.) In an editorial on February 2, his former adviser David Gergen, commenting on the response to Lehrer, said of the president: "Until credible evidence is presented to the contrary—and it hasn't been—we should believe him. But if he was lying, he has betrayed his public trust and is a scoundrel."

Less than a week later, the president addressed the American people from the White House. Peering resolutely into the eye of the television camera, Clinton, a figure of rectitude, wagged his finger four times in the manner of a stern, righteous schoolmaster as he declared, "I want to say one thing to the American people. I want you to listen to me. I'm going to say this again. I did *not* have sexual relations with that woman, Miss Lewinsky." He hesitated just a moment before saying "Miss Lewinsky," conveying the impression that his acquaintance with her was so minimal that he had difficulty even recalling her name. Striking the lectern with his finger, he added, "I never told anybody to lie, not a single time, never."

As he spoke those words, the president could not have sounded more sincere, but he talked with forked tongue. No sooner had he learned that Lewinsky was on the witness list than he instructed her to swear on oath that she had not once on her many visits to the Oval Office come to see him but had been calling on Betty Currie, his secretary. His treatment of Currie was no less reprehensible. She knew full well what had transpired, for she had abetted their affair—on one occasion sneaking Lewinsky up back stairs in the White House. But Clinton coerced her to attest that she had never seen him alone with Lewinsky and to swear that there was nothing untoward in their relationship. He pounded her with a barrage of false statements that he expected her to affirm: "You were always there when Monica was there"; "We were never really alone, right?"; "Monica came on to me, and I never touched her."

Jeffrey Toobin has written the most trenchant assessment of Clinton and Currie. He has accepted the contention of the president's attorneys that Clinton was not technically suborning perjury because Currie had not yet been summoned as a witness. Nonetheless, he has denounced how "contemptibly" Clinton treated his secretary in drawing her into "his circle of deceit," with no regard for Currie's subordinate status. "The president's willingness to use others to serve his own ends," Toobin concluded, "probably deserves greater condemnation than his sexual misadventures." He delivered this harsh judgment while acknowledging that "Clinton's right-wing enemies had...leveraged the Lewinsky affair from a personal problem to a legal and political crisis," had, indeed, "staged a banquet of excess." He further stated: "For all the piety of the authoritarians...about the importance of sexual fidelity of public persons, there remains no proof that monogamous presidents do better jobs than adulterous ones. (The evidence is actually somewhat to the contrary.)" But he added: "When Clinton was caught in that most clichéd of dilemmas—a menopausal man having an affair with a young woman from the office—he reacted not with candor and grace, but rather with the dishonesty and self-pity that are among the touchstones of his character."

Clinton earned more contempt by ordering Dick Morris to devise a poll asking the American people if they would forgive him if he confessed. Morris reported that they could tolerate his having committed

adultery but not his admitting to perjury about it. "Well," Clinton rejoined, "we'll just have to win, then." After this secret inquiry became
known, Joe Klein wrote: "This nauseating revelation seemed to encapsu-
late all the worst aspects of the Clinton administration. The President was
a man who would actually poll whether or not he should tell the truth."

With talk of impeachment heard in the land, Clinton's political advisers reminded him that although Republicans, lacking a two-thirds
majority, could not do him in, Democrats on the Hill certainly could if
they turned against him. A Democratic senator from North Dakota
alerted the White House that "you are about three days from having the
senior Democrats come down and ask for the president's resignation,"
and one of Clinton's aides has recalled: "The first seventy-two hours, the
Democrats in Congress were ready for him to go." He added: "What
changed it for them was the polling." Applause punctuated his imper-
turbably delivered January 27 State of the Union address 104 times, and
pollsters reported that affirmative responses to the president's handling
of his job had rocketed from 57 to 73 percent. In March, more than a
month after the media broke the story of the Lewinsky scandal, Clinton
had an approval rating of about 70 percent, in contrast to only 11 percent who thought well of Starr.

Clinton got more good news in April when Judge Susan Webber
Wright granted him a summary judgment throwing out Paula Jones's
frivolous suit that had begun four years earlier. The judge was infuriated
when Jones's legal team, charging that Jane Doe Number Five had been
raped by Clinton, cruelly revealed Doe's name and failed to inform the
court that the woman had sworn in an affidavit that the president had
done nothing heinous. Judge Wright also found persuasive the assertion
in Clinton's brief that Jones, after the alleged incident in the Little Rock
hotel room, had received steady raises and positive job reviews. In her
impressive opinion terminating the litigation, the judge stated that she
had seen no evidence to demonstrate that "plaintiff's reaction to Governor
Clinton's alleged advances affected tangible aspects of her compensation
terms, conditions, or privileges of employment." Though Clinton's
"alleged conduct, if true, may certainly be characterized as boorish and
offensive," she said, it provided "no basis for a claim of criminal sexual
assault" or of "workplace harassment." That spring, it seemed that the
president's travail might be nearing an end, not least because Monica

Lewinsky steadfastly refused to recant her denial under oath that her relationship with Bill Clinton had been erotic.

In late July, however, Clinton's fortunes took a sudden turn for the worse. Guaranteed that she would not be prosecuted for her earlier false testimony, which might well have resulted in a jail term, Lewinsky began to talk—and went on talking, first to Starr's lawyers, day after day, and then to a grand jury. She did more than talk. She turned over, in the FBI's words, a "Gap dress, size 12, dark blue," stained by "genetic material." At the White House in early August, the president was forced to submit to the indignity of a blood-drawing, which confirmed that his DNA matched that in the semen on Monica Lewinsky's dress. Not for two more weeks, though, when he was about to be videotaped by a grand jury, could he bring himself to confess to his wife. In his memoir, Clinton recalled, "she looked at me as if I had punched her in the gut, almost as angry at me for lying to her in January as for what I had done." She ordered him to confess to Chelsea, who would "learn that her father not only had done something terribly wrong, but had not told her or her mother the truth about it." (The president, it has been said, spent the next months sleeping alone on a couch in the executive mansion.)

On August 17, over the course of four hours in the Map Room of the White House, Clinton responded to interrogation by Starr's team of lawyers in closed-circuit testimony to the grand jury. Forced to recognize that the dress had compromised him, he finally admitted that he had engaged in "inappropriate intimate contact." He denied, though, that in his deposition in January he had lied about his relationship with Lewinsky, for their encounters "did not constitute sexual relations."

How, he was asked, could he square his admission of "intimate contact" with Bennett's assertion that "there is no sex of any kind in any manner shape or form"? Clinton replied with a feat of tightrope walking. "It depends on what the meaning of 'is' is," he offered. "If 'is' means is and never has been, that is one thing. If it means there is none, that was a completely true statement." Clinton's verbal legerdemain made him the butt of ridicule from which he has never escaped. As Nina Totenberg has pointed out, "He's trying not to commit perjury before the grand jury. That's where that stupid sentence comes from." He was carrying obfuscation "to the point of ridiculousness." Clinton, noted Jacob Weisberg in the *New York Times*, "will surely be remembered as someone who habitually played games with the truth.... The most evasive of these lines, like 'It depends on what the meaning of the word "is" is,' are destined for inclusion in *Bartletts*. Clinton is to hairsplitting legalisms what Yogi Berra is to tautological absurdities; he seems nearly to have invented the form." Yet, circuitous though his retort was, he did manage to avoid uttering a falsehood for which he could be indicted.

Having been more clever by half in his testimony that afternoon, he transformed his direct appeal to the country that night into a public relations disaster. In a televised address, he acknowledged for the first time: "I did have a relationship with Ms. Lewinsky that was not appropriate. In fact, it was wrong. It constituted a critical lapse in judgment and a personal failure on my part for which I am solely and completely responsible." He also admitted, "I misled people, including even my wife." But he also insisted falsely, "At no time did I ask anyone to lie, to hide or destroy evidence, or to take any other unlawful action."

Clinton came across not contrite or remorseful but furious and resentful. He said of the Starr investigation that it had "gone on too long, cost too much, and hurt too many innocent people." It was "past time," he said, "to move on" and "repair the fabric of our national discourse." He stated aggressively: "Now, this matter is between me, the two people I love most—my wife and our daughter—and our God.... I intend to reclaim my family life for my family. It's nobody's business but ours. Even presidents have private lives."

It did not take long for Clinton to be made aware of how grossly he had botched his opportunity. "It's bad enough that Bill Clinton defiled his presidency by having sex with an intern of the Oval Office, bad enough that he humiliated his wife and daughter," said George Stephanopoulos, who had left the White House for ABC News. "But President Clinton turned his personal flaw into a public matter when he made the whole country complicit in his cover story." Clinton, "blinded by his own self-pity," Stephanopoulos concluded, "had never displayed his flaws more clearly or in front of a bigger audience." The press was furious. "In a ghastly four-minute session, the President told the country no more than he had to," said a West Virginia newspaper. "It was a hell of a comedown from a fireside chat with F.D.R." Later, Toobin underscored the source of the president's blunder. "Clinton," he wrote, "marinated in his sense of victimhood."

On September 9, 1998, Starr gave Congress a 455-page report that, he maintained, contained "substantial and credible information that President William Jefferson Clinton committed acts that may constitute grounds for impeachment." In particular, he noted that Clinton had "lied under oath to a grand jury" and had "attempted to obstruct justice." Starr spared Clinton nothing. He gave a particularly lurid account of a March 1996 meeting: "The President inserted a cigar into Ms. Lewinsky's vagina, then put the cigar in his mouth and said: 'It tastes good.'" Analysts found fault with Starr's prurience in providing so much gratuitously graphic detail. The independent counsel, who had been appointed to scrutinize an Arkansas land speculation, used the word "Whitewater" four times, the word "sex" 581 times. "The report," said a *Washington Post* writer, read "more like a bad Harlequin romance than a legal document."

Two days later, the House of Representatives issued the report, with its salacious particulars, and on September 21, Starr released the videotape of the president's grand jury testimony—with consequences neither the independent counsel nor the Republican House anticipated. Democratic congressman Barney Frank expected a highly negative reaction, with "many people" thinking "Clinton was gone." Instead, Frank recalled, "people said, 'Oh, is this what this is about? The stupid bastard went and had oral sex with a kid? Shame on him. Now what's for dinner?'" Asked to choose between Bill Clinton and Ken Starr, most of the many millions who watched the videotape on television knew instinctively which man they preferred. More than one observer has likened the duo to Fielding's Tom Jones—a libertine and a rascal, to be sure, but oh so charming—and Blifil, his loathsome opponent, spouting morality but chillingly repellent. A prominent *Washington Post* reporter favored a different literary analogy: Starr, he said, was likely to be remembered as a counterpart of the "relentless, self-righteous Inspector Javert," the evil character of *Les Misérables*, engaged in "dogged pursuit" of Jean Valjean. Later, Nina Totenberg summed up these assessments in remarking, "There was a Cotton Mather feeling about Ken Starr." Yet if Clinton imagined that the popular response meant he was going to come away unscathed, he greatly underestimated the fierce determination of the Republican Congress to get him out of the White House.

On October 9, 1998, Henry Hyde, the silver-haired chairman of the Judiciary Committee, rose in the House of Representatives to open debate "on an historic... inquiry into whether the president has committed impeachable offenses." It was, indeed, historic, because not for more than 130 years had a president been impeached. "Shall we look further, or shall we look away?" Hyde asked. Predictably, he answered his hypothetical question by stating that "we must look further by... commencing an inquiry into whether or not the president committed impeachable acts." He maintained that "this is not about sexual misconduct any more than Watergate was about a third-rate burglary." Rather, he claimed, the House needed to resolve whether it was acceptable for presidents to lie under oath. "It is an onerous, miserable rotten duty," he concluded, "but we have to do it or break faith with the people who sent us here."

The seniority system that had elevated Hyde to the chairmanship had saddled Republicans with an implausible champion of virtue. Only a few days before his address to the House, a magazine piece titled "The Hypocrite Broke Up My Family" reported that Hyde, when forty-one, had entered into a sexual liaison with a married woman who was the mother of three children. Hyde was not the only Pecksniff on the Hill. Over the whole Republican effort to dislodge Clinton hung a thick miasma of unctuousness and partisan voracity.

Opponents of impeachment complained about the rush to judgment but differed on how to respond. Some, instead of insisting on Clinton's innocence, thought it shrewder, given all that was known, to acknowledge his defects. The Democratic leader in the House, Dick Gephardt, declared: "We're all profoundly hurt by what the president has done. He has deeply disappointed the American people, and he's let us all down." Fiery liberals, however, preferred to carry the fight to the enemy by underscoring how badly the Republicans' obsession with the scandal had skewed their grasp of reality. A Florida congressman cried: "The global economy is crumbling and we're talking about Monica Lewinsky! Saddam Hussein hides weapons, and we're talking about Monica Lewinsky! Genocide wrecks Kosovo, and we're talking about Monica Lewinsky! Children cram into packed classrooms, and we're talking about Monica Lewinsky!... The president betrayed his wife. He did not betray the country. God help the nation if we fail to recognize the difference."

Even Clinton's most ardent defenders, though, knew that they were talking into the wind, for the outcome was never in doubt. All that they could do was to threaten reprisals. "Well, you're not...going to get elected by hounding the president of the United States," warned a Harlem Democrat, "because as you judge the president of the United States, the voters will be judging you on November the 3rd." Republicans saw no reason to take him seriously because in midterm contests, the party in power almost always loses seats, sometimes dozens of them. After only two hours—all that Republicans would allow for discussion of this extraordinary step—the House voted to proceed with an investigation of possible grounds for impeachment of the president.

Overwhelmingly, the votes in the majority came from Republicans, but thirty-one Democrats—mostly conservatives facing tough challenges in swing districts—joined them. A few were genuinely indignant. A Pennsylvania Democrat who called for the president's resignation said that Clinton had mischaracterized his actions. They "were not 'inappropriate,'" he declared, but "predatory, reckless, breathtakingly arrogant." In favoring an impeachment inquiry, he asked, "If in disgust or dismay we were to sweep aside the president's immoral and illegal conduct, what dangerous precedent would we set for the abuse of power by some future president?"

These defections may have made Republicans overconfident, though they had already shown countless signs of hubris, when a number of considerations suggested caution. The 256–178 roll call fell far short of the 410–4 approval for the Nixon probe, and objections to the course they were taking were not limited to Democrats. Gerald Ford took the trouble to write a piece for the *New York Times* opposing impeachment and opting instead for a "rebuke" to the president. Most pertinently, every survey of opinion found that two-thirds of the country opposed impeachment. "Americans," Joe Klein later concluded, "had judged the Lewinsky affair a delicious, disgraceful, exploitative, and ultimately *private* act of consensual sex," and as the historian Steven Gillon wrote, "The only thing most Americans disliked more than a devious middle-aged man lying about sex was moralizing, self-righteous hypocrites telling other people how to live their lives."

Republicans saw fit to ignore these objections because they held the reins of power, and the November midterm elections promised to expand their domination of Congress. The generalissimo of the Republican campaign in 1998, Newt Gingrich, could not have been more cocksure. At a rally in suburban Atlanta, he told Young Republicans: "This fall we're going to see a surprisingly big victory almost everywhere in the country," and he informed party members on the Hill, one GOP congressman later remembered, to expect "a windfall of seats." The net gain in Congress, he predicted, might be as much as "plus forty."

The ballot counts on November 3 jolted Republicans without enlightening them. Instead of picking up more than two score seats in the House, they lost five. Still more significant was the outcome in the Senate, which would decide the president's fate in an impeachment trial. Anticipating big gains in the Senate, Republicans failed to win even one addition. Not for close to two centuries had there been such results in an election in the sixth year of a presidency. As a consequence, Republicans could not remove Clinton from office, even if every member of their party in the Senate voted to do so, unless twelve Democratic senators joined them—a highly unlikely eventuality. Simple arithmetic alerted Republicans that the time had come to settle for a resolution of censure of the president, which would have attracted a host of Democratic votes, but they refused to heed. On Election Night, Congressman Hyde concluded that the electorate had reprimanded Republicans for their fixation on Lewinsky, but he plunged ahead nonetheless.

Gingrich, though he did not slake his desire to rid the country of Clinton, took a different course. He knew that many of the GOP right-wingers in the House caucus regarded him as a false prophet and were gunning for him, so he resolved to preempt them. Three days after the election, he shocked Washington by announcing that he was resigning his post as Speaker and that at the end of the term, in a few more weeks, he would give up his seat in the House. Congressional relations assumed a more bizarre aspect when Louisiana's Robert Livingston, in line to succeed Gingrich, stunned the House by announcing that, instead of taking over the Speaker's chair, he, too, was resigning because word had gotten out that he had carried on an extramarital affair.

Led by Hyde, the Judiciary Committee, dividing largely along party lines, sent to the floor of the House four articles of impeachment. On December 11, as the entire House moved toward a decision, Clinton, speaking from the Rose Garden, made a last-second appeal for absolution.

"Looking like a whipped dog," wrote Posner later, "the President delivered still another evasive and unconvincing apology,...then walked silently back to the Oval Office, ignoring the shouts of the journalist-hounds demanding that he confess to lies." The House was unmoved. While rejecting two of the four counts, it voted to impeach Clinton—for committing perjury in his grand jury testimony and for obstructing justice by tampering with witnesses and withholding evidence.

The ensuing Senate trial, which began on January 7, 1999, had elements both of comic opera and of an overly long Hollywood film with a predictable ending. Though everyone knew from the beginning how the proceedings would play out, the Senate persisted in dawdling through thirty-seven days. In the judge's chair, Chief Justice Rehnquist had adorned his traditional black robe with four yellow stripes on each sleeve—a costume that had caught his fancy when he saw a performance of Gilbert and Sullivan's *Iolanthe*. The debate came to a melodramatic climax with an oration by a former US senator whose style was likened to that of movie idols in *Mr. Smith Goes to Washington* and *To Kill a Mockingbird*.

Nearly two weeks after the trial opened, the Mississippi Republican Trent Lott unintentionally heightened its cinematic nature by imposing a recess in order to parade the senators over to the House for a duty that had higher priority: listening to a speech by the president of the United States—the man they would shortly vote on ejecting from office. Seemingly unflappable, Clinton, in delivering his State of the Union address, gave a bravura performance. He knew that he had the tactical advantage of speaking as the messenger of good news, for every economic indicator pointed to rising prosperity. "My fellow Americans," he declared, "I stand before you to report that the state of our union is strong," a sentence that elicited thunderous applause. When he concluded, the senators, having heard him out, filed back to their chamber for still more days of chatter before each was called upon to decide, as the president's poll numbers continued to go up, whether it was wise to vote to get rid of the man.

Only at the very end of the discussion did the Senate hear a presentation of a quality measuring up to the seriousness of what was at stake, though it, too, had elements of Hollywood. On January 21, the final attorney on Clinton's defense team, Dale Bumpers of Arkansas, who had just stepped down after four terms in the Senate totaling nearly a quarter century, gave by far the most compelling exhortation of the debate. A formidable campaigner, he had defeated, in his climb to prominence, both Orval Faubus and J. William Fulbright, and he knew how to seize the moment. "Bumpers's speech," Toobin has written, "marked the high point of the trial—at once folksy and eloquent, funny and wise, heartbroken and heartfelt—in all, a great moment in the history of Senate oratory."

With "hands thrust deep into the pockets of his gray pin-striped suit," reported the *Washington Post*, Bumpers appeared to have been sent by Central Casting, an actor "with Lincolnesque features and enviable gray hair, straight as a ramrod despite 73 years, his voice a deep Ozarks blend of honey and tang, like a good barbecue sauce." The *Post* added: "Blending American archetypes—the country lawyer, the Senate orator...—he switched the channel from C-SPAN to American Movie Channel...with a beautifully aged Atticus Finch in the starring role."

Bumpers began with down-home drollery. To illustrate his point that the president should not be judged by unreasonably high standards, he spun a yarn about an evangelical preacher who asked the meeting, "Is there anybody in this audience who has ever known anybody who even comes close to the perfection of our Lord and Savior, Jesus Christ?" No one responded, so he repeated the challenge. After another prolonged silence, Bumpers recounted, "a itty bitty guy in back...kind of held up his hand." Dumbstruck, the preacher called out: "You are not saying you've known such a person? Stand up. Tell us. Share it with us. Who was it?" And, Bumpers concluded, the man stood up and said, "My wife's first husband."

In other moments of his nearly hour-long talk, the small-town Arkansan took on the persona of Jimmy Stewart looking with ineffable wonderment at the civic temples of the nation's capital. He reminded his audience that when he was in the Senate he had flown home nearly every weekend, returning "usually about dusk on Sunday evening." As the plane descended, he could see out his window "the magnificent Washington Monument," and, "after twenty-four years,...literally hundreds of times, I never failed to get goosebumps." He added: "Same thing about this chamber. I can still remember as though it were yesterday the awe I felt when I first stepped into this magnificent chamber so full of history. So beautiful."

At one point, however, he stooped to offering purple passages as maudlin as a three-hanky soaper. He did not deny that the president had "misled" and "deceived," or that "he did all of those things to his family, to his friends, to his staff, to his cabinet, and to the American people." But he asked, "Why would he do that?" He answered: "Well, he knew this whole affair was about to bring unspeakable embarrassment and humiliation on himself, his wife whom he adored, and a child that he worshipped with every fiber in his body, and for whom he would happily have died to spare her this or to ameliorate her shame and her grief."

Most of the time, he ascended to a higher plane—acknowledging Clinton's misbehavior but warning the Senate away from the course upon which it had embarked. "You pick your own adjective to describe the president's conduct," he said. "Here are some that I would use: indefensible, outrageous, unforgivable, shameless. I promise you the president would not contest any of those or any others." He also stated: "I have heard so many adjectives to describe...these proceedings—historic, memorable, unprecedented, awesome. All of those words...are apt." He then declared forcefully: "And to those, I would add the word *dangerous*—dangerous...to the political process, and...to the unique mix of pure democracy and republican government Madison and his colleagues so brilliantly crafted and which has sustained us for 210 years."

He took pains to place the president's misdeeds in context, for if Clinton had perjured himself, he had done so in response to a malicious lawsuit bankrolled by right-wing political enemies that was so worthless that it had been thrown out of court and to an inquiry by a prosecutor who had not restrained himself from any excess. Bumpers asked, "How do we come to be here?" And he replied: "We are here because of a five-year, relentless, unending investigation of the president. Fifty million dollars, hundreds of FBI agents fanning across the nation examining in detail the microscopic lives of people—maybe the most intense investigation not only of a president, but of anybody ever." He concluded: "But after all of those years...of Whitewater, Travelgate, Filegate, you name it, nothing, nothing. The president was found guilty of nothing."

Well aware of how vulnerable his former colleagues were to charges of hypocrisy, he went after the president's accusers, as the *Post* wrote, "with a warm smile and a cold shiv." The House managers of the impeachment, he noted, had said that there are "no excuses for lying." He retorted, speaking of Clinton, "Well, you put yourself in his position," after "you've already had this big moral lapse." He continued: "Sure, you say, he should have thought of all that beforehand. And indeed he should. Just as Adam and Eve should." Looking into the eyes of the senators, row on row, he added, "Just as you and you and you, . . . caught in similar circumstances, should have thought of it before." He conceded: "Here's a man who was unfaithful to his wife." But he maintained: "That is not a high crime against the United States because if it was," pointing around the chambers, "you'd be guilty, you'd be guilty, you'd be guilty—and wouldn't that be a ridiculous outcome?" In a telling phrase, he said that there was "a total lack of proportionality" in the case. "The charge and the punishment," he declared, "are totally out of sync."

Bumpers wound up by treating the Senate to a disquisition on the impeachment clause in the US Constitution, which stipulated three grounds for removal of a president. No one was contending, he pointed out, that Clinton was guilty of treason or bribery. And when the Founding Fathers added a third cause, "high crimes and misdemeanors," a perusal of the 1787 records, he asserted, revealed that they had in mind "a political crime against the state," not Bill Clinton's misdeeds. "Colleagues, this is easily the most important vote you will ever cast," he concluded. "If you have difficulty because of an intense dislike of the president—and that's understandable—rise above it. . . . If you vote to convict, . . . you're going to be creating more havoc than he could ever possibly create." It is said that speeches in the Senate do not change votes. But this address may very well have done so.

Public opinion might also have given Republican senators pause. Without question, Clinton had behaved abominably. But throughout the impeachment crisis, his high approval rating for presidential performance held steady, even though assessments of his character dropped sharply. As Michael Takiff has observed, Americans saw him as "a rogue and a scoundrel—who was good at his job," and who governed in a flush economy. "Baby boomers whose stocks and mutual bonds soared on Dow Jones thermals," in the words of one columnist, did not want to get rid of the man who presided over these palmy times. They may have recognized, too, that Clinton's unlawful responses to accusations had all taken place in the context of a bogus lawsuit and a meretricious investigation, and they certainly doubted that "lying about sex" met the criterion for removing a president from office.

Moreover, people outside the Beltway did not share Washington's absorption in the titillation over adultery in the White House. Questioned by the Pew Center on which 1998 news stories most interested them, they put the sex scandal in tenth place, not as riveting as a bout of unseasonable weather that year. Asked how they would vote if the 1996 choices were repeated, Americans gave Clinton almost precisely the same winning percentage as they had at the polls then. "It was as if the name 'Lewinsky' had never been heard in the land," wrote Joe Klein.

On February 12, 1999, Lincoln's birthday—the most sacred day of the year on the Republican calendar—the Senate approached a roll call that House Republicans had hoped would be a moment of vindication and affirmation. With the galleries packed by spectators who did not want to miss out on a historic occasion, Chief Justice Rehnquist intoned: "Senators, how say you? Is the respondent, William Jefferson Clinton, guilty or not guilty?" Each senator in turn rose to reply. On both counts, every Democratic senator voted to acquit. On the charge of perjury, ten Republicans voted with them. On the accusation of obstruction of justice, five Republicans, all from the Northeast, joined them, putting that tally at 50–50. Both results fell far short of the two-thirds (67) required for removal. In sum, Republican advocates of impeachment were not able to win a majority on either count. Accordingly, Chief Justice Rehnquist announced: "It is, therefore, ordered and adjudged that the said William Jefferson Clinton be, and...hereby is, acquitted of the charges in the said articles."

Afterward, Senator John McCain of Arizona, one of the large Republican bloc voting to remove from office a president who had appeared to be trapped, only to escape his pursuers once again, employed yet another metaphor from the movie screen in reflecting on how the melodrama had played out. "I equate...the Republican relationship with President Clinton, with that of...Wile E. Coyote and the Road Runner," he said. "Republicans are always just about to get President Clinton, and we've almost got our arms around him—and then the dynamite goes off or we run over the cliff or the train runs over us."

Every writer on the Lewinsky affair and its aftermath in the impeachment trial has stressed the terrible damage wrought to Clinton's aspirations for significant accomplishments in his second term. "The presidency is like an hourglass; the sand runs out," Stephen Hess of Brookings observed during the crisis. "The scandal has basically destroyed Clinton's sixth year, . . . and that's a terribly important year. You get into the seventh and eighth years and all the sand is at the bottom of the glass." An Associated Press reporter concluded: "He squandered the last three years of his presidency. Three years is a long time in the presidency of a talented man, and they were thrown away." Not only Clinton but those around him, commentators have noted, were slowed by the month-after-month distractions of the inquiries. "It's almost," one cabinet official stated, "as if the government adjusted to his limping."

Too much has been made of that point. The president chalked up few legislative breakthroughs in his last years in the White House less because of his dalliance with Monica Lewinsky than because there was so little of importance that he wanted enacted. When, in a State of the Union address, he offered a series of proposals, the *New York Times* characterized them as "Progressivism Lite." His White House team had a decidedly more conservative cast, with most of his liberal advisers gone and a North Carolina investment banker, Erskine Bowles, installed as chief of staff. In his first major address after the 1996 election, Clinton had asserted, "We have clearly created a new center," a statement he made with no little pride, but, some months later after observing the consequence, a columnist derided that development as "the great vanilla swamp of centrist Clintonism." In the spring of 1997, a writer for the Scripps Howard syndicate of newspapers contended: "Top analysts have increasingly been convinced that the body of President Bill Clinton, a '90s Democrat, has been taken over by the ghost of President Dwight Eisenhower, a '50s Republican. . . . Like Ike, he was good to business, and business was good to him. Some believe that Clinton made a Faustian bargain to win a second term. The good news is that he got re-elected, the bad news is that he has the soul of an elderly—and bald—Republican icon."

While liberals fussed at the president, the Speaker had applauded him. In August 1997, no longer at war over government shutdowns, Clinton and Gingrich grinned ear to ear as they hailed one another on a budget agreement that a flourishing economy made possible. The pact gave Republicans the biggest tax cut in sixteen years (with the wealthy reaping 68 percent of the benefits), the greatest reduction of the capital gains tax in history, and exemption of more than a million dollars from estate levies, as well as the hike in Medicare premiums Gingrich had been demanding.

To be sure, the president had not come away empty-handed. "In a year when the stock market landed on Mars and inflation became a fugitive," *Time* reported, "Washington embraced a new politics of abundance that gives away something to just about everyone." Clinton got $24 billion in health care for children and what one authority called "the biggest single federal investment in higher education since the GI bill." In addition, he held true to a promise he had made in his first term by persuading Congress to grant legal immigrants the welfare benefits that had been denied them earlier. In 1997, too, Congress approved a State Children's Health Insurance Program, strongly advocated by Hillary Clinton and sponsored by the Democrat Ted Kennedy and the Republican Orrin Hatch, expanding coverage for some six million children.

On several occasions, however, Clinton moved far to the right, sometimes with unfortunate consequences. Toward the end of his presidency, he approved legislation repealing the New Deal's Glass-Steagall Act of 1933 that had separated commercial from investment banking, and signed a Commodity Futures Modernization Act that sheltered over-the-counter derivatives from government regulation. Both of these measures contributed to the financial meltdown that devastated the country in the next decade. Before that severe recession ended, many billions of taxpayer dollars had been drained away to rescue Citigroup and other Godzillas fostered by these laws. Clinton, having lived through the awful times of the early twenty-first century, later acknowledged: "I very much wish now that I had demanded that we put derivatives under the jurisdiction of the Securities and Exchange Commission and that transparency rules had been observed.... That I think is a legitimate criticism."

Clinton sought, too, to expand US participation in a global market economy but failed to win over his own party members on the Hill—as well as union leaders, environmentalists, and radical activists. When he joined with Gingrich to try to renew a "fast-track" privilege confining Congress to an aye-or-nay vote on international trade deals with no power to amend, Democrats rebelled. After only 42 of 205 Democrats in the House would go along, the president had to give up. In 1999, an event that went sour focused the eyes of the world on resistance to his message. That year, Seattle provided a showplace for Clinton's vision by hosting a meeting of the World Trade Organization, but it turned out to be an embarrassment for the president. The delegates from many lands could not get to the convention hall because tens of thousands of protesters against global corporations seized control of streets, smashed store windows, and overturned police cars.

No one—least of all Bill Clinton—could have imagined on Inauguration Day 1997 that his few breakthroughs in his second term would come not in domestic affairs but in foreign policy, and they were more impressive as initiatives than for results. At the outset, the president replaced Warren Christopher as secretary of state with the US ambassador to the United Nations, Madeleine Albright—the first woman appointed to this position, the most prestigious in the cabinet. Contrary to simple-minded stereotypes of women, she proved to be the most bellicose member of the administration. She even stormed at General Powell: "What's the point of having this super military you're always talking about if we can't use it?" In part because of her influence, but also as the result of growing confidence, the president, too, became more willing to resort to arms.

Clinton targeted the government of Iraq, a regime he had initially punished in his first term. On learning that the Iraqi Intelligence Service was responsible for an attempt to assassinate George Bush with a car bomb when the former president visited Kuwait in 1993, Clinton had ordered a Tomahawk missile assault on IIS headquarters in the heart of Baghdad. In 1994, when Saddam Hussein was challenging no-fly zones, the president dispatched thirty-six thousand American soldiers to Kuwait to warn him away from another invasion. Two years later, in Operation Desert Strike, US vessels fired missiles to impede an Iraqi offensive against Kurds.

In the president's second term, he sought to bring the country's defiant dictator to heel. In his 1998 State of the Union address, he told the assembled members of Congress:

> Saddam Hussein has spent the better part of this decade, and much of his nation's wealth, ... on developing nuclear, chemical, and biological weapons and the missiles to deliver them. The United Nations weapons inspectors have done a truly remarkable job, finding and destroying more of Iraq's arsenal than was destroyed during the entire

Gulf War. Now, Saddam Hussein wants to stop them from completing their mission. I know I speak for everyone in this chamber, Republicans and Democrats, when I say to Saddam Hussein, "You cannot defy the will of the world," and when I say to him, "You have used weapons of mass destruction before; we are determined to deny you the capacity to use them again."

Later that year, Clinton signed a bipartisan resolution stating that the American goal in Iraq was "regime change," though no US ground forces would be sent.

After Saddam Hussein, in violation of the agreement terminating the Gulf War, refused to permit UN inspection of his arsenals, Clinton approved still more air attacks. Since the bombing came at the height of the impeachment imbroglio, critics accused him of following the scenario of the film *Wag the Dog* (1997), in which a president who had made sexual advances to an underage girl was able to win another term when a Hollywood spin doctor contrived a make-believe war with Albania to divert the public's attention from his misdeed. But a former Republican senator, Secretary of Defense William Cohen, stated: "I am prepared to place thirty years of public service on the line to say the only factor that was important in this decision is what is in the American people's best interest." Unchastened by the damage the missiles wrought, Saddam remained as obdurate afterward as he had been before.

Clinton wielded an iron fist in the Balkans, too, after Milošević, the Serb leader whose addiction to ethnic cleansing had not been satiated by the bloodletting in Bosnia, set out to exterminate ethnic Albanian Muslims in the breakaway province of Kosovo. In 1999, Clinton, as leader of a NATO onslaught, authorized giant Stealth aircraft to take off from bases in Missouri, fly fourteen hours to Europe, and drop 200-pound bombs, which, guided by a sophisticated global positioning system, devastated Serbian sites. This offensive marked the first time that NATO had attacked a European nation. When the Serbs still did not relent, Clinton seriously considered sending in US ground troops, as Albright advocated, but after two months of bombardment, Milošević capitulated. He did so less because of the air war than as a result of the threat of a NATO ground attack and pressure from the Serbs' historic ally, Russia. The outcome was largely cost-free for Clinton. He was not burdened by the casualties of a ground war, and no American pilot was lost, since the technologically sophisticated US planes had flown so high that the Serbs could not detect them, let alone bring them down. Not long afterward, Milošević, driven from power by his war-weary people, was extradited as a war criminal to The Hague, where he died in a prison cell.

Few questioned that Clinton had any option save force in coping with a danger that no president had ever confronted on a large scale before: terrorism. Radical Muslims, fueled by an intense hatred of Western secular culture and of US support for Israel, had followed up the bombing of the World Trade Center garage in 1993—only thirty-six days after Clinton took office—with an assault on a US Air Force barracks in Saudi Arabia in 1996 and meticulously calibrated attacks on American embassies in Nairobi and Dar es Salaam in 1998 that killed hundreds, including US Foreign Service personnel. Within days, the American people heard for the first time the name of the mastermind behind these bombings: Osama bin Laden, a wealthy Saudi whose al-Qaeda plotters were sheltered in Afghanistan by the Taliban.

In retaliation for the most recent blasts, Clinton ordered the launching of dozens of cruise missiles from American warships in the Arabian and Red Seas. Most were aimed at an al-Qaeda compound in Afghanistan, but thirteen fell on a Sudanese pharmaceutical plant in Khartoum. Clinton maintained that the factory had ties both to bin Laden and to Iraq and that it was manufacturing nerve gas, but many questioned the motive for leveling the building, which took place just three days after his grand jury testimony and his severely criticized speech on extramarital sex. "I just hope and pray," said a Republican senator from Indiana, "the decision...was made...for the right reasons, and not...because it was necessary to save the President's job." David Maraniss has written: "Far more disturbing to me than the Monica Lewinsky matter...was the bombing of the factory in the Sudan....I don't believe in the whole *Wag the Dog* theory—that a president would deliberately design some military action to divert attention from his other problems—but it comes close."

Clinton signed a memorandum in August 1999 directing the CIA to come up with a new strategy and authorizing it to murder bin Laden. Despite these efforts, al-Qaeda succeeded in bombing the destroyer USS *Cole* in the Yemeni harbor of Aden late in 2000, killing seventeen American sailors. Overall, the historian George Herring concluded,

Clinton and his advisers dealt "perfunctorily" with bin Laden's schemes. "What's it gonna take, Dick?" one counterterrorism expert asked Richard Clarke, the president's coordinator of operations. "Does al-Qaeda have to attack the Pentagon to get their attention?"

Much of the time, in formulating responses to challenges abroad, Clinton preferred to resort to diplomacy—notably so in his commitment to reconciliation in the Middle East, but that task proved to be frustrating. In September 1998, he invited Israeli prime minister Benjamin Netanyahu and the chairman of the Palestine Liberation Organization, Yasser Arafat, to confer with him at a retreat in Maryland. The resultant Wye River Memorandum provided for Israel to cede West Bank territory to the Palestinians in return for their deleting lethal anti-Israeli paragraphs from their charter. Two days after the House Judiciary Committee voted to impeach him, the president turned up in Gaza to hear the Palestinian National Council carry out its pledge to repudiate articles in its Covenant calling for abolition of the State of Israel. In subsequent negotiations during his final year in office, Clinton appeared to be making progress, but at a critical moment, Arafat balked. "You are a great man and a great president," Arafat told him as his days in the White House were drawing to a close. "The hell I am," Clinton replied. "I'm a colossal failure, and you made me one."

Years of peacemaking in Northern Ireland brought greater success, but only after disheartening setbacks. Clinton knew that it would require a very bold move on his part to win the confidence of the Irish Republican Army. In 1994, he took the grave risk of granting a forty-eight-hour US visa to Gerry Adams, the head of Sinn Féin (the IRA's political wing), though Protestant Nationalists regarded Adams as a vicious murderer. The president's action, an Irish ambassador later said, left the British "incandescent with rage." But Clinton persisted in peace efforts. In January 1995, he appointed an envoy to Northern Ireland, George Mitchell, recently retired as US senator from Maine. A brilliant choice, the former Senate majority leader quickly showed his skills as a negotiator. In February 1996, however, the IRA undid his good work by setting off a bomb in London's Docklands that killed two people.

Dismayed but not discouraged, Mitchell, with timely interventions by the president, continued to pursue a cease-fire accord between the two embittered antagonists who for decades had torn their green land apart, and at the end of seventeen months, the Americans succeeded. On April 10, 1998, Irish Catholics and Protestants signed the Good Friday Agreement disarming rival militias and pledging the two ancestral enemies to "total and absolute commitment to . . . peaceful means of resolving differences." Unhappily, the jubilation that followed news of the concordat turned out to be premature, for the pact soon fell apart, and Mitchell had to return. Not until 2007 was the promise of the agreement fulfilled. Abroad as at home, Bill Clinton found the presidency a tough and, at times, an unrewarding assignment.

Although Clinton survived the impeachment attempt, the Lewinsky scandal cast a dark shadow over the 2000 campaign. Democrats counted on Clinton's vice president to maintain party control of the White House, but Al Gore was greatly burdened by what was termed "Clinton fatigue," defined by the political analyst John Geer as "a kind of moral retrospective voting [that] had a significant impact on Gore's chances." While presidential performance ratings held fast at an exceptionally high level, a Pew survey found that only 29 percent of respondents wished that Clinton could serve a third term. No one questioned Gore's Eagle Scout probity, but numbers of Americans, especially churchgoers, saw the election as an opportunity to punish the party identified with immorality.

Consequently, Gore did all he could to distance himself from the Clinton White House. The Tennessean moved his campaign headquarters from Washington to Nashville and, in his acceptance address, made a point of saying that he was running as his "own man." Even when he spoke at a political rally in Little Rock, he did not invite the state's foremost figure. Gore created the most conspicuous breach with Clinton by choosing as his running mate Senator Joseph Lieberman. A devout Jew (the first ever on a national ticket), the conservative Connecticut Democrat was best known for the dramatic harangue he had delivered against the president's conduct on the eve of the impeachment inquiry.

In November, Gore won more than half a million more popular votes than his Republican opponent, George W. Bush, son of the former president, but the Electoral College count was very much closer. On Election Night, one of the networks projected Gore as the next president of the United States, for he had 267 of the 270 electoral votes he needed, with only Florida, where he held a lead, still counting. But when the outcome in Florida became murkier, the network retracted. Americans awakened the next morning not knowing who their president would be. They had to wait more than five weeks to find out, as officials sorted through a litter of ballots in Florida, governed by the Republican presidential nominee's brother Jeb Bush.

As was true in other states, Florida tolerated county-by-county management of election procedure—an unregulated system with no national supervision that constituted a highway accident waiting to happen. Each county was at liberty to devise its own ballot, which in 2000— with nothing less at stake than determining the leader of the greatest power on earth—resulted in a shambles, with an astonishing 175,000 votes in dispute. In a number of counties—notably in heavily Democratic areas—voters did not punch cards all the way through, leaving "hanging chads" that failed to register on machines, and in Palm Beach County a bizarre "butterfly ballot" so confused elderly Jews who thought they were voting for Gore that they marked their ballots for a minor-party candidate who was an anti-Semite.

For thirty-six days, Gore's lawyers fought their way through a maze of Florida jurisdictions in quest of a fair tally, only to encounter frustration. On November 8, the Florida Division of Elections awarded victory to Bush by a margin of 1,784 votes. Two days later, with a machine recount mandated by statute essentially completed, his margin fell to 537. Gore then requested a manual recount of the returns in four populous counties, but the partisan secretary of state turned him down and certified Bush the winner. On December 8, the Florida Supreme Court offset her edict by ordering a statewide manual recount, but one day later, in a 5–4 division, the US Supreme Court, responding to a petition from Bush's attorneys, granted a temporary stay halting that recount.

On December 12, the US Supreme Court, in a 5–4 decision in *Bush v. Gore*, ruled that in ordering a statewide recount, the Florida Supreme Court had violated the equal protection clause of the Fourteenth Amendment because counties might use varying criteria in dealing with ballots. (Two additional justices agreed that the different standards among counties created an equal protection problem, but they favored remanding the case to the Florida Supreme Court to draft guidelines.)

Furthermore, the majority opinion said, there was not enough time to establish standards before the deadline imposed by Congress. The decision resulted in a bare majority of electoral votes for Bush, just one more than the 270 he needed. In a scorching dissent, Justice Stevens denounced the majority in *Bush v. Gore* for lending "credence to the most cynical appraisal of the work of judges throughout the land." He concluded: "Although we may never know with complete certainty the identity of the winner of this year's Presidential election, the identity of the loser is perfectly clear. It is the Nation's confidence in the judge as an impartial guardian of the rule of law."

Numbers of analysts echoed Stevens, for the Court's action seemed blatantly biased and untethered in doctrine. Every justice in the majority had been appointed by a Republican, and nothing in their past opinions squared with their reasoning in this case. Geoffrey Stone, provost of the University of Chicago, observed, "No one familiar with the jurisprudence of Justices Rehnquist, Scalia, and Thomas could possibly have imagined that they would vote to invalidate the Florida recount process on the basis of their own well-developed...approach to the Equal Protection Clause." Having frequently upheld state governments when plaintiffs had sought to invoke equal protection claims, the Court, by refusing to permit Florida to determine the outcome of the election, appeared to be audaciously willful. Subsequently, the historian Sean Wilentz reflected: "The greatest irony of *Bush v. Gore* may be that conservative justices who had long railed against judicial activism had become the most activist justices in our history, or at least the most activist since the majority on the Taney Court handed down the notoriously slapdash decision in *Dred Scott v. Sandford* in 1857."

Bush v. Gore embittered millions of Americans who questioned whether the 2000 election had been fairly decided, and it opened the US Supreme Court as an institution to the most scathing criticism in the legal community since the 1930s. In the following month, on the day of Bush's inauguration, protesters marched with placards saying, "Hail to the Thief," and some of the law school commentary expressed unbridled contempt. The Harvard University law professor Alan Dershowitz wrote: "The decision in the Florida election case may be ranked as the single most corrupt decision in Supreme Court history, because it is the only one that I know of where the majority justices decided as they did because of the personal identity and political affiliation of the litigants. This was cheating, and a violation of the judicial oath." More than a decade later, one of the justices in the majority, Sandra Day O'Connor, told the editorial board of the *Chicago Tribune* ruefully: "Maybe the Court should have said, 'We're not going to take it, goodbye.'...The election authorities in Florida hadn't done a real good job there and kind of messed it up. And probably the Supreme Court added to the problem at the end of the day."

The attention lavished on *Bush v. Gore* obscured much more important reasons for Gore's defeat. In truth, once the outcome turned on disputed ballots in the quagmire of Florida's election procedures, no resolution that would have satisfied every fair-minded American was any longer achievable. It is more rewarding to ask why the virtual deadlock transpired, why Gore did not win decisively. Though some commentators pointed to the third-party candidate Ralph Nader's role as a "spoiler," most analysts emphasized a more fundamental cause for the inability of Democrats to retain control of the White House. Forty-four percent of the electorate, exit polls revealed, said that the Clinton scandals were important in determining their vote; not surprisingly, those who reported that uneasiness went overwhelmingly for Bush.

In an oral history anthology of Clinton's career, editor Michael Takiff summed up the consequences:

> Bill's dalliance with Monica...cost the nation not only what might have been done between January 1998 and January 2001, but what might have been done, and what was done instead, over the eight years that followed.
>
> Instead of responsible fiscal stewardship, endless red ink. Instead of a budget surplus bolstering Social Security or funding education and infrastructure, trillions squandered on upper-income tax cuts.... Instead of judicious use of America's armed forces, an ill-begotten, counterproductive war, entered into deceitfully and conducted unforgivably. Instead of an America respected around the world, an America reviled around the world. Instead of a commitment to slowing climate change, eight years of denial that it exists....Stem-cell research, wilderness conservation, mine safety—the list of Clinton policies repudiated by George W. Bush is practically endless.

And none of it would have happened had the president of the United States been able to control himself when a randy young woman showed him her underwear.

Allegations about extramarital sex dogged Clinton to the very end of his presidency—and beyond. In 1998, to eliminate the possibility that an appeals court might reinstate Paula Jones's suit, he settled her claim by paying her $850,000 (though without admitting guilt), but even that huge sum did not end his financial obligations. Six months later, Judge Susan Webber Wright held him in contempt of court for lying, fined him, and ordered him to pay another $50,000 to Jones's lawyers. "There simply is no escaping the fact that the President deliberately...undermined the integrity of the judicial system," she declared. "Sanctions must be imposed, not only to redress the President's misconduct, but to deter others who might...consider emulating the President of the United States." In January 2001, one day before his term was to expire, Clinton effected a plea bargain by confessing that "certain of my responses to questions about Ms. Lewinsky were false." (The Arkansas Bar Association imposed another fine, stripped him of his law license, and barred him from practicing for five years.)

After these inglorious developments, it did not seem possible that, with only twenty-four hours of his tenure remaining, Clinton could do anything further to tarnish his presidency, but he managed to pull it off. On his very last night in office, he issued 177 pardons and commutations. Cries of outrage greeted one particular pardon—of the Belgian-born financier Marc Rich, who had amassed a billion-dollar fortune through oil deals with despised rulers, notably the leaders of the apartheid regime in South Africa, but also Fidel Castro, Libya's Gaddafi, and Pinochet in Chile. On hearing that he was about to be indicted on sixty-five criminal counts—including tax evasion, fraud, racketeering, and dealing illegally with Khomeini while Americans were being held hostage in Tehran—Rich fled the country and renounced his US citizenship. The FBI placed him on its Ten Most Wanted List.

Clinton's decision to pardon the unrepentant exile seemed glaringly suspect because of the ministrations of Rich's former wife. Denise Rich had not only donated more than a million dollars to the Democratic Party and another $100,000 to Hillary Clinton's campaign for the US Senate but had pledged almost half a million dollars to building a Clinton presidential library and had even spent thousands of dollars on furniture for the Clintons' future home in a posh New York suburb. In Bill Clinton's last two years in power, she had been welcomed to the White House no fewer than ninety-six times. Jimmy Carter called Clinton's pardon of Marc Rich "disgraceful," and Joe Klein, surmising that Clinton had succumbed to Denise Rich's "emollient unctuousness" in "a final self-indulgence," concluded that "the rapacious enormity of these conceits and absolutions seemed to recapitulate Clinton's most loathsome qualities." Despite the president's last-minute *beau geste*, Marc Rich never returned to the United States.

———

Throughout his eight years in the White House, Clinton fretted over how historians would grade him after his tenure ended. Late in his first term, Dick Morris explained to him that scholars had been classifying presidents into five categories: great, near great, average, below average, failure. Clinton had started out identifying with Franklin Roosevelt, one of the only three in the top echelon. But he soon recognized that he was not confronting crises comparable to the Depression and World War II that had tested FDR. For a time, he imagined himself to be a latter-day Teddy Roosevelt, ranked "near great" despite reigning in a time of peace, but no one found that notion credible. Morris wound up his tutorial by telling him bluntly, "Right now, to be honest, I think you are borderline third tier." Clinton responded, "I think that's about right."

As it has turned out, historians have had a hard time assigning a grade because Clinton seems so elusive. Early on, writing of Clinton's governorship, David Maraniss advanced a pattern of interpretation that has endured. In his persuasive account *First in His Class*, he observed: "With Bill Clinton, it is often tempting, but usually misleading, to try to separate the good from the bad, to say that the part of him that is indecisive, too eager to please and prone to deception is more revealing of the inner man than the part of him that is indefatigable, intelligent, empathetic and self-deprecating. They co-exist." Numbers of journalists have embraced this perspective. Bill Clinton, stated *Newsweek*'s Jonathan Alter, had polar attributes, "solid and squalid; cautious and reckless; supersmart and superdumb," and a *New York Times* correspondent said of Clinton:

"One of the biggest, most talented, articulate, intelligent, open, colorful characters ever to inhabit the Oval Office can also be an undisciplined, fumbling, obtuse, defensive, self-justifying rogue.... Most of the traits that make him appealing can make him appalling in the flash of an eye."

Insiders who knew the president well have buttressed these contentions. Dick Morris has remarked: "The Sunday-morning Clinton is the one we have all seen so often on television. Pious, optimistic, brilliant, principled, sincere, good-willed, empathetic, intellectual, learned, and caring, he is the president for whom America voted in 1992 and again in 1996. But the Saturday-night Bill who cohabits within him is pure id—willful, demanding, hedonistic, risk-taking, sybaritic, headstrong, unfeeling, callous, unprincipled, and undisciplined." And, in his memoir, George Stephanopoulos characterized Clinton as a "complicated man responding to the pressures and pleasures of public life in ways I found both awesome and appalling."

When historians set out to write about Clinton, they absorbed these impressions and shared the puzzlement. After interviewing scores of people who knew Clinton, Michael Takiff felt that, like Omar Khayyam, he came out the same door that in he went. He summed up: "Principled battler for the common good? You bet. Shameless opportunist? Yup. Authoritative commander in chief? Affirmative. Feckless commander in chief? Indeed. Brilliant pragmatist? Yes. Inveterate compromiser, willing to sell out millions to get a deal? Right. A man of rare empathy? Obviously. Self-interested son of a bitch? Certainly. Liberal? Conservative? Centrist? Check, check, check."

Numbers of critics regarded Clinton as a man with no core of beliefs—a president so poll-driven that he even ordered a survey of voter attitudes to determine where he should go on vacation. "Clinton's central problem has been the lack of an inner compass," David Gergen concluded. "He has 360-degree vision but no true north." Richard Reeves called him "the flap-tongued Democratic president who seemed to know everything and believe in nothing," and Elizabeth Drew concluded: "There seemed to be something unfinished about him. Compared to many men his age, or even younger, he didn't seem quite grown up.... He didn't come across as a settled person."

Some analysts indicated that they did not believe that Clinton would even make "borderline third tier." Clinton's performance, one observer said, was "not going to put him on Mount Rushmore or probably even on one of the lower hills." The temperate columnist David Broder wrote of Clinton: "Like Nixon, he has done things of importance for the country, but, in every important way, he has diminished the stature and reduced the authority of the Presidency." Another writer titled an assessment of Clinton, "Honey, I Shrunk the Presidency."

The Lewinsky affair, in particular, impaired his standing. Senator Bob Graham of Florida, who had voted against removing the president, stated: "History should—and I suspect will—judge that William Jefferson Clinton dishonored himself and the highest office in our American democracy." Richard Posner went even further: "Clinton may be said without hyperbole to have defiled the Oval Office. . . . Imagine a President who urinated on the front porch of the White House or burned the American flag; these acts could be thought metaphors for what Clinton did." A poll of historians placed him dead last in the roster of presidents if gauged by moral behavior.

Scholars who examined dispassionately not Clinton's ethics but his legislative accomplishments found little of historic significance. Richard Norton Smith wrote: "An activist by temperament, a risk taker in his personal life, Clinton proved largely risk averse in the policy arena." The historian Douglas Brinkley recalled a conversation with Clinton at Hyde Park about "how much Roosevelt meant to him." Brinkley concluded:

He had read virtually every biography of FDR. He knew every cabinet member, knew the day on each bit of New Deal legislation. . . . One felt that he considered himself a Rooseveltian, that his hero was FDR. . . .

But when you look at the record, it's very hard to see. He seems to be the end of the New Deal tradition.

President Clinton, writers noted, carried to a climax a seismic shift to the center of the Democratic Party that began with deregulation under Carter. From a conservative perspective, George Will observed slyly that Clinton's principal accomplishment was "transformation of the party of liberalism into the party of conservatism with moist eyes." David Maraniss has concluded: "When you look at what he used his power for—at his achievements, particularly in domestic policy—I think a strong argument can be made that they are largely moderate Republican programs. The North American Free Trade Agreement (NAFTA), the balanced budget, and welfare reform are the central programs that have passed.... That's where his power went."

Clinton had gained renown as the first Democrat since FDR to win two consecutive terms, but, observers pointed out, he had failed as a party leader. He came to power with Democrats enjoying impressive majorities in both houses of Congress, and in control of a majority of state governments in the country. When his tenure ended, Republicans reigned in the Senate and the House, and they held most of the governorships. The GOP takeover of the House of Representatives ended Democratic domination that had persisted for four decades— through most of Eisenhower's years and all of Reagan's and Bush's. In 2000, the political scientist Nicol Rae summed up what had happened on Clinton's watch: "His presidency coincided with the heaviest Democratic losses at the sub-presidential level in decades.... On every electoral dimension except for the presidency, the Democrats are significantly weaker than they were when Clinton took office in 1993."

All of these many, often well-reasoned, accounts of Clinton's shortcomings ran up against one countervailing consideration: his extraordinary popularity. Despite the impeachment, Clinton ended his tenure with the highest approval rating of any president in the post-1945 era, better than that of Eisenhower or Reagan. His onetime press secretary Dee Dee Myers reflected: "People had to voice some disgust with his behavior, yet his job approval stayed so high because they thought that he was for them. There was this remarkable dual track that people, I'm particularly thinking of reporters, were proceeding along: How could this guy be such a shit and be so compelling at the same time?"

A number of scholars underscored the most conspicuous reason for his high standing: piping prosperity. Clinton presided over the greatest boom in American history, with gross domestic product growing by one-third in just eight years. From 1994 to 2000, every quarter recorded growth—a performance never before achieved. Joblessness fell from 7.5 percent to 4 percent, and inflation dropped to an almost infinitesimal 1.6 percent. Economic gains benefited the working class as they had not under Reagan, and a higher percentage of American families owned their own homes than ever before. When Clinton took office, federal deficits (totaling a staggering $290 billion in 1992) appeared to be out of control, with each year worse than the one before, but Clinton's second term brought exhilarating tidings, with an economy fueled by the dotcom revolution yielding rising revenues at a dizzying pace. In January 1998, the government announced a surplus for the first time since 1960, as it did each of the last three years of Clinton's presidency—in 2000, a stunning $236 billion. (Gross national debt, though, continued to rise.) The *New York Times* called the achievement "the fiscal equivalent of the fall of the Berlin Wall."

Some critics maintained that Bill Clinton deserved less credit for the upturn than Bill Gates, that it derived from initiatives in Seattle and Silicon Valley, not Washington, and that the president had just lucked into the surge, but Clinton sharply disputed that judgment. "If you see a turtle sitting on top of a fence post," he was fond of saying, "it didn't get there by accident." In his State of the Union address in 2000, he was able to boast: "We begin the new century with over 20 million new jobs; the fastest economic growth in more than 30 years; the lowest unemployment rates in 30 years; the lowest poverty rates in 20 years; the lowest African-American and Hispanic unemployment rates on record; the first back-to-back budget surpluses in 42 years.... We have built a new economy."

Clinton also took pride in a sizeable number of other achievements. He had enlarged the earned income tax credit that benefited low-wage workers, put through family and medical leave, expanded programs for child nutrition, doubled funding for Head Start, and persuaded Congress to establish Pell Grants to make college education more accessible. AmeriCorps enrolled 150,000 young men and women. Clinton's record on conservation was no less impressive. The political scientist Benjamin Ginsberg has pointed out that when "he was being impeached and...couldn't get anything through Congress—he couldn't have had the marigold declared the national flower—President Clinton had most of his environmental agenda written into law through rules and regulations." He set aside more land than even Theodore Roosevelt had, notably by designating Grand Staircase–Escalante in southern Utah as a national monument. He also led the country into the age of a computer-based global economy by creating the first White House website and fostering the Telecommunications Act of 1996 that subsidized Internet access for schools and libraries.

Unlike some previous presidents, Clinton did not act on the assumption that the American government was the exclusive preserve of white men. The Nobel laureate novelist Toni Morrison called him "the first Black president," remarking, "Clinton displays almost every trope of blackness: single-parent household, born poor, working-class, saxophone-playing, McDonald's-and-junk-food-loving boy from Arkansas." He chose African Americans for 18 percent of openings in the federal judiciary, a striking increase from Reagan's 2 percent, and his body language semaphored his enjoyment of the company of members of other races. Clinton not only appointed eleven women to cabinet and cabinet-level positions but allotted 28 percent of federal judgeships to women, in contrast to only 8 percent by Reagan.

Dispassionate observers as well as Clinton's champions have denied that his character flaws doomed him to mediocrity. After noting the numerous times "Clinton did what he judged to be best for the country, despite serious political opposition," the political scientist James Pfiffner has contended, "It is hard to argue that they were all merely poll-driven, craven adherence to the path of least resistance.... Despite Clinton's faults, his character led him to take some tough policy stands and achieve some significant victories." An Arkansas journalist has maintained: "There are issues throughout his career that are not negotiable with him. One of them is racial equity. He has been resolute on abortion rights. Another issue was the NRA. He stood up repeatedly to legislation offered by the National Rifle Association." When an interviewer noted that "Clinton's detractors consider him a political coward," former treasury secretary Robert Rubin responded: "I know they do. It's very common. It's an astonishing claim." He then elaborated: "Health care didn't pass, but it certainly was an act of courage to try it. NAFTA was toxic with the AFL-CIO—they were natural allies of his, and he fought for it." Rubin's successor, Lawrence Summers, pointed to "aggressive bailout responses in Mexico, in Korea, and Brazil" and to Clinton's "committing American prestige and force to Bosnia and Kosovo." He concluded: "When the stakes were high, the right decisions were made against political pressure."

Through much of the literature on Clinton, however, runs a rueful strain. The historian Matthew Dickinson has expressed the consensus of scholars: "His was a presidency of substantial accomplishments—and even more of missed opportunities." Similarly, David Gergen has reflected: "For America, the nineties turned out to be one of the brightest decades of the twentieth century, and Clinton was one of its prime movers. He will be remembered well for that. Yet, a sense of aching disappointment hangs over his presidency. How much more he could have achieved...how much went smash."

Clinton, though, never had a chance of winding up in the Valhalla of great presidents. Opposition from Republicans was relentless, and the nation was not in a heroic mood. "Clinton," observed Elizabeth Drew, "saw himself as a descendant of FDR, but he not only lacked a perceived emergency but was up against deep skepticism, even cynicism, about government.... He was the first activist President in the age of cynicism." As a journalist in *U.S. News & World Report* observed in 1997, "No president today can hope to measure up if the standard is, say, Jefferson and the Louisiana Purchase or Roosevelt and the New Deal. Clinton will see his name carved in few granite cornerstones because few are being laid. We are not in a nation-building or institution-building era." In Clinton's last year in office, polls revealed that only 10 percent of Americans wanted him to advocate more progressive policies.

In the last analysis, none of these considerations looms nearly so large as the Lewinsky episode in determining Bill Clinton's place in history. "Clinton," Jacob Weisberg wrote in the *New York Times Magazine*, "can't escape becoming a historical joke. He is now and forever our priapic President, who takes his place alongside our drunken President, Ulysses S. Grant, our napping President, Calvin Coolidge, and our treacherous president, Richard Nixon." Though Clinton asserted that he would wear his impeachment by partisan Republicans as a "badge of honor," the historian Joseph Ellis has seen the scandal as "a tin can that's tied to Clinton's tail that will rattle through the ages and through the pages of history books." As one congressman said, "There will always be an asterisk by Mr. Clinton's name." Clinton's position in the country's annals is secure not because of all he sought to do, and did, but because he is the first elected president in the more than two hundred years of the American republic to have been impeached.

EPILOGUE

THE AMERICAN PRESIDENT DEPARTS FROM both of the best-known schools of interpretation about the course of the American presidency. For most of our history, scholars have presented the chronicle as a continuous tale, with each succeeding administration adding another chapter. By contrast, I perceive a great divide—with the twentieth-century presidency markedly different from what preceded it. This cleavage may best be seen not by comparing Franklin Roosevelt to a Millard Fillmore or a Chester Arthur but by matching him with those figures in the earlier period widely thought to be "great" or "near great." Thomas Jefferson, in rationalizing the Louisiana Purchase, and Andrew Jackson, when waging the Bank War, appear to resemble latter-day chief executives. But both men spent most of their years in office striving to lessen federal intrusions, not to create anything remotely approaching a centralized Welfare State.

Abraham Lincoln, in broadly interpreting the war power and in suspending habeas corpus, seems a better fit, but Lincoln never surrendered his convictions as a Whig who had entered politics opposing Polk's assertion of national authority. The foremost constitutional history text, while accusing Lincoln of "dictatorship" in his conduct of the war, acknowledges, "In nonmilitary matters, Lincoln assumed a passive attitude of deference toward Congress." More forcefully, James Pfiffner has written:

"Despite the hagiography of presidents from the Federalist era and Lincoln, the nineteenth century did not create the high expectations that presidents would control the political agenda and deliver the country from all of its troubles. But in the early twentieth century, the Progressives raised expectations by advocating an activist central government led by a president who represented the national interest."

I have had a harder time grappling with a different contention: that it was the creation of the Executive Office of the President in 1939 during FDR's second term that produced the big fault line. Fred Greenstein, the dean of the political science guild, presented this conception starkly: "The transformation of the office has been so profound that the modern presidencies have more in common with one another in the opportunities they provide and the demands they place on their incumbents than they have with the entire sweep of traditional presidencies from Washington's to Hoover's."

Evidence sustaining this assessment is formidable, and I long found it persuasive. Indeed, I began my essay in a 1988 volume that Greenstein edited by stating flatly, "The presidency as we know it today begins with Franklin Delano Roosevelt." Furthermore, that assumption underlies my *In the Shadow of FDR*, which today, in its fourth edition, bears the subtitle *From Harry Truman to Barack Obama*. But in the years since that volume first appeared I have come to conclude that the disjuncture came not in 1933 or 1939 but in 1901, when Theodore Roosevelt succeeded William McKinley. The British journalist Godfrey Hodgson has pointed out that it was in Teddy Roosevelt's time "that the presidency first began to appear as the modern, the activist, the democratic branch of government," and TR's biographer Kathleen Dalton has written of him, "Today he is heralded as the architect of the modern presidency, as a world leader who boldly reshaped the office to meet the needs of the new century and redefined America's place in the world."

The political scientist Michael Riccards amplified this view in a broad-gauged synthesis by asserting:

TR changed the presidency and made it more of a populist, visible, and activist institution. . . . Before TR, the presidency was a national clerkship. . . . When Roosevelt . . . told the world he was off to hunt lions, he left an office very different from the one he inherited. Roosevelt created an executive branch that was more visible than Jefferson would have tolerated, more popular than Washington or Grover Cleveland would have wished, and more broadly based than Lincoln's.... His model of the presidency was quite different from what had gone before, and it had an immense influence on his younger cousin, Franklin D. Roosevelt. His years marked the beginning of the Rooseveltian presidency, of an assertive executive advocating a national domestic agenda and a powerfully positioned foreign policy.

Though the Founding Fathers had taken pains to avoid creating another George III when they framed the presidency, the office in the twentieth century took on aspects of the majesty, even divinity, that doth hedge a king. Edmund Morris captured the regal aspects of TR in the title of his biography, *Theodore Rex*, and FDR was likened to a Stuart tyrant. More recently, the philosopher Michael Novak wrote of the American president: "Hands are stretched toward him over wire fences at airports like hands extended toward medieval sovereigns or ancient prophets. One wonders what mystic participation our presidents convey, what witness from what other world, what form of cure or heightened life.... His office...evokes responses familiar in all the ancient religions of the world. It fills a perpetual vacuum at the heart of human expectations."

As the millennium approached, however, writers questioned whether this veneration of the president would carry on into the twenty-first century. In particular, they asked whether Bill Clinton had not destroyed for all time the apotheosis of the presidency. During his campaign for the White House, he had appeared on a late-night television show wearing dark glasses and tooting a saxophone, and, from that beginning, observed Joe Klein, "this was a president too familiar for comfort. Too much was known about him, and Clinton...played to it.... It is entirely possible that the Clinton era will be remembered by historians primarily as the moment when the distance between the President and the public evaporated forever." When citizens encountered the president, they addressed him as "Bill." At a forum on the MTV cable channel, a seventeen-year-old woman asked, "The world's dying to know: Is it boxers or briefs?" Instead of dismissing the question as improper, he replied, "Usually briefs."

A number of writers have maintained that the demeaning Lewinsky affair did not merely damage Clinton's reputation but also demystified the presidency. Jacob Weisberg in the *New York Times Magazine* observed: "Bill Clinton's impeachment is historic in the sense of being an event historians will puzzle over in decades to come.... What those historians will have to ponder is not how it shook the country, but why it didn't.... They will have to explain... how an impeachment could drive a President's approval rating up instead of down." He concluded: "Clinton's weathering of the Lewinsky scandal represents something that is truly historic"—nothing less than the end of "the heroic phase of the American Presidency."

Even more provocatively, Judge Richard Posner has suggested that the most enduring consequence of the Clinton farce "may be to make it difficult to take Presidents seriously as superior people." He elaborated: "For those who think that authority depends on mystery, the shattering of the Presidential mystique has been a disaster for which Clinton ought of rights to have paid with his job.... My guess is... that Americans have reached a level of political sophistication at which they can take in stride the knowledge that the nation's political and intellectual leaders are their peers, and not their paragons. The nation does not depend on the superior virtue of one man."

These judgments proved to be premature. When, only eight months after Clinton left office, terrorists leveled the World Trade towers in lower Manhattan, the nation turned instinctively to the president, vesting him with unearned virtues. "He was transformed," wrote a British journalist, "venerated as the embodiment of America" when the country rallied to him as its shield against further devastation. In the years that followed, the American people manifested an unquenched yearning for a return of the twentieth-century presidents who had once been so celebrated. More than a decade after Clinton departed, millions of television viewers watching Ken Burns's *The Roosevelts* for seven consecutive nights bore witness to the nostalgia many felt for a time when lions roamed the land.

However untrustworthy as a forecaster of the future, the Clinton presidency does have illustrative value for demonstrating what had been true throughout the twentieth century: that the evolution of the presidency has been in large part determined by its incumbents. As Stephen Skowronek, who has created the most systematic framework for comprehending the history of this nation's chief executive, has

Bridging the centuries, George H. W. Bush, Barack Obama, George W. Bush, Bill Clinton, and Jimmy Carter gather at the White House in January 2009, shortly before Obama takes the oath of office—a meeting that brings together three twentieth-century presidents with the first two of the twenty-first century. *Courtesy of the George W. Bush Presidential Library and Museum, ID P010709ED-0480*

commented, "The American presidency reflects nothing so clearly as the idiosyncrasies of personality and circumstance." To be sure, the presidency was profoundly affected by a number of impersonal forces—the decline of political parties, the imperative of controlling corporations engaged in national and overseas commerce, the revolution in communications, the enormous impact of global war. But the simile offered by George Will is apt: "The presidency is like a soft leather glove, and it takes the shape of the hand that's put into it. And when a very big hand is put into it and stretches the glove—stretches the office—the glove never quite shrinks back to what it was."

The twentieth century saw a remarkable number of presidents expand that glove, starting with Theodore Roosevelt and Woodrow Wilson, and, as Will remarked, "we are living today with an office enlarged permanently by Franklin Roosevelt." There were times when the pace slowed, notably in the 1920s and the better part of the 1970s, but there were also periods of rapid innovation, especially, with few noticing, under Harry Truman. His biographer Donald McCoy, claiming that "the American state system reached maturity during Truman's presidency," maintained, "It would be the products of Truman's administration that his successors down to the present would have to work with, especially abroad.... [Truman] played Augustus to Roosevelt's Caesar." In the last half of the century, the presidency metastasized. Early in 1965, Tom Wicker wrote: "Like the old-time Texas cattle barons on their vast domains, Lyndon Baines Johnson seems to stand a good 20 feet tall in these parts. There is nothing in the capitol that can look down on him except the Washington Monument." When Nixon flew to China in 1972, his entourage numbered three hundred—a total that seemed bloated. Only a dozen years later, when Reagan set forth to the Orient, his retinue was double that figure. And in 1998, Clinton, on his journey to China, took more than a thousand.

Theodore Roosevelt and his successors wielded enormous authority. A generation ago, one political scientist went so far as to say, "There can be no doubt that the President of the United States today is the single most powerful being in the history of the world," and David McCullough has written of the American president: "We...give him...far more power than has been held by any mortal in all history." Commenting on the Lyndon Johnson era, a foreign correspondent posted in Washington remarked that "it was...to the President, far more than to Congress or to any other agency, public or private,...that Americans looked for the carrying out of their ideals." Some political scientists have even portrayed a "presidential branch" of the national government, distinct from the executive branch.

This greatly augmented institution elicited deep concern. The United States, the Supreme Court has stated, has "no right to expect that it will always have wise and humane rulers, sincerely attached to the principles of the Constitution. Wicked men, ambitious of power, with hatred of liberty and contempt of law, may fill the place once occupied by Washington and Lincoln." After scrutinizing Lyndon Johnson's record on Vietnam, a Senate committee reported:

Already possessing vast power over the country's foreign relations, the executive...now exercises something approaching absolute power over the life or death of every living American—to say nothing of millions of other people all over the world.... The concentration in the hands of the President of virtually unlimited authority over matters of war and peace has all but removed the limits to executive power in the most important single area of our national life. Until they are restored, the American people will be threatened with tyranny or disaster.

That cry of alarm echoed James Madison's warning that "war is the nurse of executive aggrandizement." It is similarly evident in Supreme Court Justice Robert Jackson's calling the commander-in-chief clause in the Constitution "the most dangerous one to free government in the whole catalogue of powers," for it provides license to "do anything, anywhere, that can be done with an army or navy."

Too many times in the twentieth century the lions broke loose from their reservation, broad though it was. In the most glaring instance, "Watergate"—a term incorporating numerous transgressions—Richard Nixon became the only president compelled to abandon the White House ignominiously. Misdeeds, though, also scarred a number of the most esteemed presidents: Theodore Roosevelt and the Brownsville disgrace; Woodrow Wilson and the wholesale violations of civil liberties in World War I; FDR and the internment of Japanese Americans; Harry Truman and the abuses of his loyalty program; Lyndon Johnson and the deceitful pursuit of war in Southeast Asia; Ronald Reagan and the Iran-Contra dereliction.

The president, though, has not been omnipotent, even in the modern era. The Supreme Court has constrained him by decisions such as the Steel Seizure ruling, and Congress has frequently refused to do his bidding. In a period of increasingly homogeneous, ideologically driven political parties, presidents have found it dishearteningly difficult to build coalitions to enact legislation. Furthermore, departments and agencies—ostensibly in the executive branch that the president heads—have often deferred not to the White House but to the clients they are supposed to be regulating and to powerful chairs of congressional committees. In 1963, chastened by experience, John F. Kennedy declared: "The President . . . is rightly described as a man of extraordinary powers. Yet it is also true that he must wield those powers under extraordinary limitations. . . . Lincoln, Franklin Roosevelt once remarked, 'was a sad man because he couldn't get it all at once.' And nobody can."

In some reckonings, critics have expressed dissatisfaction with the presidency not because it was almighty but rather because it was feckless. The political scientist Richard Pious has noted that "between 1973 and 1993 the proportion of the public saying they had a 'great deal of confidence' in the executive fell from 29 to 12 percent," and the historian John Broesamle has written that since Nixon's second term, "the American political system [has] generally sputtered along like an ancient broken-down car," with presidents the focus of blame. Another scholar, Theodore Lowi, summed up this discontent in a harsh and oft-quoted final judgment on the presidency: "power invested, promise unfulfilled."

Sometimes, America's head of state has been perceived not as pharaoh but as vassal. "The role of the President," wrote the British historian Marcus Cunliffe, "is a strange, vulgar-lofty conception, at the very core of the American mystery. It demands solemnity and yet invites scurrility. He's almost like one of those primitive kings in Frazer's *Golden Bough* who reign in pomp until they are ritually put to death (except, maybe, that the American ruler undergoes slow torture long *before* his final extinction.)... Everything is expected of him, nothing tangible is given him, except on loan: no titles, houses, decorations. He is almost a living sacrifice to the state." Similarly, the novelist John Steinbeck said: "We give the President more work than a man can do, more responsibility than a man should take, more pressure than a man can bear.... We wear him out, use him up, eat him up.... He is ours and we exercise the right to destroy him." Cunliffe concluded: "For the foreseeable future, the quasi-monarchs briefly occupying the White House will probably come in at the iron gate but leave by the gate of the weeping willows."

Either because they regarded the president as a toothless lion or because they thought he was a ravenous beast, a number of commentators favored making Congress the dominant branch, but that notion met stern rebuffs. "I am unwilling to dismantle...the Presidency...in order to turn the leadership of this country in national affairs to the Congress," Ted Sorensen testified. "That was tried during much of the nineteenth century, unsuccessfully.... It certainly did not give us the...progressive results we have had in the twentieth century." The political scientist Andrew Rudalevige agreed. "A nation cannot meet crises, or even the day-to-day needs of governing, with 535 chief executives or commanders in chief," he wrote. "These days the flutter of a butterfly's wing in Wellington shifts the climate of

Washington; a globalized, polarized world seems to call out for endowing leadership sufficient to match its powers to the task at hand." At a time when enthusiasm for the White House was at a low point, another scholar, Aaron Wildavsky, wrote: "It has become all too easy to imagine a weakening of the Presidency. Not so. Does anyone imagine...actions will matter less to people in the future? The question answers itself. The weakening of the Presidency is about as likely as the withering away of the state." Even in the dismaying Watergate period, as the historian James Patterson observed, "the constitutional balance of American government...remained heavily tilted toward 1600 Pennsylvania Avenue."

We do well to recognize the wisdom of Alexander Hamilton's words: "Energy in the executive is a leading character in the definition of good government." No one spoke out more eloquently about the dangers of "the imperial presidency" than Arthur Schlesinger Jr., but he concluded: "An adequate democratic theory must recognize that democracy is not self-executing; that leadership is not the enemy of self-government but the means of making it work;...and that Caesarism is more often produced by the failure of feeble governments than by the success of energetic ones." As a senator, Daniel Patrick Moynihan appeared to be in a perpetual state of war with the White House, but he nonetheless said: "I am one of those who believe that America is the hope of the world, and, for that time given him, the President is the hope of America."

Over the span of the twentieth century—when they caused so much grief—presidents often gave the country cause for pride. "American Presidents," Michael Beschloss has written, "have, at crucial moments, made courageous decisions for the national interest although they knew they might be jeopardizing their careers....Without such displays of Presidential courage, America would be a lesser country—or it might not exist at all." When Teddy Roosevelt battled vested interests to preserve the nation's domain, when Woodrow Wilson sought to create a new world order, when Franklin Delano Roosevelt acted for the welfare of the impoverished one-third of a nation, when Harry Truman promoted the Marshall Plan to aid a beleaguered Europe, when Lyndon Johnson called upon Congress to grant long-overdue recognition of the civil rights of African Americans, when Ronald Reagan spoke so movingly to the sorrow over the *Challenger* disaster—at those moments, the lions were truly magnificent.

Yet the dark underside of presidential power cannot be ignored. Too often, presidents have lied to us. Too often, they have wasted the lives of our children in foreign ventures that should never have been undertaken. They are both the progenitors and the victims of inflated expectations, and when they overreach, they need to be checked. "The president," stated Theodore Roosevelt, "should be a very strong man who uses without hesitation every power that the position yields, but because of this fact I believe that he should be closely watched by the people and held to a strict accountability by them." At the Constitutional Convention in Philadelphia in 1787, as delegates debated how much authority to assign to the office of the presidency that they were creating, Gouverneur Morris said, "Make him too weak: the Legislature will usurp power. Make him too strong: he will usurp the Legislature." That is a conundrum that every generation of Americans is fated to try to resolve.

ACKNOWLEDGMENTS

DURING THE COURSE OF WELL over half a century of writing about the presidency, I have incurred many debts—to fellow historians, to students, to archivists, and to journalists who have asked searching questions.

I acknowledge with gratitude a grant from the Annenberg Foundation that motivated me to write about the twentieth-century presidency.

I thank my editor at Oxford University Press, Nancy Toff, for her encouragement, her editorial recommendations, and her skill in moving the manuscript to press, and Joellyn Ausanka for supervising the final stages of preparation of the manuscript for publication.

I am very appreciative of the many contributions of India Cooper, a superb copy editor and an exceptionally congenial colleague.

My friend and fellow historian James T. Patterson gave a careful reading to three of the later chapters and made a number of astute suggestions.

Jo Sanders did yeoman work in photocopying hundreds upon hundreds of pages of research materials, always with grace and good cheer, and at Oxford University Press, Marissa Lastres gathered illustrations.

By far my greatest debt now—as in decades past—is to the incomparable Jean Anne Leuchtenburg, whose extraordinary editorial acumen graces every page. During the years we worked together on this book, she moved from being an indispensable helpmate to becoming a collaborator.

SELECTED BIBLIOGRAPHY

THE AMERICAN PRESIDENT DRAWS UPON decades of archival research at presidential libraries (Herbert Hoover, West Branch, Iowa; Franklin D. Roosevelt, Hyde Park, New York; Harry S. Truman, Independence, Missouri; Dwight D. Eisenhower, Abilene, Kansas; John F. Kennedy, Boston, Massachusetts; Lyndon B. Johnson, Austin, Texas; Jimmy Carter, Atlanta, Georgia; as well as the collections of Theodore Roosevelt at Harvard University and of Calvin Coolidge at the Forbes Library in Northampton, Massachusetts). The book derives, too, from many years of research in hundreds of collections of the papers of cabinet officers, presidential aides, senators, representatives, governors, envoys, journalists, and other participants in the political process at archives ranging from Fairbanks, Alaska, to Tallahassee, Florida, in this country, and abroad in London and Ottawa.

But *The American President* owes a greater debt to the work of several generations of scholars. The list that follows is "selected," not a compendium of all the volumes read. It includes books that readers may wish to consult for further exploration of the saga of the American presidency.

Abshire, David M., ed. *Triumphs and Tragedies of the Modern Presidency: Seventy-six Studies in Presidential Leadership*. Westport, CT: Praeger, 2001.

Alexander, Charles C. *Holding the Line: The Eisenhower Era, 1952–1961*. Bloomington: Indiana University Press, 1975.

Alter, Jonathan. *The Defining Moment: FDR's Hundred Days and the Triumph of Hope*. New York: Simon & Schuster, 2006.

Alterman, Eric. *The Cause: The Fight for American Liberalism from Franklin Roosevelt to Barack Obama*. New York: Viking, 2012.

Ambrose, Stephen E. *Eisenhower: Soldier and President*. New York: Simon & Schuster, 1990.

Ambrose, Stephen E. *Nixon: Ruin and Recovery, 1973–1990*. New York: Simon & Schuster, 1991.

Ambrose, Stephen E. *Nixon: The Triumph of a Politician, 1962–1972*. New York: Simon & Schuster, 1989.

Ambrose, Stephen E., and Douglas Brinkley. *Rise to Globalism: American Foreign Policy since 1938*. New York: Penguin Books, 2011.

Arnold, Peri E. *Making the Managerial Presidency: Comprehensive Reorganization Planning, 1905–1996*. Lawrence: University Press of Kansas, 1998.

Arnold, Peri E. *Remaking the Presidency: Roosevelt, Taft, and Wilson, 1901–1916*. Lawrence: University Press of Kansas, 2009.

Badger, Anthony J. *FDR: The First Hundred Days*. New York: Hill & Wang, 2008.

Badger, Anthony J. *The New Deal: The Depression Years, 1933–40*. Chicago: Ivan R. Dee, 2002.

Bailey, Thomas Andrew. *Wilson and the Peacemakers*. New York: Macmillan, 1947.

Barber, James David. *The Presidential Character: Predicting Performance in the White House*. Englewood Cliffs, NJ: Prentice Hall, 1992.

Barger, Harold M. *The Impossible Presidency: Illusions and Realities of Executive Power*. Glenview, IL: Scott, Foresman, 1984.

Barilleaux, Ryan J. *The Post-modern Presidency: The Office after Ronald Reagan*. New York: Praeger, 1988.

Barilleaux, Ryan J., and Mark J. Rozell. *Power and Prudence: The Presidency of George H. W. Bush*. College Station: Texas A&M University Press, 2004.

Barilleaux, Ryan J., and Jewerl Maxwell. *Tough Times for the President: Political Adversity and the Sources of Executive Power*. Amherst, NY: Cambria Press, 2012.

Benedict, Michael Les. *The Impeachment and Trial of Andrew Johnson*. New York: Norton, 1973.

Berman, Larry. *Lyndon Johnson's War: The Road to Stalemate in Vietnam*. New York: Norton, 1989.

Berman, Larry. *The New American Presidency*. Boston: Little, Brown, 1987.

Berman, Larry. *No Peace, No Honor: Nixon, Kissinger, and Betrayal in Vietnam*. New York: Free Press, 2001.

Berman, William C. *America's Right Turn: From Nixon to Clinton*. Baltimore: Johns Hopkins University Press, 1998.

Berman, William C. *From the Center to the Edge: The Politics and Policies of the Clinton Presidency*. Lanham, MD: Rowman & Littlefield, 2001.

Bernstein, Irving. *Guns or Butter: The Presidency of Lyndon Johnson*. New York: Oxford University Press, 1996.

Beschloss, Michael. *The American Heritage Illustrated History of the Presidents*. New York: Crown, 2000.

Beschloss, Michael. *At the Highest Levels: The Inside Story of the End of the Cold War*. Boston: Little, Brown, 1993.

Beschloss, Michael. *The Crisis Years: Kennedy and Khrushchev, 1960–1963*. New York: Edward Burlingame Books, 1991.

Beschloss, Michael *Eisenhower: A Centennial Life*. New York: HarperCollins, 1990.

Beschloss, Michael. *Presidential Courage: Brave Leaders and How They Changed America, 1789–1989*. New York: Simon & Schuster, 2007.

Beschloss, Michael, ed. *Reaching for Glory: Lyndon Johnson's Secret White House Tapes, 1964–1965*. New York: Simon & Schuster, 2001.

Beschloss, Michael, ed. *Taking Charge: The Johnson White House Tapes, 1963–1964*. New York: Simon & Schuster, 1997.

Binkley, Wilfred E. *President and Congress*. New York: Knopf, 1947.

Black, Allida M. *Casting Her Own Shadow: Eleanor Roosevelt and the Shaping of Postwar Liberalism*. New York: Columbia University Press, 1996.

Blum, John Morton. *The Progressive Presidents: Roosevelt, Wilson, Roosevelt, Johnson*. New York: Norton, 1980.

Blum, John Morton. *The Republican Roosevelt*. Cambridge, MA: Harvard University Press, 1977.

Blum, John Morton. *Woodrow Wilson and the Politics of Morality*. Boston: Little, Brown, 1956.

Blum, John Morton. *Years of Discord: American Politics and Society, 1961–1974*. New York: Norton, 1991.

Borden, Morton, ed. *America's Eleven Greatest Presidents*. Chicago: Rand McNally, 1971.

Bradlee, Benjamin C. *Conversations with Kennedy*. New York: Norton, 1975.

Branch, Taylor. *The Clinton Tapes: Wrestling History with the President*. New York: Simon & Schuster, 2009.

Brands, H. W. *T. R.: The Last Romantic*. New York: Basic Books, 1997.

Brands, H. W. *Traitor to His Class: The Privileged Life and Radical Presidency of Franklin Delano Roosevelt*. New York: Doubleday, 2008.

Brands, H. W. *The Wages of Globalism: Lyndon Johnson and the Limits of American Power*. New York: Oxford University Press, 1995.

Brands, H. W. *Woodrow Wilson*. New York: Times Books, 2003.

Brendon, Piers. *Ike: His Life and Times*. New York: Harper & Row, 1986.

Brinkley, Alan. *The End of Reform: New Deal Liberalism in Recession and War*. New York: Knopf, 1995.

Brinkley, Alan. *Franklin Delano Roosevelt*. New York: Oxford University Press, 2010.

Brinkley, Alan. *John F. Kennedy*. New York: Times Books/Henry Holt, 2012.

Brinkley, Alan, and Davis Dyer, eds. *The American Presidency*. Boston: Houghton Mifflin, 2004.

Brinkley, Douglas. *American Heritage History of the United States*. New York: Viking, 1998.

Brinkley, Douglas. *Gerald R. Ford*. New York: Times Books, 2007.

Brinkley, Douglas. *The Unfinished Presidency: Jimmy Carter's Journey beyond the White House*. New York: Viking, 1998.

Brinkley, Douglas. *The Wilderness Warrior: Theodore Roosevelt and the Crusade for America*. New York: HarperCollins, 2009.

Broder, David. *The Party's Over: The Failure of Politics in America*. New York: Harper & Row, 1972.

Broesamle, John. *How American Presidents Succeed and Why They Fail: From Richard Nixon to Barack Obama*. Lewiston, NY: Edwin Mellen Press, 2014.

Brogan, D. W. *The Era of Franklin D. Roosevelt: A Chronicle of the New Deal and Global War*. New Haven, CT: Yale University Press, 1950.

Brown, Stuart Gerry. *The American Presidency: Leadership, Partisanship, and Popularity*. New York: Macmillan, 1966.

Brownlee, W. Elliot, and Hugh Davis Graham, eds. *The Reagan Presidency: Pragmatic Conservatism and Its Legacies*. Lawrence: University Press of Kansas, 2003.

Burk, Robert F. *Dwight D. Eisenhower: Hero and Politician*. Boston: Twayne, 1986.

Burke, John P. *The Institutional Presidency: Organizing and Managing the White House from FDR to Clinton*. Baltimore: Johns Hopkins University Press, 2000.

Burner, David. *Herbert Hoover: A Public Life*. New York: Knopf, 1979.

Burner, David. *John F. Kennedy and a New Generation*. Boston: Little, Brown, 1988.

Burnham, Walter Dean. *Critical Elections and the Mainsprings of American Politics*. New York: Norton, 1970.

Burns, James MacGregor. *John Kennedy: A Political Profile*. New York: Harcourt, Brace and World, 1960.

Burns, James MacGregor. *Presidential Government: The Crucible of Leadership*. Boston: Houghton Mifflin, 1965.

Burns, James MacGregor. *Roosevelt: The Lion and the Fox*. New York: Harcourt, Brace, 1956.

Burns, James MacGregor. *Roosevelt: The Soldier of Freedom*. New York: Harcourt Brace Jovanovich, 1970.

Burns, James MacGregor, and Georgia J. Sorenson. *Dead Center: Clinton-Gore Leadership and the Perils of Moderation*. New York: Scribner, 1999.

Byrne, Malcolm. *Iran-Contra: Reagan's Scandal and the Unchecked Abuse of Presidential Power*. Lawrence: University Press of Kansas, 2014.

Calabresi, Steven G., and Christopher S. Yoo. *The Unitary Executive: Presidential Power from Washington to Bush*. New Haven, CT: Yale University Press, 2008.

Campbell, Colin. *The U.S. Presidency in Crisis: A Comparative Perspective*. New York: Oxford University Press, 1998.

Cannon, Lou. *Governor Reagan: His Rise to Power*. New York: PublicAffairs, 2003.

Cannon, Lou. *President Reagan: The Role of a Lifetime*. New York: Simon & Schuster, 1991.

Cannon, Lou. *Reagan*. New York: Putnam, 1982.

Cannon, Lou, and Carl M. Cannon. *Reagan's Disciple: George W. Bush's Troubled Quest for a Presidential Legacy*. New York: PublicAffairs, 2008.

Caro, Robert. *Master of the Senate: The Years of Lyndon Johnson.* New York: Knopf, 2002.

Caro, Robert. *Means of Ascent: The Years of Lyndon Johnson.* New York: Knopf, 1990.

Caro, Robert. *The Passage of Power: The Years of Lyndon Johnson.* New York: Knopf, 2012.

Caro, Robert. *The Path to Power: The Years of Lyndon Johnson.* New York: Knopf, 1982.

Caroli, Betty Boyd. *First Ladies.* New York: Oxford University Press, 2003.

Castel, Albert E. *The Presidency of Andrew Johnson.* Lawrence: Regents Press of Kansas, 1979.

Chafe, William H. *Bill and Hillary: The Politics of the Personal.* New York: Farrar, Straus & Giroux, 2012.

Chafe, William H. *Private Lives/Public Consequences: Personality and Politics in Modern America.* Cambridge, MA: Harvard University Press, 2005.

Chambers, John Whiteclay, II. *The Tyranny of Change: America in the Progressive Era, 1890–1920.* New Brunswick, NJ: Rutgers University Press, 2000.

Childs, Marquis. *Eisenhower: Captive Hero: A Critical Study of the General and the President.* New York: Harcourt, Brace, 1958.

Clements, Kendrick A. *The Presidency of Woodrow Wilson.* Lawrence: University Press of Kansas, 1992.

Cochran, Bert. *Harry Truman and the Crisis Presidency.* New York: Funk and Wagnalls, 1973.

Conkin, Paul K. *Big Daddy from the Pedernales: Lyndon Baines Johnson.* Boston: Twayne, 1986.

Cook, Blanche Wiesen. *The Declassified Eisenhower: A Divided Legacy.* Garden City, NY: Doubleday, 1981.

Cook, Blanche Wiesen. *Eleanor Roosevelt.* New York: Viking, 1992.

Cooper, John Milton, Jr. *Breaking the Heart of the World: Woodrow Wilson and the Fight for the League of Nations.* New York: Cambridge University Press, 2001.

Cooper, John Milton, Jr. *The Warrior and the Priest: Woodrow Wilson and Theodore Roosevelt.* Cambridge, MA: Belknap Press of Harvard University Press, 1983.

Cooper, John Milton, Jr. *Woodrow Wilson: A Biography.* New York: Knopf, 2009.

Cornwell, Elmer E. *Presidential Leadership of Public Opinion.* Bloomington: Indiana University Press, 1965.

Corwin, Edward S. *The President, Office and Powers, 1787–1957: History and Analysis of Practice and Opinion.* New York: New York University Press, 1957.

Crenson, Matthew, and Benjamin Ginsberg. *Presidential Power: Unchecked and Unbalanced.* New York: Norton, 2007.

Cronin, Thomas E. *On the Presidency: Teacher, Soldier, Shaman, Pol.* Boulder, CO: Paradigm, 2009.

Cronin, Thomas E. *The State of the Presidency.* Boston: Little, Brown, 1980.

Cronin, Thomas E, and Michael A. Genovese. *The Paradoxes of the American Presidency*. New York: Oxford University Press, 2013.

Cunliffe, Marcus. *American Presidents and the Presidency*. New York: American Heritage Press, 1972.

Cunliffe, Marcus. *The Presidency*. Boston: Houghton Mifflin, 1987.

Dallek, Matthew. *The Right Moment: Ronald Reagan's First Victory and the Decisive Turning Point in American Politics*. New York: Oxford University Press, 2004.

Dallek, Robert. *Flawed Giant: Lyndon Johnson and His Times, 1961–1973*. New York: Oxford University Press, 1998.

Dallek, Robert. *Franklin D. Roosevelt and American Foreign Policy, 1932–1945*. New York: Oxford University Press, 1995.

Dallek, Robert. *Hail to the Chief: The Making and Unmaking of American Presidents*. New York: Hyperion, 1996.

Dallek, Robert. *Harry S. Truman*. New York: Times Books, 2008.

Dallek, Robert. *Lone Star Rising: Lyndon Johnson and His Times, 1908–1960*. New York: Oxford University Press, 1991.

Dallek, Robert. *Lyndon B. Johnson: Portrait of a President*. New York: Oxford University Press, 2004.

Dallek, Robert. *Ronald Reagan: The Politics of Symbolism*. Cambridge, MA: Harvard University Press, 1999.

Dallek, Robert. *An Unfinished Life: John F. Kennedy, 1917–1963*. Boston: Little, Brown, 2003.

Dalton, Kathleen. *Theodore Roosevelt: A Strenuous Life*. New York: Knopf, 2002.

Davis, Kenneth S. *FDR: Into the Storm, 1937–1940: A History*. New York: Random House, 1993.

Davis, Kenneth S. *FDR: The New Deal Years, 1933–1937: A History*. New York: Random House, 1986.

Davis, Kenneth S. *FDR: The War President, 1940–1943: A History*. New York: Random House, 2000.

De Bedts, Ralph F. *The New Deal's SEC: The Formative Years*. New York: Columbia University Press, 1964.

Devine, Thomas W. *Henry Wallace's 1948 Presidential Campaign and the Future of Postwar Liberalism*. Chapel Hill: University of North Carolina Press, 2013.

Dickinson, Matthew J. *Bitter Harvest: FDR, Presidential Power, and the Growth of the Presidential Branch*. New York: Cambridge University Press, 1996.

Divine, Robert A. *Eisenhower and the Cold War*. New York: Oxford University Press, 1981.

Divine, Robert A., ed. *Exploring the Johnson Years*. Austin: University of Texas Press, 1981.

Divine, Robert A. *Roosevelt and World War II*. Baltimore: Johns Hopkins Press, 1969.

Dodd, Lawrence C., and Bruce I. Oppenheimer, eds. *Congress Reconsidered*. Washington, DC: CQ Press, 2009.

Doenecke, Justus D. *The Presidencies of James A. Garfield and Chester A. Arthur.* Lawrence: Regents Press of Kansas, 1981.

Donald, Aida DiPace. *Citizen Soldier: A Life of Harry S. Truman.* New York: Basic Books, 2012.

Donald, Aida DiPace, ed. *John F. Kennedy and the New Frontier.* New York: Hill & Wang, 1966.

Donald, Aida DiPace. *Lion in the White House: A Life of Theodore Roosevelt.* New York: Basic Books, 2007.

Donovan, Robert J. *Conflict and Crisis: The Presidency of Harry S. Truman, 1945–1948.* New York: Norton, 1977.

Donovan, Robert J. *Eisenhower: The Inside Story.* New York: Harper, 1956.

Donovan, Robert J. *Tumultuous Years: The Presidency of Harry S. Truman, 1949–1953.* New York: Norton, 1982.

Doyle, William. *Inside the Oval Office: The White House Tapes from FDR to Clinton.* New York: Kodansha International, 1999.

Draper, Theodore. *Abuse of Power.* New York: Viking, 1967.

Draper, Theodore. *A Very Thin Line: The Iran-Contra Affairs.* New York: Hill & Wang, 1991.

Drew, Elizabeth. *On the Edge: The Clinton Presidency.* New York: Simon & Schuster, 1994.

Drew, Elizabeth. *Richard M. Nixon.* New York: Times Books, 2007.

Drew, Elizabeth. *Showdown: The Struggle between the Gingrich Congress and the Clinton White House.* New York: Simon & Schuster, 1996.

Dunn, Charles W., ed. *The Presidency in the Twenty-first Century.* Lexington: University Press of Kentucky, 2011.

Edwards, George C., III. *At the Margins: Presidential Leadership of Congress.* New Haven, CT: Yale University Press, 1989.

Edwards, George C., III. *On Deaf Ears: The Limits of the Bully Pulpit.* New Haven, CT: Yale University Press, 2003.

Edwards, George C., III. *The Public Presidency: The Pursuit of Popular Support.* New York: St. Martin's, 1983.

Edwards, George C., III, and Stephen J. Wayne. *Presidential Leadership: Politics and Policy Making.* New York: St. Martin's, 1997.

Fairlie, Henry. *The Kennedy Promise: The Politics of Expectation.* Garden City, NY: Doubleday, 1973.

Ferrell, Robert H. *Harry S. Truman and the Cold War Revisionists.* Columbia: University of Missouri Press, 2006.

Ferrell, Robert H. *Harry S. Truman and the Modern American Presidency.* Boston: Little, Brown, 1983.

Ferrell, Robert H. *The Presidency of Calvin Coolidge.* Lawrence: University Press of Kansas, 1998.

Ferrell, Robert H. *Presidential Leadership: From Woodrow Wilson to Harry S. Truman.* Columbia: University of Missouri Press, 2006.

Ferrell, Robert H. *Woodrow Wilson and World War I, 1917–1921*. New York: Harper & Row, 1985.

Fink, Gary M., and Hugh Davis Graham, eds. *The Carter Presidency: Policy Choices in the Post–New Deal Era*. Lawrence: University Press of Kansas, 1998.

FitzGerald, Frances. *Way Out There in the Blue: Reagan, Star Wars, and the End of the Cold War*. New York: Simon & Schuster, 2000.

Freidel, Frank. *Franklin D. Roosevelt: The Apprenticeship*. Boston: Little, Brown, 1952.

Freidel, Frank. *Franklin D. Roosevelt: Launching the New Deal*. Boston: Little, Brown, 1973.

Freidel, Frank. *Franklin D. Roosevelt: The Ordeal*. Boston: Little, Brown, 1954.

Freidel, Frank. *Franklin D. Roosevelt: A Rendezvous with Destiny*. Boston: Little, Brown, 1990.

Freidel, Frank. *Franklin D. Roosevelt: The Triumph*. Boston: Little, Brown, 1956.

Fried, Richard M. *Men against McCarthy*. New York: Columbia University Press, 1976.

Fried, Richard M. *Nightmare in Red: The McCarthy Era in Perspective*. New York: Oxford University Press, 1990.

Gaddis, John Lewis. *The Cold War: A New History*. New York: Penguin Press, 2005.

Gaddis, John Lewis. *The Long Peace: Inquiries into the History of the Cold War*. New York: Oxford University Press, 1987.

Gaddis, John Lewis. *Russia, the Soviet Union, and the United States: An Interpretive History*. New York: Wiley, 1978.

Gaddis, John Lewis. *Strategies of Containment: A Critical Appraisal of Postwar American National Security Policy*. New York: Oxford University Press, 1982.

Gaddis, John Lewis. *The United States and the End of the Cold War: Implications, Reconsiderations, Provocations*. New York: Oxford University Press, 1992.

Gaddis, John Lewis. *The United States and the Origins of the Cold War, 1941–1947*. New York: Columbia University Press, 1972.

Gaddis, John Lewis. *We Now Know: Rethinking Cold War History*. New York: Oxford University Press, 1997.

Gallen, David. *Bill Clinton as They Know Him: An Oral Biography*. New York: Gallen Pub Group, 1994.

Geer, John. *Politicians and Party Politics*. Baltimore: Johns Hopkins University Press, 1998.

Gelfand, Mark I. *A Nation of Cities: The Federal Government and Urban America, 1933–1965*. New York: Oxford University Press, 1975.

Genovese, Michael A. *The Power of the American Presidency, 1789–2000*. New York: Oxford University Press, 2001.

Gergen, David. *Eyewitness to Power: The Essence of Leadership, Nixon to Clinton*. New York: Simon & Schuster, 2000.

Gillon, Steven M. *The Democrats' Dilemma: Walter F. Mondale and the Liberal Legacy*. New York: Columbia University Press, 1992.

Gillon, Steven M. *The Pact: Bill Clinton, Newt Gingrich, and the Rivalry That Defined a Generation*. New York: Oxford University Press, 2008.

Ginsberg, Benjamin, and Martin Shefter. *Politics by Other Means: Politicians, Prosecutors, and the Press from Watergate to Whitewater.* New York: Norton, 2002.

Goldman, Eric F. *The Crucial Decade—and After: America, 1945–1960.* New York: Vintage Books, 1961.

Goldman, Eric F. *Rendezvous with Destiny: A History of Modern American Reform.* New York: Vintage Books, 1956.

Goldman, Eric F. *The Tragedy of Lyndon Johnson.* New York: Knopf, 1969.

Goldsmith, William M. *The Growth of Presidential Power: A Documented History.* New York: Chelsea House, 1974.

Goodwin, Doris Kearns. *The Bully Pulpit: Theodore Roosevelt, William Howard Taft, and the Golden Age of Journalism.* New York: Simon & Schuster, 2013.

Goodwin, Doris Kearns. *Lyndon Johnson and the American Dream.* New York: Harper & Row, 1976.

Goodwin, Doris Kearns. *No Ordinary Time: Franklin and Eleanor Roosevelt: The Home Front in World War II.* New York: Simon & Schuster, 1994.

Gould, Lewis L. *Four Hats in the Ring: The 1912 Election and the Birth of Modern American Politics.* Lawrence: University Press of Kansas, 2008.

Gould, Lewis L. *The Modern American Presidency.* Lawrence: University Press of Kansas, 2003.

Gould, Lewis L. *The Presidency of Theodore Roosevelt.* Lawrence: University Press of Kansas, 2011.

Gould, Lewis L. *Theodore Roosevelt.* New York: Oxford University Press, 2012.

Gould, Lewis L. *The William Howard Taft Presidency.* Lawrence: University Press of Kansas, 2009.

Graebner, Norman A. *America as a World Power: A Realist Appraisal from Wilson to Reagan.* Wilmington, DE: Scholarly Resources, 1984.

Graff, Henry F., ed. *The Presidents: A Reference History.* New York: Charles Scribner's Sons: Thomson/Gale, 2002.

Graubard, Stephen. *Command of Office: How War, Secrecy, and Deception Transformed the Presidency, from Theodore Roosevelt to George W. Bush.* New York: Basic Books, 2004.

Greene, John Robert. *Betty Ford: Candor and Courage in the White House.* Lawrence: University Press of Kansas, 2004.

Greene, John Robert. *The Limits of Power: The Nixon and Ford Administrations.* Bloomington: Indiana University Press, 1992.

Greene, John Robert. *The Presidency of George Bush.* Lawrence: University Press of Kansas, 2000.

Greene, John Robert. *The Presidency of Gerald R. Ford.* Lawrence: University Press of Kansas, 1995.

Greenstein, Fred I. *The Hidden-Hand Presidency: Eisenhower as Leader.* New York: Basic Books, 1982.

Greenstein, Fred I., ed. *Leadership in the Modern Presidency.* Cambridge, MA: Harvard University Press, 1988.

Greenstein, Fred I. *The Presidential Difference: Leadership Style from FDR to Barack Obama*. Princeton, NJ: Princeton University Press, 2009.

Halberstam, David. *The Best and the Brightest*. New York: Random House, 1972.

Hamby, Alonzo L. *Beyond the New Deal: Harry S. Truman and American Liberalism*. New York: Columbia University Press, 1973.

Hamby, Alonzo L. *For the Survival of Democracy: Franklin Roosevelt and the World Crisis of the 1930s*. New York: Free Press, 2004.

Hamby, Alonzo L. *Liberalism and Its Challengers: From F.D.R. to Bush*. New York: Oxford University Press, 1992.

Hamby, Alonzo L. *Man of the People: A Life of Harry S. Truman*. New York: Oxford University Press, 1995.

Hamilton, Nigel. *The Mantle of Command: FDR at War, 1941–1942*. Boston: Houghton Mifflin Harcourt, 2014.

Harbaugh, William H. *The Life and Times of Theodore Roosevelt*. New York: Oxford University Press, 1975.

Hargrove, Erwin C. *The Effective Presidency: Lessons on Leadership from John F. Kennedy to George W. Bush*. Boulder, CO: Paradigm, 2008.

Hargrove, Erwin C. *The Power of the Modern Presidency*. Philadelphia: Temple University Press, 1974.

Hargrove, Erwin C. *The President as Leader: Appealing to the Better Angels of Our Nature*. Lawrence: University Press of Kansas, 1998.

Hargrove, Erwin C. *Presidential Leadership: Personality and Political Style*. New York: Macmillan, 1966.

Hargrove, Erwin C., and Michael Nelson. *Presidents, Politics, and Policy*. New York: Knopf, 1984.

Harris, John F. *The Survivor: Bill Clinton in the White House*. New York: Random House, 2005.

Harrison, Cynthia. *On Account of Sex: The Politics of Women's Issues, 1945–1968*. Berkeley: University of California Press, 1988.

Hayward, Steven F. *The Age of Reagan: The Conservative Counterrevolution, 1980–1989*. New York: Crown Forum, 2009.

Herring, George C. *Aid to Russia, 1941–1946: Strategy, Diplomacy, the Origins of the Cold War*. New York: Columbia University Press, 1973.

Herring, George C. *America's Longest War: The United States and Vietnam, 1950–1975*. New York: Wiley, 1979.

Herring, George C. *From Colony to Superpower: U.S. Foreign Relations since 1776*. New York: Oxford University Press, 2008.

Herring, George C. *LBJ and Vietnam: A Different Kind of War*. Austin: University of Texas Press, 1994.

Hertsgaard, Mark. *On Bended Knee: The Press and the Reagan Presidency*. New York: Farrar, Straus & Giroux, 1988.

Hess, Stephen. *America's Political Dynasties*. New Brunswick, NJ: Transaction Publishers, 1997.

Hess, Stephen. *Presidents and the Presidency: Essays*. Washington, DC: Brookings Institution, 1996.

Hess, Stephen, with James P. Pfiffner. *Organizing the Presidency*. Washington, DC: Brookings Institution, 2002.

Hodgson, Godfrey. *All Things to All Men: The False Promise of the Modern American Presidency*. New York: Simon & Schuster, 1980.

Hofstadter, Richard. *The American Political Tradition and the Men Who Made It*. New York: Knopf, 1948.

Jamieson, Kathleen Hall. *Packaging the Presidency: A History and Criticism of Presidential Campaign Advertising*. New York: Oxford University Press, 1992.

Jamieson, Kathleen Hall, and David S. Birdsell. *Presidential Debates: The Challenge of Creating an Informed Electorate*. New York: Oxford University Press, 1988.

Johnson, Haynes. *The Best of Times: America in the Clinton Years*. New York: Harcourt, 2001.

Johnson, Haynes. *Sleepwalking through History: America in the Reagan Years*. New York: Norton, 2003.

Johnson, Lady Bird. *A White House Diary*. New York: Holt, Rinehart & Winston, 1970.

Johnson, Walter. *1600 Pennsylvania Avenue: Presidents and the People since 1929*. Boston: Little, Brown, 1963.

Juhnke, William, ed. *President Truman's Committee on Civil Rights*. Frederick, MD: University Publications of America, 1984.

Kalman, Laura. *Right Star Rising: A New Politics, 1974–1980*. New York: Norton, 2010.

Katznelson, Ira. *Fear Itself: The New Deal and the Origins of Our Time*. New York: Liveright, 2013.

Kaufman, Burton I. *The Presidency of James Earl Carter, Jr*. Lawrence: University Press of Kansas, 1993.

Keller, Morton. *America's Three Regimes: A New Political History*. New York: Oxford University Press, 2007.

Kennedy, David M. *Freedom from Fear: The American People in Depression and War, 1929–1945*. New York: Oxford University Press, 1999.

Kennedy, David M. *Over Here: The First World War and American Society*. New York: Oxford University Press, 1980.

Kirkendall, Richard, ed. *Harry's Farewell: Interpreting and Teaching the Truman Presidency*. Columbia: University of Missouri Press, 2004.

Klein, Joe. *The Natural: The Misunderstood Presidency of Bill Clinton*. New York: Doubleday, 2002.

Koenig, Louis W. *The Chief Executive*. New York: Harcourt, Brace & World, 1964.

Kraft, Joseph. *Profiles in Power: A Washington Insight*. New York: New American Library, 1966.

Kumar, Martha Joynt. *Managing the President's Message: The White House Communications Operation*. Baltimore: Johns Hopkins University Press, 2007.

Kumar, Martha Joynt., and Terry Sullivan, eds. *The White House World: Transitions, Organizations, and Office Operations*. College Station: Texas A&M University Press, 2003.

Kutler, Stanley I. *The American Inquisition: Justice and Injustice in the Cold War.* New York: Hill & Wang, 1982.

Kutler, Stanley I. *The Wars of Watergate: The Last Crisis of Richard Nixon.* New York: Knopf, 1990.

Landy, Marc, and Sidney M. Milkis. *Presidential Greatness.* Lawrence: University Press of Kansas, 2000.

Larrabee, Eric. *Commander in Chief: Franklin Delano Roosevelt, His Lieutenants, and Their War.* New York: Harper & Row, 1987.

Lash, Joseph P. *Dealers and Dreamers: A New Look at the New Deal.* New York: Doubleday, 1988.

Lash, Joseph P. *Eleanor: The Years Alone.* New York: Norton, 1972.

Lash, Joseph P. *Eleanor and Franklin: The Story of Their Relationship Based on Eleanor Roosevelt's Private Papers.* New York: Norton, 1971.

Laski, Harold J. *The American Presidency: An Interpretation.* London: G. Allen & Unwin, 1940.

Lawson, Steven F. *Black Ballots: Voting Rights in the South, 1944–1969.* New York: Columbia University Press, 1976.

Lawson, Steven F. *In Pursuit of Power: Southern Blacks and Electoral Politics, 1965–1982.* New York: Columbia University Press, 1985.

Lawson, Steven F. *Running for Freedom: Civil Rights and Black Politics in America since 1941.* Philadelphia: Temple University Press, 1991.

Leuchtenburg, William E. *The FDR Years: On Roosevelt and His Legacy.* New York: Columbia University Press, 1995.

Leuchtenburg, William E. *Franklin D. Roosevelt and the New Deal, 1932–1940.* New York: Harper & Row, 1963.

Leuchtenburg, William E. *The Great Age of Change.* New York: Time-Life Books, 1964.

Leuchtenburg, William E. *Herbert Hoover.* New York: Times Books, 2009.

Leuchtenburg, William E. *In the Shadow of FDR: From Harry Truman to Barack Obama.* Ithaca, NY: Cornell University Press, 2009.

Leuchtenburg, William E. *New Deal and Global War.* New York: Time-Life Books, 1964.

Leuchtenburg, William E. *The Perils of Prosperity, 1914–32.* Chicago: University of Chicago Press, 1993.

Leuchtenburg, William E. *The Supreme Court Reborn: The Constitutional Revolution in the Age of Roosevelt.* New York: Oxford University Press, 1995.

Leuchtenburg, William E. *A Troubled Feast: American Society since 1945.* Boston: Little, Brown, 1983.

Leuchtenburg, William E. *The White House Looks South: Franklin D. Roosevelt, Harry S. Truman, Lyndon B. Johnson.* Baton Rouge: Louisiana State University Press, 2005.

Light, Paul C. *The President's Agenda: Domestic Policy Choice from Kennedy to Clinton.* Baltimore: Johns Hopkins University Press, 1998.

Link, Arthur S. *Wilson.* 5 vols. Princeton, NJ: Princeton University Press, 1947–65.

Link, Arthur S. *Woodrow Wilson and the Progressive Era, 1910–1917*. New York: Harper, 1954.

Link, Arthur S. *Woodrow Wilson: Revolution, War, and Peace*. Arlington Heights, IL: H. Davidson, 1979.

Lowi, Theodore J. *The Personal President: Power Invested, Promise Unfulfilled*. Ithaca, NY: Cornell University Press, 1985.

Lowi, Theodore J., and Benjamin Ginsberg. *Embattled Democracy: Politics and Policy in the Clinton Era*. New York: Norton, 1995.

Manchester, William. *The Glory and the Dream: A Narrative History of America, 1932–1972*. Boston: Little, Brown, 1974.

Maraniss, David. *The Clinton Enigma: A Four-and-a-Half-Minute Speech Reveals This President's Entire Life*. New York: Simon & Schuster, 1998.

Maraniss, David. *First in His Class: A Biography of Bill Clinton*. New York: Simon & Schuster, 1995.

Mayer, George H. *The Republican Party, 1854–1966*. New York: Oxford University Press, 1967.

McCoy, Donald R. *Calvin Coolidge: The Quiet President*. Lawrence: University Press of Kansas, 1988.

McCoy, Donald R. *The Presidency of Harry S. Truman*. Lawrence: University Press of Kansas, 1984.

McCoy, Donald R, and Richard T. Reutten. *Quest and Response: Minority Rights and the Truman Administration*. Lawrence: University Press of Kansas, 1973.

McCullough, David G. *Mornings on Horseback: The Story of an Extraordinary Family, a Vanished Way of Life, and the Unique Child Who Became Theodore Roosevelt*. New York: Simon & Schuster, 1981.

McCullough, David G. *Truman*. New York: Simon & Schuster, 1992.

McElvaine, Robert S. *The Great Depression: America, 1929–1941*. New York: Times Books, 1984.

McJimsey, George. *The Presidency of Franklin Delano Roosevelt*. Lawrence: University Press of Kansas, 2000.

McPherson, James, and David Rubel, eds. *"To the Best of My Ability": The American Presidents*. New York: Dorling Kindersley, 2000.

Michaels, Judith E. *The President's Call: Executive Leadership from FDR to George Bush*. Pittsburgh: University of Pittsburgh Press, 1997.

Milkis, Sidney M. *The President and the Parties: The Transformation of the American Party System since the New Deal*. New York: Oxford University Press, 1993.

Milkis, Sidney M. *Theodore Roosevelt, the Progressive Party, and the Transformation of American Democracy*. Lawrence: University Press of Kansas, 2009.

Milkis, Sidney M., and Michael Nelson. *The American Presidency: Origins and Development, 1776–2007*. Washington, DC: CQ Press, 2008.

Millard, Candice. *Destiny of the Republic: A Tale of Madness, Medicine, and the Murder of the President*. New York: Doubleday, 2011.

Morris, Edmund. *The Rise of Theodore Roosevelt*. New York: Coward, McCann & Geoghegan, 1979.

Morris, Edmund. *Theodore Rex*. New York: Random House, 2001.

Mowry, George E. *The Era of Theodore Roosevelt, 1900–1912*. New York: Harper, 1958.

Murray, Robert K. *The Harding Era: Warren G. Harding and His Administration*. Minneapolis: University of Minnesota Press, 1969.

Murray, Robert K. *The Politics of Normalcy: Governmental Theory and Practice in the Harding-Coolidge Era*. New York: Norton, 1973.

Naftali, Timothy J. *George H. W. Bush*. New York: Times Books, 2007.

Nash, George H. *The Life of Herbert Hoover, vol. 1: The Engineer, 1874–1914*. New York: Norton, 1983.

Nash, George H. *The Life of Herbert Hoover, vol. 2: The Humanitarian, 1914–1917*. New York: Norton, 1988.

Nash, George H. *The Life of Herbert Hoover, vol. 3: Master of Emergencies, 1917–1918*. New York: Norton, 1996.

Nelson, Dana D. *Bad for Democracy: How the Presidency Undermines the Power of the People*. Minneapolis: University of Minnesota Press, 2008.

Nelson, Michael, ed. *Guide to the Presidency*. Washington, DC: CQ Press, 2002.

Neustadt, Richard E. *Presidential Power and the Modern Presidents: The Politics of Leadership from Roosevelt to Reagan*. New York: Free Press, 1990.

Nichols, David K. *The Myth of the Modern Presidency*. University Park, PA: Pennsylvania State University Press, 1994.

O'Brien, Michael. *Rethinking Kennedy: An Interpretive Biography*. Chicago: Ivan R. Dee, 2009.

Ostrogorski, Moisei. *Democracy and the Organization of Political Parties*. New York: Macmillan, 1902.

Pach, Chester J., Jr., and Elmo Richardson. *The Presidency of Dwight D. Eisenhower*. Lawrence: University Press of Kansas, 1991.

Palermo, Joseph A. *The Eighties*. Upper Saddle River, NJ: Pearson, 2013.

Parmet, Herbert S. *George Bush: The Life of a Lone Star Yankee*. New York: Scribner, 1997.

Parmet, Herbert S. *Jack: The Struggles of John F. Kennedy*. New York: Dial Press, 1980.

Parmet, Herbert S. *JFK: The Presidency of John F. Kennedy*. New York: Dial Press, 1983.

Parmet, Herbert S. *Presidential Power from the New Deal to the New Right*. Malabar, FL: Krieger, 2002.

Parmet, Herbert S. *Richard M. Nixon: An American Enigma*. New York: Pearson Longman, 2008.

Parmet, Herbert S. *Richard Nixon and His America*. Boston: Little, Brown, 1990.

Patterson, James T. *America's Struggle against Poverty in the Twentieth Century*. Cambridge, MA: Harvard University Press, 2000.

Patterson, James T. *The Eve of Destruction: How 1965 Transformed America*. New York: Basic Books, 2012.

Patterson, James T. *Grand Expectations: The United States, 1945–1974*. New York: Oxford University Press, 1996.

Patterson, James T. *Restless Giant: The United States from Watergate to Bush v. Gore.* New York: Oxford University Press, 2005.

Pemberton, William E. *Exit with Honor: The Life and Presidency of Ronald Reagan.* Armonk, NY: M. E. Sharpe, 1997.

Perlstein, Rick. *The Invisible Bridge: The Fall of Nixon and the Rise of Reagan.* New York: Simon & Schuster, 2014.

Perlstein, Rick. *Nixonland: The Rise of a President and the Fracturing of America.* New York: Scribner, 2008.

Pfiffner, James P. *The Character Factor: How We Judge America's Presidents.* College Station: Texas A&M University Press, 2004.

Pfiffner, James P. *The Modern Presidency.* Boston: Wadsworth Cengage Learning, 2011.

Pfiffner, James P. *The Strategic Presidency: Hitting the Ground Running.* Lawrence: University Press of Kansas, 1996.

Phillips, Cabell. *The Truman Presidency: The History of a Triumphant Succession.* New York: Macmillan, 1966.

Pious, Richard M. *The Presidency.* Boston: Allyn & Bacon, 1996.

Pious, Richard M. *Why Presidents Fail.* Lanham, MD: Rowman & Littlefield, 2008.

Polenberg, Richard. *Reorganizing Roosevelt's Government: The Controversy over Executive Reorganization, 1936–1939.* Cambridge, MA: Harvard University Press, 1966.

Polenberg, Richard. *War and Society: The United States, 1941–1945.* Philadelphia: Lippincott, 1972.

Polsby, Nelson W., and Aaron Wildavsky, with David A. Hopkins. *Presidential Elections: Strategies and Structures of American Politics.* Lanham, MD: Rowman & Littlefield, 2008.

Ponder, Stephen. *Managing the Press: Origins of the Media Presidency, 1897–1933.* New York: St. Martin's, 1999.

Popadiuk, Roman. *The Leadership of George Bush: An Insider's View of the Forty-first President.* College Station: Texas A&M University Press, 2009.

Posner, Richard A. *An Affair of State: The Investigation, Impeachment, and Trial of President Clinton.* Cambridge, MA: Harvard University Press, 1999.

Rae, Nicol C. *The Decline and Fall of the Liberal Republicans: From 1952 to the Present.* New York: Oxford University Press, 1989.

Rae, Nicol C. *Southern Democrats.* New York: Oxford University Press, 1994.

Rae, Nicol C., and Colton C. Campbell. *Impeaching Clinton: Partisan Strife on Capitol Hill.* Lawrence: University Press of Kansas, 2004.

Reeves, Richard. *A Ford, Not a Lincoln.* New York: Harcourt Brace Jovanovich, 1975.

Reeves, Richard. *President Kennedy: Profile of Power.* New York: Simon & Schuster, 1993.

Reeves, Richard. *President Reagan: The Triumph of Imagination.* New York: Simon & Schuster, 2005.

Reeves, Richard. *Running in Place: How Bill Clinton Disappointed America*. Kansas City, MO: Andrews & McMeel, 1996.

Reich, Robert B. *Locked in the Cabinet*. New York: Knopf, 1997.

Renshaw, Patrick. *Franklin D. Roosevelt*. Harlow, UK: Longman, 2004.

Reston, James. *Deadline: A Memoir*. New York: Times Books, 1992.

Riccards, Michael P. *Destiny's Consul: America's Ten Greatest Presidents*. Lanham, MD: Rowman & Littlefield, 2012.

Riccards, Michael P. *The Ferocious Engine of Democracy: A History of the American Presidency: From Teddy Roosevelt through George W. Bush*. New York: Cooper Square Press, 2003.

Robinson, Donald L. *To the Best of My Ability: The Presidency and the Constitution*. New York: Norton, 1987.

Robinson, Greg. *By Order of the President: FDR and the Internment of Japanese Americans*. Cambridge, MA: Harvard University Press, 2001.

Rollins, Alfred B., Jr. *Roosevelt and Howe*. New York: Knopf, 1962.

Rose, Richard. *The Postmodern President: George Bush Meets the World*. Chatham, NJ: Chatham House, 1991.

Roseboom, Eugene H. *A History of Presidential Elections*. New York: Macmillan, 1957.

Rossiter, Clinton. *The American Presidency*. New York: Harcourt, Brace, 1960.

Rovere, Richard. *The Eisenhower Years: Affairs of State*. New York: Farrar, Straus & Cudahy, 1956.

Rudalevige, Andrew. *The New Imperial Presidency: Renewing Presidential Power after Watergate*. Ann Arbor: University of Michigan Press, 2005.

Savage, Sean J. *Roosevelt: The Party Leader, 1932–1945*. Lexington: University Press of Kentucky, 1991.

Schaller, Michael. *Reckoning with Reagan: America and Its President in the 1980s*. New York: Oxford University Press, 1992.

Schaller, Michael. *The Republican Ascendancy: American Politics, 1968–2001*. Wheeling, IL: Harlan Davidson, 2002.

Schaller, Michael. *Right Turn: American Life in the Reagan-Bush Era, 1980–1992*. New York: Oxford University Press, 2007.

Schaller, Michael. *Ronald Reagan*. New York: Oxford University Press, 2011.

Schier, Steven E., ed. *The Postmodern Presidency: Bill Clinton's Legacy in U.S. Politics*. Pittsburgh: University of Pittsburgh Press, 2000.

Schlesinger, Arthur M., Jr. *The Age of Roosevelt, vol. 1: The Crisis of the Old Order, 1919–1933*. Boston: Houghton Mifflin, 1957.

Schlesinger, Arthur M., Jr. *The Age of Roosevelt, vol. 2: The Coming of the New Deal, 1933–1935*. Boston: Houghton Mifflin, 1958.

Schlesinger, Arthur M., Jr. *The Age of Roosevelt, vol. 3: The Politics of Upheaval, 1935–1936*. Boston: Houghton Mifflin, 1959.

Schlesinger, Arthur M., Jr. *The Imperial Presidency*. Boston: Houghton Mifflin, 1989.

Schlesinger, Arthur M., Jr. *Robert Kennedy and His Times*. Boston: Houghton Mifflin, 1978.

Schlesinger, Arthur M., Jr. *A Thousand Days: John F. Kennedy in the White House*. Boston: Houghton Mifflin, 1965.

Schlesinger, Arthur M., Jr. *War and the American Presidency*. New York: Norton, 2004.

Schlesinger, Arthur M., Jr., Gil Troy, and Fred I. Israel, eds. *History of American Presidential Elections, 1789–2008*. 3 vols. New York: Facts on File, 2012.

Schlesinger, Stephen C., and Stephen Kinzer. *Bitter Fruit: The Untold Story of the American Coup in Guatemala*. Garden City, NY: Doubleday, 1982.

Schulman, Bruce J. *The Seventies: The Great Shift in American Culture, Society, and Politics*. New York: Free Press, 2001.

Schwarz, Jordan A. *The Interregnum of Despair: Hoover, Congress, and the Depression*. Urbana: University of Illinois Press, 1970.

Schwarz, Jordan A. *The New Dealers: Power Politics in the Age of Roosevelt*. New York: Knopf, 1993.

Shapley, Deborah. *Promise and Power: The Life and Times of Robert McNamara*. Boston: Little, Brown, 1993.

Shaw, Malcolm, ed. *Roosevelt to Reagan: The Development of the Modern Presidency*. London: C. Hurst, 1987.

Shlaes, Amity. *Coolidge*. New York: Harper, 2013.

Sidey, Hugh. *John F. Kennedy, President*. New York: Atheneum, 1963.

Sidey, Hugh. *A Very Personal Presidency: Lyndon Johnson in the White House*. New York: Atheneum, 1968.

Sitkoff, Harvard. *A New Deal for Blacks: The Emergence of Civil Rights as a National Issue: The Depression Decade*. New York: Oxford University Press, 2009.

Sitkoff, Harvard. *The Struggle for Black Equality*. New York: Hill & Wang, 2008.

Sitkoff, Harvard. *Toward Freedom Land: The Long Struggle for Racial Equality in America*. Lexington: University Press of Kentucky, 2010.

Skowronek, Stephen. *Building a New American State: The Expansion of National Administrative Capacities, 1877–1920*. New York: Cambridge University Press, 1982.

Skowronek, Stephen. *The Politics Presidents Make: Leadership from John Adams to Bill Clinton*. Cambridge, MA: Belknap Press of Harvard University Press, 1997.

Skowronek, Stephen. *Presidential Leadership in Political Time: Reprise and Reappraisal*. Lawrence: University Press of Kansas, 2011.

Small, Melvin. *The Presidency of Richard Nixon*. Lawrence: University Press of Kansas, 1999.

Smith, Richard Norton. *An Uncommon Man: The Triumph of Herbert Hoover*. New York: Simon & Schuster, 1984.

Sobel, Robert. *Coolidge: An American Enigma*. Washington, DC: Regnery, 1998.

Sorensen, Theodore C. *Decision-making in the White House: The Olive Branch or the Arrows*. New York: Columbia University Press, 1963.

Sorensen, Theodore C. *A Different Kind of Presidency: A Proposal for Breaking the Political Deadlock*. New York: Harper & Row, 1984.

Sorensen, Theodore C. *Kennedy*. New York: Harper & Row, 1965.

Spalding, Elizabeth Edwards. *The First Cold Warrior: Harry Truman, Containment, and the Remaking of Liberal Internationalism*. Lexington: University Press of Kentucky, 2006.

Stephanopoulos, George. *All Too Human: A Political Education*. Boston: Little, Brown, 1999.

Strober, Deborah Hart, and Gerald S. Strober. *The Nixon Presidency: An Oral History of the Era*. Washington, DC: Brassey's, 2003.

Sundquist, James L. *The Decline and Resurgence of Congress*. Washington, DC: Brookings Institution, 1981.

Sundquist, James L. *Politics and Policy: The Eisenhower, Kennedy, and Johnson Years*. Washington, DC: Brookings Institution, 1968.

Takiff, Michael. *A Complicated Man: The Life of Bill Clinton as Told by Those Who Know Him*. New Haven, CT: Yale University Press, 2010.

Tananbaum, Duane. *The Bricker Amendment Controversy: A Test of Eisenhower's Political Leadership*. Ithaca, NY: Cornell University Press, 1988.

Tatalovich, Raymond, and Thomas S. Engeman. *The Presidency and Political Science: Two Hundred Years of Constitutional Debate*. Baltimore: Johns Hopkins University Press, 2003.

Tebbel, John, and Sarah Miles Watts. *The Press and the Presidency: From George Washington to Ronald Reagan*. New York: Oxford University Press, 1985.

Thompson, John A. *Woodrow Wilson*. London: Routledge, 2002.

Thurber, Timothy N. *Republicans and Race: The GOP's Frayed Relationship with African Americans, 1945–1974*. Lawrence: University Press of Kansas, 2013.

Toobin, Jeffrey. *A Vast Conspiracy: The Real Story of the Sex Scandal That Nearly Brought Down a President*. New York: Random House, 1999.

Tourtellot, Arthur Bernon. *The Presidents on the Presidency*. Garden City, NY: Doubleday, 1964.

Trani, Eugene P., and David L. Wilson. *The Presidency of Warren G. Harding*. Lawrence: Regents Press of Kansas, 1977.

Trout, Charles H. *Boston, the Great Depression, and the New Deal*. New York: Oxford University Press, 1977.

Tugwell, Rexford. *The Democratic Roosevelt: A Biography of Franklin D. Roosevelt*. Garden City, NY: Doubleday, 1957.

Tulis, Jeffrey K. *The Rhetorical Presidency*. Princeton, NJ: Princeton University Press, 1987.

Urofsky, Melvin I., ed. *The American Presidents*. New York: Garland, 2000.

Walcott, Charles E., and Karen M. Hult. *Governing the White House: From Hoover through LBJ*. Lawrence: University Press of Kansas, 1995.

Walt, Stephen M. *Taming American Power: The Global Response to U.S. Primacy*. New York: Norton, 2005.

Ward, Geoffrey C. *The Roosevelts: An Intimate History*. New York: Knopf, 2014.

Waterman, Richard W., ed. *The Presidency Reconsidered*. Itasca, IL: F. E. Peacock, 1993.

Wecter, Dixon. *The Age of the Great Depression, 1929–1941*. New York: Macmillan, 1948.

White, Theodore H. *Breach of Faith: The Fall of Richard Nixon*. New York: Atheneum, 1975.

White, Theodore H. *The Making of the President, 1960*. New York: Atheneum, 1961.

White, Theodore H. *The Making of the President, 1964*. New York: Atheneum, 1965.

White, Theodore H. *The Making of the President, 1968*. New York: Atheneum, 1969.

White, Theodore H. *The Making of the President, 1972*. New York: Atheneum, 1973.

White, William Allen. *A Puritan in Babylon: The Story of Calvin Coolidge*. New York: Macmillan, 1938.

Wicker, Tom. *George Herbert Walker Bush*. New York: Lipper/Viking, 2004.

Wicker, Tom. *JFK and LBJ: The Influence of Personality upon Politics*. New York: Morrow, 1968.

Wildavsky, Aaron B. *The Beleaguered Presidency*. New Brunswick, NJ: Transaction Publishers, 1991.

Wilentz, Sean. *The Age of Reagan: A History, 1974–2008*. New York: Harper, 2008.

Wills, Garry. *Nixon Agonistes: The Crisis of the Self-made Man*. New York: New American Library, 1979.

Wilson, Robert A., ed. *Character above All: Ten Presidents from FDR to George Bush*. New York: Simon & Schuster, 1995.

Woodward, Bob. *The Agenda: Inside the Clinton White House*. New York: Simon & Schuster, 1994.

Zelizer, Julian E. *The Fierce Urgency of Now: Lyndon Johnson, Congress, and the Battle for the Great Society*. New York: Penguin Press, 2015.

Zelizer, Julian E. *Jimmy Carter*. New York: Times Books/Henry Holt, 2010.

INDEX

———

Note: Page numbers in *italics* indicate photographs and illustrations.

Carter, Amy, *561*, 575, 599
Carter, Jimmy, *570*, *807*
  and author's background, xii
  background of, 557–58
  and the Camp David Accords,
    569–70, *570*
  Carter Doctrine, 571
  and Clinton, 798
  and deregulation, 565–66
  and diversity of administration,
    562–64
  and economic policy, 564–65
  and the energy crisis, 566–69
  and environmental protection, 564
  and Fiske, 730
  and foreign affairs, 569–73, *570*
  and governing style, 558–59, 560–62
  and Haiti, 737
  inauguration of, 557–58, 560, *561*
  intellect of, 558
  and Iran hostage crisis, 571–73,
    572, 641
  legacy of, 577–78
  and "malaise speech," 568–69
  and Panama, 686
  post-presidency of, 576–77
  and presidential debates, 555
  and Reagan, 620, 665
  reelection campaign, 573–76
  on Rich pardon, 796
Carter, Rosalynn, 560, *561*, 563, 567
Carter Center, 576
cartoons and caricatures
  Bush (G. H. W.), 677–78
  Eisenhower, *348*, 379–80
  Lyndon Johnson, *458*
  McCarthy, *348*
  Nixon, 473, *530*
  Reagan, *651*
  Roosevelt (Franklin), 166
  Roosevelt (Theodore), 30, *44*
Carville, James, 703, 705, 719
Casals, Pablo, 415
Case Act of 1972, 549–50

Casey, William, 614–15, 643–44,
  648, 653
Castel, Albert, 12
Castro, Fidel
  CIA plots against, 340, 374, 394,
    421, 549
  and Clinton pardons, 795
  and Johnson, 426
  overthrow of Batista regime, 373–74
  and Reagan's foreign policy, 612
Catholicism, 376, 443
Catt, Carrie Chapman, 114
Catton, Bruce, 12
Celler, Emanuel, 446, 449
Central America, 613–14, 648. *See also*
  specific countries
Central American Court of Justice, 82
Central Intelligence Agency (CIA)
  and Angola, 548
  and antiwar movement, 460
  and arms-for-hostages scandal, 643,
    646, 648, 649
  and Bay of Pigs invasion, 374
  and bin Laden, 789
  and Bush (G. H. W.), 656, 683
  and fall of Berlin Wall, 688
  and Haiti, 732
  and Iran, 338–39
  and Kennedy, 394, 421
  and Nicaragua, 614–15
  and Nixon, 473, 480
  origins of, 268–69
  and Panama invasion, 687
  and plots against Castro, 340, 374,
    394, 421, 549
  and Reagan, 587, 588
  and Watergate, 515, 533
Chafe, William, 180–81, 715–16, 720,
  723, 737–38, 765, 770
Chafee, John, 740, 755
Challenger space shuttle disaster,
  672–73, 811
Chamberlain, Neville, 640
Chambers, John, 95